The Soviet Union
A Documentary History
Volume I 1917–1940

The Soviet story—the revolution, Lenin, Stalinism, the Great Patriotic War, the era of Khrushchev, Brezhnev and the Cold War, and the dramatic collapse under Gorbachev—looms large in history syllabuses across the world.

This two-volume history casts fresh light on events by drawing upon the primary material that has become available since the collapse of Communist rule in 1991, much of it not previously published in English. Combining lucid narrative and analysis and a rich selection of evocative documents, it provides a lively entrée to current debate over humanity's most momentous and tragic experiment.

Structured in three parts, the book begins with revolution and civil war (1917–1921), goes on to deal with the consolidation of Bolshevik power (1921–1928) and ends by covering the upheaval through which Soviet society passed under Stalin (1928–1940).

Conceived as a companion to the highly-regarded, best-selling four-volume *Nazism 1919–1945: A Documentary Reader* by Noakes and Pridham (also published by University of Exeter Press) this book will be a valuable resource for students at all levels.

"The choice of documents is admirable: they are diverse in terms of type—ranging from government decrees to individual testimonies—and cover all major aspects of Soviet history. The degree of contextualization is well-judged. The analysis provided is balanced but never bland."
Steve Smith, Professor of History, University of Essex

To be published in 2006:
The Soviet Union: A Documentary History, Volume 2 1939–1991
paperback 0 85989 582 3 / hardback 0 85989 716 8

EXETER STUDIES IN HISTORY

General Editors: Jonathan Barry, Tim Rees and T.P. Wiseman

Modern European history titles in this series:

The Civilian in War: The Home Front in Europe, Japan and the USA in World War II edited by Jeremy Noakes (1992)

Nazism 1919–1945

> Volume 1: *The Rise to Power 1919–1934: A Documentary Reader* edited by J. Noakes and G. Pridham (new edition with index, 1998)

> Volume 2: *State, Economy and Society 1933–1939: A Documentary Reader* edited by J. Noakes and G. Pridham (new edition with index, 2000)

> Volume 3: *Foreign Policy, War and Racial Extermination: A Documentary Reader* edited by J. Noakes and G. Pridham (new edition with index, 2001)

> Volume 4: *The German Home Front in World War II: A Documentary Reader* edited by Jeremy Noakes (with index, 1998)

The Last Years of Austria-Hungary: A Multi-National Experiment in Early Twentieth Century Europe edited by Mark Cornwall (revised and expanded edition, 2002)

Nazism, War and Genocide edited by Neil Gregor (2005)

The Soviet Union
A Documentary History

Volume I 1917–1940

Edward Acton and Tom Stableford

UNIVERSITY
of
EXETER
PRESS

Paperback cover image: 'Under the Banner of Marx, Engels, Lenin and Stalin';
poster designed in 1933 by Gustav Klutsis (from the David King Collection, London).

First published in 2005 by
University of Exeter Press
Reed Hall, Streatham Drive
Exeter EX4 4QR
UK
www.exeterpress.co.uk

British Library Cataloguing in Publication Data
A catalogue record for this book is available
from the British Library.

Hardback ISBN 0 85989 715 X
Paperback ISBN 0 85989 581 5

Typeset in 11/12½ pt Bembo
by XL Publishing Services, Tiverton

Printed by Gutenberg Press Ltd, Malta

Contents

Part One: Revolution and Civil War (1917–1921)

See pages 401–410 for List of Documents

Part Two: The Period of the 'New Economic Policy' (NEP) (1921–1928)

See pages 401–410 for List of Documents

Part Three: Soviet Society under Stalin (1928–1940)

See pages 401–410 for List of Documents

See pages 401–410 for List of Documents

Acknowledgements

The first debt which Tom Stableford and I would like to acknowledge is to the team of Russian scholars at the A.M. Gorky Urals State University led by M.E. Glavatsky, who compiled the documentary collection around which this volume is built. Robert Lewis of Exeter University made a valuable contribution during the early stages of our work. Our thanks to Peter Gatrell and Steve Smith for their encouragement, to Roger Munting, Chris Read and Patrick Flood for their highly perceptive criticisms of parts of the manuscript, to András Bereznay for his fine cartography, and to Simon Baker, Anna Henderson and Tim Rees at the University of Exeter Press for their unstinting patience and good counsel. We would also like to pay tribute to Trish Stableford for expert proof-reading most gracefully done.

My own greatest debt is to Dr Francis King of the University of East Anglia. His expertise and help on every facet of commentary and documents alike have been indispensable, and he compiled the list of 'dramatis personae' with biographical details. I am grateful to the British Academy for funding his work on the project, and to the AHRB for funding a period of research leave to enable me to bring the commentary to completion. Finally, I would like to express my gratitude to Tom Stableford of the Slavonic Division at the Bodleian Library, Oxford. He was the prime mover behind the project. He translated the vast majority of the documents. And he proved the most supportive and considerate of collaborators.

Edward Acton
The University of East Anglia

The publishers would like to thank Stanford University Press for permission to reproduce, in document 16, extracts from R.P. Browder and A.F. Kerensky (eds) *The Russian Provisional Government 1917: Documents* (Stanford, CA, 1961) pp. 1386–87.

Note on Transliteration, Russian Words, Acronyms and Dates

In producing a volume of this nature, it is always difficult to decide which Russian words, acronyms and concepts to translate, and which to transliterate. In general, we have proceeded as follows:

Acronyms have been left in their Russian form except where there is a well-established English form, such as CPSU and USSR.

Words denoting specifically Russian administrative regions, weights and measures (*volosti*, *pudy*, etc.) have been transliterated and italicized, and keep their Russian plurals. An exception is the word *rayon*, which corresponds closely enough to the English word 'district' and has therefore been translated. Where Russian words have entered the English language (e.g., 'kulak'), they have been given English plurals and are not italicized. Russian words and acronyms are explained in the glossary.

Transliteration of words and names has been carried out broadly in line with the Taylorian scheme, but certain well-known names (e.g., Zinoviev) are rendered in their familiar form. Likewise, we have used the ending '-sky', as in 'Trotsky', for proper names.

Dates before 1 February 1918 are given according to the Julian Calendar (Old Style). In the twentieth century this ran thirteen days behind the west's Gregorian calendar, which Russia adopted after the revolution, declaring the day following 31 January 1918 (Old Style) to be 14 February 1918 (New Style).

Glossary of Russian Words and Acronyms

ARP — *Antifashistskaya rabochaya partiya*, Anti-Fascist Workers' Party. Phantom organization announced in 1938 by Korets and Landau. See document 197.

artel' (pl. *arteli*) — co-operative association of workmen or peasants.

ASSR — *Avtonomnaya sovetskaya sotsialisticheskaya respublika*, Autonomous Soviet Socialist Republic. Administrative division, denoting an area of a Union republic inhabited by one or more distinct national groups. ASSRs, most of which were in the RSFSR, had a greater degree of autonomy than other administrative divisions on certain legal and cultural matters.

CC — Central Committee.

Cheka (from initial Russian letters CHe Ka) — *Chrezvychaynaya komissiya*, Extraordinary Commission. Soviet political police, 1917–22. Its full title varied over time. Also known as VChK—*Vserossiyskaya ch. k.*, All-Russia Cheka.

chervonets (pl. *chervontsy*) — more stable currency introduced in USSR between 1922 and 1924. Originally the smallest denomination was 10 rubles, and this banknote was red (*chervonnyy*).

CPSU — Communist Party of the Soviet Union.

desyatina (pl. *desyatiny*) — unit of area, equivalent to 2.7 acres.

Edinstvo — 'Unity'. Small social-democratic group around G.V. Plekhanov and his paper of that name 1917–18. It was noted for its support for war to a victorious conclusion and for the Provisional Government.

GARF — *Gosudarstvennyy arkhiv Rossiyskoy Federatsii*, State Archive of the Russian Federation.

GASO — *Gosudarstvennyy arkhiv Sverdlovskoy oblasti*, State Archive of Sverdlovsk *oblast'*.

glavk (pl. *glavki*) — abbr. for *glavnyy komitet*, main committee. In early Soviet

economic organization, production and distribution of various categories
of items came under the control of *glavki*. Hence also *glavkist*, used pejoratively to describe esp. 'War Communist' methods of organization.

Glavmetall — *Glavnoe upravlenie promyshlennosti metalloizdeliy*, Main
Administration for the Production of Metal Items.

GOELRO — State Commission for the Electrification of Russia.

Gosplan — *Gosudarstvennaya planovaya komissiya*, State Planning
Commission, established 1921 to devise plans for the entire Soviet
economy, including all sectors and regions.

GPU — *Gosudarstvennoe politicheskoe upravlenie*, State Political Administration. Successor to the Cheka as Soviet political police, 1922–23.

guberniya (pl. *gubernii*) — large-scale administrative and territorial region of
pre-revolutionary Russia and the USSR before 1929.

GULAG — *Glavnoe upravlenie ispravitel'no-trudovykh lagerey i trudovykh
koloniy*, Main Administration of Corrective Labour Camps and Labour
Colonies.

Komsomol — *Kommunisticheskiy soyuz molodezhi*, Communist League of
Youth. Also known by its longer title, *Vsesoyuznyy Leninskiy kommunis-
ticheskiy soyuz molodezhi* (VLKSM), All-Union Leninist Communist
League of Youth.

Komuch — *Komitet chlenov Uchreditel'nogo sobraniya*, Committee of Members
of the Constituent Assembly—anti-Bolshevik government of Socialist
Revolutionaries (SRs) and liberals briefly established at Samara, 1918.

korenizatsiya — nativization, CPSU policy aimed at ensuring native participation and leadership in the non-Russian areas of the USSR.

KPSS — Kommunisticheskaya partiya Sovetskogo Soyuza.

kray (pl. *kraya*) — large-scale administrative and territorial region in the
USSR after the 1920s, usually inhabited by a discrete and compact national
group (see also *oblast'*).

makhorka — low-grade tobacco cultivated in Russia. See also *papirosy*.

Mezhrayonka — *Mezhdurayonnyy komitet RSDRP*, Inter-district Committee
of the RSDRP — Petrograd-based faction which merged with the
Bolsheviks in the summer of 1917.

MTS — *mashinno-traktornaya stantsiya*, machine-tractor station. Stalin-era
rural institutions which provided agricultural machinery to collective
farms and collected their produce.

Narodniks — nineteenth-century radicals who looked to the peasantry for
the solution to Russia's problems.

NEP — New Economic Policy.

NKVD — *Narodnyy komissariat vnutrennikh del*, People's Commissariat of
Internal Affairs. Largely but not solely concerned with political policing,

it took over the functions of the OGPU in 1934.

nomenklatura — literally 'schedule', list of persons deemed suitable by leading party organs to occupy responsible positions in the USSR. Regarded by some as constituting the 'ruling class' in the USSR.

NOT — *Nauchnaya organizatsiya truda*, scientific organization of labour.

oblast' (pl. *oblasti*) — large-scale administrative and territorial region in the USSR after the 1920s (see also *kray*).

OGPU — *Ob"edinennoe gosudarstvennoe politicheskoe upravlenie pri Sovete Narodnykh Komissarov SSSR*, Unified State Political Administration attached to the Council of People's Commissars of the USSR. Successor to the Cheka and GPU, operated November 1923–July 1934.

okrug (pl. *okruga*) — administrative and territorial region in the USSR after the 1920s, intermediate between *oblast'* and *rayon* (district).

papirosy — traditional Russian-manufactured cheap cigarettes, incorporating low-grade tobacco and a long tubular cardboard mouthpiece. See also *makhorka*.

Pomgol — *Komitet pomoshchi golodayushchim*, Committee to Aid the Starving. Public organization active in famine relief, 1921.

Proletkul't — *Proletarskaya kul'tura*, Proletarian Culture. Unofficial body in early Soviet Russia, associated with A.A. Bogdanov, which carried out cultural and educational activities amongst workers.

pud (pl. *pudy*) — measure of weight, 16.38 kg. or 36 lb.

rabfak (pl. *rabfaki*) — *Rabochiy fakul'tet*, workers' faculty. Further and higher educational institutions established in the 1920s to educate and train people of proletarian origin for skilled and administrative positions.

RAPP — *Rossiyskaya assotsiatsiya proletarskikh pisateley*, Russian Association of Proletarian Writers. Militant writers' organization, later known as VAPP (*Vsesoyuznaya...*, All-Union...).

RGASPI — *Rossiyskiy gosudarstvennyy arkhiv sotsial'no-politicheskoy istorii*, Russian State Archive of Socio-political History. Formerly the Central Party Archive of the CPSU Central Committee Institute of Marxism–Leninism.

RGVA — *Rossiyskiy gosudarstvennyy voennyy arkhiv*, Russian State Military Archive.

RKP(b) — *Rossiyskaya kommunisticheskaya partiya (bol'sheviki)*, Russian Communist Party (Bolsheviks). This was the official designation for the Bolsheviks from early 1918 until the end of 1922, when the USSR was formed. The party then became the *Vsesoyuznaya* [All-Union] *KP(b)*. In this volume the party has been given its familiar English designation of CPSU for the period from 1923.

RS-DLP — Russian Social-Democratic Labour Party.

RSDRP — *Rossiyskaya sotsial-demokraticheskaya rabochaya partiya*, Russian Social-Democratic Workers' Party. Founded 1898, from 1903 the party was split into Bolshevik, Menshevik and various other factions, all of which used the initials RSDRP, sometimes designating the faction in parentheses, sometimes not. After the Bolsheviks renamed themselves RKP(b) in 1918, the initials RSDRP were left to the Mensheviks and a few very small groups.

RSFSR — *Rossiyskaya sovetskaya federativnaya sotsialisticheskaya respublika*, Russian Soviet Federative Socialist Republic.

Samizdat — self-published. Term used to denote unofficial literature circulating in the USSR.

Smena vekh — 'Change of Landmarks', a collection of essays published in 1921 by anti-Communist émigré intellectuals arguing that the Soviet government should be recognized as an established fact and favouring attempts at co-operation with it.

smenovekhovtsy — supporters of the *Smena vekh* line.

smychka — bond, union. Term used to designate the alliance between workers and peasants claimed by the Soviet government during the NEP period.

SO AN — Sibirskoe otdelenie Akademii nauk.

SOTsDOO — *Sverdlovskiy oblastnoy tsentr dokumentatsii obshchestvennykh organizatsiy*, Sverdlovsk *Oblast'* Centre for Documentation of Public Organizations—a local archive.

Sovnarkom — *Sovet Narodnykh Kommissarov*, Council of People's Commissars.

Sovznak — *Sovetskiy denezhnyy znak*, Soviet currency note. Refers to the rapidly depreciating paper money issued by the Soviet authorities 1917–24.

SSR — *Sovetskaya sotsialisticheskaya respublika*, Soviet Socialist Republic, designation for one of the full 'Union republics' of the USSR.

SSSR — Soyuz sovetskikh sotsialisticheskikh respublik.

STO — Labour and Defence Council.

SVB — *Soyuz voinstvuyushchikh bezbozhnikov*, League of the Militant Godless.

TASS — *Telegrafnoe agentstvo Sovetskogo Soyuza*, Telegraph Agency of the Soviet Union. The main Soviet state news agency.

Torgprom — *Rossiyskiy torgovo-promyshlennyy finansovyy soyuz*, Russian Trade Industrial and Financial Union. Émigré organization of exiled Russian capitalists.

TsIK — *Tsentral'nyy ispolnitel'nyy komitet*, Central Executive Committee. General term which also denotes the governing body of the soviets after

June 1917. See also VTsIK.

TsK — *Tsentral'nyy Komitet*, Central Committee.

uezd (pl. *uezdy*) — administrative and territorial region of pre-revolutionary Russia and the USSR before 1929, intermediate between *guberniya* and *volost'*.

UITU — *Upravlenie ispravitel'no-trudovykh uchrezhdeniy*, Administration of Corrective Labour Institutions.

USSR — Union of Soviet Socialist Republics.

VAPP see RAPP.

VChK see Cheka.

VKP(b) see RKP(b).

volost' (pl. *volosti*) — administrative and territorial region of pre-revolutionary Russia and the USSR before 1929, generally containing several villages.

VSNKh — *Vysshiy sovet narodnogo khozyaystva*, Supreme Council of the National Economy. Established at the end of 1917 to co-ordinate all economic activity in Russia, it quickly became in effect the industrial commissariat.

VTsIK — *Vserossiyskiy/Vsesoyuznyy tsentral'nyy ispolnitel'nyy komitet*, All-Russia or, from 1924, All-Union Central Executive Committee. The VTsIK of soviets played a role in some respects analogous to a parliament in the early Soviet period.

zemstvo — local administrative body in parts of Imperial Russia 1864–1917, with some social functions, elected on limited franchise.

Zhenotdel — *zhenskiy otdel*, Women's Department of the CPSU.

ZSFSR — *Zakavkazskaya sovetskaya federativnaya sotsialisticheskaya respublika*, Transcaucasian Soviet Federative Socialist Republic, unified early Soviet republic composed of Georgia, Armenia and Azerbaidzhan.

Introduction

For historians of the Soviet Union, the period since the onset of Gorbachev's glasnost in 1986 and the collapse of communist rule in 1991 has been supremely exhilarating. Russian and other ex-Soviet scholars, freed from the shackles of Marxism–Leninism, have begun to grapple with the epic tale of the USSR. Specialists in the west, no longer working under the shadow of the Cold War and stimulated by the intellectual shift known as 'the linguistic turn', have opened up entirely fresh research areas and in some cases drastically revised conventional wisdom about the Soviet story. Meanwhile, both processes of reassessment have been fed by the release of a wealth of new archival material—political, social, economic, military and cultural. The purpose here is to bring these three ingredients together to provide non-Russian readers with a taste of the intellectual feast that is under way.

The case for doing so is strong. For three generations the USSR constituted a massive presence and an essential part of the mental furniture of humanity. Despite its disappearance from the geo-political and ideological map, much about today's world is inexplicable without an understanding of it. Equally, without such an understanding, the lessons drawn from the rise, development and failure of this first 'socialist' experiment are unlikely to be sound. Students and a wider public must have a sense of the primary sources on the basis of which Soviet history is being rewritten and which convey, as nothing else can, its flavour and smell, the distinctive ethos and culture that was the USSR. Only then will the insights of recent scholarship erase the misconceptions moulded by the Cold War and perpetuated in widely used western textbooks, fiction and journalism, be they about the explanation for Bolshevik victory in 1917, Soviet policy towards the minority nationalities, the number of victims of the terror in the 1930s, the scale of the Soviet contribution to Hitler's defeat, the process that ultimately destabilized the USSR, or the acute tension between democratic and free-market reform under Gorbachev.[1]

The format used is a documentary history which weaves a narrative commentary around and through a sequence of substantial primary sources. The narrative links the documents, sets them in context and draws attention to significant features, supported by a listing of 'dramatis personae' which provides key details on most of the hundreds of individuals mentioned. The documents—state and party papers, speeches, letters, newspaper and journal articles, diaries and memoirs—give the narrative weight, texture and nuance. Together they offer a broad entrée to recent debate and current historio-graphical developments, while the footnotes point to carefully selected and accessible secondary studies through which readers without Russian can delve deeper into the issues raised and into specialist work produced in the west, in the former Soviet Union, and, most strikingly, by direct collabora-tion between scholars from both.

The bulk of the documents are drawn from a lively collection published in Russian in the mid-1990s which contains a wealth of material unavail-able in English. That two-volume collection, *Istoriya Rossii* [*The History of Russia*]: *1917–1940* (Ekaterinburg 1993) and *Rossiya, kotoruyu my ne znali* [*The Russia We Did Not Know*], *1939–1993* (Chelyabinsk 1995), was compiled at the A.M. Gorky Urals State University under the editorial direc-tion of M.E. Glavatsky. Naturally, it reflects the preoccupations of Russian scholars and citizens in the immediate aftermath of the fall of the USSR. It foregrounds features that had been concealed by the Soviet regime and passed over in silence by official Soviet historiography; rectifies the tendency for Marxist–Leninist accounts to underplay peasant experience; gives due atten-tion to religion and repression; ponders moments—1918, 1929, 1945, the 1960s—when Soviet history might have taken a very different turn; and highlights themes that seemed most meaningful in a society undergoing the traumatic political and economic reconstruction of the early 1990s.

The Urals collection thus took for granted considerable familiarity with major features of the Soviet story. From a western perspective, it somewhat underplayed material focused squarely on long-standing controversies such as the extent of support for Lenin in 1917, the explanation for Stalin's polit-ical triumph in the 1920s, and the merits and demerits of a 'totalitarian' model for understanding the USSR. There was also relatively little material consciously addressed to questions that have moved more recently to the top

---

1 The epitome of the yawning gap between conventional wisdom and archival evidence is the contrast between the analysis of the scale of repression in the 1930s explored below, pp. 309–10, 360–1, and the discredited estimates favoured, for example, by Norman Davies' influential *Europe: A History* (Oxford 1996) or Martin Amis's high-profile novel *Koba the Dread: Laughter and the twenty million* (London 2002).

of the western agenda—discourse analysis, social and national identity construction, and changing gender roles.[2] We have therefore supplemented the collection, introducing a number of additional documents to make a rounded and free-standing whole. Concern to retain the flavour of the original, as well as space constraints, mean, however, that coverage of some important subjects has been sacrificed. Nationality issues and foreign policy, in particular, receive much less attention in Volume 1 than in Volume 2, which will run from the diplomatic antecedents of the Great Patriotic War to the final fracturing of the USSR along the national fault-lines of its fifteen Union Republics.

On the other hand, we have been able to preserve ingredients which complement current western research and are as yet inadequately addressed in standard western treatments—the multifaceted forms of lower-class evasion and resistance, new light on the scale of mass killings, the repression and survival of the Orthodox Church, the mutation of Marxist–Leninist ideology, the extent to which that ideology was internalized. One feature merits special mention. In Volume 1, documents unearthed in the Sverdlovsk archives covering the Urals region in the 1920s and 1930s bring to life the regional dimension, the concerns and fate of the regional party leadership, and the often fraught interaction between the Kremlin and the far-flung territories over which it ruled. The view from the Urals—the first and one of the largest of the new *oblasti* of the USSR, responsible for the most ambitious projects of the First Five-Year Plan, location of the largest forced-labour camps in the 1930s, and object of full-scale devastation in the Great Terror—provides a valuable counterpoint to the All-Union story. The recovery of regional perspectives is among the many advances through which ex-Soviet historians are succeeding, despite the desperate shortage of resources for higher education and research in most of the former USSR, in casting fresh light on the whole field.[3]

---

2 For illuminating discussion of the differences between the current concerns of ex-Soviet and western historians, focusing on the pre-revolutionary period, see D.L. Ransel, 'A Single Research Community: Not yet', and the forum on B.N. Mironov's new history of imperial Russia in *Slavic Review* 60 (2001) pp. 550–98.

3 There is a galaxy of Russian-language websites expanding the archival material, local and regional as well as All-Union, available on line. For some links to the growing number available in English, see, e.g., uea.ac.uk/his/webcours/russia/welcome/.

Further Reading

This selection of English-language studies provides a guide to the multi-faceted reappraisal of early Soviet history underway since the fall of the USSR

Acton, E., Rosenberg , W.G., Cherniaev, V. (eds) *Critical Companion to the Russian Revolution* (London 1997)

Applebaum, A. *Gulag: A History of the Soviet Camps* (London 2003)

Brandenberger, D. *National Bolshevism: Stalinist Mass Culture and the Formation of Modern Russian National Identity, 1931–1956* (Harvard, Mass. 2002)

Brooks, J. *Thank You Comrade Stalin! Soviet Public Culture from Revolution to Cold War* (Princeton N.J. 2000)

Davies, R.D., Harrison, M., Wheatcroft, S.G. (eds) *The Economic Transformation of the Soviet Union, 1913–1945* (Cambridge, 1994)

Figes, O. *A People's Tragedy. The Russian Revolution, 1891–24* (London 1996)

Fitzpatrick, S. *Everyday Stalinism. Ordinary Life in Extraordinary Times: Soviet Russia in the 1930s* (Oxford 1999)

Fitzpatrick, S. *Stalin's Peasants. Resistance and Survival in the Russian Village After Collectivization* (Oxford 1994)

Gatrell, P. *Empire Walking. Refugees in Russia During World War I* (Bloomington, Ind. 1999)

Getty, J.A. & Manning, R. (eds) *Stalinist Terror* (Cambridge 1993)

Haynes, M. & Husan, R. *A Century of State Murder? Death and Policy in Twentieth Century Russia* (London 2003)

Hoffman, D.L. (ed) *Stalinism. The Essential Readings* (Oxford 2003)

Hosking, G. *A History of the Soviet Union* (London 1992, revised ed.)

Jansen M. and Petrov, N. *Stalin's Loyal Executioner: People's Commissar Nikolai Ezhov 1895–1940* (Stanford, Cal. 2002)

Kotkin, S. *Magnetic Mountain. Stalinism as a Civilization* (Berkeley, Cal. 1995)

McLoughlin, B. and McDermott K. (eds) *Stalin's Terror: High Politics and Mass Repression in the Soviet Union* (New York 2003)

Martin, T. *The Affirmative Action Empire. Nations and Nationalism in the Soviet Union, 1923–1939* (Ithaca, N.Y. 2001)

Nove, A. *An Economic History of the USSR* (London 1992, revised ed.)

Read, C. *From Tsar to Soviets. The Russian people & their revolution* (London 1996)

Read, C. *The Making and Breaking of the Soviet System: An Interpretation*(London 2001)

Service, R. *Lenin: A Biography* (London 2000)

Service, R. *Stalin. A Biography* (2004)

Siegelbaum, L. H. *Soviet state and society between revolutions, 1918–1929* (Cambridge 1992)

Smele, J.D. *Civil War in Siberia: The Anti-Bolshevik Government of Admiral Kolchak, 1918–1920* (Cambridge 1996)

Smith, S. *The Russian Revolution. A very short introduction* (Oxford 2002)

Suny, R. *The Revenge of the Past. Nationalism, Revolution and the Collapse of the Soviet Union* (Stanford, Cal. 1993)

Suny, R.G. *The Soviet Experiment. Russia, the USSR and the Successor States* (Oxford, 1998)

Viola, L. *Peasant Rebels Under Stalin. Collectivization and the Culture of Peasant Resistance* (Oxford 1996)

Wade, R. *The Russian Revolution 1917* (London 2000)

Ward, C. *Stalin's Russia* (London 1999)

Maps

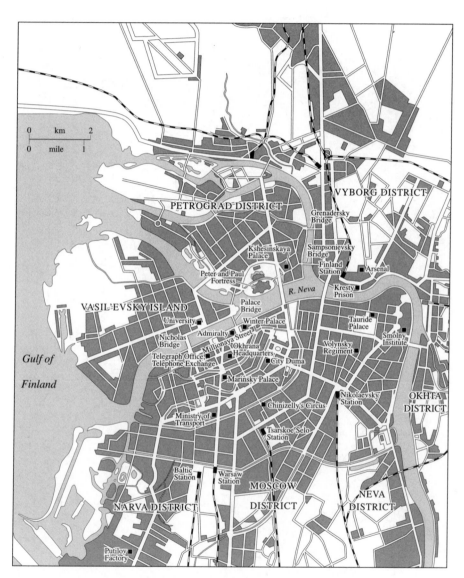

1. Petrograd, 1917: The capital and its landmarks at the time of the revolution

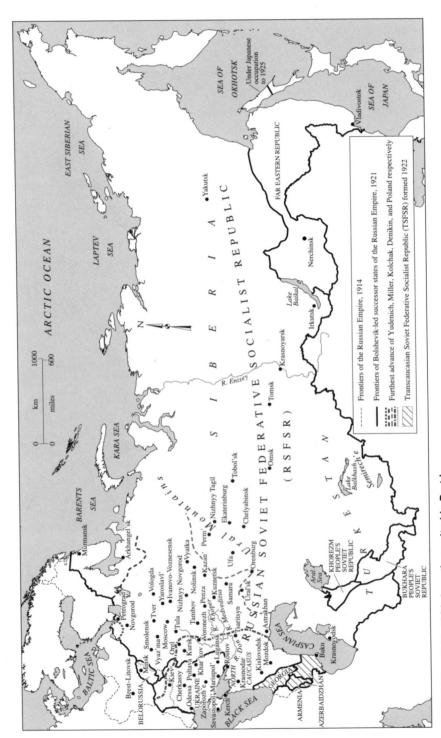

2. Civil War, 1918–1921: Locations cited in Part I

3. European Russia/Western USSR, 1918–1939: Cities, towns and villages cited in the text

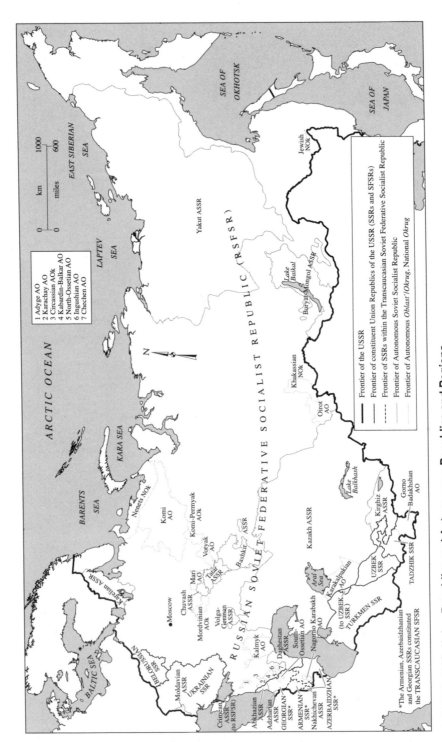

4. USSR, 1929: Union Republics and Autonomous Republics and Regions

**5. The Urals *oblast'*, 1930: Administrative districts and locations within the *oblast'*
cited in Part III**

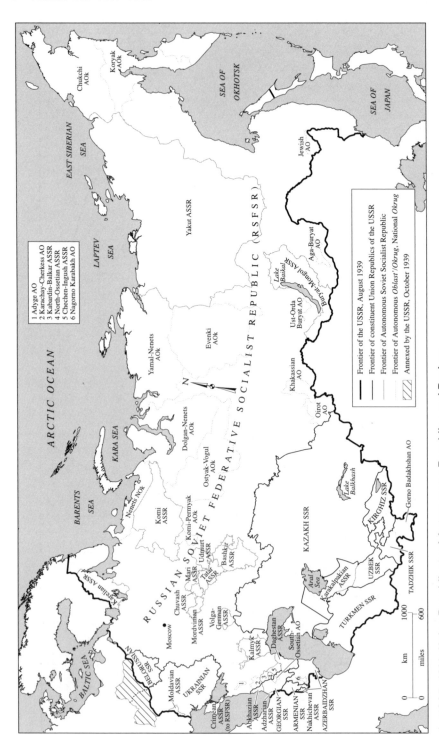

6. USSR, 1939: Union Republics and Autonomous Republics and Regions

PART ONE

REVOLUTION AND CIVIL WAR
(1917–1921)

In February 1917, Russia's 300-year old Tsarist regime was swept away by mass protest among workers and soldiers in the capital, triggering an explosion of political activity across the fallen Empire. For eight months a Provisional Government of liberals and moderate socialists struggled to contain working-class and peasant pressure for an end to the war with Germany and her allies, and for a fundamental redistribution in power and property. In October 1917, with its authority in tatters, the Provisional Government was itself overthrown in a second revolution. Power was seized by the Bolshevik party, which had been positioned by its leader, Lenin, to be the most effective vehicle for popular radicalism. The new revolutionary government promptly withdrew Russia from the war, endorsed peasant seizure of privately-owned land and proclaimed sweeping reforms. The sequel, however, was economic implosion and a bloody and destructive civil war as the privileged victims of political and social upheaval sought to reverse the verdict of 1917. The counter-revolutionary White armies failed abjectly to win popular support, and by 1921 had been crushed by the Red Army. But by then the desperate struggle to mobilize men, grain and resources had provoked mass unrest against the regime. The civil war had also nurtured the most authoritarian features of Bolshevik culture, and in 1921 Lenin entrenched a highly coercive one-party state.

1

The February Revolution and the
Provisional Government

The overthrow of the Tsar

The outbreak of war in 1914 gave the Tsar's deeply unpopular government temporary respite from the social unrest and political opposition that had confronted it in the pre-war years. From 1915, however, the number of industrial stoppages began to climb, underground revolutionary activity regained some of the momentum it had lost, and liberal politicians cautiously but openly attacked official incompetence. During the winter of 1916/17, after two and a half years of gruelling war, worsening food shortages, spiralling inflation and mounting disdain for Nicholas II and the succession of short-lived ministries he appointed, a storm of protest overthrew the regime.[1]

Wave upon wave of workers' strikes in the capital culminated in a general strike in the last days of February. Workers were joined by white-collar employees, teachers and students in mass anti-government demonstrations which converged on the city centre. With the police hopelessly over-stretched, the Tsar's survival depended on the willingness of the large number of troops garrisoned in Petrograd to implement the order he sent from the Front for the unrest to be suppressed by force. On Sunday 26 February a minority of troops opened fire, but the majority, consisting of conscripted reservists whose respect for their officers and established authority in general had reached breaking point, refused to do so and the following day soldiers streamed from their barracks to fraternize with civilians. With the autocracy helpless, socialist intellectuals and war-time labour leaders reconvened the Soviet (Council) of Workers' Deputies first established during the revolu-

---

1 For three admirable recent syntheses on the period of the revolution and the civil war, see O. Figes, *A People's Tragedy: The Russian Revolution, 1891–1924* (London 1996); C. Read, *From Tsar to Soviets: The Russian people and their revolution* (London 1996); R. Wade, *The Russian Revolution 1917* (London 2000).

tion of 1905. At the same time, the State Duma leaders, whose exasperation with the Tsar had been tempered by their alarm at the prospect of revolution, hesitantly set up a 'Provisional Committee', headed by the Duma President, M.V. Rodzyanko, a right-wing liberal, with a view to forming a new government should the old order prove beyond repair.

That momentous week in Petrograd is viewed here through the eyes of M.M. Prishvin, a writer and journalist temporarily serving as secretary to the Deputy Minister of Trade and Industry. Although Prishvin had been radical in his student days, he shared none of the exultation of the revolutionaries and workers on whose accounts of February 1917 generations of Soviet students were to be reared. He observes the sense of excitement among the lower classes as the imperial coat-of-arms is torn down and social deference is replaced by democratic camaraderie—everyone is 'Comrade' (*tovarishch*). But he despises the attempts by Social Democrats to dictate what other journalists may print and is quick to cite those who predict no good from the onset of 'socialism'.

Document 1 | Extracts from M.M. Prishvin's diary

Petrograd, 1917
26 February

No papers came out today, the 26th. The whole city is full of troops. 'Who are you guarding, then?', said some woman to a soldier. And it was obvious he didn't know the answer: the enemy, his own people. . .

Right now all of politics and state policy can be expressed in the word 'bread'. Just as at the beginning the whole life of the state lay in the word 'war', now it's 'bread!'. . . So a historian will call the first part of the epoch *War* and the second *Bread*. . .

27 February
About three this afternoon I went to the Director with my report on the Kuznetsov factory, and he said it made no difference anyway, the Ordnance management had been taken over by mutinous troops. The remand prison had been opened—the political prisoners had been let out, and so on. . . But we're still writing memos to the Ministry of Agriculture that owing to a shortage of flour and fish the coal mines of the Donetsk Basin will have to cease work; owing to a shortage of oats the Nevyansk works will have to cease timber transport. . . As we left the Ministry we looked at a big fire on the Vyborg Side—the remand prison or the Arsenal?

. . . I rang [the artist] Petrov-Vodkin, but he didn't know anything, was busy with some beautiful water-colour and was very surprised. I was trying to get to [the writer] Remizov's and had got as far as the No. 8 tram when a machine-gun opened up and then rifles from here and there; shots rang out, fire was returned, somebody was running away, somebody was laughing, just like being near the Front in the war, but much worse here in the city at night. . . Yet the telephone was still working, so I rang Remizov to tell him I hadn't been able to get there.

The porter's wife said, 'They've joined, the troops have joined!'. . . Whatever was going on was all for the best and was God's righteous anger, she said. 'Some little old man got two pounds of bread in a queue, so the poor soul just lay there with the bread in his arms. . .'

28 February
Medical units and soup kitchens are being organized at the University; all the news here says that the Duma and the Council have been dissolved and have sent a telegram to the Tsar. There was shooting near our house in the evening: a police-officer's hiding out round here somewhere. . .

There's a rumour that the Tsar's agreed to 'join'—all day people round here were saying that it all depends on the Tsar now.

1 March
It's evidently been completely forgotten that calming down the revolution depends on the Tsar. Some young student came to tell us about a meeting in the City Duma where the Social Democrats were demanding priority for the first victims. He told us excitedly that Social Democracy didn't express the people's wishes. At a meeting at the University it was obvious that the Social Democrats' manifesto—published on a single sheet alongside Rodzyanko's orders—had caused this confusion: they reckon there's two governments: the Social Democratic one and the Duma Provisional one. . .

The porter's wife opened the door for me and I wanted to dispel all my bad feelings about her joy, using her words—everybody's joined—but she said gloomily, 'Who knows whether we'll be better off from all this?' Astonished, I looked at her and asked what the matter was. She told me in minute detail that a police officer living in this building had run away, but just now some soldier with a gun had come and pestered her about where he was, and threatened her. . . What's happening in the rest of Russia is a frightening question, but nobody knows. . . Somebody says the happy feeling's just like Easter.

On the telephone they're saying Moscow's joined, Novgorod's joined. There's a rumour that the Tsar's telegram ordering suppression at all costs was just shelved. . .

2 March
The Duma's like the mouth of a volcano. There's a cooking pot under the rostrum and soldiers are eating. There's a soldiers' meeting in the Catherine Hall, and growing anger among journalists at the Social Democrats' dictatorship. . .

3 March
We went outside and listened with everybody to the news of an agreement between two committees and the new ministries' orders. A beautiful day—sunny and frosty.

March. And the people's increasing joy. There was an enormous amount of traffic on the Nevsky; illuminated Imperial coats-of-arms were being taken down, piled up in a heap and burnt. In shop windows there were announcements about the Tsar's abdication. There were processions of workers and soldiers with banners calling for a socialist republic, and they were singing the Russian version of the Marseillaise ('God Save the Tsar' no longer exists).

The chronicler Svatikov has been appointed the Mayor's assistant. . . a huge number of 'Svatikov's men' have appeared, most of them semi-literate journalists. One of them made us wait a whole hour in the Duma for a pass, while we were discussing whether to bribe him with 5 kopecks extra a line. One of them (Steklov), having received notification from the Executive Committee that it was permitting the publication of some five newspapers, informed us waiting journalists that we could print only what was being printed in *Izvestiya*. We were stunned.

5 March
Bells—the first time I've heard bells, it's Sunday. A long queue of people waiting for the morning papers. And when they came out, all day people from different parts of the city were carrying home whatever papers they could get like bunches of flowers or pussy-willows. 'Break through' and 'offensive' were the most common words. Over there, at the Front (in the State Duma), perhaps they're afraid of collapse, but here, in the rear, a real great victory's being celebrated. 'Comrades,' says the cabby, 'mind your backs, please!' 'Comrade,' says an officer to a cabby, 'take me to Liteyny.' Huge paper flowers are in vogue, and soldiers are sticking them to their chests and stomachs. . . A huge angry crowd follows a serviceman, and you can hear them saying 'Arrest him!', just because he'd said, after listening to a soap-box orator, 'Just you wait, socialism's going to cause you a lot of trouble.' You can't say everything aloud (freedom of speech?). Borodaevsky's composed an anthem, but I don't like it, so I've altered the words of 'God save the Tsar' and unconsciously hum it, but barely audibly. Then I stop myself—maybe somebody can hear me. . . and what if somebody really does?

13 March
In the bank I met an old chap, my first real Russian provincial—'Republic or monarchy?,' I asked him. 'A republic, because you can change it.' 'But what about the anointed sovereign?' 'It says in the Scriptures that there'll be anointed sovereigns from Michael to this Michael, the last Michael, and that's it. Times are different now. Men must come closer to each other and will perhaps come to know God better, 'cause they've forgotten Him, you know.'

[Source: *Literaturnaya ucheba* No. 3, 1990, pp. 88–93.]

The Petrograd Soviet, established by predominantly Menshevik and Socialist Revolutionary (SR) intellectuals and workers' leaders and convened in the Tauride Palace under the same roof as the Duma, was quickly engulfed by soldiers pouring in from one regiment after another to announce their support for the revolution. It was agreed by acclamation that the Soviet should represent soldiers as well as workers and that military units should elect deputies alongside those chosen in factories. Over the following forty-eight hours, alarm grew among the rank and file that the newly formed Military Commission, though formally acting for the Soviet as well as the Provisional Committee of the Duma, was restoring the authority of officers whose sympathy for their mutiny and for the revolution was, like that of the Duma's liberal leaders themselves, skin-deep. On 1 March radicalized soldiers demanded that the Soviet formally legitimize a drastic shift in relations between men and officers. Eager to consolidate the soldiers' allegiance to the Soviet, the Executive Committee (EC) agreed to do so, and issued the Soviet's most famous decree, Order Number One. It subordinated the Military Commission to its own authority, sanctioned the election of soldiers' committees in all units, empowered them with control over weapons, and humbled officers with strict orders to respect the dignity and civil rights of their men. The edict was addressed to the Petrograd Military District, but news of it spread rapidly after its publication by the Soviet's newspaper, *Izvestiya*. It chimed so exactly with soldiers' grievances everywhere that it triggered the immediate formation of highly assertive and radical soldiers' committees both at the Front and in garrisons across the country. The effect was to sap officers' authority and render it all but impossible for those on the political right to use force to crush the revolution.[2]

Document 2 | Order Number One

1 March 1917

The Soviet of Workers' and Soldiers' Deputies has decreed:

1) In all companies, battalions, regiments, depots, batteries, squadrons, military administrative departments and warships, committees of elected representatives from the lower ranks of the above-mentioned units are to be elected immediately.
2) In all units which have not yet elected their representatives to the Soviet of Workers' Deputies a company representative is to be selected to appear with written identification at the State Duma building by 10 a.m. tomorrow, 2 March.
3) In all political statements units must be subordinate to the Soviet of Workers' and Soldiers' Deputies and its committees.

---

2 See A.K. Wildman, *The End of the Imperial Army* Volume I (Princeton 1980), chapter 7.

4) The orders of the military commission of the State Duma must be obeyed, except where they contradict the orders and decrees of the Soviet of Workers' and Soldiers' Deputies.

5) All weapons—rifles, machine-guns, armoured cars and the like—must be at the disposal and under the control of company and battalion committees and under no circumstances issued to officers—even on demand.

6) Soldiers on duty must maintain the strictest military discipline, but off duty, in their political, civilian and private lives, can in no way be deprived of the rights enjoyed by all citizens. In particular, standing to attention and obligatory saluting while off duty are abolished.

7) Similarly, special forms of address for officers are abolished, e.g., *Your Excellency, Your Honour* and suchlike are to be replaced by *Mr General, Mr Colonel*, etc. Rude behaviour (in particular using the familiar 'thou') towards soldiers of any rank is forbidden and any violation of this, along with all misunderstandings between officers and soldiers, must be brought by the latter to the attention of company committees.

[Source: *Izvestiya Petrogradskogo Soveta rabochikh i soldatskikh deputatov*, 2 March 1917.]

With the old regime in disarray and the prestige of the Petrograd Soviet rising fast, the liberal leaders of the Duma's Provisional Committee moved to establish a Provisional Government. As they did so, Rodzyanko faded into the background and the dominant position passed to P.N. Milyukov, the leader of the main liberal party, the Constitutional Democrats (Kadets). Knowing that the Duma, elected on a restricted franchise five years earlier, lacked legitimacy among the lower classes, Milyukov and his colleagues were anxious to secure the support of the Soviet and its socialist leaders. To their delight, hastily organized talks with a delegation from the Soviet EC on 2 March revealed that the socialists were more than willing to provide support and had no wish themselves to form or even to be directly represented in the government—A.F. Kerensky was the only socialist to join the 'bourgeois' Cabinet and he secured Soviet approval by appealing over the heads of the EC to the rank and file. Moreover, rather than pressing 'socialist' demands for swift land, social and labour reform, an early peace and the immediate abolition of the monarchy, the EC concentrated instead on insisting that the new government commit itself to democratization and steps to establish civil liberty.[3] Apart from the unwelcome clause granting special guarantees to militant units of the Petrograd garrison, the new liberal government was happy to adopt the programme urged upon it.

---

3 The memoirs of one of the key Menshevik Internationalists, N.N. Sukhanov, *The Russian Revolution, 1917: A personal record*, translated and abridged by J. Carmichael (Princeton 1984), provide the most vivid account of the negotiations, pp. 16–160.

Document 3 | The composition and aims of the First Provisional Government

3 March 1917

Citizens!

The Provisional Committee of the State Duma, with the assistance and sympathy of the troops and people of Petrograd, has at present achieved such a degree of success over the dark forces of the old regime that it can set about a more durable organization of executive power.

To this end the Provisional Committee of the State Duma is appointing the following persons as ministers in the first cabinet to represent the public. Their previous social and political activity has earned them the country's trust:

Chairman of the Council of Ministers and Minister of Home Affairs: Prince G.E. L'vov
Foreign Minister: P.N. Milyukov
Minister of Defence: A.I. Guchkov
Minister of Transport: N.V. Nekrasov
Minister of Trade and Industry: A.I. Konovalov
Minister of Finance: M.I. Tereshchenko
Minister of Education: A.A. Manuylov
Procurator of the Holy Synod: V.N. L'vov
Minister of Agriculture: A.I. Shingarev
Minister of Justice: A.F. Kerensky

In its activities the Cabinet will be guided by the following principles:

1) A complete and immediate amnesty for all political and religious prisoners, including those convicted of terrorist attacks, mutiny and agrarian offences.
2) Freedom of speech, of the press, of association, of assembly, and to strike, with the extension of political freedoms to servicemen within the limits permitted by military considerations.
3) The abolition of all caste, religious and national restrictions.
4) Immediate preparation for the convening, on the principles of universal, equal, secret and direct suffrage, of a Constituent Assembly, which will establish the form of government and the Constitution of the country.
5) The replacement of the police by a people's militia with elected officers answerable to the local authorities.
6) The election of local authorities on the principles of universal, equal, secret and direct suffrage.
7) Those military units which took part in the revolutionary movement to be neither disarmed nor withdrawn from Petrograd.
8) While preserving strict military discipline on duty and during military service, the abolition of all restrictions on soldiers exercising the civil rights enjoyed by other citizens.

The Provisional Government considers it its duty to add that it does not in any way intend to use military considerations to delay the implementation of the above-mentioned reforms and measures.

Chairman of the State Duma M. Rodzyanko
Chairman of the Council of Ministers Prince L'vov
Ministers Milyukov, Nekrasov, Manuylov, Konovalov, Tereshchenko, V. L'vov, Shingarev, Kerensky

[Source: *Izvestiya Petrogradskogo Soveta rabochikh i soldatskikh deputatov*, 3 March 1917.]

The Soviet EC had agreed to support the new Provisional Government because they could see no viable alternative. The Menshevik majority on the EC, in line with their Marxist assumptions, regarded as premature any notion of a socialist government in a country as backward and poor as Russia and in a society where the working class was overwhelmingly outnumbered by peasants. Even the more radical among them were convinced that, given the acute danger of counter-revolutionary intervention from the Front, it was vital to bind the liberals and their 'bourgeois' followers to the revolution and that the surest way to do so was to allow Milyukov and his colleagues to form a government.[4] Rank-and-file opinion in the Soviet, however, was decidedly suspicious of the emergent Kadet-dominated Cabinet. When publicly announcing support for the new government, therefore, the EC did so in guarded terms and only 'in so far as' it honoured its commitment to civil liberty and the destruction of the old regime. At the same time, the socialist leaders underlined the need for discipline and order on the streets, and above all for harmony between soldiers and those officers willing to defend the revolution against the continued threat of an attempt by the right to restore the old order by force.

Document 4 | From the Executive Committee of the Soviet of Workers' and Soldiers' Deputies

3 March 1917

Comrades and Citizens!

Today the new government created from the moderate strata of society announced all the reforms which it has undertaken to implement, partly while the struggle with the old regime continues, and partly once it is finished. Some of these reforms should

---

4 See Z. Galili, *The Menshevik Leaders in the Russian Revolution: Social realities and political strategies* (Princeton 1989), pp. 45–68.

be welcomed among broad democratic circles, e.g., the political amnesty, the commitment to prepare for the Constituent Assembly, the implementation of civil rights and the abolition of nationality restrictions. We consider that in so far as the emergent government acts to further these obligations and struggle decisively with the old order, the democratic forces should render their support.

Comrades and Citizens!

The complete victory of the Russian people over the old order is approaching, but for this victory huge efforts and exceptional endurance and firmness are still needed. Disunity and anarchy must not be allowed. All instances of disorder, robbery, burglary, theft and damage of property and pointless seizure of public buildings must be stopped immediately. Anarchy and the collapse of discipline ruin the revolution and the freedom of the people.

The danger of military action against the revolution has not yet been removed. In order to forestall it, it is extremely important to ensure a spirit of co-operation between soldiers and officers. Officers to whom the interests of freedom and the progressive development of the Motherland are dear should make every effort to collaborate smoothly with the soldiers. They will respect a soldier's personal and civil dignity and be careful of his sense of honour. For their part soldiers will remember that an army's strength depends on unity between officers and men, and that not all officers should be damned because of the bad behaviour of certain individuals. For the sake of the revolution soldiers should exercise patience and ignore petty offences against democracy on the part of those officers who have joined the decisive and final struggle you are waging against the old regime.

[Source: *Izvestiya Petrogradskogo Soveta rabochikh i soldatskikh deputatov*, 3 March 1917.]

While the liberal and Soviet leaders were negotiating the formation of the Provisional Government, the Tsar was bowing to pressure from the High Command for him to abdicate. At first General Alekseev (Chief-of-Staff) and his colleagues had concurred with Nicholas's order for a punitive expedition to be sent from the Front to crush the insurrection in Petrograd. However, the version of events in the capital conveyed to Alekseev by Rodzyanko quickly led the High Command to change their minds.[5] They became convinced that the resort to force was liable to fail and to trigger civil war; that the best hope of calming the situation, limiting unrest among troops at the Front, and sustaining the war effort lay in bolstering the emergent Provisional Government; and that anti-monarchist fever in the capital had reached a pitch where no government identified in any way with

5 See T. Hasegawa, *The February Revolution: Petrograd 1917* (Seattle 1981), for what is still the best account of the February revolution in general and this interplay between the liberal leaders and the High Command in particular, pp. 473–86.

Nicholas could survive. The High Command's opinion swayed the Tsar and he resolved to step down, deciding at the last minute to do so on behalf of Aleksey, the haemophiliac Tsarevich, as well as himself, and to pass the throne to his younger brother, Mikhail. The following day Milyukov tried desperately to convince Mikhail that he should accept, but he was persuaded not to do so by other members of the Provisional Committee and the throne fell vacant.

Document 5 | The abdication of Nicholas II

3:05 p.m., 2 March 1917
GHQ Pskov
To the Chief-of-Staff

During a great struggle with an external enemy who has been trying for nearly three years to enslave Our homeland the Lord God has deemed fit to send a grave new trial upon Russia. The domestic disturbances among the people which have begun threaten to have a calamitous effect on the further conduct of a hard-fought war. The fate of Russia, the honour of Our heroic army, the good of the people and the whole future of Our beloved Fatherland demand that at all costs the war be pursued to a victorious conclusion. The cruel enemy is straining every sinew, and the hour is close when Our valiant army together with Our glorious allies will finally be able to smash the enemy. At such a decisive time in the life of Russia We have deemed it Our duty to facilitate for Our people the close unity and cohesion of all popular forces necessary for the rapid achievement of victory, and in agreement with the State Duma We have considered it right to abdicate and lay down supreme power. Not wishing to part with Our beloved son, we transfer the succession to Our brother Grand Duke Mikhail Aleksandrovich and bless him upon his accession to the Russian throne. We enjoin Our brother to run the affairs of state in complete and indissoluble unity with the representatives of the people in the legislative institutions according to the principles which they will establish, and to swear an unbreakable oath to do so. In the name of Our dearly beloved homeland We call upon all true sons of the Fatherland to carry out their sacred duty to it, to obey their Tsar at this difficult time of trial for all, and to help him, together with the people's representatives, to lead the Russian state along the path of victory, prosperity and glory.

May the Lord God help Russia!

Nicholas

Ratified by Adjutant-General Count Fredericks, Minister of the Imperial Court.

[Source: *Izvestiya Petrogradskogo Soveta rabochikh i soldatskikh deputatov*, 4 March 1917.]

The Provisional Government and popular radicalization

Among the gravest problems facing the Provisional Government when it came to office was the food shortage which had fuelled unrest in the cities and at the Front. During the war, peasants found less and less incentive to sell their grain: inflation rapidly eroded the value of rubles and as non-military manufacture declined, there were fewer and fewer goods available that peasants wanted to buy.[6] The Provisional Government's response was to proclaim a grain monopoly: all producers were to hand over their surplus grain at prices fixed by the government and affordable by consumers. In practice, however, the monopoly remained in large measure a fiction.[7] The first Minister of Agriculture, the Kadet A.I. Shingarev, was unenthusiastic, as were landowners and merchants appointed to the higher food-supply committees. Peasants on village-level committees were no keener. The price the government offered for grain, even when doubled in August, failed to keep pace with inflation and in particular with the rising price of manufactures—and the government backed away from imposing price-control on manufacturers. Coy reference in March to 'special instructions' in the case of non-compliance with the grain monopoly soon gave way to clear authorization for the use of force, but ministers remained reluctant to resort to coercion—and in any case had ever fewer troops on whom they could rely.

Document 6 | From a Provisional Government decree establishing a grain monopoly

25 March 1917

1. All grain, the harvest and fodder of previous years, of 1916 and of this year, excluding those stocks set out in Articles 3 and 4 and those necessary for the owner's provision and economic needs, are, from the time of registration, as set out in Article 5, to be at the disposal of the state and may be disposed of only through the medium of state rationing bodies...

3. Exempt from requisition are seed-corn, grain for feeding the producer, his family, and others employed by his household and dependent upon it for grain, as well as grain for economic needs (fodder)...

---

6 For a succinct analysis of the war's economic impact, see P. Gatrell, 'The First World War and War Communism' in R.W. Davies et al. (eds) *The Economic Transformation of the Soviet Union, 1913–1945* (Cambridge 1994) pp. 216–27.

7 L. Lih, *Bread and Authority in Russia, 1914–1921* (Berkeley and Los Angeles 1990), explores the continuities as well as the contrasts between the ways in which the Tsarist government, the Provisional Government and the early Bolshevik government tried to tackle the problem.

4. Local rationing committees shall be authorized to determine the standards by which grain from the 1916 harvest and previous years shall be exempted from requisitioning under the preceding article, on the basis of the following considerations. . .

5. Every owner of grain, including the consumer, is obliged to declare when so requested by the local rationing body:

a) the amount and place of storage of his available stocks

b) the number of mouths to be fed

c) the number of cattle owned and the size of the area under crops

d) The procedure and times for grain delivery are to be established by the local rationing committee. . .

8. All grain, with the exception of that mentioned in Articles 3 and 4, is to be delivered at specified times (Article 6) to the local rationing body or its agent at a fixed price. In the event of hoarded supplies being discovered, they will be requisitioned by the state at half the fixed price. . .

21. In cases when someone refuses to deliver grain voluntarily, requisitioning will be carried out according to special instructions. . .

[Source: *Sobranie uzakoneniy i rasporyazheniy pravitel'stva* No. 85, 1917, Article 487.]

When news spread to the countryside that the Tsarist regime had fallen, peasant expectations rose that, as they had demanded for generations, privately owned land would be redistributed among them. By mid-April there were reports from some areas of peasant land-seizures. The Provisional Government took alarm and frantically appealed for law and order to be respected. Having inherited minimal local administrative apparatus in the countryside, it sought to incorporate into its own administrative hierarchy committees formed by peasants at *volost'* (parish or village) level, and urged them to restrain their fellow peasants.[8] Nothing must be done, it insisted, until the Constituent Assembly had been elected and had deliberated on the land question. The Kadets recognized all property as being ultimately at the disposal of the nation, and they were more willing than liberal parties anywhere in central or western Europe to envisage far-reaching land reform; on the other hand, unlike the socialists, they insisted that private ownership of land was legitimate and that, if in the fullness of time the Constituent Assembly decided upon compulsory purchase and orderly redistribution, due compensation would have to be paid.

---

8 For an analysis of the formation of the land and food committees, see G. Gill, *Peasants and Government in the Russian Revolution* (London 1979) pp. 46–73.

Document 7 | From the appeal of A.I. Shingarev, Minister of Agriculture, to the *volost'* committees

1 May 1917

Please display prominently.

The Minister of Agriculture appeals fervently to *volost'* committees and all *volost'* citizens to prevent any kind of violence against the person and property of local landowners, farmers and peasant smallholders, and not to darken the new, free order with feelings of revenge and malice.

The property and lands of landowners, like all other domains, are national property, of which only the national Constituent Assembly will have the right to dispose. Until such time any unauthorized seizure of land, cattle, equipment, timber-felling, etc., is an illegal and unjust misappropriation of national wealth and may subsequently deprive other perhaps needier citizens.

Model farms, pedigree herds, mechanical equipment, orchards and woods should be treated with care. Such farms were established after years of hard work and at great expense. Russia is very short of model farms with pedigree herds and good seed, and so all such establishments are particularly valuable to the state and their destruction and ruin are in no way acceptable.

Only the Constituent Assembly will solve the great land question and so for now everything must remain inviolate, all the more since the instructions of the new government are making it entirely possible to settle all misunderstandings and disputes over land. . . The unauthorized seizure of others' land and property will be viewed as a violation of the rights of other citizens of free Russia and will be punished with all the severity of the law. . .

[Source: *Revolyutsionnoe dvizhenie v Rossii v aprele 1917 g. Aprel'skiy krizis: Dokumenty i materialy* (Moscow 1958) pp. 328, 329.]

In the army, the immediate impact of the February revolution was ambiguous. The formation of soldiers' committees and removal of some of the most unpopular officers did something to raise morale. On the other hand, the open struggle between the Soviet, which appealed for an early general peace 'without annexations or indemnities', and the Provisional Government's Foreign Minister, Milyukov, who was determined to fight for outright victory, encouraged impatience for an end to the fighting. When popular protest against Milyukov's policy in April forced him to resign and triggered the entry of leading Menshevik and SR figures from the Soviet EC into a coalition government (5 May), rank-and-file confidence in the government increased.[9] But so, too, did expectations of an early peace. Failure to deliver would cost the moderate socialists dear: a week earlier Lenin had articulated an increasingly radical if as yet minority alternative and succeeded in committing the Bolshevik party to champion outright opposition to the coalition.

During April and May, there were a growing number of instances of fraternization between Russian and German troops. On the Russian side, willingness to fraternize owed more to war-weariness, disdain for officers, and open debate over the issue of peace than to organized agitation by party activists.[10] But the publication of such letters as the one below, in this instance by the Bolshevik paper addressed to soldiers, *Soldatskaya pravda*, helped to spread the mood. Whereas the German authorities welcomed what they took to be evidence that the Russian army was falling apart, the Russian High Command was alarmed. Not the least of the motives behind preparations for a major Russian offensive in June was the hope that once rank-and-file attention was refocused on engaging the enemy, discipline could be restored.

Document 8 | A soldier's letter on fraternization

May 1917

Dear Comrade,

I'd like to inform you about what's going on here at the Front. On the 26th, 27th and 28th April there was no war here at the front lines, but a kind of national holiday. A river separates us and the Germans. . . Through the night everybody was at his post and discipline was very strict: apart from flares and gunfire not a sound—until dawn, when the first thing we did was wave a white flag and ask, 'Hermann, are you going to shoot?' From their side a voice said, 'No.' So, off we went to get some water, have a wash, fish, and when it got hot, stripped off and had a swim together. We also got boats and went to the other bank. As we approached the bank, the Germans ran up, grabbed the boat, hauled it ashore and said hello. Only one problem: we couldn't speak German, so we had to use sign-language. Then they took us to their dug-outs and gave us wurst, eggs, decent bread and brandy, nice and friendly as well. We'd invite them too, but we've got nothing to give them except bread. The Germans also said they were scared that our officers would arrest

9 See Z. Galili, 'The April Crisis' in E. Acton, Yu. Cherniaev and W. Rosenberg (eds) *Critical Companion to the Russian Revolution* (London 1997) pp. 62–68, for a penetrating account of Menshevik agonizing before deciding to join the coalition to prop up the tottering liberal government.

10 A.K. Wildman, *The End of the Imperial Army* Volume II (Princeton 1987) pp. 64, 73, emphasizes the lack of correlation in different parts of the army between the spirit of revolt among soldiers and a Bolshevik presence.

them. And it's true—when the Germans said they'd come over at two tomorrow afternoon, some ensign from the 9th said, 'That's great. We were supposed to catch one on reconnoitre, so when one comes over we'll send him to headquarters.' The men said then and there that, since they hadn't arrested us, we wouldn't arrest them. But if they were spies, well that'd be another matter. On the 25th when the 5th company left the trenches, the company officer ordered the Cossack artillery to open rapid fire: three shells at our own trenches and the rest at the Germans, but when the men phoned up to say we'd send half the company over to make mincemeat of them, then the firing stopped. Almost all the officers order them to fire at their own side. . .

Zhukov,
1st Company, 175th Infantry Reserves

[Source: *Soldatskaya pravda*, 18 May 1917.]

Among workers, the February revolution unleashed an almost frenzied drive to create new representative organizations—suburban, city and regional soviets, trade unions and, most energetically, factory committees. These organizations were reluctant to defer to any authority, including that of the Provisional Government, and quickly began to exert powerful influence in the 'Committees of Public Organizations', which in most towns pushed to one side the local dumas elected before the revolution on a narrow property franchise. During March and April, the level of strikes temporarily dropped away as industrialists granted significant wage increases and made efforts to accommodate factory committee and trade-union demands for improved working conditions, respectful treatment by managers and foremen and the introduction of the eight-hour day.[11] Menshevik and SR leaders encouraged moderation and established conciliation chambers under the aegis of local soviets to adjudicate industrial disputes. However, the incipient breakdown in trade which had helped to spark the Petrograd insurrection accelerated rapidly during the spring, exacerbated by severe deterioration of the railways. Shortages of fuel and raw materials as well as food led manufacturers to cut output, lay off labour and begin to resist the more ambitious claims of factory committees. During April, the minority of

---

11 Some of the cream of research undertaken in the late 1970s and 1980s into the Russian working class in the revolution is brought together in D.H. Kaiser (ed.) *The Workers' Revolution in Russia, 1917: The view from below* (Cambridge 1987). Subsequent debate over the dynamics of workers' radicalism can be sampled in R. Suny, 'Revision and Retreat in the Historiography of 1917: Social history and its critics' *Russian Review* 53 (1994) pp. 165–82, and S. Smith, 'Writing the History of the Russian Revolution after the Fall of Communism' *Europe–Asia Studies* 46 (1994) pp. 563–78.

workers who had from the start objected to the formation of a 'bourgeois' government began to attract new adherents, frustrated by national policy— by the failure to secure peace, by the continuation of a highly authoritarian managerial culture, by piecemeal, grudging concessions to factory commit- tees, and by the way rapid inflation eroded wage rises.

It was this growing radicalism which Lenin, returning from exile on 3 April, successfully tapped. He established his party as the main political vehicle and mouthpiece for workers who repudiated the Provisional Government. At the Bolshevik party conference held at the end of April he succeeded, with help from the militant rank and file and against the instincts of more moderate party leaders, in having adopted as party policy the radical critique and programme he had drawn up in his 'April Theses'.[12]

Document 9 | V.I. Lenin: *The Tasks of the Proletariat in the Present Revolution* (The 'April Theses')

4 and 5 April 1917

Theses

1) In our attitude towards the war, which under the new government of L'vov and Co. unquestionably remains on Russia's part a predatory imperialist war owing to the capitalist nature of that government, not the slightest concession to 'revolu- tionary defencism' is permissible.

The class-conscious proletariat can give its consent to a revolutionary war, which would really justify revolutionary defencism, only on condition: (a) that the power pass to the proletariat and the poorest sections of the peasants aligned with the prole- tariat; (b) that all annexations be renounced in deed and not in word; (c) that a complete break be effected in actual fact with all capitalist interests.

In view of the undoubted honesty of those broad sections of the mass believers in revolutionary defencism who accept the war only as a necessity, and not as a means of conquest, in view of the fact that they are being deceived by the bour- geoisie, it is necessary with particular thoroughness, persistence and patience to explain their error to them, to explain the inseparable connection existing between capital and the imperialist war, and to prove that without overthrowing capital *it is impossible* to end the war by a truly democratic peace, a peace not imposed by violence.

The most widespread campaign for this view must be organized in the army at the front.

Fraternization.

---

12 R. Service, *The Bolshevik Party in Revolution: A study in organizational change 1917–1923* (London 1979) pp. 53–54.

2) The specific feature of the present situation in Russia is that the country is *passing* from the first stage of the revolution—which, owing to the insufficient class-consciousness and organization of the proletariat, placed power in the hands of the bourgeoisie—to its *second* stage, which must place power in the hands of the proletariat and the poorest sections of the peasants.

This transition is characterized, on the one hand, by a maximum of legally recognized rights (Russia is *now* the freest of all the belligerent countries in the world), on the other, by the absence of violence towards the masses, and, finally, by their unreasoning trust in the government of capitalists, those worst enemies of peace and socialism.

This peculiar situation demands of us an ability to adapt ourselves to the *special* conditions of Party work among unprecedentedly large masses of proletarians who have just awakened to political life.

3) No support for the Provisional Government; the utter falsity of all its promises should be made clear, particularly of those relating to the renunciation of annexations. Exposure in place of the impermissible, illusion-breeding 'demand' that *this* government, a government of capitalists, should cease to be an imperialist government.

4) Recognition of the fact that in most of the Soviets of Workers' Deputies our Party is in a minority, so far a small minority, as against a *bloc of all* the petit-bourgeois opportunist elements, from the Popular Socialists and the Socialist-Revolutionaries down to the Organizing Committee (Chkheidze, Tsereteli, etc.), Steklov, etc., etc., who have yielded to the influence of the bourgeoisie and spread that influence among the proletariat.

The masses must be made to see that the Soviets of Workers' Deputies are the *only possible* form of revolutionary government, and that therefore our task is, as long as *this* government yields to the influence of the bourgeoisie, to present a patient, systematic and persistent *explanation* of the errors of their tactics, an explanation especially adapted to the practical needs of the masses.

As long as we are in the minority we carry on the work of criticizing and exposing errors and at the same time we preach the necessity of transferring the entire state power to the Soviets of Workers' Deputies, so that the people may overcome their mistakes by experience.

5) Not a parliamentary republic—to return to a parliamentary republic from the Soviets of Workers' Deputies would be a retrograde step—but a republic of Soviets of Workers', Agricultural Labourers' and Peasants' Deputies throughout the country, from top to bottom.

Abolition of the police, the army and the bureaucracy.

The salaries of all officials, all of whom are elective and displaceable at any time, not to exceed the average wage of a competent worker.

6) The weight of emphasis in the agrarian programme to be shifted to the Soviets of Agricultural Labourers' Deputies.

Confiscation of all landed estates.

Nationalization of *all* lands in the country, the land to be disposed of by the local Soviets of Agricultural Labourers' and Peasants' Deputies. The organization of separate Soviets of Deputies of Poor Peasants. The setting up of a model farm on each of the large estates (ranging in size from 100 to 300 *desyatiny*, according to local and other conditions, and to the decisions of the local bodies) under the control of the Soviets of Agricultural Labourers' Deputies and for the public account.

7) The immediate amalgamation of all banks in the country into a single national bank, and the institution of control over it by the Soviet of Workers' Deputies.

8) It is not our immediate task to 'introduce' socialism, but only to bring social production and the distribution of products at once under the control of the Soviets of Workers' Deputies.

9) Party tasks:
    a) Immediate convocation of a Party congress;
    b) Alteration of the Party Programme, mainly;
        (1) On the question of imperialism and the imperialist war;
        (2) On our attitude towards the state and our demand for a 'commune state';
        (3) Amendment of our out-of-date minimum programme.
    c) Change of the Party's name.

10) A new International.

We must take the initiative in creating a revolutionary International, an International against the *social-chauvinists* and against the 'Centre'.

Written 4 and 5 April 1917
Published 7 April 1917 in *Pravda* No. 26
Signed: N. Lenin

[Source: V.I. Lenin, *Collected Works* Volume XXIV (Moscow 1964) pp. 19–26.]

May and June saw the number of strikes continue to rise sharply, and ominous signs of growing popular impatience, dramatized by radical leaders at the Kronstadt naval base outside Petrograd repudiating the government's authority. Nevertheless, during these months, the alliance of Mensheviks and SRs appeared to dominate the soviets, soldiers' committees and other representative organizations of workers and peasants springing up in profusion. Their acknowledged leader, the charismatic Georgian Menshevik I.G. Tsereteli, developed a cogent case for coalition with representatives of the propertied classes. Whereas it was increasingly conventional for those on the left to use the term 'the democracy' to counterpose socialists, workers, rank-and-file soldiers and peasants to liberals and the propertied elite, Tsereteli developed a discourse designed to underline the common interest that level-headed socialists and workers shared with progressive sections of the bourgeoisie. The master term to which he struggled to give currency, against the grain of increasingly class-based metaphors, was 'all the vital forces of the country'.[13] He admitted that the government could not solve the myriad problems confronting it at once, but insisted that a solid coalition and strong state were essential to prevent either chaos and civil war or counter-revolution. In the following speech to the first Congress of Soviets, in which Mensheviks and SRs commanded a huge majority, he spelled out his rationale. It was during this speech that his confident assertion that no party had the will to rule alone was famously interrupted by Lenin.

Document 10 | **From I.G. Tsereteli's speech at the First All-Russia Congress of Soviets**

4 June 1917

For the first time before an all-Russia congress, we, the representatives of organized democracy, will give an account of the general policies we have been implementing within the Provisional Government. . .

We are told: 'You have not given us a fundamental financial reform, you have not given us a fundamental solution to the land question, you have not given us a fundamental solution to the international question of peace. . . But then you act decisively enough against those you consider to be undertaking anarchist acts. Your creative work. . . has borne no fruit, but your repressive work has been felt. . .' I tell you directly, comrades, that at the present moment we are pursuing our international policy for a general peace, and are calling for it to be underpinned by military action on our front, we are directing all our efforts towards organizing the country's food supply, straining all our efforts to find new sources of finance for the state budget. If at that moment the state starts to collapse, and what recently took place in Kronstadt breaks out all over Russia, that is, refusal to recognize a single revolutionary authority, declaring oneself to be a self-appointed supreme organization—if that starts, and if the government is not able to deal with it, then it should abandon all its legislative projects and measures in the political sphere, because it should realize that if it cannot deal with these difficulties, then all the others will be swept away by civil war and the collapse of the revolution. . . We know that in Russia at present

---

13 On the use of the language of class and social polarization, see O. Figes and B. Kolonitskii, *Interpreting the Russian Revolution: The language and symbols of 1917* (Yale 1999) pp. 104–52.

a stubborn, bitter struggle for power is going on. At the present moment in Russia there is no political party that would say: 'Give power to us, go away, we shall take your place.' There is no such party in Russia. (Lenin, from his seat: 'Yes, there is!')...

On the right they say: 'Let the left take power, then the country and we will make the appropriate choice.' On the left they say: 'Let the right take power, then the country and we will draw the appropriate conclusion.'... We understand, comrades, that there is no time for the country to learn such lessons, which would cause it to lurch right or left, we understand that only the policies we are pursuing— policies to rally all the vital forces of the country for the progressive development of the revolution—can save the country.

[Source: *Pervyy Vserossiyskiy s˝ezd Sovetov rabochikh i soldatskikh deputatov: Stenograficheskiy otchet* (Moscow and Leningrad 1930) pp. 54–67.]

What most savagely undercut the political capital of the Mensheviks and SRs was their support for the disastrous offensive launched on 18 June. Widespread mass mutiny broke out and their influence went into steep decline across the Front. Anger against and disillusionment with their leadership was as intense in the garrisons behind the lines, and nowhere was hostility greater than among soldiers in the capital. Particularly militant was the St Petersburg Machine-Gun Regiment, whose men were to play a key role in mass demonstrations on 3 and 4 July. Proud of their part in the February revolution and determined not to be sent to the Front, they were in the vanguard of demands that an all-socialist government drawn from the soviets should replace the liberal–socialist coalition. Their views were publicized in *Soldatskaya pravda*, as in the letter below, and despite the author's disclaimer about Lenin, the language of class war coincided exactly with the Bolshevik view.

Document 11 | 'Why should *I* sacrifice my life?'

June 1917

Comrades! With the blood of our brothers we've won freedom of speech—and what are we seeing now? They're shutting us up and not letting us speak. All the talking's being done by the educated and rich, who are yelling about war until total victory. But when I ask them why they don't go to the Front, if they need a war so much, and why *I*, not *they*, should sacrifice my life, they yell at me, 'You're one of Lenin's lot; you should be locked up.' I'm not a Leninist and I don't know Lenin; I'm just expressing my opinion.

Comrades! Don't forget the 27th and 28th February, when we went to get our longed-for freedom! Now we've got it, are we really going to hand it over to our enemies, the bourgeois?

Comrades! Don't worry about getting arrested, say what you think everywhere, don't let the bourgeois fool you with their fancy speeches!

K. K., a soldier of the 2nd company of the 2nd St Petersburg Machine-Gun Regiment

[Source: *Soldatskaya pravda*, 2 July 1917.]

The July Days

During the first days of July, unrest intensified in the capital and at Kronstadt, fuelled further as news reached Petrograd of the scale of the disaster at the Front. The militant mood presented the Bolshevik leadership with a growing dilemma. Activists within the party, and especially members of its Military Organization, had encouraged open and armed anti-government demonstrations and demands that non-socialist ministers resign. The party's leaders were much more cautious. They were afraid that a full-blown confrontation might prove premature and serve to strengthen the position of the government. On the other hand, they were anxious not to lose face with the more radical elements—a risk made all the greater by the huge scale of demonstrations on 3 July.

They were also emboldened by news of the (coincidental) resignation the previous day of Kadet ministers. This was triggered by government splits over how to handle Ukrainian demands for autonomy.[14] The liberals rejected moderate socialist efforts to reach a compromise with the Ukrainian leaders. The attitude of Mensheviks and SRs, once in office, towards minority national self-determination had in fact moved markedly closer to that of the Kadets. While they had accepted that Poland would become independent, they had tried to postpone final resolution of Finnish claims until the Constituent Assembly. Where other (much weaker) minority nationalist movements were concerned, they were confident that class affiliations would remain far stronger than national ones, as they had proved to be in the early months of the revolution, and had become almost as reluctant as the liberals to make far-reaching concessions.[15] That the Kadets resigned over the

---

14 For an overview of the revolution in Ukraine, which presented much the gravest national minority problem faced by the Provisional Government, see M. von Hagen, 'Ukraine' in Acton et al. (eds) *Critical Companion* pp. 728–40.

15 On the Kadet and moderate socialist approaches to the national minority issue, see R. Suny, 'Nationality Policies' in Acton et al. (eds) *Critical Companion* pp. 659–66. For the role and relative weakness of minority nationalism in 1917, see R. Suny, 'Nationality and

Ukrainian demands reflected more the underlying tension between the coalition partners over social and economic issues than profound differences over the question of the minority nationalities.

Having learned of the Kadet resignations, the Bolshevik Central Committee lent its weight to calls the next day for a mass if peaceful demonstration in favour of the transfer of power to the soviets. There are historians who, echoing the Provisional Government's charge at the time, assert that the July Days amounted to an attempt by the Bolshevik leadership to seize power. Lenin's attitude,,however, appears to have been 'wait and see' and the body to which power would presumably have been handed, the Central Executive Committee (TsIK) set up by the All-Russia Congress of Soviets in June, was dominated not by Bolsheviks but by Mensheviks and SRs.[16]

Document 12 | **An appeal by the Central and St Petersburg Committees of the RSDRP(b), the Military Organization of the CC of the RSDRP(b), the Inter-District Committee of the RSDRP (*Mezhrayonka*) and the Board of the Workers' Section of the Soviet of Workers' and Soldiers' Deputies**

4 July 1917

Comrade workers and soldiers of Petrograd!

Now that the counter-revolutionary bourgeoisie has come out openly against the revolution, let the All-Russia Soviet of Workers', Soldiers' and Peasants' Deputies take all power into its own hands. Such is the will of the revolutionary population of Petrograd, which has the right to bring its will to the attention of the presently convened Executive Committees of the All-Russia Soviet by means of a peaceful and organized demonstration.

Long live the will of the revolutionary workers and soldiers!

Long live the power of the soviets!

The coalition government, unable to carry out those tasks for which it was formed, has failed and collapsed. The revolution is faced with massive, arduous tasks. We need a new power which, together with the revolutionary proletariat, army and peasantry, will decisively set about consolidating and expanding the people's

---

Class in the Revolutions of 1917: A re-examination of categories' in N. Lampert and G. Rittersporn (eds) *Stalinism: Its nature and aftermath* (London 1992) pp. 211–42. The manner in which minority national consciousness was fostered by population displacement is explored in P. Gatrell's path-breaking study, *Empire Walking: Refugees in Russia during World War I* (Bloomington, IN, 1999), pp. 141–70.

16 Compare R. Pipes, *The Russian Revolution 1899–1919* (London 1990) pp. 385–438, with Figes, *A People's Tragedy* pp. 425–38, and the earlier thorough analysis by A. Rabinowitch, *Prelude to Revolution: The Petrograd Bolsheviks and the July 1917 Uprising* (Bloomington, IN, 1968).

achievements. Only the Soviet of Workers', Soldiers' and Peasants' Deputies can be such a power.

Yesterday the revolutionary garrison and workers of Petrograd demonstrated to proclaim this slogan: All Power to the Soviet! We call upon this movement, which has sprung into being in regiments and factories, to be turned into a peaceful, organized expression of the will of all the workers, soldiers and peasants of Petrograd.

The CC of the RSDRP
The St Petersburg Committee of the RSDRP
The Inter-Regional Committee of the RSDRP
The Military Organization of the CC of the RSDRP
The Board of the Workers' Section of the Soviet of Workers' and Soldiers' Deputies

[Source: Library of the Centre for the Political and Economic History of Russia, LIS B 31.]

The following memoir of the July Days and their aftermath, written long after the event, was by Nevsky, a leading figure in the Bolshevik Military Organization. Given the acute political tension of the early 1930s when he published it, Nevsky was unlikely to paint a picture that ran counter to the moves which Stalin and his allies were taking to establish a single orthodox version of the revolution. Nevertheless, there is an authentic tone to the memoir, and the portrayal of Lenin's attitude to lower-level activists—mild reproach combined with positive support—rings true, as does Nevsky's description of the thin line he himself trod between restraining and encouraging popular impatience.

Document 13 | Recollections of the July Days by V.I. Nevsky

1932

The events of 3–4 July 1917 in Petrograd

Dzerzhinsky, Menzhinsky and Bubnov were brought into the office of the [Bolshevik] Central Committee's Military Organization after July 1917 for 'supervision', as Ya.M. Sverdlov put it. According to Yakov Mikhaylovich [Sverdlov], some CC members thought that we, particularly N.I. Podvoysky, K.A. Mekhonoshin and I, but also M.S. Kedrov, were the main instigators of the premature July uprising and were to blame for its failure... Things soon became clear. Sverdlov informed us that the CC had proposed that he familiarize himself with the situation in the Military Organization, hence the meeting. Podvoysky and I, and somebody else, a Comrade Khitrov, I think, had already met him on Liteyny Avenue, where we were based, having left the Narva district. Yakov Mikhaylovich turned up after midnight and, after a couple of hours talking about the Military

Organization, said in a friendly way as he was leaving, 'Well, that's the end of your trial! Everything's OK! Give it all you've got, but, just one thing, please keep in touch!' 'What trial?,' I asked in astonishment. 'Well, it went up like a powder-keg!,' he added in an even more friendly manner. 'You ought to know that some comrades were extremely unhappy about you, and all sorts of things were being said. I was told to come and find out what's going on, so here I am. I'll tell you something else as well—when this was proposed, Vladimir Il'ich, meeting me shortly afterwards, said, "You do need to familiarize yourself and help them, but there mustn't be any pressure or censure. On the contrary, we ought to support them: nothing ventured, nothing gained. There's no victory without setbacks."' It is so long ago that I cannot vouch for Yakov Mikhaylovich's words, but I am giving their sense more or less correctly.

At the present time [1932] some comrades are asking who initiated the July events—the CC or the Military Organization, or whether it just flared up spontaneously.

In certain respects the question is pointless and doctrinaire: of course, the movement grew deep down among the masses who were fed up with the policies of the bourgeois government and desperate for peace. Of course, this movement, brought about by the objective conditions of the revolutionary process, was taken under the leadership of the CC through the Military Organization and the Petrograd committee; otherwise it would have ended in a complete, albeit temporary, rout for us. It was thanks to the leadership of the CC that we suffered the least conceivable losses in the circumstances.

However, there's no need now to hide the fact that all the responsible leaders of the Military Organization, i.e., mainly Podvoysky, the present writer, Mekhonoshin and Belyakov, and other activists contributed to the mood which brought about the uprising with their agitation, propaganda, and enormous influence and authority in the military units.

If my memory has failed me and I have unwittingly given the wrong names above, I can say the following about myself: although I am just a rank-and-file communist who played a small part in the revolution, my comrades will not deny that the soldiers knew me and took notice of what I said as if it was the Military Organization's instructions. And so, when the Military Organization, learning about the uprising by the Machine-Gun Regiment, sent me, as its most popular orator, to try to persuade the masses not to act, I did try, but in such a way that only a fool could have concluded that he should not act. . .

[Source: *Katorga i ssylka* No. 11–12 (1932) pp. 28–30.]

Whatever their retrospective bravado about the July Days, immediately afterwards the Bolshevik leaders and their allies were alarmed at the likely consequences. Their fears were clearly expressed in this private letter from Lunacharsky, a prominent Marxist intellectual and revolutionary orator, written (despite the eccentric form of address) to his wife, Anna.[17] In 1917 he belonged to the 'Inter-district' group of Social Democrats (the *Mezhrayonka*) which, along with Trotsky, co-operated with the Bolsheviks before formally merging with them at the end of July. Lunacharsky considered that Lenin and Trotsky had both been too willing to give in to 'spontaneity'—i.e., to endorse protest by a minority of workers and soldiers which was too ill-organized and supported by too small and politically 'backward' a part of the lower classes to overturn the government. He feared the result would be failure, demoralization and counter-revolutionary repression.

Document 14 | From a letter by A.V. Lunacharsky to his wife

5 July 1917
Petrograd

My Dear Child,

The 3rd and 4th [of July 1917] were awful. I've just sent you a telegram to let you know that at least I'm still alive. Of course you'll have got the details from the newspapers before you get this letter. I had to show solidarity with the Bolsheviks and gave the most tactful speech imaginable to the Central Executive Committee [of Soviets] in defence of them and our joint slogan. But they're not taking any notice of my advice. It's true the movement was spontaneous, but all the same it was right and in the spirit of the agreements achieved to fight against the sporadic armed outbursts to which they're being pushed by the anarchists and the dreadful condition of Petrograd's lower classes. It began on the 3rd, when I was in the City Duma, where important meetings were also going on; they passed a resolution not to oppose the armed outburst but only to try to make it as organized as possible. In this respect I tried to help. But you know what happened and how everything got out of control. Black Hundreds,* hooligans, provocateurs, anarchists and desperate people turned the demonstration into something largely absurd and chaotic. I'd foreseen this. I'd warned them at a lot of meetings and, recently, in my article 'Forward' (which I

---

17 The full series of eighty-nine letters Lunacharsky wrote in 1917 to his wife, who had remained behind when he returned from exile in Switzerland, are among the wealth of archival material currently being made available on the remarkable website funded by the Soros Foundation, auditorium.ru/books.

* Ultra right-wing organization.

sent you) that the Petrograd proletariat and the revolutionary part of the garrison, by breaking away from the rest of Russia's significantly backward democracy, are perishing and, evidently, the revolution is perishing too. Now the courageous thing to do is educate the masses and restrain them from pushing too hard in a way which is easy in Petrograd, but fatal overall. What am I to do? Trotsky and the Bolsheviks agree in word, but in deed are giving in to spontaneity—and so am I. Perhaps the awful experience of the 3rd and 4th will make people think again. Otherwise nobody will stop this rush to the precipice. Of course the war's the main reason for all this.

I do need you! You'd advise me. I really do trust your instincts. You'd both [addressing their child as well] be my sacred consolation. Will this letter get to you— and when? Will we see each other again? Yesterday death was hovering over Petrograd. I bless you, my dears. Try to be happy and live for each other. I'll send you lots of telegrams so that you won't worry too much. What's going to happen today? They're going to restore order in Petrograd. The waves are subsiding. Will there be new clashes? It's raining. I feel sick at heart. The bridges are up, you can't get to the Tauride Palace, and I feel so physically and morally tired. I was working from 10 yesterday morning till 3 this morning! May Fate take pity on Russia and mankind. I kiss and bless you both again. I want nothing so much as to see you both.

Your Dad

[Source: RGASPI, fond 142, opis' 1, delo 12, pp. 66–67.]

In part because the government denounced the Bolsheviks as agents of the enemy and succeeded in circulating evidence that Lenin had been in receipt of financial support from the Germans, many soldiers in and around the capital rallied to the Mensheviks and SRs.[18] The demonstrations died away and the Provisional Government moved to restore order. The 1st Machine-Gun Regiment was disarmed and publicly humiliated. The government tried to close much of the Bolshevik press, arrested Bolshevik and *Mezhrayonka* leaders (including Trotsky and Lunacharsky, although Lenin escaped into hiding in the semi-independent Duchy of Finland), and set up an investigation into the role of the Bolsheviks and their allies in the July demonstrations. The investigation underlined the steps taken by Bolshevik activists to involve workers and sailors from the Kronstadt naval base, and the open encouragement given by Lenin, Lunacharsky and other leaders, and it concluded that what it termed the 'armed uprising' had been orchestrated by the party's Central Committee.

---

18 For a recent analysis of the charges, see S. Lyandres, *The Bolsheviks' 'German Gold' Revisited: An inquiry into the 1917 accusations* (Pittsburgh, PA, 1995).

Document 15 | The case of Lenin et al.

22 July 1917

The Procurator of the Petrograd Court of Justice has informed the press of the following due causes for prosecuting Lenin and others.

According to information received, Ensign Semashko was both leader and initiator of the insurrection of 3rd July... Under Semashko's leadership the 1st Machine-Gun Regiment left their barracks at 10 p.m. on 3rd July and made for the Tauride Palace, where they were addressed by Zinoviev and Trotsky. On the next day, 4th July, Semashko and a group of sailors and workers went to the Regiment and started inciting their comrades to take to the streets with guns and machine-guns to demand the overthrow of the government.

On 3rd July midshipman Il'in (who calls himself Raskol'nikov) and some delegates from the Machine-Gun Regiment arrived in Kronstadt from Petrograd and spoke at a meeting in Anchor Square, calling for an armed uprising in Petrograd to overthrow the Provisional Government and transfer all power to the Soviet of Workers' and Soldiers' Deputies. In the evening the Executive Committee of the Kronstadt Soviet of Workers' and Soldiers' Deputies met under Raskol'nikov's chairmanship and passed a resolution for all units to gather armed at 6 a.m. in Anchor Square and head for Petrograd, where, together with troops of the Petrograd garrison, they would hold an armed demonstration with the slogan 'All Power to the Soviets of Workers' and Soldiers' Deputies'.

Signed by Raskol'nikov, this resolution was sent that night in the name of the head of all Kronstadt naval units to all the town's land and naval units. At a siren signal soldiers, sailors and workers, armed with rifles, began to gather on the morning of 4th July in Anchor Square, where speeches from the platform were given by Raskol'nikov and Roshal' calling for an armed uprising. At this point cartridges were given out to those assembled.

Raskol'nikov and Roshal' were the leaders of this demonstration. The number participating was about 5,000. Disembarking at the Nicholas Bridge around 11 o'clock, they all formed up into a column and under the leadership of the above moved off to Kshesinskaya's villa, on the balcony of which first Lunacharsky and then Lenin appeared, greeting the men from Kronstadt as 'the pride and joy of the revolution' and calling upon them to head for the Tauride Palace to demand the overthrow of the capitalist ministers and the transference of all power to the Soviets... On the way to Liteyny Avenue shooting began, which lasted about an hour and claimed numerous victims. In a state of agitation these units went to the Tauride Palace. They tried to arrest some of the ministers, who were in session in the palace at that moment, and the [Executive] Committee of the Soviet of Workers' and Soldiers' Deputies.

A written order had been given by the Military Organization of the Russian

Social-Democratic Workers' Party Central Committee to despatch a cruiser to Kronstadt. . . The investigation ascertained that prior to the uprising there had been systematic meetings in military units, at which speeches had been made calling for an armed uprising. Throughout April, May and June Kollontai and Ensign Semashko had visited and spoken at meetings of the Machine-Gun Regiment. They had called upon the soldiers not to send infantry regiments to the Front, not to obey the regimental committees' decisions to send soldiers to the Front, and to overthrow the Provisional Government, thereby achieving the transfer of all power to the Soviet of Workers' and Soldiers' Deputies. . .

The investigation into the Petrograd armed uprising of 3–5 July to overthrow the Provisional Government and the circumstances under which it took place have shown that it began and unfolded according to the instructions of the Central Committee of the Russian Social-Democratic Workers' Party. . .

In its investigation of the above questions the Commission of Enquiry did not in any way touch upon the political platforms of those involved and is concerned exclusively with investigating the perpetrators of a criminal act and the soundness of the basis for a prosecution. . .

[Source: *Izvestiya Petrogradskogo Soveta*, 22 July 1917.]

The combination of the Kadets' resignation on 2 July and the demonstrations of 3 and 4 July led to an acute cabinet crisis. During the next few days, the socialist ministers who remained in office drew up a Declaration (the final, somewhat toned-down version being published on 8 July) in which they promised to hasten a wide range of measures the left had expected of them since they entered the coalition in early May—the rapid convocation of the Constituent Assembly, the drastic revision of Allied war aims, energetic intervention to shore up the economy, and action both on labour legislation and on the land question. Although the Mensheviks and SRs reaffirmed their condemnation of the unrest in Petrograd and mutiny at the Front, the Declaration's radical thrust precipitated the resignation of the prime minister, L'vov. He deplored the socialists' willingness to heed opinion in the Soviet Congress, and in particular the way the Declaration tended to endorse the position of the SR Minister of Agriculture, Chernov, who had been seeking to give peasant-dominated lower-level land committees discretion over unused private land.[19]

---

19 See O. Radkey, *The Agrarian Foes of Communism: Promise and default of the Russian socialist-revolutionaries, February–October 1917* (New York 1958) chapter 5.

Document 16 | From the Programme of 8 July—Declaration of the Provisional Government

8 July 1917

. . . The Provisional Government regards as its first and major problem the application of all its strength to the struggle against the foreign foe, and to the defence of the new state order against every anarchical and counter-revolutionary attempt, without hesitating to take the most rigorous measures in its power. At the same time, it will again make it clear by its foreign policy that the revolutionary army can only go forward to the fight with the firm conviction that not a drop of the blood of a Russian soldier will be shed for foreign ends, and will again confirm the sentiments of democratic right which it has openly proclaimed to the whole world in its pacific pronouncement. With this end in view the Provisional Government, in keeping with the principles of foreign policy proclaimed in the Government's Declaration of 6 May [sic], intends to propose to the Allies to gather at a conference of the Allies during August in order to determine the general course of the Allies' foreign policy and to coordinate their actions in carrying out the principles proclaimed by the Russian revolution. Russia will be represented in this conference by members of the diplomatic corps as well as by representatives of the Russian democracy. . .

The Provisional Government will take all steps in order that elections to the Constituent Assembly take place on the appointed date (17 September). . . and that the preliminary measures be completed in advance in order to guarantee the correctness and freedom of elections. In the field of internal policy, the Provisional Government's principal problem is the introduction at the earliest possible moment of municipal and zemstvo self-government on the basis of universal, direct, equal and secret suffrage widely distributed. Attributing at the same time particular significance to the creation locally of organs of authority vested with the confidence of the entire population, the Provisional Government will immediately involve representatives of public organizations in the organization of local authority in order to form collegiate organs of regional administration, combining a number of *gubernii*.

In its desire for a consistent introduction of principles of civil equality into the life of the country, the Provisional Government will establish in the near future laws on abolishing estates [*soslovie*] as well as final liquidation of civil ranks and orders, except those granted for battle distinctions.

In order to cope energetically with the economic disorder and to take further measures for the protection of labour, the Economic Council and the Central Economic Committee, appointed by the Provisional Government, will begin their work immediately. Their tasks will consist of working out a general plan for the organization of the national economy and of labour, the working out of draft laws, and general measures to regulate economic life and the control of industry, as well as carrying them out in a planned and co-ordinated fashion. In the domain of labour policy, bills will be shortly prepared and put into effect regarding the freedom of trade unions, and regarding labour exchanges and arbitration courts. Bills are also being drafted relative to the eight-hour day, the protection of labour, and the introduction of all kinds of workers' insurance.

With regard to the agricultural question, the Provisional Government is convinced, as before, that, . . . in view of the vital requirements of our national economy and the repeatedly expressed desires of the peasants, as well as the programmes formulated by all the democratic parties in the country, future agricultural reforms must be based upon the principle of transferring the land to the toilers. On this basis a scheme of agricultural reform is being drawn up which will be submitted to the Constituent Assembly.

The measures which the Provisional Government will take in the immediate future are:

1) Complete doing away with the old agrarian policy which ruined and disorganized the agricultural communities;

2) Measures safeguarding the complete freedom of the Constituent Assembly as to the distribution of the country's land reserve;

3) Improvement of land relations in the interests of state defence and supplying the country with food by means of expanding and consolidating the network of land committees organized by the state, with well-defined legal authority in the area of deciding the current questions of agricultural-economic policy, except the basic question of the right to land ownership, which is within the authority of the Constituent Assembly; and

4) The elimination, by means of such legal regulation of land relations, of that grave danger with which the state and the future agrarian reform is threatened, such as land seizures and similar arbitrary local methods of solving the land needs which contradict the principle of the general national plan of the future land reform.

In announcing its proposed aims the Provisional Government, in its grave and responsible work, thinks it has the right to count upon the wholehearted and enthusiastic support of all the vital forces of the country. It demands of all of them sacrifice and readiness to give everything—all their strength, possessions, their very life—for the great cause of saving the country that has ceased to be the stern stepmother to the people inhabiting it, and it strives to unite all of them on the principles of complete liberty and equality.

[Source: *Vestnik Vremennogo Pravitel'stva* No. 100, p. 1. Reproduced in R.P. Browder and A.F. Kerensky (eds) *The Russian Provisional Government 1917: Documents* (Stanford, CA, 1961) pp. 1386–87.]

From the State Conference to
the Kornilov Affair

Anxious though both the moderate socialists and left-leaning liberals were
to renew the coalition, and prepared though both sides were to serve under
Kerensky as prime minister, talks dragged on for almost three weeks. The
Kadets would not endorse the Declaration of 8 July; independent liberals
would not join the socialists without the Kadets; moderate socialists ruled
out forming a purely socialist government. It was only by the device of
socialist and liberal ministers agreeing to differ on their respective
programmes that a second coalition was eventually announced on 25 July.
The socialist ministers were outnumbered two to one and their most
authoritative leader, Tsereteli, decided to stay outside the cabinet. His preoccupation had become the overriding need for a strong state and he devoted
his energies to trying to persuade the Soviet to lend the government
maximum support.[20] The new government tried to reassure moderate
socialist opinion of its commitment to further social and economic reform,
but more striking were the decrees it issued to calm mounting right-wing
impatience for the reassertion of authority. It restored the death penalty at
the Front and, in the decree below, took sweeping emergency powers.

Document 17 | **From a Provisional Government decree on combating
subversion**

2 August 1917

It is the government's duty to avert the possibility of criminal plans ripening, before
they begin to be implemented, as in wartime even a brief disruption of order
harbours great danger.

Therefore, the government, in defending the civil and political rights of all and
preserving the right of all political tendencies to exist and be openly active, will nip
in the bud the above-mentioned dangerous activities of certain persons, to which
end emergency powers will be granted at this exceptional time to the Ministers of
War and Internal Affairs. . .

1. The Ministers of War and of Internal Affairs may, with their mutual consent,
i) decree the taking into custody of persons whose activity presents a threat to the
defence of the state, its internal security and the freedom won by the revolution,
and ii) propose to the above-mentioned persons that they quit, within a specified
period of time, the borders of the Russian state, otherwise in the event of their not

---

20 See Z. Galili and A.P. Nenarokov, 'Tsereteli' in Acton et al. (eds) *Critical Companion* pp.
197–205.

departing or returning without authorization they will be taken into custody in accordance with point 1 of the present decree. . .

[Source: GARF, fond 1779, opis' 2, delo 1, ch. 3, pp. 224, 224 ob.]

Among workers, however, hostility to the Provisional Government continued to grow. The number of strikes among less skilled workers soared late in the summer, political protest being interwoven more and more closely with protest against the erosion of real wages.[21] Moreover, by August, employers were becoming resolute in resisting workers' demands and cutting back the role of factory committees; the number of lockouts was rising, motivated, according to the socialist press, by determination to discipline workers; and there was mounting alarm among workers at the prospect of mass unemployment, impoverishment and hunger. Bolshevik calls for a Soviet government committed to using state authority to maintain employment, empower workers, control prices and tax the rich struck home. The following resolution on workers' control, passed overwhelmingly at the second conference of Petrograd factory committees in mid-August, spelled out the Bolshevik case. The term 'workers' control' contained deep ambiguities. For a small minority anarchist current, it signalled the goal of abolishing traditional forms of management in private and state enterprises alike and instituting workers' democratic self-management. For most factory committees, 'control' meant workers securing the power to scrutinize and on occasion veto managerial decisions, the goal being not to take over management but to maintain production, prevent lockouts and preserve jobs. For the Bolshevik leaders, including V.P. Milyutin, who proposed this resolution, the 'control' to be exercised by factory committees within each plant was secondary to the primary aim, which was the establishment of a workers' government able to control the economy as a whole.[22]

Document 18 | Resolution of the Petrograd conference of factory committees

August 1917

Comrade Milyutin reported on the present situation and the tasks of workers' control. The basic theses of his report are expressed fully in the motion he proposed, which was adopted by an overwhelming majority.

---

21 D. Koenker and W. Rosenberg, *Strikes and Revolution in Russia, 1917* (Princeton 1989) pp. 213–38, brings home how the sharp differences between socialist and non-socialist press coverage of strikes intensified social polarization.
22 S. Smith, *Red Petrograd: Revolution in the factories, 1917–1918* (Cambridge 1983) pp. 139–67.

Resolution

1. The basic reason for the economic collapse is that the state of productive forces does not meet the demands placed upon them by the imperialist war. This is being felt particularly sharply in Russia owing to the relatively low level of development of productive forces and the inadequacies of their economic and technical organization...

The country is already plunging into the abyss of final economic collapse and death.

2. This crisis, worsening with every passing day, is being exacerbated by the policies of the bourgeoisie, which fears losing not only its political power but also its power over organized production. Not only is the bourgeoisie not organizing production, it is waging a policy of sabotage, resorting to hidden lockouts, halts in production, etc. It is consciously abetting the economic chaos with the aim of exploiting it for the cause of counter-revolution.

3. The representatives of trade and industry in the government are pursuing an analogous economic policy... Their tactics of sabotaging state power and any work aimed at regulating production, as well as their stubborn opposition to any unofficial organizations regulating economic life to a certain extent, in practice can only lead to even greater destruction. There has not been even one serious reform carried out either in the social economy or the state economy.

4. The continuation of the war, the chronic crisis of power arising from the conciliationist policies of the petit-bourgeois parties and the bourgeoisie's terror at the growing onslaught of the proletariat make it impossible to introduce even a militarized state capitalist organization of the economy, enserfing the working class to the imperialist state.

5. The continuation of the war..., on the one hand, will accelerate the process of destruction of productive forces, and, on the other hand, will lead to an extraordinary concentration of production and its centralization in the hands of the militarist state. At the same time, the continuation of the war, by proletarianizing intermediate strata on an unprecedented scale, is turning the proletariat into the serfs of the imperialist state, facilitating the absolute impoverishment of the workers, subjecting them to police repression, etc. It will therefore inevitably lead to an increase in the elements of proletarian revolution.

6. The campaign for peace through exerting pressure on the allied governments and agreements with the social-imperialists, undertaken by the soviets which have refused to make a real break with imperialism, was doomed to complete failure...

7. ... [Effective] regulation in Russia can be implemented only by an organization controlled by the proletariat and the strata of the peasantry which support it. This requires that they take control of state power, which is currently in the hands of the counter-revolutionary bourgeoisie... Moreover, it will be essential to implement a series of decisive revolutionary measures.

8. It is essential to intervene in the area of production, in order to regulate produc-

tion and distribution in a planned way. It is also essential to nationalize and centralize banking, and to nationalize the syndicated enterprises (such as oil, coal-mining, sugar, metallurgy).

9. Real workers' control must be established. The controlling bodies should be made up mainly of representatives of the soviets of workers' deputies, trade unions and factory committees...

10. Correct exchange between town and country should be organized, based on co-operatives and food committees, in order to supply the towns with essential agricultural products, and the countryside with manufactured goods, agricultural implements, machines, etc.

11. Workers' control should be developed, through a series of graduated measures, into the complete regulation of production.

12. In order to implement control... it is essential to introduce such preparatory measures as the abolition of commercial secrecy. The books of traders, industrialists and banks should be open for inspection...

13. In order to combat the financial collapse... the following measures are essential. There must be an immediate halt to the further emission of paper money and a refusal to honour state debts both external and internal, although the interests of petty investors should be taken into account. The entire tax system must be overhauled...

14. In order to increase productive forces it is essential to distribute the workforce correctly, transferring workers from sectors working for the war into sectors working for the country's needs.

15. On condition that power is transferred into the hands of the workers and the poorest strata of the peasantry..., it will be essential to introduce a general obligation to work... [which will] give the greatest possible increase in productive forces, and not just serve as a new method of fettering the workers.

16. The task of the workers' organizations (trade unions, workers' and soldiers' committees, soviets of workers' deputies) should be to encourage the adoption of these sorts of measures at the local level, to develop initiatives in that direction, to accelerate and generalize these measures onto the all-state level.

17. The introduction and implementation of all the measures outlined above will be possible only if the workers (supported by the poorest strata of the peasantry) strain all their forces to realize them, and decisively rebuff and struggle against the power of the imperialist bourgeoisie and its counter-revolutionary pressure.

There were 213 votes in favour of this resolution, with 26 against and 22 abstentions.

[Source: *Novaya zhizn'* No. 101, 15 August 1917, p. 5.]

In mid-August, Kerensky staged a State Conference in Moscow's Bolshoi Theatre, hoping to mobilize middle-ground opinion and strengthen the legitimacy of the Provisional Government. The effort proved counter-productive. Not only was the Conference met by a general strike in Moscow and boycotted by the Bolsheviks, but even in their absence the deepening social polarization was directly reflected in the confrontation between parties and organizations of left and right. The response to Kerensky's own speech indicated how rapidly the charisma he had seemed to exude in the early months of the revolution was evaporating.[23] Outspoken speeches from the right, on the other hand, notably that by the Don Cossack leader Kaledin, were met by a storm of approval from one side of the auditorium and dismay on the other.

Document 19 | From A.M. Kaledin's speech at the Moscow State Conference

14 August 1917

. . . With the profound conviction that in these times of mortal danger for the existence of our native land all must be sacrificed, the Cossacks consider that the preservation of our native land demands first and foremost taking the war to a victorious conclusion in complete unity with our Allies (shouts of 'Bravo!' and applause from the right). To this end the whole life of the country and, consequently, all the Provisional Government's activities must be subordinated. Only in such conditions will the government get the full support of the Cossacks (applause and shouts of 'That's right!' from the right). Defeatists have no place in the government (stormy applause from the right and shouts of 'Hear, hear! Bravo!'; boos from the left; all eyes are on Chernov, bent low over the table). [V.M. Chernov, the leader of the Socialist-Revolutionaries and Minister of Agriculture in the Provisional Government, had been accused in the press of collaboration with the Germans.] To save our native land we propose the following principal measures:

1) The army must be beyond politics (applause and shouts of 'Bravo!' from the right) and there must be a complete ban on all mass meetings and gatherings with their party struggles and feuds (shouts of 'That's right!' from the right).

4) Military discipline must be tightened and strengthened by the most decisive measures (noise and shouts of 'That's right!' from the right). . .

5) The Front and the Home Front must be a single whole, guaranteeing the army's fighting capability, and all measures necessary for strengthening discipline at the Front must also be applied on the Home Front (shouts of 'Bravo!' and 'That's right!' from the right).

6) The disciplinary rights of persons in command must be restored (stormy applause and shouts of 'Bravo!' and 'That's right!' from the right; noise and cat-calls

---

23 On the rise and fall of the cult of Kerensky, see Figes and Kolonitskii, *Interpreting the Russian Revolution* pp. 76–96.

from the left) and full power must be granted to the leaders of the army (applause and shouts of 'That's right!' from the right).

At a grim time of grave ordeals at the Front and of complete collapse through domestic political and economic ruin, only really firm authority can save the country from final destruction (shouts of 'Bravo, bravo!' from the right), in the hands of experienced and capable people not tied by party and group programmes (applause and shouts of 'That's right!' from the right), free from the need at every step to take account of all kinds of committees and soviets (applause and shouts of 'That's right!' from the right), and clearly aware that the source of sovereign state power is the will of the people and not of separate parties and groups (stormy applause and shouts of 'That's right!' from the right). There must be only one authority in the capital and the provinces. The misappropriation of state power by central and local committees and soviets must be immediately and abruptly terminated (a storm of protest from the left, with shouts of 'Down with Kaledin! Counter-revolutionary!'; noisy applause and shouts of 'That's right!' from the right). Russia must be united. Any kind of separatist tendency must be nipped in the bud. In the area of the management of the state the strictest economy is necessary, systematically, strictly, unswervingly and fully implemented. We must immediately set about working out and implementing a law on the obligation to work, urgently introduce norms for wage-rates and entrepreneurial profits, urgently co-ordinate agricultural and industrial prices, take the strictest and most effective measures to stop the disruption of agricultural production, which is suffering greatly from the arbitrary actions of individuals and all manner of committees violating well-established land-use and tenancy arrangements. . . The time for words has passed; the people's patience is exhausted. The great task of saving our native land must be undertaken.

(General Kaledin steps down to unprecedented uproar in the hall. The right and part of the centre applauds. There are shouts of protest and outrage from the left. The uproar takes a long time to settle down. A.F. Kerensky rises. The left rises to a man and greets the chairman-minister with a storm of applause.)

[Source: *Gosudarstvennoe soveshchanie: Stenograficheskiy otchet* (Moscow and Leningrad 1930) pp. 73–76.]

The tone struck by P.P. Ryabushinsky, speaking for Russia's commercial classes, was scarcely more conciliatory than Kaledin's. The previous week, Ryabushinsky had achieved notoriety for suggesting in a speech to other industrialists that Russian workers and soviet activists might only be brought to their senses 'by the bony hand of hunger'.[24]

---

24 M.N. Pokrovsky and Ya.A. Yakovlev (eds) *Gosudarstvennoe soveshchanie: Stenograficheskiy otchet* (Moscow and Leningrad, 1930) p. 364.

Document 20 | From P.P. Ryabushinsky's speech at the Moscow State Conference

15 August 1917

Citizens! Please allow me as a representative of commercial organizations and as a simple citizen of the Russian land to put forward a few ideas. First, let me say that the commercial-industrial world unanimously welcomed the overthrow of tsarism, and there can, of course, be no return to the past. Simultaneously, it will in the future just as sincerely welcome a republican system in Russia. It also wants the present Provisional Government to use all its power and be steadfastly strong while sincerely modest. At the present time our trade and industry are going through an extremely difficult patch.

. . . I would contend that our government, in taking the wrong path, is itself assisting the demise of our trade. If we look at the economic route Russia is travelling along, especially the state grain monopoly recently introduced without due consideration, then you will see that this undertaking. . . will cost vast amounts. At the present time 500 million rubles have already been allotted to it, which will be a great burden for the whole population of Russia. . . At the same time many people, members of the government, have pointed at the commercial class for not making the necessary sacrifices, for not being duly sympathetic to the taxes which they must shoulder (Chkheidze calls out, 'Quite so!'). That is not so. It has to be said that the commercial and industrial class has always been punctilious in paying its taxes. . . At the same time we know that there is a definite limit to taxes, because if you touch capital, the life-blood of industry, then it is not just we who will suffer but also the industrial working class and the whole of Russia. . .

Nor are we protesting against a certain level of control being imposed at such a difficult time on our industrial machine. That is completely natural, but at the same time our freedom of action must be guaranteed because an over-regulated or shackled industry does not have that initiative which is the well-spring of industrial life (an exclamation of 'Hypocrite!' from the left). We ourselves know how powerful a lever initiative is. . . Moving on now, I want to direct your attention primarily to those organizations, often unauthorized and heterogeneous, which have taken hold of all of Russia. . . If we look back, we can see that under the old regime our working class suffered terribly, but at present, I would venture to say, it is the master of the situation. If we look at trade and industry, we see that it too suffered terribly under the old regime and could not develop on even a European let alone an American scale. It was hampered by the authorities. And that is why, suffering at heart, we assisted in the removal of the old order from the state. Yet, we can at the same time see that even under the present new order, which we ourselves wanted, our trade and industry are still not on the right track. . .

I think that the present State Conference must be an assembly which will be able to clarify both our common psychology and those needs which all of Russia has, irrespective of class. . . All of this, gentlemen, obliges us to direct our attention to the make-up of the supreme power itself, because that power is the helmsman steering the country, which is being carried, perhaps, by some current or other under the influence of some pressures or other upon it. . . We realize that at present Russia is being run by an impossible dream, ignorance and demagogy. All three are dragging Russia along—to where, we do not know. So we must find the patriotic words to unite us all, in order that we, citizens, may defend Russia. . .

[Source: *Gosudarstvennoe soveshchanie* pp. 251–55.]

The political and social polarization demonstrated at the State Conference heightened expectations on all sides that there would be some kind of armed intervention from the right. While regretting the threat posed to civil liberties, a growing number of life-long liberals became resigned to or even eager for such an outcome. What has been termed a 'civil-war mentality' began to take hold.[25] The mood is captured in these exchanges by leading members of the Kadet party, several of them former or serving members of the Provisional Government.

Document 21 | From the minutes of a meeting of the Central Committee of the Constitutional Democrats (Kadets)

20 August 1917

Present: V.I. Vernadsky, G.V. Vernadsky, S.V. Vostrotin, D.D. Grimm, N.N. Glibov, A.A. Kaufman, A.V. Kartashev, F.F. Kokoshkin, Yu.M. Lebedev, A.I. Makushin, V.D. Nabokov, S.F. Ol'denburg, P.N. Milyukov, Countess S.V. Panina, A.V. Tyrkova, [A.Ya.] Timofeev, Z.G. Frenkel', A.I. Shingarev, P.P. Yurenev.

A.V. Kartashev, Minister for Religious Affairs: In trying to treat all the ills of state the authorities have so far tried only therapeutic methods, and when they have proved ineffectual, tried nothing else. And so, as a result, the country seems to be collapsing, as the authorities have not responded to its questions and demands. The army is collapsing, and servile and mutinous instincts are appearing. It is the same everywhere. . . What might the results of the authorities' inaction, of such a historic crime, be? Even those who would like to help the authorities are late in appearing. Soon nobody will be even capable of doing so and power will pass to those who are not afraid of being harsh and cruel. And the speaker himself has begun to feel that our intelligentsia are incapable of governing. The old generals in the field knew this and

---

25 W. Rosenberg, *Liberals in the Russian Revolution: The Constitutional Democratic Party 1914–1921* (Princeton 1974) pp. 204–11.

perhaps now only they could still sort out the breakdown. The government must now return to restoring elementary discipline at the Front, in spite of possible mutinies; it could still keep and follow its revolutionary programme on the Home Front. Only in this way could it justify its existence. Otherwise we wait until dictatorship comes. The Left is seething at the moment, but they will surrender meekly and be crushed.

A.A. Kaufman announced that he had heard from Mr Vikhlyaev in the Ministry of Agriculture that the government was already considering using military expeditions to requisition grain from the peasants.

A.I. Shingarev [former Minister of Agriculture and of Finance]: When you have to go down into the streets, what do you observe there? In Novaya Derevnya yesterday they simply wouldn't let Milyukov speak. Even Shingarev had had a job holding a meeting at Goryachee Pole, in the Labour Exchange, where there were only Constitutional Democrats, Bolsheviks and a few curious onlookers. In trying to find ideas and words in common, the speaker had mentioned 'homeland', and some wild-looking worker had angrily shouted, 'The worker doesn't have a homeland, just a fist!' In reminding him that in France mutual bitterness had led to heads being cut off, a sailor shouted, 'They ought to cut yours off!' At a meeting in Chinizelli's Circus a soldier proclaimed, 'We need equal wages and the bourgeois need their necks wrung!' Ignorant and embittered people, having rejected their recent leader Tsereteli, are getting close to rioting. It will come to shooting because words are useless. A dictatorship is looming. A.V. Kartashev asked rhetorically whether the Constitutional Democrats should not keep out of it all. Shingarev, too, was bothered by the same question. Even if a dictatorship after bloody shootings decided to rely on moderate forces and call upon the Constitutional Democrats to save the Fatherland, where would the party end up, having accepted such a historic mission? Even if it did manage to save the Fatherland the origin of its power would mean political suicide.

A.V. Tyrkova: The fact that the Constitutional Democrats had not conveyed to the masses that ideals of social justice were just as dear to them as political freedoms had perhaps played a part in the growth of hostility towards them. . .

Z.G. Frenkel': There has been terrified talk here about military expeditions to requisition grain, but in the provinces near the Front every military unit has been doing this all the time, whenever there have been shortages. And now there are more troops on the Home Front than at the Front. It just has to be done sensibly: for example, the Germans never requisition a cow in calf. They also use scare-tactics, but that also needs the right sort of people, and I do not see any yet. . .

N.N. Glebov: If they start using force to collect grain, there will be plunder—and then a Pugachev-style uprising. . .

P.N. Milyukov [former Minister of Foreign Affairs] finds that one cannot look upon the way events are developing in the country except as some sort of objective, physiological process; psychology plays a huge part—it can bring closer or put off the moment for surgical intervention. The choice of that moment does not depend on the Constitutional Democrats; if so much did depend on them, they could get out of the current situation with non-surgical methods. But the course of events depends on something else, not, at any rate, on the government as it is now. Its main representative [Kerensky] has evidently overstayed his welcome and has threatened that he will not give up that easily, and so forth. Around him is already beginning to crystallize the kind of milieu that usually gathers around power to serve its own interests.

Whether the cause is food riots or Bolshevik actions, life will impel society and the population to realize that a surgical operation is inevitable. This process will happen without us, but we are not neutral in our attitude to it: we acknowledge and sympathize with it to a certain extent. . .

V.D. Nabokov [former Head of Chancellery in Provisional Government]: . . . it would be extremely difficult right now to find support in the country for a bourgeois government.

A.I. Shingarev considered the continuation of the present government more beneficial both for the Party and the country than abrupt political changes.

P.N. Milyukov objected that, even if they might be beneficial for the Party, uncertain and vacillating government policies could only be harmful for the country.

F.F. Kokoshkin [former State Controller in the Provisional Government] after private meetings and arguments with Kerensky had come away with the impression of extreme uncertainty and instability in his mood and behaviour on vital issues. He is in the psychological state of Nicholas II: mistrustful and indecisive, seeming not to have his own line of conduct. Yet meanwhile his influence on government decisions could be enormous, since he has met with no resistance from the government, and the soviets would follow him quite willingly. Savinkov could make up for Kerensky's lack of political will, but Kerensky is evidently afraid of anybody's influence. These psychological facts have to be taken into consideration when assessing the overall political situation.

Yu.M. Lebedev, in characterizing governmental mistrust in its closest collaborators, reported that, in the words of peasant deputies, in the event of 'counter-revolution' by General Kornilov, etc., the government had troops with machine-guns ready; even the Bolsheviks had been drawn into it by going round the barracks.

After an exchange of opinions on the current political situation the meeting of the Central Committee was closed without formulating any conclusions or decisions.

[Source: GARF, fond 523, opis´ 2, delo 20, pp. 1–4.]

The anticipated intervention from the right took the form of the 'Kornilov affair' in the last days of August. Kornilov, appointed Commander-in-Chief by Kerensky on 19 July, was convinced of the need for a new government willing to crush left-wing agitation by force both in the army and on the Home Front and to refocus the country's energies on the war-effort. He appears to have believed that Kerensky shared his view and approved of his preparations for the imposition of martial law. In part, misunderstanding arose from the machinations of the self-appointed and eccentric go-between V.N. L'vov, who had been Procurator of the Holy Synod in the Provisional Government until late July. But it also arose from Kerensky's ambivalence.[26] At the last moment, he denounced Kornilov for treason and sought to re-establish his leftist credentials and project himself as the saviour of the revolution.

Document 22 | Kerensky's denunciation of Kornilov

The Provisional Government's address 'To All Citizens'

28 August 1917

Declaration:

On 26 August, Vladimir Nikolaevich L'vov, a member of the State Duma, was sent to me by General Kornilov demanding the Provisional Government hand over all civilian and military power to him, General Kornilov, so that he, at his discretion, could designate a new government to run the country. State Duma Member L'vov's authority to make such a proposal was later confirmed by General Kornilov in a telephone conversation with me.

Viewing the submission of this demand addressed through me to the Provisional Government as an expression of the desire of certain circles in society to use the state's difficult situation to set up in this country a system of government contrary to the gains of the Revolution, the Provisional Government deems it necessary, to protect the Motherland, freedom and the republican system, to empower me to take rapid and decisive measures to nip in the bud any attempts to infringe upon supreme state power and the civil rights gained by the Revolution.

All necessary measures to protect freedom and order in the country are being taken by me, and the population will be apprised of such measures in due course.

At the same time I order:

1. General Kornilov to hand over his duties as Commander-in-Chief to General Klembovsky, Commander of the armies of the Northern Front, which are blocking

---

26 See G. Katkov, *Russia 1917: The Kornilov Affair. Kerensky and the break-up of the Russian army* (London 1980), for a vigorous account sympathetic to Kornilov.

the way to Petrograd. For the moment, General Klembovsky is to take on the duties of Commander-in-Chief while remaining in Pskov.

2. The declaration of martial law in Petrograd and Petrograd district, where the rules for areas under martial law are to come into force. . .

I call upon all citizens to remain calm and maintain the good order necessary to save the Motherland.

To all ranks of the army and navy! I call upon you to do your duty in a calm and selfless spirit to save the Motherland from the foreign foe!

Prime Minister and Minister of Defence
A.F. Kerensky

[Source: *Kornilovskie dni* (Petrograd 1917) pp. 123–24.]

Infuriated by what seemed to him Kerensky's betrayal, and particularly by the charge of treason, Kornilov decided to break with the Prime Minister and confront him with a direct challenge. He accused the Provisional Government of bowing to Bolshevik pressure and opening the gates to the Germans; he confirmed orders for the supposedly reliable Third Cavalry Corps, made up of Cossacks and the so-called 'Savage' Division from the Caucasus, to advance on Petrograd and impose martial law; and he appealed to all true patriots to support him.[27]

Document 23 | Kornilov's appeal

Order of the Commander-in-Chief, No. 897

28 August 1917

. . . On becoming Commander-in-Chief I set out to the Provisional Government those conditions which I considered it necessary to implement to save and revive the army. Among them was the introduction of the death penalty on the Home Front.

In principle the Provisional Government approved my proposals, which I reconfirmed on 14 August at the State Conference in Moscow.

Time was precious and every wasted day threatened dire consequences, but meanwhile the Provisional Government on the one hand did not allow the implementation of my proposals and on the other even permitted specific criticism of them by the press and various organizations. Simultaneously the persecution of the High Command began, aiming at the complete breakdown of the army. At the same

---

27 On officers' attitudes see A.K. Wildman, 'Officers of the General Staff and the Kornilov Movement' in E.R. Frankel, J. Frankel and B. Knei-Paz (eds) *Revolution in Russia: Reassessments of 1917* (Cambridge 1992) pp. 76–101.

time, according to the most reliable sources, an armed uprising in Petrograd was being prepared by the Bolsheviks. There were definite indications that they intended to seize power, albeit for a few days, and announce an armistice, taking a decisive and irrevocable step towards the conclusion of a shameful separate peace and, consequently, destroying Russia. That such an intention on the part of the Bolsheviks and certain irresponsible organizations was highly likely is borne out by the fact that among them, as has been indisputably proved, are a large number of traitors and spies working for Germany and German money.

On seeing the impotence of the Provisional Government and its lack of decisiveness in taking energetic measures against persons and organizations leading Russia to certain destruction, in order to avert a catastrophe I have decided to move four cavalry divisions up to Petrograd so that, should a Bolshevik uprising actually follow, it will be decisively and sternly put down. The criminal activities of the traitors on the Home Front must be stopped once and for all.

In this I personally did not pursue any ambitious designs and had no desire to take upon myself the whole burden of personal responsibility for running the country. In agreement with a whole array of people who enjoy popular trust and of public bodies trying to save Russia, and with the help of these eminent public figures, I wanted to give Russia the powerful authorities needed to save itself from destruction and shame. All that I considered necessary was my inclusion in the New Government as Commander-in-Chief.

A Bolshevik uprising in Petrograd was planned for 28–29 August and by the 24th three cavalry divisions were already concentrated in Pskov, Velikie Luki and at Dno station. On the 24th the Head of the Ministry of Defence, Mr Savinkov, came to see me at HQ, bringing a draft of the Provisional Government's measures drawn up on the basis of my demands, and declared that, although the Government shortly intended to implement these measures, it was extremely concerned that they would cause an uprising in Petrograd and meet with strong opposition from irresponsible organizations. At the same time Mr Savinkov informed me that the Provisional Government, expecting a Bolshevik uprising, was unsure of its strength and asked me to put at its disposal a cavalry corps, to be brought up to Petrograd. For its part, the Government, on receiving information about the deployment of the above-mentioned corps, proposed to declare martial law immediately in Petrograd.

The Provisional Government's wishes, conveyed to me by Mr Savinkov, were in complete conformity with my decision and so on the same day I issued the order necessary for putting down a possible uprising in Petrograd.

On 25 August Vladimir L'vov, a member of the State Duma and former Chief Procurator of the Holy Synod, came to see me at HQ on behalf of Prime Minister Kerensky to seek my opinion on his three variants of the organization of power, viz.,

1. Kerensky's resignation from the government
2. Kerensky's continuing participation

3. The establishment by me of a dictatorship, to be announced by the present Provisional Government.

I replied that I considered the establishment of a dictatorship and the declaration of nation-wide martial law the only outcome. By dictatorship I did not mean an individual dictatorship, as I pointed to the necessity of Kerensky and Savinkov's participation. In taking this decision I declared publicly that I definitely considered and do consider a return to the old order completely impossible and that the sole task of the New Government must be the salvation of Russia and the preservation of the civil rights gained by the revolution of 27 February. On the evening of 26 August I again exchanged telegrams with Prime Minister Kerensky, who asked me to confirm what had been said in conversation with L'vov. I did not imagine that an envoy of the Provisional Government could twist the meaning of my conversation with him and replied that I did confirm it and again asked Kerensky and Savinkov to come to HQ, as I would not be able to answer for their safety if they remained in Petrograd. To this the chairman replied that he could not come out to HQ on the 26th, but would do so on the 27th. Thus, before the evening of the 26th, as may be seen from all the above, my actions and decisions were in complete accord with the Provisional Government and I had every reason to believe that the chairman and the Head of the Ministry of Defence were not playing a double game. The morning of the 27th proved me wrong. I received a telegram from the Prime Minister wherein it stated that I was immediately to hand over my duties as Commander-in-Chief to my Chief of Staff and leave immediately for Petrograd. My Chief of Staff refused to accept them. I also considered it impossible to do so prior to a full explanation being given. Throughout the 27th I was in constant telegraph communication with Savinkov, from which it became clear that the Prime Minister and Savinkov himself not only rejected the proposals made to me but also denied their very existence.

Realizing that in the current situation further vacillation was mortally dangerous and that it was too late to rescind my previous orders, I took full responsibility and decided not to hand over my duties as Commander-in-Chief in order to save the Motherland from inevitable destruction and the Russian people from German slavery. In this I was supported by all my front-line commanders and am convinced that all honest defenders of our long-suffering Motherland are with me.

Truth and justice are on our side.

I firmly believe that the Russian army, having risen from its sick-bed, will help me repulse the enemy and drive him from our borders and, having finished the war, in complete unity with our valiant Allies, will thereby help to guarantee for a Free Russia the creative work for the radiant future which it has earned through its great sacrifices in a three-year war.

I simultaneously addressed the Provisional Government as follows, 'Come and see me at HQ where your safety and freedom are guaranteed by my word, and work out with me the composition of a government of National Defence, which in securing victory would lead the Russian people to a great future worthy of a powerful and free people.'

General of the Infantry Kornilov

[Source: *Kornilovskie dni* pp. 109–14.]

In Petrograd, the left frantically mobilized to ward off the threat from Kornilov. While the outcome seemed to hang in the balance, the widening rifts between different segments of the left—between the Bolsheviks and the Mensheviks, between the growing number of radical SRs and Mensheviks and the moderate leadership of the two parties, between the moderate social-ists and Kerensky—were briefly put aside. The government positively encouraged workers to take up arms and radicals muted their criticisms of Kerensky. The Menshevik and SR leadership of the All-Russia Soviet Central Executive Committee (TsIK) desperately appealed to the soldiers reportedly marching on the capital to desert Kornilov and his cause. Aware though the moderate socialists must have been that Kerensky's popularity had rapidly faded, they portrayed him as the soldiers' hero, and anxious though they were at the advantage the Bolsheviks might wring from the situation, they dropped all talk of the party as a threat to the revolution.

Document 24 | From an appeal of the All-Russia TsIK of Soviets of Workers', Soldiers' and Peasants' Deputies

29 August 1917

Comrades—Soldiers!

Hear what we, your brothers, have to say as well. Where are you going? Who are you listening to? Who do you believe?

You have been sent to Petrograd by Kornilov. He and his crew have convinced you that there is a riot in Petrograd, that the workers and Bolsheviks are rioting, that Petrograd has betrayed the Motherland and that you must go to protect the government. It is not true. Kornilov has deceived you. . . . There is complete calm in Petrograd. Your brother workers are at work in the factories and mills, helping you to defend the Motherland and freedom.

Kornilov is bringing you here to turn your guns against the people, against the revolution and against the freedoms won by the revolution. He, Kornilov, wants to spill the blood of your brothers. He, Kornilov, wants to overthrow the Revolutionary government. He, Kornilov, plans to arrest the army's beloved leader, Kerensky. With foul treachery he, Kornilov, wants to seize power to destroy the Revolution and take away land and freedom from the people. Beware, brothers, of starting a civil war in these dark days. Do not give in to the blandishments of Kornilov, that crafty betrayer of Motherland and freedom. He has taken you from the Front, has raised the banner of fratricidal war and is not afraid of opening a front for the German armies. He wants to take Petrograd, the heart of the Revolution, destroy freedom, give back power to the enemies of the people and then deal with you. . .

Comrades, true sons of the Motherland and freedom, the whole country and people are now looking to you in hope. The foul traitor Kornilov may be among your commanders, where there are still servants of the Tsar, but we do not believe that there are traitors to the people's cause and their country among you, sons of the people.

Just remember: a Kornilov government threatens both you and us with the return of the accursed Tsarist order.

[Source: *Kornilovskie dni*, pp. 145–47.]

Fragmentation of the Provisional Government

Under the impact of the Kornilov affair, the coalition collapsed for a second time and Kerensky formed a five-man caretaker 'Directory'. It was at this moment that, desperate to shore up his radical credentials, Kerensky abandoned the Provisional Government's long-standing insistence that only the Constituent Assembly could decide upon the country's state form. He declared Russia a republic.

Document 25 | From a Provisional Government decree

1 September 1917

General Kornilov's rebellion has been suppressed, but the disturbance caused by him in the ranks of the army and the country is very great, and great danger is again threatening the fate of the Motherland and its freedom.

Considering it necessary to put an end to the uncertainty surrounding our state system, and in view of the unanimous and delighted reception of the idea of a republic voiced at the Moscow State Conference, the Provisional Government declares that the state order which the Russian state administers is a republican one and proclaims the Russian Republic.

The urgent need to take immediate and decisive measures for the restoration of the destabilized order has impelled the Provisional Government to transfer all administrative power to five of its members, headed by the Prime Minister. . .

A.F. Kerensky — Prime Minister
A.S. Zarudny — Minister of Justice

[Source: *Kornilovskie dni*, pp. 135–36.]

Kerensky's gestures, however, failed to restore the initiative to the Provisional Government. Moreover, patching the coalition together again proved almost impossible, so deep now was the left's suspicion of the Kadets. A Democratic Conference organized by the Soviet TsIK in September could not agree on whether it would be acceptable to work with Kadet ministers, and when a new cabinet was eventually formed on 22 September, the Kadet, Menshevik and SR figures included in it were only second-rank leaders.[28] Nor did the 'Provisional Council of the Republic', set up two weeks later as a forum to which the government would report in the interim before the Constituent Assembly elections (now due in November), succeed in conferring legitimacy on the new government. This so-called 'Pre-Parliament' was riven by divisions between left and right, and on its opening day Trotsky led a Bolshevik walkout.

The Third Coalition cabinet could not get to grips with the military, social and economic problems it faced. Exacerbating everything else was an increasingly desperate shortage of food. The quandary described by the new Food Minister, Prokopovich (a leading figure in the co-operative movement), differed in intensity rather than kind from that confronted by his predecessor six months earlier: the grain monopoly was inoperative and yet the government was reluctant—and probably unable—to collect grain by force.

Document 26 | S.N. Prokopovich's speech at a meeting of the Pre-Parliament

16 October 1917

Owing to an array of circumstances and difficulties over loading and unloading barges, river transport has not been used properly at all this year, and by September our [food] supplies were completely exhausted... Influenced by the complete exhaustion of supplies both at the Front and within the country, the Provisional Government was compelled to resort to extreme measures—to the doubling of [purchase] prices... We were faced with a dilemma: either try to get grain voluntarily by doubling the price, or resort directly to repressive measures—the use of military force—and use this force to take the grain from the population, because the population would not deliver grain at the old prices. We could not bring ourselves to use military force, but now if at doubled prices we still cannot get the grain we need, we shall of course be obliged to resort to military force...

The food situation is hanging by a thread which could snap at any moment, and so that it does not snap and the peasants continue to give us grain, we must say to

---

28 Galili, *Menshevik Leaders* pp. 379–91.

them that the townspeople are their brothers and that civil war between different parts of the Russian state must not take place...

[Source: S.N. Prokopovich, *Narodnoe khozyaystvo v dni revolyutsii* (Moscow 1918) pp. 36–38.]

Even gloomier was the portrait of the Army given four days later by General A.I. Verkhovsky, Minister of War.

Document 27 | A.I. Verkhovsky's speech at a meeting of the Defence and Foreign Affairs Commissions of the Pre-Parliament

20 October 1917

The Minister of War, A.I. Verkhovsky, declared that he intended to give the Commissions honest and exhaustive information about the state of the Army... Our forces number 10.2 million men. The state does not have the resources to sustain such a vast Army. This raises the question of reducing the size of our armed forces and, consequently, the basic role of these forces, which should be defensive rather than offensive... All possible reductions would amount to no more than 1.2 million, i.e., the Army would be reduced to 9 million men... The Minister of Food declared that it was possible to feed only 7 million. However, HQ would not agree to such a reduction, considering 9 million the minimum for the defence of the Front... At present the war is costing 65–67 million rubles a day... Moreover, costs have been rising continuously: in 1914—4 billion, in 1915—11 billion, in 1916—18 billion, and we are expected to go 8 billion over budget in 1917. In accordance with a demand from the Finance Ministry, work has begun on cutting the war budget, but it has proved possible to cut it by only 5 million a day, which is clearly inadequate...

The prime mover in war—the power of commanders and the obedience of the masses—has been profoundly shaken. No officer can be sure that his orders will be obeyed and his role largely comes down to one of persuasion... No attempts at persuasion work on people who do not understand what they are going to death and deprivation for. There is no point at all thinking about restoring discipline by publishing laws and regulations or by applying the death penalty, because instructions are not being carried out... As for a way out of this difficult situation—strictly speaking, there is none. Nevertheless, the Minister of War has honestly thought over and is applying all those measures which might help raise the Army's fighting efficiency by spring 1918.

The overall plan divides into several parts. Firstly, in connection with the above-mentioned cuts, I envisage calling up the 1920 recruits and putting them with the best available personnel, where they might avoid demoralization. Secondly, serious attention is being paid to sorting out discipline on the Home Front. To this end, subordination of the Home Front to the Front is being introduced; thus, all active units will have corresponding reservists at their complete disposal, with the right to inflict punishment. At the same time we must bear in mind at this point that the dissension observed between the Front and the Home Front may play a certain role: many front-line units have definitely declared that they are prepared to use force if necessary to bring the Home Front to heel...

Along with this, measures are being taken to tackle anarchy in general. To this end, the War Department is prepared to spare 100,000–150,000 fighting men and officers to form reliable militias... The ever-worsening breakdown on the Home Front shows that such a measure is more than necessary and timely... Bolshevism is continuing to sap our fighting strength... If the Bolsheviks have not yet made a bid to seize power, it is only because the representatives of the Front have threatened to suppress them... But who can guarantee that in five days' time this threat will have any force and the Bolsheviks will not make their bid? It must also not be forgotten that peace propaganda is being strongly supported by Germany, and the Minister is reliably informed that two newspapers here are getting funds from the enemy.

The only way to fight all these pernicious and corrupting phenomena is to take the wind out of their sails, i.e., to raise the question of peace ourselves, immediately... Since the concluding of peace will itself require a significant amount of time for the talks, by that time we can reckon on the restoration of the Army's fighting strength, which in turn will reflect favourably on the peace terms...

Yu.O. Tsederbaum (Martov) asked the Minister of War whether his declaration on the suppression of anarchy in the country is to be understood as the establishment of a dictatorship. The Minister replied that it is not a matter of terminology, but to fight the anarchy we also need strong, individual authority, as in the Army, and in that sense the aforesaid authority could be considered a dictatorship...

[Source: *Byloe* No. 12, book 6, 1918, pp. 28–41.]

Verkhovsky's conclusion that the government must sue for peace was regarded as treason by the Kadets: the following day they helped to persuade Kerensky to sack him.[29] By then, however, the government was confronted, as we shall see, by the Bolshevik leadership's semi-public moves to seize power. On 24 October Kerensky harangued the Pre-Parliament about the imminent uprising and demanded wholehearted support for the government against this threat. Although much of the moderate left, as well as the right, condemned Bolshevik plans, the Menshevik leaders had become convinced

---

29 Rosenberg, *Liberals* pp. 257–58.

that a purely military response, without a change in policy, would fail to shore up the government. They narrowly secured majority support for immediate peace talks and the immediate transfer of landowners' estates into the hands of local land committees. That night F.I. Dan led a socialist delegation from the Pre-Parliament to urge Kerensky to adopt the shift in policy, publicize it as widely and swiftly as possible to ensure that every soldier and every worker would know about it, and thereby, they hoped, cut the ground from under the Bolsheviks. In his subsequent account, Kerensky portrayed himself as a hard-headed realist surrounded by innocent dupes.[30]

Document 28 | From Kerensky's memoir *Gatchina*

1922

. . . Never shall I forget the following, truly historical scene. Midnight of 25 [24/25] October. In a break during a meeting of the Provisional Government a fairly stormy exchange was taking place in my office between a socialist delegation from the Council of the Republic and me. It concerned the resolution on the uprising, I had demanded that morning, which had finally been adopted by the left-wing majority in the Council. This now useless resolution was interminably long, confused and barely comprehensible to mere mortals. In essence, instead of expressing support for and trust in the government, although it did not directly refuse it, the resolution did in any case unequivocally distance the Council's left-wing majority from the government and its struggle. I indignantly declared that after such a resolution the government might as well resign the next morning and its authors and those who had voted for it would have to take all the responsibility for events, although they evidently had little idea of what was going on. Dan, no longer simply the Menshevik leader but also acting chairman of the TsIK, replied calmly and reasonably to my agitated tirade. Of course I can no longer reproduce Dan's historic declaration in his own words, but can vouch for its general sense in what follows. First of all, Dan declared that they were far better informed than I, and that I was exaggerating events under the influence of my 'reactionary staff'. He then told me that the Council of the Republic's majority resolution, which was not intended 'to flatter the government', was extremely useful and of vital importance for a 'sudden change in the mood of the masses', that its effect was 'already being felt' and that the influence of Bolshevik propaganda would 'rapidly wane'. On the other hand, according to him, in their talks with the majority leaders in the soviets the Bolsheviks themselves had expressed their willingness 'to bow to majority opinion in the Soviets' and were ready 'the very next day' to take whatever steps were necessary to put down the uprising, 'which had been sparked off against their wishes and without their sanc-

---

30 Kerensky published his most detailed account of the revolution and defence of his own record decades later, *The Kerensky Memoirs* (London 1965).

tion'. In conclusion, Dan mentioned that the Bolsheviks would disband their military headquarters 'the very next day' (always the next day!) and declared that all the measures I had taken for putting down the uprising would only 'serve to irritate the masses' and that 'by interfering' I was merely 'hampering the Soviet majority representatives from having successful talks with the Bolsheviks on putting down the uprising'. Just to complete the picture, I must add that at the very moment Dan was making this remarkable statement armed detachments of 'Red Guards' were occupying one government building after another. And almost straight after Dan and his comrades had left the Winter Palace, Kartashev, the Minister for Religious Affairs, while returning home along Millionnaya Street from a meeting of the Provisional Government, was arrested and taken straight to the Smol'ny [the former aristocratic girls' school which since July had housed the Petrograd Soviet], where Dan had returned to continue peace talks with the Bolsheviks.

I must admit that at the time the Bolsheviks did act with considerable energy and no less skill. . .

[Source: *Oktyabr'skaya revolyutsiya: Memuary* (Moscow and Leningrad 1926) pp. 170–73.]

2

The Bolshevik Seizure
of Soviet Power

The swing to the far left and the October Days

While the Kornilov affair threw the Provisional Government into disarray, it provided a major fillip to the far left and to radical workers, soldiers and sailors. By directly threatening the revolution as it was popularly conceived, the affair gave renewed momentum to their demands for socialists to take power. The following call from the Russian fortification on the Åland islands off Finland was typical.

Document 29 | '... take complete power'...

Resolution of the Soviet of Soldiers', Sailors' and Workers' Deputies of the Asv–Åland fortifications to the Soviet TsIK

30 August 1917

A general meeting of the Asv–Åland Soviet of Soldiers', Sailors' and Workers' Deputies has come to the conclusion that, now the crisis of the revolution has come, you, the Central Committee of the All-Russia Soviet, must unite with the Committees of Peasants' Deputies and the presidium of the Petrograd Soviet of Workers' and Soldiers' Deputies, take complete power and engage in a decisive struggle with the hydra of counter-revolution, and we, the whole garrison, will support you in this struggle with all available means. We are sure that you, Russia's best, will lead the Russian people, who are not afraid of any sacrifices, along the path on which the Revolution does not retreat, but affirms and expands their rights to land, freedom and war [sic]. In our opinion the left wing of the government must enter this truly democratic and authoritative body. The 'dead souls', the State Duma and State Council, must be not only abolished but dispersed, for the spirit of counter-revolution is strong if it is united, but of no significance if scattered, and we are sure that then the road to freedom and equality will be clear.

Signatures of the chairman and secretary

[Source: *Kornilovskie dni*, p. 46.]

In party-political terms, the prime beneficiary of this reaction to the Kornilov affair was the Bolshevik party. The party's repeated warnings that coalition with the representatives of 'the bourgeoisie' opened the way to counter-revolution seemed vindicated. The leaders arrested after the July Days were freed and the charge of German gold was overshadowed by what seemed the treachery of Kornilov and the High Command. In soviets across the country, the Menshevik/SR leadership which had held sway since February found it ever harder to resist increasingly militant resolutions.[31] And with the growth in the political weight of the soviets and the increase of Bolshevik influence within them, the party reaffirmed its call, briefly dropped by Lenin and the leadership after the debacle in July, for the transfer of all power to the soviets.

During September evidence of popular impatience rapidly accumulated. Direct action by peasants against private landownership became more and more common. In the army, officers found their authority in steep decline. The incidence of strikes, especially among less skilled workers, soared. Growing militancy was directly reflected in the shifting political landscape. The 'middle ground' began to crumble. As in soviet elections, so in local government elections and elections to soldiers' committees: supporters of the moderate Menshevik/SR line found themselves losing their earlier dominance and being outvoted by newly elected and more radical deputies. Within the two main socialist parties themselves, Tsereteli and Chernov, whose popularity had seemed unshakeable when they entered the Provisional Government in May, were thrown increasingly on the defensive, the former by the Menshevik-Internationalists led by Martov, the latter by the emergent Left SRs led by Natanson and Spiridonova.[32] In several cases, soviets and emergency committees set up in defiance of the government began to follow the trail blazed by Kronstadt, just as Tsereteli had feared (see document 10), to elbow aside urban dumas and other local bodies and to take power locally.[33]

---

31 For an example of the growing number of local studies confirming the shift, see H. Phillips, 'The Heartland Turns Red: The Bolshevik seizure of power in Tver' *Revolutionary Russia* 14 (2001) pp. 1–21.

32 See I. Getzler, *Martov: A political biography of a Russian Social Democrat* (London 1967), and M. Melancon, 'The Left Socialist Revolutionaries' in Acton et al. (eds) *Critical Companion* pp. 291–99. On the ideological roots of the split within the SR party, see M. Melancon, *The Socialist Revolutionaries and the Russian Anti-War Movement, 1914–1917* (Columbus, OH, 1990).

33 See N.N. Smirnov, 'The Soviets' in Acton et al. (eds) *Critical Companion* pp. 429–37; M. Melancon, 'The Syntax of Soviet Power: the resolutions of local soviets and other institutions', March–October 1917' *Russian Review* 52 (1993) pp. 486–505.

Among the Bolshevik leaders, Lenin's attitude most closely echoed popular militancy. From mid–September, he urged his colleagues that the time had come for the Bolsheviks to organize the overthrow of the Provisional Government, proclaim Soviet power and form a soviet-based government. Initially, his colleagues saw this as dangerous adventurism and reacted with scepticism and alarm, but he remained adamant and, from hiding in Finland, he continued to bombard them with letters making the case for immediate action. Lenin had no fixed plan. Sometimes he urged that the revolt start in Moscow, sometimes in Petrograd; at times he saw an armed uprising as essential, at times he insisted a simple proclamation of Soviet power would prove irresistible. Above all he piled argument upon argument—the risks of a second Kornilov putsch, of popular frustration being replaced by anarchy and despair, of the moderate socialist leaders of the TsIK postponing the planned Second All-Russia Soviet Congress, of Kerensky deliberately snuffing out revolution in Petrograd by surrendering it to the Germans, the imminence of revolution in Germany—to persuade them that to wait would be perilous and un-forgivable.

Document 30 | From Lenin's letter to the Central, Petrograd and Moscow Committees and Bolshevik members of the Petrograd and Moscow Soviets

1 October 1917

Dear Comrades,

Events are prescribing our task so clearly for us that procrastination is becoming positively *criminal*.

The peasant movement is developing. The government is intensifying its severe repressive measures. Sympathy for us is growing in the Army...

In Germany the beginning of a revolution is obvious, especially since the sailors were shot. The elections in Moscow—47 per cent Bolsheviks—are a tremendous victory. Together with the Left Socialist-Revolutionaries we have an *obvious* majority *in the country*.

The railway and postal employees are in conflict with the government. Instead of calling the Congress for 20 October, the Liberdans [Lenin's sarcastic phrase for the Menshevik leaders M.I. Liber, F.I. Dan and their followers] are already talking of calling it at the end of October, etc., etc.

Under such circumstances to 'wait' would be a crime.

The Bolsheviks have no right to wait for the Congress of Soviets; they must *take power at once*. By so doing they will save the world revolution (for otherwise there is danger of a deal between the imperialists of all countries, who, after the shootings in Germany, will be more accommodating to each other and *will unite against us*), the Russian revolution (otherwise a wave of real anarchy may become stronger *than we are*) and the lives of hundreds of thousands of people at the Front. . .

If power cannot be achieved without insurrection, we must *resort to insurrection at once*. It may very well be that right now power can be achieved without insurrection, for example, if the Moscow Soviet were to take power at once, immediately, and proclaim itself (together with the Petrograd Soviet) the government. Victory in Moscow is guaranteed, and there is no need to fight. Petrograd can wait. The government cannot do anything to save itself; it will surrender.

For, by seizing power and taking over the banks, the factories and [pro–government newspaper] *Russkoye slovo*, the Moscow Soviet would secure a tremendous basis and tremendous strength; it would be able to campaign throughout Russia and raise the issue thus: we shall propose *peace tomorrow* if the Bonapartist Kerensky surrenders (and if he does not, we shall overthrow him). We shall hand over the *land* to the peasants at *once*, we shall make concessions to the railway and postal employees *at once*, and so on. . .

[Source: V.I. Lenin, *Collected Works* Volume XXVI (Moscow 1972) pp. 140–41.]

Lenin's insistence, reinforced by radical elements lower down the party, gradually won over the Central Committee, which on 10 October committed itself to an armed rising and reaffirmed the decision six days later. However, two of his closest colleagues, Kamenev and Zinoviev, continued to dissent. To Lenin's fury, news of their opposition was published in the internationalist social-democratic paper, *Novaya zhizn'*. While they maintained the public line that the leadership had made no decision on the matter, they spelled out why they opposed the idea.

Document 31 | The protest published by Kamenev and Zinoviev in *Novaya zhizn'*

18 October 1917

In his article yesterday V. Bazarov mentioned a leaflet against a rising put out in the name of two eminent Bolsheviks, concerning which L. Kamenev says, 'In view of the intensified discussion of the question of a rising, comrade Zinoviev and I have written to our main Party organizations in Petrograd, Moscow and Finland, speaking out decisively against our Party engaging in any kind of armed risings in the near future. I have to say that I know of no Party decision naming the day for a rising. Such Party decisions do not exist. Everyone realizes that there is simply no question of something like an "armed demonstration" in the current state of the revolution. It can only be a question of an armed seizure of power, and those answerable to the proletariat cannot but realize that any movement towards a mass "rising" must involve the clear and definite consideration of an armed insurrection. Not only comrade Zinoviev and I but also a number of Party workers consider that taking the initiative for an armed uprising independently at the present moment, a few days before the Soviet congress, and with the given alignment of social forces, would be an inadmissible and fatal step for the proletariat and the revolution. There is no party, and least of all ours, within which the hopes and trust of the masses are increasingly being concentrated, that cannot but aspire to power and the implementation of its programme through state power. No revolutionary party, and least of all ours, the party of the proletariat and the poor of the cities and villages, can or has the right to reject or renounce insurrection. An insurrection against a government which is ruining the country is the inalienable right of the toiling masses, and at certain times is the sacred duty of those parties the masses trust. But, as Marx said, insurrection is an art. And this is why we consider that in the given circumstances it is now our duty to speak out against any attempt to take the initiative for an armed insurrection, which would be doomed to defeat and entail the most disastrous consequences for the Party, the proletariat and the fate of the revolution. To stake everything on an uprising in the near future would be an act of desperation, when our Party is too strong and with too great a future to take such a step.'

[Source: *Novaya zhizn'*, 18 October 1917.]

Although the party had formally decided to attempt to seize power, the organized force at its disposal was very limited, as those responsible for the Bolshevik organization in the army warned Lenin. In the days which followed, however, the Bolshevik leadership in Petrograd, with Trotsky at their head, adapted their tactics to maximize popular support.[34]

The rising was to appear defensive; it was to be led by and clearly identified with the Petrograd Soviet more than the party; and it was to be timed to coincide with the convening of and receive immediate legitimization from the Second All-Russia Soviet Congress, due on 25 October. The key organ was the Military Revolutionary Committee (MRC), which had been established by the Petrograd Soviet on 9 October to co-ordinate measures against a possible second right-wing putsch. Like the Soviet, the MRC was now dominated by Bolsheviks, and its membership overlapped with that of the party's Central Committee, which was in direct contact with it, both operating from the same building as the Soviet, the Smol'ny Institute. The MRC's first steps were taken in response to government actions: it asserted its own

---

34 The best account remains A. Rabinowitch, *The Bolsheviks Come to Power* (New York 1976).

authority over the garrison when the government moved to transfer radicalized units to the Front, and on 24 October responded with force to government attempts to close the Bolshevik press and raise the bridges linking working-class districts to the centre of the capital. But that night, impatiently urged on by Lenin, who had just arrived at party headquarters, the MRC went onto the offensive. Kerensky was unable to mobilize any significant armed force and key positions were rapidly taken over by supporters of Soviet power. Many of the groups of soldiers, sailors and Red Guards (armed detachments of radical workers) involved were mobilized on local initiative rather than under central direction.[35] The makeshift nature of the forces directed from the Smol'ny is conveyed in this memoir by P.D. Mal'kov, a Bolshevik and former sailor who served the MRC during the October Days and after the seizure of power became Commandant of the Smol'ny, from where Lenin's government initially operated.

Document 32 | The seizure of power as recalled by P.D. Mal'kov

1957

In Petrograd there was a newspaper called *Birzhevye vedomosti* [*Stock-Exchange News*], or *Birzhevka*, as we used to call it. A nasty little rag. It printed all sorts of slander against the Bolsheviks and the Baltic Fleet sailors. We often sent them resolutions of protest from Helsingfors, but they never printed them. The Baltic sailors were wondering what to do about it. A decision was taken to ask the government to close *Birzhevka*, as a libellous, bourgeois newspaper. But did the Provisional Government ever take any notice at all of our decisions?! I remembered *Birzhevka* and our resolutions—this was about 5 a.m.—and drove off to the minelayer *Amur*. I collected eight sailors and we set off to close *Birzhevka*. We drove up to the editorial office. The lads stood by the door—nobody in or out. We saw some kids running to sell the latest edition. We took the papers off them, threw them away and told the kids to clear off. Me, I went to the editor's office. I went in and told them the paper was closing. There were several people sitting there in silence. Some girl was about to start arguing with me, but I wasn't going to talk to her. 'You,' I said, 'are cultured people and write articles. The revolution's begun in Russia and you're still putting out your filthy newspaper! Get out of here and let's hear no more of you!' We sent the editorial staff of *Birzhevka* packing. Next to them in the same building are the offices of the magazine *Ogonyok*, another lousy paper. We shut that down as well. Putting somebody on guard I went off to the Smol'ny to report. This was about 7 a.m. on 25 October. I'd had no sleep for two whole days and was starving. I spotted a bakery. I went in, but they didn't want to sell me any bread because I didn't have

---

35 R. Wade, *Red Guards and Workers' Militia in the Russian Revolution* (Stanford, CA, 1984), pp. 196–207.

a ration-card. I said to them, 'Where am I supposed to get one of them?! You can see I'm a sailor. I haven't got one!' But they were sticking to their guns until some women in the shop started kicking up a fuss, 'Give him some bread, he's fighting for the revolution!'. . .

'The cadets have taken the telephone exchange,' said Podvoysky, 'and Antonov-Ovseenko's been arrested. Nobody can get through to the Smol'ny. Do something!' I left some fifteen sailors to guard the Smol'ny and set off with the rest to get the telephone exchange back. But how was I going to get there? There was no time to lose, it was a long way to the exchange and I didn't have a car. What were we going to do? We saw a tram coming. We stopped it, made the passengers get off and the lads got on. The people who'd been in the tram were making a fuss, but we hadn't got time to bandy words with them. I sat next to the tram-driver and said, 'Take us to the Peter and Paul Fortress, you!' Off he went. We'd brought our rifles with us. We got to the fortress, got hold of a cannon, hitched it onto the tram and moved off to Pochtovaya Street, where the telephone exchange was. As we went along, the gun was rumbling behind us along the road. We rode up to Pochtovaya Street, but couldn't get any further. We unhitched the cannon and pulled it along ourselves. We aimed it at the exchange and shouted to the cadets, 'Surrender or we'll open fire right now!' They put out a white flag. Out came Antonov-Ovseenko with about thirty cadets now under arrest. What could they do against artillery?! We sent them off to the Peter and Paul Fortress and occupied the exchange. The telephonists refused to work, so in their place we put sailors, who put the Smol'ny through straightaway. I set off back there. . .

[Source: *V dni Oktyabrya: Sbornik vospominaniy uchastnikov Oktyabr'skoy revolyutsii* (Moscow 1957) pp. 52–56.]

As late as the afternoon of 24 October, Trotsky, Stalin and the MRC had continued to deny categorically that they planned seizing power. They misled not only the moderate socialists but also radical SR leaders (now in the process of forming a breakaway Left SR Party), who thus far had co-operated closely, as well as provincial Bolsheviks arriving for the Soviet Congress, and indeed senior figures in the party. This letter from Lunacharsky to his wife, written just as Lenin's announcement that the Provisional Government had fallen was being telegraphed across the country, captures the mixture of exultation, anxiety and confusion amongst the Bolsheviks themselves about the likely outcome.

Document 33 | A letter from A.V. Lunacharsky to his wife

25 October 1917

. . . I'm writing on the morning of the 25th. To all intents and purposes the power struggle has begun. It's fair to say that Kerensky was the first to go on the offensive. You know from the papers what happened on the 24th, so I'm telling you only what concerns me. I spent all day in the [Petrograd] Duma, i.e., first at a special meeting of the Board and then at the Duma. I spoke at both. The Duma's the most important because you speak in public and political actions are taken there. Politically I did of course show my solidarity with the Bolsheviks. It's obvious to me that there's no hope for Russia unless all power goes to the Soviets. Well, there is another possibility—a purely democratic coalition, i.e., a front made up of Lenin, Martov, Chernov, Dan and Verkhovsky—but that would need so much good will and political wisdom on all sides that it's obviously utopian.

So, politically I've defended this idea, while in practice I've advised the city to take measures to protect the lives and property of citizens, to deal with hooligans, to stop the looting of grain and spirit stores and to set up a Red Cross organization, etc. The official proposal by the mayor [an SR] is like mine, but it's obvious from their behaviour that at this decisive moment the SRs feel closer to the Constitutional Democrats [Kadets] than to us.

I still don't know what happened in the early hours of this morning. Yesterday some provocateur killed a police inspector who'd told a crowd on the Nevsky to disperse.

The Council of the Republic's resolution might offer the feeble hope of a more or less peaceful compromise. Well, we shall see what we shall see. There's not long to wait. Today or tomorrow everything'll be sorted out on three points:

1) either the Provisional Government is completely victorious, in which case a slow but sure reaction will set in;

2) or the Petrograd Soviet is completely victorious, in which case there'll be a number of revolutionary rescue measures, but what a responsibility and what horrendous difficulties;

3) or there'll be democratic power without census [propertied] elements. The Constituent Assembly will be convened, there will be intelligent opposition from the Bolsheviks and, perhaps, their participation in a democratic government. The difficulties are enormous—yet it's still the best outcome. . .

These are really terrible times, on a knife-edge. There's a lot of anxiety and suffering, and perhaps we're threatened with an early death. All the same, I'm happy to be alive at a time of such great events when history isn't half-asleep but is flying like a bird over trackless wastes.

[Source: RGASPI, fond 142, opis' 1, delo 12, pp. 137–38.]

When the overthrow of the Provisional Government was debated in the Petrograd Soviet and then at the Second Soviet Congress, the Mensheviks and Centre/Right SRs denounced the Bolsheviks and stormed out. What had already been a large majority in favour of Soviet power thus became virtually unanimous. The Left SRs, despite fury at Bolshevik deception, elected to throw their lot in with them and accept seats on a new, Bolshevik-dominated TsIK.[36] The Congress endorsed a series of revolutionary and overwhelmingly popular decrees—on Peace, pronouncing an immediate armistice, on Land, sanctioning immediate take-over without compensation of private land, and soon afterwards, on Workers' Control and National Self-Determination—and confirmed in office a new government, the 'Council of People's Commissars' (Sovnarkom), headed by Lenin.

Lenin's first weeks in office

The new government's position was precarious. Even in towns and cities where Soviet power had already been or soon would be proclaimed, local soviets were by no means automatically willing to accept instructions from Petrograd. The government lacked organized and reliable armed force; many civil servants refused to serve it; in Moscow, the proclamation of Soviet power triggered violent, if short-lived, resistance; and across the country opponents of the new regime were vociferous in denouncing it. The day after taking office, Lenin ordered—though could only very patchily enforce—an immediate clampdown on the anti-government press.

Document 34 | The introduction of press censorship—decree of the Council of People's Commissars

27 October 1917

At an absolutely crucial moment for the Revolution, and in the days immediately afterwards, the Provisional Revolutionary Committee has been forced to apply a whole series of measures against the counter-revolutionary press of various hues. From all sides there have been immediate cries that the new socialist government has thereby violated a fundamental principle of its programme by encroaching upon the freedom of the press.

The Workers' and Peasants' Government directs attention to the fact that in our society this liberal façade is in reality a cover for freedom for the propertied classes,

---

36 On the Left SRs in October, see M. Melancon, 'The Left Socialist Revolutionaries and the Bolshevik Uprising' in V.N. Brovkin (ed.) *The Bolsheviks in Russian Society: The revolution and the civil wars* (New Haven 1997).

who have grabbed the lion's share of the press, to poison minds and sow discord in the consciousness of the masses without restriction. Everyone knows that the bourgeois press is one of the most potent weapons of the bourgeoisie. Particularly at the critical moment when the new government, a government of workers and peasants, is only just consolidating itself, it has proved impossible to leave this weapon entirely in enemy hands at a time when it is no less dangerous than bombs and bullets. That is why temporary measures for stopping the flow of filth and slander have been taken—filth and slander in which the yellow and green press would gladly drown the people's young victory.

As soon as the new order is consolidated, all administrative pressure on the press will cease and complete freedom will be established within the confines of responsibility before the courts, according to the broadest and most progressive law in this respect. However, in the belief that restrictions on the press, even at the most critical moments, are permissible only within absolutely necessary limits, the Council of People's Commissars decrees as follows:

General Statute on the Press

1. Only those organs of the press are to be closed which
   a. call for open resistance or disobedience to the Workers' and Peasants' Government;
   b. sow discord by clearly libellous distortion of facts;
   c. call for the commission of clearly criminal acts, punishable by law.
2. The closure of newspapers, temporary or permanent, may be carried out only by a decree of the Council of People's Commissars.
3. The present statute has a temporary character and will be repealed by special decree upon the onset of normal conditions of public life.

Vladimir Ul'yanov (Lenin), Chairman of the Council of People's Commissars

[Source: *Pravda*, 28 October 1917.]

Moderate and right-wing Mensheviks remained convinced that a government committed to socialism and dependent on the country's small working class was doomed to failure. This viewpoint, long argued by Tsereteli in defence of coalition with progressive liberals, was reiterated now by the 'father' of Russian Social Democracy, whom the young Lenin had once revered, Plekhanov.[37]

---

37 On the ideological gulf that opened up between Plekhanov and the Bolsheviks, see what remains the standard biography, S.H. Baron, *Plekhanov: The father of Russian Marxism* (Stanford, CA, 1963).

Document 35 | An open letter from G.V. Plekhanov to Petrograd's workers

27 October 1917

Comrades,

There is no doubt that many of you welcome the events which brought about the fall of A.F. Kerensky's coalition government and the transfer of political power to the Petrograd Soviet of Workers' and Soldiers' Deputies. I must be honest: I am grieved by these events, not because I did not want the triumph of the working class, but, on the contrary, because that is what I want with all my heart.

In recent months we social democrats have often had cause to recall Engels' remark that for the working class there could be no greater historical tragedy than to seize power at a time when it is not yet ready for it... Our working class is still very far from being capable of taking on full political power in a way that would benefit both itself and the country. To foist such power onto it is to force it along a road of very great historical misfortune, a road of supreme misfortune for Russia as well.

Among the population of our country, the proletariat comprises *not the majority but the minority*. It could successfully exercise its dictatorship only if it were the majority. No serious socialist would dispute this. It is true that the working class can rely on the support of the peasants, still the majority of Russia's population, but the peasants need land, not the replacement of the capitalist by the socialist order... Consequently, the peasantry is a completely unreliable ally for the workers in establishing the socialist mode of production... If on seizing power our proletariat wanted to accomplish a 'social revolution', our country's economy itself would condemn it to a terrible defeat.

It is said that what the Russian worker starts will be finished off by the Germans, but this is an enormous mistake. No one would deny that in the economic sense Germany is far more highly developed than Russia. The 'social revolution' is far closer for the Germans than it is for the Russians, but it is not yet on the agenda even for them. Even before the war began, all serious German social democrats, right and left, were perfectly aware of this. The war has diminished the chances of social revolution in Germany even more because of the sad fact that the majority of the German proletariat, led by Scheidemann, gave its support to the German imperialists. In Germany at the moment there is no hope of either a 'social' or a political revolution. Bernstein, Haase, Kautsky and, probably, Karl Liebknecht—all would admit it... By seizing power prematurely the Russian proletariat will not accomplish a social revolution but only cause a civil war, which in the end will force it to retreat much further than the positions gained this February and March ...

Power must rest on a coalition of all the country's vital forces, i.e., on all those classes and strata which are not interested in the restoration of the old order.

Yours, G. Plekhanov

[Source: *Edinstvo*, 28 October 1917.]

Plekhanov's viewpoint cut no ice with most Bolsheviks or Left SRs. A growing proportion of Mensheviks, too, could no longer stomach the idea of further coalition with liberals. What was contentious, however, was the option of forming a soviet-based government which included Mensheviks as well as Bolsheviks, Centre/Right SRs as well as Left SRs, and the minor socialist parties. This was the demand made by Martov and the Menshevik Internationalists and by the Left SRs; it was what most lower-ranking Bolsheviks had assumed would be the outcome of the transfer of power to the soviets; and it commanded substantial support amongst workers. On 29 October the powerful Union of Railway Employees threatened a strike to compel the different parties to come together. The Centre/Right SR leaders were deeply reluctant to compromise, and even insisted that the two most prominent Bolsheviks be excluded from the putative all-socialist coalition government. Lenin and Trotsky were every bit as reluctant, and could see no advantage in co-operating with socialists who, they argued, had shown their true colours by shoring up the Provisional Government.[38] But they were wary of refusing while the outcome of fighting in Moscow and of Kerensky's attempt to launch loyal Cossack divisions on Petrograd remained unclear. Moreover, a socialist coalition was favoured by several leading Bolsheviks, the foremost among them being Kamenev, who had just been elected chairman of the new TsIK, and V.P. Nogin, Commissar for Trade and Industry.

Document 36 | The Bolshevik debate over socialist coalition government— from the minutes of a meeting of the Petersburg Committee of the RSDRP(b)

1 November 1917

Lenin: When comrades Zinoviev and Kamenev started agitating against the uprising, they were looked upon as strike-breakers. I even wrote to the Central Committee proposing their expulsion from the Party... I wouldn't want... to be strict with them.

I look favourably on Kamenev's talks about an agreement in the Central Executive Committee, because we're not against it in principle.

However, when the Socialist Revolutionaries refused to be involved, I realized that they'd done so after Kerensky had started resisting. Things were dragging on ... in Moscow. Our people ... were getting pessimistic ... And then came the question of an agreement ...

---

38 For conflicting views on responsibility for the breakdown of negotiations, see D. Mandel, *The Petrograd Workers and the Soviet Seizure of Power* (London 1984) pp. 310–42, and G. Swain, *The Origins of the Russian Civil War* (London 1996) pp. 53–73.

The Bolsheviks were often far too nice. Had the bourgeoisie been the victor, it would have acted as it did in 1848 and 1871. Did anyone at all think that we wouldn't meet with sabotage from the bourgeoisie? It's obvious. . . even to a child. We have to apply force as well: arrest a few directors of banks and the like. Even some short-term arrests have been producing favourable results. . .

And just at the moment we come to power—a split. Zinoviev and Kamenev are saying that we haven't seized power [in the whole country]. I'm not going to just sit back and listen to this. I see it as treachery. What do they want—the start of a spontaneous bloodbath? Only the proletariat can get the country out . . . As for an agreement . . . I can't talk about one seriously. Trotsky said a long time ago that unification was impossible. Trotsky realized this and since then there's not been a better Bolshevik . . . Agree with the appeasers and they'll go and stick a spoke in the wheel . . .

They're saying that we want to 'introduce' socialism—that's absurd. . . They're telling us that we've got to 'stop', but that's impossible. . . If there's going to be a split, so be it. If they're in the majority, then take power in the Central Executive Committee and act, and we'll go to the sailors. . .

Our slogan now is: no agreement, i.e., for a homogeneous Bolshevik government.

Trotsky: We're being told we haven't got any cotton or paraffin so there's got to be an agreement, but I'm asking for the umpteenth time: how will an agreement with Gots and Dan give us any paraffin? Why are the Chernovs against us? . . . They're against us. . . because we're taking harsh measures against the bourgeoisie, but nobody knows yet what harsh measures we'll be forced to take. All that the Chernovs are capable of contributing to our work is vacillation, but vacillation in the struggle with the enemy will kill off our authority among the masses . . .

Nogin: Can we do it like this: spill blood together, but rule separately? Can the soldiers be denied power? A civil war will last for years. As for the peasants, you won't get far with bayonets . . . What'll happen if we drive off all the other parties? The Socialist Revolutionaries left the Soviet after the revolution, and the Mensheviks did too. But this means the soviets will fall to pieces. With the complete breakdown in the country such a state of affairs will end in the collapse of our party in a short time . . . Famine will pave the way for Kaledin, who's already moving against us. And by sending a telegram to the railwaymen, whom we're going to deprive of bread-ration cards, we'll really pave the way for a powerful protest . . .

[Source: RGASPI, fond 2, opis' 1, delo 25830, pp. 235–42.]

Lenin and Trotsky became increasingly assertive, insisting they would only negotiate on a coalition with the Left SRs, and this provoked Kamenev to resign as chairman of the TsIK and four of Lenin's eleven-strong cabinet, including Nogin, to resign from the Sovnarkom. With the Centre/Right SRs remaining intransigent, the pressure from the Railway Union faltering, and news that Kerensky's modest forces had been defeated, Lenin's position strengthened and the Left SRs agreed to negotiate their own entry into the Bolshevik-dominated government. Nevertheless, criticism of the new regime continued to be fierce. On the far left, former allies of Lenin, including the popular author Maksim Gorky, who co-edited *Novaya zhizn'*, warned of a yawning gulf between reality and the Bolshevik leadership's celebration of a socialist dawn and proletarian liberation. The reality, he insisted, was mindless destruction and disdain for culture among workers, themselves hopelessly outnumbered by even more ignorant soldiers and peasants.

Document 37 | M. Gorky: 'No matter who has power, I reserve my human right to be critical of it...'

19 November 1917

It says in *Pravda*, 'Gorky has started talking like an enemy of the working class.' This is not true. Addressing the most politically conscious representatives of the working class, I say this: by arousing hopes among the masses which are unrealizable in the present historical situation, fanatics and frivolous fantasists are enticing the Russian proletariat to crushing defeat and ruin, and the defeat of the proletariat will cause a prolonged and sombre reaction in Russia. Further on in *Pravda* it says, 'Any revolution, in the course of its onward march will inevitably also include a number of negative phenomena. These are inevitably connected with the breaking up of the previous, thousand-year-old state system. In the process of creating a new life, the young hero's muscular arms will infringe upon the decadent comfort of others. The petit-bourgeois philistines, the very ones Gorky has been writing about, will start to wail about the ruin of the Russian state and culture.' I cannot regard such things as the pillaging of national property in the Winter Palace, Gatchina and other palaces as 'inevitable'. I do not see the connection between 'the breaking up of a thousand-year-old state system' and the devastation of the Maly Theatre in Moscow and burglary in the dressing-room of the famous artiste M.N. Yermolova.

Without wishing to enumerate all the well-known acts of senseless violence and robbery, I assert that the responsibility for such shameful acts of vandalism lies also with the proletariat, which is clearly incapable of extirpating the vandalism in its midst. Furthermore, 'in the process of creating a new life, the young hero' is making publishing more and more impossible, as there are presses where the typesetters are earning only 35 per cent of the junior rate set by the printers' union.

The proletariat, numerically feeble amidst Russia's one-hundred-million-strong semi-literate rural population, has to realize the importance of cheaper books and the spread of publishing, but to its cost it does not. It also has to realize that it is resting on bayonets—not particularly firm ground, as everyone knows. In general, there are a lot of 'negative phenomena', but where on earth are the positive ones? Apart from Lenin and Trotsky's 'decrees', they are not obvious, and I doubt whether the proletariat has played much of a part in drafting these 'decrees'. No, if the proletariat were really involved in all these paper creations, they would look very different.

The article in *Pravda* concludes with the following lyrical question, 'When a joyous festival of the peoples brings together in a great surge of fraternity those who had previously, against their will, been enemies, will Gorky, who has so quickly defected from the ranks of the genuine revolutionary democracy, be a welcome guest at this peace banquet?'

Of course, neither the author of the article nor I will live to see this 'joyous festival'—it is a long way off, and decades of persistent, mundane cultural work will be needed to prepare for it. But at a festival where the despotism of the semi-literate masses celebrates its easy victory and—as before and as always—the human personality remains oppressed, there is no place for me. For me, that is no festival.

No matter who has power, I reserve my human right to be critical of it, and I am particularly suspicious and mistrustful of Russians in power—recently slaves themselves, they will become unbridled despots as soon as they have the chance to be their neighbours' masters.

[Source: *Novaya zhizn'*, 19 November 1917.]

An equally gloomy forecast was given by A.A. Bogdanov, a long-standing associate of Gorky and one-time rival to Lenin for the Bolshevik leadership. Bogdanov was a Marxist theoretician best known for his emphasis on the need to develop a specifically socialist culture and for his work with the Russian Proletarian Cultural Educational Association (*Proletkul't*) from 1917 to 1921.[39] He berated his brother-in-law, Lunacharsky, who had himself briefly resigned his post as Commissar for Enlightenment in protest against the wanton destruction which had outraged Gorky.

Document 38 | From a letter by A.A. Bogdanov to A.V. Lunacharsky

19 November 1917

I see nothing funny in the often absurd things which you almost always find yourselves obliged to do. Not only can I see the tragedy of our situation but also think that *you* are far from fully aware of it, so I will try to explain it in my own way.

---

39 See L. Mally, *Culture of the Future: The Proletkult movement in revolutionary Russia* (Berkeley, CA, 1990).

The root of it all is the war. It has brought about two fundamental things:
1) economic and cultural decline
2) the enormous growth of war communism.

War communism, which has spread from the Front to the Home Front, has temporarily restructured society: the multi-million commune of the Army, rations for soldiers' families, the regulation of consumption *in accordance with this*, and quotas for supply and output. The whole system of state capitalism is nothing other than the mongrel of capitalism and consumer war communism—something the present economists, who have no idea about organizational analysis, do not understand. The atmosphere of war communism has brought about maximalism. . .

Maximalism has developed more in Russia than in Europe because capitalism is weaker here and the influence of war communism as an organizational form is correspondingly stronger. The Bolshevik party was formerly a socialist workers' party, but the revolution, under military influence, has imposed tasks on it which have profoundly distorted its nature. It has had to organize the pseudo-socialist masses of soldiers (peasants taken away from production and living off the state in communal barracks). Why specifically the Bolshevik party? Seemingly simply because it has been the party of *peace*, just what the soldiers want right now. The party has become a workers' and soldiers' party, but what does that mean? There is a principle in tektology* that says: if a system consists of parts with higher and lower levels of organization, then its relationship to its environment is determined by the lower level of organization. For example, the strength of a chain is determined by its weakest link, and the speed of a squadron by the slowest ship, etc. The political position of a party made of various social classes is determined by the most backward elements. The workers' and soldiers' party is objectively just a soldiers' party. And it is striking how much Bolshevism has changed in this respect. It has adopted the logic of the barracks, their methods, culture and ideals.

Barracks logic, unlike that of the factory, is characterized by seeing everything in terms of force rather than organizational experience and work. Smashing the bourgeoisie—that's socialism. Seize power, then we can do anything. Agreement? What for? Share the spoils? Not likely! What, there is no other way? Well, all right then, let's share . . . Hey, stop! We're stronger again! We don't have to, etc. . . .

There will not be a socialist revolution in Europe now: its working class is not at that level of culture and organization, its level of maturity has been clearly shown by the history of the war. There will be a series of abolitionist revolutions: abolishing the legacy of the war, authoritarianism (oligarchy, dictatorship), debts (consequently, the hypertrophy of the *rentier* class), the remnants of national oppression, the national isolationism recreated by the war and entrenched by state capitalism, etc.—there is a great deal of work. However, in Russia the soldier-

---

* The term Bogdanov coined for his organizational theory.

communist revolution is something more opposed to, rather than approximating to, a socialist one. . .

[Source: A.A. Bogdanov, *Voprosy sotsializma* (Moscow 1990) pp. 352–55.]

The Constituent Assembly and the Third All-Russian Soviet Congress

Between mid-November and the beginning of December, the long-awaited elections to the Constituent Assembly took place. The Bolshevik party had clamoured for the elections, acknowledging no contradiction in demanding both an Assembly empowered to draw up a constitution and the transfer of all power to the soviets. Early in November, the Central Committee was optimistic that, in alliance with the Left SRs, they would command a majority. In the event, the Bolsheviks were resoundingly defeated: support for Lenin's party was concentrated among workers and soldiers, and it won only 22.5 per cent of the total vote.[40] However, this has encouraged a distorted picture of the elections in most western accounts. The elections confirmed the massive repudiation of the old order and the strength of the leftward current: socialist parties gained over 80 per cent of the vote. The Mensheviks were electorally annihilated everywhere except Georgia: the Bolsheviks outperformed them by almost 10 to 1. The Left SRs emerged grossly under-represented: although the SRs won over 40 per cent—with the Ukrainian SRs winning another 8 per cent—the establishment of a separate Left SR party had come too late for the ballot papers to enable peasants to indicate whether they preferred them or the Centre/Right SRs, who had stood by the Provisional Government. The latter still controlled much of the party's organization and were able to ensure that Left SRs, although their policies were much more in tune with popular opinion than those of the Centre/Right, secured only 10 per cent of the seats allotted to the party.

The Assembly was due to open on 28 November, but less than a quarter of the delegates had arrived in Petrograd by then and when right-wing socialists and Kadets tried to start proceedings, government forces intervened. That evening the Council of People's Commissars banned the Kadet party, accusing it of using the Assembly as cover for a planned counter-revolution.

---

40 For the best study in English, see O.H. Radkey, *Russia Goes to the Polls: The elections to the All-Russian Constituent Assembly, 1917* (Ithaca, NY, 1989). Radkey put the Bolshevik share at around 24 per cent, but the most recent Russian analysis, by L.G. Protasov, suggests the lower figure.

Document 39 | The decree on the opening of the Constituent Assembly and the banning of the Kadet party

28 November 1917

. . . The Council of People's Commissars has decreed that the Constituent Assembly will be opened as soon as there is a quorum of half, i.e., 400 out of 800 members. This decision provides the best refutation of malicious slanders claiming that the Council of People's Commissars, which relies on all the country's toiling classes, does not want to convene the Constituent Assembly. But this is exactly why the bourgeoisie could not calmly wait for the lawful convocation of the people's representatives. On the evening of 28 November a few dozen people calling themselves deputies without showing any documents, along with armed White Guards, army cadets and several thousand bourgeois and saboteur-bureaucrats, burst into the Tauride Palace.

The Constitutional Democratic Party's intention was to create a 'legal' cover for a Constitutional-Democratic and Kaledinite counter-revolutionary uprising. They wanted to present the voices of a few dozen bourgeois deputies as the voice of the Constituent Assembly. . .

All the people's achievements, including the imminent peace, are at stake. In the south is Kaledin; in the east, Dutov; and, finally, in the country's political centre, in Petrograd, a plot by the central committee of the Constitutional Democratic Party, which is continuously sending aid to Kaledin and Kornilovite officers in the south. The slightest indecisiveness or weakness on the part of the people could end in the downfall of the soviets and the cause of peace, the collapse of land reform and absolute power again in the hands of landowners and capitalists.

Fully aware of the immense responsibility now borne by Soviet power, for the sake of the people and the revolution the Council of People's Commissars declares the Constitutional Democratic Party, as organizers of counter-revolutionary revolt, to be a party of enemies of the people. . .

The political leaders of the counter-revolutionary civil war will be arrested. The bourgeois revolt will be put down at all costs . . .

Down with the bourgeoisie! There is no place for enemies of the people, landowners and capitalists in the Constituent Assembly! The country can be saved only by a Constituent Assembly of representatives of the toiling and exploited classes of the people! Long live the revolution! Long live the soviets! Long live peace!

The Council of People's Commissars

[Source: *Pravda*, 30 November 1917.]

Meanwhile, negotiations over coalition with the Left SRs had continued since early November, and an agreement under which five Left SRs joined the Sovnarkomwas reached while deputies were arriving in Petrograd.

Document 40 | The entry of the Left SRs into Lenin's government

12 December 1917

At a meeting of the Central Executive Committee of the Soviet of Workers', Soldiers' and Peasants' Deputies the following have been confirmed as members of the Council of People's Commissars:
Comrade Steinberg—People's Commissar for Justice
Comrade Trutovsky—People's Commissar for Local Government
Comrade Karelin—People's Commissar for the Property of the Russian Republic
Comrades Algasov and Mikhaylov—People's Commissars without portfolio.

Ya. Sverdlov, Chairman of the Central Executive Committee of the Soviet of Workers', Soldiers' and Peasants' Deputies.

[Source: *Izvestiya*, 15 December 1917.]

Once it was clear that the Bolsheviks and their Left SR allies would be heavily outnumbered, Lenin and the leadership in the TsIK began to downgrade the Assembly.[41] He insisted that it must come to terms with the reality of Soviet power and that new elections should be held in constituencies where delegates had already forfeited the electorate's confidence. A new date (5 January 1918) was set for the Assembly to convene, but at the same time, to underline that the Soviet order was here to stay, a third All-Russia Soviet Congress was summoned to meet three days later. The attitude of the Left SRs was not as aggressive as Lenin's, but in a declaration published just before the Assembly's opening session, they firmly reiterated their commitment to Soviet power and 'the great achievements of the October revolution'.

Document 41 | The Left SR declaration on the Constituent Assembly

5 January 1918

1) The Constituent Assembly opens at a decisive moment for the Great Russian Revolution. Having thrown off the political yoke of tsarism, toiling people have seen that the achievements of the revolution are in danger. The propertied class

---

41 See J.L.H. Keep, *The Debate on Soviet Power: Minutes of the All-Russian Central Executive Committee Second Convocation, October 1917–January 1918* (Oxford 1979), for the rapid evolution of the Bolshevik approach to the post-October constitution.

has been hindering the realization of the cherished aspirations of toiling people in every possible way. The toiling people have realized that there can be no agreement with the exploiters and that all the necessary changes in social relations can be carried out only against the wishes of the propertied classes. Realizing this, in the October revolution toiling people brought about the complete transfer of all power and the whole state apparatus to toiling people. In the struggle for the fundamental reconstruction of society, the instrument of the undivided will of toiling people has been the Soviets of Peasants', Workers' and Soldiers' Deputies. That is why the October revolution put forward and implemented the slogan: power to the soviets.

2) The Left SR faction considers it impossible to surrender the great achievements of the October revolution in the field of social reforms which have opened up not only for Russia but the whole world a new path of creative work by the toiling people for their economic and political emancipation. In recognizing that these achievements are those of the Soviets of Peasants', Workers' and Soldiers' Deputies, the faction declares decisively that it categorically speaks out in favour of the establishment of Soviet power and a Federative Soviet Republic.

3) Henceforth the Constituent Assembly cannot encroach upon this power, as its task should only be the consolidation of the achievements of the revolution and the easing of the toiling people's struggle with the propertied classes in its future creative and constructive work. . .

4) The Constituent Assembly will be doing its job properly if it can create favourable conditions for the immediate socialization of the land throughout the Russian People's Federative Republic. . .

The Constituent Assembly must work out a system of consistent workers' control as the first step on the road to the real transition from a bourgeois to a workers' economy, and from a system of capitalist exploitation of the toiling people to their liberation and the creative expression of their abilities. To this same end foreign trade, private banks and the large capital sums invested in them, the railways, all capitalist joint-stock industrial enterprises, housing stock serving as a means of exploitation and all enterprises connected with socialized land and nationalized mineral wealth will be nationalized. . .

6) At the same time the Constituent Assembly is obliged to implement the separation of Church and state, to provide universal education with free maintenance for all students at all levels, to regulate production and food supply, and to develop workers' co-operatives, etc.

7) The Left SR faction is firmly convinced that revolutionary Russia will make no concessions to the imperialists of allied or enemy countries, and, by relying on the indestructible strength of the revolutionary people and the genuine revolutionary support of the toilers of the world, will be able to achieve peace on the bases proclaimed by the Russian revolution, thereby dealing a mortal blow to international imperialism. . .

In putting the implementation of social reforms at the top of the agenda, our faction openly declares that there is no place for a power struggle within the Constituent Assembly between the Assembly and the Soviets of Workers', Soldiers' and Peasants' Deputies...

[Source: *Uchreditel'noe sobranie: Stenograficheskiy otchet* (Petrograd 1918), pp. 53–56.]

The Mensheviks could hardly have differed more sharply. In their eyes, the Constituent Assembly assumed enormous importance as a potential focus of democratic opposition against a ruthlessly repressive Bolshevik regime bent upon an attempt to introduce a socialist economy which, the Mensheviks insisted, was wildly unrealistic and doomed to disastrous failure.

Document 42 | The Menshevik declaration on the Constituent Assembly

5 January 1918

...The Constituent Assembly is gathering at a time when the whole country is enveloped in the flames of civil war and all democratic freedoms have been suppressed, when inviolability of the person and dwelling, freedom of speech, assembly, unions and even the right to strike do not exist, when the prisons are full of experienced revolutionaries, socialists and even members of the Constituent Assembly itself, when there is no justice..., when all productive forces are breaking down and going to ruin because of anarchic attempts to introduce a socialist economy into a backward country in exceptionally unfavourable foreign and domestic circumstances and the opportunity for rapid economic regeneration is being lost, thereby dooming millions of workers, deprived of organization and democratic freedom, to the torments of hunger and unemployment and uncondi-tional submission to the demands of capital in the near future, when a powerful co-operative organization is reeling under the blows of violence and the working class's fighting trade unions are going to pieces, when the country's agricultural wealth is being plundered by the wealthier elements of the rural population and the kulaks and being taken from the poorest strata of the peasantry, to whom the revo-lution promised land, when the country is breaking up into a number of completely independent states, in each of which the bourgeoisie will easily be able to exploit the rift between different sections of the Russian proletariat in order to grab for itself all the advantages in the forthcoming struggle between labour and capital, and when, finally, having brought about the total disorganization of the army, having completely exposed the Front and having thrown transport and production into complete confusion, a government, not recognized by the majority of the popula-tion, is conducting peace negotiations in such conditions and on such bases that will make revolutionary Russia a tributary of German imperialism or hand over a defenceless country to plunder by international capital. . .

The working class must demand that the supreme power of the Constituent Assembly be recognized by all the organs of power that have arisen during the civil war, giving it the whole task of establishing a Russian democratic republic, of immediately concluding peace, of giving the land to the people, of regulating trade and industry and reviving the economy in the interests and with the active participation of the toiling masses. . .

[Source: *Uchreditel'noe sobranie: Stenograficheskiy otchet* pp. 43, 44.]

The Assembly duly opened in the Tauride Palace on 5 January, although only about 470 of the 715 deputies had arrived in Petrograd. The election of Chernov as its chairman and the adoption of the Right/Centre SR agenda quickly provoked a walkout by the Bolsheviks, followed in the early hours of the next morning by the Left SRs. The palace 'guard' compelled Chernov to close the session, and later that day the TsIK declared the Assembly dissolved. The remnants of the Assembly managed to meet several times underground before eventually moving to Samara, where on 8 June they formed a short-lived government, based on *Komuch,* the Committee of Members of the Constituent Assembly. (For details of this episode, see documents 61–63 below.)

Meanwhile, a week after the Assembly's abortive opening session, the third All-Russia Congress of Soviets formally proclaimed Russia a specifically *soviet* rather than parliamentary republic.[42] The guiding principle of this new form of polity was to be that of class. The Soviet Republic was to be a republic of the lower classes: electoral rights were denied to employers, *rentiers* and entrepreneurs as well as clergymen and members of the old regime's police force. The Congress celebrated the first steps away from capitalism and towards socialism, common ownership of the means of production, workers' control and planning of the economy as a whole. While decreeing the formation of a Red Army to prevent counter-revolution at home, it reaffirmed commitment to a revolutionary and democratic peace. It repudiated imperialist domination of one nation by another and, in contrast to the Provisional Government, it portrayed the new Soviet Republic as multinational, a federation joined voluntarily by the numerous autonomous soviet national republics emerging on the territory of the fallen Russian Empire. That it was to be a multinational federation and yet to be labelled

---

42 A detailed constitution for the Russian Soviet Federative Socialist Republic (RSFSR), based on the Declaration of Rights, was adopted by the Fifth Congress of Soviets in July 1918. For text and commentary, see A.L. Unger, *Constitutional Development in the USSR* (London 1981) pp. 9–41.

'Russian' appears, in English translation, almost a contradiction in terms. However, during the Tsarist period, two different adjectives, both translated as 'Russian', had developed: *'russkiy'* and *'rossiyskiy'*. Whereas the former meant ethnically Russian, the latter embraced all the lands and peoples 'of the Russian Empire'. It was the latter term which was used for the new Republic. In principle at least, non-Russian minorities might identify with an entity that was *rossiyskiy* as they never would with one that was *russkiy*.[43]

Document 43 | From the *Declaration of the Rights of the Toiling and Exploited People* passed by the III All-Russia Soviet Congress

12 January 1918

I

1) Russia is declared a Republic of Soviets of Workers', Soldiers' and Peasants' Deputies. All central and local power resides in these Soviets.
2) The Russian Soviet Republic is established as a federation of Soviet national republics on the basis of a voluntary union of free nations.

II

In making its main task the elimination of every kind of exploitation of man by man, the complete abolition of the division of society into classes, the merciless suppression of exploiters, the establishment of the socialist organization of society and the victory of socialism in all countries, the III All-Russia Congress of Soviets of Workers', Soldiers' and Peasants' Deputies further decrees:

1) In order to implement the socialization of land the private ownership of land is abolished and all land is declared national property, and is handed over to the toiling people without redemption fees on the basis of equal land use. . .
2) As a first step towards the wholesale transfer of mills, factories, mines, railways and other means of production and transport into the ownership of the Workers' and Peasants' Soviet Republic, the Soviet law on workers' control and the setting up of the Supreme Council for the Economy are ratified to safeguard the power of the toiling people over the exploiters. The III Soviet Congress views the Soviet law on the annulment (abolition) of loans taken out by the governments of the Tsar, bourgeoisie and landowners to be the first strike against international bank and finance capital, and is confident that Soviet power will firmly follow this path until the total victory of the international workers' uprising against the yoke of capital.
3) As one of the conditions for the liberation of the toiling masses from the yoke of

---

43 The significance of the distinction is powerfully hammered home from the opening lines of G. Hosking, *Russia: People and empire, 1552–1917* (London 1997) p. xix.

capital the transfer of all banks into the ownership of the workers' and peasants' state is confirmed.

4) With the object of destroying parasitic social strata and organizing the economy, compulsory labour service for all is introduced.

5) In order to ensure that power remains fully in the hands of the toiling masses, and to remove all possibility of restoring the power of the exploiters, the arming of the workers, the formation of the socialist Red Army of workers and peasants and the complete disarming of the propertied classes are decreed.

III

1) While expressing its unswerving resolve to pluck humanity from the claws of finance capital and imperialism, which have soaked the earth with blood in the current war, the most criminal of all wars, the III Soviet Congress wholeheartedly aligns itself with the Soviet government's policy of breaking off secret treaties, the organization of wholesale fraternization with the workers and peasants of currently warring armies and, at all costs, the achievement by revolutionary measures of a democratic peace for toiling peoples without annexations and reparations on the basis of the voluntary self-determination of nations.

2) To this end the III Soviet Congress insists on a complete break with the barbarous politics of bourgeois civilization, which has built the welfare of the exploiters in a few chosen nations on the enslavement of hundreds of millions of toiling people in Asia, in colonies everywhere and in small countries. The III Soviet Congress welcomes the policy of the Council of People's Commissars, which has proclaimed the complete independence of Finland, begun the withdrawal of our troops from Persia and declared self-determination for Armenia.

IV

The III All-Russia Congress of Soviets of Workers', Soldiers' and Peasants' Deputies considers that now, at the moment of the people's decisive struggle against its exploiters, there can be no place for exploiters in any of the organs of power. Power must belong wholly and exclusively to the toiling masses and their plenipotentiary representative—the Soviets of Workers', Soldiers' and Peasants' Deputies. At the same time, in striving to create a truly free and voluntary and, consequently, a more complete and stable union of the toiling classes of all the nations of Russia, the III Soviet Congress confines itself to the establishment of the basic principles of a federation of Soviet republics of Russia, allowing the workers and peasants of each nation to make a decision independently at their own plenipotentiary Soviet congress as to whether they wish to participate, and on what bases, in the federal government and other Soviet federal institutions.

[Source: *Izvestiya*, 19 January 1918.]

Awaiting International Revolution

Securing peace was much more difficult than the Bolshevik leadership had expected. Their optimism that the formation of a socialist government, immediate announcement of a truce across the eastern front, and repudiation of secret treaties would trigger mass peace protests amongst both Allied and Central powers proved false. Instead of Trotsky as Commissar for Foreign Affairs being able, as he had envisaged, to 'issue a few revolutionary proclamations to the people of the world and shut up shop', he was compelled to hear the specific conditions insisted on by the German High Command.[44] Unable either to accept these terms, thereby endorsing a separate peace and the massive reparations and annexations which all socialists had so long denounced, or to mount effective military resistance to the German army, Trotsky momentarily stunned traditional diplomats by pronouncing a policy of 'neither war nor peace'.

Document 44 | **Statement by Trotsky at the Brest–Litovsk Peace Conference on Russia's withdrawal from the war**

10 February 1918

. . . We have heard the reports of our representatives on the territorial sub-commission and, after prolonged discussion and a thorough examination of the question, we have come to the conclusion that the hour of decision has struck. The peoples are impatiently awaiting the results of the peace negotiations at Brest–Litovsk. They are asking, when will there be an end to this unparalleled self-destruction of humanity provoked by the selfish and ambitious ruling classes of all countries? If ever the war was being fought in self-defence, that has long ceased to be true for either side. When Great Britain seizes African colonies, Baghdad and Jerusalem, that is no longer a war of self-defence; when Germany occupies Serbia, Belgium, Poland, Lithuania and Romania, and seizes the Moon Islands, that too is not a war of defence. That is a struggle for the partition of the world. Now it is clear, clearer than ever before.

We do not wish to take part any longer in this purely imperialist war, in which the claims of the propertied classes are being paid in blood. We are as implacably opposed to the imperialism of one camp as to the other, and we are no longer willing to shed the blood of our soldiers to defend the interests of one imperialist side against the other.

While awaiting the time, which we hope is not far off, when the oppressed

---

44 R. Debo, *Revolution and Survival: The foreign policy of Soviet Russia 1917–1918* (Liverpool 1979), provides a good guide.

working classes of all countries will take power into their own hands, as the working people of Russia have done, we are withdrawing our army and our people from the war. Our peasant-soldiers must return to their land, so that they can this spring culti-vate the soil which the revolution took from the landlords and gave to the peasants. Our workmen-soldiers must return to the workshops to produce there not weapons of destruction, but tools for creative labour, and together with the peasants build a new socialist economy.

We are withdrawing from the war. We are informing all peoples and all Governments of this. We are issuing orders for the complete demobilization of our armies now confronting the German, Austro-Hungarian, Turkish and Bulgarian troops. We expect and firmly believe that other peoples will soon follow our example. At the same time we declare that the terms of peace proposed by the Governments of Germany and Austria–Hungary are basically opposed to the inter-ests of all peoples. These terms will be rejected by the working masses of all countries, including even the peoples of Austria–Hungary and Germany. The peoples of Poland, Ukraine, Lithuania, Courland and Estonia regard these conditions as a viola-tion of their will, while for the Russian people themselves they represent a permanent threat. The popular masses of the entire world, guided by political consciousness or by moral instinct, reject these conditions, in expectation of the day when the working classes of all countries will establish their own standards of peaceful co-existence and friendly co-operation of peoples. We refuse to give our sanction to the conditions which German and Austro-Hungarian imperialism writes with the sword on the body of living peoples. We cannot put the signature of the Russian revolution to conditions which carry with them oppression, misfortune, and misery to millions of human beings.

The Governments of Germany and Austria–Hungary want to rule over lands and peoples by the right of armed conquest. Let them do their work openly. We cannot approve violence. We are withdrawing from the war but we are compelled to refuse to sign the treaty of peace. In connection with this statement, I am handing to the joint delegations the following written and signed declaration:

> In the name of the Council of People's Commissars, the Government of the Russian Federative Republic informs the Governments and peoples of the countries at war with us, and of the Allied and neutral countries that, while refusing to sign an annexationist peace, Russia, for its part, declares the state of war with Germany, Austria–Hungary, Bulgaria and Turkey at an end. At the same time, an order is being given for the complete demobilization of the Russian troops along the entire front.

Brest–Litovsk, 10 February 1918.
Chairman of the Russian peace delegation, People's Commissar for Foreign Affairs L. Trotsky

Members of the delegation:

People's Commissar for State Property V. Karelin. A. Ioffe, M. Pokrovsky, A. Bitsenko

Chairman of the All-Ukrainian TsIK Medvedev

[Source: L. Trotsky, *Sochineniya* Volume XVII, part 1 (Moscow and Leningrad 1926).]

The bluff did not hold. The German army resumed its advance into Russian territory. There was furious debate both between the Bolsheviks and the Left SRs and within the Bolshevik Party over the best response. Pragmatists led by Lenin argued that to save the revolution the socialist government must compromise over its ideals and bow to German demands. Radicals insisted that to sign a separate peace would be to sacrifice principle, abandon internationalism and betray fellow revolutionaries abroad, thereby undermining the very purpose of the revolution: guerrilla resistance and 'revolutionary war' must be launched and carried westward. Lenin managed to persuade a narrow majority of the Central Committee to accept German peace conditions, and thus buy a 'breathing space' for the Soviet Republic. But the price was the resignation of the Left SRs from the government, as well as N.I. Bukharin and three other 'Left Communist' Commissars, and a fateful step towards treating the security of the Soviet Republic as synonymous with the interests of international socialism.[45]

This was not how the Bolshevik leadership viewed the matter at the time. The expectation that events in Russia would be echoed by socialist revolution in the west continued to run high. In March 1919, Lenin founded the Third (Communist) International, Comintern.[46] He invited genuine revolutionary Marxists everywhere to break with the socialist parties of the Second International, compromised by support for the war and coalition with bourgeois parties. He called on them to take the Soviet Communist Party as the indispensable model for the revolutionary overthrow of capitalist regimes, to align themselves with the world's first socialist state, and to subvert the efforts its enemies were making to strangle it at birth. Trotsky's speech at a meeting held in the Bolshoi Theatre in Moscow to celebrate Comintern's foundation captured the millenarian atmosphere.

---

45 See R.J. Kowalski, *The Bolshevik Party in Conflict* (Pittsburgh, PA, 1991).

46 For a good recent introduction, see K. McDermott, *The Comintern: A history of international communism from Lenin to Stalin* (London 1996).

Document 45 | Leon Trotsky: *Great Times*

March 1919

The Tsars and the priests—the former lords of the Moscow Kremlin—never foresaw, we may imagine, that within its hoary walls would one day gather the representatives of the most revolutionary part of contemporary humanity. Nevertheless, this has happened. In one of the halls of the Palace of Justice, where still are wandering the wan ghosts of the criminal paragraphs of the Imperial Code, at this moment the delegates of the Third International are in session. Verily, the mole of history dug his tunnel well beneath the Kremlin walls.

These material surroundings of the Communist Congress are merely the outward expression, the visible embodiment of the gigantic changes that have taken place in the world during the last ten or twelve years.

In the days of the First, and again in those of the Second, International, Tsarist Russia was the chief stronghold of world reaction. At the International Socialist Congresses the Russian revolution was represented by emigrants, towards whom the majority of the opportunist leaders of European socialism adopted an attitude of ironical condescension. The bureaucrats of Parliamentarianism and Trade Unionism were filled with an unshakeable certainty that the miseries of revolution were to be the lot only of semi-Asiatic Russia, while Europe was assured of a gradual, painless, peaceful development from Capitalism to Socialism.

But in August 1914 the accumulated antagonisms of Imperialism tore to pieces the 'peaceful' cloak of capitalism, with its Parliamentarianism, its established 'liberties', and its legalized prostitution, political and otherwise. From the heights of civilization humanity found itself hurled into an abyss of terrifying barbarism and bloodstained savagery.

Notwithstanding that Marxist theory had foreseen and foretold the bloody catastrophe, the social-reformist parties were taken completely by surprise. The perspectives of peaceful development became smoke and dust. The opportunist leaders could find no work left for them but to call on the toiling masses to defend the capitalist national state. On 4 August 1914, the Second International perished with dishonour.

From that moment, all true revolutionary heirs of the Marxian spirit placed before themselves the task of creating a new International—an International of unquenchable revolutionary struggle against capitalist society. The war let loose by imperialism upset the balance of the whole of the capitalist world. All questions revealed themselves as revolutionary questions. The old revolutionary cobblers applied all their arts in order to preserve the semblance of the former hopes, the old lies, the old organizations. All was of no avail. The war—not for the first time in history—showed itself the mother of the revolution. An imperialist war brought forth a proletarian revolution.

The honour of having taken the first step belongs to the Russian working class and its veteran, battle-scarred Communist Party. By its November revolution the Russian proletariat not only opened the gates of the Kremlin to the representatives of the international proletariat, but also laid the foundation stone for the building of the Third International.

The revolutions in Germany, Austria and Hungary; the stormy tide of the Soviet movement and of civil war that has poured over Europe, crested by the martyrdom of Karl Liebknecht, Rosa Luxemburg, and many thousands of nameless heroes; these have shown that the paths of Europe are not other than those of Russia. The unity of method in the struggle for socialism, revealed by practice, has laid the ideal foundations for the creation of a Communist International, while, at the same time, it has rendered impossible the postponement of a Communist congress.

At this moment, that Congress is sitting within the walls of the Kremlin. We are witnesses of and participants in one of the greatest events in the history of the world.

The working class of the whole world has wrested the most impregnable fortress of all—that of former Imperial Russia—from its enemies. On it as its base, it is uniting its forces for the last decisive battle.

What happiness—to live and fight at such a time!

[Source: *Communist International* No. 1, May 1919, p. 40.]

The foundation of Comintern provided the catalyst which turned divisions that had long been visible within socialist parties abroad into enduring schism. Radical socialists in almost every European country as well as China broke with the relative moderation of social democracy to form a Communist party. But for all Comintern's professed internationalism and multinational composition, membership quickly came to imply allegiance to the 'socialist homeland', the USSR. The Soviet Communist Party exerted a progressively tighter grip on the organization and by the mid-1920s Comintern and the Communist movement as a whole had become subordinate to the dictates of Soviet foreign policy.

3

Bolshevik State, Orthodox Church

The formation of a socialist government made a clash with the Russian Orthodox Church inevitable. There had already been considerable tension between the Provisional Government and the Orthodox hierarchy and mainline Orthodox opinion. The February revolution, it is true, enabled reformist currents in the Church to gather momentum, and pressure had built up both from the married 'black clergy' and from sections of the laity for a greater voice and democratization of a system dominated by the 'white' celibate hierarchy. The membership of the Holy Synod, the governing body through which the state had dominated the Church since Peter the Great's time, was altered and it approved the election (women having a vote for the first time) both of bishops and of a Church Council, which met in August 1917. Thereafter, even the more adventurous Orthodox elements became concerned at the Provisional Government's agenda as it moved to subordinate parish schools to the Ministry of Education, to revoke regulations making religious instruction a compulsory part of the school syllabus, and to erode Orthodoxy's privileged position by abolishing all religious restrictions. These sources of friction, however, paled in significance before the overt hostility of the new Soviet government.[47]

Progressive opinion in Russia generally, and the socialist tradition in particular, had long regarded the Church as a bastion of reaction and a tool of the Tsarist state on which it was institutionally dependent. The Bolsheviks shared the view of the Orthodox Church as the epitome of false consciousness and cultural oppression—compared to which the Old Believers (products of the seventeenth-century schism), numerous small sects and the smaller Catholic and Protestant churches were less urgent problems and at

---

47 M.S. Shkarovskii, 'The Russian Orthodox Church' in Acton et al (eds) *Critical Companion* pp. 416–28, provides an entrée to what is becoming a lively field of research.

least had the merit of weakening Orthodoxy's hold. Its cathedrals and churches dominated the built landscape, its holy days shaped the calendar, its teaching was embedded in education, and its priests controlled the registration of births, deaths and marriages. Its ethos permeated family law, custom and a patriarchal order in which the status of women depended on that of their menfolk, and in which women were subordinate to men in terms of power, property, employment, pay and access to education. For the strong feminist current among the leadership of both the Bolshevik party and their Left SR coalition partners, a central purpose of the new government would be to overturn this entire tradition, to institute equality of the sexes, and to broaden the horizons and raise the ambitions of women.[48] Evidence of female assertiveness had grown in the last decades of Tsarism—and during the revolution itself—albeit in broad correlation with levels of urbanization and education. This increasing assertiveness and the expectation of instant action by the new government are captured in the following enthusiastic appeal to Lenin sent by a girl from Krasnoyarsk, the first Siberian centre in which local Bolsheviks succeeded in establishing Soviet power after October.

Document 46 | Letter from a schoolgirl to Lenin

No earlier than January 1918

Dear Comrade Lenin,

I'm writing from the town of Krasnoyarsk. I'm a third-year at the Krasnoyarsk provincial grammar school. You're a Bolshevik—and so am I. Please, I beg you to write an order to our grammar school so that we don't have to study Holy Writ. As our school is a bourgeois one, right from the start it has not deigned to make Holy Writ optional. Please, please write to me, as well, just a little letter will do.

Here's my address:

To:

Zhenya Zamoshchina (the Bolshevik),
Zamoshchin's flat (the Bolshevik),
68 Blagoveshchenskaya Street,
Krasnoyarsk.

Or you could send it to:
Zh. Zamoshchina,
3rd Year,
The Grammar School.

---

48 For a stimulating discussion and introduction to the literature, see B.E. Clements, 'Women and the Gender Question' in Acton et al. (eds) *Critical Companion* pp. 592–603.

I await your reply.

Zhenya Zamoshchina.

[Source: GARF, fond 130, opis′ 1, delo 47, pp. 63–63 ob.]

The proclamation of Soviet power duly triggered a broad attack on the position of the Church.[49] The land still owned by monasteries and churches was nationalized under the Land Decree; church and clerical accounts were swept up in the nationalization of the banks; the writ of the Commissariat of Education was extended even over theological institutions; the state took over the registration of births, deaths and marriages; church presses were confiscated; some major monasteries and churches, including those in the Kremlin in Moscow, were closed; and, more or less explicitly encouraged by the leadership, anti-clerical feeling found expression in local attacks on churches and Church schools, insults to religious sensitivities, and the seizure of Church property. The Church was thrown onto the defensive and opinion in the Church Council swung against democratic reformers. Within days of the Bolsheviks coming to power, to the delight of more conservative Orthodox opinion, the majority voted in favour of the restoration of the patriarchate. For two centuries the Tsarist regime had left the patriarchate in abeyance to make it easier to subordinate the hierarchy to state domination and ensure the Church loyally supported the monarchy and the existing social and political order. On 5 November the Metropolitan of Moscow, Tikhon, was elected to the office and by January 1918 he was pronouncing anathema on the new regime and its supporters, excommunicating them and calling for true believers to rally to the defence of the Church.

Document 47 | An epistle from Patriarch Tikhon

19 January 1918

From the humble Tikhon, by the Grace of God Patriarch of Moscow and All Russia, to those beloved of the Lord—pastors, arch-pastors and all loyal children of the Russian Orthodox Church.

'Deliver us out of this present evil world, according to the will of God.'

(Galatians 1:4)

The Holy Orthodox Church of Christ in the Russian land is now passing through grave times: the overt and covert enemies of the truth of Christ have raised a hue-and-cry against it and are aiming to destroy the cause of Christ and to sow

---

49 For an overview, see P. Walters, 'A Survey of Soviet Religious Policy' in S.P. Ramet, *Religious Policy in the Soviet Union* (Cambridge 1993) pp. 3–31.

everywhere the seeds of malice, hatred and fratricidal abuse instead of Christian love. Christ's commandments on love of our neighbour are forgotten and flouted: news comes to us daily of terrible and bestial slaughter of innocent people, even on their sickbeds, guilty only of doing their duty to their Motherland and of making every effort to serve the people; all of this is being done not only under cover of night but also openly, in broad daylight, with unprecedented audacity and merciless cruelty, without trial and flouting every right and all legality; these days it is being done in almost all towns and villages of our Fatherland, both in the capitals and in outlying districts (in Petrograd, Moscow, Irkutsk, Sevastopol, etc.). All of this fills our heart with woe and compels us to denounce such scum of the earth with the Holy Apostle Paul's fearsome words, 'Them that sin rebuke before all, that others also may fear' (1 Timothy 5:20).

Come to your senses, you fools, and cease your bloody reprisals, for what you are doing is not only cruel but truly satanic, for which you will suffer the fires of Hell hereafter and in this earthly life be cursed by posterity. By the authority given to us by God we forbid you the Sacraments and excommunicate you, even if you still have Christian names and even though from birth you belong to the Orthodox Church. . .

A most terrible hue-and-cry has been raised against Christ's Holy Church: the blessed sacraments that illumine human birth and Christian marriage are being openly declared unnecessary and superfluous; holy churches are being subjected to destruction by artillery (the holy cathedrals of the Moscow Kremlin) or to plunder and blasphemous contumely (the Saviour chapel in Petrograd); holy and revered abodes (like the Alexander Nevsky and Pachaevsky monasteries) are being seized by the godless lords of darkness of this age and declared some kind of national property; schools supported by the funds of the Orthodox Church, which have prepared its pastors and teachers of the Faith, are being deemed superfluous and turned into academies of unbelief or even hotbeds of vice. The property of Orthodox monasteries and churches is being seized under the pretext that it is national property, but without any justification or wish to take the lawful will of the people themselves into account. . .

And, last of all, the government that promised to introduce right and truth in Russia and guarantee freedom and order is everywhere merely displaying the most unbridled wilfulness and wholesale violence against everybody, especially the Holy Orthodox Church. Is there no end to these insults to the Church of Christ? How can this attack by its frenzied enemies be stopped?

We call upon all believers and true children of the Church to come to the defence of our insulted and persecuted Holy Mother Church.

The Church's enemies are seizing power over it and its property with deadly weapons: oppose them with a national outcry, which will stop the madmen and show them that they have no right to call themselves champions of the common good and builders of a new life at the behest of the people, for they are acting directly against the conscience of the people. And if it is necessary to suffer for the cause of

Christ, we call upon you, beloved children of the Church, we call upon you to suffer with the words of the Apostle Paul, 'Who shall separate us from the love of Christ? Shall tribulation, or distress, or persecution, or famine, or nakedness, or peril, or sword?' (Romans 8:35).

And you, brother arch-pastors and pastors, do not tarry for a moment in your spiritual activity, but with ardent zeal call your children to the defence of the now trampled rights of the Orthodox Church, quickly set up religious unions and call upon them to join, through good will not necessity, the ranks of spiritual activists who will oppose external force with the power of spiritual fervour. We firmly trust that the Church's enemies will be disgraced and dissipated by the Cross of Christ, for the promise of the Divine Crusader is immutable, 'I will build my church, and the powers of death shall never conquer it.'

Tikhon, Patriarch of Moscow and All Russia

[Source: *Tserkovnye vedomosti* No. 2, 1918, pp. 11–12.]

The very next day, the government moved to disestablish the Church, nationalize its property, abolish all its legal privileges, end its role in registering marriages and births and forbid religious instruction in all schools.

Document 48 | Decree of the Council of People's Commissars on freedom of conscience and ecclesiastical and religious societies

20 January 1918

1. The Church is separated from the state.
2. Within the Republic it is forbidden to issue any local laws or decrees which might constrain or limit freedom of conscience or establish any advantages or privileges whatsoever on the basis of citizens' creed.
3. Every citizen may confess any religion or none. Any loss of rights connected with confessing any particular creed or none is abolished.
   N.B. In all statutes reference to citizens' religious affiliation or lack thereof is abolished.
4. Religious rites or ceremonies will not accompany the activities of state or other official public bodies.
5. Freedom to perform religious rites is guaranteed in so far as it neither disturbs public order nor infringes upon the rights of citizens of the Soviet Republic. In such circumstances local authorities have the right to take whatever measures are necessary to ensure public order and safety.
6. No one is entitled to evade carrying out his or her civil duties on account of religious belief. Individual exceptions may be made by court order, provided there is some form of alternative service.

7. Religious vows or oaths are abolished. Where necessary, a solemn oath may be administered.
8. Registration of marriages and births is to be carried out exclusively by the relevant civil authorities.
9. Schools are separated from the Church. Religious education in state, public and also private general educational establishments is not permitted. Citizens may teach or study religion privately.
10. All ecclesiastical and religious societies are subject to regulations relating to private societies and unions and will not enjoy any advantages or subsidies either from the state or from its local and autonomous institutions.
11. The compulsory exaction of dues and taxes for church and religious societies, along with measures of compulsion or punishment of their fellow members by these societies, is not allowed.
12. No ecclesiastical or religious society may own property. Nor do they have rights as juridical persons.
13. All the property in Russia of ecclesiastical and religious societies is declared to be national property. According to special local or central decrees buildings and objects intended specifically for liturgical purposes may be used free of charge by the corresponding religious societies.

V. Ul'yanov (Lenin)—Chairman of the Council of People's Commissars
People's Commissars: N. Podvoysky, V. Algasov, V. Trutovsky, A. Shlikhter, P. Prosh'yan, V. Menzhinsky, A. Shlyapnikov, G. Petrovsky
V. Bonch-Bruevich—Executive Secretary
N. Gorbunov—Secretary

[Source: *Pravda*, 21 January 1918.]

The Church Council responded promptly by reaffirming the excommunication of anybody who played a part in drawing up or implementing the legislation.

Document 49 | Concerning the Council of People's Commissars' decree on separating the Church from the state—from the resolution of the All-Russia Council of the Orthodox Church

25 January 1918

The decree issued by the Council of People's Commissars on separating the Church from the state is, while purporting to be a law on freedom of conscience, a malicious attack on the whole way of life of the Orthodox Church and an overt act of persecution against it.

Any participation both in the issuing of the said hostile legislation and in attempts to implement it are incompatible with membership of the Orthodox Church and will draw upon guilty persons of the Orthodox confession the most severe ecclesiastical punishments including excommunication (in pursuit of Rule 73 of the Sacred Apostles and Rule 13 of the VII Ecumenical Council)...

[Source: *Svyashchennyy sobor pravoslavnoy Rossiyskoy tserkvi. Deyaniya.* Book 6, issue 1, (Moscow 1918) pp. 71–72.]

The new regime's drive against the Church continued alongside efforts to undermine patriarchy and emancipate women. The Family Code of October 1918 formalized numerous reforms, notably making divorce (virtually unobtainable before the revolution) relatively easy; in 1920 hospital abortion was legalized; labour protection laws and efforts to provide maternity and nursery care, despite the impoverishment of the civil war years, were designed to remove obstacles to female employment. Both the Commissariat of Enlightenment and the party's Women's Department (*Zhenotdel*) sought to enhance girls' access to education, develop women's aspirations and propagate the equality of the sexes among workers and peasants. The most radical activists, headed by Aleksandra Kollontai, Commissar for Social Security in the early months of Bolshevik rule and the party's best-known feminist theorist, looked to a vision of the future in which the family itself, along with the ownership of private property, would give way to communal provision and the social upbringing of children.[50]

Soviet policy on religion, the family and women's rights was very unevenly implemented: across much of the countryside under its nominal rule, the new regime lacked the necessary resources and personnel, and peasant resistance proved fierce in the European provinces and the Caucasus, and violent in Central Asia. From the point of view of the Church, the whole programme was unacceptable. Although Patriarch Tikhon refused to give his support to the emergent White movement, the gulf that separated the early Bolshevik state from Orthodoxy—philosophical, ideological, political, legal, institutional, cultural and social—was unbridgeable.

---

50 On the development of Bolshevik policy, see W. Goldman, *Women, the State and Revolution: Soviet family policy and social life, 1917–1936* (Cambridge 1993).

4

Soviet Power and the
Peasantry

Grain requisitioning and the Poor Peasants' Committees

The Soviet Land Decree and abolition of private land ownership had been greeted with delight in the countryside, but relations between the Bolshevik regime and the peasantry quickly deteriorated. The critical issue was grain: the problem which had bedevilled the Tsarist and Provisional Governments alike became even more acute under the Bolsheviks. Rapid industrial contraction, accelerated rather than halted by the abrupt cessation of military orders in the winter of 1917–18, ensured that the manufactured goods available were quite inadequate to restore the trade nexus between town and country. Peasants saw ever less purpose in exchanging grain for almost worthless rubles. The loss of Ukraine to the Germans, confirmed by the Treaty of Brest–Litovsk in March 1918, greatly exacerbated the problem and confronted urban areas and grain-short provinces with the spectre of starvation. Direct action seemed the only answer. The despatching of ad hoc detachments of workers, soldiers and officials was followed by organized requisitioning of supplies from the countryside. And, in sharp contrast to the Provisional Government's early reluctance to use coercion, Bolshevik decrees laid heavy emphasis on the punishment that would be meted out to those 'enemies of the people' who resisted.

Document 50 | All-Russia TsIK decree granting emergency powers to the People's Commissariat for Food

9 May 1918

Policy on foodstuffs in preceding years has shown that the disruption of fixed grain prices and rejection of the grain monopoly, allowing a bunch of capitalists the chance to feast, would make grain completely inaccessible to millions of toiling people and expose them to inevitable starvation... Not a single *pud* of grain must remain in the hands of its holders, apart from that needed for sowing and feeding their families until the next harvest. This must be implemented immediately, especially after the occupation of Ukraine by the Germans, which obliges us to make do with grain resources hardly adequate for sowing and reduced rations. . .

Realizing that only with the most rigorous accounting and equal distribution of all grain stocks can Russia extricate itself from the food crisis, the All-Russia Central Executive Committee of Soviets has decreed as follows:

1. In confirming an unwavering grain monopoly and fixed prices as well as the necessity to deal mercilessly with grain speculators and bag-traders, every owner of grain is obliged to declare any surplus, over and above that required for sowing and personal consumption, for surrender within a week of the promulgation of this decree in each *volost'*. . .

2. All toiling people and propertyless peasants are called upon to unite in a merciless struggle against the kulaks.

3. All those not delivering surpluses to grain-collecting stations or wasting them on home-made vodka are declared enemies of the people and are to be turned over to a revolutionary court where the guilty will receive no less than ten years in prison, will be ejected permanently from the commune and all their property confiscated, while home-made vodka distillers will get hard labour.

4. In the event of any surplus grain being discovered which has not been declared in accordance with paragraph 1 above, the grain will be confiscated, while one half the value of the undeclared surplus (at the present fixed prices) will be paid after its delivery to a grain-collecting point to any person reporting such hoarding, and the other half to the village commune . . .

In order to deal with the food crisis more successfully the All-Russia Central Soviet Executive Committee has resolved to grant the following powers to the People's Commissariat for Food:

1. To issue compulsory orders on the food question which can go beyond the normal competence of the People's Commissariat for Food.

2. To rescind orders by local food bodies and other organizations and institutions which contradict the plans and actions of the People's Commissar of Food.

3. To demand from the institutions and organizations of all departments the unconditional and immediate execution of the orders of the People's Commissar for Food in matters of food supply.

4. To use armed force against resistance to the seizure of grain or other foodstuffs.

5. To dissolve or reorganize food-supply bodies in the provinces in the event of resistance to the orders of the People's Commissar for Food.

6. To dismiss, remove, hand over to a revolutionary court and arrest officials and employees of all departments and public bodies in the event of their interference in the work of the People's Commissar for Food . . .

This decree comes into effect on the day of its signing and will be brought into force by telegraph.

[Source: *Sobranie uzakoneniy i rasporyazheniy rabochego i krest'yanskogo pravitel'stva* No. 35 (Moscow 1918) Article 468, pp. 437–38.]

Since the party's active support in the village was minimal, and it had lost the support of the Left SRs, whose resignation following the Treaty of Brest–Litovsk had been foreshadowed by their hostility to forced requisitioning, it proved extremely difficult both to uncover and to remove the grain required. In June 1918, therefore, the government tried to strengthen its hand by mobilizing poorer peasants against richer villagers (pejoratively dubbed 'kulaks'—exploiters), who were assumed to be hoarding grain. 'Committees of Poor Peasants' would help their urban comrades to uncover and confiscate grain reserves. Various incentives were offered to peasants to join the committees but the policy was based on the conviction, deeply rooted in Lenin's thinking in particular, that the poorer peasants would need little encouragement. He believed that social differentiation in the village had reached the point where it could readily be fanned into open class warfare in which the exploited majority would stand shoulder to shoulder with the proletariat from the city.[51]

Document 51 | The establishment of Poor Peasants' Committees—from a decree of the All-Russia TsIK on the organization and supply of the rural poor

11 June 1918

II.1

Volost' and village Poor Peasants' Committees are to be established everywhere, organized by the local Soviets of Deputies with the essential participation of food-supply bodies under the overall leadership of the People's Commissar for Food and the Central Executive Committee. All Soviets of Deputies are to implement this decree without delay. . .

II.2

All permanent and newly arrived residents of villages without exception may elect and be elected to *volost'* and village Poor Peasants' Committees, but the following are excluded: notorious kulaks, rich peasants, landlords with surplus grain and other food products, and owners of trading or industrial enterprises employing poor peasant and hired labour.

N.B.: Those employing hired labour to run farms which do not exceed the set consumption norms may elect and be elected to Poor Peasants' Committees.

II.3

Within the remit of the Committees are the following:

1. The distribution of grain, essential goods and agricultural equipment.

---

51 See Lih, *Bread and Authority* pp. 138–52, on the evolution of Lenin's thought and Bolshevik rhetoric.

2. The rendering of assistance to local food-supply bodies in the confiscation of surpluses from kulaks and rich peasants . . .

II.8

For the moment, pending a special decree from the People's Commissariat for Food, the following rules for grain distribution are to be observed:

a) Those grain surpluses, assigned by *guberniya* and *uezd* Soviets of Deputies and the corresponding food-supply organizations, taken only from kulaks and rich peasants and added to state grain reserves prior to 15 July this year, will be issued free and at the state's expense to the rural poor, in accordance with the established norms.

b) Those grain surpluses taken from kulaks and rich peasants after 15 July but before 15 August this year are to be issued to the rural poor, in accordance with the established norms, at 50 per cent off the set price.

c) Those grain surpluses taken from kulaks and rich peasants during the second half of August are to be issued to the rural poor, in accordance with the established norms, at 20 per cent off the set price. . .

Ya. Sverdlov — Chairman of the All-Russia Central Executive Committee
V. Ul'yanov (Lenin) — Chairman of the Council of People's Commissars
V. Avanesov — Secretary of the All-Russia Central Executive Committee

[Source: *Izvestiya*, 16 June 1918.]

Meanwhile, heavy penalties were decreed for those who broke the state monopoly and sought to profit from private trade in food and other goods. In official rhetoric, 'speculators' became hate-figures along with 'kulaks', although most were petty traders making a meagre living. The vehemence with which the regime hurled down threats of dire punishment reflected its lack of inhibition about using force against 'class enemies'. It reflected, too, the authorities' frustration at being unable to stamp out the black market, which continued to supply much of the food that did find its way to the cities.

Document 52 | Council of People's Commissars decree on speculation

22 July 1918

1. Those found guilty of selling, buying up, or storing for sale as a trader, foodstuffs subject to a state monopoly are liable to a penalty of not less than ten years' imprisonment with very hard labour and the confiscation of all their property.
2. Those found guilty of selling, buying up, or storing for sale as a trader rationed foodstuffs at prices above the levels fixed in state tariffs, or other goods subject

to a state monopoly are liable to a penalty of not less than five years' imprisonment with hard labour and the confiscation of all or part of their property. . .

11. Instigators, accomplices and those involved with persons engaged in the above
activities, e.g., those permitting speculators to receive and shift goods and obtain
warrants for them, providing them with storage space, railway wagons and other
means of transport, reselling duplicates and any kind of receipts, etc., will be
liable to the same punishment as the chief guilty party.

12. Attempts to commit these acts are liable to the same penalties as the acts themselves. . .

[Source: *Sobranie uzakoneniy i rasporyazheniy rabochego i krest'yanskogo pravitel'stva*
No. 54 (Moscow 1918) Article 605, p. 650.]

Peasant resistance

The Poor Peasants' Committees proved a disastrous experiment. Many of
those who joined them tended not to be poor peasants working the land but
urban migrants—destitute craftsmen and former workers, soldiers and
domestic servants—who seized upon this opportunity to secure food for
themselves and were reluctant to pass it on to urban requisitioning bodies.
In the eyes of most villagers, on the other hand, the Committees were alien
institutions which threatened their livelihood, and the great majority closed
ranks against them.[52] Lenin and the leadership had grossly underrated the
way in which the repartitional village commune and the tradition whereby
relatively well-off households were partitioned between the family's sons had
counteracted the market's tendency to stretch differentiation between rich
and poor. They had underrated, too, the resurgence of the peasant commune
during the revolution in the countryside, and the way in which villages
seizing privately owned land had sub-divided it among households, thereby
strongly reinforcing the levelling of land distribution.[53] Within weeks of their
institution, therefore, the government sought to shift the emphasis of the
Committees. Instead of representing merely the 'poor', they were also to
represent the so-called 'middle' peasant, those working the land themselves
or hiring very limited labour to support their own efforts. The regime sought
to rally middle peasants, portraying its measures as steps taken in their interest,
and reminding them that it was the 'Bolshevik-Communists' (peasants had

---

52 On the Poor Peasants' Committees, see O. Figes, *Peasant Russia, Civil War* (Oxford 1989)
pp. 184–99.
53 For an influential account of the resilience of household farming within the commune,
see T. Shanin, *The Awkward Class* (Oxford 1972); and T. Shanin, *The Roots of Otherness:
Russia's turn of century*, Vol. I (London 1985), pp. 93–102, 150–51.

reputedly begun to distinguish between the 'good' Bolsheviks of 1917 and the 'evil' Communists of 1918, the party having changed its name in March 1918) who had issued the Land Decree.

Document 53 | From a Council of People's Commissars order to *guberniya* soviets and food committees

17 August 1918

. . . The slogan aimed at organizing the poor peasantry has been misinterpreted in many localities to mean that the poor peasantry must be set against all the rest of the peasant population, both notorious kulaks and rich peasants and the numerous middle stratum of peasants, who only yesterday were going hungry and have been able to breathe freely only under Soviet power. . .

Soviet power has always aimed to unify the urban proletariat with the rural proletariat and semi-proletariat, as well as the middle-income working peasantry which does not exploit hired labour. So, in all its activities, Soviet power has striven and is striving to satisfy the needs of the middle peasantry as well as those of urban workers and the rural poor. This is the meaning of the law on the socialization of the land, which is being implemented by the leading political party, the Bolshevik-Communists, who are keeping the interests of the middle peasantry strictly in mind. . . With its decrees on tripling fixed state grain prices, organizing harvest-detachments and sending agronomists and agricultural machinery to grain-producing *gubernii* Soviet power is acting in the interests, first and foremost, of the middle peasantry . . . The satisfaction of the needs of the middle peasantry, as well as those of the rural poor, is also being pursued by Soviet power in the field of commodity exchange. As for the decree of 11 June on the provisioning of the rural poor, certain paragraphs refer directly to the middle peasantry. The note to paragraph 2 refers to attracting into the Poor Peasants' Committees not only poor peasants but also those employing hired labour without enslaving their fellow villagers; the distribution of grain and necessities, according to paragraphs 4, 5, 6, 7 and 8, must be carried out among all needy peasants, and not just rural proletarians and semi-proletarians; paragraphs 9, 10 and 11, on providing peasants with agricultural equipment on favourable conditions, have in mind both poor and middle peasants, because such equipment is, of course, needed more by the latter than by the former . . .

All *guberniya* Soviets of Deputies and *guberniya* food committees are hereby strictly instructed to co-ordinate their activities with central policy and unswervingly strive for the unification of the rural poor and the middle peasantry by guaranteeing the interests of both.

The Poor Peasants' Committees must be revolutionary bodies of all the peasantry against former landowners, kulaks, merchants and priests, and not made up only of the rural proletariat against the rest of the rural population.

Last October the alliance of the workers and peasants defeated the landowners and bourgeoisie. It is only this alliance that can guarantee land to the peasants, and factories and mills to the workers, while consolidating worker–peasant power.

The alliance of workers and peasants will also lead to the ultimate victory of socialism.

V. Ul'yanov (Lenin) — Chairman of the Council of People's Commissars
A.D. Tsyurupa — People's Commissar for Food

[Source: *Pravda*, 18 August 1918.]

Just how counter-productive the Committees proved, how much they alien-ated most villagers, and how long it took for shifts in official government policy to be implemented locally are reflected in the following plea to Lenin from peasants in the north-eastern province of Vologda.

Document 54 | Appeal to Lenin from Vologda peasants

To Commissar Lenin, the Chairman of the RSFSR
A declaration of complaint from the peasants of Kurbang *volost'*, Kadnikov *uezd*, Vologda province.

March 1919

We're hard-working middle and poor peasants and have never been bourgeois, prof-iteering speculators, drunkards, pickpockets or parasitic layabouts, either like the upper class, or like the lower class that you're standing up for now and who you're entrusting the vital rebuilding of the state to. We've worked all our lives, tirelessly and non-stop, and it's us, only us who've shouldered all the state and social burdens. The rich have wriggled out of state and social taxes, while there's nothing to take from the layabouts, who've chucked up their land and farms, haven't learned a single useful thing, have taken to extortion, theft and gambling and live off us completely. And that's the sort of people you've given power and trust to. Sitting up there in their positions of power, they haven't tried and aren't trying to raise and better the people's level of work—all they do is rob and take away what we've got through our stubborn hard work and thrift. These loud-mouthed layabouts hurt the hard-working poor peasants as well, you know. Through their slovenliness and unruliness they've turned us all against you, because it does all come from you. Why are you standing up for layabouts and scoundrels and getting at us hard-working folk through them? We hard-working middle and poor peasants appeal to you and beg you not to take away the fruits of our labour and to make the profiteering layabouts work, since they're better off than us in physical strength and youth.

We beg you to make them, compel them to work, because moral example does no good, like the story of the cook and the cat. You don't have to compel the hard-working man, he thinks up the jobs himself. Let's take four families in the village of Nekrasovo as examples: the first, the Kulikhins, have 3 allotments and 7 strong and healthy pairs of hands; they've chucked up their land and home and loll around, sponging off the commune; the second, the Kostyunenkos, are both 51 and don't have any land or a house; they've taken over the land the first lot chucked up, manured it and grown corn; the third, the Solov'evs, with 3 allotments and 7 strong pairs of hands, stay at home, play cards, loll around and don't have any grain or livestock; the fourth, Mrs Obraztsova, looks after small children and elderly parents all by herself, ploughs the land and does everything, but the Kulikhins and Solov'evs reckon they're 'poor peasants', while the Kostyunenkos and Mrs Obraztsova are 'bourgeois'; they've come and taken away their grain and livestock—their cows and horses—and then gone and landed them with all the village's taxes and things.

There's as many examples as people. And if you take a close look and study people's lives in detail, then these 'poor peasant' layabouts are a thousand times better off than us. A peasant gets his property through thrift and modesty, you know. So where's all the justice in that, then? There isn't any!

The representatives of the poor and middle hard-working peasants of the village of Nekrasovo:
Nikolay Molchanov (for Vasiliy Solov'ev, who's illiterate), A. Obraztsova, Pelageya Obraztsova, Aleksandr Kachanov.
The representatives of the poor and middle hard-working peasants of the village of Shchekotovo: (signatures follow)
The representatives of the poor and middle hard-working peasants of the villages of Bol'shaya, Nelitovo, Sukmanitsy, Kopylovaya, etc.: (signatures follow)

[Source: RGASPI, fond 2, opis' 1, delo 8952, pp. 1–1 ob.]

Lenin sent the complaint to his Commissar for Internal Affairs, G.I. Petrovsky, and the issue was taken up vigorously by Lenin's wife, N.K. Krupskaya, who worked in the Commissariat for Enlightenment. She arranged for the peasant woman who had brought the petition to Moscow, U.P. Mostakova, to see Petrovsky and was indignant to hear that at the Commissariat the peasants involved had been denounced as 'kulaks', and Mostakova had been derided for having attended a bourgeois school before the revolution.

Document 55 | Letter from N.K. Krupskaya to G.I. Petrovsky on the peasant complaint from Vologda

No later than 22 March 1919

Dear Grigory Ivanovich,
    The other day Vladimir Il'ich sent you a declaration from the peasants of

Kadnikov *uezd* in Vologda province, brought by U.P. Mostakova, whom I sent to see you.

She came to me very upset, saying that while you had spoken to her in a comradely manner, all the others had said that these peasants are kulaks and that Mostakova herself is for the kulaks because she had attended the Bestuzhev courses.

I have known Mostakova for a long time. She is a very interesting character. About the age of 11 she left home and went to Kadnikov to attend the girls' grammar school, where she lived all the time and did not get a penny from her father. She went without food, was ill, did some part-time work and got some help from the mistresses. On the courses she was victimized, as a peasant girl, by the Principal, and there were constant rows. Yet, strangely enough, she has remained a peasant even now, with peasant thoughts and concerns. The Poor Peasants' Committees are mistreating them out there. Whoever says so might be a sworn enemy of the kulaks, but it is a fact that the Poor Peasants' Committees are committing violent acts and causing disturbances. They are not made up of the poorest peasants, but of locals who have given up their farms. In them there are also former police agents from Moscow, who have gone into hiding in the countryside, former porters, janitors and various kinds of counter-revolutionary intelligentsia who have inflicted themselves on the countryside and got into the Poor Peasants' Committees. You hear this every day from people arriving from the provinces, from workers, peasants and our communists, none of whom has any direct relationship to the battle between the 'Poor Peasants' Committees' and the middle peasants.

I think—and I am convinced of this—that a significant number of so-called 'kulak' uprisings occur because the 'committees' who supply the officials are throwing their weight about in an uncontrolled fashion. Hiding behind the title of 'Soviet worker', they are turning everything and everybody against them and identifying the wish to replace the 'committee's' protégé with non-recognition of Soviet power.

I think that enough reasons for changing our attitude to the middle peasantry and for electoral accountability have been put forward at the party congress. Right now Mostakova is afraid that, instead of an inspection commission being sent to their *volost'* to expose the situation fairly, there will be a punitive expedition against those peasants who decided to turn to Lenin for help, or the local authorities will be informed and carry out reprisals.

Cases of reprisals in the provinces against those who have dared to complain to Lenin about arbitrary behaviour are not that rare. So I beg you to look into this matter with appropriate care.

I am sorry to bother you, but these 'Poor Peasants' Committees' are causing me a great deal of anguish at the moment, when one sees that instead of the organization of life a horrifying split is being created in the countryside.

Nadezhda Konstantinovna Ul'yanova

[Source: RGASPI, fond 2, opis' 1, delo 8952, pp. 2–2 ob.]

Lenin briskly ordered Petrovsky to have the matter investigated and to reprimand—but not dismiss—one of his assistants, a Cheka employee called
Pravdin, said to have insulted Mostakova.

Document 56 | V.I. Lenin to G.I. Petrovsky

No later than 22 March 1919

a) Dear Comrade Petrovsky,

Please send this telegram—or one like it—or set up an inspection commission
through the Provincial Executive Committee.
Lenin

Between 22 and 27 March 1919

b) Dear Comrade Petrovsky,

If it is true that Pravdin bawled her out as a kulak sympathizer, he needs ticking
off. Don't dismiss him, but keep an eye on him, because he's got a stupid tendency
to order people about which needs stopping.
Lenin

[Sources: V.I. Lenin, *Polnoe sobranie sochineniy* Volume L (Moscow 1965) p. 270; RGASPI,
fond 2, opis´ 1, delo 8952, p. 1.]

Petrovsky set the wheels for an investigation in motion, hoping to defuse
the row.

Document 57 | G.I. Petrovsky to M.K. Vetoshkin

A resolution on N.K. Krupskaya's letter

27 March 1919

Dear Comrade,

I am sending you this letter. I think the matter is a little more complicated than
it seemed when I passed a copy of these peasants' petition to you. Although
Mostakova does not give the impression one would expect from descriptions of her.

In view of the fact that it includes comrade Lenin's postscript which I typed on,
please do set up an investigation, send a sensible person and inform comrade Lenin.
Perhaps with this our line on the middle-peasant might calm down; in general, the
facts need looking into.

Comradely greetings,

Petrovsky

[Source: RGASPI, fond 2, opis´ 1, delo 8952, p. 2.]

Although the Poor Peasants' Committees were gradually phased out, the food supply situation became increasingly grim as the civil war gathered pace from summer 1918 onwards. Quite apart from peasant resistance and illegal trade, local authorities were reluctant to approve the removal of grain from their own area. Even relatively sympathetic critics of the regime, who supported it as the main focus for resistance to counter-revolution by the White Armies backed by foreign powers, saw it heading for disaster unless it abandoned its grain monopoly. This letter early in 1919, addressed to Lenin personally by N.A. Rozhkov, a Menshevik and former deputy minister of posts and telegraphs in the first coalition Provisional Government, spelled out the case for permitting free trade.

Document 58 | A letter from N.A. Rozhkov to V.I. Lenin urging free trade

11 January 1919

Dear Vladimir Il'ich,

I am writing this letter to you not because I hope to be heard and understood, but because I can no longer remain silent when I see a situation which seems desperate to me, and must do everything in my power, even to make a hopeless attempt. The economic, and especially the food, situation of Soviet Russia is completely impossible and getting worse every day. A final terrible catastrophe is approaching. I am not going to talk about its economic causes—I could write a special letter about these, if you so wish—rather, I am going to talk about the food question. The situation here is such that, for example, half the population of Petrograd is doomed to starve to death. In such conditions you could not remain in power, even if the Whites and the intervention were not directly threatening you. None of your threats to the barrage detachments will help: the country is in the grip of anarchy, and nobody is afraid of or listening to you. Even if they were or did, that would not be the point—the point is that your whole food policy is built on false premises. Who could object to a state trade monopoly in the most essential items, if the state could supply them in sufficient quantities! But, really, it is impossible. You neither can nor will be able to do so. Without risking your very existence, you cannot take on responsibility for something you know is hopeless.

Keep your supply system and carry on using it, but do not monopolize trade in any foodstuff, even grain. Supply what you can, but permit completely free trade, order all the local soviets to remove all import and export bans and get rid of all the barrage detachments—by force, if necessary. Without the help of private initiative in trade neither you—nor anybody else for that matter—will be able to cope with the inevitable disaster. If you do not do so, then your enemies will. In the twentieth century you cannot turn the country into a conglomeration of closed local markets; in Russia's Middle Ages, when the population of what is now Soviet Russia was twenty times smaller, it was natural, but now it is utterly absurd. You and I have grown too far apart. We probably—no, certainly—cannot understand each other. But, in my opinion, the situation is such that only your personal dictatorship can block the way and take power back from a counter-revolutionary dictator who will not be as stupid as the tsarist generals and Constitutional Democrats, who, just as before, have been stupidly taking the land off the peasants. For the time being *there is no such smart dictator*. But there will be—the Devil creates work for idle hands. You must assume the dictatorship first. It is only you who can do it, with your authority and energy. And it must be done without delay—first and foremost in the really serious area of food. Otherwise your downfall is inevitable. But you cannot, of course, stop at that. Economic policy needs a complete rethink—*with a socialist aim in view*. Yet again, this needs a dictatorship. Let the Soviet Congress deck you out with emergency powers. Economic, first and foremost—as for other policies, I will write to you some other time, if you like. It is up to you to judge and decide whether that is necessary. This letter seems, even to me, silly and quixotic on my part. Best wishes—for the first and last time, I hope.

[Source: RGASPI, fond 5, opis' 1, delo 1315, pp. 1–4.]

Lenin's reply captures key elements of his outlook that winter. He remained convinced he was in line with the flow of history. He had begun to regard what would later be dubbed 'War Communism', that is the bundle of policies the regime had adopted to deal with the economic and military crisis—grain requisitioning, rationing, wholesale nationalization of industry, attempts at strict labour discipline and increasing reliance on direct barter rather than money—as steps in the transition from capitalism to socialism. He was adamant that the food supply crisis could be ridden out by a combination of direction from above and vigorous support from below. And he remained confident that the revolution was poised to spread abroad. [54] His optimism that the overthrow of capitalism in central and western Europe was imminent was sustained by the Kaiser's flight as the war ended in November 1918, the proclamation of a German republic, and what seemed a fierce struggle by the far left to wrest control of the revolution from the moderate leaders of the German Social Democratic party.

Document 59 | Lenin's reply to N.A. Rozhkov rejecting free trade

29 January 1919

Dear Nikolay Aleksandrovich,

I was very glad to hear from you—not because of what you wrote, but because

---

54 See R. Service, *Lenin: A political life* Volume III (London 1995) pp. 52–57, 102–08.

I was hoping for a rapprochement, as we do in fact share common ground in Soviet work.

The situation is not desperate—it is just difficult. At this very moment there is real hope of improving the food situation, thanks to victories over the counter-revolutionaries in the south and east. We should not be thinking about free trade—surely it must be clear to an economist that with an absolute deficit of necessities free trade means furious and brutal speculation and the victory of the haves over the have-nots. It is not a question of going back to free trade, but onward to socialism through an improvement of the state monopoly. The transition is difficult, but despair is neither permissible nor sensible. If the non–party, sympathetic intelligentsia, instead of going on about free trade, formed emergency groups, grouplets and unions to help in the food crisis, it really would help matters and reduce hunger. As for a 'personal dictatorship', forgive me for saying so, but it is complete rubbish. In some places the state apparatus has already become enormous, excessively so, and in such conditions a 'personal dictatorship' is completely impracticable, and any attempts to establish one would only be harmful.

A turning point for the intelligentsia has come. The civil war in Germany is also a struggle over a political line: Soviet power against some 'universal, direct, equal and secret', i.e., counter-revolutionary, constituent assembly—the struggle in Germany is getting and will get into the thickest intelligentsia heads. It is clearer from a distance. Nul n'est prophète en son pays.

Here in Russia they think 'it is just the madness of Bolshevism', but history has now shown that it is the world-wide collapse of bourgeois democracy and parliamentarianism, and that there is no escaping civil war—anywhere. Fate leads the willing, but drags the unwilling; the intelligentsia will have to move to a position of helping the workers on a specifically Soviet platform. Then intelligentsia circles, organizations, committees, free unions, groups and grouplets will mushroom, offering unstinting help in really difficult food and transport situations. That way we will be able to reduce and ease the labour pains by several months. And something remarkably good and viable will be born, however severe the pains are.

Best wishes.

[Source: RGASPI, fond 2, opis' 1, delo 8492, pp. 1–2.]

Peasant resistance against the Reds was deterred from being even greater than it was by the nightmare prospect, between 1918 and 1920, of a 'White Guard' victory in the civil war and the restoration of pre-revolutionary landowning patterns. Nevertheless, even while the civil war raged, there was a powerful current of peasant opposition to Bolshevik rule, most effectively articulated by the peasant movement identified with the Ukrainian partisan leader, Nestor Makhno. A charismatic leader whose forces fought in 1918 against the rule of the German-sponsored *Hetman*, in 1919 against Ukrainian nationalists and against the Whites, and in 1920 against the Reds, Makhno became a legendary figure and symbol of peasant liberation across south-eastern Ukraine.[55] Crude and vicious though his methods were, he gathered around himself a number of anarchist activists and attempted to rally support for an explicitly anarchist vision of a Russia freed from governments of any description.

Document 60 | From the Programme Declaration of the Makhno rebels

1919

Comrade workers, peasants and rebels!

... What can we, the revolutionary rebels, usefully do to make our struggle bring us the desired fruits—real freedom and genuine equality? Act against the existing government to overthrow it and set up another 'better' one, which is what the Mensheviks and Left SRs are saying? No, no, no! Any overthrow of a government immediately brings to life another one, no better, but probably worse. It is not in the replacement of one government by another that the people will find deliverance from the shame of slavery and the yoke of capital, but in so ordering life that all power is in the hands of the toiling people themselves and is in no way handed over to some body or political party. The liberation of the toilers is the task of the toilers themselves: this slogan means not only that the toilers can liberate themselves from capitalist slavery only by their own efforts but also that their new free life can be built by them and them alone. It is revolutionary anarchism that has for a long time shown the toiling people the way to do this, and our great worker-peasant revolution is showing us brilliantly. This way is the way of independence for the worker and peasant masses, the way of their revolutionary creativity. We have experienced all sorts of state power, from the most reactionary—monarchism, to the most revolutionary—Bolshevism. All of them have shown us the impossibility of creating a free life for the people through state power... To us who are fighting for political liberation and equality the road of struggle ahead is clear. Let some government or other sit in Khar'kov or Moscow and imagine it is making a revolution. We, the children of the revolution and sons of the toiling people, will make our own freedom in our own localities. Having driven out the landowners and other parasites and oppressors from our hamlets and villages, and factory owners, bankers and other capitalists from the towns, and made their property common, we are uniting into free communes, and in a healthy and business-like manner discussing economic and social matters and jointly resolving them. If we need executive bodies to do all this,

---

55 On Makhno, see M. Malet, *Nestor Makhno in the Russian Civil War* (London 1982). His military leadership earned him the title 'Bat'ko' ('Father').

we create them, without giving them any power, but give them only specific tasks, which are their primary responsibility. . .

May complete freedom and real equality for the toilers reign on earth!

In the name of this freedom and equality let us band closer together. Let the cry rumble all over revolutionary Russia, 'Down with state and capitalist oppression! Long live the Kingdom of Truth and Freedom—Anarcho-Communism!'

Bat'ko Makhno.

[Source: *Chego dobivayutsya povstantsy-makhnovtsy*, issued by the headquarters of the insurrectionary troop division named after Bat'ko Makhno, 1919, pp. 9–16.]

5

The Other Russia: A 'Third Way' or Dictatorship?

Socialist and Kadet opposition

During 1918, mounting peasant unrest as well as disillusionment among workers, beset by industrial collapse and desperate food shortages, ensured a dramatic decline in the popularity of the Bolsheviks. In the cities, there was some recovery in support for the SRs and even the Mensheviks. Far greater was the support in rural and provincial soviets for the Left SRs, following their resignation from the government in March 1918. Yet the Bolsheviks' socialist opponents had difficulty in organizing an effective political or military challenge. In part this reflected the repressive measures taken against them by the regime in areas under Soviet control: the Mensheviks, SRs and, from the summer of 1918, the Left SRs were subject to harassment, press closures, expulsion from central and local soviets, the disqualification of election candidates, the arrest of activists, and periods of outright banning.[56] Meanwhile, in areas beyond Soviet control, the socialist opposition clashed with and was gradually crushed by emergent anti-Bolshevik regimes dominated by the right, supported by 'White' armies, and committed to reversing much of the social revolution unleashed since February 1917.

The Menshevik leadership attempted to pursue peaceful opposition within the framework of the emerging Soviet order and, while continuing to condemn the Bolshevik regime, refused to condone the use of force against it. The Left SRs, who were best placed to mobilize popular resistance, did not seek to replace Soviet power nor, at first, to dislodge the Bolsheviks. Instead they attempted to force Lenin and his colleagues to repudiate the peace treaty: in July 1918 they assassinated the German Ambassador, hoping this would rupture relations with Germany and trigger demonstra-

---

56 See V.N. Brovkin, *The Mensheviks after October: Socialist opposition and the rise of the Bolshevik dictatorship* (Ithaca, NY, 1987).

tions of support for a revolutionary war.[57] The plan failed: unpopular though Brest–Litovsk was, enthusiasm for renewed war was minimal. Disoriented by the arrest of some of their leading figures and by Bolshevik overtures to the party rank and file, the Left SRs lost momentum—although they remained a major thorn in the Bolshevik side and played an active role in strikes and peasant unrest until the party's effective suppression in 1921.

It was the Right/Centre SRs who made the most ambitious efforts to forge a socialist government to rival that of the Bolsheviks. They did so in the vast Volga–Urals region and Siberia. Although Soviet authority had briefly been established there, it was overthrown in summer 1918 when mutual suspicion erupted between the Bolsheviks and a substantial Czechoslovak legion, made up of ex-POWs heading eastward for reshipment to the western front, and the legion came out in open revolt. In Samara, one of the towns west of the Urals taken by the legion, a Committee of the Constituent Assembly (*Komuch*) was established by some seventy SR deputies of the dispersed Assembly, and it appointed a Directorate which attempted to exert governmental authority.[58]

Meanwhile a thousand miles across the Urals, in Omsk, Kadet and regionalist politicians attempted to establish a Provisional Siberian Government in defiance of Soviet power. In mid-July representatives of the two fragile anti-Bolshevik governments, both of which repudiated Brest–Litovsk and favoured restoring the zemstvos and urban dumas, attempted to reach a common position and agreed to hold a State Conference two months later. The prospects of consensus, however, looked poor. The programme of *Komuch*, which included the confirmation of the Bolshevik land decree and the retention, albeit after new elections, of soviets, was regarded as far too radical by the liberals in Omsk. They were much more responsive to the concerns of property owners expressed in this resolution.

Document 61 | From a resolution of the Congress of Representatives of Trade, Industry and Property Owners of Siberia and the Urals

Omsk, 13–19 July 1918

. . . Even during the time of the feeble administration of the Provisional Government a profound longing for a resolute and masterful state administration could be

---

57 A. Rabinowitch, 'Maria Spiridonova's "Last Testament" *Russian Review* 54, no. 3 (1995) pp. 424–46, provides an account focusing on the role of Spiridonova, who masterminded the assassination.

58 Swain, *Origins* pp. 193–245, provides a wealth of information on *Komuch*, although his view that there was great popular support for the resumption of the war against Germany is idiosyncratic. See Figes, *Peasant Russia, Civil War* pp. 162–83.

seen within responsible public and government strata, and this grew more and more as the government lost its grip, finally expressing itself in the felt need for a dictatorship as a temporary administration, guided in its actions solely by consider-ations of expediency, unfettered by any kind of public control, swift and decisive in manifesting the government's will and therefore uniquely capable of establishing a firm order in the country, finishing off the World War along with our Allies and calling a Constituent Assembly, but in conditions of a domestically regulated and externally peaceful Russia. The same thought, which has also been worrying the lower classes, seduced by the Bolsheviks' false promises of not only peace and bread, but also the halting of state collapse by decisive and firm administration, has led these classes to set up a class-based, proletarian government, which has been implementing its will in acts which, although senseless, are indisputably dictatorial.

Thus, in both currents of political thinking among the Russian people—the state and the spontaneous—it was already clear in October last year that the style of admin-istration and power-structure of the Provisional Government are indisputably obsolete and can in no way be resurrected.

Fully aware of the importance of the question for the state, the Congress proposes that, in order to save Russia from impending destruction, supreme state power, free from party and class interests, be vested in a special organ with unlimited dictatorial powers, until the favourable resolution of the fateful questions of the War, the final settling of internal discord and the calling of a new Constituent Assembly in peaceful conditions.

[Source: *Ekaterinburgskiy listok*, 6 August 1918.]

At the September State Conference, held in Ufa (east of Samara), with both fragile 'governments' threatened by the Red Army and both coming under pressure from the Western Allies and the Czechoslovaks to reach agreement, an uneasy fusion between them was effected. An All-Russia Provisional Government was proclaimed, under a five-man Directorate. In a sense it represented a resurrection of the Provisional Government of 1917: it contained two SRs (N.D. Avksent'ev, who had been briefly Minister of the Interior under Kerensky, and V.M. Zenzinov, who replaced the initial SR nominee, N.V. Chaykovsky), two liberals (General V.G. Boldyrev and V.A. Vinogradov, who replaced the initial liberal nominee, N.I. Astrov) and P.V. Vologodsky, a Siberian regionalist. It was beset by problems similar to those which had eroded the Provisional Government in 1917: it lacked popular legitimacy, had neither reliable coercive force nor substantial tax revenue, and failed to establish effective governmental authority. Moreover, its stated objectives papered over bitter divisions between socialists and liberals about land reform, private enterprise, economic regulation and the structure and political role of the military.

Document 62 | The Instrument of Formation of the All-Russia Supreme Power (excerpt)

September 1918

The State Conference—made up of members of the All-Russia Constituent Assembly and plenipotentiaries of the All-Russia Constituent Assembly Committee, the Provisional Siberian Government, the Urals *oblast'* government, the Orenburg, Urals, Siberian, Irkutsk, Semirech'e, Enisey and Astrakhan' Cossacks, the representatives of the governments of Bashkiria, Alash, Turkestan, the National Administration of Turko-Tartars of the Russian and Siberian interior and the Provisional Government of Estonia, the representatives of the Siberian, Urals and Volga urban and zemstvo congresses, representatives of the following political parties and organizations: the Socialist Revolutionary Party, the Russian Social-Democratic Workers' Party, the Trudovaya Popular Socialist Party, the Party of People's Freedom [Kadets] and the All-Russia Social-Democratic organization 'Edinstvo', and the 'Union for the Liberation of Russia'—in its unanimous desire to save the country, restore its unity and ensure its independence has resolved fully to entrust supreme power throughout the Russian state to the All-Russia Provisional Government, composed of five persons: Nikolay Dmitrievich Avksent'ev, Nikolay Ivanovich Astrov, Lieutenant-General Vasiliy Georgievich Boldyrev, Petr Vasil'evich Vologodsky and Nikolay Vasil'evich Chaykovsky.

The All-Russia Provisional Government will in its activities be guided by the following provisions, as established by this instrument:

General Provisions

1. Until the convocation of the All-Russia Constituent Assembly the All-Russia Provisional Government is the single repository of supreme power throughout the Russian State. . .

[The Duties of the Government toward the All-Russia Constituent Assembly]

The duties of the All-Russia Provisional Government are as follows:

. . .

3. It will present an account of its activities to the Constituent Assembly as soon as the Constituent Assembly declares that it has resumed operations. It will subordinate itself unconditionally to the Constituent Assembly, as the only supreme authority in the country.

[The Provisional Government's Programme of Work]

1. The struggle to free Russia from Soviet power.
2. The restoration of those *oblasti* of Russia which have broken away or become detached.
3. Non-recognition of the Brest Treaty and of all other treaties of an international character, concluded either in the name of Russia, or of its individual parts after the February revolution, by any authority other than the Provisional Government. Relations with the Entente powers will be restored in reality on the basis of our treaties.
4. The continuation of the war against the German coalition.

In the realm of domestic policy the Provisional Government is to pursue the following aims:

I. Military Matters

1. The restoration of fighting efficiency and of a single Russian army free from the influence of political parties and subordinate, through its supreme command, to the Provisional All-Russia Government. . .

II. Civil Matters

1. The organization of liberated Russia on the principle of recognition of the rights of its individual *oblasti* to wide-ranging autonomy, determined by geographical and economic, as well as ethnographic, criteria, envisaging the eventual establishment of a state organized on federal principles by a sovereign Constituent Assembly.
2. The recognition of the right of national minorities not occupying discrete territories to national self-determination in the cultural sphere.
3. The restoration in those parts of Russia freed from Soviet power of democratic urban and zemstvo self-government, with the organization of new elections as soon as possible.
4. The taking of measures for the real defence of state security.

III. Economic Matters

1. A struggle against economic collapse.
2. Assistance in the development of the country's productive forces. The attraction of private capital, both Russian and foreign, and the encouragement of private initiative and enterprise.
3. The state regulation of conditions for hiring and dismissing workers.
4. The recognition of the complete freedom of association.
5. In the area of food policy—repudiation of the grain monopoly and fixed grain-prices while retaining rationing of produce in short supply. State procurement with the participation of private and co-operative trade organizations. . .
7. In the area of land policy—without permitting such changes in existing land relations as would prevent the full resolution of the land question by the Constituent

Assembly, the All-Russia Provisional Government is leaving land in the hands of its actual users and is taking measures to resume work on the settlement of land use on the principle of the maximum increase in cultivated land and the broadening of land tenure in the light of the economic features of individual *oblasti* and districts.

[Source: *Narodovlastie* No. 1, 1918.]

Admiral Kolchak's takeover in Siberia

Within a mere six weeks, shortly after moving to Omsk, the All-Russia Provisional Government was overthrown by a military coup. Its liberal members had become increasingly frustrated at the leftward pull of the SRs. They were infuriated by the growing influence of Chernov, who arrived in Samara in late September and whom they regarded as dangerously radical: in their eyes, he and his ilk had done much to undermine the Russian army during 1917 and were liable to do the same to the emergent White army. Cossack officers arrested the SR Directors and a new regime was installed. The Kadet and right-wing leaders repudiated allegiance to the Constituent Assembly, which in view of its overwhelmingly socialist make-up had held little charm for them, and in place of the All-Russia Provisional Government they proclaimed Admiral Kolchak, the former commander of the Black Sea Fleet who had joined the Directory's Council of Ministers, Dictator of all Russia.[59]

Document 63 | A.V. Kolchak's address to the population

18 November 1918

On 18 November 1918 the All-Russia Provisional Government collapsed. The Council of Ministers has assumed absolute power and entrusted it to me, Aleksandr Kolchak, Admiral of the Russian Navy. In taking up the cross of this power in the exceptionally difficult circumstances of civil war and the complete collapse of the state I declare:

I shall not go along either the path of reaction or the disastrous one of political partisanship. I have made my main aims the creation of an army capable of fighting, victory over the Bolsheviks and the establishment of law and order so that the people may without hindrance choose the form of government they wish and implement the great ideas of freedom now proclaimed all over the world.

---

59 The best account of Kolchak's regime and the civil war in Siberia is J.D. Smele, *Civil War in Siberia: The anti-Bolshevik government of Admiral Kolchak, 1918–1920* (Cambridge 1996).

I call upon all citizens to unite and fight the Bolsheviks, to toil and make sacrifices.

Admiral Kolchak — Supreme Ruler

[Source: *Izvestiya Ministerstva zemledeliya* No. 1, 1919, p. 4.]

Right-wing local Church leaders promptly endorsed Kolchak. In this they went further than the Patriarch, who, as we have seen (documents 47–49 and commentary), though forthrightly denouncing the Bolsheviks, would not give the Whites his blessing and from 1919 recognized Soviet power while seeking to maximize the Church's independence.

Document 64 | An address from Church leaders to troops doing battle on all fronts

November 1918

Warriors beloved of Christ, valiant defenders of the Holy Church and our dear Motherland! The Supreme Church Authority, consisting of bishops, presbyters and lay people, greets you in Christian love.

Dear warriors, you can see what has become of the once strong and powerful Russian state. The country is literally perishing. Our capitals are dying from hunger and sickness. The whole horizon of Holy Russia is aglow with fire. Murder, pillage and violence are an everyday occurrence. None is sure of tomorrow and none can be sure that he will remain among the living.

God's holy churches are being defiled and the ministers of the Lord's Altar—priests and archpriests—are being subjected to violence and even death. Scientific and literary monuments are being destroyed and scholars persecuted. Darkness is about to envelop the devastated Russian land. Industry in the country has stopped, and mills and factories have come to a standstill, putting thousands of starving, unemployed people out onto the streets. All of us are hungry, cold and without clothing or shoes. What is the sense in the people having plenty of paper money when there is nothing to buy anywhere? Grief and need are knocking on every family's door. And, what is more, our world-wide shame goes beyond even this. Right now our Allies and also neutral countries are sending delegates to a peace conference taking place in Paris, the capital of France, where they will be discussing the conditions for peace, determining the frontiers of states, the losses caused by war, the international position of states, etc. The Allies have declared that Russia can take up its rightful place at this peace festival only when, albeit with their help, she can cope with the destruction and anarchy and once more has a sturdy and strong army capable of restoring order.

Dear warriors, we turn our eyes to you and cry for help: save our Motherland from destruction and shame! Return her to her former glory and might, give her, worn out with suffering, that peace and happiness of which the Russian people dreams. Help us open God's holy churches so that in them may again ascend prayers to the Lord God for world peace, your health and the prosperity of the suffering Motherland. Stand shoulder to shoulder with your Supreme Leader [A.V. Kolchak] and close ranks around him to defend the Fatherland from aggressors and traitors.

The Holy Church sends you sufferers its blessing and prays to the Lord to give you strength in the struggle with the enemy. Remember, dearly beloved, the greater the effort, the sweeter the rest and the higher the reward: from God—His Grace—and from your grateful fellow citizens—eternal glory and honour. 'Watch ye, stand fast in the faith, quit you like men, be strong' (I Corinthians 16:13), 'God is with us' (Matthew 1:23).

We who are praying for you:
Sil'vestr, Archbishop of Omsk and Pavlodar
Veniamin, Archbishop of Simbirsk and Syzran
Archpriest Vladimir Sadovsky
Professor L. Pisarev

[Source: SOTsDOO, fond 41, opis' 1, delo 117, p. 36.]

The SR members of the Constituent Assembly, meanwhile, condemned the *coup* and, despite the military's intervening to prevent them from convening a meeting of *Komuch* in Ekaterinburg, attempted to re-establish a rival socialist government.

Document 65 | Appeal by the chairman of the Congress of Members of the Constituent Assembly, V.K. Vol'sky

Not before 18 November 1918

In Omsk on 17 November a group of conspirators arrested Avksent'ev, Zenzinov and Argunov, members of the All-Russia Provisional Government. Some of the ministers, led by Vologodsky, himself a member of the government, broke the solemn oath they had signed, seized power and declared themselves the All-Russia Government, appointing Admiral Kolchak as dictator. The Congress of All-Russia Constituent Assembly members is taking up the struggle against the criminal insurgents.

The Congress resolves:
1. To elect from its membership a committee responsible to the Congress, empowering it to take all the necessary measures to put down the conspiracy, punish the guilty and restore law and order on all the territory liberated from the Bolsheviks.

2. To elect to this committee: Chernov, the chairman of the Constituent Assembly, Vol'sky, the chairman of the Congress of Members of the Constituent Assembly, Alkin, the deputy chairman of the Congress, and members of the Constituent Assembly, Fedorovich, Brushvit, Fomin and Ivanov.

3. To instruct the committee, in order to fulfil the tasks laid upon it, to enter into agreement with those members of the All-Russia Provisional Government not party to the conspiracy, *oblast'* and local authorities and administrative bodies, the Czech National Council and other leading bodies of the Allied Powers. All citizens are to obey the orders of the Committee and its representatives.

[Source: G.K. Gins, *Sibir´, soyuzniki i Kolchak* Volume II (Peking and Harbin 1921) p. 11.]

Like its predecessor, however, the putative government of the Committee failed to mobilize popular support or to forge effective military backing and Kolchak responded by denouncing the 'rebellion' and ordering its immediate suppression. Its leader, Vol'sky (who had headed the *Komuch* government), epitomized the dilemma with which the Whites' ascendancy confronted anti-Bolshevik socialists: during 1919 he went over to the Soviet side.

Document 66 | Admiral Kolchak's order for the arrest of the members of the Constituent Assembly

30 November 1918

Former members of the Samara Committee of Members of the Constituent Assembly, departmental officers of the former Samara government who have as yet not relinquished their authority despite the order to do so from the former All-Russia Government, and, siding with them, certain anti-state elements in the Ufa region close to the rear of troops fighting the Bolsheviks have been trying to foment rebellion against the state's authority. They are conducting destructive agitation among the troops, delaying telegrams from the Supreme Command, and disrupting communications between the Western Front, Siberia and the Orenburg Urals Cossacks. They have appropriated huge sums of money sent to Ataman [Chieftain] Dutov for organizing the Cossacks' struggle against the Bolsheviks, and are trying to extend their criminal activities throughout the territory liberated from the Bolsheviks.

I order:

I

All Russian military commanders to put a stop to the above-mentioned persons' criminal activities in the most decisive manner, including by force of arms.

II

All Russian military commanders above and including regimental commanders and all commanders of garrisons to arrest such persons for court-martial, and report directly to the chief-of-staff at Supreme Command.

All commanders and officers assisting the above-mentioned persons' criminal activities will be handed over by me for court-martial.

The same fate awaits any commander displaying weakness and negligence.

Admiral Kolchak, Supreme Ruler and Commander-in-Chief

[Source: G.K. Gins, *Sibir', soyuzniki i Kolchak* Volume II, p. 13.]

The ascendancy of the right was consolidated two months later in the southeast. Early in 1918, Soviet power had been established in the Don and Kuban with the active support of radicalized Cossacks recently returned from the front. Having experienced Bolshevik rule, however, and come under pressure for the redistribution of land from peasant settlers in the region, the Cossacks had risen and overthrown local soviets.[60] In their subsequent struggle to resist the advance of the Red Army, they were drawn into uneasy alliance with members of the fiercely nationalist Russian Volunteer Army raised by the Whites in the south, and in January 1919 were brought under the command of General Denikin in the 'Armed Forces of South Russia'. Denikin, like the White commanders of smaller forces in the north, General Yudenich and General Miller, recognized Kolchak's leadership and 1919 saw the Whites' scattered armies make temporary advances.[61]

Yet they were never able to mobilize more than a fraction of the number of men who fought for the Reds. [62] Indeed, in a sense the Bolsheviks were saved by the preference of the vast majority of the population, including most of their socialist critics, for the Reds over the Whites. Deep though workers' disillusionment was with Bolshevik rule, and bitterly though peasants resented the Reds' grain requisitioning, any chance the Whites would attract popular support was ruled out by the social policies they adopted. Kolchak's government smashed workers' organizations and attempted to halt and reverse peasant land seizures offering no more than vague intimations of subsequent land reform.

---

60 S. O'Rourke, 'The Cossacks' in Acton et al. (eds) *Critical Companion* pp. 498–506, provides a crisp overview.
61 For the best single volume on the civil war, see E. Mawdsley, *The Russian Civil War* (Edinburgh 2000).
62 See O. Figes, 'The Red Army and Mass Mobilization during the Russian Civil War, 1918–1920' *Past and Present* 129 (1990) pp. 168–211.

Document 67 | **The Ministry of Agriculture of the government of A.V. Kolchak on its immediate tasks (excerpt)**

January 1919

The seizures of land must be stopped. To satisfy fully the land needs of all strata of the population in the various parts of this vast state, wherein exist the most varied forms of land ownership and use, we need to work out, taking into account all the local peculiarities of the nationalities inhabiting this country, a land law which corresponds to the interests of their working people. The All-Russia Constituent or National Assembly will give sanction to this law. At present we need to start work again on the preparation of materials for land reform. A gradual transfer of land to the working population on the basis of legality is in prospect. . .

At present the Ministry has decided to work directly on the implementation first and foremost of at least a provisional granting of land to the landless population and on devising provisional regulations for land use, in conformity with the forthcoming land reform, in the interests of the economy and the working population. . .

[Source: *Izvestiya Ministerstva zemledeliya* No. 1, 1919, p. 15.]

Like the Bolshevik regime, Kolchak was confronted by desperate economic problems and the collapse of trade. Cut off from central Russia, Siberia suffered an acute shortage of consumer goods while the Urals region was starved of grain. Inflation ran out of control and the military resorted to requisitioning. Although Kolchak's civilian advisers, predominantly right-wing Kadets such as the economist G.K. Gins, objected to this denial of the market, the fragile civilian administration was at a loss.

Document 68 | **An extract from G.K. Gins's memoirs**

1921

Unbridled speculation is sapping the Home Front! That's what everybody was saying in spring 1919 when they complained about the excessive price rises, the disappearance of goods from the market and the transport abuses (bribery, false labelling of loads, etc.). In the Omsk Law Society a learned economist stated that anyone wailing about speculation is an ignoramus, because speculation is 'trade'. The Minister of Food wrote to Commander-in-Chief Lebedev that the 'fight against speculation'—in the manner it was being carried out by the military—was wrong and that what was needed was a fight against the 'fight against speculation'.

But it was impossible to convince society that speculation was harmless and that trade without it was meaningless, and the more the speculators were defended by authoritative people with education and experience, the more furiously were they attacked by the man in the street and 'the military'.

There is much that the average person, and the soldier, who is also an average person, do not understand. For example, they have not got the slightest idea about currency and exchange rates and they simply cannot grasp why goods costing a ruble in April must cost five times more in May owing to the fall in the rate for the ruble in the East and the expectation of further decline. Nor do they understand all the 'secrets' of transport.

On the other hand, the man in the street is more sensitive than the academic and bureaucratic apparatus. He cannot fail to see that goods are being deliberately hoarded and held up at stations and gets angry when nothing is done about it.

The civilian authorities were incapable of doing anything about the matter and Headquarters took up the fight against speculation all along the railway network. Purely military measures were adopted. The wholesale requisitioning of all delayed goods was declared, which brought in complaints from traders and industrialists. . .

[Source: G.K. Gins, *Sibir', soyuzniki i Kolchak* Volume II, pp. 224–25.]

6

Terror

The Cheka and the 'Red Terror' of autumn 1918

The civil war period saw extensive use of political violence and terror by Reds, Whites and independent peasant armies alike. However, whereas the brutality of the Whites and the peasant armies was most closely associated with the military itself, on the Red side it was the political police, the Cheka or 'All-Russia Extraordinary Commission to Combat Counter-revolution and Sabotage', which was most notorious. The Cheka was set up by Lenin six weeks after the Bolsheviks seized power, with the Polish-born Bolshevik Feliks Dzerzhinsky at its head. Initially envisaged as temporary, it was charged with investigating and handing over enemy agents and counter-revolutionary activists to revolutionary tribunals. It rapidly accumulated power, and from February 1918 it was authorized to deal with a wide range of culprits—German spies, profiteers, marauders, hooligans, counter-revolutionary agitators—without referring to the courts. By mid-1918 the Cheka employed approaching 40,000 in armed detachments spread across Soviet-held territory.[63]

From that summer, the Sovnarkom encouraged summary execution of suspects and explicitly included in that category active members of the Octobrist, Kadet and Right SR parties. Following the Left SRs' assassination of the German Ambassador in July, prominent Left SR Chekists, including the deputy chairman of the Cheka, V.A. Aleksandrovich, were arrested and executed. On the night of 16–17 July, Nicholas II and his family were murdered by the Cheka in Ekaterinburg in the Urals. During the period of so-called 'War Communism' (1918–21) the Cheka's reach was extended

---

63 The standard western study is G. Leggett, *The Cheka: Lenin's political police, the All-Russian Extraordinary Commission for Combating Counter-revolution and Sabotage (December 1917 to February 1922)* (Oxford 1981). For more recent work, see A.L. Litvin, 'The Cheka', in Acton et al. (eds) *Critical Companion* pp. 314–22.

ever further and lower down the social hierarchy, taking in not only right-wing and liberal political activists but socialists of other parties, petty traders and peasants. Even relatively well-disposed critics regarded terror as increasingly integral to the regime's existence. According to I.Z. Steinberg, for example, who was Left SR Commissar for Justice in the Bolshevik–Left SR coalition from December 1917 to March 1918, leader of a small Left SR group permitted to publish a journal between spring 1920 and the party's final suppression in spring 1921, and one of the few prominent Left SRs to escape abroad, terror became a system of rule.

Document 69 | I.Z. Steinberg's reflections on terror as a system

1923

It would seem that these days everyone who has either experienced or observed it knows what terror is and how it manifests itself. Day after day, month after month the citizens of revolutionary Russia have become inured and used to its increasingly severe and savage forms. What at first shook, pained and sickened us later became commonplace, inevitable and almost comprehensible, in the same way as we got used to an ever decreasing bread ration. But that is why, in answer to the question 'What is terror?', a weary person can probably no longer give an outline of the system of violence which has such a tight grip on his life. He might point out some particularly obnoxious aspect of it, e.g., the senseless arrests, the contemptuous behaviour of officialdom, the mass executions. Yet of course this is not the whole truth. Terror is not an isolated act, it is not an isolated, fortuitous, albeit repeatable instance of governmental fury. Terror is a system of violence from above, either already displayed or ready to be displayed. Terror is a legitimized plan of mass deterrence, compulsion and destruction on the part of government. Terror is a precise, well-thought-out and weighed-up schedule of punishment, retribution and threats by which the government scares, lures and obliges us to do its categorical will. Terror is a heavy shroud dropped upon the whole population of the country, a shroud woven from the suspicion, mistrust, vindictiveness and animosity of the government. *Who* is holding this shroud, *who* is stifling everyone without exception? If it is not some foreign conqueror, then can the population really be ruling itself and oppressing itself in such a way?

Of course, under such a system we are not talking about the rule of the majority. With terror, power is in the hands of a minority, an undoubted minority both aware and afraid of its isolation. Terror exists precisely because the isolated minority in power ascribes more and more people, groups and strata to the enemy camp. In any revolution this sinister, frightening figure, 'the enemy of the revolution', appears, and all its sufferings and mistakes are justly or unjustly blamed upon it. When the revolution is victorious this figure does not seem dangerous, and is depicted as some mere remote phantom, but when the revolution's fortunes look shaky, then it becomes more real, tangible and visible. As long as the revolution is led by an undoubted majority, it is not afraid of this phantom and can deal with it easily. The phantom does not take up the whole horizon. But this 'enemy of the revolution' (or 'suspect', in French revolutionary terminology) grows into a real monster occupying the whole background of the revolution, when a fearful, suspicious and isolated minority remains in power. The idea expands and expands, gradually taking in the whole country and population until finally it becomes a matter of 'everyone except the government' (and its collaborators). These are the two participants in terror.

[Source: I.Z. Steinberg, *Nravstvennyy lik revolyutsii* (Berlin 1923) pp. 20–21.]

The growth in Cheka violence was abruptly intensified in September 1918, following the assassination of two senior Bolsheviks and the attempted assassination of Lenin. The so-called 'Red Terror', which in a matter of weeks claimed at least 10,000 lives, primarily of propertied and 'bourgeois' elements under arrest, was triggered by a clamour for blood in the Soviet press and a ferocious order from the Commissar for Internal Affairs.

Document 70 | Order on hostages from Petrovsky, People's Commissar of Internal Affairs

4 September 1918, sent by telegraph

The murders of Volodarsky and Uritsky [head of the Petrograd Cheka], the attempt on the life and wounding of the chairman of the Council of People's Commissars, Vladimir Il'ich Lenin, the shooting of tens of thousands of our comrades in Finland, Ukraine, the Don region and Czecho-slavia [sic], the plots constantly being uncovered in our armies, the frank admission by Right SRs and other counter-revolutionary scum of participation in these plots, and at the same time the minute number of serious repressions and mass shootings of White Guards and the bourgeoisie by the Soviets all show there really is no terror despite constant talk of mass terror against SRs, White Guards and bourgeoisie.

A decisive end must be put to such a situation. An end must be put immediately to slackness and softness. All Right SRs known to local soviets must be immediately arrested and a considerable number of hostages taken from among the bourgeoisie and officers. Unconditional mass shooting must be carried out at the slightest sign of movement in White Guard circles. In this respect local *guberniya* executive committees must show particular initiative. Through the offices of the militia and Cheka, administrative departments must take all necessary measures to root out and arrest all those hiding behind false names, unconditionally shooting any involved in White Guard activities.

All the above measures must be carried out immediately. Any indecisiveness on the part of any local soviet organ must be reported immediately by the head of the administration department to the People's Commissar for Internal Affairs.

The rear of our armies must be finally cleansed of White Guard elements and all vile conspirators against the power of the working class and poor peasantry. There must not be the slightest hesitation or indecisiveness in the application of mass terror.

Confirm receipt of the above and pass it on to all *uezd* soviets.

Petrovsky, People's Commissar for Internal Affairs

[Source: *Ezhenedel'nik VChK* No. 1, 1918, p. 11.]

Readiness to use violence during the civil war was evident in the lower as well as the upper reaches of the party and the Cheka. Indeed, local activists could be even more outspoken and ruthless than the leadership. Witness, for example, the outburst of indignation (published in the *Ezhenedel'nik VChK* (*Cheka Weekly*) by party and Cheka officials from Nolinsk in Vyatka province, north-east of Moscow, when they read that Bruce Lockhart, a British double-agent, had been unmasked and yet was permitted to slip away.

Document 71 | 'Why are you being soft?'—letter from Nolinsk Chekists

September 1918

The Revolution teaches us. It has shown us that in a furious civil war we must not be soft. We have learned from bitter experience what it means to free the likes of Krasnov, Kolchak, Alekseev, Denikin and Co. We have also seen from the example of Volodarsky's murder what it means to go easy on 'domestic' counter-revolution. We have declared terror upon our numerous enemies, and after the murder of comrade Uritsky and the wounding of our beloved leader comrade Lenin we decided to make this terror no longer something on paper, but real. Since then, in many cities there have been mass shootings of hostages. This is good. In such matters half-measures are worst of all because they just anger the enemy without weakening him. But now we read about an action by the Cheka that stands in glaring contradiction to our whole strategy.

Lockhart, the very man who has done everything to bring down Soviet power and destroy our leaders, who has thrown about millions of pounds of British money bribing people, and who certainly knows a great deal that we need to know, has been released—and in the *Izvestiya* of the Central Executive Committee we read the following touching lines: 'Lockhart, after being unmasked, has left the Cheka in great embarrassment.'

What a great victory for the revolution! What an appalling act of terror! Now we can be quite sure that those swine from the British and French missions will stop organizing plots, because Lockhart has left 'in great embarrassment'. We say to you directly: although it hides behind 'frightening words' about mass terror, the Cheka has still not thrown off its middle-class ideology, the accursed legacy of the pre-Revolutionary past.

Tell us why you did not submit this Lockhart character to the most refined tortures to get names and addresses, as this fine fellow is bound to have plenty of them? This way we could easily have cracked open a whole lot of counter-revolutionary organizations and perhaps destroyed for the foreseeable future their source of finance, which would have been the same as destroying them; tell us why, instead of applying such tortures, the mere description of which would have terrified the counter-revolutionaries, you let him 'leave' the Cheka in great embarrassment? Or do you think that submitting a man to terrible tortures is more inhuman than blowing up bridges and food-stores in order to enlist the agonies of starvation as an ally to overthrow Soviet power? Or perhaps he had to be allowed to 'leave the Cheka in great embarrassment' so as not to incur the wrath of the British government?

But that would mean a complete rejection of the Marxist view of foreign policy. It must be clear to each one of us that British pressure on us depends on their available resources and the domestic situation there. The British will squeeze as much as they can, but the pressure will not increase by our torturing Lockhart. As for the domestic situation, it is in our interests to draw the attention of the British toiling masses to the shameful activities of their 'representatives'. Every British worker should know his country's official representative has been up to such terrible things that he, the official representative, has to be tortured. You can be sure that British workers will not approve of the system of explosions and bribes committed by this scoundrel under the orders of higher scoundrels.

You have been soft enough; give up this unworthy game of 'diplomacy' and 'representation'.

A dangerous scoundrel has been caught. Drag out of him everything you can and then pack him off to the next world.

Representative of the Nolinsk RKP (Bolshevik) (signature appended)
Representative of the Nolinsk Cheka (signature appended)
Secretary of Headquarters (signature appended)
Nolinsk Military Commissar and member of Headquarters (signature appended)

Nolinsk, Vyatka *guberniya*

[Source: *Ezhenedel'nik VChK* No. 3, 1918, pp. 7–8.]

The article's unvarnished endorsement of torture led to a reprimand from the party Central Committee, orders for the *Ezhenedel'nik VChK* to be closed, and the establishment of a top-level three-man commission, including Stalin, to examine the activities of the Cheka.

Document 72 | Decision of the RKP(b) CC concerning the *Ezhenedel'nik VChK*

25 October 1918

In No. 3 of the *Ezhenedel'nik VChK* there was an article signed by the Nolinsk Executive and Party Committees, praising torture, and the editors did not show their disapproval of the Nolinsk article.

It has been decided to censure the Nolinsk people for their article and the editors for printing it. The *Ezhenedel'nik VChK* must close down. A commission, made up of Kamenev, Stalin and Kursky, has been appointed by the Central Committee to look into the Cheka. Without weakening their fight against counter-revolution, the commission is to investigate the activities of the Chekas.

[Source: RGASPI, fond 17, opis' 2, delo 5, p. 1–1 ob.]

The upsurge in violence perpetrated by the Cheka provoked unease within sections of the party and criticism in Soviet debates and in the press. At the same time, if with increasing difficulty, non-party denunciations continued from all directions. During the Red Terror, the number of clergy shot ran into the hundreds and the regime suppressed much of the Church press and closed the Church Council. On the anniversary of the Bolshevik seizure of power, the Patriarch castigated the regime—prompting his first period of house arrest the following month.

Document 73 | Patriarch Tikhon's address to the Council of People's Commissars

26 October 1918

'All they that take up the sword shall perish with the sword' (Matthew 26:52).

We address this prophecy of our Saviour to you, the present controllers of our Fatherland, who call yourselves 'people's commissars'. For a whole year now you have held the reins of state power and are intending to celebrate the anniversary of the October revolution, but the river of blood of our brothers mercilessly murdered at your behest cries out to heaven and compels us to speak the bitter truth to you.

In seizing power and calling upon the people to trust you, what promises have you given and how have you fulfilled them?

Truly, you have given them a stone instead of bread and a serpent instead of a fish (Matthew 7:9, 10). . .

No one feels safe and everyone is living in constant fear of searches, robbery, eviction, arrest and shooting. Hundreds of innocent people are being seized, left to rot for months in prisons, and often executed without even a nominal trial. Not only those guilty of some transgression against you are being executed, but also those you know have committed no crime. These unhappy people, taken as 'hostages', are being killed in revenge for crimes committed by others who not only do not share their views, but are often your own supporters or hold views close to yours. Innocent bishops, priests, monks and nuns are being executed for nothing more than the groundless accusation of vague and indefinite 'counter-revolution'. This inhuman punishment is being made worse for the Orthodox by the deprivation of the Last Rites, and the bodies of the murdered are not even given to their relatives for a Christian burial. . .

At your incitement, lands, estates, factories, mills, homes and cattle are being taken away, and money, possessions, furniture and clothes are being stolen. At first, labelling them 'bourgeois', they robbed the well-off, and then, labelling them 'kulaks', they started robbing the more prosperous and hard-working peasants, thereby increasing the number of the destitute, although you cannot but admit that by ruining such a large number of citizens you are destroying the country's wealth and ruining the country itself. . .

You promised freedom. . .

Freedom is a great good, if it is understood properly as freedom from evil, as freedom which does not constrain others and become arbitrariness and wilfulness. But you have not given us that sort of freedom: the freedom you have given means pandering to the base instincts of the mob and no punishments for robbery and murder. You mercilessly crush every expression both of true civil and higher human spiritual freedom. Is it freedom, when without special permission no one can take home food, rent a flat or go from town to town? Is it freedom, when families, and sometimes the residents of a whole building, are evicted and their property thrown out onto the street, and when citizens are artificially divided into categories, certain of which can be starved and robbed? Is it freedom, when no one can openly express his or her opinion without fear of being branded a counter-revolutionary? Where are freedom of speech and the press, and where is religious freedom? Many brave preachers have been martyred, the voice of social and state condemnation and denunciation has been silenced, and the press, apart from the narrowly Bolshevik parts, has been completely suppressed.

Particularly cruel and painful is the violation of freedom in matters of faith. Not a day passes without the most monstrous slanders against the Church of Christ and her servants, and malicious blasphemy appearing in the press. You mock the servants of the altar, force a bishop (Bishop Hermogen of Tobol'sk) to dig trenches and send priests to do dirty work. You have laid your hands on Church property collected by generations of believers and not shrunk from violating their last will. You have closed monasteries and chapels without pretext or reason. You have blocked off access to the Moscow Kremlin, the sacred property of all believers.

'And what shall I more say? For the time would fail me to tell' (Hebrews 11:32) in order to depict all the woes which have afflicted our land. I shall not speak of the collapse of once great and mighty Russia, of the complete disruption of the transport system, of the unprecedented food shortages, of the life-threatening hunger and cold in the cities and the lack of the wherewithal to farm in the countryside. All of this is there for all to see. Yes, we are going through the terrible time of your dominion, which will remain in the people's hearts for years to come, clouding the image of God and imprinting there the image of the Beast.

It is not for us to judge secular power: any power granted by God would have Our blessing if it were truly God's servant at the service of good and were 'the minister of God, a revenger to execute wrath upon him that doeth evil' (Romans 13:4). But now to you who are using power to persecute your neighbours and destroy the innocent we extend Our word of admonition: celebrate the anniversary of your time in power by releasing those in prison and stopping the bloodshed, violence, destruction and constraint on faith; turn from destruction to establishing law and order, and give the people a longed-for, well-earned rest from internecine strife. Otherwise 'the blood of all the prophets, which was shed from the foundation of the world, may be required of this generation' (Luke 11:50) and 'All they that take up the sword shall perish with the sword' (Matthew 26:52).

Tikhon,
Patriarch of Moscow and All-Russia

[Source: *Vestnik russkogo studencheskogo khristianskogo dvizheniya* No. 89–90 (Paris 1968) pp. 19–23.]

From the other end of the ideological spectrum, Martov, the Menshevik-Internationalist leader, furiously damned the Cheka for degrading the revolution. Writing in the Menshevik party paper, *Vsegda Vpered*, briefly revived that winter, he condemned the flagrant contradiction between official rhetoric supposedly curtailing the Cheka's arbitrary power and the grim reality. Fixing upon the Cheka's execution of four Romanov Grand Dukes without trial early in 1919, he denounced the blood-letting.

Document 74 | Yu.O. Martov: 'Shame on you!'

6 February 1919

While the Soviet press has been discussing the abolition of the Chekas and the Moscow City Communist conference has agreed to remove the right to pass sentence from them, and while citizen Krylenko [in 1919, Chairman of the VTsIK Supreme Revolutionary Tribunal] states that there is not a single decree that gives them the right to execute people, the Petrograd Cheka declares with Olympian calm that it has shot four Romanovs: Nikolay and Georgiy Mikhaylovich, Dmitriy Konstantinovich and Pavel Aleksandrovich.

Not a word about the crime these people committed or what plot they hatched in those prisons where they had been incarcerated since last August, during the horrors of the Petersburg Red Terror!!

From a socialist point of view four former Grand Dukes are worth no more than any four ordinary people, but for anybody who has not replaced proletarian socialism with the bestial morality of the professional executioner, each of their lives is just as inviolable as the life of any trader or worker.

What were they murdered for? So that, after keeping them in prison for six months and constantly reassuring them that their lives were in no danger from the proletarian dictatorship, they could be taken out and shot one quiet night—without accusation or trial?

How low can you get! What pointlessly cruel vileness, what cynical compromising of the great Russian Revolution by a new stream of senselessly spilt blood!

As if the drama in the Urals—the murder of Nikolay Romanov's family—were not enough! As if that blood bath, which helped the counter-revolutionaries in their agitation in western Europe against the Revolution were not enough.

Just when European friends of the Russian Revolution need all the help they can get in their campaign against the blockade and armed intervention, mindlessly zealous terrorists are giving the Revolution's worst enemies such abundant material as the news of the pointless and motiveless murder of a few prisoners!

When they were taken hostage back in August, the Socialist Academy, which one could hardly suspect of anti-Bolshevism, protested against the arrest of Nikolay Mikhaylovich as an academic historian not involved in politics. Now even this peaceable historian, one of the very few intelligent Romanovs, has been shot like a dog.

Shame on you! And if there are communists and revolutionaries who realize the vileness of this execution, but are afraid to protest for fear of being considered sympathizers of the Grand Dukes, then double shame on them for their cowardice—the shameful accomplice of all terror!

[Source: *Martov i ego blizkie* (Paris 1959) pp. 153–54.]

Bolshevik anti-Cossack terror

While the Bolshevik leadership showed at least apparent embarrassment about the use of terror in Moscow and Petrograd, it had none where the front line of the civil war was concerned. In confronting the Cossacks, a key source of support for the Whites, the party's Organizational Bureau (set up in January 1919, alongside the Politburo, to oversee internal party administration) explicitly recommended mass terror against the wealthy.[64] The assumption was that rank-and-file Cossack resentment against the Cossack aristocracy would minimize sympathy for them, and that once the leading

---

64 On the Cossacks during the civil war, see the two volumes by P. Kenez, *Civil War in Southern Russia: The first year of the volunteer army* (Berkeley, CA, 1971), and *Civil War in Southern Russia, 1919–1920: The defeat of the Whites* (Berkeley, CA, 1977).

stratum had been eliminated, the remainder could be neutralized. Meanwhile, active steps were to be taken to encourage further immigration of poor peasant settlers who, hungry for Cossack land and hence at loggerheads with the Cossacks, were to become the base of support for Soviet power.

Document 75 | A secret circular on the attitude to the Cossacks, passed at a meeting of the RKP(b) CC Organizational Bureau

24 January 1919

Recent events on different fronts in Cossack regions—our advance deep into Cossack settlements and the demoralization of Cossack troops—oblige us to give instructions to Party workers on their work in reconstructing and strengthening Soviet power in these regions. Bearing in mind our experience with the Cossacks in the Civil War, we must realize that the only right course of action is merciless struggle against the entire Cossack leadership, annihilating each and every one of them. There must be no compromise or half-hearted measures. We must therefore

1. Conduct a campaign of mass terror against rich Cossacks and annihilate them to a man; wage merciless mass terror against all Cossacks who take part, directly or indirectly, in the fight against Soviet power. Every measure must be taken to ensure that middle-income Cossacks do not come out against Soviet power again.
2. Confiscate grain and compel them to deliver all the surplus to collection points; this applies both to grain and to all other agricultural produce.
3. Take all necessary measures to assist poor newcomers, organizing their resettlement [in Cossack territories] where possible.
4. Put newly arrived 'outsiders' on an equal footing with the Cossacks in land and all other respects.
5. Disarm them completely, shooting anyone discovered with a weapon after the surrender period has expired.
6. Distribute weapons only to reliable elements among the 'outsiders'.
7. Leave armed detachments in Cossack villages until the establishment of order.
8. Insist that all commissars stationed in Cossack settlements show absolute firmness and unswervingly implement the above instructions.

The Central Committee has decreed that the People's Commissariat for Agriculture is to work out measures with all speed for using appropriate Soviet agencies for the mass settlement of poor peasants on Cossack lands.

Central Committee of the RKP

[Source: RGASPI, fond 17, opis' 4, delo 7, p. 5.]

The bloody terror carried out among the Cossacks was counter-productive, provoking a major Cossack uprising which successfully overturned Soviet power. As the disaster was borne in upon Moscow, the assumptions behind the policy were challenged. At a full meeting of the Central Committee in March, G.Ya. Sokol'nikov, a long-standing party-member who had headed the delegation which signed Brest–Litovsk and who was to serve as Commissar for Finance from 1922, argued that a distinction must be drawn between the northern and southern Cossacks, especially in the Don and Orenburg. Resistance to the Reds had been much feebler in the north, in part because many Cossacks had limited enthusiasm for fighting outside their own locality: relations between Cossacks and the Whites were in general bedevilled by the Whites' lack of sympathy for Cossacks' aspirations to autonomy or even independence. Sokol'nikov warned that the use of terror there risked alienating potential allies.

Document 76 | From a resolution on the Cossacks passed by a RKP(b) CC Plenum

16 March 1919

Item:

Comrade Sokol'nikov raised the question of the CC's resolution on the Cossacks, stating that with respect to the Don Cossacks it is unworkable. Moreover, in the Don there is a marked difference between the north and the south, rendering our interference superfluous. With certain differences the same situation obtains among the Orenburg Cossacks.

The question of the unsuitability of the group of five [the five-man Don Bureau of the RKP(b)] to their work in the Don was also raised.

Resolved:

In view of the marked difference between the Cossacks of the northern and southern Don and, given that the northern ones might work with us, we are halting the measures against the Cossacks and not hindering their social stratification. The same applies to Orenburg and Ural'sk, with the rider that there is no north–south antagonism in Ural'sk.

The question of the group of five on the Don was passed on to the Central Committee Bureau.

[Source: RGASPI, fond 17, opis' 2, delo 11, pp. 104–104 ob.]

A month later, the Orgburo reaffirmed the distinction to be made between northern and southern Don Cossacks. However, on the recommendation of the Don party chairman, Syrtsov, renewed terror was ordered against the latter.

Document 77 | **From the minutes of the Organizational Bureau of the RKP(b) CC on the situation in the Don**

22 April 1919

1. Comrade Syrtsov reported on the situation in the Don and the Cossack uprising in Vershinsk and other districts. Some Cossacks and peasants did not participate in it. The political platform of the insurgents is 'Not against Soviet power, but against Communist commissars.' At present the insurgents are hemmed in. The Medvitsk and Khopersk Cossacks are not actively against the Communists. Mironov's Cossack division needs watching.

To be noted.

Comrade Syrtsov proposes a campaign of terror against the counter-revolutionary southern Cossacks, the resettlement of newcomers from central Russia in Cossack villages and the mobilization of the Millerovo region by arming the peasants.

Comrade Syrtsov's proposal and the Don Bureau's resolution on the Cossacks were passed, the latter with the addition of mobilization and the arming of peasants settling on Cossack lands.

The Don Bureau is to be relieved of Soviet work. A civilian administrative centre is to be created in Millerovo, and, later, Kamensk, for the Rostov *guberniya*.

Comrade Beloborodov is authorized to hold talks with the Military Revolutionary Committee of the Southern Front on the creation of a civilian administration.

The Don Bureau's personnel are to be replenished.

Comrade Shablievsky is to be brought on to the Don Bureau.

[Source: RGASPI, fond 17, opis' 2, delo 11, p. 3.]

White terror

The willingness of the Reds to employ terror was matched by the Whites. Typical was the following order on the treatment of civilians suspected of sympathizing with the Reds. It was issued by General Rozanov, who had served in the Red Army before joining the Whites and becoming Kolchak's commander in Krasnoyarsk, western Siberia.

Document 78 | **Orders from General S.N. Rozanov (Governor of the Enisey and part of the Irkutsk *gubernii*)**

27 March 1919

To commanders of units operating in rebel regions:

1. On taking brigand-held villages demand the hand-over of their ringleaders; if this is not done, but there is reliable information that such people are around, shoot every tenth villager.

2. Burn down villages that offer armed resistance to government troops; shoot all adult males; confiscate all property, horses, carts, grain and so forth for the treasury. Note: All confiscation should be carried out by order of the detachment.

3. When government troops pass through villages, if the inhabitants have an opportunity to inform them of the presence of enemies but do not do so, a collective fine will be imposed on all the inhabitants. The fines will be exacted without mercy. Note: All fines should be imposed by order of the detachment, and the sums collected handed over to the treasury.

4. On taking villages and after investigation, collective reparations must be taken unswervingly from all persons who even indirectly have aided the brigands.

5. Inform the inhabitants that for voluntarily supplying brigands not only with arms and ammunition but also with food, clothing, and suchlike, guilty villages will be burned down and property confiscated for the treasury. The population will be obliged to take away and destroy all property that might be useful to the brigands. The population is to be fully reimbursed either in money or kind requisitioned from brigands.

6. Take hostages from among the population, and if fellow villagers act against government troops, shoot them without mercy.

7. As a general rule, remember: look upon villages which aid and abet brigands openly or covertly as the enemy and deal with them mercilessly, and use their property to make up for the losses suffered as a result of military activity by that part of the population which sides with the government.

Lieutenant-General Rozanov

[Source: V.G. Boldyrev, *Direktoriya, Kolchak, interventy: Vospominaniya* (Novonikolaevsk 1925) pp. 543–44.]

Six months later, equally ruthless orders on reprisals against peasants who had revolted against Kolchak were given by another of his commanders in Siberia, General Mayakovsky.

Document 79 | General Mayakovsky's Order No. 564

30 September 1919

1. Make a detailed search of every village in the rebel area and shoot on the spot as enemies those found with weapons.
2. Using the locals' evidence, arrest all agitators, members of soviets who helped in the uprising, deserters, their accomplices and those who harboured them, and hand them over for court-martial.
3. Send untrustworthy and vicious elements to the police in Berezovsky and Nerchensk *kraya*.
4. Local authorities which have not offered adequate resistance to the bandits, have obeyed their orders or have not taken measures to liquidate the Reds on their own account are to be court-martialled. Punishments may include the death sentence.
5. Liquidate with redoubled ferocity any villages which revolt again, right up to the destruction of the whole village.

[Source: *Rodina* No. 10, 1990, p. 61.]

The scale and counterproductive impact of White and Cossack violence are spelled out in the following despairing extracts from the diary of General A. Budberg, who was responsible for food supply under Kolchak and then served in his war ministry.

Document 80 | Extract from the diary of General A. Budberg

3 May 1919

Stop the Cossack barbarism—that's my credo; I think it works far better for the Bolsheviks than all the preaching and propaganda of comrades Lenin and Trotsky. This is something that must be considered in a broader perspective, impartially, objectively and analytically. The lads think that, if they have killed and tortured a few hundred or thousand Bolsheviks and beaten up a certain number of commissars, then they have done a great job, inflicted a decisive blow on Bolshevism and brought the restoration of the old order nearer. . . The lads do not seem to realize that if they rape, flog, rob, torture and kill indiscriminately and without restraint, they are thereby instilling such hatred for the government they represent that the swine in Moscow must be delighted at having such diligent, valuable and beneficial collaborators . . .

29 May 1919

My 'pessimism' makes me think that now we can no longer deal with the uprisings in the rear by military means; we need either a miraculous change in the attitude of the population, alienated by our emergency and selfish measures, or the immediate occupation of the rear by Allied troops and the introduction there of a joint Russo-Allied administration, in which the Allied part guarantees the population's immunity from Cossack barbarism and lawlessness.

19 July 1919

The old supply system (if you can call it that) has collapsed with the cessation of all supplies. The troops are now existing on whatever they can get locally, so that down-right plundering is taking place in many instances. According to one wounded officer the peasants are saying, 'Reds or Whites—they're both swine.' Yet right now, to our disadvantage, the Red Army at the front has been given strict orders not to harm the populace and to pay set prices for everything taken. The Admiral has given the same orders and instructions several times, but with us they are not worth the paper they are written on, whereas with the Reds they are reinforced by the immediate execution of the guilty.

[Source: *Dnevnik barona Alekseya Budberga: Arkhiv russkoy revolyutsii* Volume XIV (Berlin 1924) pp. 231, 268, 325–26.]

Particularly vicious was the violence carried out against Jews, giving vent to the anti-Semitism evident on all sides and a key element in White ideology.[65] This grim memoir, published in 1990, describes the carnage of pogroms by detachments under N.A. Grigor'ev, a notorious semi-bandit leader who had fought in turn for the Ukrainian nationalists, the Hetman imposed by the Germans, the Ukrainian social-democrat Petlyura, and the Red Army, where he mutinied in May 1919 and defected to Makhno, who promptly ordered his execution.

Document 81 | **An eyewitness account of the pogroms carried out by N.A. Grigor'ev's detachments**

July 1919

When our units, hard on Grigor'ev's heels, got to Cherkassy I saw this small town in a frightful condition. Corpses had been left to rot and most homes had been ransacked. The Jewish population had suffered particularly badly. I could not help stopping by one little white house. All its windows had been smashed, the flowers

---

65 P. Kenez, 'The Ideology of the White Movement' *Soviet Studies* 32 (1980) pp. 58–83.

in the front garden had been trampled down and the fence smashed. By the door lay the body of an elderly man whose eyes had been gouged out and clumps of his beard pulled out. Beside him a disembowelled woman in a torn shirt with her breasts cut off. And, close by, the corpse of a naked girl who had obviously been raped. . .

As we pursued Grigor'ev's gangs we kept coming upon dozens of corpses buried head-first up to the waist. We established that they had been buried alive.

[Source: *Rodina* No. 10, 1990, p. 60.]

7

The Crisis of

'War Communism'

Political denunciation and popular revolt

Having briefly been confronted by the threat, in autumn 1919, that both Petrograd and Moscow might fall, the Reds regained the initiative, taking Kolchak's capital, Omsk, in November, and by December the greatest danger to the revolution appeared to have passed. That month the Seventh Soviet Congress met. Although the opposition parties had by then been reduced to too few seats in local soviets to secure any delegates to the Congress, a handful of representatives were invited to attend in a 'consultative' capacity—albeit without hope of denting unanimous endorsement of the regime.[66] Martov, speaking for the Mensheviks, defied Bolshevik heckling and boldly attacked the regime's reliance on administrative fiat and coercion and its flagrant violation of the Soviet Constitution.

Document 82 | From the Menshevik declaration made at the VII All-Russia Soviet Congress

6 December 1919

The power which, according to the constitution, should belong to the entire proletariat and working peasantry, is in fact held by just a small section of the proletariat.

Such a state of affairs, exacerbated by the total absence of freedom of the press for everybody except communists and the subordination of workers' organizations to the state, kills off at the root any sign of initiative and self-government by the masses. Not only are working people not learning statecraft and how to take full responsibility for it—they are gradually losing the skills they had previously acquired in that area. It is on this soil, on the one hand, that bureaucracy is growing at all

---

66 On the attrition of the opposition parties during the civil war, see V.N. Brovkin, *Behind the Front Lines of the Civil War: Political parties and social movements, 1918–1922* (Princeton 1994).

levels of administration, and this saps unproductively a significant portion of the energy expended by the state in the fight against famine, hunger, disease and other afflictions in our lives. All sorts of most vital measures in the areas of fuel, transport and the like are being delayed because of bureaucratic arbitrariness and incompetence, thereby losing much of their effectiveness. No amount of exhortation or admonition from on high can have any effect on this evil of bureaucratism if the masses are allowed to become increasingly convinced that administration is the exclusive preserve of a privileged caste of communists.

On the other hand, mass apathy, paralysis of any civic sense, and a readiness to leave everything to the government—all nurtured by centuries of tsarist slavery and serfdom—are thriving on the same soil. When faced with great danger from the class enemy, the masses temporarily experienced a flush of revolutionary ardour, thanks to which Soviet Russia more than once managed to repulse counter-revolution at the last minute. Now that danger has passed, the masses are sinking into torpor, and dissipation is ruining some of the fruits of that victory. Finally, this same bureaucratic degeneration of the authorities and narrow-minded degeneration of the citizenry is laying the basis for the formation of a state within a state—the transformation of the repressive and police apparatus created by the Civil War into a self-sufficient and all-powerful force. Within the last year the Cheka, originally envisaged as a temporary organ of struggle, has grown to gigantic proportions. After several attempts to confine it to strictly defined limits, subordinating it to the revolutionary courts and soviets, the government has completely capitulated to the Cheka, by handing over to it the lives, freedom and honour of the citizens. The monstrous growth of terror, the abolition of any semblance of legality and the frightful rule of arbitrary power are the result of this policy, in addition to which masses of the population are becoming extremely embittered. This is something far more dangerous to the revolution than the plots dealt with by the Cheka.

Sosnovsky: That was last year's declaration, comrades.

Martov: Last year's—and for ever and ever (noise, the Chairman rings his bell).

. . . The RSDRP sees very great danger to the revolution in the situation brought about by the virtual abolition of the Soviet constitution. The results of the most brilliant Red Army victories over the counter-revolutionary hordes will gradually come to nothing if, as has happened up to now, uncontrolled bureaucracy and the specialists in terror destroy the masses' sympathy for the revolution in those areas liberated from Denikin and Kolchak, and once again create the counter-revolutionary mood which made Denikin's job so much easier. . .

With this in mind and convinced more than ever before that real workers' power can be built only in accordance with democratic principles, in order to strengthen and develop the gains of the Revolution and ensure an economic revival, the RSDRP proposes that the following are necessary:

1. The restoration and further democratization of the Soviet constitution, making all government organs genuinely answerable to the workers and peasants, and

making their staff accountable, and the proper functioning of and regular re-elections to the soviets.

2. Equal rights for all urban and rural toilers.
3. Freedom of the press, association and assembly.
4. Inviolability of the person, guaranteed by the jurisdiction over all citizens of the same People's courts, operating according to precise laws.
5. An end to arbitrary reprisals, administrative arrests and governmental terror. (Noise and shouting in the hall.)

[Source: *Sed'moy Vserossiyskiy s˝ezd Sovetov rabochikh, krest'yanskikh, krasnoarmeyskikh i kazach'ikh deputatov: Stenograficheskiy otchet* (Moscow 1920) pp. 61–63.]

A year later, at the Eighth Soviet Congress, token opposition figures were again allowed consultative status. The Menshevik critique, delivered by Dan in the absence of Martov, who had not returned from a trip to Germany and was dangerously ill, ranged widely. In measured terms it pointed to the erosion of Soviet democracy and the flouting of the Constitution; the arrest of fellow socialists; the transformation of trade unions into institutions to mobilize rather than speak for the working class; and the perilous way in which the regime risked alienating the peasantry through continuing forced requisitioning.

Document 83 | F.I. Dan's speech at the VIII All-Russia Soviet Congress

23 December 1920

In the course of this year any observer must have been struck by the slow death of any Soviet-based system of government. This year the whole Soviet system has been paralysed from top to bottom. All of you know that in the provinces soviets have stopped meeting altogether, and to maintain at least some semblance of life, instead of meetings of deputies there have been enlarged and disparate joint meetings of soviets with factory commissions, trade-union representatives, etc. In fact, the soviets themselves have virtually never functioned as organs of state power—executive committees and presidiums have ruled autocratically in their place.

I shall dwell in particular on the withering away of our Soviet legislative body—the All-Russia Central Executive Committee (TsIK). The most important legislation has been enacted without any TsIK participation...

And now a word about administration. Everyone knows that in this country there is no separation of legislative and executive powers. The TsIK and its Presidium are the living embodiment of both one and the other. On the third anniversary of the October revolution the Presidium issued a decree on amnesty. This decree is not being applied anywhere at all, at any rate not to political prisoners. It has been applied fairly widely, but only to convicted criminals. Be that as it may, the Presidium did issue such a decree and it is natural that, given our whole state structure, it should be the Presidium, as the embodiment of the worker-peasant state, that determines the extent of the amnesty, the mode of its application, to whom it should be applied, etc. And, seeing that this amnesty was not being applied, the Central Committee of our party sent a document to the Presidium pointing to a whole list of instances where even after the amnesty our comrades were still in prison and concentration camps. (Noise in the auditorium.) Our document, in which we request the application of the amnesty decree issued by the TsIK, was sent by the Presidium for some unknown reason to the Cheka. And then a bit later a courier from the Cheka turned up at our Central Committee office with a document addressed to the Central Committee of the RSDRP. Of course, this document came into our hands as a result of clerical error. Instead of 'Presidium of the TsIK' somebody wrote 'Central Committee of the RSDRP'. So, we are now in possession of the whole truth not only about the application of the amnesty but, even better, about the relationship between the Cheka and the Presidium of the TsIK. It is not the Presidium that is giving special instructions on how to apply the act, but the head of the Cheka operations department who is permitting the Presidium of the TsIK to announce to whom the act applies.

Chairman: Your time is up.

A voice: Please go on (noise in the auditorium).

Chairman: Quiet, please! I shall take a vote. Who is for giving Dan more time? Who is against? A minority. The speaker has ten more minutes.

Dan: We are now entering a period of peaceful construction. This period is indebted to the victories won over domestic and foreign counter-revolution, in which a decisive role was played not only by the Red Army but most of all by the mood of the masses, especially the peasants. We must not forget that in its make-up the Army is a peasant one, and the behaviour of the peasants in Ukraine, the Trans-Volga and Siberia was everywhere the decisive factor because it undermined the offensives of the counter-revolutionary forces. The most telling thing was that, when the spectres of the old landowner, squire, general and civil servant appear, the Russian peasantry is invincible despite hunger, cold and deep dissatisfaction with the Soviet government. We must now say that the peasants are free from this frightful spectre, which has often helped the Soviet government by compensating for its impermissible mistakes towards the peasantry. And now, the peasants, having finally vanquished the landowners' counter-revolution and with a sense of their own worth, are not being allowed to run their own affairs and are being ordered about like a soulless, weak-willed mass. . .

It is clear that the peasantry will regard the proletariat not only as its natural friend and ally but also as its guide, and friendly relations can be established between town and country only if the highest law of Soviet power is not that coercion of which the chairman of the Sovnarkom talks so eagerly. Instead, we need a policy which deals with the fact that, like it or not, there are tens of millions of Russian peasant farms, farms based on small-scale private property, which in Marxist terminology we would call petit-bourgeois. To draw these farms into the orbit of the world socialist revolution, to draw these separate individual farms onto the capitalist [sic] track cannot be achieved by physical violence against the peasantry, but by a whole array of economic, political and cultural measures resulting from commodity circulation and economic exchange in general.

Yet what are we actually seeing? So far we have seen first and foremost the adoption of a purely coercive policy towards the peasants. Yesterday we were given figures which showed, glory be, that during the last year we extorted more than the tsarist government did in the last year of its life. In this respect I have to say that *a food policy based on violence is bankrupt*, because, although it has extorted three hundred million *pudy*, this has been done at the cost of a decrease in the sown area everywhere of almost one quarter, a reduction in livestock, the cessation of planting industrial crops, and profound agricultural decline. . . . We consider that this path of ever-deepening coercion of the peasants will be fatal. We warn you that this path of deeper and more intense coercion of the peasantry can only lead to an unbridgeable gulf between town and country. Then the peasants, no longer in fear of the Tsar and landowners, will become the basis for a bourgeois counter-revolution in Russia. Everyone who holds the interests of the revolution dear must protest against this coercion, demand that the working class be allowed broad initiative, and remember that it is far easier to build with a freely organized peasant class.

[Source: *Vos'moy Vserossiyskiy s"ezd Sovetov rabochikh, krest'yanskikh, krasnoarmeyskikh i kazach'ikh deputatov: Stenograficheskiy otchet* (Moscow 1921) pp. 34–43.]

The main SR statement focused criticism on attempts to cajole peasants into fully collectivized farms and, above all, on the continuation of forced requisitioning, the central feature of 'War Communism'.

Document 84 | From a declaration made by the Socialist Revolutionary Minority Group at the VIII All-Russia Soviet Congress

23 December 1920

The Soviet government's agricultural policy must be based on an awareness of the present importance of family farms to food production and, in so far as the individual farm is and will be for a long time the basis of agricultural production, the Soviet government and its regional bodies must try to protect and satisfy the needs of peasant economy and labour. In encouraging and supporting collective undertakings in farming, the organs of Soviet power must not in any way artificially set up collective farms and create an exceptionally cosy situation for them through additional finance, supplies, or, as often happens, using local peasant labour to work the fields. This causes hostility among most of the toiling peasantry towards the collectivization of agriculture and slows down the development of the ideas of socialist land tenure without at the same time bringing the state any tangible results in the area of food supply.

In its work on the collectivization of agriculture the Soviet government should rely on the initiative of the toiling peasantry, which expresses itself in a wide development of all kinds of agricultural co-operation (associations, *arteli*, communal ploughing, etc.) as primary forms of socialization, which will clear the way for further development.

The present difficult situation does require some state intervention to regulate agricultural production, but these measures must be careful, economically rational and, in relying on the initiative and political consciousness of the toiling peasantry, involve as little coercion as possible. In its food policy the Soviet government must move from the taking of 'surpluses', requisitioning and confiscation to the establishment of a fixed tax, necessary and sufficient to cover the sowing of the fields and the consumption of the towns and industrial centres. The government must desist—until the proper provision of the countryside with industrial products—from wholesale seizure of all grain by force. This only serves to create a hostile mood in the countryside, which can occasionally even turn into open armed uprisings, which bourgeois reactionary elements can exploit. Only the re-establishment of stable land relations on the basis of the socialization of land and the introduction of a grain tax rather than a requisitioning system can create favourable conditions for the development of agriculture and, thereby, for the development also of the country's industry.

In the industrial life of the country, as well as devising a general, single economic plan, in which the toiling masses should participate, we must also show how it is to be implemented by establishing the appropriate level of 'shock-work' and expediency. . .

The restructuring of government on the basis of mass workers' power would guarantee the Soviet republic against domestic turmoil. An essential condition for implementing Soviet workers' power is that the workers must be granted freedom of speech, of the press and of assembly, and legal guarantees for working individuals against all extra-judicial reprisals.

Long live the social revolution!

Long live its defender—the Red Army!

Long live the peasant and the worker as the true buttresses and repositories of Soviet power!

Long live the workers' economic reconstruction of Russia!

[Source: *Vos'moy Vserossiyskiy s˝ezd Sovetov rabochikh, krest'yanskikh, krasnoarmeyskikh i kazach'ikh deputatov* pp. 49—52.]

Although the Congress treated the lonely opposition spokesmen with customary disdain, there was now at last extended discussion of the crisis in agriculture. While the civil war had raged, it was the military conflict that in Bolshevik eyes was responsible for the precipitate economic decline of 1918–20, rather than the policies of 'War Communism'. Recognition that those policies were preventing recovery had been further delayed in 1920 when for a brief interlude it seemed possible the Red Army might sweep westward and ignite sympathetic revolution in central Europe. The dazzling prospect arose when the Polish army, which invaded Ukraine in April 1920, was quickly repulsed and thrown into disarray, opening the road to an advance all the way to Warsaw. Bitter disillusionment followed when Polish workers rallied not to the Red Army but to patriotic appeal, Soviet forces were driven back, and a humiliating peace was signed in October. As the prospect of early revolution abroad faded away, and with the last significant White Guard threat being crushed that autumn, the perils of pursuing 'War Communism' began to be borne in upon Lenin.

By this time, with the 1920 harvest falling to some 60 per cent of the pre-war level, rural unrest was widespread and a large-scale revolt was radiating from the central Russian province of Tambov.[67] The Tambov revolt, which had been triggered in August by resistance to forced requisitioning, was aided by Left SR activists and, from the beginning of 1921, led by the former Left SR A.S. Antonov. Antonov headed the Union of Working Peasants set up to coordinate the sprawling network of villages supporting the rebellion. In December the Union drew up a programme for the overthrow of the Bolshevik regime and the election of a new Constituent Assembly. The following leaflet, written shortly afterwards, appealed to workers to support the revolt, accusing Lenin and Trotsky of selling out to foreign capitalists and betraying the cause of true socialism.

Document 85 | **Union of Working Peasants leaflet addressed to workers**

January or February 1921

In struggle you will find your rights!

To workers

Worker, how long will you patiently endure your slavery, the dependent state into

---

67 See O.H. Radkey, *The Unknown Civil War in Soviet Russia: A study of the Green Movement in the Tambov region, 1920–1* (Stanford, CA, 1976), and O. Figes, 'Peasant Armies' in Acton et al. (eds) *Critical Companion* pp. 370–80. For a striking example of post-Soviet local initiatives to give currency to original archive documents, see the collection on the Tambov rising made available on the website of the Tambov State Technical University, www1.tstu.ru/win/kultur/other/antonov/titul.htm.

which you have fallen thanks to the deceit and the cunning of those false socialists, the Bolshevik-communists? We do not need to point out all the foul villainy with which you have already come face to face; their bayonets have forced you to look fearlessly at the way you live now. We shall just point out the most glaring, ultimate evil, that glaring contradiction between what they were saying at the start of the revolutionary struggle, when they inscribed on their banners those deeply significant slogans, not only for the Russian but also for the world proletariat: 'Dictatorship of the proletariat, dictatorship of the working people', and the miserable outcome of the battle they began with capital in the name of freeing the workers from its dead chains.

At their call, 'Struggle for a better deal for workers and peasants', you answered as one, honestly giving yourself to the struggle at the front against your accursed enemy—the capitalists—and working tirelessly at the factories on just a quarter of a loaf of bread. You could not follow the secret diplomacy carried on by Lenin and Trotsky with foreign capitalists. They have finally sold you, your factories and your railways in order to meet the conditions of their peace treaty with Poland—that is, with Allied capital. Having smothered their own bourgeoisie, they are calling in others, with even bigger appetites, to run us.

Foreigners are hardly going to agree to have socialist and revolutionary workers in their workforces. They need slaves, only slaves, and you, who are defenceless, have been sold as surplus to requirements. You have been thereby condemned to long years of slavery, dependent work, and infinite humiliation before foreign bosses.

The peasant has come out in protest against these new bosses and tyrants, the commissars, with a revolutionary struggle. He calls on you, as his flesh and blood, to join it, in the hope that this will be a common protest with the workers, and that its aim—'A free union between the working peasants and the workers, land and freedom, and an all-national Constituent Assembly'—will embrace equally the interests of workers and peasants.

Working together as a closely knit mass, we shall be able to eliminate the parasites on our backs. Through struggle we shall win our right to work and not submit to exploitation by international capital.

Worker, do not forget your friend, the peasant who ploughs the fields, now enduring his fifth month of the struggle he has launched against the Bolsheviks. Join his ranks, and victory is certain.

Tambov *guberniya* committee of the Union of Working Peasants

[Source: RGVA, fond 235, opis' 1, delo 29, p. 7.]

What shook the party's faith in the policies of 'War Communism' most severely was when peasant revolt was echoed by urban unrest. During the winter, industry was repeatedly hit by strikes, party spokesmen were howled down at workers' meetings and unable to parry hostile resolutions, and non-party Soviet delegates became outspoken in their criticism of acute food shortages and economic paralysis.[68] Lenin publicly recognized that there was little immediate prospect of substantial collectivization and acknowledged the need to provide incentives for individual peasant farmers to increase output. In early February, he recommended to a Politburo commission which had been set up to consider the issue that requisitioning should be replaced by a fixed grain tax, and that once he had paid the tax the peasant farmer should be free 'to use his surplus in local economic circulation'. The reluctance with which the party moved towards abandoning the attempt at direct distribution was reflected in the continuing avoidance of the word 'trade', with all its connotations of capitalism and exploitation. But during February *Pravda* began to carry a number of articles in support of replacing requisitioning with taxation and carefully regulated private marketing, as in the following homespun piece by O.I. Chernov, a Siberian peasant active in local co-operatives.

Document 86 | From O.I. Chernov: 'A View of the Siberian Peasantry as a Social Element'

February 1921

. . . The average Siberian peasant's ideal is something like this: to plough as much land and raise as many cattle as he can. And it is the same for everybody, i.e., to plant your foot firmly on your own piece of ground, albeit with a great deal of effort; at present there's little reason to get on somebody else's back. There are, of course, such people, but they are isolated cases. The peasant of European Russia is just the opposite. His ideal is something like this: to get richer somehow, so that he can exploit his neighbour, i.e., be a kulak or a trader or a usurer because of the stratification I mentioned earlier, and so move up a class.

So, if my premise is right, then why should we break or destroy things? There's nothing in Siberia that needs such harsh revolutionary action.

In the present situation the food agent's slogan 'Bash the kulak and be nice to the poor' does not ring true and, most important, we put up a concerted collective resistance.

---

68 On the explosive mood in Petrograd, see M. McAuley, *Bread and Justice: State and society in Petrograd, 1917–1922* (Oxford 1991) pp. 397–411. For a provincial case study, see D. Raleigh, 'A Provincial Kronstadt: Popular unrest in Saratov at the end of the civil war' in D. Raleigh (ed.) *Provincial Landscapes: Local dimensions of Soviet power, 1917–1953* (Pittsburgh, PA, 2001) pp. 82–104.

The introduction of the bonus system among the workers really tells us that we must review the methods of peasant policy.

At present the peasantry are profoundly depressed: they are convinced that they will be ruined whatever they do, so why should they bother trying to make a living; they are not taking care of their cattle, not bothering to work in the fields and are quickly going to rack and ruin. It would be a different matter if we applied the principle of a percentage tax. Then the peasants could immediately feel firm ground beneath their feet and would know that they need to work a bit more to get more in return. There would not be any of the injustices which are inevitable with the present requisition system and are messing up all the peasants' and the state's calculations.

Then up comes the question of free trade with those surpluses remaining in the peasants' hands. I think this question will be answered by life itself. We see a lot of barter, not thieving, but more acceptable, because at the moment there is no properly established apparatus for exchange of goods at all. This is what I think: firstly there should be a big state organization, which collects all the produce but leaves surpluses in the form of bonuses the peasant can do as he likes with, i.e., exchange them for what he wants, but, so that this barter is not free trade, the exchange can be done through co-operatives or specially organized shops. . .

Picture it like this: in the present situation it is as if a nappy has been put on the peasant and he has been given a nanny—who is young and inexperienced, does all his thinking, decision-making and organizing for him, promises to feed and water him, and just expects him to work. OK, the peasant would agree, but only if he got the nicest food possible for as little work as possible. But the nanny cannot feed and look after him properly, and so he starts rebelling, getting mad and might get so mad that he kills the young nanny. On the other hand, the leaders could be midwives and assist the birth of a new life without doing unnecessary violence to nature. Just weigh up the consequences of the two ways of doing things. In the first case, you get all sorts of dark, angry behaviour from the masses, all sorts of lawlessness, followed by uprisings, which might not be terrible, but reactionary forces are hiding and waiting for their chance, and then the Entente will bare its teeth. In the second case we give independence free rein, and direct it along a desirable path.

Editors' note: Published as a discussion piece.

[Source: *Pravda*, 11 February 1921.]

The foundation of the State General Planning Commission (Gosplan)

Although Bolshevik confidence in 'War Communism' became steadily more fragile, commitment in the long run to the socialist vision of planned production and distribution replacing the 'anarchy' of the market remained unshaken. That any concessions to trade would be no more than temporary was made plain by the establishment later that month of the State General Planning Commission (Gosplan), formally charged to go far beyond Lenin's early scheme to extend electricity across the country and to forge the final riposte to capitalism: a plan for the entire economy.[69]

Document 87 | **Statute on the State General Planning Commission—decree of the Council of People's Commissars**

22 February 1921

1. A General Planning Commission, attached to the Council of Labour and Defence, is established to devise a single all-state economic plan based on the electrification plan approved by the VIII Congress of Soviets, and to supervise the overall implementation of this plan.

Immediate economic tasks, especially those which should be fulfilled in the very near future, particularly in the course of 1921, should be elaborated by the General Planning Commission or its Sub-commission in the greatest detail, taking full account of existing concrete economic conditions.

2. The State General Planning Commission has the following tasks:
    a. to devise a single all-state economic plan, and the methods and order for implementing it;
    b. to examine, and to co-ordinate with the general state plan, the production programmes and planning proposals of various institutions as well as of *oblast'* economic organizations in all sectors of the economy, and to establish the order in which work will be carried out;
    c. to devise all-state measures for developing the knowledge and organizing the research necessary for implementing a plan of state economy, as well as deploying and training the necessary personnel;
    d. to devise measures for disseminating widely among the population information about the plan for the national economy, how it is to be implemented, and the corresponding ways in which labour is to be organized.

---

69 On the evolution of ideas about planning, see F. King, 'The Russian Revolution and the Idea of a Single Economic Plan 1917–1928' *Revolutionary Russia* 12 (1999) pp. 69–83.

3. In carrying out the tasks it has been set, the State General Planning Commission will have the right to communicate directly with all the highest state and central institutions and establishments of the republic.

4. Commissariats and *oblast'* and local institutions are obliged to provide the State General Planning Commission with any information and materials it may request, and also to provide necessary explanations via responsible members of staff.

5. All planning proposals arising in commissariats and departments on matters of the state economy, and production programmes to implement it, must be submitted to the State General Planning Commission for examination and co-ordination with the all-state economic plan.

6. The Presidium and the members of the State General Planning Commission are appointed by the Council of Labour and Defence. The Chairman of the State General Planning Commission is granted the right to report directly to the Chairman of the Council of Labour and Defence.

[Source: K.U. Chernenko and M.S. Smirtyukov, compilers, *Resheniya partii i pravitel'stva po khozyaystvennym voprosam* Volume I, 1917–1928 (Moscow 1967) pp. 199–200.]

The Tenth Party Congress, Kronstadt and Lenin's U-turn

This defiant declaration of faith, however, had minimal impact on immediate policy. Indeed the following month, at the Tenth Party Congress, Lenin carried through an economic U-turn which though cautiously worded seemed to point in the opposite direction: private trade was reintroduced. The *volte face* was made virtually without opposition.[70] Economic paralysis had reached a point where even the greatest enthusiasts for 'War Communism' could see no alternative. Moreover, just as the delegates were arriving in Moscow, the depth of the regime's unpopularity and the peril in which it stood was demonstrated in the most dramatic way. Direct rebellion broke out among the sailors and workers of the Kronstadt naval base outside Petrograd, hailed in 1917 as the pride and joy of the revolution.[71] An anti-Bolshevik Provisional Revolutionary Committee demanded political freedom for all socialist parties, free elections, and the replacement of requisitioning by free trade in grain.

---

70 See S.V. Iarov, 'The Tenth Congress of the Communist Party and the Transition to NEP' in Acton et al. (eds) *Critical Companion* pp. 115–27.
71 See I. Getzler, *Kronstadt, 1917–1921: The fate of a Soviet democracy* (Cambridge 1983) pp. 205–45.

Document 88 | **Resolution of a general meeting of the crew of the 1st and 2nd battleship subdivisions, Kronstadt**

1 March 1921

Having heard the reports of the crew representatives sent to Petrograd by the general meeting of ships' crews to clarify the situation there, it is resolved:

1. Since the present soviets do not express the will of the workers and peasants, there should be immediate re-elections to the soviets by secret ballot and unrestricted pre-election campaigning for all workers and peasants.
2. Freedom of speech and the press for workers, peasants, anarchists and left-wing socialist parties.
3. Freedom of assembly for trade unions and peasant organizations.
4. The convocation of a non-party conference of workers, Red Army soldiers and sailors from Petrograd, Kronstadt and Petrograd *guberniya* no later than 10 March 1921.
5. The release of all political prisoners from socialist parties and of all workers, peasants, soldiers and sailors imprisoned for involvement in worker and peasant movements.
6. The election of a commission to review the cases of those in prisons and concentration camps.
7. The abolition of all special political departments, since no party should be given privileges to conduct propaganda and receive state funds for this purpose. In their place locally elected cultural–educational commissions should be established, for which the state should provide funds.
8. All anti-smuggling roadblock detachments should be removed immediately.
9. Rations for all workers, except those in dangerous jobs, should be equalized.
10. The abolition of communist battle detachments in all military units and of the various guards posted in plants and factories by the communists. If such guards or detachments are necessary, then they are to be appointed in military units from the companies, and in plants and factories at the workers' discretion.
11. The giving of full rights over their land to the peasants, to use as they wish, and of the right to own cattle, which they should maintain and farm through their own efforts—i.e., without the use of hired hands.
12. We appeal to all military units and comrade-cadets to support our resolution.
13. We demand that all our resolutions be widely announced in the press.
14. The appointment of a travelling supervisory bureau.
15. Freedom to set up cottage industries without hired hands.

Chairman of the Brigade meeting Petrichenko
Secretary Perepelkin

Passed unanimously by the brigade meeting with two abstentions. Passed by an overwhelming majority of the Kronstadt garrison. The resolution was read out on 1 March to a meeting of 16,000 residents of Kronstadt and passed unanimously.

Comrade Vasil'ev, the chairman of the Kronstadt executive committee, and comrade Kuz'min, commissar for the Baltic fleet, voted with comrade Kalinin against the resolution.

[Sources: *Pravda o Kronshtadte* (Prague 1921) pp. 7–8; *Voprosy istorii* No. 4, 1994, pp. 16–17.]

Frantically the Bolsheviks denounced the revolt as a White-inspired plot and the Red Army stormed the base to crush the rebels. But the threat to Bolshevik authority had been made plain. It was no coincidence that at the same time as it endorsed the first steps towards what would soon become known as the 'New Economic Policy' (NEP), the Party Congress also sharply tightened political control. To halt divisions within the party and silence criticism of the leadership, a ban (supposedly temporary) was placed on the formation of intra-party factions.[72] Meanwhile, large-scale arrests of Menshevik, Left SR and SR activists effectively broke the organization of all three parties. In 1922 members of the Menshevik Central Committee were given the choice between Siberian exile or emigration, while leading SRs were put on public trial for having supposedly supported the White Armies. The USSR became a one-party state.

---

72 The classic account of intra-party opposition factions is R.V. Daniels, *The Conscience of the Revolution: Communist opposition in Soviet Russia* (Cambridge, MA, 1960).

PART TWO

THE PERIOD OF THE 'NEW ECONOMIC POLICY' (NEP) (1921–1928)

In 1921, confronted by economic desolation and mass peasant resistance, Lenin abandoned reliance on forcible grain requisitioning and shifted towards trade. The so-called 'New Economic Policy' which this U-turn represented gave its name to the period which followed. After a terrible famine, economic recovery set in and was far advanced by the time of Lenin's death in 1924. By then a new constitution had established the Union of Soviet Socialist Republics (USSR), the party's authority had been consolidated, and efforts were under way to instil a new Soviet culture. But contrary to Bolshevik expectations, western capitalism and 'bourgeois' governments had withstood the post-war unrest and the country was isolated. In the leadership struggle among Lenin's heirs, Stalin overcame Trotsky, Zinoviev and Kamenev, successfully identifying himself with the faith that, notwithstanding this isolation and the country's economic backwardness, socialism could be built in the USSR. What was needed was Bolshevik leadership, cultural transformation and the most rapid industrialization feasible. Industrial growth in 1926 and 1927 encouraged visions of a dramatic economic breakthrough, and by 1928 Stalin was poised to launch the momentous First Five-Year Plan.

8

The Economy, the Market
and Planning

From requisitioning to trade

The cornerstones of what quickly became known as the New Economic Policy (NEP) adopted in spring 1921 were the end of food requisitioning and gradual legalization of trade. Peasants would no longer see their surplus carted away without compensation. Instead they would pay a fixed tax and thereafter be free to dispose of their surplus through barter and exchange.[73] The restoration of the market and reliance on trade for profit ran directly against Bolshevik instinct and conviction—indeed, initially official proclamations tortuously avoided using the word 'trade'. For many in the party, to sanction trade seemed close to permitting the restoration of capitalism and abandoning the ideals for which the revolution and civil war had been fought. Many had accepted the policy shift only because the economic crisis of winter 1921 and the scale of peasant unrest had been so alarming: NEP had seemed the surest and perhaps the only way to defuse the explosive situation. Emotional resistance ran deep. The instinctive response of party members high and low is captured in the following possibly slightly embroidered account, by N.V. Valentinov, who had known Lenin since long before the revolution, of the reluctance Lenin encountered.

Document 89 | **'Learn to trade!'—from N.V. Valentinov's memoirs**

1956

At this point I cannot help recalling a conversation with my old friend Yu.M. Steklov, who had become editor of *Izvestiya VTsIK* (*All-Russia Central Executive*

---

73 The two best overviews of the 1920s are E.H. Carr, *The Russian Revolution: From Lenin to Stalin (1917–1929)* (London 1979), a crystal clear resumé of what is the most ambitious western study of early Soviet history, i.e., the multi-volume history by Carr and R.W. Davies; and L.H. Siegelbaum, *Soviet State and Society between Revolutions, 1918–1929* (Cambridge 1992), a superb synthesis incorporating more recent research and placing greater emphasis on the view 'from below'.

Committee News). 'Lenin,' said Steklov, 'has brought about an astonishingly bold and decisive political change. "Learn to trade!"—I thought I'd sooner cut out my own tongue than come out with such a slogan. In accepting such a directive we've got to cut out whole chapters of Marxism: they can't give us guiding principles any more. And when I.M. Vareykis said as much to Lenin, he retorted, "Please don't teach me what to put in or take out of Marxism! Don't teach your grandmother to suck eggs!"'

By virtue of his official position Steklov had to defend in VTsIK's newspaper the new economic policy that Lenin had proclaimed. This he did, but not without some resistance. As for what happened at the top when NEP was accepted, I learned from A.I. Sviderský. I had known him for years. Back in 1909–10 we both lived in Kiev and used to see each other every day in the offices of *Kievskaya mysl'* (*Kiev Thought*), where we worked. . . In 1921 Sviderský took a big job in the Commissariat of Food, and then became Deputy Commissar for Agriculture. At the Party conference in May 1921 he delivered a report approved by Lenin on the food tax, i.e., one of the cornerstones of NEP. . . When I pointed out that I had the impression that not everybody in the Party was enthusiastically following Lenin, Sviderský began to explain that, in fact, the situation was far worse, because virtually nobody agreed with Lenin. 'The only two who completely agreed were probably Krasin and Tsyurupa—all the rest said nothing or dug their heels in.' At one meeting. . . Lenin said, 'When I look you in the eye, you all seem to agree with me and say yes, but if I look away, you say no. You're playing hide-and-seek with me. In that case let me too play a parliamentary game with you. When a vote of no-confidence is taken against the head of the government, he resigns. You did this to me at the time of the Brest Treaty, even though now any fool can see that my policy was right. Now you're doing the same thing again over NEP. So I'll do what they do in parliaments and hand in my resignation to VTsIK and the Plenum. I'll stop being chairman of the Council and a member of the Politburo, and just become a journalist, writing for *Pravda* and other Soviet papers.'

'Lenin was joking, of course?'

'Not at all. He was in deadly earnest. He was banging his fist on the table, shouting that he was fed up with talking to people who didn't want to give up the revolutionary underground or their childish incomprehension of such a serious matter, and that without NEP a split with the peasantry was inevitable. Lenin's threat scared everybody so much that he immediately broke their resistance. For example, Bukharin, who had sharply disagreed with Lenin, turned in twenty-four minutes from an opponent into such a staunch defender of NEP that Lenin had to restrain him. Lenin commented sarcastically, "I've got twenty-five arguments in favour of NEP, to which comrade Bukharin wants to add another fifty. I'm afraid that with such a massive addition he'll simply swamp NEP and turn it into something I can no longer agree with. So let's stick with twenty-five. . ."'

By going furiously against the tide, Lenin masterfully whipped the Party into accepting both a policy of concessions and NEP, but a profound, undaunted resistance to all this undoubtedly still remained in the Party. . . In March 1923 (Lenin was paralysed by then) Molotov wrote in *Pravda* that despite two years of NEP 'One cannot say that we fully understand this policy or have evaluated it properly. . .' Molotov stated the simple fact that there were still Party members who considered that the system in 1918–20 was truly communist and regretted that the Party had turned away from this system to capitalism. . .

[Source: N.V. Valentinov, *Novaya ekonomicheskaya politika i krizis partii posle smerti Lenina: Gody raboty v VSNKh vo vremya NEP* (Moscow 1991) pp. 66–69.]

Having adopted it, the regime put the best possible gloss upon NEP. Although it involved abruptly dropping policies pursued since 1918, official decrees and commentary painted the U-turn as something that had always been intended. A veil was drawn over the fact that some Bolsheviks, including for a brief period Lenin himself, had come to embrace the originally ad hoc measures of 'War Communism' and the abandonment of the market as the short road to socialism.[74] Now those measures were portrayed as having been deeply regrettable temporary necessities, for which the emergency generated by the Whites' attempted counter-revolution was entirely to blame, and which the Bolsheviks had never liked. In a frantic attempt to woo peasant support, the notion of a worker–peasant union or alliance (*smychka*), epitomized by balanced exchange of goods between town and countryside, moved to the very centre of the regime's rhetoric.

NEP was also accompanied by a marked step back from the collectivist approach of the civil-war years. Individual peasants were now encouraged to seize the opportunities which the policy created. Explicit appeal was made to 'the industrious and hard-working'. For many Bolsheviks, this was an uncomfortable echo of the infamous 'wager on the sober and the strong' made by Stolypin, Nicholas II's last dynamic prime minister, who had hoped to replace the traditional repartitional peasant commune with a conservative yeomanry committed to private property.[75] The long-term Bolshevik vision, by contrast, remained common ownership and fully collectivized farming. But in the short term the market and individual profit motive were to restore

---

74 For the view that 'War Communism' was from the outset driven by ideology rather than a response to crisis, see S. Malle, *The Economic Organization of War Communism, 1918–1921* (Cambridge 1985). The best analysis of the numerous elements that made up the policy, carefully weighing the relative importance of ideological preconception and dire emergency in its formulation, is M. Sandle, *A Short History of Soviet Socialism* (London 1999) pp. 95–150.

75 P. Waldron, *Between the Revolutions: Stolypin and the politics of renewal in Russia* (London 1998), provides a good guide.

to peasants the incentive to expand the area they sowed, raise yields and maximize output.

Document 90 | 'To All Peasants'—circular from the All-Russia TsIK

23 March 1921

Why food requisitioning was necessary

The grave and destructive three-year war which Soviet power waged against tsarist generals, landowners, and Russian and foreign capitalists has ended victoriously for the workers and peasants. In that war, thanks to the heroism of the Red Army, we saved the peasants' land from seizure by the landowners, we did not let the factory owners return to their mills and factories or let foreign bourgeois states deprive Russia of its independence and plunder its wealth. The war cost us dearly and demanded great sacrifices of the workers and peasants. The requisitioning of agricultural produce was particularly burdensome for the peasants, but the Soviet government had to introduce this to feed an army of millions of soldiers, and workers on the railways and the most important industrial enterprises.

The Soviet government was well aware how burdensome food requisitioning was for the peasants, how unequally it was applied, and how inconvenient it was for the development of peasant agriculture. But it stuck by food requisitioning, realizing that the toiling peasantry would sooner forgive Soviet power all the burdens of food requisitioning for victory over the enemy, than for the removal of requisitioning at the cost of a victory for the landowners, the loss of land and the defeat and destruction of the Red Army.

Food requisitioning is abolished

Now that the onslaught by the capitalists and landowners has been beaten off and Russia, having defended in war its independence against the power of foreign capital, is speaking to the world's most powerful nations as an equal; now that mighty Britain has signed a trade agreement with us and we have the opportunity to send half of the Red Army back to peacetime work and to supply the peasantry with imported goods in exchange for part of its surpluses—now is the time to lessen the burdens on the peasantry without fear of losing the most valuable gains of the worker–peasant revolution. Henceforth, by a joint decree of the All-Russia Central Executive Committee and the Council of People's Commissars, food requisitioning is abolished and replaced by a tax-in-kind on farm produce.

Tax—making things easier for the peasants

This tax must take less than grain requisitioning did. It must be set even before the spring sowing so that every peasant can work out what portion of his harvest he must give to the state and how much will remain at his complete disposal. The tax must be collected not according to collective but individual responsibility, so that the industrious and hard-working farmer does not have to pay for his less diligent fellow villagers.

On payment of the tax, all remaining surpluses are entirely at their owner's disposal. He has the right to exchange them for the food and tools which will be delivered by the state from abroad and from its own industry to the countryside; he may barter them for food through the co-operatives at local markets and bazaars. At the same time the Soviet government still bears the responsibility of supplying essential foodstuffs to the poorest rural inhabitants, who will have no surpluses to barter.

The tax is a temporary measure

...The peasants must remember that this measure is temporary. Only frightful poverty and disorganized trade are compelling the Soviet government to take part of agricultural produce in the form of a tax, i.e., without compensation. As industry gets sorted out—the fate of peasant agriculture depends on this—and as the flow of goods from abroad in exchange for our raw materials increases, the tax-in-kind burden on the peasantry will lighten. In future, in building a socialist economy we shall be so successful that for every *pud* of peasant grain the Soviet state will in return give a much-needed product of equal value.

Let's get down to work!

The time for the spring sowing is drawing near. The All-Russia Central Executive Committee and the Council of People's Commissars call upon farmers to put everything into making sure that not a single *desyatina* is left unsown.

Every peasant must by now realize and remember that the more he sows, the more grain he will have left over for himself. But let all of worker–peasant Russia not forget that the Soviet government is now able to lighten the burden on the tillers only because the heroic Red Army drove away the enemies of the toiling people and showed the whole world that the worker–peasant state is unshakeable. If strife were to begin between the workers, peasants and the many nationalities making up our great working alliance, the foreign plunderers would always prefer to rip up their agreements with us, stop trading and start another war to reinstate the landowners and capitalists and make an enfeebled Russia easy prey for pillage and oppression.

Long live our valiant Red Army!

Long live the indissoluble union of workers and peasants!

Long live the stability of the worker–peasant Soviet government!

Long live peaceful toil, free of the power of the landowners and capitalists of Russia!

This address is to be read in all the villages, hamlets, Cossack settlements, mills, factories and Red Army units of the RSFSR.

[Source: *Izvestiya*, 23 March 1921.]

Restrictions on trade in agricultural produce were progressively lifted across the areas now back under Bolshevik rule, on the proviso that peasants must first meet the new fixed tax. The initial expectation that trade would be local and on a modest scale was rapidly overtaken by the development of a national grain market. The hated requisitioning squads were disbanded, and the role of the local 'sowing committees', set up the previous autumn, was redefined. Gone was the quixotic attempt to extend the *dirigiste* approach of 'War Communism' down to imposing precise targets and specific crops on the villages for which the committees were responsible. Their purpose now was to do what they could to respond to grim reports that the combination of forced requisitioning and the harvest failures of 1920 had left peasants in many areas with inadequate stocks for spring sowing.

Document 91 | 'On the free exchange of corn and forage'—a decree of the Council of People's Commissars

28 March 1921

The All-Russia Central Executive Committee decree of 23 March of this year has given the peasant population the right, state obligations having been fulfilled, freely to sell and buy its surplus agricultural produce.

Accordingly, the Council of People's Commissars decrees as follows:

1. To permit immediately the free exchange, sale and purchase of
   a) grain and forage in the following *gubernii*: Arkhangel'sk, Ekaterinburg, Penza, Perm', Ural', Tula, Astrakhan', Tyumen', Vitebsk, Vyatka, Vladimir, Petrograd, Vologda, Gomel', Chelyabinsk, Ivanovo, Kostroma, Kaluga, Moscow, Nizhniy Novgorod, Olonets, Pskov, Northern Dvina, Smolensk, Cherepovets, Tver', Yaroslavl', the Tatar and Chuvash Republics; Pokrovsk, Voronezh, Samara, Saratov, Kursk, Ufa, Simbirsk, Orenburg, Ryazan', Tsaritsyn, Tambov, Orel, the German colony and the Bashkir Republic;
   b) potatoes in the following: Arkhangel'sk, Samara, Petrograd, Northern Dvina, Tver', Vyatka, Orel, Moscow, Perm', Tula, Ivanovo, Ryazan', Tsaritsyn, Kaluga, Tyumen' and Bryansk;
   c) hay in the following: Voronezh, Moscow, Ekaterinburg, Saratov, Tambov, Tula, Ural, Tsaritsyn, Astrakhan', Vitebsk, Ivanovo, Cherepovets, Ryazan', Kaluga, Orel and the Tatar Republic.

N.B. In those localities (*guberniya* and *uezd*) where state obligations are being fulfilled the People's Commissariat for Food is obliged to implement this decree.

2. To permit, in the above localities, the movement of grain, forage, potatoes and hay for the purpose of exchange, sale and purchase.

3. To disband all the anti-smuggling roadblocks in the above localities on roads, railways and waterways.

N.B. Railways and waterways are to be guarded only to prevent malicious or unintentional damage.

4. This decree does not abolish the provisions for stockpiling and storing seed, set out in the regulations published in accordance with the Decree of the VIII Soviet Congress, 'On Measures for Improving and Developing Agriculture'.

5. In order to ensure maximum sowing, farmers who, as a result of selling corn or potatoes during the sowing period, are unable to sow their fields properly will be called to account by the committees overseeing sowing.

V. Ul'yanov-Lenin: chairman of the Council of People's Commissars
A. Tsyurupa: People's Commissar for Food
N. Gorbunov: Office Manager for the Council of People's Commissars
L. Fotieva: Secretary of the Council of People's Commissars

[Source: *Izvestiya*, 29 March 1921.]

Foreboding about the 1921 harvest proved all too well-placed. Drought that summer devastated a perilously weakened peasant economy, and the following winter saw horrific famine accompanied by mass cholera and typhus epidemics. Worst affected were the Volga region, the North Caucasus and Ukraine. Despite substantial famine relief from the capitalist west, it is estimated that as many as six million people died from famine and disease.[76] It was only after this catastrophe that the combination of an end to the civil war and the stimulus of NEP set the rural economy on the road to rapid recovery.

---

76 S.G. Wheatcroft and R.W. Davies, 'Population' in Davies et al. (eds) *Economic Transformation* pp. 62–64.

NEP in industry

The shift towards a fixed tax and private trade in agricultural produce was accompanied by moves away from the direct central control of industrial production and distribution. Private enterprise in small-scale manufacture, the service industries and retail trade became legal and quickly expanded, entrepreneurs or 'NEPmen' building on the black market of the 'War Communism' period. Large- and medium-scale industry, on the other hand, remained state-owned and under the broad supervision of the Supreme Council of the National Economy (VSNKh). It was here that the party saw the nucleus of a future transition to a full-scale socialist and planned economy. But for now, instead of simply responding to orders and supplies handed down from above, managers of state enterprises were to be given considerable discretion and to operate according to market principles. They were to demonstrate the superiority of state co-ordination and common ownership by mastering the requirements of the market, raising productivity and outperforming the private sector.

Document 92 | Decree of the IX All-Russia Congress of Soviets (excerpt)

28 December 1921

. . . 8. State enterprises and associations must be guaranteed a wide degree of independence in the disposal of resources allocated to them by the state and in the acquisition of raw materials, fuel, auxiliary materials, etc., and also the right to sell a proportion of their output to acquire raw materials not supplied by the state. . .

Given that NEP rejects fundamentally '*glavkist*' methods of economic management, we must fight decisively against any attempts at resurrecting such methods of managing industry. . .

12. In so far as the victory of the toiling people has granted Soviet Russia at least a temporary and unstable peace and allowed it to go from a war-footing on the domestic and foreign fronts to peace-time economic construction, the immediate task is the establishment in all walks of life of the strict principles of revolutionary legality. Strict answerability by government bodies, officialdom and citizens for the breaking of Soviet laws and the system they protect must go hand in hand with the strengthening of guarantees for the persons and property of citizens. . .

13. The so-called 'New Economic Policy', the basic principles of which were clearly set out even as far back as the first 'breathing space' of spring 1918, is based on strict accounting of the economic power of Soviet Russia. The implementation of this policy, interrupted by the combined attack on the worker–peasant state by the counter-revolutionary forces of the Russian landed gentry and bourgeoisie and European imperialism, became possible only after the military destruction of these counter-revolutionary attempts at the beginning of 1921. Now that the struggle

between communist and private enterprise has gone onto an economic footing, in the market, the nationalized industry, concentrated in the hands of the workers' state, must, by adapting to market conditions and methods of competing within it, win a dominant position for itself.

[Source: *Vserossiyskiy s˝ezd Sovetov rabochikh, krest'yanskikh, krasnoarmeyskikh i kazach'ikh deputatov: Stenograficheskiy otchet, 22–28 dekabrya 1921* (Moscow 1922) pp. 247–51.]

Over the following two years, the regulations governing 'trusts' (as the semi-autonomous state enterprises were known) were elaborated. They reflected the novel balance the regime was seeking to strike between developing Soviet industry according to centrally identified priorities and subjecting enterprises to the discipline of the market. Managers were to be state employees, appointed by VSNKh and subject to its directions. But they were to bear the responsibility of virtual owners, answerable in law for the well-being and assets of the enterprise. They were to draw up their own business plan, but within the constraints of the government's broad priorities for production in each branch of industry. Each trust was responsible for its own financial balance, but should a trust make a loss, VSNKh could recommend that the Treasury cover the shortfall. Managers were free to negotiate with buyers, but they had to give priority to state orders. They were to set their own prices, but VSNKh might impose below-market prices.

Document 93 | On state industrial enterprises operating on the basis of commercial accounting (trusts)—from a Sovnarkom and VTsIK decree

10 April 1923

Preamble

1. State trusts are defined as state industrial enterprises to which the state has granted operational independence, each according to their individual statutes, and which operate on a commercial profit-and-loss basis.

State trusts are responsible for their obligations only within the limits of the property at their disposal...

The Treasury is not responsible for their debts...

IV. The financing of trusts

... 20. If a trust's year-end balance shows a loss and it becomes necessary to restore the statutory capital, then the Supreme Council of the National Economy may...

make a representation to the Council for Labour and Defence on the expediency of making up the loss at the expense of the State Treasury. . .

V. The trust's management and auditing bodies are:
  a) The Supreme Council of the National Economy
  b) Its Management Board
  c) The Audit Commission

A. The Supreme Council of the National Economy

. . . 28. Under the Supreme Council of the National Economy's jurisdiction are:
. . . b) Appointment and removal of members of the Management Board, the Audit and Liquidation Commissions. . .
c) The scrutiny and ratification of budgets and of the business plan for the coming year on the basis of the production plan for the relevant branch of industry approved by the Council for Labour and Defence, as well as ratification of the accounts and the balance for the previous year. . .
f) The distribution of the previous year's profit according to the rules stipulated in Section VI.
g) The authorization of changes in the statutes, the amount of statutory capital and of the liquidation of the trust by a ruling on these questions—to be ratified by the Council for Labour and Defence.
h) Authorization to spend capital reserves.
i) Authorization to the Management Board to introduce substantive changes in the approved production plan and to join syndicates and other commercial/industrial associations. . .

29. The Supreme Council of the National Economy is not to interfere in the day-to-day administrative and operational work of a trust's Management Board.

B. The Management Board

31. In carrying out their duties the chairman and members of the Management Board must display the prudence of a careful owner and bear a disciplinary, criminal and civic responsibility for both the integrity of the property entrusted to them and the business-like conduct of affairs. . .

37. The Management Board can spend above its approved budget in exceptional circumstances, but must account to the Supreme Council of the National Economy both for the necessity for such expenditure and its consequences. The latter body must be informed within three days of such expenditure. . .

VI. Depreciation, capital reserves and the distribution of profits

. . . 45. All a trust's profits are to go to the Treasury with the exception of a deduction of no less than 20 per cent for the trust's capital reserves. . . and deductions for bonuses to members of the Management Board, workers and staff. The size of the deductions for capital reserves, as well as the sums payable as bonuses are to be determined on an annual basis by a decree of the Supreme Council of the National Economy, while the amount of profit which must be paid to the Treasury is to be determined by the Supreme Council of the National Economy in agreement with the People's Commissariat for Finance. . .

VII. Taxes, prices and indents

. . . 48. All trusts must be members of an exchange and register their wholesale transactions on that exchange. Trusts' output is to be sold at prices agreed with the buyer. Compulsory selling prices of goods intended for free sale may be set in necessary circumstances only by decrees of the Supreme Council of the National Economy and the Council for Labour and Defence.

49. A trust's output may be supplied at below-market prices (but not lower than cost price and inclusive of average profit) by decision of the Council for Labour and Defence via the Supreme Council of the National Economy. . .

50. In matters of buying and selling, trusts are obliged, all things being equal, to give priority to state bodies and co-operative unions acting as purchasing agents.

[Source: *Sobranie uzakoneniy i rasporyazheniy raboche-krest'yanskogo pravitel'stva* No. 29, 1923, Article 336, pp. 558–68.]

Subjecting nationalized industry to market constraints did not, in the eyes of the leadership and party economists, mean abandoning what they saw as its massive superiority over private enterprise. Even while industry was in the condition of near paralysis that was the legacy of the civil war and 'War Communism', enthusiasts waxed eloquent about the potential gains in efficiency to be made by workers in a socialist state. At the macro level, rationally planned production would outperform capitalism, cursed by its in-built conflict and waste, while at the micro level, at the level of the individual enterprise, workers would reach far higher levels of productivity. Unlike workers exploited by capitalism, Soviet workers were working for the common good. They were overseen by a workers' government, so the argument went, and guided by managers whose interests and ethos were the same as their own and in whom they trusted. Their welfare was protected by both the state and by powerful communist trade unions. Every improvement in efficiency and increase in output benefited them, their families and their fellow workers, and they knew it. They would therefore embrace improvements in technique, time-keeping and organization. Unlike capitalist workers, for whom the intensification of labour associated with 'Taylorism', the American movement for the scientific organization of labour based on precise time-and-motion studies, was experienced as an intensification of exploitation, Soviet workers would eagerly welcome such advances.[77] Socialist man would work in full harmony with and adjust his rhythm to those of the machine—the vision whose nightmare potential E. Zamyatin depicted in his dystopian novel *We* (on Zamyatin, see document 118).

The following extract is by P.M. Kerzhentsev, a theatre critic and journalist who had been a member of *Proletkul't* and was among those enthusiasts of NOT (*Nauchnaya organizatsiya truda*, or scientific organization of labour) who placed primary emphasis not on the role of managerial discipline but on workers' own enthusiasm and creativity.

Document 94 | P.M. Kerzhentsev: Favourable Conditions for the Scientific Organization of Labour (NOT) in our Country

Excerpt from *NOT: The Scientific Organization of Labour* (1923)

NOT requires the application of scientific methods and principles to human labour, measured systems in work, a strict plan in organizing the economy, accuracy, accounting, calculation and so forth.

In other words, the scientific organization of labour is a union in practice between scientific achievements and the organization of labour in production and administration. For this reason NOT is very much in harmony with the transition period, and will, of course, truly flourish in the epoch of communism, when there will no longer be the profound gulf we see now between our theoretical scientific achievements and their practical manifestation.

We can therefore say that NOT, the scientific organization of labour, is by its very nature a discipline which is particularly close to the proletariat when constructing a socialist economy. For us now it is especially important to unite life and practice with science, and to make all our work conscious, accurate and systematic.

This is the first of the favourable conditions for NOT in the USSR. In spite of all the failures and disappointments, objectively NOT in our conditions will develop ever further, and under communism its achievements will manifest themselves to the maximum extent.

A second favourable circumstance is the existence of the dictatorship of the workers, which provides opportunities for scientific investigations, especially those related to questions of work and production, to proceed freely, undistorted by the

---

77 On Bolshevik attitudes to Taylorism and the development of NOT, see R. Stites, *Revolutionary Dreams: Utopian vision and experimental life in the Russian Revolution* (Oxford 1989) pp.145–64.

mercenary requirements of the capitalists.

Moreover, it is precisely thanks to the dictatorship of the proletariat and our centralized economy that the principles of NOT can be widely applied in our country in full measure, which is quite impossible in capitalist conditions.

The very presence of capitalism fundamentally contradicts the central idea of the scientific organization of labour, the principle of the planned organization of the economy. Capitalist competition and the anarchy of production can never be reconciled with the idea of a single plan.

On the other hand, a whole series of problems connected with the organization of labour (for example, questions of rest and feeding at work, questions of professional training and selection, etc.) can be posed and resolved correctly only in a country where the greatest attention is paid to the interests of the working class. A science of labour can be created only where they who labour directly govern the state and its economic life.

The widespread interest in problems of NOT and the ongoing concern with all the questions connected with it are certainly not just empty fashions. Our striving to reorganize the country's economy is very closely linked with questions of NOT. The working masses will instinctively try to deal with such problems as how to work with less expenditure of energy and greater productivity, how to organize the machine, the factory, the national economy, and the state in order to avoid friction and superfluous effort, unnecessary strain, and wastage of material resources.

With regard to NOT, the proletariat sees this new discipline not as an enemy, but as an ally. This is a massive advantage compared with the situation which faced, and still faces, the Taylorists in the West. There, the working class has taken a hostile attitude to Taylor and his system, and the trade unions have waged a stubborn struggle against all innovations proposed by Taylor. And they have been quite right in this. Thanks to this opposition the principles of NOT abroad have filtered into industry only with great difficulty.

In this respect we are in a completely different situation. Any improvement in production will directly, albeit not immediately, be reflected in an improvement in the position of the working class, in an increase in the productivity of industry as a whole, in an improvement in the country's economy, in a strengthening of the dictatorship of the proletariat. Therefore our proletariat will always welcome all scientific improvements in the sphere of labour and production.

These are some of the basic features which will affect positively the future of NOT in our country. One does not need to be a prophet to say that NOT will be developed genuinely scientifically only where the proletariat has triumphed. And our Soviet Union will soon achieve so much in this sphere that the Americans will be coming to learn from us.

[Source: E.B. Koritsky (ed.) *U istokov NOT: Zabytye diskusii i nerealizovannye idei*
(Izdatel'stvo Leningradskogo universiteta, Leningrad 1990) pp. 123–25.]

Economic recovery

In practice, agriculture began to recover before industry. A major step in restoring peasant confidence and encouraging commerce was the introduction of a stable currency. 'War Communism' had seen the ruble come close to losing its value entirely. In July 1922, a new currency, backed by gold, the *chervonets*, was introduced, but it was issued only in limited numbers and large denominations. The old *Sovznak* ruble remained in circulation for most purposes, still depreciating rapidly in value and thereby severely discouraging private trade and bedevilling the drive to have enterprise managers adopt careful cost-accounting and learn to respond to clear market signals. The market was placed on much firmer footing in March 1924 when the old currency notes were withdrawn and replaced by small-denomination notes and coins of the stable *chervonets*. This made it possible to complete the gradual replacement of the agricultural tax-in-kind introduced in 1921 by a money tax. As the Commissar for Finance predicted at the time, the combination of the need to secure cash to pay the tax and greater confidence in currency stability quickened peasant involvement in the market, increased their incentive to diversify their output where profitable and to seek non-farm sources of income, and at the same time raised their purchasing power and thus demand for manufactures.

Document 95 | From an interview with G.Ya. Sokol′nikov, People's Commissar for Finance

1 February 1924

This year's most important financial measures will be the currency reform and the changeover in the single agricultural tax from a tax-in-kind to a cash tax. Both measures are very closely connected. Abandoning the tax-in-kind in the countryside is being done in the interests of both the rural and national economies. For the peasant farmer the switch to a cash tax means complete freedom of choice in finding the most advantageous way to pay the tax. The peasant, no longer obliged to pay the tax in grain, might direct his farm predominantly in the direction of developing those cultures which will give the best returns according to market conditions, or he might gather the means to pay by ancillary trade and seasonal work. Finally, all of the costs connected with collecting the tax-in-kind and the frictions and misunderstandings resulting from differing conditions, etc., will completely disappear.

In autumn 1923 the peasantry already made good use of the opportunity to pay in cash rather than in kind, so that in 1923 tax-in-kind revenues amounted to only about 20 per cent of the total. However, paying in cash did prove difficult for the peasantry because of currency instability, i.e., the *Sovznak* banknotes with which the tax was mainly paid. With the fall in the exchange rate both the peasantry and the Soviet state lost out. Thus, the creation of a stable currency is a matter of considerable urgency...

This currency reform will be a turning point in our economic development...

With a stable currency workers will receive a stable wage, not losing its value because of a falling ruble. In exchange for their produce the peasantry will get reliable money which can be saved without fear of devaluation. Rural turnover will benefit from a stable currency. The prices of urban-produced goods in the countryside will fall, since one of the reasons for their rising is village shops marking up to cover the fall in the value of the money. State trading and co-operative organizations will also be able to lower their prices and establish more reliable accounting procedures, not messed up by the falling value of money. There is no doubt that the easing of trading turnover will increase the flow of goods to the towns, and in urban markets prices will be a better expression of value. In short, stable prices will be the bridge between town and countryside...

This currency reform will also undoubtedly have a favourable effect on our international standing...

[Source: *Izvestiya*, 1 February 1924.]

Peasant demand for industrial products was at first desperately weak and when in 1923 it began to grow, state industry forced industrial prices up so sharply that it fell away again. This was the 'scissors crisis', christened by Trotsky, the two price blades parting and widening ever further. By the end of the year, however, the terms of trade had been steered back more in agriculture's favour, demand revived and industrial output began to climb. During the mid-1920s, NEP saw both agricultural and industrial output increase rapidly. By 1926 the grain crop had returned to pre-war levels and there was a sharp increase in non-grain production. After a slower start, industrial expansion was very rapid indeed in 1924 and 1925, approximately reaching overall pre-war levels by 1926/27.[78]

Stalin's act of faith in building socialism in an isolated country

Despite economic recovery, however, attitudes within the party towards NEP remained deeply ambivalent. Even those most impressed by the speed

---

78 For a summary of the vigorous debate over the comparison between pre-war and late NEP figures, see M. Harrison, 'National Income' in Davies et al. (eds) *Economic Transformation* pp. 41–42.

of the recovery, and by Lenin's advocacy, regarded reliance on the market and small-scale peasant farming as temporary. All were convinced that in principle private enterprise and the individual profit motive were morally objectionable, economically inferior and historically doomed. The socialist future lay with common ownership, large-scale production, and a planned economy. All were convinced, too, that the absolute *sine qua non* for the transition to socialism was industrialization.[79]

Russian Marxists viewed the productive power of modern industry as the prerequisite for socialism. It alone would provide the economic base for the wealth, leisure, mass education and cultural richness which they associated with full-blown socialism and the communist utopia beyond. It was through industrialization, too, that a social structure in which petit-bourgeois peasants predominated would give way to one characterized by a mass working class committed to common ownership and social production. Moreover, international isolation and the recurrent threat from a hostile capitalist world required that the USSR build an industrial base comparable or superior to that of the other great powers to retain military security and ideological independence.

The key problem, given the country's poverty and low level of productivity, was one of investment. To construct and equip new factories, mines, hydro-electric dams, railways and roads would involve massive investment. During the first years of NEP, Bolshevik hopes remained high that much of this capital could be drawn from the west. In 1921 Britain signed a modest trade agreement with the USSR, implying recognition even though full diplomatic recognition came only in 1924. This fed the leadership's optimism that western loans and direct investment, carefully supervised by the Soviet government, which would retain a monopoly over foreign trade, could provide the necessary resources. In November 1924, however, what had seemed a breakthrough in commercial relations with the west, a much more ambitious draft Anglo-Soviet trade treaty negotiated by the British Labour government, was repudiated by the Tories. The prospect of significant funds from abroad faded rapidly. With investment available neither from the comradely western socialist governments the Bolsheviks had expected to emerge, nor from foreign capitalists, the regime was face to face with the question the Mensheviks had pressed on Lenin in 1917. How could a wretchedly poor, peasant-dominated country build socialism on its own, lacking as it did both the modern productive power and the huge proletariat that Marx had seen as the prerequisite?

---

79 On the industrialization debate, see M. Lewin, *Political Undercurrents in Soviet Economic Debates* (London 1975).

It was in this context that, the following month, Stalin began to insist that it was indeed possible to do so. He made this act of faith the centrepiece of a prolonged polemic against Trotsky, denouncing him for denigrating Soviet potential and for portraying the USSR, should relief not come from abroad, as doomed to degeneration. In a manner that had already become his hall-mark, Stalin presented his ideas as those of Lenin (who had died in January 1924), using carefully slanted quotations—in this case one from a 1915 article of Lenin's that he would reiterate tirelessly—to substantiate his claim.[80]

Document 96 | From Stalin's Preface to *The Road to October*

17 December 1924

. . . The second specific feature of the October Revolution lies in the fact that this revolution represents a model of the practical application of Lenin's theory of the proletarian revolution.

He who has not understood this specific feature of the October Revolution will never understand either the international nature of this revolution, or its colossal international might, or the specific features of its foreign policy.

'Uneven economic and political development,' says Lenin, 'is an absolute law of capitalism. Hence, the victory of socialism is possible first in several or even in one capitalist country taken separately. The victorious proletariat of that country, having expropriated the capitalists and organized its own socialist production, would stand up *against* the rest of the world, the capitalist world, attracting to its cause the oppressed classes of other countries, raising revolts in those countries against the capitalists, and in the event of necessity coming out even with armed force against the exploiting classes and their states.' For 'the free union of nations in socialism is impossible without a more or less prolonged and stubborn struggle of the socialist republics against the backward states'. (See 'On the Slogan for a United States of Europe', August 1915.)

The opportunists of all countries assert that the proletarian revolution can begin—if it is to begin anywhere at all, according to their theory—only in industrially developed countries, and that the more highly developed these countries are indus-trially the more chances there are for the victory of socialism. Moreover, according to them, the possibility of the victory of socialism in one country, and one in which capitalism is little developed at that, is excluded as something absolutely improb-able. As far back as the period of the war, Lenin, taking as his basis the law of the uneven development of the imperialist states, counterposed to the opportunists his theory of the proletarian revolution about the victory of socialism in one country, even if that country is one in which capitalism is less developed.

---

80 Lenin, *Selected Works* Volume V (Moscow 1968) p. 141.

It is well known that the October Revolution fully confirmed the correctness of Lenin's theory of the proletarian revolution.

How do matters stand with Trotsky's 'permanent revolution' in the light of Lenin's theory of the victory of the proletarian revolution in one country?

Let us take Trotsky's pamphlet *Our Revolution* (1906).

Trotsky writes:

'Without direct state support from the European proletariat, the working class of Russia will not be able to maintain itself in power and to transform its temporary rule into a lasting socialist dictatorship. This we cannot doubt for an instant.'

What does this quotation mean? It means that the victory of socialism in one country, in this case Russia, is impossible '*without* direct state support from the European proletariat', i.e., before the European proletariat has conquered power.

What is there in common between this 'theory' and Lenin's thesis on the possibility of the victory of socialism 'in one capitalist country taken separately'?

Clearly, there is nothing in common.

[Source: J.V. Stalin, *Problems of Leninism* (Peking 1976) pp. 129–31.]

Stalin's act of faith did not in itself point or commit him to any specific recipe for securing the necessary resources for industrialization. In common with all the party leaders, he took it for granted that the peasantry and rural sector would in some fashion provide the bulk of the necessary capital as well as the new labour that would be required. But in the mid-1920s he attacked Trotsky and the so-called 'Left Opposition' in the party for their supposedly anti-peasant approach. He resisted the demand of their most prominent economist, E.A. Preobrazhensky, that peasant living standards must be urgently squeezed, even if it involved hardship ('primitive socialist accumulation' to match the 'primitive capitalist accumulation' graphically described by Marx), to fund comprehensive planning based upon large-scale investment in heavy industry.[81] In the same breath, Stalin denounced Trotsky both for exaggerating Soviet dependence on events abroad and for underrating the potential and importance of the 'first peculiar feature of October', the alliance between workers and peasants. And in the mid-1920s Stalin broadly supported the approach of Bukharin, the Politburo member who became the boldest champion of NEP.

---

81 Preobrazhensky published his lectures on the subject in expanded form at the end of 1924: see *The New Economics*, translated by B. Pearce (Oxford 1965).

Bukharin and the celebration of NEP

For Bukharin, the need to maintain harmony (the *smychka*) between workers and the 'workers' state', on the one hand, and the peasantry on the other was axiomatic.[82] This involved sustaining market relations, and thus maintaining balance both in the terms of trade between industry and agriculture and in investment in heavy industry and the light industries supplying manufactures for peasant consumption. And he argued that this represented more than a forced pause: it offered the surest route to socialism. The socialist sector would gradually outgrow the private, benefiting from the advantages of planning, but a form of planning that took full account of and channelled rather than disrupted the dynamism of the market. Given that, unlike in a capitalist country, the commanding heights of the economy—heavy industry, the banks, foreign trade—were firmly in the hands of the socialist state, the most individualistic of peasant efforts could be harnessed to building socialism. On the one hand, taxation and careful regulation of prices would be used to cream off significant investment funds from those who acquired most wealth. On the other, peasant demand for manufactures would provide the vital stimulant which would expand state/socialist industry. Far from fearing the emergence of a rural bourgeoisie and being anxious at the prospect of individual peasant households flourishing and acquiring wealth, everything must be done to foster peasant enterprise, initiative and economic development. All peasants, rich and poor alike, said Bukharin in a phrase that would come back to haunt him, must 'enrich' themselves.

Document 97 | **N.I. Bukharin: '... enrich yourselves, accumulate, develop your farms...'**

From Bukharin's report to a conference of Moscow party activists: 'On the New Economic Policy and Our Tasks'[83]

17 April 1925

... Among the working class and within our party we find comrades whose attitude towards the peasantry resembles narrow craft unionism: what, they ask, has the countryside to do with us? This way of thinking must be abandoned, for there is nothing so harmful at the present moment as failure to understand that our industry depends on the peasant market.

Socialist industry depends on quantitative and qualitative changes in peasant

---

82 For the fullest exposition, see S. Cohen, *Bukharin and the Bolshevik Revolution* (New York 1973).

83 For a full English translation, see N.I. Bukharin, *Selected Writings on the State and the Transition to Socialism*, translated and edited by R.B. Day (New York 1982), pp. 183–88.

demand. And what does demand from the peasant economy mean? The peasant economy presents two kinds of demand: consumer demand, i.e., demand for textiles, cottons, etc., and productive demand, i.e., demand for agricultural implements and for all kinds of means of production.

What determines the agricultural sector's consumer demand, i.e., what determines, say, the quantity of textiles demanded by the peasantry? It depends on the condition and rate of development of the peasant economy.

The effective demand of the peasantry is determined primarily by the state of the peasant economy, its level, and the development of its productive forces. This demand will expand in proportion to the extent that *productive* demand develops, i.e., to the degree that the peasantry improves its economy, moves it forward, introduces more and better equipment, raises the level of farming techniques, improves methods of cultivation, etc., etc. It is quite clear from this that a process of *accumulation* is needed in the peasant economy, so that rather than everything being wasted and consumed, part of the resources will be used for the purchase of agricultural implements, etc.

Even now certain remnants of war-communist relations can be found in our country, which are hindering our further growth. One of these is the fact that the prosperous upper stratum of the peasantry, and the middle peasants, who are also striving for prosperity, *are currently afraid to accumulate*. This leads to the position where the peasant is afraid to buy an iron roof for fear that he will be declared a kulak; if he buys a machine, he makes certain that the communists do not see it. Advanced technology has become a matter for conspiracy. Thus, on the one hand the prosperous peasant is unhappy because we prevent him from accumulating and hiring labourers; on the other hand the village poor, the victims of overpopulation, sometimes grumble at us for preventing them from hiring themselves out to this same prosperous peasant.

An excessive fear of hired labour, fear of accumulation, fear of a capitalist peasant stratum, etc., can lead us to adopt an incorrect economic strategy in the countryside. We are too eager to tread on the toes of the prosperous peasant. But this means that the middle peasant is afraid to improve his farm and lay himself open to heavy administrative pressure; while the poor peasant complains that we are preventing him from selling his labour power to the rich peasant, etc.

. . . Overall, we need to say to the entire peasantry, to all its different strata: enrich yourselves, accumulate, develop your farms. Only idiots can say that the poor must *always* be with us. We must now implement a policy which will result in the disappearance of poverty.

[Source: N.I. Bukharin, *Izbrannye proizvedeniya* (Moscow Izdatel'stvo politicheskoy literatury, 1988) pp. 195–96, 197.]

Like all Bolsheviks, Bukharin remained firmly wedded to the ultimate vision of collective farming. But, he insisted, to contemplate imposing collectivization by force would be madness. To do so would be to destroy the *smychka*, set the party at loggerheads with the peasantry and revert to the impasse of 'War Communism'. Instead, the poor and middle peasantry must be gradually won round, and the key mechanism to do so was the plethora of small credit and trading co-operatives which were being created in their thousands by village communes. Citing the enthusiasm Lenin had shown for co-operatives in his last years,[84] Bukharin argued that commercial co-operatives would demonstrate to the peasantry the advantages of pooling their resources. Co-operatives formed to secure credit, purchase implements and organize sales would gradually extend their activity to purchasing substantial agricultural machinery, establishing small-scale processing plants and factories, and eventually hiring or buying tractors: strip farming would be exposed as manifestly inefficient and the advantages of collective farming on open fields would be irresistible.

The strength of Bukharin's approach in the mid-1920s was that where the peasantry were concerned it seemed hard-headedly realistic. He acknowledged just how limited at present the influence of the party in the countryside was. The early years of NEP had seen a fall in the initial burst of energy the regime had devoted to expanding rural education and health provision, the participation rate in rural soviets was derisory, and rural party membership extremely low. In this situation his refusal to believe that party propaganda could persuade the peasantry of the superiority of collective or state farms—and in the mid-1920s remarkably little progress was made even in drawing up blueprints for forming collective farms—seemed sober and well-founded. His approach took fully on board just how powerful had been the resurgence of the traditional repartitional peasant commune, and just how wedded peasant households were, for the time being, to farming their strips of land independently within it.[85] Bukharin's approach aroused respect rather than enthusiasm among party members but his portrayal of peasant attitudes and motivation was difficult to deny, as is shown in the following letter from a long-term social democrat and revolutionary, who at this time was himself an individual peasant farmer.

---

84 See Lenin, 'On Cooperation' in *Collected Works* Volume XXXIII (London 1964) pp. 467–75.
85 See D. Atkinson, *The End of the Russian Land Commune, 1905–1930* (Stanford, CA, 1983) pp. 233–312, and for an earlier account that remains valuable, D. Male, *Russian Peasant Organization before Collectivization* (Cambridge 1971).

Document 98 | From P.A. Zalomov's letter to the Society of Former Political Prisoners

18 December 1924

The land-hungry in particular hate the state farms. They desperately want work and blame central government for cutting back coal production in the Donbass. In their opinion the 'reform', i.e., the October Revolution, gave them nothing, and they want some other sort of reform which would give them all work. They don't want tsarism, landowners and capitalists, but, in their opinion, the helm of state is in incompetent hands, hence all the calamities. . . Of course, those peasants who prior to the Revolution owned purchased land want private land ownership. The peasants' greatest wish is a bit more land and a guaranteed wage as well. . . If we judge the mood of the peasants by the decrees of Soviets, conferences and the like, we don't see the true face of the peasant. . . All the resolutions are compiled by Party comrades and reflect their opinions and wishes. The majority of peasants can't make sense of the resolutions and are prepared to 'vorte' [sic!] as much as you like and for whatever you like. 'Vorting' against isn't usually allowed, and 'unanimous' can mean 75 per cent abstaining. In general, there is complete indifference to the resolutions. The peasant comes to life only when. . . somehow or other his economic interests are affected. . .

Here in the Kursk *oblast'* you can buy a cow for 20 rubles because of the fodder shortage, and some peasants and even 'proletarians' want to export livestock and are angry that central government won't allow it. And we're not talking about some kulaks or other, but about poor peasants, albeit poor peasants who got used to speculating during the Revolution. . . I often tell them about the value of crop rotation, of growing sugar beet, etc., but some just dismiss it as 'old wives' tales', while those who do understand talk about the impossibility of collective work because of the extreme individualism of most peasants. . .

[Source: *Izvestiya TsK KPSS* No. 7, 1991, pp. 174–75.]

Where Bukharin's vision of NEP proved less easy to realize in practice than in theory, even during the brief period in the mid-1920s in which party policy broadly conformed to it, was in maintaining balanced terms of trade between agriculture and industry. His premise was that the price paid for grain must always be sufficient to ensure the peasantry marketed food and industrial crops in sufficient quantities to satisfy the needs of consumers, industry and export. But the urgency of industrialization gave the regime the most powerful incentive to tilt the terms of trade the other way and reduce the price paid to the peasantry. For the less the state paid for rural produce, the lower the cost of food and the wage bill for industrial workers and for state employees in general, the cheaper the raw materials for industry, and the greater the funds available for industrial investment. Moreover, predicting how the peasantry would react to price shifts was fraught with difficulty—in particular where the all-important grain market was concerned. Harvest forecasts were bedevilled by the combination of huge regional variations and the vagaries of the weather. Even if the size of the harvest had been broadly predictable, no 'norm' in terms of what proportion of the annual grain harvest was marketed had been established since the upheavals of the war, revolution, land reform, civil war, 'War Communism' and famine. Unlike commercial farmers, most households only expected to sell a small proportion of their grain harvest and if the price seemed inadequate in a given season many might decide not to sell at all. The regime was taken aback, too, by how quickly peasants in some areas responded to price increases for industrial crops, livestock and dairy produce, abruptly increasing their output and sale of these and cutting the amount of grain they marketed.[86]

To complicate matters further, the authorities were determined throughout the mid-1920s to cut industrial prices, extending price controls ever wider, even when the demand for goods clearly exceeded supply. The rationale was both to maintain pressure for increased industrial efficiency and to make manufactures affordable to peasants. But the result was a recurrent 'goods famine': there were shortages in manufactures and, especially far from industrial centres, they were often not available at all. A goods famine made peasants hesitate to part with grain even for apparently satisfactory prices, further compounding the difficulty of manipulating prices successfully. And on top of all this, peasant commercial behaviour was repeatedly jolted by abrupt oscillations in public rhetoric—about the speed of industrialization, about 'kulaks', the emergence of a rural bourgeoisie and the place of the peasantry, about the danger of war, and about price policy itself.

The pressure to accelerate industrialization

At no stage, therefore, was the smooth market equilibrium envisaged by champions of NEP established, and by the same token the form of planning envisaged by Bukharin, carefully operating within the constraints of the market, did not take firm root. Instead, as soon as industrial recovery gathered speed, pressure began to mount—notably from regional leaders such as those of the Urals—for investment projects on a scale that could all too easily

---

86 The most lucid guide to NEP remains A. Nove, *An Economic History of the USSR* (London 1992, revised ed.) pp. 78–158.

upset the equilibrium. Non-party economists found themselves, as in this discussion by L.N. Yurovsky of the Finance Commissariat, constantly looking over their shoulders at a much more ambitious, comprehensive and, in their view, rash form of planning which would ultimately prove incompatible with the market.

Document 99 | From L.N. Yurovsky's article *On the Problem of the Plan and Equilibrium in the Soviet Economic System*

1926

The very term 'planned economy' may evidently have a double meaning, i.e., it can designate two different concepts, depending on the system within which the plan will be carried out. . .

Planning the economy in the Soviet economic system, influencing the prices of raw materials, deliveries and imports, and the direction of capital construction. . . does not mean supplanting the commodity economy, but regulating it.

. . . Owing to the significance of the material resources concentrated in the hands of the state and the large scale of Soviet economic organizations, many transactions which in less centralized systems take place between different economic subjects take place in our case within a single economic subject. That is, they become a matter of administrative direction and not of a market transaction. . . Consequently, some peculiar methods for regulating the economy also operate. But administrative directions become improvident if they are made without reference to value correlations laid down by the market, and the market in any case remains as a criterion and a regulator, as long as all objects of consumption are realized within it, because in the end every product becomes an object of consumption, which is why it is produced. . .

We have repeated more than once that the planning principle in the current Soviet economic system must not only be implemented with reference to market equilibrium, but even have as its aim the establishment of the kind of equilibrium that establishes itself spontaneously in the conditions of a capitalist economy. . .

The absence of equilibrium can evoke two types of reaction. One consists in taking measures to restore equilibrium. The other consists in attempts to get by without restoring equilibrium by introducing into the economy a new non-market principle.

A shortage of goods indicates unsatisfied demand. But if there is no possibility of satisfying demand, then the latter cannot be made the regulator of the territorial distribution of goods, because this regulator works properly only up to the point where the quantity of goods is sufficient to satisfy the market. It is far from easy to find another regulator, as [the need for one] always appears at moments when a shortage is being experienced in some sector of the economy. This regulator is 'planned distribution' (not to be confused with planned economy), which in its complete form comes in the guise of distribution by ration-cards, and in its incomplete form takes a variety of guises, in particular planned deliveries. Planned deliveries, as we all know, means the Union-wide distribution of goods in short supply in the form of quotas assigned by special plans for certain localities. Here is not the place to dwell on the question of which is better—to put the scarce goods onto the market or to regulate the market in the above fashion. But it is perfectly obvious that however brilliantly the People's Commissariat departments given the job carry it out—and so far we have not seen any brilliance in this area—they can only draw up a plan of supply based on such general and conditional coefficients as size of population and general standard of living, or such data as those given to local bodies on the inadequacy of earlier quotas. One can hardly regard this element of pseudo-planned economy (pseudo-planned *vis-à-vis* a commodity economy) as anything more than a measure brought about by need, to be abolished once the shortages disappear and economic equilibrium is established.

If. . . equilibrium is upset and not restored, then one cannot try to solve the problem, bypassing monetary equilibrium, with just one single regulatory measure. The task requires ever new measures, the last of which completes the chain and provides a real solution, moving not towards market equilibrium but away from it. This measure is the elimination of the market and the establishment in the corresponding sphere of complete, strictly planned distribution, totally disregarding the demands of the 'law of value'. . .

[Source: *Vestnik finansov* No. 12, 1926, pp. 19–21.]

Within VSNKh, too, there were conflicting voices for and against the industrial policies identified with NEP. By the mid-1920s, the Supreme Council had developed a substantial apparatus, its own industrial planning agency, and eight *glavki* overseeing different branches of state industry. Its chairman since 1924, Dzerzhinsky, former head of the Cheka and OGPU, became increasingly frustrated by features of the management of state enterprises that would haunt Soviet industry in later decades—the mutual distrust between managers and the central agencies, misinformation sent from enterprises to the centre, and mountains of paperwork imposed by the centre on managers. He wrote the following letter in July 1926, days before his sudden death and replacement by V.V. Kuybyshev, a champion of much more ambitious rates of investment. Dzerzhinsky urged that instead of managers being guided by wasteful and excessive supervision and cross-checking from above, they should be subjected to the market discipline of self-financing and openness.

Document 100 | From a letter by F.E. Dzerzhinsky to VSNKh executives

1 July 1926

From my fact-finding mission to the Southern Engineering Trust, Southern Steel and elsewhere in the south I came away with the firm conviction that our present system of management is useless. It is based on universal mistrust, demanding from subordinate bodies all sorts of reports, forms and information. It relies on averages for entire trusts, depersonalizing the basic units, the factories. It engenders endless paperwork and red tape, has a pernicious effect on any real work and is immensely wasteful of resources and effort. This system must be abandoned. With this system we do not know in fact what is going on, and instead of a plan linking everything in an agreed direction and pace we have a chaotic free-for-all. . . The factories still do not know what their costs are. Instead of being an organizing force in this sector our system has been making no headway.

There is only one answer: we must make a 180° turn and introduce a system based on trust. It is impossible to run industry without trusting those to whom one entrusts the given task, teaching them and learning from them, helping them and carefully choosing Soviet industrial cadres suited to a system based on trust.

It follows from this that we need a little more personal contact (from Main Administration [*glavk*] to trust to factory); the reduction of correspondence and report-writing to the bare minimum; the replacement of bureaucrats by people who know and can learn the job; frequent visits by leading personnel to the factories themselves; all factories to go over to commercial accounting, i.e., to balanced finances in factories and fixed relationships with the trusts, so that the factory's financial affairs are transparent not only to the factory, trust and the Supreme Council of the National Economy, but also to the public at large. . .

All the issues I have raised in this note must be dealt with urgently in order to arrive at some practical measures. This work must involve economic executives on the widest scale. These are the lines along which we should be waging our campaign for economy in industrial management. It should save us tens of millions and bring in hundreds of millions of rubles. . .

[Source: RGASPI, fond 76, opis' 2, delo 270, pp. 16–18.]

As late as 1927 it was still just possible for non-party members to express, without immediate danger, much more jaundiced views of the entire experiment with state-owned industry. The following letter, sent to the industrial journal *Predpriyatie* (*Enterprise*) albeit without expectation of publication, expresses scorn for the whole notion of socialist industry being able to match capitalism's efficiency and power of innovation. Its author, V.E. Grum-Grzhimaylo, was a prominent mining engineer with extensive experience of the pre-revolutionary metallurgical industry. He had been on the faculty of both the St Petersburg Polytechnic Institute and Urals University, was a corresponding member of the Academy of Sciences, and at the time of writing worked for the ferrous metals council attached to VSNKh. His scepticism and counsel of caution—he was dismissive of Urals leaders' plans for the development of a massive industrial base to rival that of Ukraine[87]—clashed directly with growing enthusiasm within the party for accelerated state-run industrialization.

Document 101 | From V.E. Grum-Grzhimaylo's letter to the journal *Predpriyatie* (not intended for publication)

March 1927

You are asking me how to bring prices down? Why are our prices high? What is wrong with Soviet industrial organization? By asking you are raising the old argument about the advantages and disadvantages of so-called state socialism or the command economy—one that dozens of writers have been arguing for and against for decades.

I am not an economist, writer, politician or courtier; I am an industrialist, who has seen a lot in his time, and I am going to write frankly about what life has taught me. . .

You hear it said that only in America can shoe-shine boys become millionaires. That is wrong. The merchants of Moscow came up from nowhere. Their millions were earned not by highway robbery or sharp practice, but by sheer hard work. Who advanced them? Life, not some office. In an office they would have died quietly and come to nothing.

An acquaintance of mine had the opportunity to have a good talk to the late Moscow millionaire Solodovnikov. He asked him why and how he'd got rich. Solodovnikov went up to a table, took out an exercise book and said, 'These are all my accounts. If you want to get rich, don't bother with accountants and clerks. Your business should all be in your head and you shouldn't handle any more than your head can hold. . .'

So far I have written only about the memory, efficiency, ability to work, thoroughness and honesty of the successful. But apart from this such people have always tried big ideas and new methods—either of their own or ones learnt from life; in doing so they have shown characteristic persistence and common sense. They have worked out beforehand the possibility of failure and loss—and then gone for it.

They dared to try an idea out, did not give up on a loss-maker so long as it was

---

87 J. Harris, *The Great Urals: Regionalism and the evolution of the Soviet system* (Ithaca, NY, 1999) pp. 124–26.

not based on error, and always saw it through, however hard it was to sort things out. You can only work like that at your own risk and responsibility. Command industry usually rules out risk-taking. To take risks you have to apply for special credit. If not, any failure brings up the question of wasting public money. Hence the audits, accounts, angry words and nervous strain. All this makes it so hard to try out new ideas and methods that factory engineers avoid initiative and just draw their wages.

Let us assume something has been achieved in a factory. If the factory has a single owner, who knows everything and everybody, then the person behind this achievement immediately gets a bonus, which encourages him to work harder and his mates to make some effort to achieve something in their turn. So, the achievement quickly bears real fruit. In a private enterprise run by a managing director and a board, things are worse and the achievement is probably hushed up. It is not always in the manager's interest to promote a subordinate. In the best instance, the author of the idea will get praise from a manager who will also claim to have 'done his bit'. In a government factory the ladder is already crowded with managers, consultants and inspectors. The new idea will find plenty of authors, and the real inventor often just gets lost among those who claim the 'initiative' for the idea. This is being taken even further at present. Alongside the real administrators there are red directors, trade unions, factory committees and cells crammed with layabouts. They all want their share of credit for the achievement, too. So, this is what you read in the papers, 'A new achievement by the workers of such-and-such factory. . .' What have the workers got to do with it? Nothing, it is just the way they write these days. . . The ideas man is now lost among all those who 'also did their bit'. 'What on earth made you do it?!' says the one just drawing his wages. 'So much effort and worry. What a fool!' 'You're right. That's the last time,' says the inventor.

And you want to bring down prices with industry organized like that?. . .

There has been a lot of talk recently about worn-out equipment and out-of-date factories, and the need for capital investment in factories, etc., etc. On the basis of my own experience I can tell you straight that it is a load of rubbish. The equipment is not half as bad as the maintenance and management. They appoint as director somebody who has nothing to do with the factory, knows nothing about production and how his machines work. He is given a production programme and thousands of inspectors over him to check on its implementation. What can the poor man do? He bashes the programme out until the factory stops working from so many breakdowns and accidents. Then he moans about the equipment being worn out. . .

How do you bring down prices under such crazy conditions in industry? It would be better to ask those who devised the system.

Capitalism was not thought up. Life produced it. It is far from perfect and has no end of faults, but there is corn among the weeds. Pull the weeds up, but do not damage the corn. Capitalism preserves the true, upright bearers of divine truth, the creators of new ideas, the teachers and nurturers of mankind, and does not give feeble nonentities a chance...

What are you going to put in its place?

[Source: *Arkhiv muzeya istorii Ural'skogo universiteta*, O.F. 3038.]

Among workers a very different form of dissatisfaction with NEP became increasingly pronounced. Here it was attacked not for its failure to reward the innovations and talent of the ambitious or outstanding few, but for its failure to cater sufficiently for general workers' needs. Although economic recovery revived urban life, working-class wages and living and working conditions improved painfully slowly. Housing in the major cities remained overcrowded and insanitary, medical provision was rudimentary, and the NEP years were marked by significant levels of unemployment. Efforts to cut costs, tighten discipline, intensify labour and raise productivity were widely experienced as oppressive and all too like the pressures of capitalism.[88] From the factory floor, there was a blatant mismatch between the grinding struggle for daily life and the party leadership's high-flown rhetoric about and debate over the building of socialism. The following letter, from an outspoken worker in eastern Siberia to V.M. Molotov, who was then in the Central Committee's Secretariat and closely allied with Stalin, conveys something of working-class frustration with NEP.

Document 102 | From a metalworker's letter to Molotov

14 November 1926

... The 'transitional' moment has already turned into a prolonged period of construction, which has started weighing heavily upon the workers. None of your campaigns have any effect in reality, of course they look good in the figures in your reports, you can see that in *guberniya* A, x-amount was sown in 1923 and y-amount in 1926, but I can see only one thing: that I get 280 kopecks a day, when my flat costs 10 rubles a month, lighting 3–5 rubles, poor quality boots from the co-operative 20–25 rubles, 400 grams of white bread 11–13 kopecks, cigarettes 20 kopecks a packet, meat 35–40 kopecks, etc. You read about retail prices going down (there was a campaign about that, as well): butter's gone down by 1½ kopecks a kilo, but I need 100 grams. Of course it's good that it's cheaper, but this doesn't count for my 100 grams, but only for somebody who buys 16 kilos. Well, divide 1½ kopecks

---

88 For two case studies, see W. Chase, *Workers, Society and the Soviet State: Labor and life in Moscow, 1918–1929* (Urbana and Chicago 1987), and C. Ward, *Russia's Cotton Workers and the New Economic Policy* (Cambridge 1990).

by 10 and see what sort of a reduction I get? You would say that's a piffling amount! It might be a piffling amount for you, but my life depends on such piffling amounts! You might say that all this is petty trivia and that it's far more important to understand Engels' theses on the possibility of social revolution in one country, whether in 1905 Lenin had Russia in mind when he wrote on the same topic and who understands him better, Trotsky or Kamenev, Zinoviev or you and Stalin. Yes, it is important no doubt, but to us our stomachs are also important, and while you sit there arguing, my family could starve to death. And I'll be left naked and sick from overwork!!! We should be saying to you, 'Clear off or get down to work and stop making so much hot air about who wrote what and who understands it best!' You remind me of all those medieval religious debates. . . We can't make head nor tail of it, but just want to work and have full stomachs. So, comrade Molotov, I'm not a Party member, but have just put down openly and frankly all my observations in this letter. I don't care about any repression and I'm not afraid of your GPU—I was in prison in 1908 and wasn't scared then!. . .

I'll tell you where I work at present and what I do; I won't hide anything and am telling you straight that things are bad for us workers despite our resolutions at meetings. There we just go through the motions: they bring forward the resolutions and we raise our hands to get it over with because we're hungry and want to get things done at home, help our wives, etc. I'm telling you again—I'm not afraid of repression (and, by the way, I'm not one of your troublemakers, but a disciplined factory worker, you can check if you like). That's all for now.

Fraternally yours,

L.N. Kalinin, a metalworker,
Water Transport Workers' Club,
Vladivostok

[Source: *Kommunist* No. 5, 1990, p. 82.]

Rank-and-file worker opinion had little prospect of directly affecting party policy. The leadership had taken a variety of steps designed to ensure that influence flowed the other way. The trade unions were now in party hands and served increasingly as conduits for party policy, a rapid recovery in membership being ensured by making them responsible for the modest but expanding system of social insurance as well as cultural and educational opportunities. Moreover, the effect of high levels of unemployment and keen competition for jobs was to divide workers, in particular pitting thoroughly urbanized workers against peasant migrants, and to limit the scope for united working-class pressure. On the other hand, from 1923 the leadership launched a sustained drive to recruit workers both into the Komsomol and directly into the party itself: by 1928 half a million had enrolled, attracted by the party's socialist mission as well as the improved opportunities for promotion and higher education which membership provided. While many of the new recruits were deferential and biddable, some were not. In the wave of strikes against cost-cutting in 1925, party members were often prominent, albeit directing their criticism at management and specialists rather than at the party itself. The differentials in pay, clothes and lifestyle enjoyed by these 'bourgeois' elements were keenly resented. The sharpest animus, expressed in this letter from a Komsomol member in northern Ukraine, was felt against so-called 'NEPmen', the private traders and small-scale entrepreneurs who flourished during the mid-1920s.[89]

Document 103 | From a letter from a member of the Young Communist League to the Central Committee of the CPSU

30 August 1926

The following often demands to be asked: why at present is the Communist Party not paying any attention to, or rather, is it not halting the spiralling growth of NEP? It has already done what it was supposed to do, and it's time it was written off precisely because co-operation can replace this NEP. I reckon it's time to pay the maximum amount of attention to this question, the question of abolishing NEP, because it's horrible to see here in this Soviet state people so fat they can't get through a door, but mainly because it's time to stop this shameless cheating and the existence of people living off the labour of workers and peasants. . . I really don't think that this NEP is any real use to us as a Soviet state; admittedly, it was useful once, but now it's harmful. . .

A.E. Zaporozhets,
Member of the Komsomol,
Naumovka,
Koryukov district,
Konotop *okrug*.

[Source: *Kommunist* No. 5, 1990, p. 80.]

---

89 For discussion of the controversial proposition that working-class and rank-and-file party pressure in Moscow played at least some part in Stalin's sharp 'leftward' turn in 1928, see J. Hatch, 'The "Lenin Levy" and the Social Origins of Stalinism: Workers and the Communist Party in Moscow, 1921–1928' *Slavic Review* 48 (1989) pp. 558–77.

In the higher reaches of the party, impatience with the prevailing version of NEP, and demands for heavier taxes on better-off peasants, higher wages for workers, and dynamic planning for industrial expansion, was initially articulated, as we have seen, by the so-called Left Opposition, whereas the dominant group accepted Bukharin's caution. But from 1926, at the very time that Stalin and his allies were sidelining Trotsky and the left, they were themselves coming to share a similar vision of a dramatic industrial breakthrough. In part Bukharin's willingness to abandon his earlier emphasis on building socialism at 'a snail's pace' arose from the sheer speed of recovery: 1926 in particular saw a bumper harvest and a steep rise in industrial output. This expansion encouraged trust directors and party leaders in each region, too, to press the case for ambitious increases in investment and development. Their pressure found expression in the upper reaches both of VSNKh and of the party itself: regional leaders were strongly represented on the Central Committee and Stalin's readiness to support their growing demands did much to secure him their backing. A major additional stimulus came with the so-called 'war scare' of 1927: shock in April at the massacre of Chinese Communists by their erstwhile Nationalist allies was followed in May by alarm when the British broke off diplomatic relations with the USSR and relations with France became severely strained. With Stalin and Bukharin loudly warning of the danger of imminent capitalist aggression, possibly via Poland, the urgency of military–industrial development took on even greater impetus.

Crucial to the shift in attitude of Stalin, Bukharin and the party leadership as a whole was their mounting confidence that the dynamism latent in economic planning could now be set in motion. Until 1926 it had been critics of Bukharin and Stalin's caution who had expressed greatest optimism about the opportunity to achieve unprecedented rates of industrial expansion now that the commanding heights of industry were in state hands and planned growth within reach. Trotsky, who had long urged that Gosplan be given real power to plan the growth of the state sector of the economy, had argued in 1925 that the USSR could aspire to a rate of industrial growth twice or three times the relatively rapid 6 per cent of pre-war Russia. In the next two years that confidence rapidly spread as Stalin and Bukharin moved from denouncing the left as 'super-industrializers' to themselves indulging a tantalizing vision of what was becoming possible. Moreover, massively increased investment in heavy industry could be accompanied, so they argued, by a simultaneous improvement in the quality of life of both workers and the majority of peasants—a far more attractive proposition than the initial squeeze on living standards which Trotsky and the left had seen as unavoidable. Both central and regional party leaders—those from the Urals prominent among them—egged on economic experts to make the most of socialist potential. They then derived further encouragement as optimistic economists in both Gosplan and VSNKh began to elbow aside the more cautious and to vie with each other to forge the most compelling and inviting Five-Year Plan. The sense of dramatic and irreversible momentum was captured by Stalin's speech at the Fifteenth Party Congress in December 1927.

Document 104 | I.V. Stalin: *The Rate of Development of Our Large-Scale Socialist Industry*

December 1927

a) The growth of the output of large-scale nationalized industry, which constitutes over 77 per cent of *all* industry in the country: whereas in 1925–26 the increase in output (calculated in pre-war rubles) of large-scale nationalized industry over that of the preceding year amounted to 42.2 per cent, in 1926–27 to 18.2 per cent, and in 1927–28 will amount to 15.8 per cent, the State Planning Commission's rough and very conservative five-year estimates provide for an increase in output during five years of 76.7 per cent, with an average arithmetical annual increase of 15 per cent and an increase in industrial output in 1931–32 to *double* the pre-war output.

If we take the gross output of all industry in the country, both large-scale (state and private) and small industry, then the annual, average arithmetical increase in output, according to the State Planning Commission's five-year estimates, will be about 12 per cent, which will be an increase in total industrial output in 1931–32 of nearly 70 per cent compared with the pre-war level.

In America, the annual increase in total industrial output for the five years 1890–95 was 8.2 per cent, for the five years 1895–1900 — 5.2 per cent, for the five years 1900–05 — 2.6 per cent, for the five years 1905–10 — 3.6 per cent. In Russia, for the ten years 1895–1905, the average annual increase was 10.7 per cent, for the eight years 1905–13 — 8.1 per cent. *The percentage of annual increase in the output of our socialist industry, and also in the output of all industry, is a record one, such as not a single big capitalist country in the world can show.*

And that is in spite of the fact that American industry, and especially Russian pre-war industry, were abundantly fertilized by a powerful flow of foreign capital, whereas our nationalized industry is compelled to base itself on its own accumulations. And that is in spite of the fact that our nationalized industry has already entered the period of reconstruction, when the re-equipment of old factories and the erection of new ones has acquired decisive importance for increasing industrial output. *In the rate of its development, our industry in general, and our socialist industry in particular, is overtaking and outstripping the development of industry in the capitalist countries.*

b) How is this unprecedented rate of development of our large-scale industry to be explained?

Firstly, by the fact that it is nationalized industry, thanks to which it is free from the selfish and anti-social interests of private capitalist groups and is able to develop in conformity with the interests of society as a whole.

Secondly, by the fact that it is conducted on a larger scale and is more concentrated than industry anywhere else in the world, thanks to which it has every possibility of beating private capitalist industry.

Thirdly, by the fact that the state, controlling nationalized transport, nationalized credit, nationalized foreign trade and the general state budget, has every possibility of directing nationalized industry in a planned way, as a single industrial enterprise, which gives it enormous advantages over all other industry and accelerates its rate of development many times over.

Fourthly, by the fact that nationalized industry, being industry of the biggest and most powerful kind, has every possibility of pursuing a policy of steadily reducing production costs, of reducing wholesale prices and cheapening its products, thereby expanding the market for its products, increasing the capacity of the home market and creating for itself a continuously increasing source for the further expansion of production.

Fifthly, by the fact that nationalized industry is able for many reasons, one of them being that it pursues the policy of reducing prices, to develop under conditions of gradual rapprochement between town and country, between the proletariat and the peasantry, in contrast with capitalist industry, which develops under conditions of increasing enmity between the bourgeois town, which bleeds the peasantry white, and the decaying countryside.

Lastly, by the fact that nationalized industry is based on the working class, which is the leader in all our development, thanks to which it is able more easily to develop technology in general, and the productivity of labour in particular, and to apply rationalisation to production and management, with the support of the broad masses of the working class, which is not and cannot be the case under the capitalist system of industry.

All this is proved beyond doubt by the rapid growth of our technology during the past two years and the rapid development of new branches of industry (machines, machine tools, turbines, automobiles and aircraft, chemicals, etc.). It is also proved by the rationalization of production that we are carrying out, *along with* a shorter working day (a seven-hour day) and *along with* a steady improvement in the material and cultural conditions of the working class, which is not and cannot be the case under the capitalist system of economy. *The unprecedented rate of development of our socialist industry is direct and indubitable proof of the superiority of the Soviet system of production over the capitalist system.*

Lenin was right in saying, as far back as September 1917, before the Bolsheviks had captured power, that after establishing the dictatorship of the proletariat we can and must 'overtake and outstrip the advanced countries *economically as well*' (Vol. XXI, p. 191). *The Party's task: to maintain the achieved rate of development of socialist industry and to increase it in the near future with the object of creating the favourable conditions necessary for overtaking and outstripping the advanced capitalist countries.*

[Source: J.V. Stalin, *Works* Volume X (Moscow 1955) pp. 307–10.]

Although Stalin made no reference to it, during the weeks before the Congress the leadership were suddenly becoming aware of a momentous crisis with the potential to destroy this tantalizing vision. The amount of grain procured by the state, on which depended provision for the cities, export earnings to secure machinery, and thus the entire investment drive, was falling drastically short of expectations. The party's response to the crisis was to precipitate the abandonment of NEP and the onset of 'revolution from above'.

9

The State, the Party and the Leadership Struggle

The Constitution of the USSR

The manner in which the party fought the civil war, and responded to the economic crisis and popular unrest which accompanied it, left a permanent imprint on the form taken by Bolshevik rule. The party retained a monopoly on political organization and propaganda, the remnants of its rivals being suppressed and the SR and Menshevik leaders imprisoned or exiled. It retained, too, the vastly expanded range of administrative responsibilities it had accumulated during the civil war. Alongside the policy-making and vote-winning functions it shared with parties in multi-party systems, its officials now operated as the core hierarchy charged with ensuring government policy was implemented. Through the development of what became known as the *nomenklatura* system, party committees oversaw appointments to all significant public posts—including all branches of the state's executive, legislative, judicial, civil, police, cultural, military and economic apparatus—maintaining lists of politically acceptable candidates for posts within their purview.

At the same time, the expression of dissent within the party became increasingly difficult. The temporary ban on the formation of 'factions' approved in the face of the trauma of winter 1921 became permanent. Party cells were dominated by the agenda and in large measure the recommendations of the local committee, and the local committee was itself increasingly bound by instructions from above. The same process set in all the way up the committee ladder. Moreover, the key link in the chain of command through which authority was exercised, the committee secretary, who increasingly gained ascendancy over his own committee, was more and more often put in post not by election from below but appointment from above. The effect was to accentuate the centralized and unitary structure of the party, reinforcing the influence of the Moscow leadership over party officials belonging to every nationality and every region of the country.[90] Lenin and all the most prominent Bolsheviks protested against this 'bureaucratization' of the party. Yet it became permanent, conditioning both the Soviet constitutional structure and the party leadership struggle of the 1920s.

Where the constitution was concerned, the key issue was the reintegration of those non-Russian areas which had enjoyed a period of independence before being brought back under Bolshevik rule at the end of the civil war: Ukraine and Belorussia to the west, the three Caucasian republics of Azerbaidzhan, Armenia and Georgia to the south, and, politically and militarily less urgent, the Central Asian republics of Khiva and Bukhara and the far eastern territories.[91] It was axiomatic for the Bolsheviks that, although each had been recognized as a separate state, now that they were back under communist rule they should form a union with the giant RSFSR, a step towards a world union of soviet socialist republics. Resistance to such a union would be reactionary bourgeois nationalism and would be overridden. On the other hand, the party had long condemned the subjection of one nationality to another as a reflection of class domination, and specifically denounced Great Russian oppression of the national minorities of the former empire. The civil war had also revealed the gulf of incomprehension in minority national areas between an overwhelmingly Russified officialdom and urban working class, on the one hand, and the majority of the population in non-Russian areas on the other. Simply to ride roughshod over national sensibilities and make these areas once again undifferentiated provinces of a Russian state would be to provoke national resentment and identify Soviet and Great Russian rule as one and the same thing.

The unitary structure of the party, underpinned by the *nomenklatura* system, provided the Bolshevik leaders with a way to square the circle. It made it possible to adopt a novel form of ethnically based federal constitution. The five republics would retain their territorial integrity and national character, and indeed the right to secede from the federation, yet none would exercise that right and break away because all would be ruled by (local) members of the unitary and centralized Communist Party of the Soviet Union (CPSU), as it was renamed.

However, during 1922 and 1923 there was furious controversy over the

---

90 G. Gill, *The Origins of the Stalinist Political System* (Cambridge 1990) pp. 23–198, provides a cogent analysis.

91 The ageing but most influential western account is R. Pipes, *The Formation of the Soviet Union: Communism and Nationalism* (Cambridge, MA, 1997, new ed.). For a deeper analysis, especially of the development of policy towards national minorities and 'autonomization' within the RSFSR, see J. Smith, *The Bolsheviks and the National Question, 1917–1923* (London 1998).

terms of this federation. Stalin, in his role as Commissar for Nationalities, pressed for a solution which would absorb the five Soviet republics into the RSFSR. This would reduce them to the same status as the small 'autonomous republics' set up within the RSFSR, in line with the 'Declaration of Rights' of January 1918 (see document 43), none of which had ever enjoyed independence. Even among the Bolsheviks now ruling the five independent Soviet republics, 'autonomy' in this form provoked hostility. There was fierce opposition in Ukraine, and in Georgia the local Central Committee boldly rejected Stalin's proposals.

Document 105 | From the minutes of a meeting of the Central Committee of the Communist Party of Georgia

15 September 1922

Agenda Item:
1. Comrade Stalin's theses on declaring the Soviet republics to be autonomous.

Resolved:
1. Unification by means of declaring the independent Soviet republics to be autonomous, as proposed in comrade Stalin's theses, is to be considered premature.

We consider the unification of economic efforts and general policy to be necessary, but all the attributes of independence are to be retained.

Voting:
CC members for: 5
CC members against: 1 (comrade Eliava)
Candidate members for: 6
Candidate members against: 0
Of those present 19 for, 6 against: comrades Ordzhonikidze, Enukidze, Kirov, Sokol'nikov, Gogoberidze, Kakhiani.

Comrade Mikha Tskhakaya abstained. The secretary of the CC is to canvass the opinions of absent members: comrades Orakhelashvili, Eshba, Toroshelidze, Kalandadze, Gogiya, Gegechkori.

Comrade Mdivani is to canvass those CC members who are in Moscow: comrades Okudzhava, Dumbadze and Tsintsadze.

2. For the time being the above question is not to be put to the broad mass of Party members.

Signed: Sabashvili, secretary of the CC
Confirmed: Nazaretyan

[Source: *Izvestiya TsK KPSS* No. 9, 1989, p. 196.]

For Stalin, this was unacceptable. It amounted to fellow Bolsheviks placing their allegiance to their nationality above their allegiance to the proletariat and party. It was evidence of bourgeois remnants among the supposed vanguard of world socialism. He had no compunction, as a Georgian himself whose prior loyalty to class and party was unquestioning, in insisting that such attitudes should be tackled head-on. A week later he wrote to Lenin reiterating his forthright views on the constitutional question.

Knowing that Lenin considered military, diplomatic and economic integration essential for the defence and development of the socialist oasis, Stalin tried to persuade him that there were only two alternatives: formal absorption of the five republics into the RSFSR, no less subordinate to the Russian federal bodies than were the thirteen autonomous republics that already existed, or acceptance that they really were authentically independent countries. He also warned that unless nationalists within the party—'consistent social-independents'—were firmly dealt with, before long the party would fragment along national lines. On the other hand, if the 'regions', as he liked to label the five republics, were promptly promised autonomy within an expanded RSFSR, their respective Communist Party Central Committees (and thus the communist-controlled Central Executive Committees of their respective soviets) could be coaxed into endorsing the plan for absorption within the RSFSR by the time of the All-Russia Soviet Congress scheduled for December.

Document 106 | I.V. Stalin: '… the replacement of fictitious independence with real internal autonomy for the republics…'

22 September 1922

Dear Comrade Lenin,

We have reached a position where the relations between the centre and the regions, i.e., complete chaos and the absence of any order, are becoming unbearable. Conflicts are breaking out, arguments and irritation are turning our so-called unified federal economy into a fiction, and hindering and paralysing all economic activity throughout Russia. It is a simple choice: either real independence, meaning non-interference by the centre, their own People's Commissariat for Foreign Affairs, their own foreign trade body, their own Concessions Committee, their own railways, with common questions being settled by negotiations and agreements between equals and the decrees of the All-Russia Executive Committee, the Council of People's Commissars and the RSFSR's Council of Labour and Defence not being binding for the independent republics—or real unification of the Soviet republics into one economic unit with the formal extension of the power of the Council of People's Commissars, the Council of Labour and Defence and the RSFSR's All-

Russia Executive Committee to the Councils of People's Commissars, Central Executive Committees and economic councils of the independent republics, i.e., the replacement of fictitious independence with real internal autonomy for the republics in matters of language, culture, legal system, domestic affairs, agriculture and the like.

One should bear in mind that:

1. The decisions of the Council of People's Commissars, the Council of Labour and Defence and the RSFSR's All-Russia Executive Committee are not formally binding for the independent republics. However, these institutions countermand the decrees of the central institutions of the independent republics at will. This evokes protests from the latter against the 'illegal actions' of the central institutions in Moscow.

2. In such cases the interference of the Central Committee of the Russian Communist Party usually takes place after the central bodies in the peripheral areas have already issued their decrees, which are then countermanded by the central institutions in Moscow. This creates red tape, hampers economic activity, and in the peripheral areas causes incomprehension among non-Party people and irritation among communists.

3. During the four years of the Civil War, when the intervention obliged us to make a show of Moscow's liberalism on the national question, despite ourselves we ended up nurturing among communists some real and consistent social-independents who demand real independence in every sense and see the interference of the Central Committee of the Russian Communist Party as Moscow's deceit and hypocrisy.

4. We are at a stage of development when form, law and constitution cannot be ignored, when the younger generation of communists in the regions refuses to see the independence game as a game. It insists on taking words about independence at face value, and demands that we implement the constitutions of the independent republics to the letter.

5. Right now if we do not make the formal relationships between centre and periphery correspond to the real relationships, in which the periphery should defer unconditionally to the centre on all fundamentals, i.e., if we do not immediately replace formal (fictitious) independence with formal (but real) autonomy, then within a year it is going to be incomparably harder to defend the real unity of the Soviet republics.

At present it is a question of how not to 'offend' the nationalists, but within a year it will probably be a question of how to avoid a split in the Party over this matter. Uncontrolled 'national' politics in the periphery work against the unity of the Soviet republics, and formal independence assists that work. Here is one of many examples: it turns out that recently the Georgian Central Committee—without the knowledge of the CC of the Russian Communist Party—decided to allow the Ottoman Bank (Anglo-French capital) to open a branch in Tiflis. This would undoubtedly have led to the financial subordination of Transcaucasia to

Constantinople (the Turkish lira has already become dominant and is squeezing out Georgian and Russian money), yet the Central Committee's decisive veto, taken at comrade Sokol'nikov's insistence, has caused, it turns out, a storm of protest among Georgian national-communists.

My plan is this:

1. The question of Bukhara, Khiva and the as yet non-Sovietized Far Eastern Republic should be left open, i.e., do not declare them autonomous for the time being.

2. As for the remaining five independent republics (Ukraine, Belorussia, Georgia, Azerbaidzhan and Armenia), it is expedient to declare them autonomous so that by the time of the All-Russia Soviet Congress the Central Executive Committees of these republics will themselves voluntarily have declared their desire to enter into closer economic relations with Moscow on the basis of autonomy (I already have declarations by the CCs of the Azerbaidzhani and Armenian CPs about the desirability of autonomy, and a declaration from the Georgian CP CC on the desirability of retaining independence. . .)

[Source: *Izvestiya TsK KPSS* No. 9, 1989, pp. 198–200.]

Lenin rejected Stalin's bald 'either/or' and insisted instead on the formation of a new federation which the five republics and the RSFSR would enter together. An agreement on this was formally adopted at the December Congress. Unlike Stalin's plan, the new state was not to be called 'Russian', even in the non-ethnic sense used in the 1918 Declaration of Rights and constitution of the RSFSR (see document 43), but the 'Union of Soviet Socialist Republics', a decisive step, the new constitutional preamble asserted, to 'the union of toilers of all countries into one World Soviet Socialist Republic'. Unlike in Stalin's plan, the 'Union' republics, as the six founding members became known, retained a status above that of the 'autonomous republics' within the RSFSR, as their leaders insisted they should. On the other hand, in terms of the distribution of power between Moscow and the republics, the distinction between Lenin's 'federation' and Stalin's 'autonomy' was minimal. The detailed constitution elaborated during 1923 firmly asserted that in most fields the 'All-Union' bodies had binding authority over those of the constituent republics.[92] Only in cultural and linguistic policy did the republican governments exercise considerable autonomy. Moreover, in several key areas, notably that of the GPU and state security, there was no separate RSFSR institution but rather, in a manner that echoed Stalin's vision, one all-union authority radiating outwards from Moscow.

---

92 See Unger, *Constitutional Development* pp. 45–76, for the full text and lucid commentary.

Document 107 | From the Treaty on the Formation of the USSR

30 December 1922

The Russian Socialist Federative Soviet Republic (RSFSR), the Ukrainian Socialist Soviet Republic (UkSSR), the Belorussian Socialist Soviet Republic (BSSR) and the Transcaucasian Socialist Federative Soviet Republic (ZSFSR: Georgia, Azerbaidzhan and Armenia) have concluded the present treaty on unification into a single union state, the 'Union of Soviet Socialist Republics', on the following bases:

1. The USSR, in the person of its supreme bodies, will have responsibility for:
   a. representation of the Union in international relations;
   b. changes to the external boundaries of the Union;
   c. the conclusion of agreements on accepting new republics into the Union;
   d. the declaration of war and the conclusion of peace;
   e. the conclusion of foreign-state loans;
   f. the ratification of international treaties;
   g. the establishment of systems of foreign and domestic trade;
   h. the establishment of the bases of and a general plan for the entire economy of the Union, and also the conclusion of concessionary agreements;
   i. the regulation of transport, post and telegraph services;
   j. the establishment of the bases for organizing the armed forces of the USSR;
   k. the establishment of a single state budget for the USSR, of a currency, monetary and credit system, and also a system of Union, republic and local taxes;
   l. the establishment of the basic principles of land tenure and land use, likewise the exploitation of mineral wealth, forests and water resources throughout the territory of the Union;
   m. general Union legislation on resettlement;
   n. the establishment of the foundations of the judicial system and legal procedures, and also civil and criminal Union legislation;
   o. the establishment of fundamental labour laws;
   p. the establishment of the basic principles of public education;
   q. the establishment of general measures to protect the people's health;
   r. the establishment of a system of weights and measures;
   s. the organization of Union statistics;
   t. legislation on Union citizenship with respect to the rights of foreigners;
   u. the right of general amnesty;
   v. the abolition of any decrees by the Soviet Congresses, Central Executive Committees and Councils of People's Commissars of any of the Union republics which infringe the Union treaty.

2. The supreme body of the USSR is the Congress of Soviets of the USSR, and,

in the periods between congresses, the Central Executive Committee of the USSR. . .

11. The executive body of the Central Executive Committee of the Union is the Council of People's Commissars of the USSR (USSR Sovnarkom), which is to be elected by the Central Executive Committee of the Union for the term of office of the latter. . .

12. In order to establish revolutionary legality throughout the USSR and to unify the efforts of the Union republics in the struggle against counter-revolution, a Supreme Court, attached to the Central Executive Committee of the USSR is to be set up with the task of overall judicial control. A unified body, the State Political Administration (GPU), attached to the USSR Sovnarkom, is to be established, the chairman of which is to have a consultative vote on the USSR Sovnarkom. . .

21. A single Union citizenship is established for citizens of the Union republics. . .

25. The ratification, alteration and supplementing of the Union treaty is solely within the competence of the Congress of Soviets of the USSR.

26. Each of the Union republics retains the right freely to secede from the Union.

[Source: *I s˜ezd Sovetov Soyuza Sovetskikh Sotsialisticheskikh Respublik: Stenograficheskiy otchet s prilozheniyami* (Moscow 1923), appendix 1, pp. 4–7.]

Cultivating the allegiance of national minorities

While the terms of the agreement were being hammered out, relations between Lenin and Stalin became severely strained and Lenin briefly entertained the possibility of far greater devolution of power. Matters were brought to a head by further friction between Stalin and his allies, on the one hand, and the Bolshevik leadership in Georgia on the other.[93] Stalin had for some time been urging that the three Caucasian republics—Azerbaidzhan, Armenia and Georgia—should form a Transcaucasian Federation, itself to be incorporated into the new Soviet state. In part his motive was to ensure that the Turkic Azeri people of Azerbaidzhan, despite their ethnic and religious connections with Turkey in the west and the Azeris across the border in Persia, were successfully bound into the emergent Soviet federation, and in part to provide a context in which the titular nationality of each of the three republics would be called to account by the others for their treatment of their own minorities. In the eyes of the Georgian leader-

---

93 On the background, see R.G. Suny, *The Making of the Georgian Nation* (Bloomington, IN, 1988), pp. 209–19.

ship, however, the putative federation amounted to a further slight on Georgian status. Although they had agreed to it in the spring, in October their leader, B. Mdivani, discovering that Lenin had become less than enthusiastic, had them try (unsuccessfully) to repudiate the agreement. Stalin sent his Georgian ally, G.K. Ordzhonikidze, to discipline the recalcitrant comrades and in the course of his visit Ordzhonikidze not only browbeat the party leadership in Georgia but physically struck one of their number.

In Lenin's mind, this otherwise trivial incident crystallized the dangers of what socialists had long condemned as 'Great Russian chauvinism', and the tendency for non-Russians who identified with Moscow to be every bit as arrogant in their treatment of the minorities as Russians themselves. By December his health, undermined by a major stroke in March, had suffered a severe relapse and, as in the summer, he was being urged to cease work. But at the turn of the year, while Stalin was recommending the agreement to the Soviet Congress, Lenin frantically dictated a number of memoranda (his so-called 'Testament') expressing his alarm. Behind Stalin's attitude and impatience for a 'united apparatus', which would inevitably be completely dominated by Russians, he saw the arrogant ethos of the Russian state bureaucracy which the Bolsheviks had inherited from the Tsarist regime. He placed maximum emphasis on the urgency of each minority national republic's being able to devise rules governing language so as to empower non-Russians and prevent the abuses of Russian chauvinism.

Document 108 | V.I. Lenin: *The Question of Nationalities or 'Autonomization'* (excerpt)

30/31 December 1922

. . . From what I was told by Comrade Dzerzhinsky, who was at the head of the commission sent by the CC to 'investigate' the Georgian incident, I could only draw the greatest apprehensions. If matters had come to such a pass that Ordzhonikidze could go to the extreme of applying physical violence, as Comrade Dzerzhinsky informed me, we can imagine what a mess we have got ourselves into. Obviously the whole business of 'autonomization' was radically wrong and badly timed.

It is said that a united [state] apparatus was needed. Where did that assurance come from? Did it not come from that same Russian apparatus which, as I pointed out in one of the preceding sections of my diary, we took over from tsarism and slightly anointed with Soviet oil?

. . . It is quite natural that in such circumstances the 'freedom to secede from the union' by which we justify ourselves will be a mere scrap of paper, unable to defend the non-Russians from the onslaught of that really Russian man, the Great Russian chauvinist, in substance a rascal and a tyrant, such as the typical Russian bureaucrat is. . . It is said in defence of this measure that the People's Commissariats directly concerned with national psychology and national education were set up as separate bodies. But there the question arises: can these People's Commissariats be made totally independent? and secondly: were we careful enough to take measures to provide the non-Russians with a real safeguard against the truly Russian bully? I do not think we took such measures although we could and should have done so.

I think that Stalin's haste and his infatuation with pure administration, together with his spite against the notorious so-called 'nationalist-socialism', played a fatal role here. In politics spite generally plays the basest of roles...

I think that in the present instance, as far as the Georgian nation is concerned, we have a typical case in which a genuinely proletarian attitude makes profound caution, thoughtfulness and a readiness to compromise a matter of necessity for us. The Georgian [Stalin], who is neglectful of this aspect of the question, or who carelessly flings about accusations of 'nationalist-socialism' (whereas he himself is a real and true 'nationalist-socialist', and even a vulgar Great Russian bully), violates, in substance, the interests of proletarian class solidarity, for nothing holds up the development and strengthening of proletarian class solidarity so much as national injustice; 'offended' nationals are not sensitive to anything so much as to the feeling of equality and the violation of this equality, if only through negligence or jest, on the part of their proletarian comrades. That is why in this case it is better to over-do rather than under-do the concessions and leniency towards the national minorities...

What practical measures must be taken in the present situation?

Firstly, we must maintain and strengthen the union of socialist republics. Of this there can be no doubt. This measure is necessary for us and it is necessary for the world communist proletariat in its struggle against the world bourgeoisie and its defence against bourgeois intrigues.

Secondly, the union of socialist republics must be retained for its diplomatic apparatus...

Thirdly, exemplary punishment must be inflicted on Comrade Ordzhonikidze (I say this all the more regretfully as I am one of his personal friends and have worked with him abroad)...

Fourthly, the strictest rules must be introduced on the use of the national language in the non-Russian republics of our union, and these rules must be checked with special care. There is no doubt that our apparatus being what it is, there is bound to be, on the pretext of unity in the railway service, unity in the fiscal service and so on, a mass of truly Russian abuses. Special ingenuity is necessary for the struggle against these abuses, not to mention special sincerity on the part of those who undertake this struggle. A detailed code will be required, and only the nationals living in the republic in question can draw it up at all successfully. And then we cannot be sure in advance that as a result of this work we shall not take a step backward at our next Congress of Soviets, i.e., retain the union of Soviet socialist republics only for military and diplomatic affairs, and in all other respects restore full independence to the individual People's Commissariats.

It must be borne in mind that the decentralization of the People's Commissariats and the lack of co-ordination in their work as far as Moscow and other centres are concerned can be compensated for sufficiently by Party authority, if it is exercised with sufficient prudence and impartiality; the harm that can result to our state from a lack of unification between the national apparatuses and the Russian apparatus is infinitely less than that which will be done not only to us, but to the whole International, and to the hundreds of millions of the peoples of Asia, which is destined to follow us on to the stage of history in the near future. It would be unpardonable opportunism if, on the eve of the debut of the East, just as it is awakening, we undermined our prestige with its peoples, even if only by the slightest crudity or injustice towards our own non-Russian nationalities. . .

[Source: V.I. Lenin, *Collected Works* Volume XXXVI (Moscow 1966) pp. 605–11.]

Lenin's warnings were not made public for forty years. And the idea he floated of drastically decentralizing all but military and diplomatic power was only considered under Gorbachev a generation later than that. Nevertheless, the regime's approach towards the nationality issue was broadly guided by considerations like his. It was axiomatic that class divisions were primary, national sensibilities and allegiances decidedly secondary. And at no stage was there any question of permitting the minority republics to exercise their formal right to secede. But unlike multinational empires of the past, the Soviet leaders did not regard the suppression of national consciousness, language and customs as the surest way to build supranational identity and allegiance. On the contrary, they (Stalin no less than Lenin) were concerned to ensure that Soviet power was regarded positively by national minorities. In part this was because of the need to entrench party support across the vast Union. When the USSR was formed, the great majority both of party members and of state officials were Russians. Only by enrolling and promoting native cadres could communist rule put down roots. But in part, too, it was guided by confidence that, provided the new order demonstrated that it could accommodate national sensibilities, the deeper, objective common interests of workers would prevail and bind the different nationalities together.

From the very foundation of the new state, the language, culture and education of the minorities were energetically fostered and ambitious non-Russians recruited into the local party and state apparatus in the policy known as *korenizatsiya*. The USSR became what western historians have labelled 'the Affirmative Action Empire', sponsoring the codification and teaching even of languages which till now had no written form.[94] Even where there

---

94 See T. Martin, *The Affirmative Action Empire: Nations and nationalism in the Soviet Union, 1923–1939* (Ithaca, NY, 2001).

was already a well-established cultural tradition, as in Ukraine, home to much the largest minority, the policy involved a profound transformation and break with the Russification pursued by the Tsarist regime. In this speech to V.Ya. Chubar', a Ukrainian whose appointment to head the Russian-dominated Ukrainian Sovnarkom in July 1923 epitomized the policy, outlines the challenges involved. He emphasizes resistance within the party, which in the early 1920s was everywhere predominantly Russian. But he also points to the potential the policy had in legitimizing Soviet rule outside the ranks of the party. He urges that energetic steps be taken to draw into the process the non-party Ukrainian intelligentsia, prominent members of which had signalled their willingness to support the new order now that it was committed to Ukrainianization in the 'Declaration of the 66' made to the Ukrainian Party Congress earlier in the year.[95]

Document 109 | **From the report of the head of the Ukrainian SSR Sovnarkom, V.Ya. Chubar', at the plenum of the Ukrainian CP CC on Ukrainianization**

6–8 October 1924

We need to divide the whole practical question of Ukrainianization into three parts. Firstly, there is the introduction of the Ukrainian language into everyday use, into schools, institutions and so forth. The decree of the [Ukrainian] Sovnarkom, published in August of last year, should address this part of the task. Of course, many comrades cannot remember it, and Soviet institutions also cannot remember it. As a result it has turned out that the introduction of the Ukrainian language has not proceeded as rapidly as it should have done. We can now say that to a large extent lower-level Soviet personnel and lower-level technical workers have studied the Ukrainian language, whereas the personnel of the leading organs have not studied it. Our CC plenum provides the best example of this. (From the audience: And you're speaking in Russian!)

Yes, . . . there was a resolution of the plenum to the effect that all comrades who could do so should speak in Ukrainian, but to speak on your own to an entire hall of people who do not understand Ukrainian is an unacceptable position. . . But, comrades, this phenomenon can be observed not only in the central Soviet apparatus and the CC. The same thing is happening everywhere. . .

Our cadres are inadequately prepared, and we have insufficient material for introducing the Ukrainian language. The dictionaries are deficient, we have few textbooks, overall there is a whole host of obstacles to the study of Ukrainian. For this reason at the moment we should be cautious in the way we push it. First and

---

95 J.E. Mace, *Communism and the Dilemmas of National Liberation: National communism in Soviet Ukraine, 1918–1933* (Cambridge, MA, 1983), pp. 86–119.

foremost, we should intensify our work on training personnel and teaching staff in order to introduce the use of the language as it is actually spoken... This basic task requires a more attentive attitude to this question; it requires us to abandon the approach that very many comrades adopt: Ukrainianization, they say, just means teaching secretaries and clerks; it is not a task for the entire party. My first suggestion for the introduction of Ukrainian would be this: we must reconsider the timescales for learning Ukrainian and ensure firm Party leadership of the work on Ukrainianization. Within the Party there still has not been any broad study of work on Ukrainianization. The study which was carried out on the central Soviet institutions shows that of the 599 leading personnel studied, 302 knew Ukrainian, which is about 52 per cent. Most of these comrades, presumably, only know it to the extent that they can distinguish it from Chinese. That, in general, covers the leading personnel of our institutions. Among the Party staff only 46 per cent know the language... In view of this, even the leading and rank-and-file non-party members of staff who have learned Ukrainian do not speak it. They reason more or less as follows: 'Since the authorities are not learning the language and the Party people do not speak it, this means they are not taking it too seriously; it means that this is another one of those Bolsheviks' schemes which will probably be abandoned in a month or two.'

The second aspect of our task is to develop culture, literature and so on. In this respect our state publishing houses have made significant steps forward. *Chervony shlyakh* [Red Path] has significantly increased its output of Ukrainian literature. Demand is increasing. The same is true in the villages. When you go to a village, you immediately hear complaints that there are not enough books. Demand for books is increasing and so is the output of books in Ukrainian. Over the half year from 1 January to 1 July 1924, 52 per cent of the total number of books published by the State Publishing House were in Ukrainian. Since July there has been further movement in this direction, and 80 per cent of the output is now in Ukrainian. In the recent period many small pamphlets have been published. These are readily accessible to a mass audience—to workers and peasants—Leninist literature and so forth. In this respect we have achieved something. But as far as our textbooks are concerned, the translation of textbooks into Ukrainian, especially for institutions of secondary and higher education, is being held back because of a lack of suitably qualified people. This will require long-term work. This can only be done over a lengthy period of time, and in this sphere the support of our Ukrainian educational institutions, the Academy of Sciences and other Ukrainian bodies, will become even more important.

Now on to the third aspect—which is the recruitment and advancement of Ukrainian personnel. Little has been done in this respect. It is enough to look at each organization. Not enough is being done to draw people in. I think we need to think about this, in order to use the forthcoming re-elections to the soviets and the Party conference for a more careful approach to personnel selection, to supplement our leading bodies with Ukrainian Party members, and also to bring in non-Party Ukrainians. At our Party conference the 'Declaration of the 66' was made public. The Ukrainian intelligentsia are signing up to it in all *gubernii*. These forces are disparate, they have no organization, nobody is bothering with them in order to make use of them, to draw them into Soviet public life. It is possible to draw them into our work, even if only through some kind of practical club; we can get them to give lectures and so on. We should note that in all these cases our staff are negligent about this matter, and for this reason we have not managed to do anything. What are we doing about this in the localities? This question gets a cool reception there as well, and so although there was a temporary upsurge, it has come to nothing. This is a big question which needs to be studied and dealt with attentively.

These are the three aspects. The inculcation of the language, the recruitment of staff, and the development of culture. All these three aspects require a great deal of attention on the part of the Party.

[Source: *Natsional'ni vidnosini v Ukraini u XX st.*, pp. 114–16. Reproduced on history.univ.kiev.ua/ukrbooks/doc1921_85.html.]

The speed with which the policy of *korenizatsiya* shifted the balance in favour of the local linguistic group was remarkable. In the case of Ukraine, within a decade Ukrainian and Ukrainians had replaced Russian dominance in education, in literature and the press, and in the main urban political institutions, including the party.[96] The creation of a mosaic of national territories, it is true, itself generated friction since within each were minority ethnic groups which felt disadvantaged in relation to the titular nationality. And Moscow was permanently wary, especially in the case of the Union Republics, lest the policy breed nationalism and resistance: in the Great Terror of the late 1930s the leadership of each republic was devastated in part on the basis of that charge. On the other hand, that the USSR resisted for six decades the nationalist tide which overwhelmed and reshaped central Europe owed much to the policy.[97]

---

96 G.O. Liber, *Soviet Nationality Policy, Urban Growth, and Identity Change in the Ukrainian SSR 1923–1934* (Cambridge 1992). In the case of the party, Liber notes, much of the intake was of Russified Ukrainians who defined themselves as Ukrainian but whose native tongue was Russian, pp. 92–100.

97 See R. Suny, *The Revenge of the Past: Nationalism, Revolution and the Collapse of the Soviet Union* (Stanford, CA, 1993) pp. 20–97, for an influential analysis.

Trotsky's critique and defeat

Although Stalin strongly endorsed *korenizatsiya*, his estrangement from Lenin, deepened as we shall see when he offended Krupskaya, reached the point where Lenin resolved to seek his removal as General Secretary. In a postscript added to his Testament on 4 January 1923, Lenin recommended that Stalin be replaced by someone 'more tolerant, more loyal, more polite and more considerate to comrades, less capricious. . .', and primed Trotsky to work with him in bringing this about.[98] But in March 1923, before his influence could be brought to bear on who might succeed him, a further stroke permanently deprived Lenin of the power of speech. Trotsky, deceived and outmanoeuvred by the 'triumvirate' of Zinoviev, Kamenev and Stalin, declined to use the ammunition Lenin had given him until it was too late to do so.

Only in the autumn did Trotsky launch a direct challenge to the trio, albeit in a confidential letter to the leadership. Besides reiterating his demand for dynamic, planned expansion of state-owned industry, he attacked the bureaucratization of the party, appointment from above, and smothering of debate. His message was in line with concerns Lenin had expressed before his fateful stroke: that bureaucratization concentrated too much power in the hands of the Secretariat; that few of those recruited to the party since the revolution had sufficient mastery of Marxism or confidence to contribute significantly to policy formation and all too many were passive or careerist; and that the party's future depended on the continuing influence of its pre-revolutionary core, the 'Old Bolsheviks'.

Document 110 | **From L.D. Trotsky's letter to members of the Central Committee and Central Control Commission of the CPSU**

8 October 1923

Top Secret.

. . . 10. In the very worst period of War Communism the appointment of people to posts within the Party was not even one tenth as commonplace as it is today. It has now become the rule for *guberniya* committee secretaries to be appointed. This makes the secretary, in effect, independent of the local organization. If there is any opposition, criticism or dissatisfaction the secretary gets himself transferred by courtesy of the centre. . . Appointed by the centre and thereby virtually independent of

---

98 M. Lewin's classic account, *Lenin's Last Struggle* (London 1975), should be tempered with the less sympathetic treatment in the final volume of R. Service's trilogy, *Lenin: A political life* Volume III, pp. 256–316.

the local organization, the secretary is in turn a source of further appointments and removals within the *guberniya*. The secretarial machinery, created from the top downwards and increasingly self-sufficient, pulls all the threads together. The participation of rank-and-file Party members in the actual creation of the Party organization is becoming increasingly illusory. In the last eighteen months or so a special kind of 'secretarial psychology' has come into being, the main feature of which is the conviction that a secretary is capable of solving all and any problems without any knowledge of the facts of the matter. . . . Such a practice is all the more harmful, in that it dissipates and kills off any sense of responsibility.

11. The X Party Congress took place under the banner of workers' democracy. Many of the speeches made at the time in defence of workers' democracy seemed to me exaggerated and to some extent demagogic, owing to the incompatibility of a fully fledged workers' democracy and a dictatorship. But it was crystal clear that the War Communism system had to give way to a broader and livelier Party community. However, the regime that in its essentials had already come into being before the XII Party Congress, and has subsequently become established and fully formed, is much farther from workers' democracy than the regime during the harshest times of War Communism. The bureaucratization of the Party machinery has developed to an unprecedented extent through the application of methods of secretarial selection. Even during the darkest hours of the civil war, we debated in our Party organizations and even in the press about the use of specialists, about a partisan and a regular army, about discipline, etc., etc. Now there is no trace of such a frank exchange of opinions on matters that really concern the Party. There is now a broad stratum of Party workers entering the machinery of state or Party who flatly refuse to form their own Party opinion, or, at least, to express it openly. It is as if they think that the secretarial hierarchy is the apparatus which creates Party opinion and decisions. Beneath this stratum of people without their own opinions lies the broad mass of Party rank-and-file, for whom any decision takes the form of a call or command. Among this basic mass of the Party there is an extraordinary amount of dissatisfaction. It is well founded and derives from a variety of causes. This dissatisfaction is not being resolved by a frank exchange of opinions at Party meetings and by rank-and-file pressure on the Party organization (the election of Party committees, secretaries, etc.). Instead, it is swelling below the surface, and will later develop into abscesses. While the official, i.e., secretarial, machinery of the Party increasingly gives a picture of the Party as an organization which has achieved almost automatic uniformity, ideas and opinions on the most acute and pressing problems bypass the official Party machine, creating conditions for illegal groupings within the Party.

12. An orientation towards old Bolsheviks was officially adopted at the XII Congress. It is perfectly obvious that these cadres of old Bolsheviks with underground experience are the revolutionary leaven of the Party and its organizational backbone. We can and must, by using all the normal Party and ideological measures, assist in the selection of old Bolsheviks, so long as they have other essential

qualities, for leading Party posts. But the means by which this selection is now being carried out—by direct appointment from above—contain even greater dangers, in that the old Bolsheviks are being split into two groups from above with the help of the criterion of 'independence'. Old Bolshevism, as such, is becoming, in the eyes of the Party as a whole, somehow responsible for all features of the current regime within the Party and for its serious mistakes in the sphere of economic construction. We must not forget that the overwhelming majority of Party members consists of young revolutionaries without underground experience, or of people who have come over from other parties. The current growth of dissatisfaction against the self-sufficient secretarial machine, which identifies itself with old Bolshevism, may have—if things continue to develop along these lines—extremely serious consequences for maintaining the ideological hegemony and organizational leadership of Bolsheviks with underground experience in our present Party with its half a million members.

13. A menacing symptom is the Politburo's attempt to base the state budget on the sale of vodka, i.e., to make the income of the workers' state independent of any successes in economic construction. Only a decisive protest within and without the CC has halted this attempt, which would have dealt a savage blow not only to economic work, but to the Party itself. However, the CC has still not ruled out the idea of the further legalization of vodka. There is no doubt that there is an inner connection between the self-sufficient character of a secretarial organization increasingly independent of the Party, and the tendency to create a budget as far as possible independent of the successes or failures of the Party's collective construction. . .

[Source: RGASPI, fond 17, opis' 2, delo 685, pp. 53–68.]

A week later, Trotsky's charges were echoed when forty-six prominent party members wrote to the Central Committee, demanding both a restoration of inner-party democracy and the implementation of coherent planning for industrial expansion. Despite denouncing the action as a breach of the 1921 ban on factionalism, the leadership was forced to allow public debate on the issues and itself to come out strongly against the bureaucratization of the party. However, every attempted remedy—the Secretariat's 'recommending' rather than appointing candidates for key posts; energetic steps to shift the balance of membership away from white-collar to blue-collar workers and to purge 'unworthy' members; the expansion of the Central Committee—depended for success on the existing secretarial hierarchy. Yet it was precisely that hierarchy whose power was at issue. Far from checking centralization, the effect of each palliative was further to increase the power of the Secretariat as a whole and the General Secretary in particular.

In the course of 1924, Trotsky's position became steadily weaker as the number of prominent party members sympathetic to him dwindled and he was increasingly seen as embittered and divisive. His civil-war reputation as a harsh disciplinarian as well as his evident leadership ambitions undermined his credibility as a critic. Despite the potential appeal of the left's demands for rapid industrial growth, Trotsky's frankness about the initial squeeze on living standards that would be needed appealed neither to senior party members nor to rank-and-file workers. His strictures about Stalin and Bukharin cosseting the richer peasantry stirred fears that his adventurism might jeopardize the *smychka* between workers and peasants. And at the same time, the leadership succeeded in overlaying his reputation as Lenin's closest ally with the image of a vain ex-Menshevik whose insistence on the necessity of world revolution betrayed a lack of faith in the Soviet Union's future. By the time that Lenin's Testament and recommendation that Stalin be demoted was read to an expanded (and astonished) meeting of the Central Committee, in May 1924, Trotsky was in no position to exploit it. Zinoviev and Kamenev argued passionately that Stalin had mended his ways, and it was agreed that the document should not be published.

The defusing of Lenin's Testament and the defeat of the 'United Opposition'

Once Trotsky had been defeated and, in January 1925, had resigned as War Commissar, Zinoviev and Kamenev became increasingly suspicious of Stalin's growing power, and themselves began to take up many of the themes of Trotsky and the forty-six. They criticized the inadequate pace of industrialization, denied the possibility of achieving the construction of socialism in one country, and attacked Stalin's increasingly dominant position within the leadership. But by the time they did so openly, at the Fourteenth Congress in December 1925, their supporters—the core of whom formed the delegation from Leningrad, where Zinoviev still controlled the party machine—were massively outvoted.

Document 111 | From L.B. Kamenev's speech at the XIV Congress of the CPSU

1925

. . . We are against creating a theory of a 'leader' and against making a 'leader'. We are against a position where the Secretariat, which in reality embraces both policy and organization, stands above other political bodies. We are in favour of our highest bodies being internally organized in such a way that we have a genuinely sovereign Politburo, bringing together all our Party's political figures, and that the Secretariat is subordinate to it, concerned with the technical implementation of its resolutions.

(Noise from the hall.) We cannot consider it normal and think it harmful for the Party if the situation continues whereby the Secretariat embraces both policy and organization and in effect determines policy beforehand.

. . . (Noise from the hall; someone calls out, 'That's what you should have started with!'). . . You seem to think that I should have started by saying that I personally think that our General Secretary is not the figure who could unite the old Bolshevik staff around him. I do not think this is the fundamental political question. . . I do think that, if the Party had adopted (noise from the hall) a definite political line and had clearly dissociated itself from the deviations which part of the CC is now supporting, this question would not have arisen now. Please let me finish. It is because I have said it more than once to comrade Stalin and to a group of Leninist comrades that I am saying it again now: I have come to the conclusion that comrade Stalin cannot fulfil the role of unifier of the Bolshevik staff. (Voices from the hall: 'You're wrong!' 'Rubbish!' 'That's the whole point!' 'The cards are on the table!' More noise. The Leningrad delegation applauds. Shouts of 'We're not giving you the top job', 'Stalin! Stalin!' The delegates stand to greet comrade Stalin. There is stormy applause and shouts of 'The Bolshevik staff must unite where the party has united.')

Evdokimov, from the floor: 'Long live the Russian Communist Party. Hurrah! Hurrah!' (Delegates stand and shout, 'Hurrah!' Extended stormy applause.)

Evdokimov, from the floor: 'Long live our Party's CC! Hurrah!' (Delegates shout 'Hurrah!') 'The Party is supreme! That's right!' (More applause and cheering.) Voices shout. 'Long live comrade Stalin!!!' (There is long, stormy applause and cheering.)

Chairman: 'Comrades, please calm down. Comrade Kamenev will now finish his speech.'

Kamenev: 'I began this part of my speech with the words "We are against a theory of leadership and creating a leader!" With these words I shall end my speech.' (Applause from the Leningrad delegation.)

Someone calls out, 'Who do you propose, then?'

The chairman announces a ten-minute break.

[Source: *XIV s˜ezd VKP(b)* (Moscow 1926) pp. 274–75.]

The Congress demoted Kamenev from full to candidate membership of the Politburo, and early in 1926 Zinoviev and his allies lost control of the party in Leningrad, Stalin's ally S.M. Kirov taking over as First Secretary. By spring 1926 Zinoviev and Kamenev were sufficiently desperate to mend their fences with Trotsky, forming with him what became known as the United Opposition. At an expanded meeting of the Central Committee in July 1926, together they attacked the Stalin–Bukharin leadership across the whole range of issues confronting the party. They denounced the demise of inner-party democracy; the pitifully low level of workers' wages; inadequate taxation of

NEPmen and richer peasants; the desultory approach towards encouraging collective farming; the absence of an ambitious Five-Year Plan for rapid industrialization; the absurdity of claiming it was possible to build socialism in one (backward) country; and what they labelled Comintern's opportunist and defeatist policy of compromising with reformist, social-democratic parties abroad. But in the eyes of the great majority on the Central Committee, this new alliance of sworn enemies looked insincere. Parts of their critique hit home: regional leaders on the Central Committee, too, were impatient for increased investment, but in practice they found the current leadership increasingly responsive to their demands and there seemed little reason to break ranks with the solid majority behind Stalin and Bukharin. Stalin successfully portrayed the Opposition as disloyal to the party and Zinoviev was dropped from the Politburo.

All aspects of the confrontation continued to be argued out with maximum reference to Lenin's words, each side combing his works for passages seeming to endorse their side of the argument. Lenin's Testament, too, continued to rumble through the dispute. To parry the United Opposition's charge that Lenin had become deeply hostile to Stalin towards the end of his life, Bukharin worked with the dead leader's sister, Mariya, to use her inside knowledge in Stalin's defence.[99]

Document 112 | 'Vladimir Il'ich had an extraordinarily high opinion of Stalin...' —a text compiled by N.I. Bukharin for M.I. Ul'yanova

1926

In view of the systematic attacks on comrade Stalin by the opposition minority in the CC and the ceaseless assertions that Lenin had virtually completely broken with Stalin, I feel duty-bound to say a few words about Lenin's attitude to Stalin, because throughout the last stages of V.I.'s life I was with him.

Vladimir Il'ich had an extraordinarily high opinion of Stalin, to such an extent that at the time of both the first and second strokes V.I. gave the most intimate jobs to Stalin, emphasizing that it was to Stalin he was speaking.

At the worst times of his illness V.I. did not summon any member of the CC or want to see anybody—he called only Stalin. So the speculation that V.I.'s relations with Stalin were worse than those with other people is the direct opposite of the truth.

[see Document 113 for source]

---

99 By October 1927 Stalin was confident enough not only himself to read to the Central Committee Lenin's recommendation that he be replaced as General Secretary, but to have his speech on it reported in *Pravda*. R. McNeal, *Stalin: Man and ruler* (London 1988) pp. 109–11.

Document 113 | **M.I. Ul'yanova: 'Vladimir Il'ich had a very high opinion of Stalin'—a declaration to the Presidium of a full plenary of the CC and CCC of the CPSU**

26 July 1926

The opposition minority in the CC has recently been making systematic attacks on comrade Stalin, even going so far as to mention a complete break between Lenin and Stalin in the last few months of V.I.'s life. In order to establish the truth, I consider it my duty to inform comrades briefly about relations between Lenin and Stalin during the period when V.I. was ill. (I won't mention here the time preceding his illness, concerning which I have evidence of the most touching relationship between V.I. and Stalin—about which CC members know as well as I do.) At that time I was always at his side, and carried out numerous tasks at his request.

Vladimir Il'ich had a very high opinion of Stalin. It is significant that in spring 1922, when he had his first stroke, and also in December 1922, when he had the second stroke, V.I. called Stalin in and asked him to undertake the most intimate tasks, tasks that you would entrust only to somebody you particularly trusted, that you knew to be a true revolutionary and a close comrade.

Moreover, Il'ich emphasized that it was Stalin he wanted to talk to, and not anybody else. Generally, throughout this period of his illness, while he had the chance to talk to his comrades, it was comrade Stalin he called in most, and during the worst periods of his illness he did not call for any CC members, except Stalin.

There was one incident between Lenin and Stalin which comrade Zinoviev mentioned in his speech and which took place not long before Il'ich lost the power of speech (March 1923), but it was a purely personal matter with no political import. Comrade Zinoviev is well aware of this, and referring to it is quite pointless. This incident happened because Stalin, who on doctors' orders had been asked by the CC Plenary to see to it that Il'ich, then very ill, was not given any political news, so as not to upset him and make his condition worse, scolded members of his household for telling him such news. Il'ich, who heard about this by chance—and always disliked such mollycoddling treatment—rebuked Stalin. Comrade Stalin apologized, and that was the end of the matter. Obviously, if Il'ich had not been so ill at the time, he would have reacted differently.

This incident is documented, and I can produce the documents immediately if the CC requires them.

I can therefore affirm that all the Opposition's talk about relations between V.I. and Stalin does not correspond to reality at all. These relations were and remained very close and comradely.

[Source: RGASPI, fond 17, opis' 2, delo 246, vypusk 4, p. 104.]

Mariya Ul'yanova came to regret the account she had given of Lenin's attitude towards Stalin. She subsequently made a fuller record of her recollections. It is a striking document. Although it was evidently written once Stalin was firmly in the ascendancy, it refers to him in a matter-of-fact way, with neither deference nor awe. The innocuous details about Lenin's convalescence and her uncertainty about whether or not Krupskaya saw Lenin's furious letter to Stalin ring true. And strange as the account of Lenin's asking Stalin to provide him with poison should he become incurably ill may seem, it is not out of line with other evidence. Lenin had told Krupskaya long before that he preferred poison to paralysis.[100]

Document 114 | M.I. Ul'yanova: '… I did not tell the whole truth… about Vladimir Il'ich's attitude to Stalin'

[Found among M.I. Ul'yanova's personal papers after her death. The exact date of this document cannot be established.]

In my declaration to the CC Plenary I wrote that V.I. had a high opinion of Stalin. This is, of course, true. Stalin is a good organizer and a major figure.

It is also beyond doubt that I did not tell the whole truth in that declaration about Vladimir Il'ich's attitude to Stalin. The purpose of the declaration, written at the request of Bukharin and Stalin, was to shield him somewhat from Opposition attacks by referring to relations with Il'ich. They were gambling on V.I.'s last letter to Stalin, where the matter of breaking off relations was raised. The immediate cause of this was personal—V.I.'s anger that Stalin had dared to be rude to Nadezhda Konstantinovna [Krupskaya].

This was an entirely personal matter, but at the time I thought Zinoviev, Kamenev and others wanted to use it for political and factional purposes. But later on, comparing it with a number of things V.I. had said, his political testament, Stalin's general behaviour after Lenin's death and his 'political' line, I began more and more to understand Il'ich's real relationship with Stalin in the last period of his life. I feel it my duty to say something about this, if only briefly. . .

I had the opportunity to observe V.I.'s relationship with his closest colleagues, members of the Politburo, in summer 1922 during V.I's first illness, when I almost never left his side.

Even before then I had heard that V.I. was rather unhappy with Stalin. I had been

---

100 See R. Service, *Lenin: A biography* (London 2000), for the best account of Lenin's private life and psychology and for this point, pp. 439, 445–46. See also D. Volkogonov, *Lenin: Life and legacy* (London 1994), a study which epitomizes how Soviet historians escaped from the veneration in which Lenin was held until the fall of the USSR: Volkogonov cites a letter from Stalin to the Politburo in March 1923 describing his resistance to Lenin's renewed pressure for poison, pp. 425–27.

told that, on hearing of Martov's illness, V.I. asked Stalin to send him some money. 'You want me to waste money on an enemy of the workers! Find yourself another secretary to do it,' Stalin said.

V.I. was really upset about this, and angry with Stalin. Were there other reasons for V.I.'s dissatisfaction? Clearly there were. Shklovsky, who was in Berlin at the time, told me about V.I.'s letter to him. It was clear from the letter that V.I. felt that he was being undermined. By whom and how remain a mystery.

In the winters of '20–'21 and '21–'22 V.I. felt very bad. His headaches and inability to work really bothered him. I am not sure exactly when, but round about then V.I. said to Stalin that he would probably end up paralysed and got Stalin's word that he would help him get and take potassium cyanide. Stalin promised. Why should V.I. have asked Stalin? Because he knew he was as hard as nails and quite devoid of sentiment. There was nobody else he could turn to with such a request.

In May 1922, after his first stroke, V.I. asked Stalin to fulfil that promise. V.I. had decided at that time that he was finished, and asked to see Stalin briefly. He was so insistent that one could not refuse. Stalin stayed with V.I. for literally only about five minutes, no longer. When he left Il'ich, he told Bukharin and me that V.I. had asked him to get hold of some poison, because the time had come to fulfil his earlier promise. Stalin had promised to do so. V.I. and Stalin had embraced and Stalin left his room. After talking the matter over, we decided we must try to cheer V.I. up, so Stalin went back to V.I. He told him that, after talking things over with the doctors, he was convinced that all was not lost, so it was not yet time to fulfil his promise. V.I. brightened up noticeably and agreed, although he said to Stalin, 'Are you being honest?' Stalin answered, 'Have you ever known me be anything else?' They parted and did not see each other again until V.I. began to recover, as he was not allowed any meetings with his comrades. . .

When he got back to work again in autumn 1922, V.I. often met Kamenev, Zinoviev and Stalin in the evenings in his study. I sometimes tried to get them to leave in the evenings, remembering the doctors' warnings about them staying too long. They joked and said that their meetings were just chats, not business.

V.I. was very unhappy with Stalin over the question of the nationalities in the Caucasus. His correspondence with Trotsky on this is well known. V.I. was terribly angry with Stalin, Ordzhonikidze and Dzerzhinsky. This really troubled V.I. throughout the rest of his illness.

Then came the conflict which arose from V.I.'s letter of 5 March 1923 to Stalin, which I will quote below. It happened like this. The doctors kept insisting that V.I. should not discuss affairs of state. They were worried most of all about N.K., who was so used to sharing everything with him that she would sometimes, involuntarily, blurt something out. The Politburo gave Stalin the job of checking to ensure that doctors' orders were obeyed. On apparently hearing about some conversation N.K. had had with V.I., Stalin phoned her and, assuming it would not get back to

V.I., told her pretty sharply that she was not to talk business with V.I., or she would be hauled up before the Central Control Commission. N.K. was extremely upset by this call: she was beside herself, weeping, rolling around on the floor, etc. After a few days she told V.I. about it, adding that she and Stalin had made up. Prior to this Stalin really had phoned her and tried to smooth over the bad impression his words and threats had made upon her. But she had also told Kamenev and Zinoviev about the row over the phone, and had obviously referred to the Caucasus business as well.

One morning Stalin called me into V.I.'s study. He looked very agitated and distressed. He said, 'I haven't slept all night. Who does Il'ich take me for, talking to me as if I were some traitor! I love him with all my heart! Please tell him that.' I felt sorry for Stalin because he really did seem genuinely upset.

Il'ich called me in for something and I told him, by the way, that all the comrades sent their best wishes. 'And?' V.I. objected. 'And Stalin asked me to send you a special greeting and to say that he really does love you.' Il'ich smiled ironically, but said nothing. 'Shall I give him your regards?', I asked. 'Give them,' said Il'ich rather coldly. 'But Volodya,' I went on, 'Stalin is a clever man, you know.' 'He's not clever at all,' said Il'ich, pulling a face.

I did not go on, but a few days later V.I. found out how rude Stalin had been to N.K. and that Zinoviev and Kamenev both knew. In the morning, very upset, he called in his stenographer, having asked first whether N.K. had gone off to the People's Commissariat for Education. He was told she had. Volodicheva came in and V.I. dictated the following letter to Stalin:

TOP SECRET. PERSONAL.
Dear Comrade Stalin,
You have had the temerity to phone my wife and insult her. Although she has agreed with you to forget what was said, Zinoviev and Kamenev learned about it from her. I am not prepared to forget slights against me so easily and, needless to say, I consider slights against my wife to be slights against me. I therefore ask you to consider whether you are prepared to retract and apologize or would prefer to terminate relations between us.
Yours respectfully,
Lenin.

V.I. asked Volodicheva to send the letter to Stalin without mentioning it to N.K., and to give a copy in a sealed envelope to me.

But when she got back home, N.K. knew by V.I.'s face that something was wrong, and asked Volodicheva not to send the letter. She said she would talk to Stalin herself and ask him to apologize. That is what N.K. says now, but I have the impression that she did not see the letter, and it was sent to Stalin, as V.I. had wished. Stalin delayed in replying to V.I., then they [probably N.K. and the doctors] decided not to give V.I. the reply, as he had taken a turn for the worse, so V.I. never did know about the reply in which Stalin apologized.

But, as V.I. was not irritated with Stalin, there is one thing I can say with assurance: when V.I. said 'He's not clever at all', he said it without any irritation whatsoever. What he told me was his opinion, definite and thought out. This does not contradict the fact that V.I. valued Stalin as a man of action, but he thought it necessary that there should be something to restrain some of his particular ways. This was why V.I. thought that Stalin should be removed from the post of General Secretary. He said this clearly in his political testament, in his characterizations of several comrades, which he made just before he died and which never did reach the Party. But of that another time. . .

[Sources: RGASPI, fond 14, opis' 1, delo 398, pp. 1–8; V.I. Lenin, *Polnoe sobranie sochineniy* Volume XLV (Moscow 1965) pp. 361, 362.]

In October 1926, the full text of Lenin's Testament was published in *The New York Times* by Max Eastman, an American admirer of Trotsky. Although Trotsky had not encouraged it, he had earlier given Eastman much of his information and, in the eyes of Stalin and the majority on the Central Committee, was plainly responsible. At an explosive meeting of the Politburo a week later, Stalin labelled the Opposition a 'social-democratic deviation'. Turning to Stalin, Trotsky responded: 'The First Secretary poses his candidature for the post of the grave-digger of the revolution.'[101] The next day Trotsky was dropped from the Politburo.

Unable to make any inroads at the summit of the party, the United Opposition tried to mobilize support among the rank and file. But there, too, they made little headway. The more isolated the Opposition appeared, the easier it was for local committees to ensure they received a hostile reception when they attempted to visit party cells and factories. Between 1926 and 1927 Stalin, Bukharin and the current leadership adopted those of the Opposition's demands that had potential appeal to working-class members— the rise in wages, the pressure on NEPmen and richer peasants, more energetic encouragement of collectivization, and preparation for an inspiring plan for industrial breakthrough. At the same time, they successfully glossed the Opposition's criticisms as the embittered and divisive product of frustrated ambition, and its denial of the possibility of building socialism in one country as deeply unpatriotic and virtually betrayal. Where foreign policy

---

101 See the second volume of I. Deutscher's classic trilogy, *The Prophet Unarmed: Trotsky 1921–1929* (Oxford 1970) p. 196.

was concerned, they rebuffed the charge that Bukharin and Stalin had led Comintern to desert the cause of revolution and feebly resigned itself to a prolonged period of capitalist stabilization. When Soviet diplomacy was rocked in April 1927 by Chiang Kai-shek's massacre of Chinese communists, which destroyed the policy of co-operation with the Chinese nationalists, and in May by Britain's severing of diplomatic relations with the USSR, Stalin implied that Trotsky welcomed the setbacks. Amidst acute alarm and a full-scale war scare in the Soviet Union, Stalin spoke of a united front 'from Chamberlain [British Foreign Secretary] to Trotsky', and damned the Opposition's criticisms of Comintern policy as treacherous.

That summer, the United Opposition drew up a comprehensive, twelve-chapter Platform, initially signed by thirteen members of the Central Committee, for submission to the Fifteenth Party Congress scheduled towards the end of the year. They passionately denounced the Stalin–Bukharin group, spelling out in detail and with copious reference to Lenin their charge that the party and the revolution were being led astray.

Document 115 | From the draft Platform of the Bolshevik–Leninists (the Opposition) at the XV Congress of the CPSU

1927

The systematic destruction of inner-Party democracy has been under way in recent years, in spite of the Bolshevik Party's entire past and in spite of the direct resolutions of a series of Party congresses. The genuine elective principle is in fact dying out. At every step Bolshevism's organizational principles are being perverted. The Party rules are systematically changed to increase the rights of the higher bodies and reduce those of the basic Party units. The terms of office of *oblast'*, district and *guberniya* committees are being extended to a year, to three or more years. The senior members of *guberniya* committees, executive committees, trade-union committees, etc., are virtually irremovable (for three, five or more years). The right of every Party member and every group of Party members 'to bring fundamental disagreements before the court of the whole Party' (Lenin) has in fact been abolished. Congresses and conferences are called without the preliminary free discussion of matters by the whole Party that existed in Lenin's time, and demands for such discussions are seen as a breach of Party discipline. . . . The dying out of inner-Party democracy is leading to the dying out of workers' democracy in general—in the trade unions and in all other non-Party mass organizations. . . .

Every comrade and every group of comrades must have the opportunity to defend his point of view to the Party in the press, at meetings, etc. . . . . Workers on the shop floor, advanced proletarian Communists, popular among both the Party and non-Party masses, must make up the decisive majority in the whole Party machine. This should not be composed entirely of salaried staff and should be regularly replenished from among the workers. The budget of local organizations (including *guberniya* ones) must be made up mainly from membership subscriptions. Local organizations should be accountable to the Party masses for their income and expenditure on a regular basis, not only in word, but in deed. The Party's present excessive budget must be reduced several times, as must the number of paid personnel. A significant amount of Party work can and must be done voluntarily by Party members after their productive or other work. One way to replenish the Party apparatus regularly is systematically to send some of the comrades on the Party staff to work in industry or in some other lowly post. We must fight against the irremovability of secretaries. There must be a maximum time limit set for secretarial and other such jobs.

N.I. Muralov
Kh.G. Rakovsky
L.B. Kamenev
L.D. Trotsky and others.

[Source: *Arkhiv Trotskogo* Volume IV (Moscow 1990) pp. 147–48, 152–53.]

When the leadership refused to circulate the Platform along with other material for the forthcoming Congress, the Opposition tried themselves to organize its printing and dissemination. The OGPU intervened and arrested some of those involved for engaging in what they claimed was a counter-revolutionary plot. In October, citing police evidence of the Opposition's collusion with foreign enemies, Stalin successfully urged the Central Committee to expel Trotsky and Zinoviev from their number.

The climax came on the tenth anniversary of the revolution, 7 November 1927. Their leaders expelled from the Central Committee, blocked from making their case to the Party Congress, and vilified ever more crudely in the press, the Opposition made a desperate attempt to mobilize demonstrations in their support. They failed dismally. And the small minority of party members who remained sympathetic found themselves drowned out by hostile voices, laced with anti-Semitic jeers about Trotsky, Zinoviev and Kamenev. This *cri de coeur* is conserved in the Trotsky Archive:

Document 116 | I.M. Arkhipov's declaration to his CPSU cell, the 2nd Moscow Freight Depot

11 November 1927

Dear Comrades,

Very sadly I have to write these lines to you, since unheard of things have been going on in our cell which have never happened before. Very sadly, at present I have to report the appearance of completely anti-Party and anti-worker groups who behave like this: on 7 November this year, just as a demonstration was gathering by the Aleksandrovsky Station, the leaders of the world proletariat, comrades Trotsky, Kamenev and Muralov, came to see us and were met by the cheers of workers from the Krasnaya Presnya district. At that very moment a group of layabouts, organized in advance, of a really fascist type, including such members of our Party cell as Eydenov, Korolev and others, hurled themselves at our leaders' car and tried to drag them out of it. As a dedicated Party member who always defends workers' interests, I joined in the fight against them and when Eydenov climbed onto comrade Trotsky's car to thump him, I dragged this out-and-out fascist from our cell off by the collar.

When the car carrying the leaders of the world revolution drove off, these fascists pelted them with apples, buns, dirt and anything they could get their hands on. The fascists in our cell, Eydenov, Korolev and others, took a direct part in all this. When we went back to our group, I remarked to Eydenov, 'Only fascists do that sort of thing.' Then Korolev punched me in the head just because I had done the duty of an honest worker and Party member in defending the leaders of the world's proletariat and the duty of any honest worker, even if he's not a communist, in defending the leaders.

We went back to our group where a big row had started about what had happened. Despite my loyalty in the conversation, more than once I heard Korolev threatening to do me over.

So I think this sort of thing is unacceptable in a Party cell and ask you to discuss it and draw the necessary conclusion, since I reckon the leaders of the working class are cut off from the masses, but do not want to break their links and appear among them, regardless of the danger. So this is the conclusion you can draw: that the working class, which has been misinformed and has become confused, wanted to meet its real leaders, Trotsky, Kamenev and others, at the demonstration, but an organized bunch of layabouts and fascists stopped them doing so.

For my part I consider it my duty to declare that this sort of thing must be stopped, because they are leading the working class astray, and reliance on these layabouts might lead to the destruction of all the gains of October. As for our cell and the organized group of layabouts in it, I blame everything on our secretary, who condones such goings-on, and the consequences will be blamed on people higher up who have given these layabouts this job to do, since the working class has never tolerated and cannot tolerate this sort of thing and has always cut down with cold steel anybody stopping its cause advancing.

No thug is going to stop the Opposition, the only defence of Leninist ideas, from inculcating in the working class its true class interests and ways to struggle, because that's what comrade Lenin said.

Arkhipov, member of the CPSU since 1917.

Copies to Trotsky, Muralov and the Central and Moscow Control Commissions.

N.B. Our cell secretary did not think it necessary to discuss my declaration. For over one month I have not been able to get it onto the agenda. Arkhipov.

[Source: *Arkhiv Trotskogo* Volume IV (Moscow 1990) pp. 260–61.]

A week later Trotsky and Zinoviev were expelled from the party and in January 1928, by which time Zinoviev and Kamenev had recanted and sought readmittance, Trotsky was exiled to the small, remote town of Alma Ata in Central Asia. A year later he was deported from the USSR.

10

Soviet Power and the
Intelligentsia

The devastation of the cultural intelligentsia

The combination of revolution, socio-economic upheaval and the consolidation of Bolshevik rule during and after the civil war traumatized the country's cultural elite. The ordeal tore the heart out of what since the mid-nineteenth century had been known as (and called itself) 'the intelligentsia', artists and scientists, musicians, poets and playwrights, novelists and journalists, teachers and academics of all disciplines. The market, journals and institutions on which its elite members had depended for financial security collapsed. Their deeply rooted sense of moral responsibility for the country and the people—the *narod*—was shattered by the revolution from below and the violence and destruction of the civil war. And to their bewilderment the radical regime which replaced the familiar target of their criticism, the repressive and reactionary Tsarist autocracy, treated them as conservative enemies and imposed a censorship far tighter and more effective than that of the old order.

The party leadership regarded the intelligentsia as the mouthpiece for the different classes into which society was divided. 'The intelligentsia are so called,' Lenin had explained long before the revolution, 'just because they most consciously, most resolutely and most accurately express the development of class interests and political groupings in society as a whole.'[102] With only a very small minority of the intelligentsia wholeheartedly endorsing the October revolution, the new authorities regarded the majority with deep suspicion. Whether they knew it or not, so party orthodoxy held, they were propagators of ideas and values that were in essence counter-revolutionary, defending the bourgeois and petit-bourgeois society the new order was replacing. This did not mean that the Bolshevik leaders were cultural nihilists: Lunacharsky, the first Commissar for Enlightenment, was among a group of

102 Lenin, *Collected Works* Volume VII (London 1961) p. 45.

Bolsheviks who resigned (temporarily) from the government in protest against the destruction of ancient monuments during the violence which followed the proclamation of Soviet power in Moscow. Moreover, to shore up Soviet culture and education Lenin and his colleagues were anxious to 'win over' those among the intelligentsia whose attitudes were sufficiently plastic. The leadership was aware, too, of the need to harness the expertise of much more widely educated and skilled strata even if they were not automatically sympathetic to the new order. By spring 1918, Lenin was pressing hard for active steps to persuade managers, engineers, specialists and experts in the economy, industry, and administration—who began to be known as the 'technical' intelligentsia by analogy with the 'cultural' intelligentsia—to accept the new regime and work under it. With the onset of NEP, the relative privileges and favourable differentials granted to them grew markedly.

Among humbler party members, attitudes towards the non-party intelligentsia were often intensely hostile. Unlike Lenin, Trotsky, Bukharin and much of the leadership, who themselves belonged to the very small cultural elite—as late as 1900 the total number of graduates (overwhelmingly men) was no more than 85,000 in a population of some 135 million[103]—party members drawn from socially less educated backgrounds resented the intelligentsia's sense of superiority and tended to see their cultural refinement as itself evidence of alien class affiliation. This hostility towards educated strata extended far beyond the cultural elite. Within the economy and administration, specialists, engineers and technical experts also attracted rank-and-file party and wider lower-class resentment. Their privileges and what was seen as a supercilious air offended the idealism of party members old and new, and especially of militant members of the rapidly growing Komsomol. Red Army warriors returning triumphantly to civilian life and eager to reap the rewards of victory were scornful of these relics of the bourgeois order. With the expropriation and flight of most landowners, industrialists and property owners, the cultural and technical intelligentsia together became, as it were, a surrogate for the hated privileged classes of Tsarist society.

During the first decade after the revolution, therefore, there was an underlying tension in the regime's treatment of the intelligentsia, efforts to secure their loyalty running concurrently with steps to control or silence them. The much more rigid conditions of the 1930s have led many historians to portray the Soviet government in the 1920s as 'extraordinarily accommodating and tolerant toward the intelligentsia',[104] although it has been forcefully argued

---

103 V.R. Leikina-Svirskaya, *Intelligentsiya v Rossii vo vtoroi polovine XIX veka* (Moscow 1971) pp. 69–70.

104 R.G. Suny, *The Soviet Experiment: Russia, the USSR and the successor states* (Oxford 1998) pp. 199–200.

that where the cultural intelligentsia are concerned the broad trajectory across the decade was in the direction of tighter restrictions.[105] But in the first years after the revolution, direct party intrusion and censorship, though already extensive in some fields—the list of books banned was formidable—were haphazard and unsystematic.

Initially there were occasional, limited opportunities for leading intellectuals deeply hostile to the entire Marxist project to ruminate in public about the revolution. The following extract from a lecture by Nikolay Berdyaev is a good case in point. Berdyaev had been a prominent member of the group of intelligentsia who in 1909 published a highly controversial set of essays— *Vekhi (Signposts)*—in which they denounced their fellow intelligentsia for having sacrificed the spiritual values of humanity on the altar of materialism and a fantasy notion of historical progress.[106] In 1918, several of the contributors collaborated on a second volume, *Out of the Depths*, reflecting on what they saw as the tragic fulfilment of their warnings about Russia's future.[107] For Berdyaev, whose religious convictions became increasingly strong, the 'prophet' of the revolution was Fedor Dostoevsky. He saw Dostoevsky's famous portrait of the medieval Grand Inquisitor arresting and condemning Christ in *The Brothers Karamazov* (1880) as a brilliant anticipation of the way in which socialism would ape and deride true religion.[108] The excerpt from Berdyaev below captures the unbridgeable gulf between Bolshevik assumptions and his diagnosis that the materialistic socialist project was the product of Russia's moral illness. By the time *Out of the Depths* had been printed in the autumn, civil war was raging and there was no chance that the book, edited by the right-wing Kadet P.B. Struve, would be allowed to circulate. Part of Berdyaev's contribution, however, was published that summer and in the next two years, during which he became professor of philosophy at Moscow University, he managed to pursue the same theme in lectures and in the short-lived semi-formal philosophical academies he was involved in until 1922.[109]

---

105 C. Read, *Culture and Power in Revolutionary Russia: The intelligentsia and the transition from tsarism to communism* (London 1990).

106 *Landmarks*, edited and translated by M.S. Shatz and J.E. Zimmerman (Irvine, CA, 1986). For a close analysis of the controversy, see C. Read, *Religion, Revolution and the Russian Intelligentsia 1900–1912* (London 1979).

107 *Out of the Depths (De Profundis)*, edited and translated by W.F. Woehrlin (Irvine, CA, 1986).

108 F. Dostoevsky, *The Brothers Karamazov*, translated by D. Magarshack (Harmondsworth 1958) pp. 288–311. 'The Grand Inquisitor' has been called the greatest chapter in literature.

109 J. Burbank, *Intelligentsia and Revolution: Russian views of Bolshevism 1917–1922* (Oxford 1986) pp. 193–208.

Document 117 | N.A. Berdyaev: 'Socialism will never succeed'

From a lecture given around 1919–20 in Moscow.

In human history nothing has really succeeded and there are grounds to think that it never will. . .

Neither the fundamental ideas and goals by which our epoch lives will succeed, nor will socialism, which they will try to implement and which will probably play a major role in the period of history which we are now entering. In the attempt to realize it, socialism will not turn out to be what the socialists are aiming at. It will reveal new inner contradictions in human life, which will make it impossible to attain the goals set by the socialist movement. It will never bring about that liberation of human labour, which Marx wanted to achieve by fettering it; it will never lead to prosperity and achieve equality, but merely create a new enmity between people, a new alienation and new, unheard of, forms of oppression. . .

The path of freedom is hard and tragic, because there is truly nothing more crucial, heroic and painful. Any path of necessity and compulsion is easier, less tragic and less heroic. That is why throughout history humanity has constantly been seduced by the idea of replacing paths of freedom by paths of compulsion. . . In the past this temptation produced the historical Inquisition; now it is producing the religion of socialism, which is nothing other than the religion of the Grand Inquisitor, based on substituting paths of compulsion for paths of freedom and lifting from humanity the burden of tragic freedom. It is on this stage that the drama of history is being played out with the constant struggle between freedom and compulsion, and the constant swing from one principle to the other. . .

History has not been able to solve the problem of Man's individual fate, which constitutes the theme of Dostoevsky's brilliant discoveries and is linked to the metaphysics of history. This problem of individual fate is insoluble within the confines of history. The tragic conflict between an individual fate and the fate of the world, of the whole of humanity, cannot be resolved within these confines. That is why history must come to an end. The world must enter an elevated reality and integrated time wherein the problem of humanity's individual fate will be solved and the tragic conflict between this and the fate of the world will find its outcome. History is primarily fate and must be understood as such, as tragic fate. A tragic fate, like any tragedy, must have a final act, a dénouement. In tragedy catharsis is unavoidable. History has no endless development in our time, it is not governed by natural laws, precisely because history is fate. Such is the ultimate conclusion and outcome of the metaphysics of history. The fate of humanity, which we must trace through all periods of history, cannot be resolved within the confines of history. The metaphysics of history teaches us that what cannot be resolved within the confines of history can be resolved outside them. This is the greatest argument in favour of history's not being meaningless, but having a higher meaning. If it had only an imma-

nent earthly meaning, then it really would be meaningless because all the fundamental difficulties connected with the nature of time would either be insoluble, or
the solutions would be fictitious, illusory and untrue. This relatively pessimistic
metaphysics of history breaks with the illusions connected with the deification of
the future and deposes the idea of progress, but reinforces hopes for and trust in a
solution to all the pains of history in the prospect of eternity, the prospect of eternal
reality. This pessimistic metaphysics of history is more optimistic, in the ultimate
and deeper sense of the word, than the optimistic doctrine of progress, which is
cheerless, and lethal to all that is living. Some kind of inner change must happen,
after which world history, as if cast up from the depths of the spirit, will appear not
in the perspective of the destructive flow of time, but in the perspective of eternity,
in the perspective of celestial history. It will return to the depths as a moment in the
eternal mystery of the Spirit.

[Source: N.A. Berdyaev, *Smysl istorii: Opyt filosofii chelovecheskoy sud'by* (Berlin 1923),
pp. 237–248.]

To make ends meet, members of the cultural intelligentsia were compelled
to take what work they could, however humbling or mundane, as well as
to share in compulsory heavy labour. With their wealthy patrons and clients
expropriated and/or fleeing into exile, independent presses, theatres and
galleries in dire straits, and universities and established cultural bodies starved
of funds and unable to pay a living wage, their livelihood imploded. During
the civil war, creative *intelligenty* (members of the intelligentsia) set up a
variety of semi-formal networks around co-operative bookshops, lending
libraries, reading and discussion circles and associations—both to sustain a
forum for their work, and to help supplement incomes shrivelling to nothing.
In one year, starvation carried off seven of the forty-five members of the
Academy of Sciences, the most prestigious academic institution in the
country.[110]

The following extract from a 1921 article by the novelist E. Zamyatin
conveys the combined impact of sheer impoverishment and a regime determined to make all conform to a rigid 'neo-Catholic' understanding of the
world. Although Zamyatin was able to publish a number of scathingly critical pieces in the ephemeral literary collections which the rapidly shrinking
number of independent publishers struggled to issue until late 1922 (this
particular one was printed in Prague), he could not publish any of his most
substantial works. The new Soviet censors rejected the novel for which he

---

110 J.C. McClelland, 'The Professoriate in the Russian Civil War' in D. Koenker, W.
    Rosenberg and R. Suny (eds) *Party, State and Society in the Russian Civil War*
    (Bloomington, IN, 1989) p. 260.

is best known, *We*, written in 1920 and eventually published in New York without his permission in 1924, a classic anti-utopian portrayal of a repressive modern urban society in which individuals were reduced to characterless numbers, their lives regimented by clockwork obedience to machinery and dictatorship.[111] Here he imagined how the talent of the greatest figures in pre-revolutionary Russian *belles lettres* would have been stultified in the new Soviet Russia, deprived of the time to write and in any case prevented from publishing anything unacceptable to the new orthodoxy. And he warned that Russian literature would atrophy until the new authorities were less terrified of having ordinary people hear 'heretical' ideas.

Document 118 | E. Zamyatin: 'I am afraid...'

1921

Any writer who cannot become smart has to go to work in an office, briefcase in hand, if he wants to stay alive. These days Gogol' would be running to the Department of Theatre with his briefcase; Turgenev would undoubtedly be translating Balzac and Flaubert for *World Literature*; Herzen would be giving lectures for the Baltic Fleet; Chekhov would be working for the Commissariat of Health. Otherwise, in order to live—to live as a student did five years ago on forty rubles— Gogol' would have to write four *Government Inspectors* a month, Turgenev three *Fathers and Sons* every two months, and Chekhov a hundred stories a month. It sounds like a bad joke, but unfortunately it is not. These figures are real...

But even this is not the real point: Russian writers are used to going hungry. Nor is it a question of paper: the real reason for this silence is not bread or paper. It is something much harder, tougher, made of iron. The point is that real literature can exist only when it is written not by dependable and reliable office workers, but by madmen, recluses, heretics, dreamers, rebels and sceptics. So, if today a writer must be sensible, devoutly Catholic, and useful, he cannot, like Swift, lash everybody, he cannot, like Anatole France, smile at everybody—there can be no literature cast in bronze, but just paper which will be read today and used to wrap bars of soft soap tomorrow.

I fear that we shall have no real literature until they stop treating the Russian people as a child whose innocence must be protected. I fear that we shall have no real literature until we cure ourselves of a kind of neo-Catholicism which no less than the old fears heresy. If this illness is incurable, I am afraid Russian literature has only one future—its past.

[Source: *Dom iskusstv*, sbornik 1 (Prague 1921).]

111 E. Zamyatin, *We*, translated by N. Ginsburg (London 1972).

While much of the non-Bolshevik cultural elite was demoralized, reduced to silence or had joined the huge emigration, in 1921 a minority current ran the other way. The most famous expression of reconciliation with the new regime was a collection of essays entitled *Smena vekh* (*Change of Landmarks*), a deliberate jibe at *Landmarks*.[112] In it several prominent intellectuals apologized for their failure to grasp the positive aspects of Bolshevism. The thrust of their message was that whatever the social and cultural damage wrought by the Bolshevik regime, it had held together the great bulk of the Russian empire—and, as was shown by western alarm when the Red Army briefly threatened Warsaw in 1920, restored respect for Russia. Reason and the demands of great-power status were destined to drive the regime in a direction sympathetic to Russian patriots, and the adoption of NEP pointed the same way. Initially published abroad (in Prague), the collection's pretensions to supersede *Landmarks*, to represent a further chapter in the intelligentsia's repentance and realism, caught the attention of and for the most part infuriated the émigré cultural elite. From the point of view of the regime, however, there were advantages in allowing some scope for its partisans, the so-called *smenovekhovtsy*. Their language and logic were alien to the Bolsheviks, but the underlying message could be read as a vote of confidence in the new order and might help to reconcile educated strata who had remained in Russia and attract useful émigrés to return to live and work in the Soviet Union. In 1921 and 1922 considerable publicity was given to debates among protagonists of *Smena vekh*, two small editions of the book itself were published in the provinces, and their émigré paper *Nakanune* was permitted to open an office in Moscow. In parallel, a literary journal, *Novaya Rossiya*, later *Rossiya*, run by another group of intellectuals inclined to come to terms with the new order, was sanctioned and reached a circulation of 15,000 at its height in 1924. The following extract from the contribution of S.S. Chakhotin, a writer who had worked for the Whites during the civil war, conveys the flavour of *Smena vekh*.

Document 119 | S.S. Chakhotin: 'We are going to Canossa!'*

1921

Now we are not afraid of saying, 'We are going to Canossa! We were wrong and mistaken. Let us not be afraid to admit it both for our own and others' sake.'

Bolshevism with its extremes and horrors is a disease, but at the same time a natural, albeit unpleasant, condition of our country in the process of its evolution.

---

112 Burbank, *Intelligentsia and Revolution* pp. 222–37.
* A reference to Emperor Henry IV's archetypal capitulation to Pope Gregory VII at Canossa in 1076.

Not only the whole of Russia's past but we ourselves are to blame for the country's falling ill. An unnecessary illness, perhaps, but now it is too late to sigh and squabble: our country is sick, its illness is taking its course, and we, the Russian intelligentsia, the brains of the country, do not have the right to stand aside and wait and see whether the crisis ends in recovery or death. It is our duty to help heal the wounds of our sick motherland and care for it lovingly, regardless of attacks of feverish delirium. It is clear that the sooner the intelligentsia set about working energetically for the cultural and economic revival of Russia, the sooner the patient will regain all its strength, the fever will abate, and the renewal of its organism will be completed all the more easily.

People ask me, 'But how!? Go to the Bolsheviks, go along with them? But that means accepting that you were wrong and sanctioning their victory.' Yes, it does mean going to Canossa. This admission will not humiliate us or break our spirit. We have fought honestly hitherto, because we considered it our duty. Events have shown us that we were wrong, that our path was leading in the wrong direction. And, recognizing this and seeing what our country's interests demand from us, we are ready to admit our error and change direction.

So will we become communists or Bolsheviks, as some seem to think? Of course not. As a practical doctrine in the current circumstances communism remains for us the same utopia as before, but it can and must change if it wants to join the real world, and in many respects we, the intelligentsia, can assist the process.

After every illness an organism is seen to have new energy, a fortified metabolism, a better state of health and strength. Within the disease itself there are frequently the basis and source of recovery. And so I must fearlessly admit that within Bolshevism itself, along with plenty of ugly features, there are undoubtedly healthy elements and positive features, which are difficult to deny. Firstly, history obliged the Russian 'communist' republic, despite its official dogma, to take upon itself the national task of holding together a Russia on the verge of collapse, along with the restoration and strengthening of Russia's weight in international affairs. It was strange and unexpected to observe how, when the Bolsheviks were approaching Warsaw, all corners of Europe spoke with fear, but also with a certain respect, not about the 'Bolsheviks', but about Russia, and its renewed appearance on the world stage.

One must also admit that another positive feature of Soviet power was that (again, in spite of its theories) it was compelled to create a disciplined army. That is the first precondition for the existence of any state, however offensive it may be to say this after the innumerable victims of 'the Great War to end all wars'.

We should consider the third undoubted plus in what the Bolsheviks are doing to be that they really have made it impossible to return to the past, that sad, dark past which was the primary source of the indigence, ignorance and bitterness of the people, of the unpreparedness and flabbiness of our intelligentsia, and of all the evil which has befallen Russia recently. Although at great cost, this danger has, fortunately, been removed for ever. There is now the chance to lay the foundations on a new rational basis of a new Russian state system, rather than piling new, disjointed superstructures on top of old, archaic and absurd foundations.

Moreover, even the fact of the destruction itself has some positive features: matters have made us give up our Russian carelessness and the hope that someone some-where will do something for us. On the edge of a precipice everybody must wake up and find a way out, think quickly and cope—or perish. For the first time that most effective of instincts, the healthy instinct of self-preservation, has been goaded into action on a colossal scale in the once slumbering masses; we are sure that the full meaning of this biological impulse will express itself in future in the lives of the Russian people, in a significant and positive rebuilding of the Russian character, and, if so, that alone might justify the sacrifices and losses of our time.

Finally, let us be objective and admit that among those in whose hands the fate of Russia lies, some are endowed with realism and are not enemies of evolution. The logic of events is forcing them inexorably to give up positions which are unworkable in practice and take up ones more in accordance with real life. The acceleration and completion of this process for the good of Russia and of progress will depend on what our intelligentsia do. People will object, 'That's just optimism!' 'Yes, it is,' we shall reply, 'but not groundless optimism.' Moreover, if we have to achieve at all costs and in difficult conditions the task we have set ourselves, the salvation of Russia, then we do need optimism, an attitude of mind which gives us cheerful assurance of our own strength and the feasibility of our tasks.

So, we are going to Canossa, i.e., we admit we lost the game, we went the wrong way and that our actions and calculations were mistaken. . .

[Source: *Smena vekh* (Prague 1921) pp. 159–61.]

The Bolsheviks' commitment to expanding education provided some common ground with *intelligenty* employed in schools and universities, who needed a *modus vivendi* with the new authorities if they were to keep their jobs and pursue their vocation. On the other hand, even the relatively pragmatic approach of Lunacharsky involved repeated clashes over demo-cratization of the student body and decision-making, over pedagogic methods and the syllabus, over institutional autonomy and trade-union inde-pendence, and over finance. The conflicts involved were epitomized by the establishment from 1920 of Workers' Faculties (*rabfaki*), new departments set up within universities to provide intensive tuition to prepare the chil-dren of workers and peasants for higher education proper. All too often *rabfak* students appear to have struggled to meet the academics' requirements, which fed their resentment and the militancy of the many recruited to Komsomol. However, although teachers and academics alike found them-selves increasingly on the defensive, there were too many unresolved policy issues for the new authorities to impose any single template. Moreover, the grim conditions and desperate financial straits of schools and universities made all too real the danger that the education system would be suspended altogether. Late in 1921, with academics even at Moscow University, which weathered the civil-war years much better than most universities and schools, threatening to go on strike, the government made conciliatory moves to explore ways of improving conditions and increasing rations for academics.

Document 120 | On improving life for academics—from a Sovnarkom decree

6 December 1921

In order to make the best use of the country's academic resources to rebuild the economy and also to ensure that scientific workers have the opportunity to work undisturbed and regularly, the Council of People's Commissars, after hearing a draft bill put forward on 6 December by the Central Commission on Improving Life for Academics, has resolved:

1. To establish a special supplementary academic ration in addition to the current forms of remuneration for scientific workers. . .
3. Determination of the size of the academic ration and the establishment of distribution criteria for different categories of scientific worker depending on their qualifications is to be left to the Central Commission on Improving Life for Academics.
4. To establish bonuses for academic, teaching and popular educational work, based on a special ration drawn up by the Central Commission on Improving Life for Academics.
5. To introduce the supplementary academic ration on 1 January 1922. . .
9. To oblige the Central Commission on Improving Life for Academics to take immediate steps to establish, in agreement with the appropriate government departments, a simplified procedure for granting permission for academics to go abroad.
10. To oblige the Central Commission on Improving Life for Academics, in agreement with the appropriate government departments, to establish a procedure whereby academics may receive publications from abroad.

A. Tsyurupa acting for the chairman of the Council of People's Commissars
N. Gorbunov, office manager of the Council of People's Commissars, L. Fotieva, secretary

[Source: *Sobranie uzakoneniy i rasporyazheniy rabochego i krest'yanskogo pravitel'stva* No. 1, 1922, Article 5, p. 3.]

The deportations of September 1922

In the face of a strike by academics in the major universities early in 1922, the government adopted a similar tone and the protest was quickly called off. Slowly material conditions in education improved, but in the course of 1922, alongside continuing efforts to increase collaboration with the cultural intelligentsia, harsher measures were taken against those reckoned incurably hostile. The replacement of the Cheka by the GPU (State Political Administration) announced in a TsIK statute on 6 February 1922 marked a (temporary) tightening of discipline within the political police and an end to summary executions. But the GPU retained a wide-ranging remit for combating anti-state agitation and organization, including that of suspect *intelligenty*. The continuity with the practices of the Tsarist secret police in dealing with political 'undesirables' is exemplified by the following decree. It formally sanctioned the use not only of deportation abroad but also of 'internal exile' to provincial backwaters to live under police surveillance cut off from the political and cultural mainstream, a sentence imposed on many revolutionaries before 1917.

Document 121 | 'On Administrative Exile'—VTsIK decree

10 August 1922

The All-Russia Central Executive Committee resolves:

1. With the aim of isolating people involved in counter-revolutionary activities, in relation to whom permission for isolation of longer than two months has been sought from the Presidium of the All-Russia Central Executive Committee, and in those cases where it is possible not to resort to arrest, administrative exile abroad or to a particular region of the RSFSR is established.
2. The consideration of questions concerning the exile of individual persons is to be entrusted to a Special Commission of the People's Commissariat of Internal Affairs, headed by the People's Commissar of Internal Affairs, with representatives of the People's Commissariat of Internal Affairs and the People's Commissariat of Justice approved by the Presidium of the All-Russia Central Executive Committee.
3. Decisions on the exile of each individual person must be accompanied by detailed statements of the reasons for exile.
4. The decision on exile should indicate the district and period of exile.
5. The list of regions used for exile is to be approved by the All-Russia Central Executive Committee on the recommendation of the Commission.
6. The period of administrative exile cannot exceed three years.
7. Persons subject to administrative exile lose their active and passive voting rights during the period of exile.

8. Those exiled to a particular region come under the supervision of the local unit of the GPU, which decides on the place of residence within the region of the exiled person.

9. Escape from the place of exile, or on the way to it, will be punished by the courts in accordance with Article 95 of the Legal Code.

The People's Commissariat of Internal Affairs is to publish detailed instructions to its local organs on the basis of this decree.

Chairman of the All-Russia Central Executive Committee M. Kalinin
Secretary of the All-Russia Central Executive Committee A. Enukidze

[Source: *Sobranie uzakoneniy i rasporyazheniy rabochego i krest'yanskogo pravitel'stva* No. 51, 1922, Article 646, pp. 813–14.]

Later that month there was a major police swoop against prominent *intelligenty*, between 160 and 200 of whom were deported at the end of September.[113] During the summer the Politburo had considered detailed lists of 'anti-Soviet' academics, specialists and writers from Petrograd and Moscow, although exactly how the list of those selected for deportation was settled upon is not clear. Among them were ex-Kadets and SRs and many academics, including the rector of Moscow University, M.M. Novikov. The list also included several of those who had been part of the short-lived Public Committee to Aid the Hungry (Pomgol) set up in July 1921 to mobilize voluntary and foreign help against the famine and promptly closed the following month, on Lenin's orders, under suspicion of crystallizing criticism of the regime. Although the interrogation of the arrestees amounted to little more than a formality, the OGPU archives reveal the bureaucratic precision with which the suspects were questioned and the sophistication and irony with which they responded. The languages of the two sides, as Berdyaev's case shows, were irreconcilable. To Berdyaev, the questions posed were crude attempts to incriminate him. His interrogator doubtless saw plenty of damning evidence, not only in his polished denial of any class affiliation, his measured verdict on *Smena vekh*, and his claim not to have followed the first major show trial, that of SR leaders, that summer, but even in the most basic information he supplied regarding his social origins, occupation and employment record.

---

113 See the study by S. Finkel, 'Purging the Public Intellectual: The 1922 expulsions from Soviet Russia' *Russian Review* 62 (2003) pp. 589–613.

Document 122 | Record of the interrogation of N.A. Berdyaev

Secret Department of the GPU, 18 August 1922

I, the undersigned, interrogated as accused, declare:

1. *Surname*: Berdyaev.
2. *Name and patronymic*: Nikolay Aleksandrovich.
3. *Age*: 48.
4. *Social class*: former noble from the city of Kiev.
5. *Address*: Flat 3, 14 Bol'shoy Vlas'evsky, Moscow.
6. *Occupation*: writer and academic.
7. *Marital status*: married.
8. *Property ownership*: none.
9. *Political affiliation*: none.
10. *Political convictions*: I am a supporter of Christian community, based on Christian freedom and Christian equality, which cannot be brought about by any political party, i.e., I do not agree with either bourgeois society or communism.
11. *General Education*: university, higher. *Specialism*—philosophy.
12. *Nature and place of employment*:
    a. *Prior to the 1914 war*—I had no employment and lived off my literary work.
    b. *Prior to the February revolution of 1917*—I had no employment and was involved in academic work.
    c. *Prior to the October revolution of 1917*—I had no employment.
    d. *From the October revolution until my arrest*—I worked in the Main Archive Administration; in 1920 I was given the post of teacher at Moscow State University, gave lectures at the State Institute of the Word and am an active member of the Russian Academy of Artistic Sciences.
13. *Previous convictions*: in 1915 I was taken to court over an article against the Synod and charged with blasphemy. In 1920 I was arrested by the Cheka, but was released. P.S.: From 1900 to 1903 I was exiled to Vologda on political grounds.

Testimony on the essence of the case

Q. Citizen Berdyaev, what are your views on the structure of Soviet power and the system of the proletarian state?

A. My convictions do not allow me to take a class stance, and therefore I consider the ideologies of the nobility, the peasantry, the proletariat and the bourgeoisie to be equally narrow, limited and self-interested. My standpoint is that of Man and Mankind, a level to which all class distinctions and parties should raise themselves. I would consider my own personal ideology to be aristocratic, not in the caste sense, but in the sense of rule by the best, the most intelligent, talented, educated and noble. Democracy I consider a mistake, because it is based on the domination of the majority. . . . Moreover a view of society and knowledge of nature may be based on the spiritual rebirth of humanity and the people. I do not believe in the wishes of the authorities and a material road to rebirth. I do not think we have a proletarian state in Russia because the majority of Russians are peasants.

Q. Tell me your views on the role of the intelligentsia and this so-called 'community'.

A. I think the intelligentsia's job in all areas of culture and society is to defend the spiritual principle by subordinating the material principle to the idea of spiritual culture. It should be the bearer of scientific, moral and aesthetic awareness. I think there should be interaction and co-operation between elements of community and elements of state power. . .

Q. Tell me what you think about such methods of fighting Soviet power as the professors' strike.

A. I do not know enough about the matter to judge. If the professors are fighting for the interests of science and knowledge, then I think their struggle is just, but if it is exclusively economic, then I think it is mistaken.

Q. Tell me what you think about *Smena vekh*, Savinkov and the trial of the SRs.

A. My attitude to the *Smenovekhovtsy* is mainly negative. I have only read their book of essays, and found that it abounded with phrases, but was insufficiently knowledgeable about Russian life. [See Chakhotin's article from *Smena vekh*, document 119.] I agree with its critical attitude to the emigration and foreign attempts to change the course of Russian life by force. I am against what Savinkov is trying to do. I have not been following the trial of the SRs. I think the harsh sentence is mistaken and do not sympathize with it.

Q. Give me your views on Soviet higher education policy and your attitude to the reforms.

A. I am not in sympathy with the policy of the Soviet government regarding higher education in that they violate academic freedom and constrain the freedom of earlier philosophy.

Q. What are your views on the prospects of the Russian émigrés?

A. I think the position of most of them is difficult and, as far as I know, their point of view is based on ignorance and incomprehension of the course of Russian life. I have a negative attitude to partisanship and have never belonged, nor ever will belong, to any party. I do not sympathize with any of the existing parties.

Nikolay Berdyaev
Interrogator: Bakhvalov.

[see Document 124 for source]

Document 123 | The GPU's conclusion on Berdyaev's exile

19 August 1922

I, Bakhvalov, of the 4th Secret Department of the GPU, having investigated Case No. 15564 against Nikolay Aleksandrovich Berdyaev, aged 48 and from a Kiev noble family (temporarily resident in Moscow), find the following:

From the moment of the October revolution to the present he has not only not become reconciled to the worker–peasant government which has existed in Russia for five years but also has not for one moment ceased his anti-Soviet activities. Moreover, Berdyaev actually increased his counter-revolutionary activities at the moment when the RSFSR was facing the greatest external difficulties. . . Therefore, in accordance with para. 2f of the Statute on the GPU of 6 February 1922, in order to prevent further anti-Soviet activities by Nikolay Aleksandrovich Berdyaev, I propose that he be expelled from the territory of the RSFSR *immediately.*

Taking into consideration citizen Berdyaev's request to the GPU collegium to be allowed to go abroad at his own expense, he is to be released for seven days to put his personal and work affairs in order, under obligation to report to the GPU on the expiry of this period and thereafter immediately go abroad. . .

Bakhvalov, Assistant Director of the 4th Secret Division of the GPU

Agreed by I. Reshetov, Director of the 4th Division

Agreed by Samsonov, head of the Secret Division of GPU, and Unshlikht, Dep. Chairman of GPU.

[see Document 124 for source]

Document 124 | From the minutes of the session of the (judicial) collegium of the GPU

21 August 1922

Item: Case No. 15564. Nikolay Aleksandrovich Berdyaev, accused of anti-Soviet activity. Arrested 17 August and held in prison. Report by comrade Bakhvalov. Confirmed by comrade Unshlikht.

Resolved:

In accordance with para. 2f of the Statute on the GPU of 6 February 1922, to be deported from the territory of the RSFSR.

To be released for seven days, under obligation to report to the GPU on the expiry of this period.

Ezerskaya, secretary of GPU

[Source for documents 122–24: V.A. Mazur and M.E. Glavatsky, *Istoriya Rossii 1917–1940* (Ekaterinburg 1993) pp. 201–03.]

The novelist M.A. Osorgin later gave a Kafkaesque account of his deportation.[114] He had been a member of Pomgol and editor of its weekly bulletin, *Pomoshch'*, and was a close friend of Berdyaev, with whose family he was sharing a dacha outside Moscow that summer. He scorned the sheer ignorance of the officials he dealt with, for whom the names of illustrious members of the intelligentsia meant nothing at all.[115] He recalled the absence of any attempt even to pretend his fate hung on legal niceties or evidence, and the expectation that the deportees themselves would form a working group to make the necessary arrangements for their departure. Describing the broken spirit of his colleagues in the Writers' Union, of which he had been vice-president since 1918, he conveyed, too, the gloom and fear that hung over those left behind.

Document 125 | M.A. Osorgin: 'How we were exiled'—from his memoirs

There was a rumour going round Moscow that the leadership was not in complete agreement about exiling us. We knew who was 'for' and who 'against'. It was a pity that Trotsky was 'for'. Later on, when he was exiled himself, he was probably 'against'!

So, after the first wave of panic had passed, many of us were even congratulated: 'You're lucky, you're going abroad.' All the same, as I approached the GPU building, where I had already been imprisoned twice, both in the 'Death Ship' and in the 'Special Section', it was with a sinking feeling. Before, I had been driven there, this time I was walking under my own steam. Yet it turned out that it was not so easy to get into that terrible building voluntarily! 'Where do you think you're going, comrade!'

'I've been called in.'

'Your pass, please!'

'I don't have a pass, somebody rang me and told me to come in.'

'No pass, no entry!'

'But I've come to see the investigator!' They did let me into the offices, but then refused to deal with me for half an hour.

'What are you doing here?!'

I replied quietly, 'You're supposed to be arresting me.'

'We can't without permission.'

'What am I supposed to do then? Go and get permission.' They spent ages tele-

---

114 There is a good collection of Osorgin's fiction and memoirs edited and translated by D.M. Fiene in M.A. Osorgin, *Selected Stories, Reminiscences, and Essays* (Ann Arbor, MI, 1982).

115 Figures for 1920 show over half the officials in the Cheka had no more than elementary education and a bare 1 per cent had higher education. A.L. Litvin, 'The Cheka' in Acton et al. (eds) *Critical Companion* p. 318.

phoning and finally got a bit of paper, and some toy soldier let me in.

We were interrogated in several rooms by several investigators. Apart from the intelligent Reshetov, all of these interrogators were ignorant, arrogant and did not understand us at all; we were just some comrade Berdyaev, or comrade Kizevetter, or Mikhail Novikov.

'What was your job?'

'I was a rector of a university.'

'What are you, a writer? What do you write, then? You say you're a philosopher, but what do you actually do?'

The interrogation was a model of bureaucratic simplicity and logic. Actually, there was nothing to interrogate us about, because we had not been accused of anything. I asked Reshetov, 'What are we actually accused of?'

He replied, 'Just drop it, comrade, it's not important! It's no use asking pointless questions.'

Another investigator shoved a bit of paper at me, saying, 'Sign here to show you've been informed of your detention.'

'No, I'm not signing that. Reshetov told me over the telephone that I did not have to bring my bedding in with me.'

'Just you sign, and you'll see, I'll give you another document.'

In the other document it simply said that on the basis of my interrogation (which had not yet taken place) I had been sentenced to exile abroad for three years. And some article or other had been filled in. 'What interrogation? There hasn't been one!'

'That'll come later, comrade, when we've got time. It will make no difference to you anyway.' Then there was the third document, in which it said simply that, if I agreed to leave at my own expense, I would be released with the obligation to quit the RSFSR within five days. Otherwise I would be kept in the Special Section until deportation.

'How would you like to leave? Voluntarily and at your own expense?'

'I don't want to leave at all.'

He was surprised. 'How can you not want to go abroad? I advise you to go voluntarily, or else you'll be stuck in here for a long time.' There was no argument; I agreed to go voluntarily.

Something else was written down—on a bit of paper our crime was set out: 'Unwillingness to be reconciled and work with Soviet power'.

I think that with regard to the majority of us this accusation was wrong and senseless. Does not submission mean reconciliation? Were any of those academics and writers at that time thinking of plotting and fighting against Soviet power? No, they were thinking about how many herrings they got in their academic rations! Inner intransigence? Well, why did they exile only fifty people out of a hundred million? Unwillingness to work? They all worked as well as they could in their own way, but as for working with the government—it was enough for me to have worked with the Famine Relief Committee created by the government for emergency joint work—it was a matter of luck that I did not end up getting shot.

In short, if you must go, then go, since it has to be done quickly and voluntarily. On the whole, they were quite polite to us; it could have been worse. In an interview with a foreign journalist, Leon Trotsky put it like this: 'We've exiled these people because there were no grounds for execution, but we just couldn't tolerate them.' Again I cannot vouch for the exact words of the then dictator, who was later exiled himself, although there were grounds for executing him.

But it is easy to say 'go'. What about a visa, a passport, transport and foreign currency?

It dragged on for more than a month. The all-powerful GPU proved powerless to help us leave our country 'voluntarily'. Germany would not provide visas if we were being compelled to leave, but promised to provide them quickly if we ourselves requested them. And so it was suggested that we who were about to be exiled form a working group with a chairman, office and delegates. We gathered, had meetings, discussed things and did things. They were obliging enough (how else could they get rid of us?) to provide a car for our representative, issued papers and documents at his request, changed rubles into foreign currency, and provided red passports for us and family members accompanying us. Among us were those with old connections to the business world—only they were able to get a separate carriage in Petersburg, although the GPU insisted on providing an observer, even though he didn't have a ticket; they put him in the next carriage. We got a hotel in Petersburg, and somehow managed to reserve all the decent berths on a German steamer bound for Stettin. All this was very complicated, and the Soviet machine was not geared up for such undertakings at that time. Worried that all this trouble might persuade them to 'liquidate' us instead, we were in a hurry to get away. Meanwhile, we had to survive, get hold of something to eat and sell everything so that we did not arrive in Germany completely penniless. Many begged to be allowed to remain in the RSFSR, but only one or two managed it.

I have made myself describe all this in 'gentle tones'. But I have to add that people were destroying their way of life, leaving behind their libraries and everything that had served them in their work over the years, without which continued intellectual activity was unimaginable, and they were leaving behind friends, like-minded people—and Russia. For many leaving was a real tragedy: no Europe could entice them; their whole life and work was bound up with Russia, a link inseparable from the meaning of life. You cannot express this in gentle tones, so I shall leave it out.

But I shall be less gentle in recalling the last sitting of the Writers' Union a day or two before our departure. A significant proportion of those being exiled were in the Union, and four were on the Board. Our exile did of course upset people and evoked general sympathy, and, of course, it also evoked faint-heartedness—everyone was afraid for himself. Those leaving were busy with things, and I was the only one of them to turn up at the meeting, because I was supposed to be the chairman. There were some minor matters, but we soon dealt with them. On the agenda for the next meeting was the question of replacing resigning members of the Board, especially the two deputy chairmen (N. Berdyaev and me; the chairman, B. Zaytsev, had been sent abroad earlier). Closing the meeting, I thought, 'Now somebody's going to stand up, propose a vote of thanks and ask me to give the Board's greetings to all who are leaving! Five years of working together, almost all the same people, always friendly and always independent! Better left unsaid. The Union must remain, but, even if only for a brief moment, we all desperately need to show our feelings. There's nothing wrong with that, we're all one family!'

Then we stood up and pushed our chairs back. I remember brushing some cigarette ash off my sleeve. Then somebody mumbled, 'Well, there it is!' Then one or two left, with me following slowly behind, and not a word was spoken. In the lobby I hurried to be the first to put my coat on. We had, by the way, said our goodbyes earlier and had even made after-dinner speeches. Anyway, who could even doubt the goodwill of old friends?

[Source: M.A. Osorgin, *Vremena* (Paris 1955) pp. 180–85.]

Just how closely the Politburo was involved in drawing the line between potentially sympathetic *intelligenty* and those regarded as irredeemable—and just how sensitive the Bolshevik leadership remained about the Mensheviks and other rivals embarrassing them despite tightening censorship—can be seen from the following message Lenin sent Stalin during his illness late in 1922. The issue was how to deal with N.A. Rozhkov, a senior Menshevik with whom, as we have seen (documents 58 and 59), Lenin corresponded during the civil war. Lenin insisted that pro-Bolshevik statements made by Rozhkov should not be brandished in the newspapers, be it by Steklov, editor of *Izvestiya*, or anyone else. Such declarations, he acknowledged, had been extracted under pressure from the Petrograd Cheka and its chair, S.A. Messing. With a frankness that would become increasingly rare among the leadership, he drew directly the analogy between Rozhkov's pragmatism and the way in which the Bolsheviks and Mensheviks alike had temporized in the face of Tsarist repression. In particular he recalled the revolutionaries' willingness, in order to take seats in the Tsarist Duma and use it to publicize their ideas, to swear fealty to a monarch and constitution they intended to overthrow.

Document 126 | V.I. Lenin: '... Rozhkov is a man of strong and straight-forward convictions'

For the CC Plenum of 13 December 1922

Comrade Stalin!

To understand our disagreements over Rozhkov correctly, we have to remember that the matter has already been raised several times in the Politburo. On the first occasion Trotsky spoke in favour of putting off exiling Rozhkov. On the second, when, under pressure from Messing, Rozhkov gave us a new formulation of his ideas, Trotsky spoke in favour of exiling him, because he thought that the reformulation was not only worthless, but that it clearly showed the insincerity of Rozhkov's views. I completely agree with Zinoviev that Rozhkov is a man of strong and straightforward convictions, and is deferring to us in his dealings with Messing and making all sorts of declarations against the Mensheviks solely for precisely the same reasons that we once pledged allegiance to the Tsar on entering the State Duma. So, if we ask Steklov or anybody else to make use of Rozhkov's declarations (e.g., as a 'challenge' to the Mensheviks), firstly, it will not hit the target and, secondly, it will put us to shame, because the Mensheviks will say straight out that they, just like us, always argued in favour of signing under pressure any oath of allegiance: in such a 'duel' with the Mensheviks we would be the losers.

This is what I propose: firstly, exile Rozhkov abroad; secondly, if this does not happen (e.g., because Rozhkov deserves mercy for reasons of age), there should be no public discussion about broadcasting declarations extracted from Rozhkov under duress. In that case, we shall just have to wait, albeit for a few years, until Rozhkov makes a sincere declaration in our favour. Until then I would suggest sending him to, say, Pskov, where he can be made comfortable and given a job. But he needs to be kept under strict supervision, because this is a man who is our enemy, and will probably remain so to the end of his days.

Lenin. Recorded over the telephone by Lidiya Fotieva.

[Source: RGASPI, fond 2, opis' 2, delo 1344, p. 1 ob.]

The 'fellow travellers' and the party in the 1920s

For those non-party *intelligenty* who were permitted to continue publishing in the USSR, the dilemmas of the 1920s were acute. That they had been spared exile suggested they retained some room for independent work; on the other hand, the party's tolerance of dissent was clearly severely limited. These 'fellow travellers' of the proletarian revolution, as Trotsky labelled them, were represented in every cultural sphere from fine art and theatre to history and social science. The following letter from A.V. Chayanov, a highly original agrarian economist specializing in the study of the peasantry, points to the narrow line they trod. Chayanov was one of the few prominent members of Pomgol to remain at liberty after its closure in summer 1921. During the mid-1920s he and a group of non-Marxist agronomists developed an analysis of rural Russia that directly contradicted Marxist analyses. They insisted on the stability of the self-employed family farm of the 'middle peasant'; they denied that its prevalence was being undermined by the market or that the middle peasantry was polarizing between kulaks and poor peasants; and they underlined the potential for rural economic development without collectivization. Only at the end of the decade, when debate over 'kulak sabotage', rural differentiation and the urgency of collectivization became politically explosive, was he forced to abandon this work, which a generation later was taken up with enthusiasm in western historiography and sociology.[116]

Chayanov's letter is written to E.D. Kuskova, another prominent member of Pomgol, but one of the many who had been deported in 1922—having narrowly escaped execution earlier in the year for supposedly using the Committee as a base for spying on behalf of foreign enemies. She was now living in Berlin. Like Chayanov, Kuskova and her husband, S.N. Prokopovich, who as we have seen (document 26) was a member of Kerensky's government in 1917, were champions of the co-operative movement, which they saw as the prime vehicle for rural economic development. Here Chayanov expresses his hope that non-Marxist economists like himself will at least for the time being have scope to criticize government economic policy; he envisages highlighting the vital contribution made by non-party *intelligenty*; and he speculates that the regime's eagerness to encourage and give confidence to western investment, which he regards as sure to grow, might lead it to allow some non-party figures into government.

Document 127 | A.V. Chayanov to E.D. Kuskova on economic 'intervention'

1923

If we are still dreaming of saving Russia, then we have to intervene. But how to intervene and what to intervene with—that is the difficult thing to fathom. On a small scale, we probably can. By this I mean journalism. Russia and the USSR have to be clearly and firmly distinguished. We have to measure the processes under way in the economy and the assistance given to these processes by the intelligentsia

---

116 Chayanov's work was brought to the attention of the English-speaking world in the 1960s. See D. Thorner, B. Kerblay and R.E.F. Smith (eds) *A.V. Chayanov on the Theory of Peasant Economy* (Homewood, IL, 1966).

working with the Soviet government. . . We need objectivity, which will show more clearly how the Soviet government is hampering economic growth—this is something we shall do as long as we can. . . Yet this is all small beer. It is not satisfactory and does not bring the end any nearer. As for what to do on a grander scale I have no idea. This is what still rather vaguely occurs to me: I shall write about intervention—not military but economic. In the future the penetration of foreign capital seems inevitable. We cannot extricate ourselves on our own. . . This kind of intervention has got stronger, since with a money economy in Russia pressure from the West will always be more real. If the *chervonets* is to be quoted in the West, any stable bank could threaten and cause alarm. This is much more frightening than Wrangel' or any military campaigns! Should we not also make use of these economic opportunities opening up to the West? Should we not add political concessions to the economic concessions we are making to the West, which might mean that one by one non-Soviet people, albeit working within Soviets, enter the Soviet government? How can we put this into practice? We have to agree among ourselves, i.e., all those who understand what to do in Russia and can accept the new Russia. We need private influence on Western statesmen. . .

[Source: GARF, fond 5865, opis' 1, delo 548, pp. 3–6.]

During the mid-1920s there was widely publicized controversy over the role of 'fellow travellers', the latitude they should be allowed, and the extent to which the party should be forging a distinctive 'proletarian' culture. Pressure for the party to adopt a more militant policy came from various groups of activists sympathetic to the now enfeebled *Proletkul't*, though unlike Bogdanov and his supporters they strongly favoured the assertion of direct party control over culture. Most vocal were writers and critics belonging to the so-called All-Union Association of Proletarian Writers (VAPP). High culture, they argued, was as much a site for class struggle as the economy itself. Just as bourgeois political and economic power were being superseded by that of the proletariat, so the artistic and intellectual domination of cultural works permeated by capitalist individualism must be broken by work expressing the collectivism of the socialist world view. It was intolerable that bourgeois *intelligenty* should continue to be given scope to publicize their class-alien ideas. Resources should be concentrated on supporting party intellectuals committed to developing the literature, art, history and social science essential to consolidating proletarian hegemony.

This was not the view of Lunacharsky and the leadership of the Commissariat of Enlightenment, nor was it shared by members of the Politburo, all of whom became involved in the debate, Lenin, Trotsky and Bukharin most energetically. They were less confident about there being the potential, in the foreseeable future, for a specifically proletarian high culture; they underlined how brief a time the proletariat, especially in backward Tsarist Russia, had had in which to develop such a culture; they urged the priority of providing mass education rather than cultural experimentation; and though they concurred on silencing actively hostile intellectuals, they emphasized the use the party could make of the abilities of fellow travellers.

The flavour of the conflict can be sampled from the following exchange in spring 1924 at one of a number of discussions on the issue. P.N. Sakulin, one of the best-known pre-revolutionary intellectuals to affiliate himself closely with the party, argued the case for latitude for academics and intellectuals. Confident that his own loyalty was not in question and rather disingenuously asserting that most academics and intellectuals broadly supported the new regime, he made the classic liberal case that freedom of debate would maximize intellectual progress. In a manner that was rapidly becoming standard practice for all sides in any debate, he eagerly cited Lenin in confirmation of his view.

Document 128 | P.N. Sakulin: Contribution to the debate on the future of the intelligentsia

6 April 1924

I mainly have in mind the psychology of academics. For them creative freedom has always been dearest. . . In his mental work the intellectual must feel free. If not, his life loses all meaning.

Despite its victory the Party could not expect or demand an instant change of heart from them. I think the intelligentsia would demean itself if it were immediately to jump on the victor's bandwagon. The intelligentsia were psychologically on the side of the Revolution, but were waiting to see what practical conditions would be created for their creative work. Their attitude to the new system depended on how their working conditions changed. Even those who were able to grasp the great meaning of what was happening, and were ready to play whatever part they could in the creation of the new life, could not avoid attaching importance to the conditions necessary for them to carry out their tasks in life. To be historically fair, one must admit that during War Communism, which has since been abolished in the course of events, the position of the intelligentsia was very difficult. I remember the agitation in intellectual circles after the publication of the well-known appeal to academics [in *Kommunisticheskiy trud*, 14 December 1920]. It is a very valuable document. It spoke about the high goals the worker–peasants' government set itself. These goals were not rejected by at least the majority of those to whom the appeal was directed. However, it abolished the freedom of academic teaching and research, and instituted an ideological and methodological dictatorship. Its authors justified their standpoint as transitional, and hoped that, once the class struggle on Earth ceased, the restrictions would no longer be necessary. But we have to work, i.e., think, right now. The demands set out were in profound conflict with the psychology of scientific creativity. From the history of human civilization we know that external pressure on creative thought has never brought the desired results. This is not just some liberal slogan, but an indisputable axiom. . .

Anatoliy Vasil'evich Lunacharsky has said that recent government policy could be formulated in Vladimir Il'ich Lenin's words: it should operate not by compelling people, but by convincing them. We (in so far as I have the right to speak for a certain part of the intelligentsia) warmly welcome such a principle. This is the only correct method of influence when it is a matter of such complex phenomena as academic and artistic work. A particular ideology naturally aims for supremacy and will use all means at its disposal. But it should win not by external compulsion but by its intrinsic superiority. One must not claim a monopoly on truth. It cannot be decreed, but must be developed and broadcast. This is particularly true in relation to university and higher education, which is all about teaching, research and academic competition. We have to believe that young working-class students will be able consciously and critically to make sense of what they are being taught. If there are disputed questions in the academic world, let them be mulled over by the young. It is much safer because in the end life is stronger than lesser ideologies. History and the logic of life will prevail. We must put an end to the prejudice often found in the actions of ruling groups and surround the intelligentsia with an atmosphere of trust. . .

[Source: *Sud'by sovremennoy russkoy intelligentsii* (Moscow 1925) pp. 14–19.]

The relative openness of the mid-1920s was reflected by Sakulin's speech being published along with other contributions. However, his view was scorned even by party heavyweights wary of the militant line of VAPP. Bukharin, whose star was then in the ascendant, was scathing about Sakulin's style and language, with its traditional 'self-deceiving' rhetoric about serving the people, and false notion that there could be a class-neutral form of culture and education. He rejected any implication that somewhere—in Tsarist Russia, under the Provisional Government, in a society dominated by bourgeois power—there had been greater effective freedom than in the USSR. All social orders impose constraints on ideas that are hostile to them, he argued, and the logical extension of Sakulin's line would be to offer freedom even to the militantly monarchist, anti-Semitic and anti-socialist 'Black Hundred' gangs of the late Tsarist period. In particular Bukharin repudiated the case for removing constraints on the academic and cultural elite. Whereas a humble village schoolteacher, still equipped with nothing but the books of the nineteenth-century Tsarist educational reformer K.D. Ushinsky, might sincerely believe education had nothing to do with politics and class conflict, it was hardly possible for an eminent professor to do so.

Document 129 | N.I. Bukharin: Contribution to the debate on the future of the intelligentsia

6 April 1924

We know full well and are not afraid to say that at the beginning of the October Revolution it was the worst part of the intelligentsia that came over to our side, along with some of the most highly qualified, such as Timiryazev, who was exceptional in the breadth of his thought. But such white ravens could be counted on the fingers of one hand. Most of the honest intelligentsia were against us. Why? Because they shared the views which the esteemed Pavel Nikitich [Sakulin] here still holds. . . He asks: Where did you begin? You encroached upon the freedom of academic research. But was there academic freedom under the tsar? I ask you, how many Bolshevik professors were there even under Kerensky? How did you understand freedom of research? You understood freedom of research within the bounds of those concepts and systems the sociological structure of which was tolerable to the prevailing order. But just think, within the bounds of our regime we permit freedom of research. From this point of view we have just the same bounds, so why do you say that was freedom and this is not?

   P.N. Sakulin tells us that we consider it our duty to propagate particular views and that we want the hegemony of Marxism. And I ask you, why do you think we are trying to implant ourselves in one field after another, until we can take them over? Because we have a very powerful weapon in our hands, which will enable us to build what we want. Why did the tsarist government permit all sorts of values, but simply would not tolerate Marxist ones? Was it not because they were a time bomb under the old order? We can allow some village school-mistress, who has seen nothing but a pair of old boots and Ushinsky's books, to say in her defence that she was just doing cultural work, but when an eminent professor says that he does not count, is remote from politics and should be allowed to teach against Marxism, it is not acceptable because it has not been thought through. Freedom to teach is, one might say, a kind of sophistry, because it is not just a matter of individual propositions or facts. When it is a matter of elaborating a world view, we come up against the fact that this system is a particular instrument which not only develops on a particular base but also serves as a means of struggle. . . In the ideological skirmish which is taking place here, there are differing approaches to a class matter. The whole of Pavel Nikitich's speech from start to finish was full of fetishistic concepts and old phraseology. Forgive me, but I simply cannot stomach such phraseology. 'The people', and 'we want to serve the people'. They are all empty words. When you talk about 'the people', I must ask you what you mean by 'the people'; when you talk about 'good', I must ask you what you mean by 'good'; when you talk about 'freedom', are you also demanding freedom for the Black Hundreds? (Applause.)

You say that now you would not find a single person who would say he is working against us; even with a secret ballot we would probably get a majority. So, you conclude, give us creative freedom. But I have to say clearly that in our scheme of things, our fundamental concern is correct leadership. We will never be able to adopt the position that everything can sort itself out, and if people want to believe in God, then let them. That is not how to run the country. We do not have a communist society yet, and until we do, we are obliged to concern ourselves with the fate of the country. We do not want to apply the *Smena vekh* brakes. Everybody must be made to realize that those ideologues who think that communism will retreat are wrong. That we will never do! We will never give up our communist goals! We need the intelligentsia cadres to be trained ideologically in a particular way. Yes, we will turn out intellectuals, we will manufacture them, just as in a factory. I am saying that if we have set ourselves the task of attaining communism, then we must imbue everything decisively with that goal. Comrade Sakulin says that we must raise educated people. That is right. But not just educated people, but the sort of educated people who will work for communism. Tell me, is there any regime which would not do the same? Where would you find educational institutions—higher, secondary or elementary—which are not producing a certain type of cadre? Such countries and such educational institutions do not exist. The only distinction is that we are training different people to build a different kind of system. We think like builders or architects, and not like people who say that one should keep out of politics.

[Source: *Sud'by sovremennoy russkoy intelligentsii* pp. 20–29.]

Bukharin pulled no punches on the role of the party and its unswerving commitment (contrary to the idle hopes of the *smenovekhovtsy*) to building a new socialist society. The party, guided by its scientific understanding of social development, would fulfil its vanguard role and consciously forge new intellectuals imbued with revolutionary Marxist ideology. On the other hand, however, while Bukharin was much more sympathetic than the rest of the Politburo to the notion that ultimately a distinctive proletarian high culture would emerge, he would not lend his support to VAPP and those demanding that a tightly drawn new orthodoxy be immediately imposed on literature and culture in general.[117] Although authentically proletarian and socialist culture would in the end prevail, it would take time to form. For now, he insisted that just as under NEP socialist forms of production must

---

117 S. Cohen, *Bukharin* pp. 201–08; see J. Biggart, 'Bukharin's Theory of Cultural Revolution' in A. Kemp-Welch (ed.) *The Ideas of Nikolai Bukharin* (Oxford 1992) pp. 148–58, for a less sympathetic view of Bukharin.

exert their superiority in competition with private production, so competing views on and forms of literature should be permitted. The formal resolution on literature, which was drafted by Bukharin and adopted by the Central Committee and published in July 1925, drew an analogy with the party's approach to the family. That summer saw the early stages of a prolonged debate and widespread consultation through local soviets over a new Family Code which envisaged the imposition of no one model. However, no amount of protest, especially from peasant women and married women, would deflect the party from pressing its vision of female emancipation. The new Code further weakened the status of marriage, making divorce even easier than under the reforms of 1918 and conferring the same property and alimony rights on women in de facto as in legal marriages.[118] Likewise, where literature was concerned, the 'free competition' encouraged came with the proviso, underlined in the resolution, that throughout it was for the party to set the bounds beyond which 'freedom' became counter-revolutionary.

Document 130 | From the Central Committee resolution on literature

1 July 1925

. . . 4. So long as the class struggle in general does not cease in our country, it will certainly not cease on the literary front. In class society there neither is, nor can there be, any neutral art, although the class content of art in general, and of literature in particular, can take infinitely more diverse forms than, for example, the class content of politics. . .

6. The proletariat, while conserving, strengthening and extending its leadership, must occupy corresponding positions in a whole range of new sectors of the ideological front. The penetration of dialectical materialism into completely new areas (biology, psychology, the natural sciences in general) has already begun. In the same way, sooner or later positions will need to be won in the sphere of literature.

7. It should, however, be borne in mind that this task is infinitely more complicated than the other tasks to be solved by the proletariat. Within the confines of capitalist society the working class could prepare itself for a victorious revolution, build its cadres of leaders and develop a magnificent ideological weapon for political struggle. But it could neither solve scientific or technical questions, nor could it, as a culturally oppressed class, develop its own literature, its own artistic form, its own style. If the proletariat already has infallible criteria for assessing the socio-political content of any literary work, it still does not have definite answers to all questions concerning artistic form.

---

118 See Siegelbaum, *Soviet State and Society* pp. 149–56, on western analysis of the debate and Code.

8. The above considerations should determine the policy of the leading party of the proletariat in the field of literature. First and foremost, they are concerned with the following questions: the relationship between proletarian writers, peasant writers and the so-called 'fellow travellers' and others; party policy towards the proletarian writers themselves; questions of criticism; questions of style and form in artistic productions and ways of devising new artistic forms; and, finally, questions of an organizational nature. . .

12. The above, overall, determines the tasks of *criticism*, which is one of the major educational tools in the hands of the party. Without relinquishing the positions of communism for one minute, nor retreating a single step from proletarian ideology, revealing the objective class content of various literary works, communist criticism should struggle relentlessly against counter-revolutionary phenomena in literature, and unmask *Smena vekh*-ist liberalism, etc. At the same time it should display the greatest tact, caution and patience towards all those literary strata which might side with the proletariat and those who will do so. Communist criticism must exclude from its language any sense of issuing literary commands. This criticism will have a deep educational significance only when it relies upon its *ideological* supremacy. Marxist criticism must decisively drive out all pretentious, semi-literate and self-satisfied communist arrogance from its midst. Marxist criticism must set itself the task of study, and must rebuff all tendencies towards hack writing and ad libbing in its own midst.

13. While it can discern without error the social and class content of literary currents, the party as a whole certainly must not bind itself to any particular tendency in the area of *literary form*. In guiding literature as a whole, the party cannot support any particular literary faction (defining these factions in terms of differences in their views on form and style) any more than it can pass resolutions to determine the structure of the family, although it certainly leads and must lead the construction of the new way of life in general. A style conforming to the epoch will be created, but it will be created by different methods, and the solution to this question is not yet apparent. Any attempts to commit the party in this direction in the current phase of the country's cultural development should be rejected.

14. For these reasons the party should express itself in favour of free competition between various groupings and currents in this field. Any other solution to this question would be a state-bureaucratic pseudo-solution. Similarly, any party resolution or decree granting a legal monopoly on literary publishing to any particular group or literary organization would be just as inadmissible. While giving material and moral support to proletarian and proletarian–peasant literature and helping 'fellow travellers', etc., the party cannot grant a monopoly to any one group, even if it were the most proletarian in its ideological content. That would ruin proletarian literature first and foremost.

[Source: *Izvestiya TsK RKP(b)* No. 25–26, 1925, pp. 8–9.]

The controversy surrounding the intelligentsia, technical and cultural alike, was carried on with copious references to the wider tensions within the leadership over the direction of NEP. During the mid-1920s, partisans of VAPP were freely labelled 'Trotskyists' and accused of sharing the adventurism of the Left Opposition. As heavy emphasis on gradualism and a 'snail's pace' approach to socialism began to lose favour from 1926 and 1927, however, militancy against the intelligentsia gathered momentum. From 1928, both the cultural and the technical intelligentsia were to be caught up in a series of show trials, wave upon wave of denunciation and purge, and a so-called 'cultural revolution'.

11

Church and State

Lenin's caution over attacks on religion

As we have seen, the Bolshevik regime was deeply contemptuous of the ideas, the rituals and the social deference of Russian Orthodoxy, and within weeks of the October revolution the Church was disestablished. The evident sympathy of many priests and bishops for the White cause during the civil war, and the active support of a minority, deepened hostility between government and hierarchy. However, while regarding the clergy as equivalent to the most reactionary elements of the cultural intelligentsia, high-ranking Bolsheviks were cautious about how best to eradicate the religious loyalties of the laity. They regarded popular faith—'the opium of the people', as Marx had called it—as the product of ignorance, Tsarist and bourgeois repression, and the malign influence of the clergy, and something from which it was the party's role and duty to liberate the masses. On occasion, Lenin and his colleagues had no compunction about recommending the exemplary massacre of priests. But they were well aware that attempting simply to suppress the Church could prove counterproductive, and rather than weakening the prestige and influence of the clergy was liable to arouse sympathy.[119]

During the civil war, with the Whites attempting to win peasant support by advertising their alliance with the Church, it had seemed foolhardy for the new regime to go out of its way to offend popular religious sensibilities. The new party programme adopted in March 1919 urged party activists to campaign to overcome popular religious prejudice but to tread carefully and avoid feeding religious illusions by handling the matter abrasively. Equally, it seemed unwise to add fuel to the waves of popular unrest which broke out as the White threat receded and which triggered the adoption of NEP.

---

119 On the evolution of the new regime's approach, see A. Lukkanen, *The Party of Unbelief: The religious policy of the Bolshevik Party, 1917–1921* (Helsinki 1994).

Although popular respect for the Orthodox clergy had declined steeply in the late Tsarist period, and the Church's hold had been steadily eroded by new sects and rival Christian denominations as well as the resilience of the Old Believers, religious faith and practice were deeply rooted among the overwhelming majority of the Russian peasantry.[120] The case for caution seemed even greater in non-Russian areas brought back under Soviet power where minority national and ethnic loyalties were closely bound up with native religious institutions and traditions—notably those of the independent eastern-rite churches of Georgia and Armenia as well as Islam in Azerbaidzhan and Central Asia.

Rank-and-file Bolshevik attitudes, however, especially in Komsomol and among party members who had served in the Red Army, tended to be more strident than those of the leadership, especially where Russian Orthodoxy was concerned. The following memo sent by Lenin to Molotov and the Central Committee's Secretariat reflects this dialogue over tactics. In 1921, the period of Easter, the most sacred feast in the Orthodox calendar, celebrated even by those with little formal contact with the Church, coincided with 1 May, international labour day, which the new regime had proclaimed a national holiday. Lenin was anxious to ensure that party activists did not use the coincidence to lampoon and denigrate religion.

Document 131 | V.I. Lenin: '... avoid at all costs offending religion'

Sometime between 9 and 21 April 1921

Comrade Molotov,

If I am not mistaken, there was a letter or CC circular in the papers about May Day that said, 'Unmask the lies of religion', or some such thing. We must not do that. It is not very tactful. Precisely around Easter we must recommend something else: do not unmask lies, but avoid at all costs offending religion. You need to put out another letter or circular. If the Secretariat does not agree, then take it to the Politburo.

[Source: V.I. Lenin, *Polnoe sobranie sochineniy* Volume LII (Moscow 1965) p. 140.]

Lenin was conscious that there would be those in the Secretariat who would disagree with him. Rather than simply instruct Molotov, he gave him the option of referring the issue to the Politburo—though in practice, as was usually the case, Lenin's word was enough, and the Secretariat acted promptly.

---

120 On the pre-revolutionary period, see G. Freeze, *The Parish Clergy in Nineteenth-Century Russia: Crisis, reform, counter-reform* (Princeton 1983).

How far activists were able or willing to stick to the narrow line Lenin urged is another matter. The revised circular's claim about the growing popularity of May Day in the countryside appears to have been sheer bravado.

Document 132 | Instruction from the RKP(b) CC to all *guberniya* committees to avoid offending mass religious sentiments

21 April 1921

The CC considers it necessary to address all Party organizations once again on the matter of May Day. While organizing it, emphasizing its international character and pointing out how different May Day is in Soviet Russia from other countries, special attention must be paid to the fact that this is a people's holiday, which involves not only the conscious cadres of the urban working class, organized in the Party trade unions, but also the countryside. The history of this festival in Russia shows that the rural population has been taking an increasing part in it, thereby showing solidarity with the urban working class and strengthening ties between rural labourers and the proletariat. Precisely because the May Day holiday is taking on this character in our country, we must take care to avoid anything on that day which might alienate us from the broad working masses. As May Day coincides with the first day of the Christian Easter, the CC is reminding you under no circumstances to permit any action which would offend the religious sentiments of the mass of the population. This instruction applies in both town and country. May Day must become, and will become, a festival for the toiling peasantry. The sooner this happens, the greater will be our support from this peasantry.

[Source: *Pravda*, 21 April 1921.]

Famine and the campaign to confiscate Church property

The following year there was a head-on clash between the hierarchy and the regime. In the face of the mass famine of 1921–22, the government decided—with anything but reluctance—to requisition Church valuables to fund famine relief and the purchase of emergency grain from abroad. The decree authorizing the confiscation ordered that it be done systematically and openly, that parishioners be permitted to witness the confiscation, and that accounts be published to demonstrate that the funds released were to be devoted entirely to famine relief.

Document 133 | VTsIK resolution on confiscating Church property

26 February 1922

Because of the desperate need rapidly to mobilize all the country's resources which can be used to battle with the famine in the Volga region and get the fields sown, the All-Russia Central Executive Committee, in addition to the decree on the confiscation of museum property, has resolved:

1. Within one month of the publication of this decree, local soviets are to take from Church property granted for use by groups of believers from all religions on the basis of inventories and agreements all valuable items made from gold, silver and precious stones, the confiscation of which will not substantially affect worship, and transfer them to the People's Commissariat for Finance especially for the Central Famine Relief Committee.

2. In order that this measure be carried out according to plan, and the above-mentioned valuables registered accurately and transferred to the organs of the People's Commissariat of Finance expressly for the Central Famine Relief Committee, commissions are to be formed in every *guberniya* made up of responsible representatives of the *guberniya* executive committee, the *guberniya* department for famine relief and the *guberniya* finance department, under the chairmanship of a member of VTsIK.

3. The examination of the agreements and the actual removal of the precious items according to the inventories is to take place in the presence of representatives of the groups of believers to whom the use of the above-mentioned property had been granted.

4. The confiscated property is to be placed in a special fund and in a special account and is to be used exclusively to help the starving, as set out in the special instruction devised by the Central Famine Relief Committee in agreement with the People's Commissariat for Finance and the Commission for Registering, Confiscating and Collecting Valuables.

5. The Central Famine Relief Committee will periodically publish details in the press of all items confiscated from Church property and how they have been spent. The local press must publish an itemized list of valuables confiscated from local churches, chapels, synagogues, etc., specifying the churches.

[Source: *Izvestiya*, 26 February 1922.]

The Patriarch roundly condemned the decree, his epistle appearing in the Church's increasingly impoverished and restricted gazette. The government had paid scant attention to his efforts to encourage collections for famine relief, and had denounced the hierarchy for its supposed selfish hoarding of wealth and callous disregard for mass hunger. The sticking point on which

Tikhon focused was the issue of chalices and other consecrated articles. To sell them and thus allow them to be misused and abused was to break Church law, to desecrate holy things and to commit sacrilege.

Document 134 | Patriarch Tikhon: Epistle 'To All the Orthodox Faithful'

28 February 1922

Amid all the terrible misfortunes and sufferings heaped upon our land for our lawlessness, the greatest and most awful is the famine which has gripped a huge area with millions of inhabitants.

As long ago as August 1921 rumours of this terrifying disaster were reaching me, so I, considering it my duty to come to the aid of my suffering flock, sent an epistle to the heads of the individual Christian Churches—the Orthodox patriarchs, the Pope, the Archbishop of Canterbury and the Bishop of New York—calling upon them in Christian love to begin collecting money and provisions, and send them to those starving in the Volga regions. It was then that I founded the All-Russia Church Famine Relief Committee and in all churches and among believers collections were begun to help the starving. But such a Church organization was branded as superfluous by the Soviet government, which demanded that all the funds gathered be handed over to the government committee. However, in December the government proposed that money and food donations be collected to help the starving through the Church administrative bodies (the Holy Synod, the Supreme Church Council, the Diocesan Council and the Rural and Parish Council).

Wishing to render all possible assistance to the starving in the Volga regions, I found it possible to allow rural and parish councils and communities to sacrifice for the starving valuable ornaments and non-liturgical objects. The Orthodox population was informed of this on 13 February this year by a special appeal, which the government allowed to be published and distributed among the people. But immediately after this, following harsh attacks in the government press on the spiritual leaders of the Church, on 26 February VTsIK decreed the confiscation of all Church valuables to help the starving, including consecrated vessels and liturgical items. From the Church's point of view such an act is an act of sacrilege, and I consider it my sacred duty to explain the Church's attitude to this act and also inform the faithful. Because of extreme circumstances I have permitted the sacrifice of unconsecrated and non-liturgical Church items. Even now I call upon all believers to make such sacrifices, with the proviso that they come from love of one's neighbour and will prove to be of real help to our starving brothers. But I cannot approve of the removal of consecrated items from churches, even through voluntary sacrifice. Their use for non-liturgical purposes is forbidden by Canon Law and punishable, as sacrilege, by excommunication for lay members or defrocking for priests.

[Source: *Tserkovnye vedomosti* No. 6–7, 1922, p. 2.]

When confiscations began, there were instances of vigorous obstruction by priests and laity: in Petrograd, the Metropolitan followed Tikhon's injunction and was arrested and subsequently executed for leading the resistance. For a moment the regime hesitated, the Central Committee issuing instructions to regional committees for a pause to allow activists to persuade parishioners to accept that the confiscations were necessary.

Document 135 | **'In view of the difficulties which have arisen…'—coded telegram from Moscow to the Urals Office of the RKP(b) CC**

Moscow, 19 March 1922

A copy to go to the Ekaterinburg *guberniya* committee.

In view of the difficulties which have arisen in the matter of confiscating Church valuables the CC proposes that, until further instructions from the CC, the confiscation of Church valuables be halted. At present all efforts should be concentrated on preparatory and explanatory agitational work. The CC will send further directives on 20 March.

Molotov
Secretary of the RKP(b) CC

[Source: V.A. Mazur and M.E. Glavatsky, *Istoriya Rossii 1917–1940*, p. 226.]

However, in Lenin's view the resistance cast the hierarchy in the worst possible light and ensured it would not be supported by most peasants. He therefore saw this as an ideal moment to cut away the authority of the clergy. His enthusiasm has been interpreted by some historians as evidence that the purpose of the confiscation was to legitimize an offensive against the Church.[121] Lenin's reference to the regime's desperate shortage of funds and the need to present a plausible front at the international conference in progress at Genoa, and his evident expectation of huge takings from wealthy monasteries, suggest otherwise. But certainly he was eager to inflict maximum damage on the Church, explicitly endorsing Machiavelli's advice about the need for brutal government measures to be as swift and harsh as possible.[122]

121　D. Pospielovsky, *The Russian Church under the Soviet Regime* (New York 1984) Vol. I, pp. 93–99. See Pospielovsky's three-volume *History of Soviet Atheism in Theory and Practice, and the Believer* (London 1987–88) for the Church's ordeal under the Soviet regime.

122　Robert Service cites this as one of the instances in which Lenin's violence may have been exacerbated by his ill health—he was too ill to attend the Politburo the following day. Service, *Lenin: A political life* III, pp. 246–47.

His call for the chair and deputy chair of the GPU, Dzerzhinsky and Unshlikht, to give the Politburo weekly briefings on the activities of the Patriarch foreshadowed Tikhon's subsequent house arrest. He was insistent that Trotsky, who was in charge of anti-religious propaganda, should not be publicly identified with the process in any way for fear the clergy would make use of Trotsky's Jewishness to manipulate peasant anti-Semitism. He saw M.I. Kalinin, the senior party figure with the most authentic Russian peasant background, as the ideal spokesman.

Document 136 | V.I. Lenin: 'Now is the time to teach this lot...'

19 March 1922

TOP SECRET

Under no circumstances are copies to be made and every member of the Politburo, as well as comrade Kalinin, is to make comments on the document itself.

It is now, and only now, when people are being eaten in the famine areas and hundreds, if not thousands, of corpses are strewn along the roads, that we can (and so must!) confiscate Church valuables with merciless, unrelenting energy, without shrinking from crushing whatever resistance we meet. It is now, and only now, that the vast majority of peasants are either for us or at least are not capable of supporting at all decisively that handful of Black-Hundred priests and reactionary urban middle-class types who are able to, and want to, try a policy of violent resistance to the Soviet decree.

We must at all costs conduct the confiscations of Church valuables as decisively and quickly as possible, thereby ensuring ourselves a fund of several hundred million gold rubles, bearing in mind the colossal wealth of some monasteries. Without this fund any state work in general, any economic construction in particular, and any defence of our position at Genoa are completely unthinkable...

A sensible writer on matters of state correctly observed that, if attaining a certain political goal necessitates resorting to a series of cruel acts, they should be undertaken as energetically as possible in the shortest possible time, because the people will not tolerate cruelty over a long period...

So I have come to the definite conclusion that now is the time to inflict the most decisive and merciless defeat on the Black-Hundred clergy and crush it. I would envisage our plan of action as something like this:

Any such measures should be officially announced only by comrade Kalinin. Not at any time or under any circumstances should comrade Trotsky publicize it either in the press or in any other way. The telegram already sent out by the Politburo about a temporary halt to confiscations should not be rescinded. It is useful to us because it will make our opponents think that we are vacillating and that they have managed to scare us off. (Of course, our enemy will find out about the secret telegram soon enough, precisely because it is supposed to be secret.). . . I think it expedient not to touch Patriarch Tikhon himself, although he undoubtedly stands at the head of this whole slave-owners' revolt. As for him, we must send a secret directive to the GPU, so that all this character's connections are observed and revealed as accurately and fully as possible, particularly at the present moment. Dzerzhinsky and Unshlikht must report on this to the Politburo in person once a week.

At the Party congress we should set up a secret meeting of all or almost all delegates together with the head personnel from the GPU, the People's Commissariat for Justice and the Revolutionary Tribunal. At this meeting there should be a secret congress resolution saying that the confiscation of valuables, especially from the wealthiest monasteries and churches, must be done with merciless decisiveness, not flinching from anything, and as rapidly as possible. The greater the number of reactionary priests and bourgeois we manage to shoot in this campaign, the better. Now is the time to teach this lot that they had better not even think about putting up any resistance to us for decades to come.

To see that these measures are carried out as swiftly and successfully as possible, at the congress, that is, at the secret meeting, we should appoint without publicity a special commission, which must include comrades Trotsky and Kalinin, to make sure it is in charge of the whole operation, while running it, not in the name of the commission, but of the Party and government as a whole. The very best and most responsible Party workers are to be appointed to carry out the job in the wealthiest monasteries and churches. . .

[Source: RGASPI, fond 2, opis´ 1, delo 22947.]

The orders duly sent out across the country by Molotov four days later closely followed Lenin's instructions. Unlike the TsIK decree published in February, by which soviet bodies were given the key role, here the emphasis was explicitly on the local party secretary, the secret police, and Agitprop, the Secretariat's agitation and propaganda section, which was charged with preparing the ground. Lenin's concern that Trotsky be kept out of the limelight was matched by the Secretariat's euphemistic instruction that the 'national composition' of official commissions should not be such as to feed chauvinism, i.e., should include no Jews. In line with Lenin's insistence since the revolution that the party should try not to offend the religious sensibilities of ordinary peasants, there was special emphasis on proceeding with care in poor rural parishes. And, to maximize support from parishioners and such priests as might be won over, the issue of famine relief was throughout to be kept centre-stage.

Document 137 | **'Set up secret organizing commissions for confiscating valuables...'—coded telegram from Moscow to the Urals Bureau of the RKP CC at Ekaterinburg**

Sent 23 March, received 24 March 1922

Top secret. In addition to the telegram of 19 March you are to set about the unswerving and immediate implementation of the CC of the RKP's resolution of 20 March.

1. Set up secret organizing commissions for confiscating valuables in the *gubernii* immediately, which must certainly include either the *guberniya* committee secretary or the head of Agitprop, and also a brigade or divisional commissar or head of the political section. Please note: In the most important *gubernii* the confiscations are to take place as quickly as possible, but in less important ones later on, after the news about confiscations in the Petrograd and central *gubernii* has spread all over Russia.

2. Alongside these secret preparatory commissions set up official commissions or departments attached to the Famine Relief Committees for formal receipt of valuables by agreement with groups of believers and the like. Make very sure that the national composition of the official commissions gives no cause for chauvinistic agitation.

3. In every *guberniya* conduct an unofficial week of agitation and preliminary organization for confiscation of valuables, combining it as far as possible with the two-week campaign for aid to the starving. Choose the best agitators and, in particular soldiers. The nature of the agitation should have nothing to do with the struggle against religion and the Church, but should be directed entirely towards helping the starving. At the same time create a split among the clergy by encouraging decisive initiatives from, and by giving state protection to, those priests who come out in favour of confiscation...

4. If necessary, especially if Black-Hundred agitation goes too far, organize a demonstration, involving armed soldiers, with banners with something like 'Church valuables—to save lives of the starving' on them. As far as possible do not touch eminent priests, but get the *guberniya* political section to send them official warning that, if there are any excesses, they will be the first to answer for them.

5. Alongside agitational work there must be organizational work: preparing the necessary apparatus to record the confiscated material so that this work is completed in the shortest possible time. It would be best to start the confiscations from a church where there is a loyal priest. If there is no such priest, start from the most important church, having got everything thoroughly ready beforehand (post communists on all neighbouring streets, do not allow crowds to form; a reliable unit, preferably of special forces, must be at hand, etc.). The confiscation of valuables should be done first in the city churches, starting with the wealthiest. Deal very carefully with rural churches in poor parishes, having thoroughly explained the whole situation. In the

gubernii and the centre allow loyal clergy to help the Famine Relief Committees with recording the confiscated Church valuables, informing everyone that the people will be able fully to check that not a single item of Church property will be used for any purpose other than helping the starving.

6. In those *gubernii* and *uezdy* where local conditions and thorough preparatory work will make confiscation possible without excesses, the *guberniya* committee of the RKP(b) should be fully responsible for carrying out confiscations. . .

8. The CC yet again emphasizes the absolute secrecy of all preparatory and organizational work. The Central Commission is to be informed regularly on the progress of work, deadlines and any measures taken.

Molotov, Secretary to the CC of the RKP.

Austrina, encoder.

Decoder and destroyer of original — signature illegible.

[Source: SOTsDOO, fond 1493, opis' 1, delo 74, pp. 2, 7–8 ob.]

Divisions in the Church and Patriarch Tikhon's apology

By the time of the clash over consecrated articles, the party leadership—Trotsky foremost among them—had become aware that there were severe fissures within the Orthodox Church which might usefully be exploited. A number of clergy considered Tikhon's policy towards the new regime fruitless and even unpatriotic, and some actively supported the confiscation policy. When Tikhon was restricted to house arrest for his opposition, several of the leaders of what was to become known as the 'Living Church' persuaded him to delegate his authority temporarily and then, without his sanction, proclaimed the establishment of a new governing body.[123] The Politburo decided to cultivate the split and for a brief period local party authorities were instructed to favour this reformist current which sought a rapprochement with the new regime in a manner somewhat analogous to the *smenovekhovtsy*: Trotsky called the policy 'an ecclesiastical NEP'. During 1923 and 1924, with this official help, the so-called 'Renovationists' wrested control of a majority of parishes from the traditionalists. By favouring the Renovationists the regime hoped to weaken the authority of the clergy as a whole, and undoubtedly succeeded in doing so. Moreover, the Renovationists themselves rapidly split, the more innovative reforms favoured by some—measures which a minority in the Church had pressed for before the revolution, including greater lay participation, an end to the

---

123 See P. Walters, 'The Renovationist Coup: Personalities and programmes' in G. Hosking (ed.) *Church, Nation and State in Russia and Ukraine* (London 1991) pp. 250–70.

steep hierarchical division between the married 'black' clergy and their 'white' superiors, and the adoption of modern spoken Russian in religious services—alienated others and were unpopular with the rural laity. When, within a year, the regime withdrew its tactical support for the Renovationists, both the number of parishes they controlled and the prestige of their leaders rapidly dwindled. The result, however, was to leave Orthodox reformers demoralized without restoring the authority of Tikhon and the conservative hierarchy.

The regime maintained its pressure on them, denouncing Tikhon— 'Citizen Belavin', as Soviet officialdom liked to call the Patriarch—for the activities of émigrés who had organized a Church council in Yugoslavia which explicitly supported the overthrow of the Bolsheviks. In June 1923 Tikhon publicly apologized for his attitude towards Soviet power and explicitly repudiated expatriates claiming to speak for the Church.

Document 138 | Patriarch Tikhon: '… from now on I am not an enemy of Soviet power'

Address to the Supreme Court of the RSFSR, composed under pressure from the CPSU CC Commission for Separating Church from State

16 June 1923

In making this declaration to the Supreme Court of the RSFSR I consider it my pastoral duty to declare as follows:

Having been brought up in a monarchical society, and being under the influence of anti-Soviet persons until my arrest [in 1922], my attitude towards Soviet power was genuinely hostile. Moreover, my passive hostility sometimes turned into active hostility, such as my address on the Brest–Litovsk Treaty in 1918, my anathematizing of the government in the same year and, finally, my proclamation in 1922 against the confiscation of Church valuables. Apart from a few minor inaccuracies all my anti-Soviet activities are set out in the Supreme Court's prosecution statement. In admitting that the Court is right to institute proceedings against me in accordance with the articles of the Criminal Code on anti-Soviet activity indicated in the prosecution statement, I repent of these actions against the state and request that the Court lift the sanctions against me, that is, release me from detention. Moreover, I declare to the Supreme Court that from now on I am not an enemy of Soviet power. Finally and decisively, I dissociate myself from both foreign and domestic monarchist and White Guard counter-revolution.

Patriarch Tikhon (Vasiliy Belavin)

On 25 June 1923 the Supreme Criminal Court, comprising comrades Karklin (chairman), Galkin and Chelyshev, decided as follows:

Citizen Belavin's plea is to be granted and, in accordance with Articles 161 and 242 of the Criminal Procedural Code, the sanctions adopted against him for avoidance of trial and investigation—detention—are to be lifted.

[Source: *Izvestiya*, 27 June 1923.]

Metropolitan Sergiy's celebration of Soviet loyalty and the protest of imprisoned archbishops

After Tikhon's death in 1925, the regime refused to allow a new Patriarch to be appointed and continued to accuse the Church of identifying with outspoken émigré critics. The hierarchy, albeit with much heart-searching and division, were edged further and further along the path that Tikhon had begun to tread. Following the damage done by the Renovationist split, and with the most prominent bishops under arrest, it was becoming increasingly difficult to administer the Church as a unified, country-wide institution. Only an abrupt change of the hierarchy's attitude, the regime made plain, might ease the pressure. The incentive to find a *modus vivendi* was increased by the contrast with the regime's less abrasive treatment of sectarians and Old Believers, and the evidence of energetic religious activism at parish level during the 1920s. In 1927, the acting head of the Church, Metropolitan Sergiy, made a long, formal statement, published in *Izvestiya*, in which he affirmed the Church's loyalty to the Soviet state without any of the qualifications and caveats to which Tikhon had tried to cling. He even spoke of gratitude to the regime for its concern for the spiritual needs of the Orthodox. The statement was issued against the background of the 1927 war-scare triggered by the souring of relations with Britain and France, intensifying Sergiy's anxiety to underline the Church's rejection of the outspoken—if increasingly divided—émigré clergy.

Document 139 | From the address of the Provisional Patriarchal Synod

29 July 1927

From Sergiy, by the Grace of God Metropolitan of Nizhniy Novgorod, the Deputy Patriarchal *locum tenens* and the Provisional Patriarchal Holy Synod, to Right Reverend arch-priests, priests beloved of God, honest monks and all the faithful of the Holy All-Russia Orthodox Church who 'rejoice in the Lord'.

One of the concerns of our late Holy Father Patriarch Tikhon before his passing was to settle relations between our Orthodox Russian Church and the Soviet government and thereby give the Church the chance for a fully lawful and peaceful existence. On his death-bed the Holy Father said, 'I should have lived another three years.' And, of course, if his unexpected passing had not cut short his work, he would have seen the matter through. Unfortunately, various circumstances, especially the actions of the Soviet state's foreign enemies, in which not only lay members of our Church took part but also their leaders awakened a natural and justifiable mistrust on the part of the government towards Church figures in general. This hampered the efforts of our Most Holy Father, and he was not to see his efforts crowned with success in his lifetime.

Now the lot of being the provisional Deputy head of our Church has fallen to me, the unworthy Metropolitan Sergiy, and also the duty of carrying on the work of the deceased by trying my best to settle Church affairs peacefully. My efforts in this direction, shared between the Orthodox arch-priests and myself, have not been fruitless: since the establishment under me of the Provisional Patriarchal Holy Synod, hopes of putting Church affairs in order have been growing, as has confidence in the possibility for us of a peaceful life and activity within the law.

Now, as we have almost reached our goal, attacks by foreign enemies have not ceased: assassination, arson, raids, bombing and other signs of underground activity are taking place before our very eyes. All of this is disturbing the peace and creating an atmosphere of mutual mistrust and all kinds of suspicions. It is therefore all the more necessary for our Church and all the more obligatory for all of us to whom Her interests are dear, for all of us who wish to lead Her along the path of a legal and peaceful existence, to show right now that we Church leaders are not on the side of the enemies of our state and the senseless weapons of their intrigues but on the side of our people and our government.

Testifying to this is indeed the primary aim of this epistle from myself and the Synod. We hereby notify you that in May of this year at my invitation and with official permission a Provisional Patriarchal Holy Synod, composed of the signatories to this letter, was organized. . . Now our Orthodox Church in the Soviet Union has a fully legal central administration not only in Canon Law but also in civil law. We hope that legalization will gradually spread to the lower levels of Church administration, i.e., diocesan, *uezd*, etc. It is hardly necessary to explain the importance and consequences of the change which has taken place in the position of our Orthodox Church, its clergy, Church leaders, institutions. . .

Let us then offer up grateful prayers to the Lord, who has shown His favour to our Church! Let us as one express our gratitude to the Soviet government for its attention to the spiritual needs of the Orthodox population, and at the same time assure the government that we will not abuse that trust.

In setting about our Synodal work with God's blessing, we are fully aware of the magnitude of the task facing us, and all representatives of the Church. We must show not merely in word but in deed that not only those indifferent to, or apostate from, Orthodoxy, can be true citizens of the Soviet Union, loyal to Soviet power. So can the most ardent believers, for whom the Church with all its dogma and traditions, with all its canonical and liturgical structure, is as dear as life itself. We want

to be Orthodox and at the same time recognize the Soviet Union as our civil homeland, the joys and successes of which are our joys and successes, and its failures our
failures. . .

Though Orthodox we remember our duty to be Soviet citizens 'not only for fear
of punishment, but also for conscience's sake', as the Apostle taught us in Romans
8:5. And we hope that with God's help and your good offices and support this task
will be achieved.

What is perhaps standing in our way is only what prevented the organization of
Church life on principles of loyalty in the first years of Soviet power. This is an
insufficient awareness of the full significance of what has taken place in our country.
Our affirmation of Soviet power seemed to many to be some kind of misunderstanding, accidental and therefore transient. They were forgetting that for the
Christian nothing is accidental and that always and everywhere we see the Hand of
God in everything, leading each people to their pre-ordained destiny. For such
people, who do not wish to see the 'signs of the times', it might seem that one cannot
break with the old regime or even with the monarchy without breaking with
Orthodoxy. Such an attitude in certain Church circles, which expressed itself, of
course, in both word and deed, aroused the suspicion of Soviet power and slowed
down the efforts of our Most Holy Patriarch to establish peaceful relations between
the Church and the Soviet government. It was not for nothing that the Apostle
instilled in us that 'we may lead a quiet and peaceable life' (1 Timothy 2:2) only by
submitting to the lawful authority; otherwise we must leave that society. Only
dreamers in their studies might think that such a huge society as our Orthodox
Church with all its organization could quietly exist hidden away from the government. Now that our Patriarchate, in implementing the wishes of the late Patriarch,
is irrevocably and decisively taking the loyal road, people who feel that way will
either have to restrain themselves and, leaving their politics at home, bring only faith
to church and work with us only in the name of faith or, if they cannot restrain
themselves, at least not get in our way, by keeping out of things for the time being.
We are sure that they will very quickly return to work with us, having realized that
only our attitude to the government has changed, while our faith and Orthodox
Christian life remain unshakeable.

In the present circumstances the problem of the members of the clergy who went
abroad in the emigration is a particularly acute one. The strongly anti-Soviet statements of some of our arch-priests and priests did as we know oblige our late Patriarch
to abolish the Synod-in-Exile (5 May 1922). But this Synod still continues to exist
with the same political attitudes, and recently its pretensions to power have even
split the émigré Church community into two camps. In order to put an end to this
we have demanded from émigré clergy a written undertaking of their complete
loyalty to the Soviet government in all their public activities. Those who do not
give such an undertaking or betray it will be removed from the body of clergy under
the Moscow Patriarchate. In distancing ourselves thus, we think that we are safe

from any unexpected events abroad. On the other hand, our decree will perhaps oblige many to consider whether it is time for them to re-examine their attitude to Soviet power, in order not to break with their own native Church and homeland. . .

In conclusion, we earnestly beg all of you, Right Reverend arch-priests, priests, brothers and sisters, each in your place, to help us with your sympathy for our task, with your zeal for God's work, with your dedication and obedience to the Holy Church and especially with your prayers for us to the Lord, that He may enable you successfully and worthily to carry out the task laid upon us to the glory of His Holy Name, to the benefit of our Orthodox Church and the salvation of us all.

May the blessings of our Lord Jesus Christ, the love of God, the Father, and the Holy Spirit be with you all. Amen.

Patriarchal *locum tenens* Sergiy, Metropolitan of Nizhniy Novgorod. Members of the Provisional Patriarchal Holy Synod: Serafim, Metropolitan of Tver'; Sil'vestr, Archbishop of Vologda; Aleksiy, Archbishop of Khuta, head of Novgorod diocese; Anatoliy, Archbishop of Samara; Pavel, Archbishop of Vyatka; Filipp, Archbishop of Zvenigorod, head of Moscow diocese; Konstantin, Bishop of Sumy, head of Khar'kov diocese; Sergiy, Bishop of Serpukhov, Synod office manager.

[Source: *Izvestiya*, 19 August 1927.]

Although the regime clearly welcomed the tone it had imposed on Sergiy, the commentary which *Izvestiya* published alongside his statement was contemptuous: all he had done was to postpone what remained an inevitable break between Church and people.

Document 140 | Among the clergy

From an *Izvestiya* editorial published in response to the address of the Provisional Patriarchal Synod

19 August 1927

. . . We wish to draw your attention only to the political aspects of the document, which its authors clearly consider to be a most important one. Politically, the matter is very clear. The working class and the peasantry have driven the White Guards out of the workers' state. Along with the White Guards the Black-Hundred clergy either emigrated or was chased out—all those Evlogiys, Platons, Antoniys or whatever else they call themselves. . . Orthodoxy for them is just a way of returning power to the landowners and capitalists, and, at the same time, returning the gold mitres, sparkling chasubles and huge incomes to the arch-priests of the Church. . . Between the White Guard flocks and their clergy there is complete unanimity on this point. That is how the priests, Church and Orthodoxy of our worker–peasant state wanted things to remain. Who can forget the frenzied curses which Patriarch Tikhon heaped upon Soviet power when it was fighting the capitalist world, and when it decided to use part of the Church's plundered wealth to feed the hungry?

However, back in 1921 a far-seeing section of the clergy realized that such a policy, such an overt alliance with the exploiters would bury the Church in the eyes of the workers and peasants, drive the last nail in its coffin, threaten to deprive the clergy of all its income and make its profession unnecessary for all working people. A section of the clergy made a very clever move by renouncing Patriarch Tikhon and accepting Soviet power as divinely ordained.

Tikhon's people resisted for a long time. They did not break with the Black-Hundred clergy of the White Guard emigration and tried to help the agents of Nikolay Nikolaevich, that comic pretender to the broken Romanov crown. But the result was a constant fight against their flock, against those workers and peasants who had remained in the Church. All that was good and healthy was turning against the Church. The Church's anti-Soviet policy was hurting the Church itself, not Soviet power. So Tikhon's lot had to drape themselves in Soviet colours. . . All the in-fighting and squabbling that broke out among various groups of the clergy in general, and Tikhon's own people in particular, after Tikhon's death is of little interest. Only the dullest and most backward members of the clergy were incapable of seeing and understanding that a political alignment with the flock, the working people, was the only way the Church could keep what it had left, especially the income still provided by the simple souls in its flock. That outburst of indignation which spread throughout the whole country, town and countryside, when the thick-skulled British government insolently began to prepare for war, and acts of terrorism began against the leading fighters of the proletariat and peasantry—that outburst of indignation showed even the thickest of Tikhon's lot that they could delay no longer, as it would be fatal for them. In their own interests, they had hastily and completely to dissociate themselves from all those Evlogiys, Chamberlains, Lianozovs and their hired assassins and incendiaries.

A political alignment with the flock, an adoption of Soviet colours forced on them by the mood of the workers and peasants, and an attempt to postpone a complete break between Church and people—that is the basic significance of the address from the clergy we have printed.

[Source: *Izvestiya*, 19 August 1927.]

Parts of the Church found it impossible to accept Sergiy's abject submission: it was in part because many priests and bishops refused to disseminate his statement that the regime published it in *Izvestiya*. The following carefully reasoned renunciation came from a group of imprisoned archbishops. They were among some 400 clergymen incarcerated in what was the first large labour camp set up by the regime, on the Solovki Islands in the White Sea where an ancient monastery and churches were used as barracks.[124] The previous year they had strongly endorsed Sergiy's refusal to give ground and they were now fiercely critical of his change of stance.

Document 141 | A message from the archbishops imprisoned in the Solovki camp

27 September 1927

1. We approve of the fact that the Church's highest body has sent an address to the government with its assurance of the Church's loyalty to Soviet power in all matters concerned with civil legislation and administration.

Such assurances, made more than once for the Church by the late Patriarch Tikhon, have not dispelled government suspicions, so the repetition of such assurances now seems expedient.

2. We quite sincerely accept the purely political part of the epistle, namely:
   a. We consider that parish clergy and other churchmen should obey all laws and government orders which concern the civil organization of the state.
   b. We consider that moreover they should not take part—either directly, covertly or overtly—in plots and organizations which aim to overthrow the existing order and type of government.
   c. We consider it completely inadmissible that the Church should appeal to foreign governments with the aim of inciting them to armed intervention in the Union's internal affairs for a political revolution in our country.
   d. We quite sincerely accept the law forbidding political activity to ministers of religion. We believe that ministers of religion, both in their open public Church work, and in the intimate sphere of pastoral influence on the consciences of the faithful, should neither approve nor criticize the actions of the government.

3. But we cannot accept and approve the epistle in full for the following reasons:
   a. Paragraph 7 (on the Church's subordination to civil authorities) is expressed so categorically and unconditionally that it could easily be seen as the complete merging of Church and state. The Church cannot undertake the obligation, regardless of the form of government, to consider 'its joys and successes our joys and successes, and its failures our failures', because any government can make senseless, unjust or cruel decisions, to which the Church may be obliged to submit, but cannot welcome or approve.

The eradication of religion is part of the present government's programme

---

124 See W.C. Fletcher, *The Russian Orthodox Church Underground, 1917–1970* (Oxford 1971) pp. 50, 54, 131–35.

and to this end a number of laws have been made. The government's successes in this respect cannot be seen by the Church as its own successes.

b. The epistle expresses 'our gratitude to the Soviet government for its attention to the spiritual needs of the Orthodox population'. Such an expression of gratitude from the mouth of the head of the Russian Orthodox Church cannot be sincere, is not worthy of the Church and arouses righteous indignation in believers' hearts, because hitherto the government's attitude to the spiritual needs of the Orthodox population has been expressed only in all kinds of restrictions on the religious spirit and its manifestations: the defilement and destruction of churches, the closing of monasteries, the confiscation of holy relics, the ban on teaching children Holy Writ, the removal from public libraries of religious literature and restrictions on priests' civil rights. How little attention the government has been paying to religious needs at present in its promise to legalize Church institutions is best shown in the article in the government organ *Izvestiya*, which is offensive to the sentiments of believers.

c. The Patriarchate's epistle unreservedly accepts the official version and lays all the blame for the bitter clashes between Church and state on the Church, on the counter-revolutionary attitude of the parish clergy, expressed in words and deeds, although of late there has not been a single trial where the political crimes of priests have been publicly and openly proven. At the same time innumerable bishops and priests are kept in administrative detention in prison, in exile and labour camps purely for their Church activities (the struggle against 'Renovationism') or for reasons often unknown to the victims themselves. The real reason for the struggle, so onerous for both Church and state, is the task of eradicating religion which the present government has set itself. It is the government's fundamentally negative attitude to religion which obliges the state to view the Church with suspicion, whatever political statements the Church makes, and does not allow the Church to accept laws that are aimed at its destruction.

d. The epistle threatens priests who have left with the emigration with removal from the body of clergy under the Moscow Patriarchate for their political activity, i.e., it imposes clerical punishment for political crimes. This contradicts the decree of the All-Russia Council of 1917–1918, adopted 3–16 August 1918, which clarified the canonical unacceptability of such punishments and rehabilitated all persons defrocked for past political crimes (Arseniy Matsievich, the priest Grigoriy Petrov).

4. Finally, we find the epistle of the Patriarchal Synod incomplete, reticent and, therefore, inadequate.

The law separating Church and state has two sides: by preventing the Church from interfering in the political life of the country, it guarantees non-interference from the government in its internal life and the religious activity of its institutions.

Nevertheless, this law is being continually flouted by the security services. The supreme Church authorities, while guaranteeing the loyalty of the Church to the state, will have to declare openly to the government that the Church cannot accept interference in purely Church matters by a state which is hostile to religion.

[Source: *Otechestvennaya istoriya* No. 6, 1992, pp. 134–36.]

While the institution of the Church—its hierarchy, clergy, churches, monasteries and publications—suffered enormous attrition and public humiliation during the 1920s, priests and congregations, especially in rural Russia, proved resilient. Making use of the traditional village assembly, peasant co-operatives and even village soviets, activists were often able to deflect official policy.[125] Moreover, to the further frustration of the most militantly atheist groups within the party, the resources committed to anti-religious propaganda were modest. Despite a number of high-profile poster campaigns, public debates, exhibitions and the opening of museums of atheism to expose Orthodox 'deception' and 'mystification',[126] at local level and in schools little time or effort was devoted to anti-religious teaching.[127] Pressure for such propaganda from activists brought together in 1924 in the 'League of the Godless', headed by the Bolshevik historian and member of the Central Committee E.M. Yaroslavsky, made limited impact on the policy pursued by the Commissariat of Enlightenment. In 1928, however, with the onset of the 'cultural revolution', the initiative passed to militants.

---

125 On religious politics in the countryside in the 1920s, see G. Young, *Power and the Sacred in Revolutionary Russia: Religious activists in the village* (University Park, PA, 1997).
126 See P. Kenez, *The Birth of the Propaganda State: Soviet methods of mass mobilization, 1919–1929* (Cambridge 1985) pp. 65–69, 183–85.
127 See L.E. Holmes, 'Fear No Evil: Schools and religion in Soviet Russia, 1917–1941' in Ramet (ed.) *Religious Policy in the Soviet Union* pp. 125–57.

PART THREE

SOVIET SOCIETY UNDER STALIN (1928–1940)

The period of the First Five-Year Plan (1928–32) saw Soviet society undergo traumatic upheaval. In 1929, when peasant refusal to part with grain for the inadequate price offered by the state imperilled the entire industrialization Plan, Stalin resorted to forced collectivization. Planners, intellectuals and those party leaders, headed by Bukharin, who urged restraint, were rendered helpless. In a millenarian atmosphere of 'cultural revolution', militant activists silenced moderate voices and clamoured for a radical 'proletarian' orthodoxy in all spheres of life. Collectivization gravely disrupted production and triggered a calamitous famine in 1932–33, though it did secure for the regime a permanent grip on the grain supply. Industrial expansion and urbanization was dramatic but was accompanied by severe set-backs and appalling deprivation. By 1934, with the Second Five-Year Plan (1933–37) achieving more balanced growth, the regime moved to stabilize society, enhanced the authority of managers and officials, curbed militant activists and imposed rigid, centralized party censorship. Urban living standards improved and 1936 saw the introduction of the so-called Stalin Constitution in celebration of apparent stabilization. What followed, however, was a series of economic reversals and the Great Terror of 1937–38. Friction with Japan and mounting tension with Nazi Germany made rearmament an immediate priority in the Third Five-Year Plan (1938–42), and by 1940 there was intense public resentment as the regime sought to tighten labour discipline through a series of draconian decrees.

12

Collectivization
and the Peasantry

The defeat of Bukharin

The years 1928 and 1929 saw the rupture of NEP and the onset of a period of momentous economic, social and cultural upheaval and transformation.[128] The trigger for what Stalin labelled the 'great turn' was the decline in the supply of grain from the countryside. The tension between the increasingly ambitious rate of industrial investment adopted in 1926 and 1927 and the maintenance of adequate incentives for peasants to market their grain reached breaking point. In January 1928, with the amount of grain state agencies had managed to buy falling disastrously short of what was needed, the Politburo agreed on temporary emergency measures to extract more.

When Stalin and Molotov set about implementing the Politburo's decision in areas deemed grain-rich—they both personally toured the Urals and Siberia—they did so in a far more coercive manner than Bukharin and others on the Politburo had envisaged.[129] They mobilized wave upon wave of central, provincial and district officials of state and party to halt trade, close local markets, impose steep quotas, search out hidden grain stores, and compel peasants to sell by accelerated tax collection and the imposition of swingeing fines. Poor peasants were encouraged to support police and party–state search parties in exchange for a proportion of the grain collected, while protests by local officials and party members, and resistance of any kind by peasants, were denounced as 'kulak'-inspired treachery.

After a brief pause when the immediate grain shortfall had been met,

128 The best guide to the historiography and the controversies that surround the period is C. Ward, *Stalin's Russia* (London 1999, 2nd ed.); for the two most influential social historians, see M. Lewin, *The Making of the Soviet System: Essays in the social history of interwar Russia* (London 1985), and S. Fitzpatrick, *Everyday Stalinism: Ordinary Life in Extraordinary Times. Soviet Russia in the 1930s* (Oxford 1999).
129 See J. Hughes, *Stalin, Siberia and the Crisis of the New Economic Policy* (Cambridge 1991), for a close analysis.

during which Stalin ostensibly agreed an end to emergency measures and made gestures of regret for the 'excesses' of the campaign, the programme of virtual requisitioning was resumed in April. Rumours spread across the country of a return to 'War Communism', there were ominous instances of peasant resistance, and peasant confidence in NEP and the stability of the market was shaken to the core. At this point the Stalin–Bukharin alliance, which when it smashed the United Opposition just months earlier had seemed so solid, split apart. Bukharin clung to the belief that accelerated industrial investment could be combined with a stable grain trade via skilful manipulation of grain prices, the price for other agricultural produce, and tax rates. Stalin and his allies were becoming increasingly convinced that a watershed was being reached and that the party must find a way to secure an unshakeable grip on grain supplies or the emergent Five-Year Plan would be thrown into jeopardy. As they saw it, either the peasantry must be made to part with their grain at prices laid down by the state or the vast resources needed for investment would be frittered away in paying peasants whatever price they insisted upon.

Because Bukharin and those sympathetic to him, headed by M.I. Tomsky, the trade-union chief, and A.I. Rykov, the chairman of Sovnarkom, occupied key posts and controlled much of the press (Bukharin himself headed the editorial board of *Pravda*), the depth of the emergent split was not clear to those further down the hierarchy. The following outspoken letter to the Politburo came from the Deputy Commissar of Finance, M. Frumkin. Frumkin's gloomy memo condemned the way the extraordinary measures had alienated the great majority of the peasantry, stifled legitimate criticism within the party, made a mockery of law by announcing ludicrously high fines, undermined the market mechanism, smothered the incentive for middle peasants to improve their output, and used coercion rather than incentives, technical improvement and enlightenment to try to expand state and collective farms. The Finance Commissariat was throughout the 1920s strongly committed to maintaining market equilibrium and at loggerheads with the more and more ambitious investment plans developed by VSNKh under Kuybyshev. Whereas Bukharin shared many of Frumkin's anxieties, Stalin was dismissive. The breach between the two over how to respond to the letter left them no longer on speaking terms.

Document 142 | M.I. Frumkin: '...the sentiment in the countryside... is opposed to us'—from a letter to the CPSU Politburo

5 June 1928

...The deterioration in our domestic situation is primarily connected with the countryside, with the position of agriculture. We must not close our eyes to the fact

that the sentiment in the countryside, apart from a small section of the poor peasants, is opposed to us, and that this mood is already beginning to spread into urban
areas. . . In ascribing exceptional importance to the role of the countryside in the
present crisis, I consider it my duty to direct the Politburo's attention to those matters
which are uppermost in the minds of hundreds and thousands of Party members and
about which they talk at every opportunity. I hardly need to point out that our
current difficulties do not stem solely, or even mainly, from our mistakes in planning the economy. . .

At a meeting of the Urals *oblast'* committee attended by some thirty to forty
comrades, comrade Molotov expressed his attitude to the countryside like this:
'We've got to hit the kulaks in such a way as to make the middle peasants stand to
attention.' This was not an accidental formulation. In his report on the grain-
procurement expedition he accused everybody who did not agree with this line of
pandering to the kulaks. . .

A new line on the middle peasants has been taken by the whole Party. They keep
on talking about a union with the middle peasants, but in reality we are pushing
them away from us. . .

The line taken lately has led to the main mass of the middle peasants being without
hope, without prospects. Fear of being branded a kulak has paralysed all stimuli to
improve their farms. . .

What needs to be done soon:

1. Establish revolutionary legality. Making outlaws of the kulaks has resulted in
   a lawless attitude to all peasants. In the 11th year of Soviet power it is
   completely unacceptable for the authorities to issue decrees which are formally
   laws, but which in essence merely make a mockery of the law, e.g., a fine of
   100–200 rubles for weevils or not keeping a dog on a lead.
2. The questions of agricultural production and the extent to which it is
   marketed must retain the importance given to them by the XIV Party
   Congress and the XV Party Conference. . .
3. We must therefore struggle against the kulaks by reducing what they have
   accumulated, increasing taxes and by freeing the poor and middle peasants
   from the kulaks' economic (and, consequently, political) influence. We must
   not support the kulaks with our meagre credits, but nor must we 'de-kulakize'
   or wreck their farms, which we will need for some years to come. Therefore
   attention and assistance to individual farms over the coming year should take
   first place, not tenth place. . .
5. There should be maximum help to the poor peasants joining the collective
   farms, and by strengthening these collectives they should be drawn into real
   (not a pseudo-) socialized economy.
6. State farms should not be expanded by shock or super-shock tactics. . .
7. Re-establish, or rather, open the grain markets. . .
8. Increase grain prices by 15–20 kopecks, while lowering other farm produce

prices sufficiently to keep the general agricultural price index at the present level. . .

9. Fight harder against illegal home distilling, which wastes so much grain.
10. Make the People's Commissariat for Agriculture's priority the development of field-crop cultivation, in particular grain production, to which it has hitherto paid little attention.
11. Give individual farmers, not just collective farms, the chance to get machinery. . .

[Source: *Literaturnaya gazeta*, 26 December 1990.]

Bukharin became alarmed at Stalin's tightening grip on the leadership. In June and July he met three times with Kamenev, whom he had so recently joined in humiliating. He now confessed to his dismay about Stalin, this new 'Ghengis Khan'. In September, his dissent over policy towards the peasantry became public. Far from seeking to steady the economy in the face of the repeated grain shortfall, Stalin and Kuybyshev called for further acceleration in the rate of investment. Peasant resistance, which they portrayed as the product of 'kulak' manipulation, must be broken for good and maximum support given to the rapid development of collective farms. Bukharin responded on 30 September with a major article in *Pravda*, 'Notes of an Economist'.[130] Though he stood by the ambitious investment plans endorsed in 1927, still believing they were compatible with balanced trade between town and country, he repudiated even greater ambitions as 'Trotskyist' adventurism. And he rejected reliance on coercion, whether it be to extract adequate grain or to accelerate the replacement of family farms by collective and state farms.

With the conflict over policy now inseparable from the clash over leadership, supporters of the Stalin–Bukharin alliance were forced to choose between them. On 8 October, the Politburo reprimanded Bukharin for publishing the 'Notes' and by the following month Stalin had established a clear majority in the Central Committee. In explaining Stalin's rapid victory, primary emphasis has been laid on the manner in which Stalin exploited his control of the Secretariat, the bureaucratization of which critics of the left had so long attacked, and the number of second-rank officials whose careers depended on his approval, as well as on his close alliance with the head of the OGPU.[131] This, however, was not the sole source of the majority he built around the issue. His supporters were not simply placemen willing to

---

130 Bukharin, *Selected Writings* pp. 301–30.
131 For a clear exposition, see Gill, *Origins* pp. 113–98.

endorse whatever course he cared to choose. The twists and turns in Stalin's attitude to the economic dilemmas of the 1920s, whether arising from cynical manoeuvring or changes in his own understanding of what was possible, closely mirrored majority opinion among them. He was highly sensitive to the hopes and anxieties, the pride and prejudices of the party.

In the mid-1920s, his caution had matched the dominant mood of a party which was still recovering from peasant rebellion and near catastrophe at the end of the civil war. By 1928, his confidence in a dramatic escape from the frustrations of NEP had more appeal among senior Bolsheviks than did Bukharin's emphasis on compromise. For regional party leaders, vying with each other to maximize the share allocated to their own *oblast'* of the huge investment programme taking shape in the draft Five-Year Plan, Stalin's message was much the more attractive. It was hardly surprising that Molotov should have got a ready hearing for the speech to the Urals *oblast'* committee which so shocked Frumkin (see document 142): they were straining every sinew to win the leadership's backing for their bid to have included in the Plan a series of vast projects to develop heavy industry in the Urals. Nor could the language of Bukharin—or Frumkin—match the appeal within the party of that used by Stalin, Molotov and their allies: a final reckoning with 'kulaks' and the class-alien elements flourishing under NEP, a historic industrial breakthrough towards socialism, and the overriding importance of party unity. The abrupt defeat of the Bukharinist leadership's hold on the critical Moscow party organization in October epitomized the combination of bureaucratic in-fighting and political conviction that delivered victory to Stalin.[132]

By November, he knew he had a majority on both the Politburo and the Central Committee. In the following speech to a full meeting of the latter, he used Frumkin's June letter and a second letter sent in November to condemn Bukharin's line and those who sympathized with it. Confident that his audience would back him, he dismissed evidence of peasant unrest, accusations that middle peasants were being alienated, protest about the use of force to expand state and collective farms, and the call to moderate industrial investment as bourgeois–liberal, alarmist and reactionary. Endorsing the sinister label that had gained currency during the year, he attacked those who propagated such views as part of a 'Right deviation'.

---

132 See C. Merridale, *Moscow Politics and the Rise of Stalin: The Communist party in the capital, 1925–1932* (London 1990) pp. 47–67. For a recent commentary playing down Stalin's cynicism and arguing the logic and rationality of the often brutal positions he adopted, see E. van Ree, *The Political Thought of Joseph Stalin: A study in twentieth-century revolutionary patriotism* (London 2002).

Document 143 | I.V. Stalin: *Combating Deviations and Conciliation towards Them*—from a speech at the Plenum of the CC of the CPSU

19 November 1928

Are there spokesmen of the Right deviation among our Party members? There certainly are... I think that in this respect the palm should go to Frumkin. (Laughter.) I am referring to his first letter [June 1928] and then to his second letter, which was distributed here to the members of the CC and CCC [November 1928]...

Let us take the 'basic propositions' of the first letter.

1) '*The sentiment in the countryside, apart from a small section of the poor peasants, is opposed to us.*' Is that true? It is obviously untrue. If it were true, the bond would not even be a memory. But since June [the letter was written in June] nearly six months have passed, yet anyone, unless he is blind, can see that the bond between the working class and the main mass of the peasantry continues and is growing stronger. Why does Frumkin write such nonsense? In order to scare the Party and make it give way to the Right deviation.

2) '*The line taken lately has led to the main mass of the middle peasants being without hope, without prospects.*' Is that true? It is quite untrue. It is obvious that if in the spring of this year the main mass of the middle peasants had been without economic hope or prospects they would not have enlarged the spring crop area as they did in all the principal grain-growing regions... Here again he is trying to scare the Party with the 'horrors' of hopeless prospects in order to make it give way to his, Frumkin's, view.

3) '*We must return to the XIV and XV Congresses.*' That the XV Congress has simply been tacked on here without rhyme or reason, of that there can be no doubt. The crux here is not in the XV Congress, but in the slogan: Back to the XIV Congress. And what does that mean? It means renouncing 'intensification of the offensive against the kulak' (see XV Congress resolution)... [I]n calling for a return to the XIV Congress, Frumkin is rejecting the step forward which the Party made between the XIV and XV Congresses, and, in rejecting it, he is trying to pull the Party back...

4) ... When Frumkin speaks of maximum assistance to the poor peasants entering collectives, he is in point of fact turning away from, evading, the task set the Party by the XV Congress of developing the collective-farm movement to the utmost. In point of fact, Frumkin is against developing the work of strengthening the socialist sector in the countryside along the line of collective farms.

5) '*State farms should not be expanded by shock or super-shock tactics.*' Frumkin cannot but know that we are only beginning to work seriously to expand the old state farms and to create new ones. Frumkin cannot but know that we are assigning for this purpose far less money than we ought to assign if we had any reserves for it. The

words 'by shock or super-shock tactics' were put in here to strike people with 'horror' and conceal his own disinclination for any serious expansion of the state farms. Frumkin, in point of fact, is here expressing his opposition to strengthening the socialist sector in the countryside along the line of the state farms.

Now gather all these propositions of Frumkin's together, and you get a bouquet characteristic of the Right deviation.

Let us pass to Frumkin's second letter. In what way does the second letter differ from the first? In that it aggravates the errors of the first letter. The first said that middle-peasant farming was without prospects. The second speaks of the 'retrogression' of agriculture. The first letter said that we must return to the XIV Congress in the sense of relaxing the offensive against the kulak. The second letter, however, says that 'we must not hamper production on the kulak farms'. The first letter said nothing about industry. But the second letter develops a 'new' theory to the effect that less should be assigned for industrial construction. Incidentally, there are two points on which the two letters agree: concerning the collective farms and concerning the state farms. In both letters Frumkin pronounces against the development of collective farms and state farms...

There can be no doubt that this theory [of 'retrogression'] is the invention of bourgeois experts, who are always ready to raise a cry that the Soviet regime is doomed. Frumkin has allowed himself to be scared by the bourgeois experts who have their roost around the People's Commissariat of Finance, and now he is himself trying to scare the Party so as to make it give way to the Right deviation...

Frumkin says that 'we must not hamper production on the kulak farms'. What does that mean? It means not preventing the kulaks from developing their exploiting economy... It means allowing a free rein to capitalism in the countryside, allowing it freedom, liberty...

It follows, then, that we must now go over from the *socialist* slogan—'ever-increasing restrictions on the capitalist elements' (see the theses on the control figures)—to the *bourgeois–liberal* slogan: do not hamper the development of capitalism in the countryside...

What does giving the kulak a free hand mean? It means giving him power... For it must be understood, after all, that you cannot but restrict the development of kulak economy if you take power away from the kulaks and concentrate it in the hands of the working class...

Capital construction in industry. When we discussed the control figures we had three figures before us: the Supreme Council of National Economy asked for 825,000,000 rubles; the State Planning Commission was willing to give 750,000,000 rubles; the People's Commissariat of Finance would give only 650,000,000 rubles. What decision on this did the Central Committee of our Party take? It fixed the figure at 800,000,000 rubles... Frumkin defends the figure of 650,000,000 rubles not out of stinginess, but because of his new-fangled theory of 'feasibility', asserting in his second letter and in a special article in the periodical of the People's Commissariat of Finance that *we shall certainly do injury to our economy if we assign to the Supreme Council of National Economy more than 650,000,000 rubles for capital construction*. . . It means that Frumkin is against maintaining the present rate of development of industry, evidently failing to realize that if it were slackened this really would do injury to our entire national economy.

Now combine these two points in Frumkin's second letter, the point concerning kulak farming and the point concerning capital construction in industry, add the theory of 'retrogression', and you get the physiognomy of the Right deviation.

[Source: J.V. Stalin, *Works* Volume XI (Moscow 1954) pp. 281–88.]

The following months only widened the rift. With Bukharin and his allies isolated in the Politburo and resigning from most of their key posts, the rest of the leadership drove further and harder down the road they had rejected. The shift in power was mirrored in the regions: in the Urals, I.D. Kabakov successfully ousted the First Secretary, N. Shvernik, over the issue of the tempo of local industrial expansion (January 1929), and proceeded vastly to expand the investment ambitions for the *oblast'* in what became known as 'the Great Urals plan'.[133] There could be no question about where Kabakov's sympathies lay and he epitomized the majority on the Central Committee, of which he had been a member since 1925: his ideological vision, his regional agenda and his personal ambition all pointed squarely to support for Stalin. The already hugely ambitious targets of the draft Five-Year Plan were revised steeply upwards, and new 'minimal' and 'optimal' versions of the Plan prepared for the party conference due in late April 1929. At the same time, continuing shortfalls in grain procurement were met by intensification of what Stalin approvingly called the 'Urals–Siberian method of grain collection'.[134] Peasants who failed to meet quotas were subjected to punishments ranging from fines, through expulsion from co-operatives to confiscation of property, and local officials responsible for failure were denounced and dismissed. Official analysis of the grain crisis focused more and more closely on the inadequacy of small-scale, non-collective farming, on the one hand, and supposed 'kulak' sabotage and politically motivated hoarding, on the other. Stalin warned that the closer the breakthrough to socialism drew, the more frantically the enemies of socialism would fight and the more intense class struggle would become.

---

133 Harris, *The Great Urals* pp. 70–104.
134 See Y. Taniuchi, 'Decision-Making on the Urals–Siberian Method' in J. Cooper et al. (eds) *Soviet History 1917–1953* (Basingstoke 1995) pp. 78–103, which points up the contrast between Bukharin's allies, anxious that adequate grain be acquired but critical of the methods used, and the more ruthless attitudes of Kabakov and other regional leaders.

At the Central Committee plenum preceding the Sixteenth Party Conference in April, Bukharin spelled out his grounds for dissent on what he sensed might be the last occasion to do so. Although his supporters were massively outnumbered by those behind Stalin, his responses to heckling were robust—the jibes from A.I. Mikoyan in the extract below are only a sample of the sneers thrown at him. Perhaps because support among the leadership for breakneck industrialization was now so fierce, he did not make lower investment targets as such part of his argument. He concentrated instead on what he saw as increasing and suicidal reliance on 'extraordinary measures' rather than the market to secure grain. The need to introduce food rationing in January 1929 confirmed him in the view that force could not extract sufficient quantities and would rapidly undermine production as peasants took fright. As for the notion that class struggle would become more intense the closer socialism approached, it was to his mind an absurd theory which contradicted his entire vision of the *smychka* between workers and peasants and of a relatively harmonious route to socialism.

Document 144 | **N.I. Bukharin: '... the small producer has turned from a grain-seller into a grain-deliverer...'—from a speech at a plenary meeting of the CC and CCC of the CPSU**

18 April 1929

Bukharin: Comrades, I urge you to pay the greatest attention to my speech, as I believe that this is the last speech I shall make at a plenary meeting as a member of the Politburo...

The notorious 'theory' that the closer we get to socialism the more bitter the class struggle must be, and the greater must be the number of difficulties and contradictions heaped upon us—this 'theory' has now received full recognition within the Party. Comrade Stalin outlined it at the July plenary, and comrade Kuybyshev in particular developed and 'deepened' it with genius. I consider that this 'theory' brings together two completely different things. It mixes a temporary phase of exacerbation in the class struggle—we are going through one such phase at the moment—with the general course of development. It elevates the fact of this present exacerbation to some kind of inevitable law of our development. According to this strange theory, the nearer we move towards socialism, the more the difficulties pile up and the harsher the class struggle gets. At the very gates of socialism we must evidently either begin a civil war or lie down and starve...

The bases of the so-called economic difficulties at present facing us seem to me to lie in a certain violation of fundamental economic proportions, and primarily in the violation of the correct relationship between industry and agriculture. I really must emphasize that this proposition should not be understood as saying that the tempo of industrial development we have chosen is too rapid. One might have thought so a while ago. A closer analysis has shown that this is not the crux of the matter. The point is that we can develop at our future tempo, the one we have chosen, or maybe an even more rapid one, only under certain conditions. The specific condition is that we must have an upsurge in agriculture, as the basis for industrialization, and a rapid economic turnover between town and country.

Moreover, delays in adopting certain measures led us to commit several mistakes. (I consider the main ones to be: an inflexible price policy; excessive taxation of agriculture prior to the reform; unsystematic swings in policy; extraordinary measures which were forced on us at first as a result of previous mistakes; and a degree of blockage in commodity circulation.) These mistakes meant that agriculture, the grain sector, did not grow, but rather contracted. The quantity of food grain harvested, its gross volume, fell. . .

The position can be put in the following way: had we paid attention in recent years to the state of the grain sector, we could, in one, two or three years, have got a massive increase in construction, on a firm rather than an unstable basis. We could have advanced with a firm international economic position, with a good foreign currency position, with gold, with reserves, with an active balance of trade and payments, with a stable exchange rate, with the prospect of a painless transition to genuine parity. Instead, we have ended up with inevitable difficulties. Please note, comrades, that our difficulties started to manifest themselves most starkly when those sources which had kept us going for a certain period of time dried up, and we all saw that we could not get any further with them. That moment coincides with the greatest difficulties. But once it had turned out like that, once those difficulties had become an objective fact, we slipped further and further into extraordinary measures.

A Voice: That's the whole point—you missed the chance.

Mikoyan: What a prophet!

Bukharin: In my opinion it is you, Comrade Mikoyan, who proved to be a poor prophet. I see that you made some remarkable predictions in your polemic with Pyatakov!

(Comrade Mikoyan's response could not be heard.)

I can tell, Comrade Mikoyan, that you are clearly very unfamiliar with the Greek philosophers and the Jewish prophets, but I am not responsible for your ignorance in these matters.

A Voice: This means that prophets are not much good at collecting grain.

Bukharin: On the matter of prophets, I should say that when I asked Comrade Mikoyan about the food situation in Moscow, he explained that it was 'all right', and that the problem arose because the people ate too much.

Mikoyan: Stop lying.

Bukharin: When I asked Comrade Mikoyan before the November Plenum how things stood with the winter sowing, Comrade Mikoyan replied: 'Actually, you're just spreading panic. The peasants are sowing with great enthusiasm at night, by lamplight!' In fact, it turned out that there was a significant drop in winter sowing.

So, as far as prophecy is concerned, Comrade Mikoyan, I would not cast the first stone, if I were you!

Mikoyan: We're doomed, we're doomed, the whole time.

Bukharin: I have never said that we are doomed.

Mikoyan: What do you mean, you have never said it? You never said it to Pyatakov, you never said it to Kamenev, you never said it to me?

Bukharin: What are you on about?

Mikoyan: You never said it?

Bukharin: That we're doomed? I said that *you* are making great efforts in that direction, but you still won't manage to wreck things. (Laughter.)...

I think that if we could put the agricultural situation in a nutshell, we could put it like this: at present the small producer has turned from a grain-seller into a grain-deliverer. Consequently the basic form of the bond has been broken, a form which for a long time should have remained the main, decisive form—that of market relations... And here we see a chain of events. This is where we find the root of the new 'extreme measures': so-called self-taxation, boycotts and a whole new swathe, overt or covert, of extreme measures...

I feel that comrades clearly overestimate the potential for influencing the bulk of the peasantry without market relations. I would put it like this: they overestimate the possibility of direct influence on the small and very small peasants and are jumping into a more distant phase of development in our economic relations...

Market links as a form will be with us for many years to come. I would even say that market links will for many years be the decisive form of economic link. Yes, decisive!...

[Source: N.I. Bukharin, *Problemy teorii i praktiki sotsializma* (Moscow 1989) pp. 253–81.]

Bukharin's resounding defeat in April, and the formal adoption of the 'optimal' version of the Five-Year Plan (backdated to October 1928), marked the onset of the 'great turn'. By the end of the year, Bukharin had been dropped from the Politburo and Stalin's ascendancy became entrenched: he stood head and shoulders above his remaining colleagues and the growing practice among his supporters of eulogizing his leadership had become a full-blown public cult.[135] Promising figures on the rate of industrial expansion in 1928–29, and continuing pressure from regional leaders, encouraged Stalin and his allies to raise targets even further. April's 'optimal' figures became 'minimal', and the Five-Year Plan was now to be accomplished in four. Most ominous of all was the mounting enthusiasm, destined

---

135 J. Brooks, *Thank You, Comrade Stalin! Soviet Public Culture from Revolution to Cold War* (Princeton 2000), explores the cult in the context of the official Soviet discourse that developed in the press.

to cast a shadow over the rest of Soviet history, for forced-pace collectivization.[136]

Forced collectivization and 'dekulakization'

During the summer, there was a remorseless increase in the pressure against
'kulaks' and in favour of state and collective farms. Encouragement from the
centre was seized upon by provincial activists. Whether from conviction or
out of eagerness to please Moscow, they vied with each other in claiming a
surge of enthusiasm from middle as well as poor peasants and hailing dramatic
progress in enrolling peasants in collective farms.[137] A chain reaction between
centre and periphery was set in motion: the leadership in Moscow was
emboldened by the response from below; it publicized instances of dramatic
progress; officials in more passive provinces and districts were spurred into
action; the early-comers strove to report even greater achievements; enthusiasm in Moscow soared. And at every level, from the Politburo through
regional committees to the humble village party cell, it became ever harder
for those with reservations to protest against the coercion used; to point to
the depth of hostility not only from richer peasants but from the vast mass
of 'middle peasants' and even many of the poorest; to expose how often
reports of successful 'collectivization' amounted to little more than signatures cajoled from peasants; and to warn about the lack of adequate
machinery, preparation and managerial knowledge to establish effective
large-scale farms.

Such protestations were overwhelmed by the enthusiasm that the 'great
turn' unleashed. That collective farms working open fields would be more
productive than household farms working scattered strips had always been a
fundamental Bolshevik assumption. The possibility of bringing about the
transformation not over decades, as had been almost universally assumed as
late as 1928, but now, this winter, overnight, was tantalizing. The current
dearth of tractors and other machinery would surely be rapidly overcome by
the glittering promises of the Five-Year Plan. And in regions such as the
Urals, already suffering mounting labour shortage as new construction and

---

136 For four of the most illuminating studies, see R.W. Davies, *The Socialist Offensive: The
collectivization of Soviet agriculture, 1929–1930* (London 1980); Lewin, *Making of the Soviet
System*; S. Fitzpatrick, *Stalin's Peasants: Resistance and survival in the Russian village after
collectivization* (Oxford 1994); and L. Viola, *Peasant Rebels under Stalin: Collectivization and
the culture of peasant resistance* (Oxford 1996).
137 See J. Hughes, *Stalinism in a Russian Province: Collectivization and dekulakization in Siberia*
(New York 1996), for the view, not widely shared, that the regime succeeded in mobilizing a significant measure of support among poorer peasants.

mining projects multiplied, there was eager anticipation that collectivization would make a large pool of surplus rural labour available to industry. Peasant reluctance and even overt resistance, it was argued, were rooted in the opposition of wealthy peasants who had supposedly grown rich under NEP: greedy, selfish, exploitative 'kulaks' and foolish poorer peasants duped by them. Immediate collectivization seemed a permanent solution to recurrent grain crises both because output would soar and because collective farms would be in the socialist sector under firm party and state guidance. Collecting grain would no longer involve choosing either to submit to 'kulak blackmail' over prices or to mount drastic coercive requisitioning campaigns. It would become automatic.

Between May and November 1929, it was Molotov rather than Stalin who led enthusiasts at the centre, but that month the leader hailed the mass movement of middle peasants in favour of collectivization, the enormous economic benefits that would follow, and the need for a decisive campaign against the 'kulaks'. In mid-November the same Central Committee plenum which expelled Bukharin from the Politburo resolved to recruit 25,000 industrial workers to go to the countryside and take the lead, alongside party officials, returning Red Army men, and committed peasants, in establishing collective farms.[138] Early in December the Politburo set up a Commission to fix targets for collectivization in different regions, provide guidance on how far peasant livestock and household plots as well as field strips should be socialized, and lay down how 'kulaks' were to be dealt with. Stalin exercised his weight in particular over the latter issue, making the following landmark speech to a conference of agricultural specialists and officials. With the full authority of a leader whose genius had been trumpeted in every forum on the official occasion of his fiftieth birthday six days earlier, he spurned the idea favoured by some on the Commission and at the conference that repentant 'kulaks' could enter collective farms. He backed ruthless treatment for them all.

Document 145 | I.V. Stalin: '... we must smash the kulaks, eliminate them as a class'—from a speech at a conference of Marxist agrarians

27 December 1929

To launch an offensive against the kulaks means that we must smash the kulaks, eliminate them as a class. Unless we set ourselves these aims, an offensive would be mere declamation, pinpricks, phrase-mongering, anything but a real Bolshevik offensive. To launch an offensive against the kulaks means that we must prepare for

---

138 See L. Viola, *The Best Sons of the Fatherland: Workers in the vanguard of Soviet collectivization* (Oxford 1987).

it and then strike at the kulaks, strike so hard as to prevent them from rising to their feet again. That is what we Bolsheviks call a real offensive. Could we have undertaken such an offensive some five years or three years ago with any prospect of success? No, we could not.

Indeed, in 1927 the kulaks produced over 600,000,000 *pudy* of grain, about 130,000,000 *pudy* of which they marketed outside the rural districts. This was a serious force to be reckoned with. How much did our collective farms and state farms produce at that time? About 80,000,000 *pudy*, of which about 35,000,000 *pudy* were sent to the market (marketable grain). Judge for yourselves: could we at that time have replaced the kulak output and kulak marketable grain by the output and marketable grain of our collective farms and state farms? Obviously, we could not.

What would it have meant to launch a determined offensive against the kulaks under such conditions? It would have meant certain failure, strengthening the position of the kulaks and being left without grain. That is why we could not and should not have undertaken a determined offensive against the kulaks at that time, in spite of the adventurist declamations of the Zinoviev–Trotsky opposition.

But today? What is the position now? Today, we have an adequate material base for us to strike at the kulaks, to break their resistance, to eliminate them as a class, and to replace their output by the output of the collective farms and state farms. You know that in 1929 the grain produced on the collective farms and state farms has amounted to not less than 400,000,000 *pudy* (200,000,000 *pudy* less than the gross output of the kulak farms in 1927). You also know that in 1929 the collective farms and state farms have supplied more than 130,000,000 *pudy* of marketable grain (i.e., more than the kulaks in 1927). Lastly, you know that in 1930 the gross output of the collective farms and state farms will amount to not less than 900,000,000 *pudy* of grain (i.e., more than the gross output of the kulaks in 1927), and their output of marketable grain will be not less than 400,000,000 *pudy* (i.e., incomparably more than the kulaks supplied in 1927).

That is how matters stand with us now, comrades.

There you have the change that has taken place in the economy of our country.

Now, as you see, we have the material base which enables us to replace the kulak output by the output of the collective farms and state farms. It is for this very reason that our determined offensive against the kulaks is now meeting with undeniable success.

That is how an offensive against the kulaks must be carried on, if we mean a genuine and determined offensive and not mere futile declamations against the kulaks.

That is why we have recently passed from the policy of restricting the exploiting tendencies of the kulaks to the policy of eliminating the kulaks as a class.

[Source: J.V. Stalin, *Works* Volume XII (Moscow 1955) pp. 174–76.]

On 5 January 1930, the Politburo adopted a formal resolution that collectivization be drastically accelerated. Whereas the Plan approved in April 1929 had envisaged some 10 per cent of the peasant population being collectivized by 1933, now there was to be total collectivization in some of the main grain areas by late 1930 to early 1931, and in the other grain regions by spring 1932. The resolution committed the party to 'eliminating the kulaks as a class' though it did not spell out exactly what was to become of them. Many local officials did not wait for more detailed instructions. Exhorted by the centre, eager to excel in achieving the party's goals, anxious to reach some kind of local stability in time for the spring sowing, and apprehensive about the potential scale of peasant resistance, they threw their efforts into a once-and-for-all crash programme. Even before a further Politburo Commission deliberating on the 'kulak question' had reported, provincial and district party officials raced ahead with frantic and often chaotic campaigns to identify 'kulaks' in their villages, confiscate their land and property, and evict them from their houses.

The following resolution from the bureau of the Urals *oblast'* committee conveys something of the frenetic way in which regional party organizations approached the huge task confronting them. The trigger for the resolution was an urgent telegram from the first secretary, Kabakov, who was on the Politburo's Commission on the 'kulak question'. The local leaders set up a sub-committee which among a host of duties was charged to provide, within five days, target figures for the number of 'kulaks' to be evicted from each of the 168 sprawling districts into which the *oblast'* was divided. The procedure mirrored Moscow's approach to supervising what amounted to a form of social revolution across the vastly varied regions of a country covering nearly a sixth of the earth's surface. Global figures based on formulaic class categorization were rendered even more crude by dividing them up among sub-areas according to scarcely less arbitrary political considerations and rough-and-ready socio-economic statistics. Just how arbitrary and haphazard a form 'dekulakization' took was shown a week later when the Politburo Commission, having come under strong regional pressure to do so, agreed guide figures far higher than those on which the Urals regional bureau had been operating. The Commission indicated approximate numbers to be placed in each of three categories, distinguished according to intensity of opposition, and in mechanistic fashion set overall ceilings on the number to be labelled 'kulak': 2–3 per cent of households in non-grain areas and 3–5 per cent in grain areas.[139] For the Urals this suggested a figure some ten times greater than that originally assumed.

---

139 Davies, *Socialist Offensive* pp. 232–43.

Document 146 | '… the kulaks are to be evicted…'—from Minute 61 of a closed session of the Politburo of the Urals *oblast'* committee of the CPSU

22 January 1930

Special file. Top secret. No copies to be made.

Item: Telegram from comrade Kabakov on the kulaks.

Resolved:

1. Confirm the text of the telegram on behalf of the secretaries of the *okrug** committees and the chairmen of the *okrug* executive committees…

3. Instruct a group from the *oblast'* committee within five days:

   a. To draw up special instructions for making production inventories and estimates for the transfer and use of confiscated kulak property by the collective farms.

   b. On the basis of the household, economic and political characteristics of each *okrug* and the rate of collectivization, to determine concretely those *okruga* and districts from which the kulaks are to be evicted, reckoning on 10–15,000 people across the *oblast'*.

   c. Ascertain the *okruga*, districts and number of kulaks to be resettled in remote northern forest regions (Tobol'sk, Obdorsk, Ivdel', the Northern Upper Kama *okrug*, etc.).

   d. To draw up a plan for using the kulaks on logging, land and other work and their possible incarceration in concentration camps…

5. To send directives through the local Party, Komsomol and Soviet channels and the organs of the OGPU on getting the entire apparatus ready so that they can be sure of conducting a successful campaign against the kulaks.

6. To send instructions through Party and Soviet channels on revising and strengthening the composition of the soviets.

7. To run a political campaign among workers on the shop floor to pass resolutions and statements approving Party and government measures for destroying the kulaks as a class.

8. To instruct the Urals Collective Farm Union to give out directives throughout the collective farm system on the active participation of collective farm organizations in destroying the kulaks. Approval of the draft letter to be obtained from the *oblast'* committee of the Party.

P. Zubarov, Secretary of the Urals *oblast'* committee of the CPSU

[Source: SOTsDOO, fond 4, opis' 8, delo 54, p. 9.]

---

* The administrative subdivision between *oblast'* and district, abolished later in 1930.

The language of 'kulaks' and class division played a vital role in enabling officials at all levels to cling to the fiction that collectivization was overwhelmingly voluntary. Any opposition was categorized as that of 'kulak elements' and thus by definition not indicative of the attitude of the great mass of middle as well as poor peasants. The fiction remained unshaken even though the scale and intensity of protest led party officials to provide emergency armed backup for the groups of officials, workers, and students cajoling peasants into voting for and signing up to collectivization. The following resolution by the party committee of Sverdlovsk *okrug* typifies the precautions taken. It reflects, too, the ever greater pressures on the committee secretary, the key party official at every level, who is made personally responsible for ensuring adequate detachments of armed workers are available and somehow doing so without affecting industrial and agricultural output.

Document 147 | **'Get... ready for battle...'—circular from the CPSU**
Sverdlovsk *okrug* committee

6 February 1930

Urgent. Top secret. Return within 24 hours.

In carrying out the policy of destroying the kulaks as a class it is possible that kulak elements in the countryside might try to bring together all malcontents in certain regions with a view to forming bands against Soviet power. Although it rejects in advance that any possible bandit actions could be successful, as a precaution the *okrug* committee proposes to district committee secretaries that within three days of receipt they take personal responsibility for checking on the feasibility of mobilization plans for forming communist detachments. Each district committee must make sure that these communist detachments are brought up to the requisite strength in such a way that they are undoubtedly ready for battle, while at the same time ensuring that if the detachments are formed and used in fighting, the withdrawal of CPSU members does not impact on production. Therefore the lists of members of these detachments should be reviewed immediately, adding those members of the CPSU whose departure would not affect production, but selecting them so that all members of the detachment are able to take part in battle operations, i.e., no invalids. In addition, it is essential to check each detachment's courier communications system to ensure rapid muster and complete readiness.

Measures are to be taken to ensure that all Party members enlisted in the detachment are immediately brought up to battle-readiness by the training units of the Society for Assisting Defence, Aviation and Chemical Construction, so that, should the detachments be required, they are effective fighting units. There should be military training for all communists, as those not enlisted in the detachments will be the immediate reserve for replenishing the communist detachments, should this be necessary.

On request from the GPU, with *okrug* committee sanction (by telephone), district committee secretaries must immediately gather detachments. These will operate under the command of a detachment commander, on instruction from the GPU. Get the communist detachments' mobilization plan ready for battle in accordance with the instructions in this letter and inform the *okrug* committee of implementation after three days.

These measures must in no way hinder the implementation of the economic plans for industry and agriculture.

Potaskuev — Chief Secretary of the CPSU

[Source: SOTsDOO, fond 4, opis´ 8, delo 54, p. 38.]

Peasant resistance was widespread, sustained and multiform. It was fuelled by the high-handedness and ignorance of party officials and agents installed to run the new collective farms; by the creation of vast collectives which removed the management far from the traditional village and alienated peasants even further; by peasant fury at being ordered to surrender livestock to the collective, outrage at the frontal assault on religion, priests and churches that accompanied the campaign, and horror at violent 'dekulakization' of fellow villagers, neighbours and friends. There were thousands of cases of peasants carrying out assaults on groups of collectivizers, night-time attacks, assassinations and arson.[140] Ukraine saw by far the largest number of peasants involved, but in the Urals there were almost a thousand recorded acts of resistance in 1930 alone. For the most part, though, the local authorities looked able to mobilize too much force to make armed struggle an option, and peasants resorted to varieties of passive resistance from local demonstrations and disrupting meetings called to institute collectivization, to deceiving collectivization teams, disobeying simple instructions, feigning confusion and, on a massive scale, slaughtering livestock for barter or consumption rather than see it taken over by the collective farm.

The risk became alarming that the spring sowing would be seriously disrupted and the new farms unable to function; even worse was the danger that the thousands of reports of individual 'incidents' would snowball into a threat to the stability of the whole regime. On 2 March Stalin published in *Pravda* an article entitled 'Dizzy with Success', blaming over-zealous local officials for going far beyond their remit and defying party policy by resorting to coercion. Officials were dismayed and peasants delighted by the sudden green light that Stalin gave for peasants to withdraw from the collective farms. There followed a massive exodus. In the Urals region, the proportion of

---

140 Viola, *Peasant Rebels* pp. 100–31.

collectivized households fell in March and April from 76 per cent to 32 per cent, and across the country the proportion fell from 57 per cent in March to 21.5 per cent in September.[141]

Yet once grain collections resumed in the autumn, the violence and coercion of the spring returned. Though the harvest was good, initial reports exaggerated just how good and the authorities imposed enormously ambitious procurement targets to maximize exports. The 'Urals–Siberian' method of extracting grain from the peasantry was again widely employed, and procurement squads found that newly collectivized peasants were considerably easier to manage than individual householders. They, too, tried to evade the quotas imposed but found it much harder to do so given the party's greater presence, closer monitoring of what was grown, and leverage over the politically appointed farm management. With encouragement from the centre, collectivization resumed alongside forcible grain requisitioning. Although the pace was now more moderate, heavy pressure had to be brought to bear on the peasantry before they would consent, and across the country activists made use of the device of isolating and exiling likely opposition ringleaders as 'kulaks'. The (implausibly precise) exile numbers reported to the Politburo Commission overseeing the process, which was headed by A.A. Andreev, chair of the party's Control Commission, showed a considerably greater number for 1931 than 1930—the Urals being by some way the largest recipient. Only from 1933, when the main grain-growing regions had been overwhelmingly collectivized and harassment, discrimination and rates of taxation had made independent households barely viable, would the annual number decline. By the end of the decade, when households outside collectives had been reduced to a small residue, it is estimated the exile total reached over one million families.

Document 148 | Report on the number of evicted kulaks

1931

TOP SECRET to comrade Andreev.

1. Total evictions in 1930	113,013 families	551,330 persons
2. Total evictions in 1931	243,531 "	1,128,198 "
Total evicted in 1930 and 1931	356,544 "	1,679,528 "
Of which: Sent in from other *oblasti*	245,403 "	1,157,077 "
Resettled within their *oblasti*	111,141 "	522,451 "
Total	356,544 families	1,679,528 persons

141 Davies, *Socialist Offensive* pp. 442–43.

3. Evicted kulaks have been resettled in the following areas

1. Northern *kray*	58,800	families	288,560	persons
2. Urals *oblast'*	123,547	"	571,355	"
3. Kazakhstan	50,268	"	241,331	"
4. Western Siberian *kray*	69,916	"	316,883	"
5. Eastern Siberian *kray*	28,572	"	138,191	"
6. Far Eastern *kray*	9,694	"	48,269	"
7. Yakutia (Aldan)	1,366	"	7,157	"
8. Leningrad *oblast'*	6,884	"	31,466	"
9. Nizhniy Novgorod *oblast'*	1,497	"	6,316	"
10. North Caucasus *kray*	3,000	"	15,000	"
11. Ukrainian SSR	3,000	"	15,000	"
Total	**356,544 families**		**1,679,528 persons**	

[Source: RGASPI, fond 17, opis' 120, delo 52, p. 59.]

While the motive for 'dekulakization' was to pre-empt and destroy resistance to collectivization, it also offered opportunities to respond to industry's urgent need for new labour. In the early years of the Bolshevik regime, the prevailing ethos, in line with European left-wing critiques of traditional penal policy, was that prison and corrective labour should be designed first and foremost to reform the transgressor. During the 1920s, however, this ethos gave way to more and more emphasis on those who broke socialist law making their contribution via forced labour (see document 161 below). This applied *a priori* to class enemies such as those convicted of belonging to the 'kulak element'. In the course of 1930, as it became clear that tens of thousands of able-bodied men and women would be available for forced labour, industrial managers began to press for suitable exiles to be assigned to their enterprises. Andreev's Commission, which included the OGPU chief, G.G. Yagoda, was responsible for overseeing the transfer of 'kulak' families within and between regions. In practice its control was extremely loose and calls by it and by Sovnarkom for those bidding for labour to ensure basic provisions for exiles were widely ignored. As the following document of summer 1931 shows, at the front of the queue, encouraged by Kabakov, were the major Urals coal, steel and non-ferrous metal trusts. The request for no fewer than 50,000 'special migrants' to work in the timber industry reflected the virtual impossibility of getting voluntary labour to stay for any length of time working in grim conditions in remote regions of the *oblast'*.

Document 149 | **From the minutes of comrade Andreev's Commission on the Kulaks**

8 July 1931

TOP SECRET

Chairman: comrade Andreev

Present: comrades Yagoda, Evdokimov, Nikolaev, Kogan, Verman, Smol'yaninov, Figatner, Bal'yan

1. *Eastern Coal's applications*

To satisfy Eastern Coal's applications:

  a) 1,000 families of special migrants for Cheremkhovo. Satisfy application using Bashkir special migrants. Despatch dates: 30 July–1 August.

  b) 500 families of special migrants for Bokuchacha, using internal Eastern Siberian special migration. Despatch dates: 15–25 July.

  c) 2,000 families of special migrants for Anzherka-Sudzhenka, using Bashkir special migrants. Despatch dates: 18–24 July.

  d) 3,000 families of special migrants for the Prokop'evsk district, using Bashkir special migrants. Despatch dates: 25 July–3 August.

  e) 500 families of special migrants for the Minusinsk district, using internal Western Siberian special migration. Despatch dates: 15–20 July.

2. *Ural Coal's applications*

To satisfy Ural Coal's applications:

  a) 1,100 families of special migrants from Nizhniy Novgorod *kray* for Kizelovsk district. Despatch dates: 2–4 August.

  b) 1,100 families of special migrants from Nizhniy Novgorod *kray* for Chelyabinsk district. Despatch dates: 5–7 August.

3. *Eastern Steel's applications*

To satisfy Eastern Steel's applications for 18,200 families to work in the following enterprises:

  a) 5,000 families of special migrants from the Moscow *oblast'* for Kuznetskstroy. Despatch dates: 20 July–1 August.

  b) An extra 1,000 families of special migrants from the Central Black Earth *oblast'* for Sinarstroy. Despatch dates: 9–11 July.

  c) 5,000 families of special migrants from Tatariya for Magnitogorsk. Despatch dates: 16 July-5 August.

  d) 500 families of special migrants from the Moscow district for Vysokogorsk Ore Administration. Despatch date: 2 August.

  e) 1,200 families of special migrants from the Moscow district for Bakal'sk Ore Administration. Despatch dates: 3–6 August.

  f) 1,000 families of special migrants from the Moscow district for Goroblagodatsk

Ore Administration. Despatch dates: 7–9 August.

g) 500 families of special migrants from the Moscow district for Zlatoust Ore Administration. Despatch date: 10 August.

h) 1,000 families of special migrants from Nizhniy Novgorod *kray* for Sinarsk Ore Administration. Despatch dates: 30 July–1 August.

i) Comrade Trakhter, director of Tagilstroy, to be reprimanded for refusing to accept the 3,000 special migrants sent at his request from Ukraine. Consequently, they had to be re-routed to other work.

Eastern Steel must within twenty-four hours provide a specific application, stating when it will accept the special migrant families to Tagilstroy. The OGPU is to ensure that the application is dealt with.

4. *Non-Ferrous and Gold's Applications*
To satisfy Non-Ferrous and Gold's applications:
1. In the Urals:

a) 400 families of special migrants from the Nizhniy Novgorod *kray* for Kalata. Despatch date: 2 August.

b) 200 families of special migrants from the Nizhniy Novgorod *kray* for Tagil. Despatch date: 3 August.

c) 400 families of special migrants from the Nizhniy Novgorod *kray* for Karabash. Despatch date: 4 August.

d) 800 families of special migrants from the Nizhniy Novgorod *kray* for Ural Platinum. Despatch dates: 5–6 August.

2. In Western Siberia:

a) 400 families of special migrants using internal Western Siberian special migration for the Mariynsk district. Despatch dates: 15–20 July.

b) 200 families of special migrants using internal Western Siberian special migration for the Ol'khovsk district. Despatch dates: 15–20 July.

3. In view of the disgraceful arrangements made for families of special migrants already transported from Aldan, as a result of which 4,000 people, family members, have still not been accommodated and are living on the railway tracks near Bol'shoy Never railway station, Aldan's application for another 1,000 families is to be rejected.

5. *Union Peat's Application*
Of the 50,000 families of special migrants sent to the Urals for Ural Timber 5,000 are to be sent to work on peat in the Urals in August.

6. Kulaks cannot be used at peat workings in the Central districts, at Avtostroy and Soyuzstandartstroy in the Donbass. Applications refused.

7. *Union Timber's Applications*
a) In view of the poor use made at logging camps of the labour of those special

migrants already transported to Union Timber, the latter's application for 17,000 families of special migrants for the Northern *kray* is to be refused.

b) Comply with the supplementary application from the Vel'sk district of the Northern *kray* for 3,000 families of special migrants for logging work for the Moscow and Leningrad areas.

[Source: RGASPI, fond 17, opis´ 120, delo 52, pp. 1–4.]

Famine

The disruption and demoralization of forced collectivization, the expulsion or flight of many of the most able peasant farmers, the drastic decline in livestock and acute shortage of tractors and other machinery, exacerbated by adverse weather, resulted in a steep fall in the harvests of 1931 and 1932. Requisitioning quotas, however, remained brutally high as the party strove to maintain export levels to pay for vital capital goods imports and to feed the rapidly burgeoning urban population. The result was to leave both individual householders and collective farmers struggling, in the worst months, to find enough to eat. The theft of grain, especially in the form of scavenging from collective farms, soared. In the eyes of many collectivized peasants, the collective farm fields, which they had sown and harvested, were fair game given the derisory prices paid for requisitioned grain. As conditions became more and more desperate, farm managers and indeed local officials in many places proved sympathetic or were themselves implicated in 'theft' to provide for their own workforce. Concern at the disruption and cost of theft mounted; police and judicial officials pressed for action; and in August 1932 a draconian decree, reputedly drafted by Stalin himself, was issued. In time-honoured fashion the harsh measures were presented as being in response to demands from loyal workers and peasants, drawing a veil over the fact that most of the theft was by collective farmers themselves. Stealing could be punished by death ('the highest degree of social protection') and the minimum penalty was to be ten years' imprisonment. There were at least 55,000 convictions (many of them women and children) and 1,000 executions in the last months of 1932, and twice as many in 1933.[142]

---

142 Viola, *Peasant Rebels* pp. 222–23.

Document 150 │ **From a TsIK and Sovnarkom decree: 'On the protection of the property of state enterprises, collective farms and co-operatives and the strengthening of public (socialist) property'**

7 August 1932

Complaints from workers and collective farmers about theft have increased recently: theft from trains and barges and of co-operative and collective-farm property; similarly, complaints have increased about violence and threats from kulak elements against collective farmers who do not wish to leave the collective farm. . .

The Central Executive Committee and the Council of People's Commissars of the USSR consider that public property (state, collective farm and co-operative) is the basis of the Soviet system, is sacred and inviolable and those threatening it must be looked upon as enemies of the people. Consequently, a resolute struggle against those stealing state property is the primary duty of the organs of Soviet power.

Therefore, and in response to the demands of workers and collective farmers, the Central Executive Committee and the Council of People's Commissars of the USSR decree as follows:

I

. . . 2. The application of the highest degree of social protection as a measure of legal repression against theft from trains and barges—execution by firing squad and confiscation of all property or, if there are mitigating circumstances, confiscation of property and a minimum of ten years' imprisonment. . . 3. Amnesties will not apply to criminals sentenced for the theft of goods in transit.

II

. . . 2. The application of the highest degree of social protection as a measure of legal repression against theft of collective-farm and co-operative property—execution by firing-squad and confiscation of property or, if there are mitigating circumstances, confiscation of property and a minimum of ten years' imprisonment. 3. Amnesties will not apply to criminals sentenced for the theft of collective-farm and co-operative property.

III

. . . 2. The application of legal repression against violence and threats against collective farms and collective farmers by kulak and other anti-social elements—from five to ten years' deprivation of freedom in a concentration camp.

3. Amnesties will not apply to criminals sentenced in such cases.

M. Kalinin, chairman of the TsIK of the USSR
V. Molotov (Skryabin), chairman of the Sovnarkom of the USSR
A. Enukidze, secretary of the TsIK of the USSR

[Source: *Sobranie zakonov i rasporyazheniy raboche-krest'yanskogo pravitel'stva Soyuza SSR* No. 62 (Moscow 1932) Article 360, pp. 583–84.]

So dreadful were conditions in the village—especially for those who ran the risk of being denounced as 'kulaks'—that even the truly abysmal urban conditions of 1930–33 seemed preferable. Alongside victims of 'dekulakization' were many more families who chose 'self-dekulakization' and sold or abandoned their property rather than risk being forcibly exiled. They joined the massive tide of migrants who left the countryside in search of safety, work and food in the cities. The scale of urban migration amounted to a virtual social revolution, running in the early 1930s at three million per year. The influx, which dwarfed the number of 'special migrants' formally assigned to industrial enterprises, was welcomed by industrial managers as they struggled to find the necessary labour to meet soaring construction and production targets. But cities already barely able to absorb the annual migration of one million in the late NEP period were overwhelmed; overcrowding became sordid and degrading; rudimentary health and welfare organizations could not cope; and the rationing system introduced in 1928 was stretched to breaking point. In late 1932, during a brief pause in pressure for additional labour from industrial managers, the regime sought to stem the tide and return unwanted peasants to the countryside. The system adopted—a sinister echo of the Tsarist policing method abolished in 1917—was to introduce internal passports.

Peasants had no automatic right to a passport and had to apply for them before migrating, enabling the police and local authorities to slow sharply the rate of urban migration. In the cities and other designated 'passport regime' areas, all residents were required to secure a passport and urban registration card. This gave the police a powerful tool of social control, enabling them to expel not only unauthorized peasant migrants but all those deemed 'harmful elements', from 'socially alien' strata disenfranchised under the constitution—former propertied elements, priests, White Army officers—to 'labour shirkers' with no sanctioned job, vagrants, prostitutes and those with a criminal record, political or civil.[143] Of comparable long-term significance was the requirement that each passport holder identify his or her nationality. The requirement corresponded to the regime's policy of acknowledging and affirming the significance of national differences. But it made immutable an aspect of each individual's identity which might otherwise have remained far more plastic, especially among a generation which was destined to be the subject of massive social flux, migration, urbanization and military devastation, and with the onset of Nazi invasion in 1941 was to prove highly responsive to transnational, Soviet patriotic appeal.[144]

---

143 P.N. Hagenloh, '"Socially Harmful Elements" and the Great Terror' in S. Fitzpatrick (ed.) *Stalinism: New directions* (London 2000) pp. 295–300.
144 Y. Slezkine, 'The Soviet Union as a Communal Apartment' *Slavic Review* 53 (1994) pp. 415–52.

Document 151 | **The establishment of a single Union passport and compulsory registration of passports—from a TsIK and Sovnarkom decree**

27 December 1932

In order to keep better account of the population of cities, workers' settlements and new towns and to move out persons not connected with production or work in government establishments or schools and not involved in socially useful work (excluding invalids and pensioners), and also to clear these populated areas of kulaks, criminal and other anti-social elements who have taken refuge there, the TsIK and Sovnarkom resolve as follows:

1. To establish across the USSR a single passport system according to the passport statute.
2. To introduce across the USSR in the course of 1933 a single passport system, with obligatory registration of residence, starting with Moscow, Leningrad, Khar'kov, Kiev, Odessa, Minsk, Rostov-on-Don, Vladivostok. . .
4. To authorize the governments of the Union Republics to bring their own legislation into line with the above resolution and the statute on passports.

M. Kalinin, chairman of the TsIK of the USSR
V. Molotov (Skryabin), chairman of the Sovnarkom of the USSR
A. Enukidze, secretary of the TsIK of the USSR

[Source: *Sobranie zakonov i rasporyazheniy raboche-krest'yanskogo pravitel'stva Soyuza SSR* No. 84 (Moscow 1932) Article 516, pp. 821–22.]

As famine bit deeper and deeper in the winter of 1932–33, the measures taken to restrict migration became increasingly violent. Hardest hit were the main grain-producing areas stripped bare by requisitioning, most notoriously Ukraine and the North Caucasus, from where the following OGPU report was sent early in 1933.[145] The euphemisms used had become standard. The negative labels 'White', 'kulak', 'counter-revolutionary', 'sabotage' and 'insurgency' were rolled together almost indiscriminately, reflecting the authorities' sense that these categories overlapped and shared a desire to undermine the regime. The 'explanatory work' alluded to included heavy reliance on threat and coercion. The focus on 'escapees' conveyed the false

---

145 The most graphic account is R. Conquest, *The Harvest of Sorrows: Soviet collectivization and the terror famine* (London 1986), although his view that the regime deliberately fostered famine is no longer convincing. See the persuasive corrective by M.B. Tauber, 'The 1932 Harvest and the Famine of 1933' *Slavic Review* 50 (1991) pp. 70–89, and the exchange in *Slavic Review* 51 (1992) pp. 192–94.

impression that migration was restricted to 'kulaks' under police supervision rather than a cross-section of desperate peasants. From Stalin downwards, the regime stoutly denied the very existence of the famine, and officials who broke the taboo risked punishment and dismissal.[146] The nearest this report came to acknowledging the truth was its passing recognition that the number escaping rose where there was 'the greatest grain procurement pressure'.

Document 152 | **E.G. Evdokimov: '...stop the escapes...'—from a message telegraphed to the OGPU deputy-chairman in Rostov-on-Don**

1933

No. 141256: the question of the struggle against escape was raised by me immediately after my arrival in the North Caucasus region—on the basis of data from a number of regions on the increasing number of escapes, which have reached epidemic proportions in some areas. At the end of November and several times thereafter I gave categorical orders to the operational sectors, the *oblast'* departments, the Mountain district departments of the transport militia and the *kray* militia to take a variety of decisive measures to stop the escapes. At that time the measures taken on the ground fell into the following basic categories:

1. An agency has been mobilized to deal with mass escapes, especially of White Guard kulak elements, and especially to unmask the organizers and agitators who are encouraging and provoking escape. Demoralizing work, and explanatory work, is being carried out, and appeals are being made, etc.
2. Measures have been taken and the question of increasing mass explanatory work is constantly being raised, so as to organize public resistance to the escapes. The question has been raised at the *kray* committee level, which has issued special directives to the localities.
3. The transport militia, besides operational and agitational work, have created mobile groups on the transport system, operational detachments at the points and in the regions where fugitives gather and travel, particularly towards Ukraine and Transcaucasia. This has even gone as far as checking travellers purchasing tickets.
4. Cordons have been set up by the militia, along with party and Soviet activists on the main routes used by fugitives, particularly those leading to the Black Sea, the Transcaucasian and Black Sea coasts at the border with Abkhazia and also in Dagestan at the border with Azerbaidzhan, as well as the main passes into Transcaucasia. Of those kulaks detained, the counter-revolutionary element have been arrested, the rest have been filtered, and individuals, after processing, have been sent back to where they came from for demoralizing and explanatory work.

---

146 For the sustained impact of official denial on popular memory of the famine, see C. Merridale, *Night of Stone: Death and memory in Russia* (London 2000) pp. 196–233.

Leaving without permission being granted by the village soviet or the collective farm is forbidden, but this does not work, since they run away without permission.

5. In the cities an agency has been mobilized for discovering fugitives and preventing possible counter-revolutionary active and diversionary work in enterprises and new building sites on the part of fugitives who have settled in towns. Measures have been taken to use agents and guards to protect the most important strategic points, state installations and major enterprises, particularly those with military significance. A number of anti-escape operations have been conducted in the towns.

6. Our main efforts have been directed against organized insurrectionary counter-revolution, and its instigating and organizing role in escapes. As you are aware, in the Kuban an important insurgency organization has been discovered in the Kurgan and other parts of the North Caucasus *kray*—the case of Colonel Popov and others. In connection with this case, work has been discovered on organizing escapes with a view to sabotage, the formation of insurrectionary groups of fugitives in the Black Sea area. . . In addition to this, from other cases which have been completed it has also been established that counter-revolutionaries have been working to concentrate fugitives in remote forested mountain regions, as well as in cities. As a result of the measures we have taken in the *kray* (as well as operations in Shakhty, Taganrog, Rostov and elsewhere) our organs have detained 7,534 persons from this fugitive element.

. . . In November and December the number escaping rose in certain places and Cossack settlements. This was particularly so in the settlements where there was the greatest grain procurement pressure. Now we can observe:

1. Compared with November and December the number escaping in January has dropped. However, in individual regions and Cossack settlements it still continues. We have established that there is a concentration of fugitives in the Azov flats, and we are preparing an operation. We are also preparing an operation in Rostov. In certain places it has been observed that fugitives have been seen returning. . .

Evdokimov.

[Source: V.A. Mazur and M.E. Glavatsky, *Istoriya Rossii 1917–1940*, pp. 267–68.]

Coming on top of the violent drive for collectivization, the onset of the famine bred even more brutal maltreatment of those who fell foul of the authorities. When compliant peasants were on the brink of starvation, and even rural officials and urban workers subsisted on desperately low rations, officials showed ruthless indifference to the plight of exiles uprooted and deposited in the growing network of special settlements. The bewilderment of those caught up in the net of 'dekulakization' and facing famine is painfully apparent in the following *cri de coeur* from one of the victims, 'settled' in the Urals district of Nadezhdin, east of Perm. Fedosiy Matveevich Loboda wrestles with the tension between his pride at having served in the Red Army and solidarity with 'staunch builders of socialism' on the one hand, and his own treatment on the other. He has imbibed much of the regime's discourse: he identifies with the Soviet Union, he venerates its Constitution, he freely echoes condemnation of 'kulak types', and calls for 'proper camps' for those causing real damage, and he is desperate to shed the stigma of having been deprived of voting rights.[147] He is adamant—whether sincerely or disingenuously it is impossible to be certain—that the Moscow authorities have 'no idea what is going on in the provinces' and about the injustice meted out to those like himself. And he accepts that as a result of his social background he may have his faults. On the other hand, he protests against the notion that a man is to blame for being born the son of a 'kulak', and he pulls no punches in describing local economic chaos, the utter callousness of local officials, and the growing number dying of hunger.

Document 153 | **'I was born into a kulak family'—letter from Fedosiy Matveevich Loboda of the Tractor Division, resettled at 173 km along the Perm railway, to the Bureau of the CC of the Bolshevik Party**

22 August 1932

I was born into a kulak family. I served in the Red Army for over two years at the time of War Communism, and after the Civil War in 1925–26 served in the territorial system. In addition, from 1924 to 1930 I worked in village institutions and in 1928–29 even worked as a teacher. In all, I have served the Soviet state loyally for more than five years, and the Constitution of the Union says that anybody not from a working family but who has served five years is not deprived of voting rights. Unless my memory fails me that is the case. Even if I did have my faults, that was the result of my background and not from malice. Anyway, I don't consider it a fault to have been born into a kulak family. There was nothing I could do about that and there are many more in my position. While in the Red Army I managed

---

147 For a path-breaking analysis of the diary and emerging self-definition of a young worker whose father had been dekulakized, see J. Hellbeck, 'Fashioning the Stalinist Soul: The diary of Stepan Podlubnyi, 1931–9' in S. Fitzpatrick (ed.) *Stalinism: New directions* pp. 77–116. For rejection of the view that new Soviet workers internalized the identity and characterization attributed to them in official discourse, see D.L. Hoffman, *Peasant Metropolis: Social identity in Moscow 1929–1941* (Ithaca, NY, 1994).

to get a bullet in the head and because it didn't kill me, I'm now in the Urals. Take War Communism: desertion by a Red Army soldier was considered a grave offence, for which you could get the highest measure of social defence—you could be shot. A lot of men then didn't serve in the army, went over to Makhno or Grigor'ev, did well out of pillaging, and are now serving as the mainstay of socialism in the villages. What's your opinion? Are they loyal? No! I am not a communist, I am a person without rights, but I would never trust them. When they have the chance they just loll about, which is dangerous. I was in the Red Army, was a civil servant in Nikolaev [Ukraine] and rooted out such evil, but now I'm stuck in the Urals, wondering whether I'll survive tomorrow or starve to death, and there's an epidemic here. I was born in 1899, never had land or a farm—and I'm a kulak! The Communist Party doesn't look at things in such a way. It looks at life properly, but what is it doing about the injustices happening in the provinces? I have already written many times about the injustice of the deprivations I am suffering, but always get some routine answer in Ukrainian about managing, and still have not been given any reason for it. That's the answer I got to my statement from the public prosecutor of the Bashtansk region [Ukraine]. Just imagine this: I have been sent away by the GPU as the son of a kulak, and locally they accuse me of being dangerous for collectivization because I'm the son of a kulak and am a kulak at heart. I have a family—a wife and two children, and the elder one needs to start school. I live in communal barracks, where there are some real kulak types, and in such surroundings the children, despite themselves, are picking up bad habits. Surely they're not going to be accused of being born into the son of a kulak's family and having an anti-Soviet nature just because they've ended up by chance in such surroundings?! No, that's downright wrong. The children need to be moved away from here, they could be made into staunch builders of socialism, but for them to be here is a big mistake, in my opinion. If I am wrong about this, show me and I shall change my mind. Anyway, there are many dependants here whose presence is simply harmful, as they need feeding and cannot do anything useful. The Urals need workers, not dependants. Down in the steppe area these dependants could feed themselves and be of some use to the Union. As for those causing real damage, there are proper camps for them where they could be sorted out. Before harvest there were big lay-offs here, people could not get work and were starving to death. You just come and take a look at these exile settlements—many have already cleared off or died, while 75 per cent of those left are all swollen up, and the main reason is starvation. This is a typical scene: a young man goes somewhere to get a bit of bread or even steal it, because hunger makes people into wolves, but collapses by the roadside, dies and just lies there like a log of wood. When they bring in a consignment of wood, they do a thorough stock-take. If it reveals that the person bringing it in is guilty of losing some logs, he is answerable for it. But the dead can just be left to lie there, and nobody's to blame. You can ask the commandant's office to tell you how many people they've got, how many have escaped and how many have died. They'll tell you, but the figures won't bear any relation to the truth. When I was brought here, there were a lot of people, but now? Why do they lay a man off and not give him any work? He will just die, he can't work or get any bread to eat, and to buy it at the market you need money, a lot of it. Why are they dragging people from one place of work to another where they just starve? This is the answer many people here get: 'I'm free, I can get food without queuing, but you're a saboteur.' People stand for days on end and still get nothing, even though there is work. This really needs looking into and rooting out. We need to set up proper socialist re-education, not just clamp-downs. The centre has no idea what is going on in the provinces. There's a lot I could tell you, but I just haven't got time to write it all down. I do not bother telling the commandants, because most of them would just say, 'I'll bang you up and you can starve there.' That's not re-education. It is very damaging, because the children will soon pick up that way of thinking. Throughout the Nadezhdin district eleven people have had their voting rights restored. You mean to tell me that they could find only eleven people who were good workers?! At our timber centre there's not a single one, and there are three exile settlements here. If you go to the commandant's office, they just say that, if you want your rights back, you've got to get a reference from the economic managers; you go to one of them for a reference and they say, 'We've got no orders and we don't know if we can give you one.' I would ask the centre to come and investigate this settlement and see things for themselves. I don't expect you'll want to believe me, because all the information you get, presumably, says everything is fine. Please just insist on one thing: let them tell you why so many have scarpered or died. I bet you won't get a straight answer. The young need taking away from here, and the dependants, and the workers need feeding, and there'll be a clear result: the production programme will be fulfilled properly.

The canteen boils some fish, but that's all there is, and so workers have bread and fish and the water in the brook's free, but for some reason there's canteen staff.

I haven't taken a single day off and have done my quota, and got 250 grams of vegetable oil for one year, but some have not even got that much. Where are the calories in that?! The co-operative needs looking into properly.

Do not take what they tell you on trust—by the end of the Five-Year Plan you need to come and check up on things.

This letter will seem very bold, but the only hope rests in the centre. The programme will not be fulfilled by filing reports, but by actual work to implement it, and for this we need enough bread, a bit of oatmeal, even without the fat.

Fedosiy Loboda, a settler.

[Source: GASO, fond 4, opis' 10, delo 174, pp. 25–26.]

The horrendous picture painted by Loboda is given striking confirmation by the following report to Kabakov from the key local official in the Nadezhdin district, the party secretary M.A. Zhdanov. Zhdanov, a new appointee sent in to replace one of the tens of thousands of local officials sacked during collectivization—for overzealous 'dekulakization' in 1930, maltreatment of migrants, and above all for 'foot-dragging' over grain procurements in 1931 and 1932—was charged with bringing social and economic stability to the 'special migrants' exiled to the district. His readiness to castigate the inhumanity and inefficiency of his predecessors suggests Kabakov had been vigorously passing the blame to his subordinates in a manner that became standard practice.

Document 154 | **From a letter from M.A. Zhdanov, secretary of the Nadezhdin district CPSU committee, to I.D. Kabakov, concerning special migrants**

31 March 1933

Dear Ivan Dmitrievich,

In sending you the Nadezhdin district committee's resolution, which was adopted in connection with the *oblast'* committee's decision on the question of special migrants in the Nadezhdin region, I am to inform you of the following:

1. The treatment of special migrants throughout 1932 was really barbaric and criminal. This is clearly illustrated by the fact that there were 10,000 deaths and 6,500 deserters in 1932.
2. The systematic failure to deliver food in the second half of 1932 led to marked emaciation.
3. Even now housing is in a dreadful condition (windows frequently lack glass, houses are not insulated, there are often no stoves).

It is my profound conviction that these people's living conditions could be significantly better if the district organizations put their minds to it.

In order to improve the existing situation and implement your instructions in this regard, we intend to do the following:

1. We must make use of the 6,000 hectares set aside for sowing by the exiles. But we can ensure this only if we get some help with seeds. Comrade Rapoport has had 1,500 quintals of seed sent to us. Moreover, he has also allowed about 700 hectares to be set aside for growing vegetables. In order to sow the planned 6,000 hectares, we need additional seed for approximately 4,000 hectares. We request that we be given the permission of the *oblast'* executive committee's Party group to make use of the 1,500 quintals we have in reserve and ask comrade Rapoport, if we are allowed to keep the 1,500 quintals of grain, to send a further 2,500 hectares' worth of corn and vegetable seeds.
2. We ask to be allowed to buy cattle for the special migrants in one of the Urals

districts. In particular, we think this can be done in the Gari district. At present
the exiles are being given wages for the last few months and the present situation
is that, once they have got the money, the kulaks run away in greater numbers,
because, having the money but not having anything to buy in the forest, they
naturally head for the town to buy food.

Since the number of cattle in our region is small and the demand amongst
special migrants to purchase cattle is extraordinarily high, there have been spec-
ulative hikes in the price of cattle both on the part of individual and collective
farmers. A cow now costs 2,500–3,000 rubles round here.

3. We also ask for goods and food to be sent to the forest at commercial prices.

4. Comrade Rapoport has helped us a great deal. He has done this by sending people
to organize those unable to work into a variety of non-statutory craft workshops.
We have snatched up this offer. After talking to the comrades who arrived today
we have decided in the first instance to organize the following:

a. Cooperage.

b. Production of children's toys.

c. Production of pottery.

d. Basket-weaving, furniture-making and bast shoe-making.

But since neither our industrial co-operatives, nor any other organizations in
our region have taken this matter seriously, nobody has any funds for it.
Specifically: in two or three weeks' time we could organize large-scale cranberry
picking; in summer we could organize large-scale mushroom gathering, pickle
them in barrels made by ourselves, and feed not only our own people but perhaps
elsewhere (the locals say that there are so many mushrooms around here that
there are more than enough for the Nadezhdin district). We would like to ask
you and comrade Rapoport just to help us get started. When we have barrels,
children's toys, mushrooms and cranberries, we think we will have more than
enough funds and money.

5. Moreover, we hope that in the current year, along with work on the mechanization of logging, we will be able to bring the special migrants' settlements up
to the required standard. To do this we ask you for just one thing: we need glass,
in order to fit double-glazing in the houses. We can find the rest ourselves.

Yours,
Zhdanov

[Source: SOTsDOO, fond 4, opis´ 11, delo 198, pp. 49–51.]

The following OGPU report, written at the height of the famine, paints an
even more graphic picture of the callous handling of prisoners arriving at a
labour camp in the Urals, east of Sverdlovsk. It is relieved only by the outrage
expressed by the OGPU officials themselves, and that is overlaid by their

sense of helplessness in the face of the brutality, debauchery, nepotism and incompetence they describe running all the way from the local camp officials to the district procurator's office.[148]

Document 155 | From a report on Nizhneturinsk labour camp by Milovanov, head of the district department of the OGPU, and plenipotentiary Ermakov

7 April 1933

Between January and 6 April 1933 the number of deaths in the Nizhneturinsk labour camp has reached 2,200. It has risen entirely as a result of prisoners newly arrived from Magnitogorsk, Perm and other labour camps. These arrived here on 20 February 1933 severely emaciated, brought in completely bare coal trucks. The trucks presumably had not been heated en route, as they arrived covered with snow on the inside and were iced up. Insufficient water had been provided. As a result some of the prisoners had died in the wagons...; on 20 February among the consignment from Magnitogorsk there were 18 corpses on the train, 15 died during disembarkation and 60 died during that same night.

Moreover, the management of Nizhneturinsk camp were simply not prepared for the reception and settlement of the newly arrived prisoners: the barracks had not been prepared, nor had food, water or medical provision. The weakened arrivals were housed in the still unfinished barracks, 180–200 each in a section meant for 45–50, and in barracks meant for 300 they put up to 1,800. The sick were put on the floor because there were not even any plank beds, let alone bunks, because they had not yet been made. The dead were laid face down with the dying on top of them, and piles were built in this way. Water was running down the walls of these barracks, the floor was damp and there was no medical provision because the senior doctor, Stepanov, regarded it with indifference, and did not allow anybody else to interfere. The newly arrived prisoners were issued 300 grams of bread per week, but not on time, and there was not enough water—sometimes there was none for days on end. On 20 February medical attendant Giaynulin reported four dead, whom he sent to the morgue, where, on being undressed by senior orderly Kutyuk, two were found to be still alive. These he put in a bath, and they survived another ten hours.

When two cases of typhoid appeared, Stepanov did not take adequate measures to prevent its spread. He called the prisoners lousy scum, etc., did not bathe them, did not isolate the prisoners from the same dormitory, did not disinfect their clothes, waited for it to increase and once there was an epidemic, he said with an ironic smile, 'There's nothing we can do about it now. There'll be 500 cases.' With the

---

148 For the fullest recent account of the horrors of the whole network of concentration camps, see A. Appelbaum, *Gulag: A history* (London 2003).

arrival of Doctor Mirov from the *oblast'*, Stepanov declared, 'No good'll come of this.' Mirov acted decisively, got everybody in the bathhouse in five days, repeated this five days later, mobilized all the medics to fight the typhoid and reduced its incidence.

Stepanov used to be a doctor with officer's rank in a cavalry regiment of the tsarist army.

These outrages are undoubtedly the direct result of nepotism among the camp management, namely, the director, Lyapunov, the head of supplies, a kulak's son called Oshchurkov, the assistant director of education, Luzyanin, and staff from the *oblast'* Administration for Corrective Labour Institutions [UITU] and the *oblast'* procuracy. . .

After the arrival of the transported prisoners, at the beginning of March, a commission to investigate the outrages came from the *oblast'* UITU. It was headed by Zyryanov (assistant deputy director of the *oblast'* UITU), along with Petrovykh from the UITU production sector, Andryukov from the administrative sector, assistant *oblast'* procurator Sirotkin, and Popov, the senior investigator at the *oblast'* procurator's office. During the investigation several times, day and night, Zyryanov woke Oshchurkov up and sent him for wine, which he fetched on demand. . . This group investigating the outrages carried on like this for about a week. On 13 or 15 March they gathered in the flat of the assistant director of the education section, Luzyanin, for a drinking session, at which they drank themselves senseless. . . Even before the arrival of the transported prisoners Ermakov, deputy director of the *oblast'* UITU, spoke at a meeting of the Party group of the district executive committee. Instead of demanding concrete assistance for Lyapunov to deal with the arrival of the prisoners, he declared to the local authorities that there was no real problem, the arrival of the prisoners would mean high death rates, and nobody should be surprised. . .

The beatings at the camp continue: on 20 January Mikhail Naumov, one of the guards, pistol-whipped a prisoner known as Eremek because he and others kept on asking for water. . . The occurrence of the above outrages is just a continuation of prior goings-on, and with such nepotism among the camp management, the *oblast'* UITU camp management and the *oblast'* procurator's office, it is very difficult to eradicate. . .

[Source: SOTsDOO, fond 4, opis' 11, delo 198, pp. 3–6.]

By May 1933, the government had reached the conclusion that further 'dekulakization' and mass deportations must be halted. The disruption of agriculture was proving too great, the organization of resettlement too burdensome, the increasingly high-handed processes by which charges and arrests were made too disorderly, the impact of the famine too grave.

Moreover, by then the danger of provoking mass protest no longer appeared a necessary risk. A substantial majority of households had been collectivized, and those that remained independent accounted for a small proportion of agricultural output. Provided local resistance gathered no wider momentum, the main 'battle' seemed won.

The secret party instruction issued on 8 May signalled no let-up in general pressure against 'kulaks' and explicitly reiterated Stalin's dictum that class struggle would intensify as the final reckoning approached. But the shift in emphasis was clear. The procedures for arrest were to be sharply tightened and strictly restricted to the legal and police authorities, and the procuracy and OGPU themselves were to observe rigorously the 1922 statute [see Chapter 10, p. 223]. The huge rise in the number in prison was to be abruptly halted by eliminating imprisonment on remand for petty crimes. Above all, in place of mass deportations, 'dekulakization' was henceforth to be reserved for targeted enemies: regional officials seeking permission to exile tens of thousands were abruptly ordered to cut the numbers by some 90 per cent.

Document 156 | '… we no longer need the mass repressions…'— from instructions to all Party and Soviet workers, all organs of the OGPU, the courts and the Procuracy

8 May 1933

Secret. Not to be published.

The CC and Sovnarkom consider that, as a result of our successes in the countryside, the moment has come when we no longer need the mass repressions which are hurting not only the kulaks but also individual farmers and some collective farmers. It is true that demands for mass evictions from the countryside and the use of harsh repression are still coming from some *oblasti*. The CC and Sovnarkom have applications for the immediate eviction of about 100,000 families from some *oblasti* and *kraya*. The CC and Sovnarkom have evidence that disorderly, mass arrests are still being made by Party workers in the countryside. The arrests are being made by collective-farm chairmen, collective-farm management, chairmen of village soviets, Party group secretaries, district and *kray* plenipotentiaries, in fact by anybody who feels like it, but actually does not have the authority to do so. It is therefore not surprising that in such a disorderly situation those bodies with the right to make arrests, including organs of the OGPU and especially the militia, are losing their sense of proportion and often making senseless arrests on the principle of 'Arrest first and sort it out later.'

What does all this mean?

It means that out there in the provinces there are still quite a few comrades who have not grasped the new situation and are still living in the past.

It means that despite this new situation, which requires that the centre of gravity be shifted to mass political and organizational work, these comrades are still clinging onto outworn styles of work, which no longer correspond to the new situation and threaten to weaken the authority of Soviet power in the countryside.

It would appear that these comrades are willing to replace and are already replacing political work among the masses to isolate kulak and anti-collective elements with GPU and militia Cheka-style 'operations', without realizing that such behaviour, should it take on a mass nature, could reduce our Party's influence in the countryside to zero. These comrades apparently do not understand that in the new situation the method of mass evictions of peasants outside their *kray* has already outlived itself and that eviction can be applied only partially or specifically and then only to the ringleaders or organizers of the struggle against collective farms.

These comrades do not realize that in the new situation the method of disorderly mass arrests, if one can even call it a method, is counterproductive, diminishing the authority of Soviet power, that the arrests must be limited and strictly controlled by the appropriate bodies and that arrest must apply only to the active enemies of Soviet power. The CC and Sovnarkom have no doubt that these and similar mistakes and deviations from the Party line will very soon come to an end.

It would be wrong to assume that this new situation and the need to move on to a different style of work mean the end of or any kind of easing off of the class struggle in the countryside. On the contrary, the class struggle in the countryside will inevitably become more intense. It will become more intense because the class enemy can see that the collective farms have won, that his last days are here—and in desperation he is bound to resort to the sharpest methods of struggle against Soviet power. There can therefore be no question whatsoever of easing off the struggle with the class enemy. On the contrary, our struggle must be greatly intensified and our vigilance heightened. It is, consequently, a matter of stepping up our struggle against the class enemy. But the point is that stepping up the struggle against the class enemy and liquidating it using the old methods of working are impossible in the new situation because these old methods have outlived themselves. It is therefore a matter of improving the old methods of struggle, of rationalizing them and of making our blows more accurate and organized. Finally, it is a matter of ensuring that every blow we strike is politically prepared in advance and is reinforced by activity from the broad masses of the peasantry. Only by improving our style of work in this way can we achieve the final destruction of the class enemy in the countryside.

The CC and Sovnarkom are in no doubt that all Party–Soviet and security–judicial organizations will take on board the new situation brought about by our victories and re-organize their work in accordance with the new conditions of struggle. The CC and Sovnarkom have decreed as follows:

I

On ending the mass eviction of peasants

All mass evictions must cease forthwith. Eviction is permissible only in individual or special circumstances and then only of those households the members of which are waging an active struggle against the collective farm and organizing a boycott of sowing or grain deliveries. Eviction is permissible only from the following *oblasti* and in the following maximum numbers:

Ukraine	2,000 holdings
N. Caucasus	1,000 holdings
Lower Volga	1,000 holdings
Middle Volga	1,000 holdings
Central Black-Earth region	1,000 holdings
Urals	1,000 holdings
Gor'ky *kray*	500 holdings
E. Siberia	1,000 holdings
Belorussia	500 holdings
Western *oblast'*	500 holdings
Bashkiria	500 holdings
Transcaucasia	500 holdings
Central Asia	500 holdings
Total	12,000 [sic] holdings

II

On regulating the making of arrests

1. Unauthorized arrests by executive-committee chairmen, district and *kray* representatives, village soviet chairmen, chairmen of collective farms and collective-farm unions, Party group secretaries, and so on are to be forbidden.

Arrests may be made only by organs of the procuracy, the OGPU and the militia. Investigators may make arrests only with the procurator's prior consent.

Arrests made by militia chiefs must be confirmed or annulled by district OGPU executives or procurators through the proper channels and within 45 hours of the arrest.

2. The procuracy, OGPU and militia are to be forbidden from imprisoning people on remand for trivial crimes. Imprisonment on remand may be employed only for persons accused of crimes of counter-revolution, terrorism, sabotage, brigandage and robbery, spying, leaving the country, smuggling, murder, grievous bodily harm, large-scale misappropriation and embezzlement, professional speculation, foreign currency dealing, counterfeiting, malicious hooliganism and professional recidivism.

3. OGPU organs must seek prior consent from the procuracy when making arrests, except for cases of terrorism, bombing, arson, spying, desertion, political brigandage and counter-revolutionary, anti-Party groupings.

This will come into force only in six months' time in the Far East, Central Asia and Kazakhstan.

4. The Procuracy of the USSR and the OGPU must unswervingly observe the 1922 procedures on procuratorial supervision of arrests and detention carried out by the OGPU. . .

V. Molotov (Skryabin), Chairman of the Council of People's Commissars
I. Stalin, secretary of the CC of the CPSU

[Source: SOTsDOO, fond 4, opis' 11, delo 181, pp. 149, 149 ob.]

This secret circular was followed by a marked reduction in mass deportations and as the terrible famine receded some semblance of order began to return to the countryside. But collectivization left the Soviet countryside traumatized. Besides the five to seven million victims of famine and up to six million victims of 'dekulakization', the most basic rhythms of the lives of tens of millions of peasant men, women and children had been violently broken. The destruction of their economic independence was accompanied by an assault on their entire culture, religion and traditional village institutions. Some idea of the impact on the dwindling minority in the countryside left outside the collectives is given by this heart-rending plea by a 12-year-old girl from a village in Ivanovo *oblast'*, north-east of Moscow.[149] Addressed to Stalin, it includes the jingle which spread the slogan of the late 1930s, 'Thank you, Comrade Stalin, for a Happy Childhood', and stands in the long Russian tradition of appealing directly to the Tsar, adopting the regime's self-congratulatory rhetoric while simultaneously painting a picture of utter destitution.

Document 157 | '... we haven't got anything to eat'—a schoolgirl's letter to Stalin

13 January 1937

Hello, Dear Comrade Stalin. Our beloved leader, teacher and friend of the whole happy Soviet land. Dear Comrade Stalin, I'm sending you warm and sincere greetings and wish you success in your life and hope that you are always well. I want to tell you about my unhappy life.

Dear Comrade Stalin, I heard you saying on the radio that children have very good lives in the Soviet Union, go to school and that the school doors are always open wide to them. That's true, of course, Dear Comrade Stalin.

Dear Iosif Vissarionovich, me and my brother Aleksandr aren't able to go to school, because, Comrade Stalin, we haven't got anything to eat. The Kurilov village

---

149 On the experience of childhood in the 1930s more widely, see L. Siegelbaum and A. Sokolov, *Stalinism as a Way of Life* (New Haven 2000) pp. 256–420.

soviet took away our horse and cow back in 1935. So we've been living for two years now without a cow or a horse. Now at present we haven't got any livestock at all because the village soviet taxed us when they shouldn't have done. They reckoned my father was working as a carrier, which isn't true. One tax was 900 rubles and altogether it came to more than 2,000. We can't pay such big taxes. There are eight of us in our family, Comrade Stalin: six kids, the oldest is a girl of 14 and the youngest a little lad of 2.

Dear Iosif Vissarionovich, we didn't join the collective farm because my father is an invalid. He fought in two wars, his health's gone and so he just can't work on the collective farm. Things aren't going too well for us on our own, they're pretty bad really. We get along somehow. At present we don't have any land—that went to the collective farm in 1936.

Comrade Stalin, I'm in the fourth year at school and my brother's in the second. The rest don't go to school because they're too little. Dear Comrade Stalin, it's ever so difficult for us to go to school, because we haven't got anything to eat and have got really bad anaemia.

Dear Comrade Stalin, I want to tell you how well I've been doing at school: for the first quarter I got 'excellent' in seven subjects and 'good' for the other three. But I want to and I'll try to get 'excellent' in everything in the third quarter. If I had something to eat, Comrade Stalin, I could do even better.

Nobody in my year's joined the Pioneers. But I've told the group leader that I want to join the Pioneers, so they've put me down for the Stalin team in the sixth year, Comrade Stalin.

Dear beloved leader, Comrade Stalin, I think and hope that you'll give us some help. Please don't ignore us.

> Comrade Stalin,
> Thank you, Comrade Stalin
> For our happy lives!
> For our happy childhood,
> For our wonderful days.

So, our beloved leader Comrade Stalin, I've told you about my life. I hope that you, beloved leader of a happy land, won't ignore my plea. Please do answer, Dear Comrade Stalin. I'm waiting to hear from you.

Nina Vasil'evna Shevtsova (I'm 12),
Ileikino,
Kurilov village soviet,
Ivanovo *oblast'*,
Makar'ev-on-Unzha.

[Source: *Kommunist* No. 1, 1990, pp. 95–96.]

The collective farm and peasant apathy

Life for those within a collective farm, though less desperate than for Nina
Shevtsova and her siblings, remained grim even after the famine of 1932–33
receded. Collective farm wages were derisory and the new farms were widely
hated. Peasant resistance belies the notion of a 'totalitarian' regime so powerful
that its will could not be frustrated. In particular, the peasantry wrung from
the regime two permanent concessions. Instead of the wholesale socialization envisaged at the height of the collectivization drive of 1929–30, the
version of the collective farm that prevailed was the so-called '*artel*' model.
Pioneered after the revolution, it had been regarded as only a staging post
to full socialization. Each household was permitted to retain a small plot of
land for its own use together with some livestock, and local collective farm
markets where they could sell any modest surplus were legalized. But this
did nothing to soften peasant hostility to collective farms, or overcome their
apathy in working collective land, which, despite the legal fiction of collective ownership, they experienced as the property of an alien institution.[150]

For the regime, the danger was that as a result of peasant apathy the
economic devastation wrought by the initial disruption of collectivization,
the slaughter of livestock and the steep decline in output in 1931 and 1932
would become permanent. Its response, despite misgivings among some local
officials, was to tighten monitoring of and control over collective farming
and to pressurize, harass and, with dizzying speed, to sack and replace local
agricultural officials and collective-farm chairmen. Peasant foot-dragging,
the 'teething problems' of new farm structures, and the inevitable hiccoughs
in the introduction of tractors, combine harvesters and other new machinery
could be overcome, it was assumed, by vigorous, hands-on supervision. Farm
managers would supervise the workforce; Machine Tractor Stations (MTSs)
controlling essential machinery would supervise farm managers; the MTS
management and workforce would themselves be supervised by political
departments attached to each MTS; and the OGPU, answering to the
Politburo, would oversee the entire rural economy.

The following document from a Urals OGPU official—one of a sequence
sent every five days during sowing in May and June that year—gives a sense
of the mammoth supervisory task involved in just one *oblast'*. It conveys the
dire level of motivation among the peasantry. And, addressed to OGPU
headquarters in Moscow, it suggests how inadequate punitive investigation
and central intervention was as a method of dealing with the bewildering
variety of problems confronting Soviet agriculture.

---

150 See the detailed study by R.W. Davies, *The Soviet Collective Farm, 1929–1930* (London
    1980).

Document 158 | **Note on sowing from Tuchkov, Urals OGPU, to G. Yagoda, OGPU deputy chairman, and others**

14 May 1933

13 May 1933 in Urals *oblast'* 94,157 ha sown. Of 9,155 collective farms 8,213 have started sowing. Shown in seed transportation: 55 per cent exchanged, 47 per cent state loan. 262 quintals of rye sent from Krasnopolyansk commune in exchange for grain elevator. Wheat not issued. No sowing done. Measures taken by Political Division. In Borodulino collective farm (Sverdlovsk) 130 quintals of wheat after rubbish removed, not enough to sow 14 ha. In Belozerskoe because of bad organization field teams sitting in offices, young people in fields. Bukhvalov, director of Zaikovo MTS, drunk for two days. Not managing work. Tractors not fulfilling quotas. Answering to Party bodies. In repair shops of Krasnopolyansk MTS kulaks running the management did not ensure quality of repair work. 25 tractors out of action. 713 hours standstill. Team leader Chinov and tractor driver Shusharin arrested. Rest making up time. Of 3,104 tractors available 2,402 involved in sowing. In Varna 11 tractors out of action because of poor repairs and overloading with trailers. Tractor drivers to blame. 18 tractors sent for repair in Troitsk. 2 in Foki MTS, enquiry under way. In Berezovsky MTS 3 tractors out of action because of poor repair jobs. 12 tractors despatched by Stalingrad factory took over month to get to Ust' Uyskoe MTS. Transport police establishing who to blame. Stepnoe MTS wasted 1,200 kg of fuel, no responsibility, lack of fuel pipes. Tractor driver Kalinin used 820 kg for hectare and half. On Chernushka 'Dawn of Brotherhood' collective farm 5 tractor drivers took 13 days to plough 15 ha, using 1,400 kg of fuel. Reason: waterlogged soil, skidding, pointless trips, choice of field.

Quality of sowing: in Krasnopolyansk teams of 'Collective Farm Way' sowing unsorted, untreated wheat seed; soil not turned, seed left on surface. On 'Red Ploughman' collective farm in Kachar 6 ha sown with millet and then wheat on top. On 'Toiler' in Kizil'skoe 75 kg sown instead of 90, 12 of millet instead of 20. Bredy has vermin problem—fleas—on 220 ha. MTS dealing with it. Mass absences of collective farmers in Belozerskoe region because of production difficulties. 2000 *pudy* issued. 'October Path' collective farm in Varna using carrion. Collective farmers not working through exhaustion and swellings. District seed centre sent out 11 quintals of waste as food. Analogous situation in Shadrinsk. Crowds of peasants from neighbouring regions gathering for last three days on fields of Shadrinsk state grain farm to collect surrogate foodstuffs. Marked anti-Soviet feelings have been noticed. Measures being taken against gatherings. Removal of anti-Soviet elements.

Tuchkov, deputy plenipotentiary of Urals OGPU

[Source: SOTsDOO, fond 4, opis' 11, delo 188, pp. 87–88.]

The lengths to which the leadership went to try to convince regional and local officials that Moscow's eyes were everywhere is epitomized by the following document sent to Kabakov in Sverdlovsk. The General Secretary himself, as well as Molotov, head of government since 1931, purportedly takes the keenest interest in *makhorka*, the low-grade tobacco grown in the Urals, setting out in detail the precise steps needed to ensure the target for the *oblast'* is met.

Document 159 | **V.M. Molotov and I.V. Stalin: '... complete *makhorka* planting by 20 June...'**

6 June 1933

To the secretary of the Urals *oblast'* committee of the CPSU and the chairman of the *oblast'* executive committee. The secret section of the Urals *oblast'* committee of the CPSU.

Your district is behind in *makhorka* planting, which you evidently consider of secondary importance. The Sovnarkom and Central Committee consider fulfilling the plan in *makhorka* planting a matter of great state importance and oblige you to take measures to ensure complete fulfilment of the plan for planting and appropriate processing of *makhorka*. To this end: first, complete *makhorka* planting by 20 June; second, check land allocation for *makhorka* so that manured land is allocated; third, organize *makhorka* processing to the same standard as that of the basic industrial crops to ensure the completion of triple weeding and pruning over the whole area by July; fourth, in view of the usual significant losses of *makhorka* seedlings particular attention is to be paid to sowing and processing, ensuring that pruning and thinning are done, along with hoeing the land between the crops over the entire sown area; fifth, introduce the organization on a wide scale of special *makhorka* planting and processing teams within the landworkers' brigades; sixth, prepare barns and dryers well in advance; seventh, in every instance assist collective and individual farmers sowing *makhorka* with ploughing. Inform of measures taken.

Molotov, Stalin.
6/6/1933

[Source: SOTsDOO, fond 4, opis' 11, delo 81, p. 55.]

13

Industrialization
and the Working Class

Accelerating the First Five-Year Plan

Ill-prepared and chaotic though collectivization was, the momentum gathered in the autumn and winter of 1929–30 further inflated the economic ambitions of both the regional and the central leadership. Despite the abrupt reversal triggered by Stalin's 'Dizzy with Success' article in March 1930, that summer the firm expectation remained that collectivization would be largely complete in the course of the First Five-Year Plan. The regime's grip on grain supplies, it seemed, would now be unshakeable, guaranteeing the flow required both to feed a rapidly expanding industrial workforce and to sustain the exports necessary to finance the import of machinery. Preparations for the Sixteenth Party Congress, due in June 1930, saw the pattern of the previous two years repeat itself. Optimism soared: the exhortations of the leadership, the demands for investment and promises of increased production made by competing commissariats and regional officials, the beguiling projections produced by the central planners, and the pervasive atmosphere of euphoria over a break-neck industrial drive all pointed the same way. In May, for example, the Central Committee endorsed plans for the creation of a huge metallurgical base in the Urals which, though not quite on the scale Kabakov and his colleagues bid for, dwarfed the vision entertained just two years earlier.[151] Stalin's report to the Central Committee duly listed a battery of new targets for growth far above the already wildly ambitious plans adopted the previous year. Any notion that midway moving of targets was arbitrary or made nonsense of planning was dismissed as the pedantry of 'hopeless bureaucrats'.

---

151 Harris, *The Great Urals* pp. 101–04.

Document 160 | From the political report of the CC to the XVI CPSU Congress

27 June 1930

The Central Committee's work in this sphere [of economic construction] has proceeded mainly along the lines of amending and giving precision to the five-year plan by accelerating tempo and shortening time schedules, and along the lines of checking the economic organizations' fulfilment of the assignments laid down.

Here are a few of the principal decisions adopted by the Central Committee amending the five-year plan in the direction of speeding up the rate of development and shortening time schedules of fulfilment.

In the iron and steel industry: the five-year plan provides for the output of pig iron to be brought up to 10,000,000 tonnes in the last year of the five-year period; the Central Committee's decision, however, found that this level is not sufficient, and laid it down that in the last year of the five-year period the output of pig iron must be brought up to 17,000,000 tonnes.

Tractor construction: the five-year plan provides for the output of tractors to be brought up to 55,000 in the last year of the five-year period; the Central Committee's decision, however, found that this target is not sufficient, and laid it down that the output of tractors in the last year of the five-year period must be brought up to 170,000.

The same must be said about *automobile construction*, where, instead of an output of 100,000 cars (lorries and passenger cars) in the last year of the five-year period as provided for in the five-year plan, it was decided to bring it up to 200,000. . .

State farm development: the five-year plan provides for the expansion of the crop area to be brought up to 5,000,000 hectares by the end of the five-year period; the Central Committee's decision, however, found that this level was not sufficient and laid it down that by the end of the five-year period the state farm crop area must be brought up to 18,000,000 hectares.

Collective-farm development: the five-year plan provides for the expansion of the crop area to be brought up to 20,000,000 hectares by the end of the five-year period; the Central Committee's decision, however, found that this level was obviously not sufficient (it has already been exceeded this year) and laid it down that by the end of the five-year period the collectivization of the USSR should, in the main, be completed, and by that time the collective-farm crop area should cover nine-tenths of the crop area of the USSR now cultivated by individual farmers. (Applause.). . .

It may be said that in altering the estimates of the five-year plan so radically the Central Committee is violating the principle of planning and is discrediting the planning organizations. But only hopeless bureaucrats can talk like that. For us Bolsheviks, the five-year plan is. . . merely a plan adopted as a first approximation, which has to be made more precise, altered and perfected in conformity with the experience gained in the localities, with the experience gained in carrying out the plan. . .

The Central Committee is of the opinion that the reconstruction of the technical basis of industry and agriculture *under the socialist organization of production* creates such possibilities of accelerating tempo as no capitalist country can dream of.

[Source: J.V. Stalin, *Works* Volume XII (Moscow 1955) pp. 355–59.]

Migration and forced labour

A key ingredient in the industrialization drive was the massive mobilization of under-utilized labour. As we have seen, collectivization played a crucial, if largely unplanned, role here. Above all, it triggered the exodus of millions of peasants in search of non-agricultural work. But it also saw large numbers forcibly exiled to labour settlements, labour camps and prison. This coincided with a rapid increase in the use of forced labour as a standard legal punishment for virtually all forms of crime. As we have seen in the previous section, the increasing stress on ensuring that both short- and long-term prisoners contributed to the labour force was seized upon by economic managers and regional leaders such as those in the Urals who were unable to recruit nearly enough voluntary labour. Shorter-term sentences took the form of periods of unpaid labour without deprivation of liberty; heavier penalties involved periods in labour camps and colonies. The following article in *Pravda* by N.V. Krylenko, the RSFSR's chief prosecutor and from 1931 Commissar for Justice, published in the middle of the First Five-Year Plan period, underlined the emphasis on summary justice and putting offenders to work on 'socialist construction'.

Document 161 | **N. Krylenko: '… develop the system of forced labour to the maximum extent'—from his article 'On Certain "Theories" in the Field of Criminal Law and Policy'**

March 1930

Hitherto the practical bases of criminal practice have had two points of departure: the practice of deprivation of liberty as the basic method of fighting crime and the practice of implementing this deprivation of liberty according to the principles of so-called 'dosage', that is, of determining, of 'weighing up', the dosage of deprivation for a term of one day to ten years in accordance with the 'seriousness of the crime'. The legislative practice of the last year has, it is true, introduced a number of correctives to these two principles.

On the basis of a resolution of the RSFSR Council of People's Commissars of 29 May 1929, deprivation of liberty for a period of less than a year is no longer practised. It is proposed to develop the system of forced labour to the maximum extent. A number of measures have been introduced to use the labour of persons sentenced to a term of more than three years for socially necessary work in special camps in remote regions. Nevertheless, the basic principle which obliges courts as before to 'weigh up' the deprivation of freedom on the basis of the 'seriousness and degree of danger' of the crime has remained untouched. That is, the principle which was characterized back in 1924 by comrade Pashukanis, one of the best Marxist theoreticians, as 'the essentially stupid idea that the seriousness of every crime can be weighed on some kind of scales and expressed in months or years of imprisonment' is still sacrosanct (*A General Theory of Marxism and Law*, p. 126).

At the same time the practical absurdity of the idea that one can combat crime and the criminal's 'ill will' by 'weighing out' two years' deprivation of liberty for one and four years' for another and the pointlessness of subsequent arguments in the Courts of Appeal (should he be given 2 or 2.5 years?) has been shown by life itself.

We have contrasted the idea of 'just deserts' and retribution with an obligation upon the court in every concrete case of combating criminal behaviour to seek the most expedient measures in order to:

1. protect our social collective against repeated dangerous acts by a particular criminal, not according to the 'seriousness' of the crime but primarily according to the criminal's character;

2. use the fact of the court sentence to have a certain effect on the environment. . .

[Source: *Pravda*, 17 March 1930.]

The opening of Soviet archives has brought some clarity to the much-disputed size of the sprawling network of labour settlements, labour colonies, labour camps and prisons under the concentration camp administration or GULAG.[152] The number held in prison stood at 800,000 at its peak in 1933 and repeatedly approached half a million; by the end of the decade, the number consigned to 'special settlement areas' was about a million, and the number in labour colonies and camps, where life expectancy was pitifully low, exceeded 1.6 million—a total in 1939 of some three million. Moreover, since there was a steady flow in and out of detention the overall number to pass through the hands of the OGPU (NKVD from 1934) and GULAG was much greater. The forced labour at its disposal gave the OGPU/NKVD a

---

152 See J.A. Getty, G.T. Rittersporn and V.N. Zemskov, 'Victims of the Soviet Penal System in the Pre-War Years' *American Historical Review* 98 (1993) pp. 1017–49; S. Wheatcroft, 'The Scale and Nature of German and Soviet Repression and Mass Killings, 1930–45' *Europe–Asia Studies* 48 (1996) pp. 1319–53; S. Wheatcroft, 'Victims of Stalinism and the Soviet Secret Police: The comparability and reliability of archival data—not the last word' *Europe–Asia Studies* 51 (1999) pp. 315–45. In particular, see pp. 340–42 for a dissection of the implausible figures in N. Davies, *Europe: A history*, referred to above, p. xviii, fn 1.

significant economic base of its own and, although it is not easy to weigh with precision, the economic contribution made by forced labour was clearly significant, notably in the hardest manual labour involved in developing some of the major industrial complexes thrown up from scratch, and in mining and timber in the most inhospitable regions of the north and east.[153]

Shock workers

At the other end of the spectrum from those forced to work were a minority of workers who threw their energies with passionate enthusiasm into the drive to 'build socialism'. This almost missionary zeal was most evident in the atmosphere of revolutionary upheaval of the early part of the First Five-Year Plan period. The break with NEP and adoption of the Plan, broadcast through posters, the press and factory meetings, struck a real chord and succeeded in mobilizing the hearts and minds of a vocal minority. Rank-and-file workers were at last to receive their due as the inferior status of manual labour was repudiated in favour of an egalitarian society in which all working people would pull together to forge a new world. Some enthusiasts, as we have seen, volunteered to assist with imposing collectivization while others vied to increase productivity, raise norms and exceed planned targets. Small groups of workers, initially often with little encouragement from management, trade unions or local party officials, formed 'shock brigades' to act as models of responsibility, initiative and self-discipline, to experiment with new methods and rationalize production, and to urge each other on by engaging in 'socialist competition'.[154]

The following recollections of V.Ya. Shidek, a worker involved in construction in the Kuznetsk Basin in western Siberia which was to provide coal for the massive new metallurgical centre based on iron ore in the Urals, capture something of the ethos. His story was selected for a collection of individual accounts (published in 1934) carefully designed to celebrate the achievement at Kuznetsk, create role models and inspire emulation, and his resilience despite bereavement strains credibility. Yet, composed while Shidek was still fully engaged in the huge construction project, its tone and texture are in line with a wealth of testimony about the committed minority: the pioneering spirit of shock workers, their stoicism in the face of physical

---

153 For the view that forced labour played a major role in Soviet industrialization, especially during the Great Patriotic War, see E. Bacon, *The GULAG at War: Stalin's forced labour system in the light of the archives* (London 1994) pp. 123–44.

154 For two key studies, see V. Andrle, *Workers in Stalin's Russia: Industrialization and social change in a planned economy* (Hemel Hempstead 1988), and H. Kuromiya, *Stalin's Industrial Revolution: Politics and workers, 1928–1932* (Cambridge 1988).

hardship, their work ethic, pride at making innovations and rationalizations, pleasure in time and again overfulfilling quotas and targets, disdain for 'kulaks' as well as the occasional teams of foreigners they encountered, and readiness to denounce inadequate managers even if they belonged to the party.[155]

Document 162 | From the memoirs of construction team leader V.Ya. Shidek

1929–31

In October 1929 we—a gang of six bricklayers—arrived at the Kuznetskstroy site.

The train got in in the evening. At that time Kuznetsk station just consisted of two wagons and two lines. Paraffin lamps on posts flickered here and there.

'Where's the site?' we asked.

'Over there,' they said, pointing north, 'at the foot of the hill the other side of the swamp.'

Loading up our knapsacks, we set off in that direction, northward to where the light of a few electric bulbs twinkled.

When we got to the Upper Settlement, we spotted some mud huts and settled ourselves for the time being in a stuffy little room.

After a couple of days we were shifted to better barracks, where we settled in and got down to work.

First I'll tell you how we lived.

We lived in barrack No. 14 in Lower Settlement, all six of us in one room. They put a stove in and hired a woman to cook our lunches and dinners. At that time there was just one separate canteen, and that was in a mud hut. There was no system, we weren't given spoons—we had to take our own, and if you didn't have one you had to slurp it and mop up with a bit of bread. The pots were washed up at the same table where we ate. The woman who washed up would bring her bucket, put it on the table, wash everything up and then move on to another table.

On the site work finished at five in the evening. We stopped work at a signal. The foreman-carpenter would bang one axe against another, others had a rail hanging from a post that they would bang. Off home we went, had a wash, a bite to eat and we'd start reading the paper. Then people would start talking and arguing. Most of the arguments were about the international situation. There was a lot of talk about the Americans who were supposed to work at Kuznetskstroy with us.

At the time none of us was in the Party or the Komsomol, but we weren't religious either and didn't celebrate the religious holidays, unlike a lot of the navvies.

---

155 For a detailed case study of the chaos, oppression and liberation of labour on the great construction projects of these years, see S. Kotkin's study of Magnitogorsk, one of the most ambitious undertakings of the Great Urals Plan, *Magnetic Mountain: Stalinism as a civilization* (Berkeley, CA, 1995).

We were very particular about cleanliness. We slept on trestle beds, but as soon as any bedbugs showed up, we killed them immediately. In the morning we all shook out the bedding. In the barracks we had a collection of portraits of the leaders and historical pictures. There were balalaikas and an accordion, too.

Over tea me and the lads used to have almost daily production meetings in the barrack.

Now I'll tell you how we worked.

We started with the administration block. First we heated the gravel. We had to pour concrete when it was freezing, and since there were no stoves, we used to pour boiling water over the gravel. We put the concrete on cross pieces, and to stop the foundations freezing they were covered with felt and tow and concreted.

They set us a quota of 500 bricks, but we pushed that up to 1,000. We tried to work faster and so didn't stop for a smoke. You needed a couple of minutes to roll your own with *makhorka*—and that was dozens of bricks' worth. So we smoked only *papirosy* and that was on the job.

After the administration block we worked on the stores, the meat store, the Works Industrial School, the Garden City homes and then in the fire-brick shop.

I remember working on the Works Industrial School, where we were laying red bricks. By the end of 1930 we were supposed to have finished 40 per cent of the building, but we had done the full 100 per cent.

We used the Western method and the rest the 'Russian Orthodox' method; the Western method is almost like that of the Central Institute of Labour. We made several suggestions for rationalization on the job. The first one was moulds for the door and window apertures and corner-irons for the corners. The second was the three-quarter brick. This was important, and using such a brick saved about 25 per cent in dressing. The third was introducing asbestos and slag slabs to replace building materials in short supply: planks, blocks, etc. The fourth was special boxes for pouring the mortar.

In December 1930 we finished the Works Industrial School building and went on to the fire-brick shop and started work on the fireproof cladding—something we'd not done before. We couldn't get into the swing of it at first. But we soon did and instead of the 165-brick quota, we were churning out 1,200.

Then misunderstandings started with the management. They started meeting us in our own and other shops.

Why? We were putting forward a counter-plan and wrecking their plans and charts. We were using up ten days' material in a couple. We'd ask for more, but they couldn't get hold of it and started getting uppity. We wouldn't give in. There was a squabble. I've never given in and didn't intend to. That's what led to a row.

Teplov, clerk of the works and an old contractor, was there. He'd brought his gang of workers from Moscow. They were a bunch of kulaks, who were neither able nor willing to do as much as we did. When we started putting the pressure on, they turned against us and threatened to do us in, etc.

They soon got rid of Teplov and made Oleynikov, a communist, boss. He was no good. He was against the counter-plan, argued with Frankfurt, and our relations with him soon got worse. There was something else involved.

Frankfurt had known our brigade virtually since the first day he arrived at the site. Whenever he came to the fire-brick shop, he always came to us first, had a chat, asked us about everything and only then went to see the head of the section.

We soon unmasked Oleynikov as an opportunist and he was expelled from the Party.

Then they put Teplov's kulaks into our brigade, making it up to sixty people. They tried to disrupt the brigade, but we fought with them and managed to improve some of them.

In May 1931 we were transferred to coke-oven cladding, which is very complicated and none of our bricklayers had ever done such work. Some Frenchmen were working on it and had set up a quota of half a tonne. The planning department raised this to 0.8 of a tonne. But when I worked it out, I realized that however difficult the work was, we could do a tonne—and we did.

The Frenchmen looked askance at us, thought we were crazy and got annoyed when we put forward yet another counter-plan—for 2.2 tonnes. Then we exceeded that figure, and got up to 3.8 tonnes.

The French downed tools several times and stormed off because they couldn't manage to supervise us.

We made gains on the deployment of the workforce. Where the French used six men, four were enough for us. Since we were supposed to do what the French said, we'd start off with six, but as soon as the French had gone, we immediately sent the pair of them off to work somewhere else.

The French finally cleared off completely and we built the shop without them.

At this point we had a competition with Obolensky's Donbass brigade. It was hard for me to keep up with them. His team was made up entirely of young men, instructors from the Central Institute of Labour courses, while my lads were all old fellows who'd never seen such brickwork.

Day and night for two months on end the writers Panferov and Il'enkov watched us work. What they wrote about us wasn't bad, although they missed bits out. There were seventy-four men in our brigade, working in three shifts. There is no writer who could grasp, understand and learn it all.

'When *don't* you work?' Panferov used to ask me.

What was I supposed to say? When we were trying to finish the first battery as a gift to the XVI Party Conference, I didn't leave the kiln for four days on end and didn't go home. A rail served as a pillow for my rest, although to make it softer, I covered it with canvas gloves.

Just before this my wife fell ill, so I sent her off to Tomsk, leaving our 3-year-old and a 7-year-old at home. Then, on the second day after I'd gone, my youngest son fell ill and died suddenly. Under the pressure of work I had forgotten about the kids. I went home on the fifth day and found that my youngest son had died, while the oldest was wandering around the site looking for me. The neighbours had also been wandering around looking for me, but couldn't find me. The little corpse was already starting to smell. I had no choice but to bury him, and afterwards had to go and get drunk. I drank to victory and grief.

Then we worked on a blast furnace, where things went wrong straightaway. At the Komsomol air injector there were some Komsomol members working in competition with us without us knowing it, until they surprised us. 'You've lost, Shidek,' they said.

They started denouncing our brigade and threw down a challenge. A couple of days later there was a shock-workers' meeting, where they swore at us and put us to shame. They promised to make some sort of cart and to tow us around in it.

I turned to *Rabochaya gazeta* [party newspaper] for help. They helped us and at injectors No. 5 and 6 we overfulfilled our quota by 370 per cent. We got accommodation as a prize. We moved from the barracks to stone building No. 6, where we were given a room each.

Afterwards we were moved to the rolling shop, where we've been working ever since. I'm no longer a team leader, because I was made deputy director for production meetings recently.

I don't like the work yet. I work and work but don't see any results: you lay a brick and can see what you've done. I'd be glad to go back to the shop floor. I miss the lads as well.

Quite a few people don't like us. Why? We've been given a lot of praise. But if they praise one team, the others will lose heart.

At the time when we produced 3.8 tonnes at the coke oven, many people thought one tonne was an achievement. They'd get annoyed at us, but I didn't care. We were doing our job and getting paid for it.

We need to sort out the competition. The more they laugh at us, the harder we work: we're not going to let ourselves be laughed at.

It can't be done without offence. If it can't be done with kindness, then we have to get at people, and worry the life out of them. People need shaking up. If they get shaken up, they give up their old ways and start doing things differently.

If we pick on somebody, let him get angry, but then he will start trying to catch us up—let him.

[Source: *Kuznetskstroy v vospominaniyakh* (Novosibirsk 1934) pp. 93–97.]

As Shidek's account suggests, shock brigades tended rapidly to become diluted or bogged down. On the one hand, other workers, both new recruits from the countryside and older skilled workers, resented the additional pressure which their heroics placed on the rest of the workforce. From 1930 the dynamism and image of the early shock workers was swamped as millions enrolled as shock workers not from genuine commitment but for form's sake and for the rewards that membership could bring. On the other hand, trade unions, managers and party officials increasingly took over spontaneous worker efforts not only to try to generalize and capitalize on them but also to tame and control them. Their efforts to increase productivity and raise expectations were, of course, in principle welcome. Large wage increases, honorary awards and public praise would continue to be heaped on shock brigades and outstanding workers. In the mid-1930s the most famous symbol of this was Aleksey Stakhanov, a coal miner who produced fourteen times the norm and was accorded massive publicity and quickly emulated by 'Stakhanovites' in other industries.[156] But the Stakhanovite movement would be orchestrated and controlled in a manner that set it apart from the spirit of the early stages of the First Five-Year Plan. From 1931, the boisterousness and potential disruption of spontaneous worker enthusiasm was increasingly at odds with what became the primary preoccupation of the regime's labour policy: discipline.

Labour discipline and labour turnover

Worker productivity—output per man/woman—was the key variable in successive Five-Year Plans. It was confidence that new machinery, energy sources and techniques would unleash a mighty leap in productivity that underpinned the huge optimism behind the industrialization drive. Yet, far from soaring as new machinery came on line, output per worker rose only very modestly in many branches of the economy and in some fell drastically. It could scarcely be otherwise. The main body of workers, who were neither idealists nor forced labourers, had very low levels of industrial skill and the millions pouring in from the countryside were entirely lacking in training or experience of the rigour and rhythms of life in a factory or on a construction site. Many reacted to harsh and unfamiliar working conditions by small-scale, more or less deliberate insubordination and carelessness, slipshod work practices, indulgence in drink and absenteeism. Motivation and even energy levels were also undermined by sheer undernourishment, especially during the First Five-Year Plan period. Rationing, as we have seen, had been introduced in 1929, and by 1930, long before the desperation of the famine, workers were experiencing acute deprivation. This simple plea for help was addressed to Kalinin, formally head of state in faraway Moscow, by a Urals worker.

---

156 See the close study by L. Siegelbaum, *Stakhanovism and the Politics of Productivity in the USSR, 1935–1941* (Cambridge 1988).

Document 163 | **To the 'father of the working people'—a worker's letter to M.I. Kalinin**

February 1930

Dear Comrade Mikhail Ivanovich,

The worker's life is hard. Our wives give us nothing to eat, they go off at five in the morning for bread, meat, potatoes and get back home about four without all they went out for. I am always hungry and our children go barefoot and hungry and every day it gets worse and worse—the peasants bring nothing to market, so what are we going to do? Our hopes are on you. A worker from the Lenin Works who respects you. Help us.

[Source: V.A. Mazur and M.E. Glavatsky, *Istoriya Rossii 1917–1940*, p. 261.]

In these conditions, to forge a disciplined and diligent workforce out of a ballooning working class in which experienced cadres, themselves confronted by new and complex machinery, were being swamped by raw recruits from the countryside, presented a formidable challenge. The regime's response was a major shift in rhetoric and policy in 1931. The First Five-Year Plan had been launched with a wave of attacks on managers and specialists suspected of harbouring alien class sympathies and constituting latent support for Bukharin and the 'Right deviation' (see below, documents 173–76 and 182–86). 'Bourgeois specialist-baiting' and denunciation by workers was positively encouraged from 1928, and many were harassed or arrested and put on trial for offences ranging from deliberate falsification of reports to poor-quality output and 'wrecking'. The disruption which resulted created mounting concern among the planning agencies and industrial commissariats and they pressed for the tide to be stemmed. To continue to undermine the position of specialists, alarmed party officials and managers protested, was incompatible with the discipline drive, given their direct involvement in monitoring labour performance and implementing measures designed to raise productivity.

In a landmark speech on 23 June 1931, Stalin signalled a sharp change in policy. The specialists trained under the old regime, he announced, had seen the light and could now be trusted, especially as they were rapidly being outnumbered by the influx of so-called 'red' specialists, tens of thousands of selected workers, most of them party members, taken off the factory floor and promoted into technical and managerial positions either following crash courses or without formal qualifications. The authority, status and privileges of the white-collar strata now began to be energetically buttressed. Managers were armed with a panoply of other powers, including in most industries the introduction of the piece-rate system of wage payment, to impose discipline. A decree of November 1932 spelled out their authority to dismiss unsatisfactory workers, to withdraw ration cards, to evict them from factory housing, and to deprive them of social benefits.

On the face of it, the decrees hurled down from above suggest a working class helpless before the state's determination to harness it to the industrialization drive. In reality, however, the increasing harshness of labour legislation reflected less the regime's ability to impose its will on a helpless society than the leadership's intense frustration. This disparity between the appearance of omnipotence and the reality, in industry as on the collective farm, is one of the factors that has eroded the notion that Stalin's regime achieved 'totalitarian' control over society. Admittedly, collective protest by workers was kept to a minimum. The trade-union leadership was firmly in the hands of party appointees. Deep fissures within the working class— between established cadres and the influx of rural migrants, between young and old, between skilled and unskilled, between the enthusiasts and the majority—which were further exacerbated by widening pay differentials from 1931, militated against the creation of new, independent organizations. In any case, strike action or attempts at co-ordinated opposition of any kind were rapidly dealt with by the ubiquitous OGPU/NKVD. Yet the state proved unable even to approximate the degree of day-to-day control to which it aspired or to approach the level of discipline achieved by industrial capitalism.

What prevented it from doing so was the fact that, despite their lack of independent collective organizations, workers retained a rudimentary amount of autonomy and bargaining power. This was guaranteed by the enormous demand for labour entailed in the over-ambitious targets of successive Five-Year Plans. The effect was to compel managers to compete with each other in order to secure and retain labour, thereby limiting their ability to discipline their workers. They had to be highly selective about implementing punitive labour legislation and were strongly inclined to reach an unofficial *modus vivendi* with their workforce, turning a blind eye to work practices that ran directly counter to the regime's intent. Certainly individual workers were subject to arbitrary mistreatment, but if the management of one factory was too heavy-handed, a worker could move on and sign up in another where the demands made on him or her were less exacting, wages higher, or conditions better.[157] As the following 1931 report from the Commissariat of Labour lamented, during the First Five-Year Plan period, the rate of labour turnover was astronomically high—disrupting production plans, absorbing

---

157 For the best analysis, see D. Filtzer, *Soviet Workers and Stalinist Industrialization: The formation of modern Soviet production relations, 1928–1941* (London 1986).

massive managerial and administrative resources, and constantly under-mining efforts to instil new skills and habits—and it continued to bedevil labour policy throughout the decade.[158]

Document 164 | From a report of the People's Commissariat of Labour's Administration for Manpower Supply to the Board of the Commissariat

The scale of labour turnover is clear from the following figures: between May and August 1931, at twenty-six priority construction sites, 124,140 workers were taken on and 102,492 left. Thus, these construction sites spent time and money on the recruitment of 124,000 people, but actually increased their workforce by only 22,000.

The situation at the following sites, in particular, should be noted:

Site	May–August 1931 Hired	Left	Manpower on 1 September 1931
Petrovsky Factory	3,313	2,960	4,422
Makeevka Metallurgical Plant	5,352	5,116	6,046
Dneprostroy	10,431	8,795	15,384
Dneprozavodstroy	15,439	14,148	13,364
Khar'kov Tractor Factory	13,351	13,969	8,354
Svir'stroy	8,534	8,413	7,708

It is interesting to note that at three of these sites, labour turnover was also high before, as the figures for the special quarter of 1930 show:

Site	October–December 1930 Hired	Left	Manpower on 1 January 1931
Petrovsky Factory	2,388	2,021	5,941
Makeevka Metallurgical Plant	5,732	4,379	7,016
Khar'kov Tractor Factory	16,290	13,604	14,140

Labour turnover at these construction sites reflects not only extremely poor accommodation and living conditions, but also wage equalization and extremely poor work organization and labour utilization.

[Source: *Industrializatsiya SSSR 1929–1932gg: Dokumenty i Materialy* (Moscow 1970) pp. 441–42.]

---

158 Nove points out, *Economic History* p. 198, that the average worker in the coal industry in 1930 left his employment three times.

The rate of labour turnover and level of labour indiscipline was intensely frustrating for Moscow. During 1932 it became impossible, behind closed doors, for the leadership to deny a mounting economic crisis.[159] Failure to reach targets in one sector had knock-on effects on another and reverberated across the whole of industry. Major projects scheduled for completion by the end of the plan period remained unfinished: in the Urals by 1932 less than 10 per cent of those begun during the First Five-Year Plan had been completed.[160] Alongside the drive for labour discipline there was mounting criticism of and pressure on managers, officials and regional party leaders. Central Committee resolutions such as the following one of October 1932 condemned the shortfalls, laid the blame firmly at the door of management as well as labour, and signalled a shift of emphasis away from starting myriad gigantic new projects towards concentration on completion, delivery and meeting output targets.

Document 165 | 'On ferrous metallurgy'—from a resolution of a CPSU CC Plenum

2 October 1932

. . . 2. However, the successes listed above are wholly inadequate when compared with the tasks placed on the iron and steel industry by the growth of the USSR's economy. The 1932 plan, which was approved by the XVII Party Conference— 9m tonnes of pig iron, 9.5m tonnes of raw steel and 6.6m tonnes of rolled steel—is not being met. The iron and steel industry continues to lag behind the general level of the country's productive forces, limiting the development of the whole of the engineering industry and holding up reconstruction and the pace of new construction in transport and agriculture. . .

3. The Plenum of the Central Committee considers that the main reason for the deterioration of the performance of the iron and steel industry during the summer months of this year has been the not wholly satisfactory, and sometimes totally unsatisfactory, economic, administrative and technical management by factory managements, corporations, the Main Administration for Iron and Steel and the People's Commissariat for Heavy Industry. . .

The Central Committee also notes the weakness of Party and trade-union work in iron and steel plants; as a result there has been a deterioration in labour discipline, a weakening of socialist competition and the shock-worker movement, and a deterioration in the attention paid to the daily living needs of the workforce. Transport difficulties have also played a role in the failure to complete the plan for iron and

---

159 The full scale of the industrial crisis is brought out by R.W. Davies, *Crisis and Progress in the Soviet Economy, 1931–1933* (Basingstoke 1996).
160 Harris, *The Great Urals* p. 129.

steel during the summer months; these have resulted in breakdowns in the supply of ore, coal, limestone and fireproof and building materials. . .

[Source: *Resheniya partii i pravitel'stva po khozyaistvennym voprosam. Tom 2: 1929–1940* (Moscow 1967) pp. 399–403.]

The Five-Year Plans

In the face of the crisis of 1932, the regime took immense care in preparing and publicizing the outcome of the First Five-Year Plan. The Plan had been constantly, relentlessly used to provide popular motivation and to urge workers on. It had become the organizing 'myth' of the entire industrialization drive. It was therefore essential that the best plausible gloss be placed upon the statistics gathered and that they carry conviction. At the beginning of 1933, the Politburo issued a stern warning against any piecemeal dissemination of results.

Document 166 | **'. . . only with Gosplan's permission'—from the minutes of Politburo meeting No. 129**

1 February 1933

Present:

Members of the Political Bureau of the CPSU, comrades Kalinin, Kuybyshev, Molotov, Stalin. Candidate member of the Political Bureau, comrade Mikoyan.

Members of the Central Committee of the CPSU, comrades Bubnov, Zelensky, Kviring, Knorin, Komarov, Krupskaya, Kubyak, Lebed', Lomov, Lyubimov, Manuil'sky, Pyatakov, Strievsky, Sulimov, Shvarts, Shvernik, Yakovlev. Candidate members of the Central Committee, comrades Bulat, Kalmanovich, Kiselev, Kosarev, Krinitsky, Mezhlauk, Nikolaeva, Osinsky, Perepechko, Polonsky, Popov, Serebrovsky, Sokol'nikov, Unshlikht, Chutskaev, Eliava, Yagoda. Members of the Presidium of the Central Control Commission, comrades Antipov, Belen'ky, Vermenichev, Enukidze, Nazaretyan, Royzenman, Sol'ts, Ul'yanova, Yaroslavsky.

Item:

. . . 17. On the results of the fulfilment of the First Five-Year Plan (comrade Kuybyshev)

Resolved:

1) Prior to the official publication by USSR Gosplan of the results of the fulfilment of the First Five-Year Plan, forbid all departments, republics and *oblasti* to publish any other summary works of any kind, whether composite, sectoral or district, so that even after official figures are published all works dealing with the results can be published only with Gosplan's permission.

2) Oblige all institutions to present to USSR Gosplan all available materials and studies on the results of the fulfilment of the First Five-Year Plan to be used by Gosplan and to coordinate the methodology used in their compilation.

I. Stalin,
Secretary of CC

[Source: RGASPI, fond 17, opis' 3, delo 914, p. 5.]

By placing great emphasis on industrial figures, and in particular heavy industry, while drawing attention away from light industry and agriculture, as well as from issues of quality as opposed to volume, the regime was able to present the outcome as a massive success. The following selective figures, based on those of the 1930s, were published during the last years of the USSR, in the period of glasnost and perestroika. They acknowledge the huge growth that did take place but also bring out clearly the wild gyrations between different sectors of the economy, the massive shortfall below the super-targets of 1930 and 1931, and the dire setback of 1932–33.[161]

Document 167 | **Percentage rates of growth of gross output in USSR industry, 1928–1933**

	Years of the First Five-Year Plan				
Index	1928/29	1929/30	1930/31	1931/32	1932/33
Initial variant	21.4	18.8	17.5	18.1	17.4
Optimal variant	21.4	21.5	22.1	23.8	25.2
Annual plans	21.4	32.0	45.0	36.0	16.5
Actual achievement	20.0	22.0	20.5	14.7	5.5

[Source: *Izvestiya SO AN SSSR*, No. 12, 1984 (Series *Ekonomika i prikladnaya sotsiologiya*, issue 3, p. 56); O.R. Laṭsis, *Vyyti iz kvadrata* (Moscow 1989) p. 239.]

161 For the most authoritative western assessment, see Davies et al. (eds) *Economic Transformation* pp. 242–58.

Document 168 | Industrial production in the First Five-Year Plan

Type of production	Actually produced in 1928	Targets for the final year of the 5-year plan		Actually produced in 1932	Year-plan targets actually achieved	
		Set at 16th Party conference and 5th congress of Soviets, 1929	Raised in 1930		Initial	Raised
Oil, million tonnes	11.6	22	45–46	21.4	1934	1952
Iron, million tonnes	3.3	10	17	6.2	1934	1950
Tractors, 000s	1.3	53	170	48.9	1933	1956
Cars, 000s	0.84	100	200	23.9	1935	1937
Combine harvesters 000s	—	0	40	10	—	1937
Woollen cloth, million metres	86.8	270	—	88.7	1957	—

[Source: O.R. Latsis, *Vyyti iz kvadrata* (Moscow 1989) p. 239.]

The grim reversals of 1932–33 induced the leadership to revise sharply downwards the investment targets outlined in early drafts of the Second Five-Year Plan (1933–37) which had been eagerly supported by regional leaders.[162] There was now a substantial increase in resources devoted to light industry and consumer goods. Above all, what differentiated the new Plan was the emphasis on 'realism', on cutting waste, on raising quality, on close monitoring of the use of investment funds, and on reaching output targets. Managers and officials responsible either for misusing capital or for producing faulty goods were made criminally liable, and underfulfilment became grounds for dismissal and removal from the party. It was now that a permanent tension became entrenched between the authorities at the centre and officials in the party, state and managerial hierarchies.

Officials and managers responsible for achieving targets in a region, branch or enterprise tried to ensure those targets were low or at least feasible, to maximize the inputs and resources assigned to them, and to report sustained success. This led them to bend the rules, strike illicit deals with suppliers of fuel and raw materials, and tolerate monstrous waste and the production of faulty and even useless goods to meet gross output targets. The result was

---

162 See E. Zaleski, *Stalinist Planning for Economic Growth, 1933–1952* (Chapel Hill, NC, 1980), for a lucid commentary.

the formation of informal 'family circles' linking officials within and among different hierarchies. In seeking to ensure that 'their' Republic, commissariat, *oblast'* or enterprise secured scarce labour and raw materials, officials in the party, state bureaucracy, enterprise management and indeed the procuracy and OGPU/NKVD colluded in unofficial networks designed to conceal failures, circumvent unwelcome directives, evade scrutiny and hoodwink or win over emissaries sent from Moscow.[163] And these networks of the regional or local *nomenklatura*, characteristically headed by the senior party official (in the case of Urals *oblast'*, Kabakov stood at the centre of just such a 'family circle'), were lubricated by patronage, nepotism, bribery and embezzlement.

To regional and local officials and managers, these practices seemed unavoidable and indeed necessary. The targets now imposed on them were impossible to achieve: the lavish estimates they had given of the output that massive investment during the First Five-Year Plan would yield were coming home to haunt them. The centre made it ever clearer that to cite 'objective' obstacles to target achievements—inadequate resources and skills—was unacceptable and reminiscent of the ill-fated 'Right deviation'. Since chronic shortages of labour and raw materials were inevitable given the excessive level at which overall output targets were set, it seemed essential to show initiative in securing what was needed locally. But the effect was to link senior officials in networks which, if uncovered, might appear to Moscow not only as corrupt and deceitful malpractice but as deliberate defiance.

The Stalin Constitution

In the mid-1930s, the tension between centre and periphery remained largely submerged because economic output rose fast. For the *nomenklatura* and workers alike, these were the best of the Stalin years. Food supply became sufficiently regular for rationing to be ended in 1935. Although overcrowding remained desperate, more investment was put into workers' living conditions. Health and social security provision, on which the regime prided itself as establishing the model for the fully developed socialist future, improved markedly. Millions benefited from the mass literacy campaigns and there was a huge increase in enrolments for education at all levels. Every effort was made to encourage workers to acquire new skills through a wide range of training schemes, and differentials were deliberately widened to reward skilled workers. The combination of full employment and a rudi-

---

163 The networks and their relationship with Moscow are explored in G. Rittersporn, *Stalinist Simplifications and Soviet Complications: Social tensions and political conflicts in the USSR, 1933–1953* (Chur 1991).

mentary but wide-ranging education, health, social security and pension system for workers was celebrated in the new Constitution drawn up in 1936. The text, drafted in large part by Bukharin, was less flamboyant than its predecessors of 1918 and 1924, aiming, according to Stalin, to be simple and concise. The onset of the Great Terror (see below, documents 191–96) just as the Constitution was being promulgated would cast the sickliest pall over the political rights it proclaimed in Articles 125, 126 and 127 and the direct elections to the Supreme Soviet it introduced.[164] But there was widespread (controlled) consultation, nationwide meetings and press discussion over its terms, and the unique range of welfare rights and provision it aspired to, as well as its guarantee both of employment and of equal rights for women, lent it iconic status.[165]

Document 169 | From the 1936 USSR Constitution

CHAPTER X

FUNDAMENTAL RIGHTS AND DUTIES OF CITIZENS

ARTICLE 118. Citizens of the USSR have the right to work, that is, are guaranteed the right to employment and payment for their work in accordance with its quantity and quality.

The right to work is ensured by the socialist organization of the national economy, the steady growth of the productive forces of Soviet society, the elimination of the possibility of economic crises, and the abolition of unemployment.

ARTICLE 119. Citizens of the USSR have the right to rest and leisure.

The right to rest and leisure is ensured by the reduction of the working day to seven hours for the overwhelming majority of the workers, the institution of annual vacations with full pay for workers and employees and the provision of a wide network of sanatoria, rest homes and clubs for the accommodation of the working people.

ARTICLE 120. Citizens of the USSR have the right to maintenance in old age and also in case of sickness or loss of capacity to work.

This right is ensured by the extensive development of social insurance of workers and employees at state expense, free medical service for the working people and the provision of a wide network of health resorts for the use of the working people.

---

164 See J.A. Getty, 'State and Society under Stalin: Constitutions and elections in the 1930s' *Slavic Review* 50 (1991) pp. 18–36. Plans that these elections should be competitive were abruptly abandoned in autumn 1937.

165 For a detailed commentary, see Unger, *Constitutional Development* pp. 77–138. On the consultation process, see Siegelbaum and Sokolov, *Stalinism as a Way of Life* pp. 158–201.

ARTICLE 121. Citizens of the USSR have the right to education.

This right is ensured by universal, compulsory elementary education; by education, including higher education, being free of charge; by the system of state stipends for the overwhelming majority of students in the universities and colleges; by instruction in schools being conducted in the native language, and by the organization in the factories, state farms, machine and tractor stations and collective farms of free vocational, technical and agronomic training for the working people.

ARTICLE 122. Women in the USSR are accorded equal rights with men in all spheres of economic, state, cultural, social and political life.

The possibility of exercising these rights is ensured to women by granting them an equal right with men to work, payment for work, rest and leisure, social insurance and education, and by state protection of the interests of mother and child, prematernity and maternity leave with full pay, and the provision of a wide network of maternity homes, nurseries and kindergartens.

ARTICLE 123. Equality of rights of citizens of the USSR, irrespective of their nationality or race, in all spheres of economic, state, cultural, social and political life, is an indefeasible law.

Any direct or indirect restriction of the rights of, or, conversely, any establishment of direct or indirect privileges for, citizens on account of their race or nationality, as well as any advocacy of racial or national exclusiveness or hatred and contempt, is punishable by law.

ARTICLE 124. In order to ensure citizens freedom of conscience, the Church in the USSR is separated from the state, and the school from the church. Freedom of religious worship and freedom of anti-religious propaganda is recognized for all citizens.

ARTICLE 125. In conformity with the interests of the working people, and in order to strengthen the socialist system, the citizens of the USSR are guaranteed by law:

a) freedom of speech;
b) freedom of the press;
c) freedom of assembly, including the holding of mass meetings;
d) freedom of street processions and demonstrations.

These civil rights are ensured by placing at the disposal of the working people and their organizations printing presses, stocks of paper, public buildings, the streets, communications facilities and other material requisites for the exercise of these rights.

ARTICLE 126. In conformity with the interests of the working people, and in order to develop the organizational initiative and political activity of the masses of the people, citizens of the USSR are ensured the right to unite in public organizations— trade unions, co-operative associations, youth organizations, sport and defence organizations, cultural, technical and scientific societies; and the most active and politically most conscious citizens in the ranks of the working class and other sections of the working people unite in the Communist Party of the Soviet Union (Bolsheviks), which is the vanguard of the working people in their struggle to strengthen and develop the socialist system and is the leading core of all organizations of the working people, both public and state.

ARTICLE 127. Citizens of the USSR are guaranteed inviolability of the person. No person may be placed under arrest except by decision of a court or with the sanction of a procurator.

ARTICLE 128. The inviolability of the homes of citizens and privacy of correspondence are protected by law.

[Source: J. Stalin, *On the Draft Constitution of the USSR: Constitution (Fundamental Law) of the Union of Soviet Socialist Republics* (Moscow 1945) pp. 76–79.]

The labour decrees of 1938 and 1940

Following the rapid increase in industrial output and gradual recovery of agriculture in 1934 and 1935, 1936 saw a series of major economic setbacks. This coincided with growing international tension and a huge increase in defence investment. The regime's response was to redouble attempts to root out what were seen as the causes of the economic problems: criminal negligence and deliberate sabotage by officials and managers in the economy, the state administration and the party on the one hand, and indiscipline by rank-and-file workers on the other. The culmination of the drive against the former, as we shall see (documents 194–96) played a major role in the Great Terror. Where the latter was concerned, the late 1930s saw further intensification of the administrative and legal measures introduced in 1932 to tighten labour discipline. The prime concern remained the rate of labour turnover. Full social insurance benefits were made conditional on a long period of service in one enterprise, and maternity leave was reduced from 112 to 70 days. In 1938 a stricter system of work-record books was instituted, and managers were ordered to refuse employment unless the employee could produce a satisfactory work-book with details of and explanation for his/her previous changes of employer.

Document 170 | **On the introduction of work-record books—from a Sovnarkom decree**

20 December 1938

The Council of People's Commissars of the USSR decrees as follows:

1. From 15 January 1939 the introduction for all workers and employees in state and co-operative enterprises and institutions of work-record books, to be issued by the administration of the enterprise or institution.
2. They are to contain the following information about the bearer of the work-record book: surname, name, patronymic, age, education, profession, work-record, details of moves from one enterprise or institution to another and reasons for them, as well as any bonuses or awards.
3. The format of the work-record book is to be confirmed.
4. The work-record books are to have a standard format throughout the USSR. The contents of the work-record book are to be in Russian and the language of the given Union or autonomous republic. . .
5. On starting work, workers and employees are obliged to present their work-record books to the administration of the enterprise or institution. The administration is permitted to hire workers and employees only on presentation of their work-record books.

   Persons starting work for the very first time are obliged to present the administration with a certificate from the local authority or village soviet affirming their previous occupation.

[Source: *Direktivy KPSS i sovetskogo pravitel'stva po khozyaystvennym voprosam* (Moscow 1957) p. 544.]

Eighteen months later, evidently exasperated by the limited impact of this measure, and by severe labour shortages, the first of a series of three draconian decrees was issued—purportedly by request of the trade unions. Its grim provisions were to cover white- as well as blue-collar workers and it was to take immediate effect. First, the working day, proudly cut to seven hours in 1927, as trumpeted in the 1936 Constitution, was lengthened to eight hours, and the working week was lengthened from five out of six to six out of seven days. Second, it became a criminal offence, punishable by prison sentence, to change jobs without specific authorization, and employers were given tight guidelines severely restricting the granting of such permission. Third, absenteeism (arriving more than twenty minutes late for work on two occasions was subsequently defined as enough to break the law) was to be punished by a period of up to six months of compulsory labour at 75 per cent normal pay rates—and cases were to be heard within a maximum of five days of being reported. Employers who failed to report cases of absenteeism or of workers who left without permission, or who took on such workers, were themselves to be subject to criminal prosecution.

Document 171 | **Edict of the Presidium of the Supreme Soviet of the USSR on the move to an eight-hour working day, a seven-day working week and the prohibition of workers and staff leaving their enterprises without authorization**

26 June 1940

In accordance with representations from the All-Union Central Council of Trade Unions, the Presidium of the Supreme Soviet of the USSR decrees as follows:

1. An increase in the length of the working day for workers and employees in all state, co-operative and public enterprises and institutions: from seven to eight hours in enterprises with a seven-hour working day; from six to seven hours at places with a six-hour working day, excluding professions with dangerous working conditions, as specified in the schedules established by the Sovnarkom of the USSR; from six to eight hours for the non-manual employees of institutions, and from six to eight hours for persons who have reached the age of 16 years.

2. A change from a six-day week to a seven-day week—the seventh, Sunday, being a rest day—in all state, co-operative and public enterprises and institutions.

3. Unauthorized leaving by workers and employees of state, co-operative and public enterprises and institutions is forbidden, as is unauthorized moving from one enterprise or institution to another. Permission to leave an enterprise or institution or to transfer from one enterprise or institution to another can be granted only by the enterprise director or the head of the institution.

4. It is established that the director of an enterprise or head of an institution has the right and duty to give permission for a worker or employee to leave an enterprise or institution in the following instances:

   a. When the worker or employee, according to the findings of a medical board, can no longer do his former job because of illness or disablement and the administration cannot find other suitable work in the same enterprise or institution, or when a pensioner awarded an old-age pension wishes to stop work.

   b. When a worker or employee must stop work as a result of starting at an institution of further or higher education. Time off for female workers and employees for maternity leave is retained in accordance with existing law.

5. It is established that workers or employees leaving state, co-operative and public enterprises and institutions without authorization are to be brought before a court and, subject to sentence by a people's court, are liable to imprisonment for a period of two to four months.

   It is established that for absence from work without good cause, workers and employees in state, co-operative and public enterprises and institutions are to be brought before a court, and, on the sentence of a people's court, may be punished by up to six months' corrective labour at their place of work with 25 per cent of

their wages deducted. In connection with this, immediate dismissal for unauthorized absenteeism is abolished.

People's courts are instructed that all cases covered by this article are to be
heard within five days and sentences are to be carried out immediately.

6. It is established that directors of enterprises or heads of institutions who fail to
refer cases of persons leaving their enterprise or institution without authorization, or of persons guilty of absenteeism without good cause, are to be prosecuted.
It is also established that directors of enterprises or heads of institutions who hire
people who have left their enterprise or institution without authorization and are
hiding from the law are to be prosecuted.

7. The above comes into force on 27 June 1940.

M. Kalinin, chairman of the Presidium of the Supreme Soviet of the USSR.
A. Gorkin, secretary of the Presidium of the Supreme Soviet of the USSR.
Moscow, Kremlin

[Source: *Izvestiya*, 27 June 1940.]

As with earlier decrees, there was widespread evasion and collusion by
employers and workers. Moreover, so generally was this intrusive use of the
criminal law seen as objectionable that at first procurators and judges, too,
proved very reluctant to implement it—and that despite the fear and tension
in the aftermath of the Great Terror of 1937–38. Together with sharply dete-
riorating living standards, resentment against increasing privileges for officials
and intelligentsia, and rumours of severe setbacks in the Finnish war of
1939–40, popular hostility to the legislation of the late 1930s created a level
of popular discontent that dismayed the NKVD.[166] The following article,
claiming evidence of mass enthusiasm, was part of a furious campaign to
compel implementation. Only the Nazi onslaught of June 1941 lent retrospective legitimation to a measure almost universally detested.

Document 172 | From K. Gorshenin: 'An edict in action'

26 July 1940

A month has passed since the publication of the Presidium of the Supreme Soviet's
edict 'On the move to an eight-hour day, a seven-day working week and the prohibition of workers and staff leaving their enterprises without authorization'.

In the last month people's judges of the RSFSR have already investigated a fair
number of cases of infringement of labour discipline. . . The people's court of sector

---

166 See the ground-breaking discussion in S. Davies, *Popular Opinion in Stalin's Russia: Terror,
propaganda and dissent* (Cambridge 1997).

1 of Moscow's Proletarian District sentenced a certain Cherkasov, an electrician from a wiring factory, to six months' corrective labour for absenteeism on 28 June. Cherkasov is only 20, but in the last eighteen months he has been sacked from four factories for absenteeism and refusal to work. . .

Among those sentenced by the people's courts are a few remnants of defeated hostile classes. In the Tovarkovo region of Tula *oblast'* the people's court prosecuted one Semenikhin. A former kulak, Semenikhin had already been tried and served a sentence of five years in prison. At work he was not conscientious, took time off and flitted from enterprise to enterprise. On the last occasion Semenikhin had simply walked out from a geological prospecting group.

After the trial of one Gerasimov, who disorganized production at the Lobanov spirits factory in the Tula *oblast'*, a worker at the factory, comrade Molchanov, declared, 'I was present at the session of Gerasimov's trial where that layabout was sentenced. We honest workers were outraged to hear the wiles and excuses of this disorganizer of production. . . All the workers greeted the sentence of the court with great joy.'

K. Gorshenin, People's Commissar for Justice of the RSFSR

[Source: *Pravda*, 26 July 1940.]

14

'Cultural Revolution'
and the Intelligentsia

The Shakhty Case

The maelstrom of collectivization and industrialization had an impact on the relatively privileged white-collar, non-manual strata of Soviet society that was scarcely less profound than that on the peasantry and working class. From early in 1928 these strata, who had come to be known collectively by the label 'intelligentsia', once reserved for the cultural and artistic elite, became directly caught up in the intra-party struggle developing between supporters of Stalin and those of Bukharin. Stalin appears to have quite deliberately sought to unleash the pent-up frustration that NEP had generated within the party and among workers against the intelligentsia, regarded as privileged remnants of the old order and protégés of the expropriated bourgeoisie whose loyalty to the Soviet cause was viewed with deep suspicion. This ensured that instead of providing potential support for and strengthening the position of the relative moderation identified with Bukharin, the non-party technical and cultural intelligentsia were thrown onto the defensive and association with them became a political liability. A millenarian atmosphere was fostered in which militant activists went onto the offensive, in industry and economic management as well as all areas of cultural life, against the 'bourgeois deformities' of NEP.[167]

The catalyst for what contemporaries called the 'cultural revolution' was the trial, amidst massive publicity, of fifty-three mining engineers and technicians, including three Germans working on contract, from the Shakhty region of the Donbass.[168] On 10 March the front page of *Pravda* announced

---

167 See S. Fitzpatrick (ed.) *Cultural Revolution in Russia, 1928–31* (Bloomington, IN, 1978), for a highly influential collection of essays.
168 For the position of the technical intelligentsia and the ramifications of the affair, see K.E. Bailes, *Technology and Society under Lenin and Stalin: Origins of the Soviet technical intelligentsia 1917–1941* (Princeton 1978), and N. Lampert, *The Technical Intelligentsia and the Soviet State: A study of Soviet managers and technicians 1928–1935* (London 1979).

the sensational discovery of a far-flung counter-revolutionary plot to undermine the economy. The public prosecutor denounced a conspiracy to
destroy the Soviet coal industry, supposedly involving every device from
direct arson to fiendishly clever sabotage and deliberate maltreatment of
workers, and purportedly orchestrated by former mine owners co-operating
with foreign agents and White Guard émigrés.

Document 173 | The 'Shakhty Case'—report of the Procurator of the Supreme Court of the USSR

9 March 1928

A counter-revolutionary organization, which aimed to disorganize and destroy the
coal industry of the Shakhty region of the Don Basin in the northern Caucasus has
been uncovered by the OGPU with the full co-operation of the workers.

The command centre of this organization, as confirmed by the indisputable facts
of the investigation, is abroad and is made up of former capitalist mine owners and
shareholders of the Don Basin coal mines, who have close links with individual
agents of certain German firms and Polish counter-intelligence.

A detailed analysis of numerous occurrences which disorganized production
(fires, explosions, damage to machinery and mineshaft blockages) led to the discovery
of the counter-revolutionary criminals. The subsequent arrest of the criminals, and
the testimonies of the accused, of witnesses and of expert opinion provided us with
abundant material which enabled us to establish exactly the make-up, aims, means
and methods of a disparate conspiratorial organization.

Apart from former capitalist mine owners and shareholders, the organization had
lured in a group of specialist engineers, technicians, foremen and office workers.
Moreover, it turned out that they had systematically been receiving payment from
their former bosses and special sums from foreign espionage agents, and that many
of them had previously been White counter-intelligence agents.

The investigation established that the work of this counter-revolutionary organization, which has been going on for some years, consisted in malicious sabotage
and undercover disruptive activity, in undermining the coal industry by irrational
construction, unnecessary capital expenditure, the lowering of quality and the raising
of costs, as well as the direct destruction of mines, pits, factories, etc. In all of this,
in the event of the intervention they were constantly counting on, the criminals'
intention was to organize a catastrophic industrial collapse, sharply lower the
country's defence capabilities and thereby help the interventionists overcome the
resistance of the Workers' and Peasants' Red Army.

The completely objective facts of the investigation have established that wherever members of the organization, in their capacities as engineers and office workers,
were able to bring the economic management of the enterprise under their influence, the following invariably happened: rich seams and profitable pits which might

have given tens of millions of *pudy* of good coal were put out of action, flooded and intentionally blown up and blocked off. Conversely, unprofitable mines with poor-quality coal were developed. This was clearly useless and damaged locomotives.

In order to undermine industry and discredit the socialist rationalization of production a very finely tuned system of sabotage was developed and introduced under the guise of production rationalization. Unnecessary equipment was purchased from abroad, sometimes antiquated, sometimes so new that it could not be used in the technical conditions of the Southern coalfield. For example, coal-cutters, suitable only for hard seams, were bought in America, and used in soft seams. Orders were placed especially so that they could not be fulfilled in time. Completely unnecessary machines were often ordered, and individual parts of machines were ordered at different times. Wherever the counter-revolutionaries managed to put their people into positions of power, the re-equipping of mines was done with delib-erate negligence, leading to all sorts of misfortunes, accidents and destruction. It has been established that wherever the sabotage organization managed to put its people into positions of power, the state of production and the finances of the enterprises declined catastrophically. The plotters tried in every way to worsen the workers' conditions at the mines. Housing was not repaired and dangerous work was under-taken with criminal negligence and direct flaunting of the elementary rules of safety. Workers were often underpaid, insulted and deliberately provoked to take strike action. 'Inconvenient' workers were dismissed. The plotters also wormed their way into the engineering and technical section of the trade union, which enabled them to remove recently promoted workers, communists and honest specialists, committed to the cause of socialist construction, from leading positions and their jobs.

The investigation established that the organization's participants were financed by the White Guard centre abroad.

The criminals have been arrested and are being held in accordance with Articles 58/11 and 58/7.* At the end of the investigation the matter will be referred to the Supreme Court of the USSR.

[Source: *Pravda*, 10 March 1928.]

---

* Article 58 of the Criminal Code of the RSFSR was the notorious article dealing with sabotage, subversion, espionage and counter-revolutionary crimes. Paragraph 7 dealt with economic crimes, and paragraph 11 specified the death penalty for participating in any organizational or preparatory work deemed to have subversive or counter-revolutionary aims.

Although the case itself did not open until May, and although Rykov, Kuybyshev and others publicly counselled caution in assuming that disloyalty among technical *intelligenty* was widespread, that assumption quickly gained ground. The following report from the Moscow party organization conveys the violent hostility against and contempt for specialists on the factory floor. The account of the mood among party members and workers is lent credibility by the nuanced reference to the recently disgraced United Opposition.

Document 174 | The 'Shakhty Case'—report by the Information Division of the Moscow Committee of the CPSU

15 March 1928

The mood among communists is perfectly healthy. All comrades are demanding the harshest measures against the counter-revolutionaries. Some comrades are demanding that immediate steps be taken to increase supervision of local specialists and to check defects in the work of particular specialists. Party members at the Il'ich factory have spoken of the need to watch the work of specialists with greater vigilance, and in particular to take an interest in the work of the former owner in the trust. They also think it necessary to check the non-fulfilment of orders for equipment from abroad. Comrades think that the affair is not confined to the Don Basin and that attention should be paid to local disorders, in particular, the disorder in the fire service. This has been noted at the 'Red Proletarian' works, once owned by Tsindel'.

Instances of harassment of specialists have been observed in some factories. At the Armature factory there had been cases of specialist-baiting before, and now they are saying, 'Half of them ought to be shot.' At the No. 8 Mouldings factory the workers are saying, 'There's no need for such a fuss, we can manage without them.' The Party cell at Moscow Construction is saying that there ought to be a purge of specialists on the staff.

One also hears this sort of thing: 'Some of the Opposition's ideas on Thermidor elements in the country have been proved right, but the Opposition drew the wrong conclusions.' From expelled members of the Opposition one hears, 'The Opposition was absolutely right in its assessment of the forces in the country' (Verman and Lipkin of the 'Paris Commune' factory); 'Those are the people we need a second October against' (Ermirov of the 'Il'ich' factory); 'Those running the economy everywhere, and especially in our factory, have fallen under the influence of specialists.'

Non-Party workers are demanding no less severe measures: 'Off with their heads! Hang the counter-revolutionaries! Shoot the lot without trial!' There is considerable dissatisfaction that it has taken so many years for the authorities to uncover the plot ('Red Proletarian', 'Paris Commune', No. 8 Mouldings, 'New Dawn', the Tsindel' works). The fact that they failed to notice it for so long shows that the communists were being insufficiently vigilant, so tried and tested communists should be used for economic work ('New Dawn'). 'The GPU isn't worth a light. The Cheka would've done a better job.'

The mood among specialists is generally rather subdued. There are fears that a new wave of harassment of specialists and repression among the intelligentsia has begun. Fears have been voiced that the extensive publicizing of these facts will engender negative attitudes to all specialists ('New Dawn'). There have been protest meetings by specialists, passivity in other cases and the appearance of national-chauvinist attitudes among others ('What's happened in the Don Basin is the result of too many non-Russian engineers working there'). Negative attitudes towards bringing in specialists from abroad have been expressed.

Some also spoke out against repressive measures being taken against specialists. Dr Nechaev of the Timiryazev hospital said, 'Even judging from the papers, they have been having problems everywhere—and as a result they are piling all the blame onto our heads.'

[Source: B.A. Starkov, 'Perekhod k "politike razgroma" (Shakhtinskoe delo)', *Istoriki otvechayut na voprosy* Issue 2 (Moscow 1990) pp. 255–56.]

The trial itself, the publicity surrounding it, the death sentence pronounced on eleven of the accused (five of whom were executed), and the widespread wave of denunciations against specialists, accompanied by local show trials apeing the Shakhty case, bore out Dr Nechaev's fears. Here V.E. Grum-Grzhimaylo, the mining engineer who as we have seen served on the ferrous metals council attached to VSNKh in the 1920s (see document 101), spells out some of the effects. The regime's motive for making entirely false accusations, he asserts, is to find a scapegoat for the inherent deficiencies of the non-capitalist economy. For patriotic reasons like those of the *smenovekhovtsy* (see document 119) Grum-Grzhimaylo had up to this point been willing to take a senior role in what he saw as an experiment which, though doomed, would ultimately trigger a healthy capitalist reaction. Now, however, he offered his resignation (he died later the same year), insisting that the destruction of trust—'mistrust erected into a principle'—made it impossible to continue. The letter circulated in *samizdat* and appeared in the émigré press: had it been published in the USSR his frank admiration for capitalism and contempt for socialism would have confirmed suspicion about the attitude of specialists.

Document 175 | The 'Shakhty Case'—from V.E. Grum-Grzhimaylo's letter of resignation to V.I. Mezhlauk, head of *Glavmetall* at VSNKh

June 1928

I most humbly request to be released from my post as chairman of the Ferrous Metals Council. . . Real sabotage is just a myth and what took place was just trickery. How did the Bolsheviks react to this? Calmly? As if it were simple trickery? No. They have blown up the Shakhty affair and created from it an imaginary threat to disrupt industry. They have put the whole intelligentsia under suspicion, arrested numerous engineers and are instituting a whole series of court cases. What are their reasons for acting in such a way? There could be two reasons for the Bolsheviks' nervous attitude:

1. The Bolsheviks were frightened of betrayal, really did lose their heads and begin to do stupid things, but I reject this version in no uncertain manner.
2. The first and unquestionable defeat suffered by the Bolsheviks on the industrial front has not been recognized by them as a defeat of the way of running industry they have adopted. They do not have the courage to do so and have jumped at the Shakhty trial as a possible way of justifying their own failures.

Once every action of a specialist is looked at from a procurator's point of view, and all technical specialists are under suspicion, paralysis of the administrative machine is inevitable. . .

What should I, who can see clearly where we are headed, do? I am an honest man. Should I write, speak out, publish? There is neither freedom of speech nor a free press. . . All that is left is to shut up and pretend to be doing your job—as they say, we are just cogs—and wait for the inevitable disaster.

. . . The whole intelligentsia have been turned into time-serving salary-drawers, forced by hunger to be obedient slaves. That is why nobody is speaking out. . .

Will it be honest of me to say nothing and carry on working in ferrous metals if I am convinced that the institution can work properly only with the complete trust of government bodies?—and with mistrust erected into a principle it cannot work properly. . .

It is quite clear that an honest and independent man must not work in such conditions. He is obliged to give up his responsibilities, once he is convinced that without trust that institution cannot work in a healthy fashion. These are the reasons for my resignation.

Grum-Grzhimaylo, mining engineer

[Source: *Bor'ba za Rossiyu* No. 128 (Paris 1928) pp. 3–7.]

That figures such as Grum-Grzhimaylo should have been dismayed by the Shakhty 'revelations', and rank-and-file party members and workers incensed, suited Stalin and his allies admirably in the intensifying struggle with Bukharin, Rykov and more cautious leaders. The charge of politically motivated sabotage in industry matched the claim that the grain crisis arose from the politically motivated activity of 'kulaks'. It handed the initiative to advocates of a decisive industrial, social and political breakthrough. It gave credibility to the suspicion of broad sympathy between the 'Right deviation' and the anti-party attitudes and treacherous activities of privileged elements left over from the old order. It lent weight to Stalin's growing insistence that the closer the USSR came to socialism, the more viciously class enemies would fight to halt progress.

This raises the issue of Stalin's role in promoting the Shakhty affair. The case appears to have begun with complaints against managers and engineers by mine workers in the region, but the initiative for pressing it forward and bringing it to the attention of Moscow was taken by the OGPU chief in the North Caucasus region, E.G. Evdokimov. The fact that he was a friend of Stalin's, and that Stalin quoted and spoke up for him when members of the Politburo protested against the initial arrests, suggests the General Secretary saw and welcomed the political potential of the case. Here Evdokimov commends the OGPU agent responsible for the investigation and interrogation—despite the fact that the show trial had been marred by two witnesses repudiating their signed confessions and a third refusing to confess at all.

Document 176 | The 'Shakhty Case'—from E.G. Evdokimov's recommendation for an award to be given to OGPU agent K.I. Zonov

November 1928

Comrade Zonov attached particular importance to a number of technical defects which resulted in accidents, flooding and the like. Sensing that indisputable sabotage activity was going on here, comrade Zonov began a lengthy, serious and extremely complex agent's investigation not only of particular shortcomings, but of all the activities of the Shakhty mine management and the entire staff of specialists. As a result of this work comrade Zonov became convinced that there was a diversionist organization in the Shakhty district, and further work on his results led him to conclude that this organization had centres in Khar'kov, Moscow and abroad. Extremely skilled investigative work completely confirmed comrade Zonov's conclusions.

Throughout the whole immense process of agents' and investigative work into the Shakhty case not only was comrade Zonov the main leading figure but he also directly conducted the work at its most difficult moments.

1. Comrade Zonov personally worked out the plan of the entire 'operation' in

the Shakhty case.

2. More than once during the investigation he went to the spot (to Shakhty) giving valuable instructions to those involved in the Shakhty case at grass-roots level.

3. Comrade Zonov personally conducted all the initial interrogations of those arrested, which assisted the course of further investigations.

4. He also conducted all the general interrogations of the prime suspects.

5. The confession of Gavryushenko, giving the basic evidence which played a decisive role in the case, was extracted exclusively as a result of extremely skilled interrogation, conducted personally by comrade Zonov.

6. The expert opinion which provided such great help in uncovering the sabotage was selected and appointed by comrade Zonov personally. He participated directly in the work of the commission of experts, and used the experience he gained in working in the Supreme Economic Council to great effect.

E. Evdokimov, Plenipotentiary representative of the North Caucasus *kray* and Dagestan ASSR OGPU.

[Source: GARF, fond 3316, opis' 2, delo 628, p. 20.]

The 'cultural revolution'

The explosive response to the Shakhty 'revelations' in March reflected and accelerated mounting tension among cultural as well as technical *intelligenty*. Radical intellectuals, students and activists took up the cry for a decisive party-led struggle against 'bourgeois' traitors and false fellow travellers. Echoing the regime's rhetoric and paralleling the drive against 'kulaks' in the countryside, they took it upon themselves to 'ascribe' the class position of suspects. The Marxist notion that an individual's class was defined by his or her relationship to the means of production was diluted and overlaid by focus on family background and former occupation: the discovery of parents from the nobility, bourgeoisie or clergy became grounds for exposure.[169] Those accused of indifference to and alienation from the demands of socialist construction and cultural revolution saw their reputations, their posts and even their liberty put at risk. Non-Marxists were 'unmasked' and purged for their class affiliation, while Marxist scholars, teachers, lawyers and even architects and town planners vied with each other in their enthusiasm for establishing firm party leadership and militantly revolutionary policy in every

---

169 On the way in which Soviet class categorization mutated in the 1920s and 1930s, see S. Fitzpatrick, 'Ascribing Class: The construction of social identity in Soviet Russia' in Fitzpatrick (ed.) *Stalinism: New directions* pp. 20–46.

field. From philosophy to the sciences and from music to theatre, a new 'front' in the class war was opened and a frantic search made for truly 'proletarian' approaches.

In some fields, notably history and the social sciences, the initiative and main thrust of change remained throughout in the hands of the party leadership. The link between Lenin and Stalin, between Russia's backward economic development and the possibility of building socialism in one country, between October and the 'second revolution' were themes that became too politically sensitive to be left to scholars. So too, once the 'extraordinary measures' of 1928 and gathering war against 'kulaks' were under way, did developments in the countryside and the controversy over class differentiation among the peasantry. In many fields, however, the drive behind the 'cultural revolution' came in large part 'from below', from activists and enthusiasts.

Cinema provides an example. On many of the aesthetic, commercial and stylistic issues debated by practitioners during the 1920s, no clearly defined party line existed. But from 1928 Marxist theorists of every stripe strove to outdo others in clamouring for the establishment of a hegemonic party line (and in seeking to secure appropriate funding to pursue it) while mining the works of Marx, Lenin and current party leaders for quotations with which to support their own view of what that line should be. Typical of the language used was the following letter from a group of film directors to a Party Conference on Cinema held days after the dramatic announcement of the Shakhty affair. Among those signing was S.M. Eisenstein, whose *Battleship Potemkin* had earned him an international reputation in 1926 and whose *October* was released the day the Conference opened. The resolution adopted at the Conference duly affirmed the vital role of art in general and film in particular as 'the sharpest instrument of the proletariat in the struggle against the hostile opposition remnants of the old world'.[170] The exact nature of the appropriate party line was furiously debated between 1928 and 1931, many of the radicals of 1928 quickly falling from favour. But the overall trend was towards heavy emphasis on ideological content, a drastic narrowing in freedom to experiment with form and style, and ever tighter control by the mushrooming apparatus of the Central Committee.

---

170 R. Taylor and I. Christie, *The Film Factory: Russian and Soviet cinema in documents, 1896–1939* (Cambridge, MA, 1998), p. 208. For the best overview of the development of Soviet cinema in the period, see P. Kenez, *Cinema and Soviet Society: From the revolution to the death of Stalin* (New York 2001).

Document 177 | '…we need a *Red Culture Officer*…'—from a letter by a group of film producers

16 March 1928

In all spheres of the work of the state the revolution has established a single leadership and a single plan. This is one of the greatest achievements of the proletarian revolution, allowing a firm ideological dictatorship to be exercised on all fronts of socialist construction. Has this opportunity been seized in cinema? No. If in the economic management of the cinema we have only a retarded monopoly (there is a multiplicity of film-making organizations, which in the nature of things pushes them into an unhealthy competition, etc.), then in the ideological sphere, which ultimately is the reason why the entire cinema industry exists, we have nothing at all.

There is no planned ideological leadership. The way Soviet film production is organized does not differ much from bourgeois film production, since production is either the result of small-scale initiatives by individuals working with, or not working with, other social organizations or, at best, the result of state orders on anniversaries.

This happens because all cinema production is actually carried out not by cultural but by commercial organizations which cannot govern themselves on the ideological plane.

To implement a single ideological plan we need an authoritative body to plan cinema productions.

The Central Repertory Committee does not satisfy this need, because it is neither a governing, nor a planning, body, but simply accepts films or production plans already created by others.

For this responsible work we need a *Red Culture Officer*. The guiding body must first and foremost be a cultural and political body directly connected to the CC of the CPSU.

For such an organization ideology will not be the mysterious blue or rather 'red' bird which the present leadership tries in vain to catch by the tail. Ideology is not the 'philosopher's stone', but a set of specific steps in the construction of socialism, analysed and brought together by the Party at every given moment as a set of specific practical theses. The cinematographic expression of these theses must set a legal limit on the metaphysical speculations of ideology 'as such'.

So, a body directly attached to the CC Agitprop Department needs to be created, which will in an organized way set exhaustive cultural and political tasks for the film-producing organizations.

This will enable us to overcome the chaotic swings in the repertoire of the film-producing organizations, which are merely the productive and economic expression of the directives they have received, which stress commercial profitability.

Only this sort of demarcation between two bodies, a political–planning body and an economic–executive one, will dialectically produce healthy conditions for the growth of Soviet cinematography.

To give such a body full authority in practice, it is essential that film producers be widely involved. As in the past, so in the future, they will be the cultural force responsible for implementing these tasks. . .

The greatest danger for Soviet cinematography would be for a situation to arise where the Party's interest in the film industry, which has been heightened by this Party conference, just fades away once the conference is over. This may well happen if the implementation of conference resolutions is not carried out by well-chosen personnel, as happened after the theatre conference, where its good intentions remained hanging in the air.

The body we are proposing must be a permanent militant body, paying unflagging attention to the cinematographic area of the cultural front.

Aleksandrov, Kozintsev, Trauberg, Popov, Pudovkin, Room, Eisenstein, Yutkevich.

[Source: *Iskusstvo kino* No. 4, 1964, pp. 14–15.]

The combination of intellectual upheaval, hectic institutional experiment and 'class-based' purge transformed education and academic life. Relative moderates in the Commissariat of Enlightenment were overtaken by radicals: Lunacharsky himself was dropped in 1929. The mass enrolment of adult workers, a stupendous growth in student numbers, the expulsion of children of 'bourgeois' parents, and wave upon wave of dismissals of ideologically suspect faculty brought the university system to the point of collapse. The Academy of Sciences, whose independence had survived relatively unscathed till the late 1920s, was now subjected to drastic restructuring. Most dramatic was the attack on leading historians in the Academy, denounced for supposedly concealing major archival material in the Academy's library as well as for anti-Marxist propaganda.[171] The following exchange between S. Kirov, party First Secretary in Leningrad, and Yu.P. Figatner, heading a commission of inquiry, on the one hand, and Stalin and the Politburo, on the other, conveys the rapid sequence of events in the 'Platonov' affair. The chief prosecutor, Krylenko, was brought in and over the following year 115 arrests were made, including those of S.F. Platonov, E. Tarle and other prominent historians who were convicted of conspiring to restore constitutional monarchy and were sent into administrative exile. As in other fields, however, the scholar-bureaucrats who initially benefited from the upheaval and took up the cry for the exclusive hegemony of the party line rapidly fell

---

171 See J. Barber, *Soviet Historians in Crisis, 1928–32* (London 1981) pp. 31–41, for a close analysis.

from grace. Most prominent in this instance was the Marxist historian M.N. Pokrovsky, co-opted onto the commission to pursue the case (see document 179), rather than the lesser-known academician of the same name among those to be investigated (see document 180). Control of the Academy passed to VSNKh (and later the Commissariat of Heavy Industry, the most powerful of the three commissariats into which VSNKh was subdivided in December 1931) under Ordzhonikidze, signalling its direct subordination to an agenda set by the political leadership.

Document 178 | **The case of academician S.F. Platonov of the Academy of Sciences—coded telegram from Leningrad to I.V. Stalin and G.K. Ordzhonikidze**

20 October 1929

Urgent.

According to our agents' evidence, the library of the Academy of Sciences contains an uncatalogued collection, which contains the original manuscripts of the abdications of Nicholas and Mikhail, the archives of the CC of the SRs, the CC of the Constitutional Democrats, and Metropolitan Stadnitsky, two bundles of manuscripts from the dissolution of the Constituent Assembly, materials on emigration in 1917, an appeal of the Soviet opposition in 1918 and other materials. Only five people, including Academicians Ol'denburg and Platonov, know about this. There is reason to believe there is similar material in the archives of Pushkin House, the Tolstoy Museum and the Archaeography Commission.

We consider it expedient to confiscate the material in the following way: Sergo [Ordzhonikidze], as People's Commissar of the Worker–Peasant Inspectorate, sends the following telegram to Figatner: 'I suggest the commission, in checking the administration of the Academy of Sciences, familiarizes itself with the contents of the materials in the uncatalogued collection in the library of the Academy of Sciences, with the contents of the library and archive of Pushkin House, and with the materials of the Archaeography Commission and the Tolstoy Museum. You are personally responsible for sending materials of historical and political significance to Moscow.'

It is essential to bear in mind that the academicians might deny the existence of such archives. We cannot in any way whatsoever reveal the sources of our information. Be aware that the Academy is due to meet on 28 October. There is concern that these materials may be stolen or destroyed. Confiscation of these materials may give us some new leads. . .

A reply is urgently required no later than Monday, for fear that the materials are stolen or destroyed. Inform the OGPU of your agreement to the carrying out of this operation under the supervision of Figatner's commission.

Figatner and Kirov.

[see Document 180 for source]

Document 179 | **The case of academician S.F. Platonov of the Academy of Sciences—from the CPSU Politburo minutes**

5 November 1929

To be returned within 24 hours.

Top secret.

To comrades Rykov and Kaganovich—section (a), to Krzhizhanovsky—section (b), to Krylenko—section (c), to Figatner and Pokrovsky—all sections

Item:
. . . 20. The Academy of Sciences.

Resolved:
20.

   a) Tomorrow (6 November) inform the press about the discovery of the materials in the Academy of Sciences and announce Ol'denburg's dismissal, entrusting the editing of the text of the announcement to a commission composed of comrades Rykov, Kaganovich, Figatner and Pokrovsky. The commission to be convened by comrade Rykov.

   b) Comrade Krzhizhanovsky is to secure Platonov's dismissal from his work in the Presidium of the Academy of Sciences within one week, having discussed appropriate measures together with the Party group in the Academy.

   c) To instruct comrade Figatner's commission, with the involvement of comrade Krylenko, to consider the question of prosecuting those guilty of concealing documents. . .

I.V. Stalin, secretary of the CC

[see Document 180 for source]

Document 180 | **The case of academician S.F. Platonov of the Academy of Sciences—coded telegram from Yu.P. Figatner in Leningrad to I.V. Stalin and G.K. Ordzhonikidze**

1 December 1929

Top secret: to be returned within 48 hours.
Urgent.
No copies to be made.

The commission of enquiry, having acquainted itself with the materials, and after interrogating several persons, considers it necessary immediately to begin an official investigation in accordance with Article 78, in the first instance with regard to Platonov, Ol'denburg, Sreznevsky, Pokrovsky, Andreev, Molass and Druzhinin.

   It is not excluded that Article 58/11 may also apply during the course of the investigation.

I urgently request assent to begin an official investigation by the procurator's office, in effect, the OGPU. The investigation will be carried out under the overall supervision of our commission.

Figatner.

[Source for documents 178–80: V.A. Mazur and M.E. Glavatsky, *Istoriya Rossii 1917–1940*, pp. 308–10.]

In literature, the 'cultural revolution' saw the Association of Proletarian Writers (RAPP) and even more radical groups able at last to launch the attack on bourgeois individualism they had been urging on the party throughout the 1920s (see document 130). Authors were exhorted to engage fully in the construction of socialism, to address themselves to issues of immediate relevance, to commit themselves to their own 'planned' literary output. There was a full-blown cult of the machine, while individual heroes—and even individual authorship—were denounced as self-indulgent, elitist, bourgeois. The change in climate here was dramatic but also unpredictable. Poets, playwrights and novelists who had managed to publish elements of their work during the 1920s suddenly found it much harder to do so. Yet the precise limits of tolerance remained capricious. A case in point was M.A. Bulgakov, a major interwar Soviet novelist and playwright who would become best known for *The Master and Margarita*. In October 1928 Bulgakov's play *Flight*, despite praise from prominent figures including Lunacharsky, was abruptly banned for depicting the White Guards during the civil war in too favourable a light. Late the following year, he was able to stage *Crimson Island*, boldly exploring censorship, only to be told after it provoked furious controversy that he must make drastic alterations. When he refused, Stalin himself intervened, insisting on milder changes.[172] The following letter, written a month later, expresses Bulgakov's exasperation: because of Stalin's personal approval, some of his work of the 1920s continued to appear, but his finest work of the 1930s, including *The Master and Margarita*, remained unpublished and many other leading literary figures were reduced to 'the genre of silence'.

Document 181 | **M.A. Bulgakov: 'The fight against censorship... is my duty as a writer...'—from a letter to the Soviet government**

28 March 1930

The fight against censorship, whatever form it may take and under whatever govern-

---

172 A. Kemp-Welch, *Stalin and the Literary Intelligentsia, 1928–39* (London 1991) p. 54.

ment it may exist, is my duty as a writer, as are my calls for freedom of the press. . .
That is one of the features of my creative work, and that alone is sufficient to ensure
that my works do not exist within the USSR. It is with this first feature that all the
other features of my satirical stories are connected: the dark, mystical colours in
which the innumerable deformities of our life are depicted, the poison which fills
my language, the profound scepticism about the revolutionary process which has
been happening in my backward country, which I contrast with my favourite Great
Evolution, and most importantly the depiction of the terrible features of my people,
which long before the revolution caused immense suffering for my teacher M.E.
Saltykov-Shchedrin.

It goes without saying that the Soviet press has not even thought of taking any
notice of this at all, obsessed as it is with its unconvincing protestations that M.
Bulgakov's satire is 'SLANDER'.

Only once, just when I was beginning to get well-known, was it noticed with a
hint of haughty surprise, 'M. Bulgakov WANTS to be the satirist of our era'
(*Knigonosha*, No. 6, 1925). The verb, alas, is in the present tense, when it should be
in the pluperfect: M. Bulgakov HAD BECOME A SATIRIST at a time when any
real satire (i.e., touching on forbidden topics) had become absolutely unthinkable
in the USSR. . .

And, finally, the characteristics of my work to be found in the ruined plays *The
Days of the Turbins* and *Flight*, and in my novel *The White Guard*, are an unfailing
depiction of the Russian intelligentsia as the best social stratum in our country. In
particular, it is the depiction of a gentry-intelligentsia family cast during the Civil
War by the immutable will of history into the White Guard camp, in the traditions
of *War and Peace*. . . But in the USSR such a depiction leads to the author, just like
his characters, being branded as a White Guard enemy, despite his efforts TO RISE
DISPASSIONATELY ABOVE RED OR WHITE, and, as everyone knows, once
you have that label in the USSR, you can consider yourself finished. . .

[Source: M.A. Bulgakov, *'Ya khotel sluzhit' narodu. . .': Proza, P'esy, Pis'ma. Obraz
pisatelya* (Moscow 1991) pp. 603–04.]

Stalin and the show trials of 1930 and 1931

During the 'cultural revolution', pressure on the intelligentsia as a whole and
on the technical intelligentsia in particular was intensified by two further
major show trials, of the 'Industrial Party' in November–December 1930
and of the 'Menshevik Union Bureau' in March 1931. The accused were
more prominent men than those in the Shakhty affair. The eight indicted in
the 'Industrial Party' trial were leading figures in key industrial research insti-
tutes and sections of VSNKh and Gosplan. The fourteen indicted in the

'Union Bureau' trial were economists and officials in Gosplan, the State Bank, the Trade Commissariat and other parts of the economic apparatus, most of whom had earlier been Mensheviks or Menshevik-Internationalists. They were charged with economic wrecking, sabotage and espionage on behalf of foreign and émigré organizations in preparation for armed intervention. In addition to supposedly using their positions to disrupt the Five-Year Plan—the 'Industrial Party' was denounced for deliberately inflating targets, the 'Union Bureau' for deliberately deflating them—both were also charged with involvement in a conspiracy to undermine and disorganize food supply.

There appear to have been three main motives for the trials: to identify and pillory scapegoats for the dire conditions and economic setbacks of 1930–31; to tar critics of the leadership, both within and outside the party, by association with treacherous 'enemies of the people'; and to pre-empt any attempt by members of the intelligentsia to 'exploit' their economic and technical expertise to question party directives or resist party control.[173] The following three letters by Stalin convey his mind-set. Like much of the evidence coming to light on the show trials and political repression of the later 1930s, they also demonstrate his personal involvement and just how closely he studied and orchestrated the investigations, interrogations and main contours of the judicial proceedings themselves.

In the first extract, he moves seamlessly from the macro-economic problems of summer 1930 to investigation into counter-revolution and wrecking—returning in the latter part of the letter to issues of economic management. Having read the transcripts of interrogations under way since July, he orders three arrests—two ex-Menshevik-Internationalists, N.N. Sukhanov (the superb chronicler of 1917, who worked in the Soviet economic apparatus in the 1920s) and V.A. Bazarov (a prominent economist in Gosplan), as well as a liberal professor of the old regime, L.K. Ramzin (a leading engineer and Director of the Institute of Thermal Technology)—drawing no distinction between revolutionary socialists and a former Kadet sympathizer. The use of psychological as well as physical torture to extract confessions is signalled by Stalin's offhand instruction that Sukhanov's wife be 'pressed': as in the Shakhty trial, both cases would rest on the testimony of the accused—there was no other written evidence. His insistence that all the relevant 'evidence' be circulated to the Central Committee was to ensure that the leadership had a unanimous view of the matter and to make it quite plain that to entertain doubts about the guilt of the accused was tantamount to association with them. His derogatory reference to Kalinin refers to the

---

173 Lampert, *Technical Intelligentsia* pp. 38–55.

claims by one of the accused (N.D. Kondrat'ev) that he had had conversations with him.

Document 182 | Documents on the 'Case of the Industrial Party'—I.V. Stalin to V.M. Molotov

No earlier than 23 August 1930

1. The figures for the last ten months show a 26 per cent growth in state industry (instead of 32 per cent). Not a comforting result. You talk about an industrial and financial counter-plan and a Central Committee proclamation. I think we could have tried anything, just to achieve 30–32 per cent growth. I am afraid it is too late to talk about it now—all the same, no big changes can be brought in before October (end of the financial year). But perhaps we can try? Yes, let's. We certainly ought to try.
2. We have another four to six weeks left to export grain: from the end of October (perhaps even earlier) American grain will start coming onto the market on a massive scale, which will be hard for us to stand up against. If in the next six weeks we don't export 130–150 million *pudy* of grain, our foreign currency situation could become simply desperate. I repeat: we must force grain exports with all our might.
3. Sukhanov, Bazarov and Ramzin must be arrested. We need to press Sukhanov's wife (a communist!) a little, because she must have known about the outrages that have been going on at their place. Absolutely all the evidence (principal and additional) ought to be distributed to the members of the CC. That Kalinin is in the wrong is beyond all doubt. Everything the evidence says about Kalinin is the bare truth. The CC must be informed of all of this, to teach Kalinin not to get mixed up with such scoundrels in future...

[Source: L. Kosheleva and others, compilers, *Pis'ma I.V. Stalina V.M. Molotovu 1925–1936 gg.* (Moscow 1995) p. 198.]

The next extract, from a letter Stalin wrote a week later, refers to preparations being made for a third trial, that of the 'Toiling Peasants' Party'. This further imaginary conspiratorial organization was supposedly led by Kondrat'ev, a prominent economist who had been a deputy minister in the Provisional Government and worked in the Soviet Commissariat of Finance in the 1920s, supposedly included A.V. Chayanov (see document 127), and was supposedly closely linked to the 'Industrial Party' and 'Menshevik Union Bureau'. Details of the fictitious plot and interrogation of Kondrat'ev and others were included in the substantial dossier circulated, as Stalin had demanded, to the Central Committee. The third trial, however, did not proceed, possibly because of difficulty in forging a plausible case and in persuading those arrested to 'humiliate themselves politically', and instead the accused were convicted in closed session. The third paragraph suggests that Molotov raised the issue of punishing party members associated with the accused. The assured domination of Stalin and his allies is reflected in his reply, mulling over the fate of Rykov and Kalinin, fellow members of the Politburo and respectively head of the government (chairman of the Sovnarkom) and state (chairman of the TsIK of the USSR). Three weeks later Stalin resolved to remove Rykov from Sovnarkom and put Molotov in his place.

Document 183 | Documents on the 'Case of the Industrial Party'—I.V. Stalin to V.M. Molotov

2 September 1930

. . . 2. It makes sense to publicize the Kondrat'ev 'case' in the papers *only* if we intend to put this 'case' before a court. Are we ready for that? Do we think it necessary to turn this 'case' over to the courts? It would certainly be difficult to get by without a trial.

By the way, cannot the accused gentlemen consider admitting their *mistakes* and generally humiliating themselves politically, at the same time admitting the stability of Soviet power and the correctness of our collectivization methods? That would not be bad. . .

3. About prosecuting Communists who assisted the Gromans and Kondrat'evs, I agree, but what then is to be done about Rykov (who *unquestionably helped them*) and Kalinin (who has clearly been implicated in this 'affair' by the *scoundrel Teodorovich*)? We need to think about this.

[Source: L. Kosheleva and others, *Pis'ma I.V. Stalina V.M. Molotovu 1925–1936 gg.*, p. 211.]

The third letter, to V.R. Menzhinsky, head of the OGPU, brings home most clearly Stalin's detailed mapping of the kind of confessions to be secured. It shows how chance or even absurd statements wrung out of the accused became embedded in the case when the General Secretary fastened upon them. The supposed leader of the group of émigré capitalists whom Stalin identifies as the 'driving force' behind the interlocking counter-revolutionary organizations, P.P. Ryabushinsky (see document 20), had in fact died in 1924: only after the indictment had charged Ramzin with being in communication with him in 1928 did the *non sequitur* come to light. Stalin seized in particular on the issue of impending foreign military intervention. The fact that there is no evidence of any such planning by the Polish,

Romanian or western governments might be taken as proof that Stalin was simply and deliberately fabricating a threat. However, just a month earlier in private correspondence with Molotov, without reference to the impending trials, he underlined his conviction that a Polish–Romanian–Baltic bloc would launch an attack on the USSR as soon as it possibly could.[174] The language used—unquestioningly identifying the USSR, the Bolshevik party, and his leadership with the cause of socialism; making steadily fainter the distinction between critics within the party, hostile social groups at home, and foreign enemies abroad; and blurring the line between actual and potential opposition, conscious and unconscious hostile acts—was not a collection of metaphors to be set aside at will. This was the language in which the Stalinist leadership communicated behind closed doors; it was the language affirmed and reaffirmed in every document they read, speech they made, proposal they advanced; it was the language in which they thought.[175]

Document 184 | Documents on the 'Case of the Industrial Party'—from a letter by I.V. Stalin to V.R. Menzhinsky

Early–mid October 1930

Written on the envelope: 'To Comrade Menzhinsky, OGPU. Strictly personal. From Stalin.'

Comrade Menzhinsky!

I have received your letter of 2 October and the enclosed materials. Ramzin's testimony is very interesting. I think the most interesting thing in it is the question of intervention in general and, in particular, its timing. It seems they were reckoning on an intervention in 1930, but had put it off to 1931 or even 1932. That is important and highly likely. It is even more important because it comes from the primary source, i.e., from the group of Ryabushinsky, Gukasov, Denisov and Nobel', who represent the most powerful socio-economic group of all the groupings existing either in the USSR or in the emigration—the most powerful both in terms of capital and in terms of links with the French and British governments. It may appear that the Toiling Peasants' Party or the 'Industrial Party' or Milyukov's 'party' are the driving force. But that is wrong. The driving force is the group of Ryabushinsky, Denisov, Nobel' and the like, i.e., *Torgprom*. The Toiling Peasants'

174 L.T. Lih, O.V. Naumov and O.V. Khlevnyuk (eds) *Stalin's Letters to Molotov 1925–1936* (New Haven 1995) pp. 208–09.

175 For a sustained analysis of the way in which the distinctive discourse shared by the party leadership developed during the 1930s, see the detailed commentary in J.A. Getty and O.V. Naumov, *The Road to Terror: Stalin and the self-destruction of the Bolsheviks, 1932–1939* (New Haven 1999).

Party, the 'Industrial Party' and Milyukov's 'party' are at the beck and call of *Torgprom*. The information coming from *Torgprom* about the timing of any intervention is even more interesting. For us the question of greatest interest is the idea of intervention in general and, in particular, its timing.

These, then, are my suggestions:

a) Make the question of intervention and its timing one of the key points in the new, forthcoming testimony of the leadership of the Toiling Peasants' Party, the 'Industrial Party' and, especially, Ramzin:

1) why did they postpone the intervention in 1930?

2) was it because Poland was not yet ready?

3) perhaps it was because Romania was not yet ready?

4) perhaps it was because the border states had not yet closed ranks with Poland? Why did they put it off until 1931?. . .

6) why 'might' they put it off until 1932, etc., etc.?

b) Involve Larichev and the other members of the 'CC of the Industrial Party' in the case and question them severely about it, after you have let them read Ramzin's testimony;

c) Interrogate Groman as severely as possible, as according to Ramzin's testimony, on one occasion he declared in the 'Unified Centre' that the intervention had been put off until 1932;

d) Give the treatment to Messrs. Kondrat'ev, Yurovsky, Chayanov and the like, who are craftily trying to dissociate themselves from the 'interventionist tendency', but are (undoubtedly) pro-intervention, and interrogate them severely about the timing of the intervention (Kondrat'ev, Yurovsky and Chayanov must know about it equally as well as Milyukov, to whom they went for a 'chat').

If Ramzin's testimony is **confirmed and made more specific** by the testimonies of the other accused (Groman, Larichev, Kondrat'ev and Co.), it will be a real success for the OGPU, because in some form or another we will make the material we manage to get available to the parties of the Comintern and the workers of all countries. We will run the widest possible campaign against the interventionists and will succeed in paralysing and undermining any attempts at intervention in the next year or two, which is not unimportant for us. Do you understand? Regards.

[Source: RGASPI, fond 558, opis' 1, delo 5276, pp. 1–5.]

The final paragraph makes ominously plain Stalin's ascendancy over Menzhinsky and the OGPU leadership. The following letter makes equally clear the subordination of the procuracy and the judiciary. After urging that the case be heard not by the Supreme Court of the RSFSR but by that of the USSR, of which he was Procurator, P.A. Krasikov asks for close guidance by 'the political body which is directing the trial'.

Document 185 | **Documents on the 'Case of the Industrial Party'—**
P.A. Krasikov to I.V. Stalin

30 October 1930

Top secret
Personal
To: the General Secretary of the CC of the CPSU.

Dear Iosif Vissarionovich,

   According to TASS of 27 October the case of Ramzin and others, a case of exceptional importance, is being handed over to the Supreme Court, but without any clear indication as to which Supreme Court will be given the case to hear. Both in content—its significance means that this case is for broad consumption within the USSR and abroad—and formally, in accordance with the Constitution, we must mean the Supreme Court of the USSR, regardless of the composition of the audience and the state prosecution at the trial, as was the case in the Shakhty trial.

   If you are in agreement with my opinion, please ensure that I am sent the materials and CC resolutions relating to this question which will be needed to guide the Procuracy. I hope you will also find it expedient to keep me in constant touch, in so far as the interests of the case require it, with the political body which is directing the trial. . .

(Krasikov)

Pass on in compiling the indictment (I.V. Stalin)

[Source: V.A. Mazur and M.E. Glavatsky, *Istoriya Rossii 1917–1940*, p. 314.]

Stabilizing the intelligentsia

The Menshevik trial in spring 1931 marked the high point both of 'specialist-baiting' in industry and of the wider upheaval of the 'cultural revolution'. That summer the regime instituted a major change in policy towards the intelligentsia. The initial shift, and the most effective pressure for change, came from within industry. Stalin's fellow Georgian Ordzhonikidze, appointed to head VSNKh in November 1930 and thus responsible for meeting the soaring targets in heavy industry, opened the way for planners and managers in the major industrial branches of the economy to express their alarm both at their own insecurity and at the decline in morale, authority and willingness to take the initiative among specialists and engineers. The Politburo was persuaded of the need to stabilize the position of specialists and Stalin's speech of 23 June, referred to above, signalled the change. The following Central Committee resolution endorsed a flurry of moves to enhance specialists' prestige, security and incentives. New tribunals were to institute brisk reviews of—and for the most part reverse—sentences passed on specialists. Enterprise managers were to be empowered to veto intervention against specialists by the militia, OGPU and procuracy. And a series of measures were to be taken to improve the rewards and material well-being of specialists, notably in terms of housing.[176]

Document 186 | CPSU CC resolution: 'On the work of technical staff in enterprises and the improvement of their working conditions'

10 July 1931

Secret. Not for publication.

With a view to improving working conditions for engineering and technical staff in enterprises and institutions, the CC of the CPSU confirms the following proposals from the Supreme Economic Council of the USSR:

1. Enterprise and institution managers, and Party and trade-union bodies are to increase the authority of engineering and technical staff and implement in full the rights and duties of engineers to manage production...

2. Engineering and technical staff are to be given the opportunity to show wide initiative in rationalizing and improving production processes by permitting risk-taking...

3. Enterprise and institution managers are in every way to encourage specialists to show inventiveness in their work, intelligent leadership, energy, and initiative, by rewarding them, publicizing their achievements in the press and in particularly outstanding cases proposing engineering and technical staff for awards.

4. The cases of specialists tried and sentenced to hard labour for allowing defects and mistakes in their work and for breaking labour law are to be reviewed. In the cases of convicted specialists who have shown dedication to the cause of socialist construction in their work, their convictions are to be overturned, and expunged from their work-records.

   In order to implement this resolution, special commissions are to be formed at enterprises and institutions made up of representatives of the People's Commissariat of Justice, the enterprise management and the... bureau of the trade union, who are to complete their work on reviewing these cases within a month. The above commissions' decisions are to be binding...

7. The following measures are to be taken to improve the living conditions of engineering and technical staff:

   a. Places in educational institutions are to be guaranteed for the children of engineering and technical staff on the same basis as those of industrial workers.

---

176 See Lampert, *Technical Intelligentsia* pp. 135–48, on the scale of material and symbolic privileges they enjoyed. Their wages and material conditions were in fact already markedly better than those of the vast majority of industrial workers, but the emphasis on parity of treatment underlined their enhanced social standing.

b. Places in rest-homes and sanatoria are to be guaranteed for engineering and technical staff on the same basis as for industrial workers.

c. Sickness benefits are to be paid to engineering and technical staff during illness on the same basis as to industrial workers.

d. Supply conditions for both engineering and technical staff and their families are to be equal to those of industrial workers.

f. Engineering and technical staff are to have equal rights to living space with industrial workers. Existing housing co-operatives for engineering and technical staff are to be put onto the same basis as workers' housing co-operatives. . .

When establishing norms for living space, take account of the necessity for specialists to work at home to raise their qualifications, and grant them the right to additional space on the same basis as managerial staff. . .

9. Extend point 5 (a., b., and c.) of the resolution of the CPSU CC and the Sovnarkom of the USSR of 3 June 1931 to all of the Soviet Union:

a. The militia, criminal investigation police and procuracy are forbidden to interfere in the productive activity of factories or to conduct investigations into questions of production without special permission from enterprise managements or higher bodies.

b. The existence of official OGPU offices in factories is inexpedient.

c. Party organizations are not to countermand, alter or delay factory directors' operational instructions.

[Source: RGASPI, fond 17, opis' 3, delo 835, p. 25.]

The rehabilitation of specialists and enhanced authority and autonomy of managers did not go so far as to establish any firm distinction between economic failures, on the one hand, and criminal 'wrecking' on the other. During the mid-1930s, regional and local party leaders, NKVD operatives and the procuracy repeatedly reacted to economic setbacks, industrial accidents and manifest waste by placing the blame on directors or specialists or both, and demonstratively dismissing and arresting them. And Stalin, Molotov and the Politburo majority by no means accepted that arrest and prosecution as a response to economic failure was either unjustified or inherently counter-productive. In April 1933 they even backed a further high-profile show trial, that of Metro-Vickers personnel charged with espionage and wrecking electric power stations. On the other hand, despite being charged with working for Great Britain, in this case the engineers were not executed and the trial did not trigger a renewed wave of denunciations. In several instances where such accusations were made, Ordzhonikidze and his Commissariat successfully challenged them as unwarranted. In the Urals *oblast'*, the procurator and many of his office were sacked in 1933 on these grounds; a year later the regional NKVD was sharply reined in and reprimanded for another such attack; in 1936, Kabakov and the party leadership in Sverdlovsk, who had sought to disguise their own lack of enthusiasm for the Stakhanovite movement by sanctioning over 200 trials of managers and specialists for resisting Stakhanovism, were taken to task by Moscow.[177]

The change in policy towards the technical intelligentsia in the early 1930s was followed by progressive moves to stabilize the intelligentsia generally. The licence which between 1928 and 1930 the Central Committee had given for radical institutional experiment and for euphoric dreams of the imminent transcending of all that was bourgeois, from the market to religion and the state, was rapidly curtailed. The notion that the family was destined to 'wither away' was repudiated and earlier attacks on it gave way to emphasis on parental responsibility and authority. In the face of soaring rates of divorce and abortion, the laws governing both were sharply tightened, and at the same time there was rapid improvement in maternity benefits and a new emphasis on the provision of crèches and nursery schools to encourage parenthood.[178] Along with this 'retreat' from the more radical social policies of the 1920s, there was a drive to bring to an end the denunciations and purges of the period of 'cultural revolution'. Many non-party scholars and writers were rehabilitated, and life became more secure and more predictable. In literature, RAPP was disbanded and there was a reversion to respect for traditional literary values and significant parts of Russia's pre-revolutionary literary heritage. There was a new emphasis on the leading role of the Russians, depicted as 'elder brothers' among the peoples of the USSR. Although the policy of promoting native cadres within each minority republic (*korenizatsiya*) continued, an elevated status began to be accorded to Russian culture and history.[179]

The sequel to the 'cultural revolution' did not amount in any sense to intellectual liberation or even a return to the narrow parameters of the 1920s. Instead, centralized party control much tighter and more effective than under NEP was established. As militants had eagerly demanded at the height of their influence, 'Marxism–Leninism' was to be treated as the guide to all knowledge. Contrary to their expectations, however, the key to that guide was to be provided not by them but by the party leaders, who became the

---

177 On efforts to protect management and technical intelligentsia, see O. Khlevnyuk, 'The People's Commissariat of Heavy Industry' in E.A. Rees (ed.) *Decision-making in the Stalinist Command Economy* (London 1997) pp. 94–123; Harris, *Great Urals* pp. 146–69.

178 The classic treatment of the shift in social and cultural policy is N.S. Timasheff, *The Great Retreat: The growth and decline of communism in Russia* (New York 1946). For more recent analysis, see Goldman, *Women, the State and Revolution*.

179 On the incipient tension between *korenizatsiya* and the new emphasis on Russian superiority, see Martin, *Affirmative Action Empire*.

guardians of Soviet culture and whose agenda (and tastes) were imposed even over issues relatively remote from politics and economics. The overriding purpose of literature, for example, was to be its contribution to constructing socialism, affirming the Soviet path, describing the progress made and the inevitability of triumph, and providing heroic models for emulation. All authors were gathered into a new Union of Soviet Writers, formally insti-tuted in September 1934 under the direct control of the Central Committee. At the Union's founding Congress, the opening speech was by A.A. Zhdanov, a close ally of Stalin's who had recently been appointed a Secretary to the Central Committee and had special responsibility for ideology and political education.[180] He took as his theme Stalin's description of writers as 'engineers of human souls' and spelled out the new literary orthodoxy by which all must abide: 'socialist realism'.[181]

Document 187 | **From Zhdanov's speech to the founding congress of the Union of Soviet Writers**

1934

Under the leadership of the Party, with the thoughtful and daily guidance of the Central Committee and the untiring support and help of Comrade Stalin, a whole army of Soviet writers has rallied around the Soviet power and the Party. And in the light of our Soviet literature's successes, we see standing out in yet sharper relief the full contrast between our system—the system of victorious socialism—and the system of dying, mouldering capitalism. . .

In our country the main heroes of works of literature are the active builders of a new life—working men and women, men and women collective farmers, Party members, business managers, engineers, members of the Young Communist League, Pioneers. Such are the chief types and the chief heroes of our Soviet literature. Our literature is impregnated with enthusiasm and the spirit of heroic deeds. It is opti-mistic, but not optimistic in accordance with any 'inward', animal instinct. It is optimistic in essence, because it is the literature of the rising class of the proletariat, the only progressive and advanced class. Our Soviet literature is strong by virtue of the fact that it is serving a new cause—the cause of socialist construction.

Comrade Stalin has called our writers engineers of human souls. What does this mean? What duties does the title confer upon you? In the first place, it means knowing life so as to be able to depict it truthfully in works of art, not to depict it in a dead, scholastic way, not simply as 'objective reality', but to depict reality in its revolutionary development.

---

180 On Zhdanov's role in the 1930s, see J.A. Getty, *Origins of the Great Purges: The Soviet Communist Party, 1933–1938* (Cambridge 1985) esp. pp. 92–112.

181 On socialist realism, see K. Clark's study, *The Soviet Novel* (London 1991).

In addition to this, the truthfulness and historical concreteness of the artistic portrayal should be combined with the ideological remoulding and education of the toiling people in the spirit of socialism. This method in *belles lettres* and literary criticism is what we call the method of socialist realism.

Our Soviet literature is not afraid of the charge of being 'tendentious'. Yes, Soviet literature is tendentious, for in an epoch of class struggle there is not and cannot be a literature which is not class literature, not tendentious, allegedly non-political. . .

To be an engineer of human souls means standing with both feet firmly planted on the basis of real life. And this in turn denotes a rupture with romanticism of the old type, which depicted a non-existent life and non-existent heroes, leading the reader away from the antagonisms and oppression of real life into a world of the impossible, into a world of utopian dreams. Our literature, which stands with both feet firmly planted on a materialist basis, cannot be hostile to romanticism, but it must be a romanticism of a new type, revolutionary romanticism. We say that socialist realism is the basic method of Soviet *belles lettres* and literary criticism, and this presupposes that revolutionary romanticism should enter into literary creation as a component part, for the whole life of our Party, the whole life of the working class and its struggle consist in a combination of the most stern and sober practical work with a supreme spirit of heroic deeds and magnificent future prospects. Our Party has always been strong by virtue of the fact that it has united and continues to unite a thoroughly business-like and practical spirit with broad vision, with a constant urge forward, with a struggle for the building of communist society. Soviet literature should be able to portray our heroes; it should be able to glimpse our tomorrow. This will be no utopian dream, for our tomorrow is already being prepared for today by dint of conscious planned work. . .

Comrades, the proletariat, just as in other provinces of material and spiritual culture, is the sole heir of all that is best in the treasury of world literature. The bourgeoisie has squandered its literary heritage; it is our duty to gather it up carefully, to study it and, having critically assimilated it, to advance further.

[Source: *Problems of Soviet Literature: Reports and speeches at the First Soviet Writers' Congress* (Moscow 1935) pp. 18–22.]

A short list of novels was recommended by the Union as models of the correct structure, approach and above all message: the certain victory of socialism over capitalism. The literary intelligentsia were thus feted and celebrated at the same time as they were corralled and censored by the political authorities. Gorky, who had been initially so critical of the Bolshevik revolution (see document 37) and had spent most of the 1920s abroad before returning permanently to the USSR in 1933, was made the subject of a major cult and became the figurehead of Soviet writers. But as is conveyed by his own flowery endorsement of the regime, written to K.E. Voroshilov, Commissar for Defence, on the occasion of the seventeenth anniversary of the revolution, the rapprochement between intelligentsia and regime was on the latter's terms.

Document 188 | A.M. Gorky to K.E. Voroshilov

Not before 8 November 1934

Dear Kliment Efremovich,

My 'fine words' to you were said not only because of the 'formal' occasion of the 17th Anniversary of the October Revolution, but also according to my rights as a Soviet citizen not opposed to the Party's magnificent work, truly delighted with the work of its tireless leaders and truly loving and respecting them. Believe me, I do not say fine words to the wicked—I am not like that. Finally, I do feel that I, probably more than most others, can see how the cultural-revolutionary activity of the nanny-Party of 170 million children is bringing them up strong and successful not with fairy tales but with the deeds and the stern, invincible truth of its Cause. . .

[Source: *Izvestiya TsK KPSS* No. 8, 1991, p. 157.]

The improvement in status and privileges of specialists and managers in the early 1930s was extended to all sections of the rapidly expanding Soviet intelligentsia. The tendency evident under NEP for the higher ranks in the party, the state apparatus, the police, the army, the economy and the cultural field alike to acquire a wide range of privileges, including special access to rare consumer goods and better housing, rapidly accelerated. The shift was clearly registered in terms of access to education, where discrimination in favour of the children of workers by current occupation, at its height from 1928 to 1931, was dropped and at the end of the decade, in contravention of the Constitution, school fees were introduced for upper-secondary and tertiary education. In the mid-1930s, the Central Committee would adopt as party policy the goal that all Soviet citizens be raised to the educational and cultural level of the *intelligenty*. The intelligentsia, the great majority of whose members were now drawn from peasant and proletarian backgrounds, had good reason to identify with the Soviet system.[182] Though internally steeply stratified from humble village school teachers and trainee technicians at the base to the '*nomenklatura*' at the summit, they constituted the prime beneficiaries from and major source of support for the new order.

---

182 The remarkable speed and scale of upward social mobility that accompanied Stalin-style industrialization is explored in S. Fitzpatrick, *Education and Social Mobility in the Soviet Union, 1921–1934* (Cambridge 1979).

15

The Great Terror

The scale of the Great Terror, 1937–1938

Notwithstanding their status, it was these upper tiers of the Soviet social pyramid who were to be, in proportionate terms if not absolutely, the main victims of the Great Terror of 1937–38. Whereas a small fraction of the peasantry and working class were caught up in the mass executions of those years, the impact was so great among the intelligentsia broadly defined that, in the upper reaches, few social circles remained unaffected. The period of butchery remains the feature of Soviet history for which historians have had greatest difficulty in assembling a rounded and satisfactory explanation. The conditions that made it possible are not difficult to identify: the erosion of institutional, legal and social constraints on state and police power; the tendency of the understaffed regular police to rely on crude, indiscriminate methods of keeping order, launching intermittent 'sweeps' to arrest likely criminals, speculators, beggars, gypsies, prostitutes, vagabonds and even the ubiquitous 'street' children made orphans by two decades of social upheaval, and the blurring of the line between regular and political policing; the current of brutality and cheapening of life fed into the political culture by war, civil war, famine and the violence of collectivization; tight censorship of the media, information and public debate; the concentration of decision-making in the hands of a small elite convinced of the party's historic destiny, moral justification and ideological infallibility; and the dominant position of a murderous leader seemingly without qualms about taking human life. Emphasis has recently also been placed on the role played by popular opinion, once the centre had triggered a demand for unmasking enemies; the prevalence of belief in anti-Soviet conspiracy and in deliberate abuse and wrecking by officials; and the undiminished intensity of popular hatred for supposed allies of the pre-revolutionary upper classes.[183] A 'post-Enlightenment' strain

---

183 P.N. Hagenloh, "'Chekist in Essence, Chekist in Spirit": Regular and political police in

of scholarship is currently labouring the European-wide Enlightenment roots of the regime's increasing readiness to use both state welfare and violent 'cleansing' to refashion society.[184] Though taken for granted by historians of Carr's generation, and almost self-evident to historians of socialist ideology, the point has become somewhat obscured by emphasis on specifically Bolshevik and Stalinist ingredients. What remains much less easy to pinpoint are the precise motives prompting the leadership to sponsor mass killings.

The case has been made for a variety of different explanations: Stalin's cynical and ruthless desire to place his absolute personal domination beyond question;[185] a 'conspiracy mentality' among Stalin and his lieutenants which made them genuinely fear attempts by rival elements in the party to challenge or displace them;[186] the leadership's concern in the face of impending war to destroy any potential for the formation of a 'fifth column';[187] the leadership's wish to discipline and establish effective control over regional party leaders inclined to develop 'family circles' lubricated by nepotism and corruption and insufficiently responsive to Moscow's orders;[188] the leadership's wish, in the face of mounting economic crisis, to lash out at party and state personnel responsible for economic planning and management who were held responsible for repeated setbacks in industry and agriculture;[189] pressure from Ezhov and local NKVDs, personally endorsed by Stalin, to eliminate marginal 'socially harmful elements' considered responsible for high levels of law-breaking and common crime.[190] This abundance of

the 1930s' *Cahiers du Monde Russe* 42 (2001) pp. 447–76; G. Rittersporn, 'The Omnipresent Conspiracy: On Soviet imagery of politics and social relations in the 1930s' in Lampert and Rittersporn (eds) *Stalinism* pp. 101–20; R.T. Manning, 'The Great Purges in a Rural District: Belyi Raion revisited' in J.A. Getty and R.T. Manning (eds) *Stalinist Terror* (Cambridge 1993) pp. 168–97; R.W. Thurston, *Life and Terror in Stalin's Russia, 1934–1941* (New Haven 1996) pp. 137–63.

184 See D.L. Hoffman, 'European Modernity and Soviet Socialism' in D.L. Hoffman and Y. Kotsonis (eds) *Russian Modernity: Politics, knowledge, practices* (New York 2000); P. Holquist, 'State Violence as Technique: The logic of violence in Soviet totalitarianism' in D.L. Hoffman (ed.) *Stalinism: The essential readings* (Oxford 2003) pp. 129–56; and Kotkin, *Magnetic Mountain* pp. 18–23.

185 This lies at the heart of what was long the most influential treatment, R. Conquest, *The Great Terror: A reassessment* (London 1990).

186 Getty and Naumov, *Road to Terror* pp. 258–61.

187 O. Khlevnyuk, 'The Objectives of the Great Terror, 1937–1938' in Hoffman (ed.) *Stalinism* pp. 83–104, and also in C. Read (ed.) *The Stalin Years: A reader* (London 2003) pp. 104–18; O. Khlevnyuk, 'The Reasons for the "Great Terror": The foreign–political aspect' in S. Pons and A. Romano (eds) *Russia in the Age of Wars 1914–1945* (Milan 2000) pp. 159–69.

188 Rittersporn, *Stalinist Simplifications*; Getty, *Origins of the Great Purges*.

189 R.T. Manning, 'The Soviet Economic Crisis of 1936–1940 and the Great Purges' in Getty and Manning (eds) *Stalinist Terror* pp. 116–41; Harris, *The Great Urals* pp. 146–90.

190 Hagenloh, '"Socially Harmful Elements"' pp. 286–308; Holquist, 'State Violence as Technique'.

possible motives, plausible in themselves but mutually incompatible as master explanations, has made it difficult to construct a narrative which gives due weight to each, explains their interconnection and accounts for the wild trajectory of terror. According to the following annual figures collected by the secretariat of the GULAG, the number of executions rose steeply in the most violent years of the collectivization drive, peaking at over 20,000 in 1930; fell sharply to under 3,000 in 1932 and down to 1,118 in 1936; and then soared to over 350,000 in 1937 and almost 330,000 in 1938, before dropping by 99 per cent to below 3,000 in 1939 and 1,649 in 1940.[191]

Document 189 | Cheka–OGPU–NKVD convictions, 1921–1940

Compiled 11 December 1953

This table was compiled by V.P. Popov on the basis of information prepared by Colonel Pavlov, acting head of the First Special Section of the MVD [Ministry of the Interior] of the USSR.

Popov made two significant errors in his table. In column 8 for 1937 he has put 'convicted by OGPU collegia', which had ceased to exist in 1934. Figures for people sentenced by the Special Conference of the USSR NKVD, in column 9, are given from 1924, but it was not formed until 5 November 1934, so the numbers in question should apply to the OGPU–NKVD, which was operating during that period. On one sheet, the following has been written in pencil: 'Total sentenced for 1921–1938: 2,944,879 people, of whom 30 per cent (1,062,000) were criminals'. Note: dots indicate that the category in question is not applicable for that year; dashes indicate no data were available.

Year	Total sentenced	Punishments				By whom sentence passed			
		Capital punishment	Camps and prison	Exile and deportation	Other	Tribunals and courts	OGPU	NKVD Special Conferences	3-man Commissions
1921	35,829	9,701	21,724	1,817	2,587	35,829	...	...	...
1922	6,003	1,962	2,656	166	1,219	6,003	...	...	...
1923	4,794	414	2,336	2,044	—	4,794	...	...	...
1924	12,425	2,550	4,151	5,724	—	3,059	—	9,366	—
1925	15,995	2,433	6,851	6,274	437	—	2,284	9,221	4,490

---

191 The most recent analysis suggests under-reporting of executions by some regional NKVDs in 1937–38, which may mean that the totals for the period of 1937–38 were up to 25 per cent higher than these figures. S. Wheatcroft, 'The Scale and Nature of German and Soviet Mass Killings' p. 1351, footnote 37.

Year	Total sentenced	Punishments				By whom sentence passed			
		Capital punishment	Camps and prison	Exile and deportation	Other	Tribunals and courts	OGPU	NKVD Special Conferences	3-man Commissions
1926	17,804	990	7,547	8,571	696	—	2,323	13,102	2,379
1927	26,036	2,363	12,267	11,235	171	—	3,434	15,947	6,655
1928	33,757	869	16,211	15,640	1,037	—	3,756	25,844	4,157
1929	56,220	2,109	25,853	24,517	3,741	—	10,262	37,197	8,761
1930	208,069	20,201	114,443	58,816	14,609	—	9,072	19,377	179,620
1931	180,696	10,651	105,683	63,269	1,093	—	13,357	14,592	152,747
1932	141,919	2,728	73,946	36,017	29,228	49,106	6,604	26,052	60,157
1933	239,664	2,154	138,903	54,262	44,345	214,334	—	25,330	—
1934	78,999	2,056	59,451	5,994	11,498	32,577	12,588	1,003	32,831
1935	267,076	1,229	185,846	33,601	46,400	118,465	—	29,452	119,159
1936	274,670	1,118	219,418	23,719	30,415	114,383	—	18,969	141,318
1937	790,665	353,074	429,311	1,366	6,914	39,694	45,060	17,911	688,000
1938	554,258	328,618	205,509	16,842	3,289	95,057	—	45,768	413,433
1939	63,889	2,552	54,666	3,783	2,888	—	50,868	13,021	—
1940	71,806	1,649	65,727	2,142	2,288	—	28,894	42,912	—

[Source: *Otechestvennye arkhivy* No. 2, 1992, pp. 28, 29.]

Opposition and repression, 1933–1936

A central reason for controversy over the motivation for the Terror is the mismatch between the monstrous scale of repression and the shortage of evidence of organized opposition. The strongest such evidence was uncovered not on the eve of the Great Terror, but half a decade earlier, in 1932. In that year Trotsky, who since his deportation in 1929 had published the *Bulletin of the Opposition* to mount a sustained critique designed to recapture the party from Stalin, made his most concerted, though stillborn, effort to rebuild an organization in the USSR. One of his contacts, made via his son L. Sedov in Berlin, was his longtime ally I.N. Smirnov, who urged a new united bloc bringing together both 'left' and 'right' opponents of Stalin.[192]

More ominous, because it originated from within the USSR and among current party members, was the discovery of the most elaborate domestic

---

192 J.A. Getty, 'Trotsky in Exile: The founding of the Fourth International' *Soviet Studies* 38 (1986) pp. 24–35.

critique of the leadership composed in the whole Stalin period, the so-called 'Ryutin platform'. Running to almost 200 pages, it was written in spring and summer 1932 by a group initially led by M.N. Ryutin, who had been a Moscow district secretary in the 1920s before being expelled from the party for refusing to recant his 'Right deviation' views and opposition to the collectivization drive. *Samizdat* copies of the platform, which spoke for an organized 'Union of Marxist–Leninists' within the party, circulated in several cities. Like Trotsky's abortive efforts, the Ryutin group was swiftly snuffed out by the OGPU and those implicated were expelled from the party and sentenced to prison. Nevertheless, the group's activities caused the leadership serious alarm. What made it so dangerous in their eyes was that the platform was based on an appeal to a rival reading of Leninism. It assumed the primacy of the party and accepted much of the same language and purpose as the regime, and yet it rejected Stalin's leadership and policies root and branch.

Document 190 | **Stalin and the crisis of the dictatorship of the proletariat— from the Platform of the 'Union of Marxist–Leninists' (the Ryutin group)**

1932

Stalin will undoubtedly go down in history, but his 'celebrity' will be that of Herostrates. Limited and crafty, ambitious and spiteful, treacherous and envious, hypocritical and insolent, boastful and stubborn—Khlestakov and Arakcheev, Nero and Count Cagliostro—that is the ideological, political and spiritual face of Stalin. . .

Just like Louis Bonaparte, Stalin has achieved results: his revolution has been accomplished and his most undisguised and deceitful personal dictatorship is in place. The main cohort of Lenin's comrades-in-arms has been removed from leading positions: one part is in prison or exile; another, the capitulators, despised and demoralized, is dragging out a pathetic existence in the ranks of the Party; the third, having become completely corrupt, has turned into faithful servants of the 'leader'-dictator. In the last four to five years Stalin has beaten all records for political hypocrisy and unprincipled intrigue.

From being one of the tools of socialist construction, planning has become a way of disrupting the economy and leading it into a state of anarchy and chaos. The decisive advantage of socialist construction over capitalism—planning, foresight, calculation and assessment—has disappeared. Moreover, in such conditions, plus turns into minus, because, while under capitalism the law of value (albeit by crises and great losses every two or three years) creates conditions (of course, very limited ones within the framework of private property) for the development of new productive forces or at least for halting their decline, under a planned economy year by year reckless plans may disorganize the economy over a longer period and push the country into complete paralysis and famine, as is happening at this very moment. . .

Stalin's economic policy, despite the fact that in recent years we have built dozens of huge factories, mills, power stations, etc., with the latest technology, has not only led the country into an unparalleled economic crisis but also discredited the very foundations of socialist construction, knocking us back economically some twelve to fifteen years. . .

Terror, given our unprecedented degree of centralization and the strength of our apparatus, operates almost automatically. In terrorizing others, everyone at the same time terrorizes himself, and in forcing others to dissemble, everyone is himself forced to do a certain amount of this 'work'. . .

The entire elite of leading Party workers, from Stalin down to *oblast'* committee secretaries, is in the main fully aware that it is breaking away from Leninism, doing violence to those within and outside the Party and destroying the cause of socialism, but is so confused and trapped within a vicious circle that it is no longer capable of escape. The mistakes of Stalin and his clique have turned into crimes. . . In fact, they look upon the Party as their fiefdom. They are not working for the Party, but the Party is working for them. . . The Party does undoubtedly have a small seam of middle-aged, subjectively honest members who nonetheless continue to believe sincerely in the correctness of Stalin's policies. How are we to explain this? Among a significant proportion of Party members with little or no theoretical baggage and limited theoretical horizons there is a tradition of supporting the CC, because 'the CC is always right'. . . These Party members cannot explain the gigantic contradictions between the declarations of the Stalinist leadership and reality, but are terrified of any 'deviations', have got used to voting for the CC and so try not to notice these contradictions. . . All their explanations for the contradictions of our real life come down to the inevitable difficulties of socialist construction or the inevitable deficiencies in any major undertaking. . .

Stalin's reckless 'ultra-left' policies are absolutely inevitably leading to the restoration of capitalism. . . The Party and the vast majority of the working class are against Stalin and his clique. These disparate and terrorized forces simply need to unite. . . and begin to work to remove the Stalinist leadership. . .

In concrete terms, all the measures necessary for getting the Party and the country out of this dead-end crisis can be reduced to the following:

In Party matters:

1. The elimination of the dictatorship of Stalin and his clique.
2. The immediate removal of all the heads of the Party apparatus, the setting of new elections for Party bodies on the basis of real inner-Party democracy and the creation of firm guarantees against usurpation of Party rights by the Party apparatus.
3. An immediate extraordinary Party congress.
4. The Party's decisive and immediate return on all questions to the standpoint of Leninist principles.

In Soviet matters:

1. Immediate new elections to the soviets with a decisive and effective abolition of patronage.
2. The replacement of the judicial apparatus and the introduction of strict revolutionary legality.
3. The replacement and a decisive purge of the GPU apparatus.

On industrialization:

1. The immediate cessation of anti-Leninist methods of industrialization, playing with tempos, funded by robbing the working class, salaried staff and the countryside, and by direct and indirect, overt and covert unbearable taxes and inflation. Industrialization should be carried out on the basis of a real and continuous increase in the welfare of the people.
2. Investment in capital projects should be brought into conformity with the overall state of available resources within the country.

On agricultural matters:

1. The immediate disbandment of all forcibly created and inflated collective farms. Collectivization should be genuinely voluntary, on the basis of mechanization and all-round assistance to the collective farms.
2. The immediate creation of all necessary real conditions, and the provision of assistance, for the development of individual poor and middle peasant farms.
3. The elimination of all loss-making state farms, retaining those which we are really able to make into genuine model socialist enterprises.
4. The transfer of all stocks of large-scale machinery from the liquidated state and collective farms to local agricultural societies. . .
6. The immediate cessation of grain procurement and the procurement of other products by the current method of robbing the countryside. The holdings of individual farmers and their long-term right to use the land must be safeguarded.

In trade matters:

1. The cessation of agricultural exports at very low prices.
2. The cessation of industrial consumer goods exports at very low prices.
3. The return to a Leninist policy on pricing. Decisive price reductions. The restoration of co-operatives and their rights. . .

The living standards and civil rights of the workers and peasants:

. . . 3. Restoration of old rights and of Leninist policies in trade-union work. . .
4. Immediate cessation of the reckless policy of dispossessing the kulaks in the countryside, which in fact is directed at the entire population of the countryside.

[Source: *Izvestiya TsK KPSS* No. 8, 1990, pp. 202–03; No. 11, p. 185; No. 12, pp. 186–89, 195–99.]

In 1932 the possibility that criticism within the party would gather momentum and create a threat to the regime's stability and their own position seemed tangible to the Stalinist leadership. They were well aware that the violence, social dislocation and deprivation of the First Five-Year Plan period provided fertile soil for disillusionment and loss of confidence among the party rank and file and for much more widespread unrest. If tapped into by an effective and articulate alternative leadership, the potential for a dangerous challenge seemed manifest. Had there been a consistent correlation between threats to the existing leadership and the levels of repression to which it resorted, the Ryutin group might have been expected to trigger the most savage response. Yet it was not until much later in the decade, when evidence of organized opposition was minimal and social conditions, though grimmer than in the mid-1930s, were less desperate than in 1932, that mass summary executions for supposedly political crimes were instituted.

As the economic shocks and dreadful famine of 1932–33 receded, the leadership conveyed growing confidence that they had weathered the storm of collectivization and the harshest period of industrialization. The Seventeenth Party Congress in February 1934 was known as the Congress of Victors and, with living standards beginning to improve markedly, there was a palpable reduction in tension that year. For historians who see a master plan behind the terror, the end of this interlude came on 1 December 1934 with the assassination of the Leningrad First Secretary, Kirov, at his headquarters in the Smol'ny building. The circumstances surrounding the assassination, from the level of incompetence of the local NKVD to the untimely death of almost all those involved in the investigation, has led the majority of western historians to conclude that Stalin himself was behind the murder. Stalin, they argue, had reason to eliminate Kirov because he was too moderate and too popular within the party, possibly even being groomed by some as a replacement for the General Secretary. For Robert Conquest, for long the most influential historian of the Great Terror, the assassination was the opening move in an elaborate plan by Stalin to terrorize the upper echelons of the party and society at large.[193] It afforded a pretext, so the argument goes, to legalize summary executions and it provided the ideal crime around which conspiracy charges could be and, over the next five years, were fashioned against all of Stalin's potential enemies.

More recently, this view has been challenged both in Russia and in the west, notably by J. Arch Getty.[194] Numerous weaknesses in the case against

193 R. Conquest, *Stalin and the Kirov Murder* (London 1989).
194 See J.A. Getty, *Origins* pp. 207–10; J.A. Getty, 'The Politics of Repression Revisited' in Getty and Manning (eds) *Stalinist Terror* pp. 40–62; Getty and Naumov, *Road to Terror* pp. 141–47.

Stalin have been pointed out: the high risk he would have run that those through whom he supposedly acted, presumably including the NKVD chief Yagoda, with whom his relationship rapidly deteriorated, would reveal the plot; the initial failure to convict the first prominent suspects, Zinoviev and Kamenev, of direct responsibility for the crime; the long lapse of time between this supposed opening step in Stalin's planned campaign of terror and the vortex of 1937 and 1938; the numerous moves between 1934 and 1937 which pointed towards stabilization and relaxation of tension; and the failure of the commission of inquiry established under Gorbachev in the 1980s to arrive at a verdict.[195] Yet much turns on the issue. If Stalin's guilt is conclusively proven, it would indicate an additional level of conscious deceit and hypocrisy in his dealings with his loyal colleagues that, as we have seen, cannot otherwise be detected from his letters or from Politburo minutes, and it would lend weight to the notion that his personal agenda provides the core motivation for the Great Terror. By the same token, if he was not involved doubt is cast on much about the version of events popularized by Conquest.

One of the pieces of evidence in dispute is the draconian decree below, issued immediately after Kirov's death. Protagonists of the theory that Stalin organized the assassination find the speed of its issue deeply suspicious and claim it had been composed before the assassination. Others suggest Stalin drew it up as he rushed to Leningrad on hearing of the assassination and that it was an almost instinctive response in direct line with the leadership's reaction to the attempted assassination of Lenin in 1918, to the shooting of a Soviet diplomat in Warsaw in 1927, and to the frantic emergency steps taken to deal with 'kulaks' during collectivization.

Document 191 | Decree of the USSR TsIK on *in camera* hearings

1 December 1934

The TsIK of the USSR decrees the introduction of the following changes into the current criminal procedural codes of the Union Republics on the investigation and examination of cases dealing with terrorist organizations and terrorist acts against those working for the Soviet government:
1. Investigations must take no more than ten days.
2. The charges must be conveyed to the accused twenty-four hours prior to the hearing.

---

195 D.P. Koenker and R.D. Bachman (eds) *Revelations from the Russian Archives* (Washington, DC, 1997), the translated version of the 1992 Library of Congress exhibition of new documents on Soviet history, includes a selection of relevant material, pp. 69–84.

3. Cases are to be heard *in camera*.

4. Appeals and pleas for pardon are not permitted.

5. Sentences to the highest measure of punishment [execution by firing squad] are to be carried out immediately after the sentence is pronounced.

M. Kalinin, chairman of the Central Executive Committee of the USSR

A.S. Enukidze, secretary of the Central Executive Committee of the USSR

[Source: *Izvestiya*, 5 December 1934.]

The vigilance demanded by the regime after Kirov's assassination made it highly probable that any significant opposition activity would be discovered. The NKVD provided regular reports on the political mood, based on its network of informers, and drew attention to behaviour, talk, slogans, songs, jokes and graffiti that ran counter to the Marxist–Leninist orthodoxy the regime sought to generalize.[196] Yet the *samizdat* opposition literature and calls to action that have come to light in Central Committee archives suggest a scale of organization and level of sophistication far inferior to that of the Ryutin group of 1932. The following example was found in November 1935 on the walls of the student washroom at the Rubezhansky Institute of Chemical Technology in the Donetsk *oblast'* in Ukraine. According to the NKVD, it was the work of a group of eight students, one of them a former member of the party, three former members of Komsomol, and most of them in their first year. It wove together in fairly haphazard fashion student-specific and broader protests—against socialist realism, Stakhanovism and mass impoverishment.

Document 192 | A.M. Budov: 'Do not let socialism be built on the bones of the proletariat'

November 1935

BOLSHEVIK REALISM

Whoever said that Soviet literature contains only real images is profoundly mistaken. The themes are dictated by the CC of the Party, headed by Stalin. The CC of the Party deals harshly with anybody who tries to depict the real state of affairs in their literature.

Is it not a fact that all of you now reading these lines saw people dying in the streets in 1932? People, swollen with hunger and foaming at the mouth, lying in their death throes in the streets.

---

196 The striking portrait of currents of popular, as opposed to intelligentsia, opinion that ran counter to official rhetoric drawn by S. Davies, *Popular Opinion in Stalin's Russia*, is based on these reports.

Is it not a fact that whole villages full of people perished in 1932? Does our literature show any of these horrors, which make your hair stand on end? No. The CC of the Party has closed the door on that.

Let us remember how collectivization took place in the initial stages. Do you remember the article *Dizzy with Success*, round about 1930, when 'mistakes' were made in implementing collectivization? They were over-eager, so to speak.

Even peasants from lower than average strata were counted as kulaks. Many innocent people were exiled or just shot. Grain was taken away from the peasants and they were forced to eat oil-cakes and bread with chaff.

Where will you find such appalling things depicted in Soviet literature? You call it realism?

At present we are all suffering from malnutrition: stomach problems, mass anaemia, nervous disorders.

One has to ask: writers, why are you falsifying things in the name of BOLSHEVIK REALISM? You are artists, why are you prostituting yourselves. Show it like it is!

Do not let socialism be built on the bones of the proletariat!!!

THE MATERIAL WELL-BEING OF THE WORKING CLASS

We can often read in the Soviet press how in the last five or six years the material well-being of the working class has significantly improved. They write in glowing colours of Stalin as 'most wise', 'dearly beloved', 'the great genius', 'our own', etc., etc.

But has the material position of the working class improved? Is it so? You can judge for yourselves from the figures below.

I want to remind you of the rises in prices for goods produced in the Soviet Union, as well as the rises in wages in recent years:

PRICES

	1930	1935
White bread/kilo	6 kopecks	1 ruble 50 k: a rise of 2,500%
Sugar/kilo	60 k	4 r 50 k: a rise of 800%
Pair of shoes	25–30 r	100–120 r: a rise of 400%

WAGES

	1930	1935
Coalface worker	100–120 r	300–350 r
Mining engineer	200–250 r	600–650 r
Labourer	35–40 r	110–120 r: an average rise of 300%

STUDENTS!

You are society's cultured stratum. You are the leading politically aware group. Approach these articles critically. Assess their veracity and respond to them as you compare reality around you. You must synthesize, and your analysis and synthesis must find expression in the publications you create.

Note everything negative and write about it; only in this way will the 'bosses' from the CC and Stalin pay any attention to the proletariat.

Eighteen years of privations must be rewarded with a new policy directed at really improving the material well-being of the working people.

RESPOND TO MY NEWSPAPER. THE TIME HAS COME FOR STUDENTS, INDIVIDUALLY AND COLLECTIVELY, TO FIGHT FOR A BETTER LIFE!

THE STAKHANOVITE MOVEMENT

What does breaking a record mean? It means pushing yourself physically to the limit. This is what characterizes the Stakhanovite movement. So why disagree, why reject it? You students were recently producers. You know full well what this 'PRODUC-TIVE ENTHUSIASM' is. The proletariat, wishing to provide for its material needs, is trying not to let its wages lag behind the furious price-rises. It keeps breaking records, sparing no effort just to get more money. It is all very well thought out. For every extra ton of coal, bonus payments are doubled and tripled. All sorts of rewards are thought up. There may be no fines, but the bonus payments work both ways. If you do not keep up with the quotas, your pay is docked.

It is stupid to think that the Stakhanovite method will raise your pay. For most people it will not. The vast majority of engineering and technical personnel in the Donbass coalfield get less than average. You are being fooled by the newspapers—those Stakhanovite earnings are just for isolated individuals.

Never mind, just keep working. Have a rotten life. Let your grandchildren have a rotten life, so that your great-grandchildren can have a bit of a break.

At the cost of privations now, the CC and Stalin are trying to build socialism for future generations.

The unlucky ones are those building socialism by the sweat of their brows, and the lucky ones are only those who will be living in a socialist society.

FIGHT FOR HIGHER GRANTS!

We get a grant of 93 rubles. The question arises: can you live on that? No. The canteen costs a lot more. The first course is 25 k, the second 95 k, bread is 30 k, a total of 1 r 50 k, i.e., 4 r 50 a day or 135 rubles a month. You cannot live like that. When will our 'most wise', 'most brilliant' and 'own' leaders get this into their heads?

STUDENTS, FIGHT FOR REAL IMPROVEMENTS IN YOUR LIVES!

USE ALL MEANS TO CHANGE POLICIES TO BETTER THE LIVES OF WORKING PEOPLE IN REALITY!

DO NOT LET SOCIALISM BE BUILT ON THE BONES OF THE PROLE-TARIAT.

[Source: RGASPI, fond 17, opis' 120, delo 272, pp. 9–13.]

In the first half of 1936, Stalin instructed N.I. Ezhov, a protégé of L.M. Kaganovich's whose personnel work for the Central Committee had secured him rapid promotion in the 1930s and who had become head of the increasingly powerful Party Control Commission in 1935, to follow up scattered NKVD reports of former followers of Trotsky maintaining contact with him abroad. Ezhov, with Stalin's active encouragement, soon claimed to have uncovered a sprawling conspiratorial organization, directed by Trotsky, with the personal involvement of Zinoviev and Kamenev. This 'Trotskyite–Zinovievite United Centre' had supposedly been responsible for Kirov's assassination and had planned the murder of Stalin and much of the Politburo. In August, sixteen former opposition figures, headed by Zinoviev, Kamenev and Smirnov, were publicly tried for treason, terrorism and assassination, condemned to death, and executed.

The massive publicity given to the case, and the feverish debate within the party over how best to uncover remaining Trotskyites, triggered a rash of denunciations to the NKVD. Public organizations of every kind, from trade unions to professional organizations and the Union of Soviet Writers, hurried to hail the verdict. To withhold support for resolutions heaping praise on Stalin and damning the 'fascist hirelings' was perilous; to oppose, suicidal. With the political and ideological definition of a 'Trotskyite' becoming ever less precise, a record of past affiliation with anyone 'unmasked' was becoming more and more dangerous. In the following letter to Ezhov, G.E. Osipov denounced a prominent party member in Sverdlovsk, B.V. Didkovsky, on the grounds that he had admitted to being a personal friend of one of those convicted in the show trial, S.V. Mrachkovsky. The connection had been investigated during the verification of party cards and purge/expulsion of idle or politically suspect members during 1935, without costing Didkovsky his party membership. Now, however, it placed him in peril of being numbered among the 160 lesser figures arrested and executed for association with the crimes unmasked in the trial.

Document 193 | Letter to N.I. Ezhov from citizen G.E. Osipov

August 1936

On reading in the paper the charges against the fascist hirelings L. Trotsky, Zinoviev and Co., I could not react calmly—I just do not know how to express my outrage—I felt such hatred towards these scoundrels that I fell to thinking about how all honest Party and non-Party Bolsheviks should keep an eye on their friends and acquaintances: how they breathe, how they live and what they do, in order completely to unmask all traces of Zinovievism—and there are plenty, I suspect.

I want to describe one case: I find it incomprehensible and if anyone needs to know about it, let them look into it. B.V. Didkovsky, a member of the CPSU since

March 1917, a former head of the Geological Trust and very close friend of the Trotskyites S.V. Mrachkovsky and S.I. (I think) Ufimtsev, works in the Sverdlovsk Party organization. In the *oblast'* Party archives there is a leaflet from 1921 signed by Ufimtsev, Didkovsky and other members of the Workers' Opposition; when Didkovsky's case was looked into by the Sverdlovsk city committee of the CPSU on 9 December 1935, he admitted that he was a personal friend of and connected with Mrachkovsky, Ufimtsev and other Trotskyite leaders, that he shared the Trotskyite platform and had never dissociated himself from it either in the press or publicly... As head of the Urals Geological Trust, he led it to ruin. He lost the country millions, did not find any useful minerals for the country, and surrounded himself with strange characters whom he protected in all kinds of ways. He bought a house for the White Guard G.G. Kitaev at the trust's expense, and used to lend money from a special fund to an alien element, Shapiro, for all sorts of purposes...

In 1932, 1933 and 1934 Didkovsky was literally the whole time in Moscow and Leningrad, supposedly on business trips, and then was often in Ufaley, a nest of Trotskyites in the Urals. It cannot be excluded that he was using all this for contacts...

I am profoundly convinced that right up to the present he has not rejected Trotskyism, but has just hidden it...

Please let me know, if all of the above is familiar to you and I am wrong, and maybe B.V. Didkovsky deserves the trust of the Party and the government, then there will be no misunderstandings on my part. I must add that everybody who knows Didkovsky's case is surprised that he still has not been unmasked as a Trotskyite.

The facts are all true, but please do not reveal my name...

[Source: SOTsDOO, fond 4, opis' 104, delo 571, pp. 22–24.]

The major components of the Great Terror

The process which led from the denunciation and arrest of Old Bolsheviks and former oppositionists to the elimination of vast swathes of the current, loyalist *nomenklatura*, was in part cumulative. At the same time as the definition of what constituted a 'Trotskyite', a 'Zinovievite' or an 'enemy of the people' became blurred, so too did the distinction between the charge of being directly responsible for opposition or wrecking and the charge of having failed to detect and root out such activity. Suspicion of sabotage and conspiracy was fed by a sharp slowdown in the industrial economy in 1936, exacerbated by a very poor harvest and dramatized by a variety of major and highly publicized industrial accidents. In January 1937 a second major show trial saw seventeen prominent figures, including G.L. Pyatakov,

Ordzhonikidze's Deputy at the Commissariat of Heavy Industry, accused of wrecking and spying for Trotsky and the German government. Pyatakov had been a high-profile associate of the United Opposition in the mid-1920s and in the aftermath of the Zinoviev–Kamenev trial was acutely vulnerable to denunciation. But the growing emphasis on industrial sabotage by prominent officials began to imperil members of the hierarchy whose political records were unblemished.[197]

Summer 1937 saw the onset of denunciations of the highest officials below Politburo level, the chief republican, *kray* and *oblast'* party secretaries. They had provided the mainstay of Stalin's majority on the Central Committee, had heartily endorsed the attack on former oppositionists, and regarded themselves as part of a homogeneous and loyal Stalinist elite. Yet they were now virtually swept from the scene. Kabakov was among those arrested, interrogated and shot; by mid-summer the majority of his colleagues on the Sverdlovsk *oblast'* committee, linked to him through countless ties, were in prison.[198] By 1939, of the 139 full and candidate members of the Central Committee elected in 1934 seventy per cent had been arrested and shot, and the party leadership of every Union Republic, every autonomous republic and every region was devastated. Along with the top ranks went thousands of officials associated with and patronized and protected by them through the semi-licit 'family circles' that had taken root during the 1930s. The leadership in every field and every organization—the planning agencies, the commissariats, industrial management, the trade unions, Komsomol, education, the NKVD itself—was decimated. So too were the ranks of the cultural intelligentsia, those affiliated with the 'leftism' of 1928–31 being as easily 'unmasked' as their opponents. The attrition in the Presidium of the Writers' Union was even greater than that for the Party Central Committee.

The prime purpose of Stalin's original 1936 instruction to Ezhov may have been political: to demolish remnants of earlier opposition factions. But if so, the effect was to set in motion a much larger snowball of local denunciations. The process was driven by mounting fear, NKVD pressure, mutual suspicion among groups of officials and *intelligenty*, and the resentment of juniors against seniors and of workers and peasants against privileged strata above them. Officials, professionals and managers in all hierarchies were at risk of being 'exposed' by the police, by their peers and by their subordi-

---

197 See O. Khlevnyuk, *In Stalin's Shadow: The Career of 'Sergo' Ordzhonikidze* (Armonk, NY, 1995), on Ordzhonikidze's inability to ward off attacks on his Commissariat and his eventual suicide.

198 Harris, *Great Urals*, draws skilfully on the NKVD interrogation files on Kabakov and his colleagues. Kabakov himself was among those executed. In 1934 the Urals *oblast'* had been divided into three smaller *oblasti*—Chelyabynsk, Obsko–Irtyrshsk and Sverdlovsk—and Kabakov became party secretary of the latter.

nates: economic failures, dysfunctions, corruption and deception, as well as residual professional and intellectual independence, became accepted as evidence of counter-revolutionary crime and sabotage. Whereas those higher up the hierarchy were habitually accused of 'Trotskyist' motives and connections, humbler rural officials were arrested and tried for sheer incompetence and/or abuse of power.[199]

In the course of summer 1937, at least four new terror initiatives, two of them of mass proportions, were launched.[200] They were so disparate in kind that they are not easily explained in terms of extended planning by Stalin, and yet he personally authorized each. They were not simply the product of cumulative momentum, although local responses did raise the number of victims far above those originally envisaged by the Kremlin. A proposition currently finding renewed favour among historians is that the overarching motive behind them was preparation for war and an all-encompassing pre-emptive strike against any potential source of internal opposition liable to take advantage of military crisis.

By 1937, so the argument runs, war seemed imminent. Continuing friction with Japan in the Far East was matched by Hitler's alarming drive to restore German military might and expand eastward. Neither Comintern's abandonment of its radical policy of 1928–34 and attempt to forge 'Popular Fronts' with non-Communist parties, nor the USSR's joining the League of Nations (1934) and championing international collective security, had led to effective alliances with the western powers. Accordingly, at the same time as defence expenditure soared, Stalin initiated mass terror 'as a means of eliminating a potential "fifth column"'.[201] The evidence for this as a general explanation is not entirely compelling: much cited are retrospective justifications for the Great Terror couched in these terms by Soviet leaders, notably Molotov, offered many years later at a time when it was plausible and psychologically understandable to portray actions of the late 1930s as preparation for the Great Patriotic War. At the time, however, rather than seeing impending foreign attack as the overriding issue, the leadership wove it in among a host of other issues supposedly addressed by the Terror. Moreover, when the carnage was curtailed at the end of 1938, the international scene was markedly darker than it had been at the time the violent repression began, the Munich crisis (September 1938), progressive dismemberment of Czechoslovakia, and mounting German pressure on Poland stretching across the autumn and winter of 1938–39. As war in Europe became a reality in

---

199 Fitzpatrick, *Stalin's Peasants* pp. 296–312.
200 See the rich collection of essays in B. McLoughlin and K. McDermott (eds) *Stalin's Terror: High politics and mass repression in the Soviet Union* (New York 2003) Part 2.
201 Khlevnyuk, 'Objectives of the Great Terror' p. 102.

autumn 1939, with Hitler invading Poland and Soviet troops moving into eastern Poland, as provided for under the terms of the Nazi–Soviet Non-Aggression Pact of August 1939 (see Volume II), and the USSR attacking Finland in November, the execution count fell to below 1 per cent of the colossal number carried out in 1937 and 1938. However, while there are grounds for scepticism that elimination of a potential 'fifth column' was the primary motivation for the Great Terror, there is no doubt that international tension coloured the atmosphere in which it was perpetrated.[202]

The first of the four new terror initiatives was the denunciation for treason of key figures in the High Command in May 1937. In June, Marshal Tukhachevsky and seven others were tried and summarily shot, and there followed a purge of the officer corps in which some 10,000 were arrested and another 23,000 dismissed. Here there is evidence that German intelligence successfully fed misinformation, raising Stalin's fears of concerted military opposition developing.[203] That it was because of the prospect of early war that Stalin responded in the manner he did, at enormous cost in terms of military expertise and international prestige, seems dubious.

The second sudden hurricane of summer 1937, and, in terms of sheer numbers of deaths caused, the core of the Great Terror, was triggered by the instruction which Stalin sent on 3 July to Ezhov and the First Secretary of every republic, *kray* and *oblast'*. They were ordered to instigate a major sweep of 'former kulaks and criminals' who had returned from periods of detention or exile and were supposedly instigating anti-Soviet crimes and economic sabotage. Ezhov elaborated the instruction in the now notorious NKVD order 00447, the dreadful document below. Here the categories to be dealt with were greatly extended to include those with a suspect political or social background—including former White Guards, bureaucrats, members of non-Bolshevik socialist parties, active sectarians, churchmen 'and so forth', and the most 'active' of those still in exile or detention, as well as returnees, were to be repressed. Guide figures were listed for the numbers to be arrested and executed in each *oblast'*, arrived at in response to (even larger) estimates provided by regional leaders. The notion that the motive here was fear of a 'fifth column' sits uneasily with the leadership's contemptuous view of these categories as 'marginal'.[204] Neither Stalin's instruction of 3 July nor NKVD order 00447 cited fifth-column potential or approaching

---

202 See the analysis by G. Roberts, 'The Fascist Threat and Soviet Politics in the 1930s' in Pons and Romano (eds) *Russia in the Age of Wars* pp. 147–58.

203 On the scale of attrition in the Red Army, see R.R. Reese, 'The Red Army and the Great Purges' in Getty and Manning (eds) *Stalinist Terror* pp. 198–214.

204 For a thoughtful discussion, which presses the fifth-column fear as the trigger, see D. Shearer, 'Social Disorder, Mass Repression and the NKVD during the 1930s' *Cahiers du Monde Russe* 42 (2001) pp. 505–34.

war as the motive. As yet no convincing explanation for the timing of Stalin's murderous move has been advanced.[205] Doubtless the tension and mounting butchery surrounding the offensive against former oppositionists and current leaders in some sense conditioned the sudden instigation of mass, almost blind, terror, and, as we have seen, the institution of emergency troikas to issue summary verdicts was in line with the decree following Kirov's assassination (document 191) and earlier emergency action. But its focus on former 'kulaks' is less easily explained: with the loudest clamour directed against officials and educated strata using their position for sabotage or to spy for foreign enemies, scattered and dispossessed peasants hardly constituted the obvious suspects.

Document 194 | 'On operations to repress former kulaks, criminals and other anti-Soviet elements'—from a draft operational order of the People's Commissar for Internal Affairs

30 July 1937

The organs of state security are faced with a task—mercilessly to crush this anti-Soviet gang, to defend the Soviet working people from their counter-revolutionary machinations and, finally, once and for all put an end to their foul subversive work against the bases of the Soviet state.

I accordingly ORDER THAT FROM 5 AUGUST 1937 OPERATIONS TO REPRESS FORMER KULAKS, ACTIVE ANTI-SOVIET ELEMENTS AND CRIMINALS MUST BEGIN IN ALL REPUBLICS, *KRAYA* AND *OBLASTI*.

Be guided by the following in organizing and conducting operations:

I. THOSE GROUPS TO BE REPRESSED

1. Former kulaks who have returned after serving out their punishment and are still conducting active anti-Soviet subversive activity.
2. Former kulaks who have escaped from camps or labour colonies, and also kulaks who have evaded dekulakization, and who are conducting anti-Soviet activity.
3. Former kulaks and socially dangerous elements who have been in insurgent, fascist, terrorist and bandit groups, have served out their punishment, have hidden from repression, have escaped from imprisonment and have renewed their anti-Soviet criminal activity.
4. Members of anti-Soviet parties (SRs, Georgian Mensheviks, Mussavatists, Ittihadists and Dashnaks), former Whites, former tsarist policemen and civil

---

205 J.A. Getty has pointed to the interplay between the order and preparations for new elections in 1937, suggesting that the leadership sanctioned the bloody purge to allay the anxieties of local party leaders that elections would prove destabilizing. J.A. Getty, '"Excesses are not permitted": Mass Terror and Stalinist Governance in the Late 1930s' *Russian Review* 61 (2002) pp. 113–38.

servants, members of punitive expeditions, bandits and their accomplices, dealers and returnees from emigration, those who have hidden from repression or have escaped from imprisonment, and are continuing to conduct their anti-Soviet activity.

5. The most dangerous and active participants in those White Cossack insurgent organizations, fascist-terrorist and espionage–diversionary counter-revolutionary groups which are now being destroyed, who have been uncovered by investigations and confirmed by materials from agents. Elements from these categories, currently detained on remand, for which investigations have been completed but which have yet to come before a court, are to be repressed.

6. The most active anti-Soviet elements from among former kulaks, members of punitive expeditions, bandits, Whites, active sectarians, churchmen and so forth who are now in prisons, camps, and work camps and colonies and are still undertaking active anti-Soviet activity there.

7. Criminals (bandits, robbers, re-offending thieves, cattle and horse thieves) conducting criminal activity and still involved in criminal circles.

   Elements from these categories, currently detained on remand, for which investigations have been completed but which have yet to come before a court, are to be repressed.

8. Criminal elements in camps and work colonies carrying on criminal activity within them.

II. ON THE PUNISHMENTS TO BE USED AGAINST THE REPRESSED AND THE NUMBER LIABLE TO REPRESSION

1. All kulaks, criminals and other anti-Soviet elements subject to repression fall into two categories:

   a. To Category 1 belong the most hostile of the elements enumerated above. They are to be arrested immediately and once their cases have been examined by a three-judge panel—SHOT.

   b. To Category 2 belong all the less active, but nonetheless hostile, elements. *They are to be arrested and sent to a labour camp for eight to ten years, and the most malicious and socially dangerous among them, on the decision of a three-judge panel, are to be kept in prison for the same period.*

2. According to data provided by Union republic, *kray* and *oblast'* NKVDs, it is confirmed that the numbers liable to repression are as follows:

	Cat. 1	*Cat. 2*	*Total*
1. Azerbaidzhan SSR	1,500	3,750	5,250
2. Armenian SSR	500	1,000	1,500
3. Belorussian SSR	2,000	10,000	12,000
4. Georgian SSR	2,000	3,000	5,000

	Cat. 1	Cat. 2	Total
5. Kirgiz SSR	250	500	750
6. Tadzhik SSR	500	1,300	1,800
7. Turkmen SSR	500	1,500	2,000
8. Uzbek SSR	750	4,000	4,750
9. Bashkir ASSR	500	1,500	2,000
10. Buryat–Mongol ASSR	350	1,500	1,850
11. Dagestan ASSR	500	2,500	3,000
12. Karelian ASSR	300	700	1,000
13. Kabardino–Balkar ASSR	300	700	1,000
14. Crimean ASSR	300	1,200	1,500
15. Komi ASSR	100	300	400
16. Kalmyk ASSR	100	300	400
17. Mari ASSR	300	1,500	1,800
18. Mordovian ASSR	300	1,500	1,800
19. Volga German ASSR	200	700	900
20. N. Ossetian ASSR	200	500	700
21. Tatar ASSR	500	1,500	2,000
22. Udmurt ASSR	200	500	700
23. Chechen–Ingush ASSR	500	1,500	2,000
24. Chuvash ASSR	300	1,500	1,800
25. Azov–Black Sea *kray*	5,000	8,000	13,000
26. Far Eastern *kray*	2,000	4,000	6,000
27. W. Siberian *kray*	5,000	12,000	17,000
28. Krasnoyarsk *kray*	750	2,500	3,250
29. Ordzhonikidze *kray*	1,000	4,000	5,000
30. E. Siberian *kray*	1,000	4,000	5,000
31. Voronezh *oblast'*	1,000	3,500	4,500
32. Gor'ky *oblast'*	1,000	3,500	4,500
33. Western *oblast'*	1,000	5,000	6,000
34. Ivanovo *oblast'*	750	2,000	2,750
35. Kalinin *oblast'*	1,000	3,000	4,000
36. Kursk *oblast'*	1,000	3,000	4,000
37. Kuybyshev *oblast'*	1,000	4,000	5,000
38. Kirov *oblast'*	500	1,500	2,000
39. Leningrad *oblast'*	4,000	10,000	14,000
40. Moscow *oblast'*	5,000	30,000	35,000
41. Omsk *oblast'*	1,000	2,500	3,500
42. Orenburg *oblast'*	1,500	3,000	4,500
43. Saratov *oblast'*	1,000	2,000	3,000
44. Stalingrad *oblast'*	1,000	3,000	4,000

	Cat. 1	Cat. 2	Total
45. Sverdlovsk *oblast'*	4,000	6,000	10,000
46. Northern *oblast'*	750	2,000	2,750
47. Chelyabinsk *oblast'*	1,500	4,500	6,000
48. Yaroslavl' *oblast'*	750	1,250	2,000
Ukrainian SSR			
1. Khar'kov *oblast'*	1,500	4,000	5,500
2. ...			
3. ...			
4. Donetsk *oblast'*	1,000	3,000	4,000
5. Odessa *oblast'*	1,000	3,500	4,500
6. Dnepropetrovsk *oblast'*	1,000	2,000	3,000
7. Chernigov *oblast'*	300	1,300	1,600
8. Moldavian *oblast'*	200	500	700
Kazakh SSR			
1. N. Kazakh *oblast'*	650	300	950
2. S. Kazakh *oblast'*	350	600	950
3. W. Kazakh *oblast'*	100	200	300
4. Kustanay *oblast'*	150	450	600
5. E. Kazakh *oblast'*	300	1,050	1,350
6. Aktyubinsk *oblast'*	350	1,000	1,350
7. Karaganda *oblast'*	400	600	1,000
8. Alma-Ata *oblast'*	200	800	1,000
NKVD camps	10,000	—	10,000

3. These confirmed figures are for orientation purposes. However, Union republic, *kray* and *oblast'* NKVDs do not have the right to exceed them on their own accounts. Should the situation require an increase in the number, Union republic, *kray* and *oblast'* NKVDs must submit an appropriate application, with justification, to me.

A reduction in these numbers, as well as the transfer of people scheduled for repression in Category 1 into Category 2 and vice versa, are allowed.

4. The families of persons sentenced under both categories, as a rule, are not to be repressed—with the following exceptions:

   a. Families the members of which are capable of anti-Soviet activity. Members of such families, with the special permission of a three-judge panel, may be sent to a camp or work colony.

   b. The families of people repressed in Category 1 living in a border region are to be moved outside the border zone to the interior of the *kray*, *oblast'* or republic.

c. The families of people repressed in Category 1 living in Moscow, Leningrad, Kiev, Tbilisi, Baku, Rostov-on-Don, Taganrog and in the Sochi region, Gagra and Sukhumi are to be removed from these areas to other regions of their choice, excluding border zones.

5. All families of persons repressed in the first and second categories are to be registered and kept under systematic surveillance.

III. RULES FOR CONDUCTING OPERATIONS

1. The operation is to begin on 5 August 1937 and end within four months. . .
2. The contingents belonging to Category 1 are to be repressed first.
   The contingents belonging to Category 2 are not to be repressed until further orders.

IV. INVESTIGATIONS

1. An investigation is to be held for each arrested individual or group. The investigation is to be carried out in a simplified and accelerated fashion. During the investigation all the criminal links of the accused should be uncovered.
2. After the investigation the case is to be sent for consideration by a three-judge panel. The case files should contain the following: arrest warrant, search report, evidence gathered from the search, personal documents, the questionnaire on the person arrested, intelligence material, interrogation report and a brief statement of the charges.

V. ORGANIZATION AND WORK OF THE THREE-JUDGE PANELS

. . . 5. The three-judge panels are to take minutes of their meetings, in which are also to be recorded the sentences passed in relation to each of the accused. The minutes of the panel session are to be sent to the leader of the operational group to carry out the sentence. . .

VII. OPERATIONAL MANAGEMENT AND ACCOUNTABILITY

1. I have put overall responsibility for conducting the operation on my deputy, the head of the Main Administration for State Security, Corps Commander comrade Frinovsky.

N. Ezhov, People's Commissar for Internal Affairs of the USSR and General Commissar for State Security.
Confirmed: M. Frinovsky

[Source: *Trud*, 4 June 1992.]

The Politburo formally endorsed Ezhov's targets, voted funds to cover the process, and identified in broad terms the use to be made of the new influx into labour camps of those designated to 'Category 2'.

Document 195 | 'Confirm the proposed NKVD draft...'—from Minute No. 51 of the CPSU Politburo

31 July 1937

442—the NKVD question

Top Secret

1. Confirm the proposed NKVD draft of the operational order for the repression of former kulaks, criminal and anti-Soviet elements. . .

5. Release 75 million rubles to the NKVD from the Sovnarkom reserve fund for expenses incurred in conducting the operation. . .

7. All kulaks, criminals and other anti-Soviet elements sentenced in Category 2 to terms in labour camps are to be deployed as follows:

    a) on the NKVD GULAG sites currently under construction.

    b) in the construction of new labour camps in remote areas of Kazakhstan.

    c) in the construction of new camps, specially organized for logging work using prisoners' labour. . .

11. Release a loan of 10 million rubles to the NKVD GULAG from the Sovnarkom reserve fund for organizing camps and carrying out the preparatory work. . .

12. Request that *oblast'* and *kray* committees of the CPSU and Komsomol, in those *oblasti* where camps are being organized, make the necessary numbers of communist and Komsomol members available to the NKVD to bring the camp administration and guards up to strength (as required by the NKVD).

13. The People's Commissariat of Defence is to recruit 240 commanders and political officers from the Workers' and Peasants' Red Army to bring the officer corps of the armed guards of the newly formed camps up to strength.

14. The People's Commissariat of Health is to provide the NKVD GULAG with 150 doctors and 400 medical attendants for the newly formed camps.

15. The People's Commissariat of Forestry is to provide the GULAG with ten leading forestry specialists and fifty graduates of the Leningrad Forestry Academy.

I.V. Stalin, secretary of the CC

[Source: *Trud*, 4 June 1992.]

Month-by-month records in Tomsk *oblast'* in Siberia demonstrate that some 60 per cent of the huge number of executions in 1937–38 were concentrated in the five months following the order.[206] It is not clear from which

---

206 S. Wheatcroft, 'The Scale and Nature of Stalinist Repression and its Demographic Significance: On comments by Keep and Conquest' *Europe–Asia Studies* 52 (2000) p. 1159.

social strata the victims duly reported by the local NKVD—which far exceeded both Ezhov's limits and the additional 48,000 executions sanctioned by Stalin in January 1938—were predominantly drawn. NKVD records, although greatly improved by the introduction of passports and urban registration cards, fell desperately short of a 'totalitarian' ideal, and were markedly better on those in positions of responsibility than on workers, let alone peasants.[207] Some historians assume that the order's focus on 'socially harmful elements' was duly implemented, that those arrested were mainly drawn from existing police lists of former 'kulaks' and criminals as well as those with a record of some form of opposition, and that these 'mass operations' were quite separate from the purges of officialdom.[208] Others point to evidence that most names were provided by denunciation at mass meetings in farms and factories, that few of those listed had previous criminal records, that here, too, it was on those in positions of authority in the state and party, rural as well as urban, and on the intelligentsia in general and not on peasants or workers at large that the Great Terror left its deepest imprint.[209] If this view is vindicated by further local archival research, it suggests that the response to NKVD order 00447 became caught up in the assault on officials.

That assault was given additional fuel by a third terror initiative: Stalin's order of 3 August 1937 sent to district party committees to prepare and publicize show trials of local rural officials unmasked as wreckers. Though accounting for a relatively small number of the victims of the Terror, the number of trials appears to have run into the hundreds, Stalin repeatedly pressing personally for execution of the convicted.[210]

Of much greater numerical significance was a fourth component, a series of decrees the same summer directed at members of suspect national minorities.[211] At least nine minorities—Poles, Germans, Finns, Estonians, Latvians, Koreans, Chinese, Kurds and Iranians—were affected. In this case, international security does appear to have been the overriding preoccupation. Those summarily uprooted and decimated by executions were concentrated in the Soviet borderlands and specifically in the narrow strips around the country's periphery. The regime appears to have become increasingly anxious as the

---

207 For two views, see Hagenloh, '"Socially Harmful Elements"' pp. 295–300, and Thurston, *Life and Terror* pp. 59–106.
208 Hagenloh, '"Socially Harmful Elements"' pp. 300–02.
209 Manning, 'Great Purges in a Rural District' pp. 191–96; Fitzpatrick, *Stalin's Peasants* pp. 201–03.
210 M. Ellman, 'The Soviet 1937 Provincial Show Trials: Carnival or terror?' *Europe–Asia Studies* 53 (2001) pp. 1221–33.
211 For a clear account, see M. Jansen and N. Petrov, *Stalin's Loyal Executioner: People's Commissar Nikolai Ezhov 1895–1940* (Stanford, CA, 2002) pp. 93–100.

1930s progressed that minorities here, especially those with cross-border ethnic ties, posed a security risk. And during the period of the Great Terror, suspicion extended even to members of these nationalities scattered within the heartland of the USSR. A decree of 9 August 1937 issued by Ezhov against Poles, the victimized minority group that has been most closely studied, foreshadowed decrees for 'national operations' against all the suspect national minorities. Recent attempts to disaggregate the executions of 1937–38 estimate that while NKVD order 00447 may have accounted for over half the number, the national operations accounted for more than one third.[212] When the Soviet Union occupied eastern Poland in 1939 and Estonia, Latvia and Lithuania in 1940, there were echoes of 1937–38 in the treatment of the political, economic and cultural elites of the new territories—mass deportation and executions. The version of 'ethnic cleansing' that formed part of the Great Terror would be reenacted even more closely in the brutal punishment of victimized minorities in the latter stages and aftermath of the Great Patriotic War (see Volume II).

The fate of Bukharin

The last of the three major show trials took place in March 1938. The victim who has attracted most attention is Bukharin. Although he steadily denied some charges and gave ambiguous answers on many others, he was to be the model for Arthur Koestler's classic dramatization, *Darkness at Noon*, in which the senior Bolshevik protagonist is persuaded as a final service to the party to admit guilt for acts he never committed. Bukharin spent a year under arrest and investigation. As late as December 1937 he still had some hope of escaping death and wrote a long letter to Stalin raising the possibility that instead of execution he might be exiled with his family to America, where, he said, he would champion the validity of the trials and 'wage a mortal war against Trotsky'.[213] By the time he wrote the following letter to his wife, he was braced for the worst and concerned for her, for his baby son, and for his former wife, Nadya.

---

212 See the forceful discussion by T. Martin, 'The Origins of Soviet Ethnic Cleansing' *Journal of Modern History* (1998) pp. 813–61.
213 Getty and Naumov, *Road to Terror* pp. 559–60.

Document 196 | N.I. Bukharin—from a letter to his wife on the eve of his trial

15 January 1938

My beloved, darling Anna,

I'm writing to you on the eve of my trial, and am writing with a definite aim, which I cannot stress enough: whatever you read, whatever you hear, however horrible the things said to me or by me—put up with them ALL bravely and calmly. Prepare the whole household. Help everybody. I fear both for you and for others, but especially for you. Don't feel any malice. Just remember that the great cause of the USSR lives on, which is the main thing, while individual fates are transient and miserable in comparison. An enormously testing time awaits you. I beg you, my dear, to do everything you can and strain every nerve NOT to give in. Don't talk carelessly to anybody. You know my situation. You are the dearest and closest person to me. And I beg you by everything good that we have shared to make a supreme effort and strain every nerve to help yourself and the family GET THROUGH this terrible phase. I don't think father or Nadya should read the papers for a while: let them as it were SLEEP through it. As it's more obvious to you, see to it that there are no unexpected shocks. If I'm asking this of you, then believe me, I've gone through it all, both this request and what's going to happen, as great and major interests demand it. You know what it's costing me to write such a letter, but I'm writing it knowing full well that I've no other choice. This is the main thing, the fundamental thing, the decisive thing. You can understand what these few short lines mean. Do as I ask and keep a hold of yourself: be STONY, like a statue.

I'm very worried FOR YOUR SAKE and, if YOU were allowed to write to me or say a few comforting words about the above, my heart would feel a bit lighter.

I beg and implore you, my dear friend. I've got a second request—ridiculously small, but very important to me.

You'll be given three manuscripts:
a) A big 310-page philosophical work called 'Philosophical Arabesques'.
b) A little book of poems.
c) The first seven chapters of a novel.

They need re-typing, three copies of each. Father will help you do the poetry and the novel (the poetry does have a PLAN; even if it looks chaotic you can make sense of it; each poem needs a separate page).

The main thing is not to lose the philosophical work, which I've worked hard on and put a lot into: it's a very MATURE thing compared with my previous efforts and, unlike them, DIALECTICAL from start to finish.

There's ALSO the book the first part of which I wrote at home (Socialism and the crisis of capitalist culture). Do try to rescue it because I haven't got it and it'd be a shame if it were lost.

If you get the manuscripts (a lot of the poems are about YOU and you'll be able to tell how attached I am to you), and if you're allowed to send me a few lines or words, DON'T FORGET TO MENTION MY MANUSCRIPTS AS WELL.

This isn't the place to go on about my feelings, but you can tell from what I've written how very much I love you. At such a difficult time do help me by doing the first thing I asked. Whatever the outcome of the trial is, I'll see you afterwards and kiss your hand then.

Goodbye, my love.

Your Kol'ka

P.S. I've got your picture with the baby. Give Yurka a kiss from me. I'm glad he can't read. I'm also very worried about our daughter. Tell me something about our son—he'll have grown into a little boy now, and doesn't know me. Give him a hug from me.

[Source: *Rodina* No. 8–9, 1992, p. 68.]

The cultural impact of the Great Terror

The Great Terror did not put an end to scattered voices of opposition. And those uncovered—such as the following trenchant leaflet by two young Moscow physicists—tended to assume the superior virtue of socialism and appeal to the proletariat. But what was silenced was overt dissent at any level from within the party.

Document 197 | **M.A. Korets and L.D. Landau: Leaflet—'Overthrow this fascist dictator and his clique...'**

23 April 1938

Workers of the world, unite!
Comrades!

The great cause of the October revolution has been basely betrayed. The country is awash with blood and filth. Millions of innocent people have been thrown into prison, and nobody knows when it will be his turn. The economy is disintegrating. Famine is rearing its head. Can you not see, comrades, that Stalin's clique have carried out a fascist coup? Socialism remains only on the pages of the utterly mendacious press. In his rabid hatred of real socialism Stalin is on a par with Hitler and Mussolini. In destroying the country in order to preserve his own power, Stalin is turning it into easy pickings for a brutalized German fascism. The only way out for the working class and all the working people of our country is a decisive fight against Stalinist and Hitlerite fascism, a fight for socialism.

Organize yourselves, comrades! Do not be afraid of the NKVD butchers. They are only capable of beating up defenceless prisoners, seizing unsuspecting innocent people, looting national property and holding ludicrous trials for non-existent conspiracies.

Comrades, join the Anti-Fascist Workers' Party (ARP). Get in contact with its Moscow committee. Organize ARP groups in your factories. Collect material for underground work. Prepare a mass socialist movement by agitation and propaganda.

Stalinist fascism endures only because we are not organized. The proletariat of our country, which overthrew the power of the tsar and the capitalists, can overthrow this fascist dictator and his clique.

Long live May Day—the day of the struggle for socialism!

Moscow Committee of the Anti-Fascist Workers' Party

[Source: *Izvestiya TsK KPSS* No. 3, 1991, pp. 146–47.]

The deadening impact of the Great Terror on intellectual life was epitomized by the publication in November 1938 of the *History of the CPSU(B) Short Course*. Composed under Stalin's direct supervision, it wove a seamless web between a Marxist reading of world history, a Leninist reading of the Russian revolution, and a Stalinist account of everything that had happened since. It vilified not only all opponents of Bolshevism but also the leading opposition figures within the party—Trotsky, Bukharin and all of Lenin's main lieutenants—as 'White Guard pygmies', traitors from the start. And it became for two decades the obligatory dogmatic text from junior school to professorial level.[214]

Document 198 | '… unified guidance on the history of the Party…'—from a CC decree

14 November 1938

The publication of the *History of the Communist Party of the Soviet Union (Bolsheviks) Short Course* is an extremely important event in the ideological life of the Bolshevik Party. With the appearance of the *Short Course* the Party has acquired a powerful new Bolshevik ideological weapon and an encyclopaedia of the basic ideas of Marxism–Leninism. This course in the history of the Party is a scientific history of Bolshevism. It expounds and generalizes the Communist Party's immense experience, which no party in the world could or can equal.

The *History of the Communist Party of the Soviet Union (Bolsheviks) Short Course* is an extremely important means through which Party members can master Bolshevism and arm themselves with Marxist–Leninist theory, i.e., with a knowledge of the laws

---

214 *History of the Communist Party of the Soviet Union (Bolsheviks)* (Moscow 1939).

of social development and political struggle. It is a means of raising political awareness among Party and non-Party Bolsheviks and a means of raising Marxist–Leninist propaganda to the appropriate theoretical height.

In producing the *History of the Communist Party of the Soviet Union (Bolsheviks) Short Course* the CC of the CPSU proceeded from the following desiderata:

1) It was necessary to give the Party unified guidance on the history of the Party, guidance representing the interpretation, officially approved by the CC of the CPSU, of the main questions in the history of the CPSU and Marxism–Leninism, allowing no arbitrary interpretations. The publication of the *Short Course*, as approved by the CC of the CPSU, has put an end to arbitrary and confused expositions of Party history and to the multitude of viewpoints and the arbitrary interpretations of major questions in Party theory and history which were to be found in several earlier textbooks on Party history. . .

[Source: *VKP(b) v rezolyutsiyakh i resheniyakh s˝ezdov, konferentsiy, plenumov TsK*, 6th edition, part 2 (Moscow 1941) p. 678.]

In November 1938, Stalin and Molotov called a halt to the Great Terror. The troikas which had been responsible for the great majority of the executions were instructed to stop their work. Ezhov was replaced by L.P. Beria as head of the NKVD. Although the regime was apologetic only for disorderly aspects of the Terror, not for the Terror itself, much of the blame was popularly laid at Ezhov's door. In April 1939, the party leadership in Sverdlovsk asked for permission to change the name of its 'Ezhovsk' district to 'Molotovsk'.[215]

If a major aim of the Great Terror was to overcome endemic waste and poor-quality production, to remedy the inherent malfunctions of the Stalinist form of 'planning', or to compel regional and local officials to obey Moscow to the letter, it had failed dismally. A decree of 1940 would vehemently reaffirm once again the equation between poor-quality work and sabotage on the part of those in positions of responsibility. Nor had the Great Terror done anything to reverse the trend of the regime's becoming more and more closely associated with the white-collar elite rather than the working class it claimed to represent. Between 1939 and 1941 the successive purges of the party—peaceful in the mid-1930s, bloody in 1937 and 1938—gave way to rapid recruitment, with membership doubling by the outbreak of war with Germany, and it was among white-collar workers that the new members were overwhelmingly concentrated.

While mass terror was curtailed at the end of 1938, this did not signal a

---

215 Getty and Naumov, *Road to Terror* p. 538.

shift in the brutalized political culture of the leadership. The following circular from the beginning of 1939 underlines the use made of physical torture to extract confessions from suspects. Stalin's explicit encouragement that it be employed on those who have 'not yet come clean' takes guilt for granted.

Document 199 | I.V. Stalin: '... the use of physical coercion by the NKVD has been allowed by the CC of the CPSU since 1937...'

From a telegram to secretaries of *oblast'* committees, *kray* committees, CCs of national communist parties, people's commissariats of internal affairs and NKVD directorate heads

10 January 1939

The CPSU CC would like to explain that the use of physical coercion by the NKVD has been allowed by the CC of the CPSU since 1937... It is well known that all bourgeois intelligence services apply physical coercion against the representatives of the socialist proletariat, and apply it in the most outrageous forms. The question arises as to why the socialist intelligence service must be more humane towards inveterate bourgeois agents and sworn enemies of the working class and collective farmers. The CC of the CPSU thinks that the use of physical force must henceforth be used, in exceptional circumstances, against manifest enemies of the people who have not yet come clean, as a perfectly correct and expedient method.

[Source: *Izvestiya TsK KPSS* No. 3, 1989, p. 145.]

Even after the Great Terror was over, the fate that could still befall Soviet *intelligenty* who passed into the hands of the NKVD was horrific. This is graphically conveyed in the following declaration addressed to Molotov at the beginning of 1940 by V.E. Meyerhol'd, one of the greatest Soviet theatre directors. A party member since 1918, Meyerhol'd fell foul of tightening cultural control in 1936. He was among the thousands of leading intellectuals hounded out of his post during the Great Terror for heresy, in this case so-called 'formalism', a flexible category embracing almost any departure from the increasingly rigid demands of 'socialist realism'.[216] His theatre was closed in 1938, and he was arrested in 1939 and subjected to excruciating torture before his death in 1940.[217]

---

216 Among the subsets of the Soviet intelligentsia, it should be noted that the cultural/artistic elite suffered proportionately much less than party, state, economic and military elites or the intelligentsia as a whole. See J.A. Getty and W. Chase, 'Patterns of Repression among the Soviet Elite in the Late 1930s: A biographical approach' in Getty and Manning (eds) *Stalinist Terror* pp. 225–46.

217 S. Wheatcroft, *Australian Slavonic Papers* I, no. 1.

Document 200 | From V. E. Meyerhol′d's declaration, addressed to V.M. Molotov

2 January 1940

When the investigators started using their physical methods on me, the prisoner, and then combined them with the so-called 'psychological attack', these both terrified me so much that my inner nature was fully revealed. . .

My nerves seemed to be very close to the surface, my skin as tender and sensitive as a baby's and my eyes capable of floods of tears because of the unbearable physical and emotional pain. Face down on the floor I found myself capable of wriggling, writhing and yelping like a dog being whipped by its master. A guard who took me away from one such interrogation asked me, 'Have you got malaria?' My body proved capable of nervous trembling. When I lay on my bunk to get some sleep after an eighteen-hour interrogation, just to go to another in an hour's time, I was woken by my own groans and tossing and turning, just like patients dying of fever.

Fear generates terror, and terror demands self-defence. 'Of course, death is easier than this!', says the victim of interrogation to himself—as I, too, did, and started incriminating myself in the hope that they would lead me to the gallows. And that's what happened: on the last page of my 'case' (No. 537) were the terrible numbers of those paragraphs from the criminal code: 58, subsections 1 and 2.

Vyacheslav Mikhaylovich, you know my shortcomings (do you remember once saying to me, 'Are you trying to be original in everything!?'), and the person who knows another's shortcomings knows him better than one who admires his merits. Tell me, do you really believe that I am a traitor (an enemy of the people), that I am a spy, that I am a member of a Rightist–Trotskyite organization, that I am a counter-revolutionary, that in my art I propagated Trotskyism, that in the theatre I (consciously) carried out hostile work, in order to undermine the bases of Soviet art?

It's all in No. 537, where the word 'formalist' (in the field of art) has become a synonym for 'Trotskyite'. In case No. 537 it turns out that I. Ehrenburg, B. Pasternak, Yu. Olesha (he is also a terrorist), Shostakovich, Shebalin, Okhlopkov, and so on, are all Trotskyites. . . I shall finish the rest of my declaration in ten days' time, when I'm given a form.

Continuation of the declaration
13 January 1940, Butyrki Prison, Moscow

One more dreadful circumstance contributed to my not being able to hold out, losing all control over myself, and being in a dulled, stupefied state of mind. This was that just after my arrest on 20 June 1939 I became deeply depressed by the nagging idea that 'it must be right'. I began to convince myself that for my sins, condemned from the podium of the first session of the Supreme Soviet, the

Government felt that the punishment meted out to me (the closure of the theatre, the breaking up of the troupe, the cessation of work on the theatre I had planned on Mayakovsky Square) was inadequate, and that I had to endure yet another—the one being inflicted on me by the NKVD. 'It must be right,' I kept saying to myself, and my self split into two persons. The first half started looking for the second's crimes, and, not finding any, started to invent them. The investigator was a very experienced assistant in this regard, and we began to concoct them together, in close co-operation. When my fantasy had run out of steam, the investigators began pairing them up (Voronin + Rodos, Voronin + Shvartsman) and cobbling reports together, some of which were rewritten three or four times. Eventually I collapsed, from hunger (I could not eat anything), from lack of sleep (for three months), night-time palpitations and hysteria (I wept floods of tears, and trembled as if feverish). I had sunk, my features had aged ten years, and this scared the investigators. They started looking after me assiduously. At that time I was in the 'internal prison' (it has a good medical section). I was fed intensively. But this only helped me externally, physically, while my nerves were still in the same state, and my mind remained dulled, stupefied, because the sword of Damocles was still hanging over me. The investigator kept threatening me, 'If you don't write something (meaning—make it up!?), we'll beat you again. Only your head and right hand will be left alone, the rest of your body we'll reduce to shapeless bloody shreds.' So I signed everything before 16 November 1939. I now retract my confessions, as they were beaten out of me. I beg you, as head of the Government, to save me and give me back my freedom. I love my Motherland and will devote all my strength to it in the final years of my life.

Vs. Meyerhol'd-Raykh

Footnote to both parts of the declaration of 2 January 1940:

They have been beating me here, a sick, 66-year-old man. I was put face down on the floor and beaten on the back and heels with plaited rubber; then, sitting on a chair, beaten violently on the legs (from above, with great force), and in places between the knees and thighs. And, over the following days, once these parts of my legs were swollen from massive internal bleeding, they beat these red–blue–yellow bruises all over again with the rubber plait. The pain was so intense, it was as if boiling water was being poured directly onto these painful, tender parts of my legs (I screamed and wept from the pain). I was beaten on the back with that rubber, and I was beaten about the face with swings from above. . .

Vs. Meyerhol'd

[Source: *Sovetskaya kul'tura*, 16 February 1989.]

16

Church and State

The 'cultural revolution' of 1928–31 was accompanied by a dramatic and violent ratcheting up of attacks on the Orthodox Church and religion in general. The change in tone began in 1928 and the pressure, both on religious institutional life and activity and on individual believers, became increasingly frenetic from 1929.[218] 'The League of the Militant Godless', as Yaroslavsky's organization was renamed, grew rapidly when membership was made automatic for those joining Komsomol. It campaigned furiously to close churches, arrest priests or force them to stop administering the sacraments, purge religious believers from schools and universities, flood the education system and media with anti-religious propaganda and break the back of religion. The stereotype energetically propagated was of the religious believer resenting the 'great turn', clinging to backward customs, ignorance and superstition, and obstructing the working people and the building of socialism. The following newspaper report in the Urals follows a recurrent pattern—the fusion between priest and White Guard, the indignation of loyal workers at 'their' sneering at 'our' efforts, and the spontaneous demand that such 'counter-revolutionary attacks' be halted, the local church closed, and measures taken against churchgoing workers.

---

218 For two recent studies that throw a great deal of light on the anti-religious drive, see D. Peris, *Storming the Heavens: The Soviet League of the Militant Godless* (Ithaca, NY, 1998), and W. Husband, *Godless Communists: Atheists and society in Soviet Russia, 1917–1932* (De Kalb, IL, 2000).

Document 201 | **'Echoes of the Civil War'—a note in _Ural'skiy rabochiy_ (_Urals Worker_)**

March 1929

A few days ago in the Ashinsk club there was a lecture on culture and everyday life. A priest, Karsky, a former White Guard officer, turned up at the lecture and showered the speaker with questions. So, a special debate on an anti-religious topic was organized the next day. The White Guard Karsky, of course, mobilized his Church 'activists' and at the debate citizens heard not only a White Guard officer in a cassock, but also a 'worker', Ivan Pavlovich Kuznetsov, a steel worker who is head of the Church council.

Here the church fraternity put their cards on the table. Karsky crudely avoided the majority of questions, to which he simply had no answer, and directed his main attack against Soviet power, exploiting our difficulties with flour and textiles. One citizen remarked to the White Guard priest that he had undoubtedly lopped off quite a few workers' heads when he was an officer, to which the 'quick-witted' priest replied, 'And how many heads did your revolution cost?!' This counter-revolutionary outburst outraged many workers, who discussed it at a meeting. 'We must put a decisive end to counter-revolutionary attacks by clergymen,' said the workers. The workers demanded the closure of the church and the transfer of the building to one of the cultural institutions of the settlement. The workers also sharply criticized Kuznetsov's sabotage and demanded his expulsion from the trade union.

I. Chelombiev

[Source: _Ural'skiy rabochiy_, 17 March 1929.]

It was in part under pressure from the Militant Godless League that the notorious decree of April 1929, imposing much tighter rules governing religious practice, was issued. The restrictions spelled out in Articles 17, 18, 22 and 58 were so sweeping that religious groups were forbidden virtually any activity other than worship itself.

Document 202 | **'On Religious Organizations'—from a decree of the VTsIK and Sovnarkom of the RSFSR**

8 April 1929

. . . 4. Religious societies or groups may go about their business only after the society or group has registered with the appropriate administrative department (section or part) of the local executive committee, city soviet, _volost'_ executive committee or town soviet of a town which is not the administrative centre of a district or _uezd_. . .

17. Religious societies may not:
   a) set up mutual aid funds, co-operatives, producers' associations and generally use the property under their control for any purposes other than satisfying religious needs;
   b) provide material support for their members;
   c) organize either special children's, young people's, women's and other meetings or general biblical, literary, needlework, labour or religious education meetings, groups, circles and sections, or organize trips and children's playgrounds, open libraries and reading rooms, organize sanatoria or medical help.

   Only books essential to the operation of the cult in question may be kept in Church buildings and premises.

18. Religious teaching of any kind is not allowed in state, public and private educational institutions. Such teaching is permissible only on the special theological courses run by Soviet citizens with the permission of the NKVD of the RSFSR, and in the Autonomous Republics—with the permission of the central executive committee of the Autonomous Republic in question. . .

22. Religious congresses and the executive bodies they elect have no juridical person and, moreover, may not:
   a) organize any fund-raising bodies whatsoever for collecting voluntary donations from believers;
   b) organize any non-voluntary collections of funds;
   c) own any religious property, receive it by agreement or acquire it by purchase or renting for the purpose of religious meetings;
   d) conclude any deals or agreements whatsoever. . .

36. The transfer of a religious building currently in use by believers to other purposes (i.e., its abolition as a religious building) is permissible only by a resolution, with explanation, of the central executive committee of an Autonomous Republic, or of the *kray, oblast'* or *guberniya* executive committee, if the said building is required for state or public purposes. Such a decree is to be communicated to the believers constituting the religious society. . .

37. If the believers constituting a religious society appeal against the decree within a fortnight of being informed of it to the Presidium of the All-Russia TsIK, then the whole question of the abolition of the religious building passes into the hands of the Presidium of the All-Russia TsIK. An agreement with believers loses its force and the religious building is removed from their use only after the corresponding confirmation of the resolution by the Presidium of the All-Russia TsIK. . .

57. In religious buildings or premises specially adapted and conforming to technical construction and health regulations, gatherings for prayer of believers, united into groups or societies, may take place without informing or seeking permission from government bodies.

In buildings not specially adapted, gatherings of believers for prayer may take place with the notification of: in rural localities—the village soviet; in urban localities—the police department; and in the absence of either—the administrative division.

58. No religious services or ceremonies of any kind are permissible in any state, public, co-operative and private establishments and enterprises. This prohibition does not apply to religious rites requested by the dying or seriously ill, held in specially isolated places in hospitals or prisons, or to the performance of religious rites at cemeteries and crematoria.

59. Religious processions, and the performance of religious rites and ceremonies in the open air are allowed with special permission for each occasion. . . Such permission is not required for religious services associated with funerals.

60. Religious processions which are an integral part of a service, and which take place around the religious building both in urban and rural locations, do not require special permission from or notification of government bodies, so long as these processions do not disrupt normal street traffic. . .

M. Kalinin: chairman of the All-Russia TsIK
A. Smirnov: deputy chairman of Sovnarkom
A. Dosov: deputy secretary of the All-Russia TsIK

[Source: *Sobranie uzakoneniy i rasporyazheniy raboche-krest'yanskogo pravitel'stva RSFSR* No. 35, 1929, Article 353.]

That summer, the Constitution was altered in the same direction. Whereas in 1918, the propagation of both religious and anti-religious ideas had been sanctioned, it now became illegal to try to convert or press religious views on others. The ban was experienced as most oppressive not by the Orthodox Church but by denominations and sects committed to proselytization. Moreover, militants now targeted non-Orthodox believers as much as the Orthodox. As this article in the Urals press emphasizes, the relative tolerance experienced in the 1920s by sectarians, Baptists and Old Believer congregations (of which the region had one of the largest concentrations) gave way to fierce attack.[219]

---

219 See I.K. Paert, 'Popular Religion and Local Identity during the Stalin Revolution: Old Believers in the Urals, 1928–41' in Raleigh (ed.) *Provincial Landscapes* pp. 171–93.

Document 203 | '… stop sabotage by churchmen and sectarians…'—from
V. Borisov: *An Important Amendment to the Constitution of
the RSFSR*

July 1929

Today a number of amendments have been introduced by the Congress of Soviets
to the Constitution (Fundamental Law) of the Soviet state. In particular, the content
of Article 4 has been altered. This Article formerly said, 'To guarantee genuine
freedom of conscience for the working people, the Church is separated from the
state and schools from the Church, but freedom of religious and anti-religious propaganda is recognized for all citizens.' The contents of this Article have been very
widely interpreted by clergymen… In the Nozhevsk region of the Sarapul *okrug*
priests have been agitating against the collective farms. They have been quoting the
Commandments and 'scripture' to confirm that 'the collective farm is godless and
collective farmers will be punished by God…'. What sort of 'religious propaganda'
is this? It is open agitation against the policies of the Soviet government. And how
many instances are there of priests insinuating anti-Soviet propaganda into their 'religious propaganda' at any gathering of people 'lawfully and in accordance with the
Constitution'? The sectarians have made particularly wide use of the imprecise
wording of Article 4. When they were building the Sarapul shoe factory, the
construction trust's representative, a sectarian, preached his sect's ideas among the
workers. He illegally promoted those who joined his sect. The sectarians had their
own travelling agents, conducted meetings in the villages and had their own book-
peddling 'propagandists'. Sectarians and churchmen entrenched themselves in the
village of Marakushi, deep in the forests of the Foki region of Sarapul *okrug*. At the
time of re-elections to the soviet, in order to disrupt an election meeting, they
announced a believers' meeting, threatening Divine retribution on those who did
not turn up…

In order to stop sabotage by churchmen and sectarians and really to separate the
Church from the state, the Congress of Soviets has introduced an amendment into
Article 4 of the Constitution. The new wording of this article is: 'To guarantee real
freedom of conscience for the working people the Church is separated from the
state and schools from the Church, but freedom of religious confession and of anti-
religious propaganda remains for all citizens.'

The new version in no way restricts believers in the profession of their belief. It
remains a personal matter for every citizen whether to profess any religion or not.
But this new wording does introduce restrictions against the activities of churchmen
and sectarians. The freedom to conduct religious ceremonies and services remains
in force. However, because of this Article churchmen and sectarians may not
conduct missionary activity or religious propaganda. This Article allows no other
activity beyond ministering to religious needs.

[Source: *Ural'skiy rabochiy*, 7 July 1929.]

During the 'cultural revolution' the number of churches closed rose steeply. For anti-religious zealots, they represented the most visible symbol of the enemy, of the old ways and of opposition to Soviet power. They were also the most tangible target. The Militant Godless League eagerly collected statistics on the rate of closures: the following report appeared in its monthly journal *Antireligioznik* (*The Antireligious*), the only one among its many publications which included even a pretence of serious and scholarly material.

Document 204 | The closure of churches

August 1929

The statistical information sub-division of the Central Council of the League of Militant Godless (SVB) has summarized the information on the number of religious buildings closed in the first half of 1929. To a limited extent the information was drawn from reports and communications of the Councils of the SVB, but most of it was taken from the local press.

The available information is far from full: the press has not reported every closure, and moreover the Central Council does not receive all local newspapers by a long way. It is inevitable that many cases of closure of religious buildings will be missed. Only those instances of closure are included which took place as a result of workers' demands and excluded are instances of closure for administrative reasons (dilapidation, hindrance to traffic, etc.). No attention has been paid to the closure of sectarian religious buildings as these are not significant: such places of worship are usually not special religious buildings. Also excluded are all unclear and vague comments (like 'is being closed' or 'is to be closed' without concrete reference to an actual closure). In the report 'urban' churches refers to religious buildings in settlements of an urban type, and also buildings in new towns or attached to enterprises. By Christian churches are meant Orthodox churches, cathedrals and chapels as well as Polish Catholic and Lutheran churches.

Throughout the USSR in the first half of this year 423 churches (243 urban, 180 rural) have been closed in fulfilment of resolutions passed by working people. Moreover, there have been applications, which have not yet received final assent, as they are awaiting approval from various executive committees, to close 317 religious buildings, of which 154 are urban and 163 rural. This figure does not include the numerous resolutions 'we demand closure', 'we consider it necessary' or press comments such as 'ought to be closed', 'is earmarked for closure', etc., which have not been accompanied by formal applications.

As we can see, reports from the Union Republics are extremely incomplete. Our papers are being even more careless about providing information on how closed religious buildings are being redeployed. The details are as follows:

Closed religious buildings have been used in the following ways:

1. Cultural needs (clubs, reading rooms, houses of the people, red corners   156
   [propaganda centres], houses of sport and exercise, theatres, cinemas,
   museums)
2. Children's educational needs (all kinds of schools, technical colleges,   38
   kindergartens, crèches, etc.)
3. Production and trade purposes (co-operative shops, warehouses,   14
   granaries, fire stations, workshops, mills, power stations, etc.)
4. Medical (surgeries, hospitals, medical attendant and veterinary points, etc.)   10
5. Taken down for use as building materials, regardless of purpose   26
   (e.g., for schools, hospitals, etc.)
6. Other (housing, canteens)   9
7. Unknown and partially unused (e.g., owing to lack of resources for
   re-equipment etc.)   171

Information on religious buildings closed throughout the USSR:

Union Republics	Urban			Rural		
	Churches	*Mosques*	*Synagogues*	*Churches*	*Mosques*	*Synagogues*
RSFSR, including autonomous *oblasti* and republics	180	3	15	106	13	—
Belorussia	1	—	—	2	—	—
Ukraine	16	—	19	20	—	8
Transcaucasia	2	—	—	—	29	—
Turkmenistan	4	—	1	—	—	—
Uzbekistan	2	—	—	—	1	—
Totals	205	3	35	128	43	8

It is interesting to compare this year's figures with those for the first half of 1928, when, according to the data of the information department, 219 religious buildings were closed. Even if this information is also incomplete, nonetheless a significant growth can be discerned in the movement to close down these opium dens during the current year.

The movement to close religious buildings this year has spread rapidly amongst the working people of the Union, but in a very large number of instances workers' resolutions have not been carried out properly, in places owing to extreme indifference, carelessness and a bureaucratic attitude to matters of this type on the part of local institutions and organizations. Consequently, in many cases demands to close religious buildings have been ignored, because churchmen have managed to organize bunches of believers, who have managed to bring together groups to keep the religious buildings in use, despite the hostile attitude towards religion of the vast majority of working people in the place in question.

In a number of cases the closure of religious buildings has met with great resistance from churchmen, who have used every guile to defend their positions, in particular forgery, slander, threats, while in some instances they have even resorted to religious fanaticism (Rykovo, where stones were thrown at a workers' demonstration).

There have been instances of churches being burnt down and church windows being broken after closure, and of attempts to beat up active atheists.

In a significant number of cases, the closure of religious buildings has happened spontaneously, at the unanimous request of the working people. In a number of villages churches have been closed immediately following the adoption of a resolution on closure at a village gathering, because there were almost no opponents of closure to be found, or because there were none at all.

[Source: *Antireligioznik* No. 9, 1929, pp. 106–07.]

As the drive for mass collectivization gathered momentum the following winter, so too did the campaign against religion. In the countryside, there was overt and sometimes violent resistance to moves to close the village church, confiscate the bell and icons, and drive out the priest. In March 1930 over 500 cases of mass disturbances triggered in this way were reported.[220] The resistance, combined with intense foreign criticism, prompted Stalin, in his 'Dizzy with Success' article in *Pravda* that month, to reproach local activists not only for coercing peasants into collective farms, rather than winning their voluntary consent, but also for overstepping the mark in the methods they used to close churches. However, just as forced collectivization resumed after a brief pause, so too did the closure of churches, their demolition or conversion for other use, and the expulsion of parish priests. The most spectacular destruction was the dynamiting of the Cathedral of Christ the Saviour in Moscow in 1931. Despite the efforts of the Militant Godless League to gather statistics, there is no clear picture of the rate of attrition. By some accounts, within four years, the number of churches had been reduced by more than half. Thereafter the pace slowed until the period of the Great Terror, when there was a further wave of closures among the fraction of churches still functioning. Ezhov's drastic instruction of July 1937 (see document 194) included among those slated for repression churchmen and 'active sectarians' in prison camps and colonies along with other 'anti-Soviet elements', and the much-thinned ranks of priests and bishops suffered further losses. Between the census of 1926 and that of 1937, the number of

---

220 Viola, *Peasant Rebels* pp. 39–40, 135–37.

priests and ministers fell from 79,000 to 31,000.[221] The number of Orthodox parish priests executed or imprisoned in the 1930s may have been over 35,000.[222] All denominations—the Armenian and Georgian churches, Old Believers and sectarians, Protestants and Catholics, Muslims and Jews—came under repeated attack, although the greatest victim was the Orthodox Church. By the end of the decade, only a small fraction of the 54,000 Orthodox churches in existence at the outbreak of World War I were still open.

The assault on visible demonstrations of faith, on the ability of religious denominations to train and consecrate new priests, and on formal religious instruction to children was at its most vigorous between 1928 and 1932. Membership of the Militant Godless League in those years rose from half a million to over five and a half million and there was a massive increase in anti-religious agitation and propaganda. The League's output of anti-religious literature soared, by one count from twelve million pages in 1927 to 800 million three years later.[223] Thereafter, however, the League's membership and activity subsided along with the 'cultural revolution', and so too did the militancy with which the press and local officials pressed the campaign against religion. After a brief upsurge, active teaching of atheism slipped rapidly down the list of priorities in the school curriculum. Although the restrictive decree of 1929 remained in force, the League had to endure the formal confirmation of religious liberty in the Constitution of 1936 and the restoration of voting rights to priests. The population census taken in 1937—which remained unpublished, so dramatic were the population losses it revealed—included a question on religious affiliation which revealed that two-thirds of the rural population and one-third of the urban population were believers. The attempt to eradicate belief appears to have been much less successful than the militants had expected. This report in *Antireligioznik*, which after a brief resurgence in 1937–38 had shrunk further in size and confidence,[224] conveys the frustration of the League's enthusiasts at the ambivalent attitude among local Soviet officials even before the outbreak of the Great Patriotic War. Once the country was in mortal danger of defeat, as we shall see in Volume II, the regime would seek a partial rapprochement with the Church, and anti-religious propaganda would temporarily be muted.

221 Fitzpatrick, *Stalin's Peasants* pp. 204–05.
222 Pospielovsky, *History of Marxist–Leninist Atheism and Soviet Anti-religious Policies* (Basingstoke 1987) p. 68.
223 Ibid., pp. 60–68.
224 J.S. Curtiss, *The Russian Church and the Soviet State, 1917–1950* (London 1965) p. 205.

Document 205 | **Elections to the soviets and the unmasking of churchmen— from an article by P. Efimov**

May 1938

Churchmen try in every way to deceive the workers. They try to worm their way into the confidence of people working for the village soviet or proclaim themselves friends of Soviet power so as to play their snake-like tricks more easily. That is what churchmen did in the Dedovichi region of Leningrad *oblast'*. In the Yaskov village soviet the priest of Trinity Church sent a letter to the village soviet fawningly thanking Soviet power for allowing him to vote and offering his help in explaining electoral law to the 'laymen' of his parish.

Some of the people in village soviets just do not realize that there are a lot of sworn enemies of our socialist construction hiding among churchmen and sectarian preachers. For example, in the Kayasula region of Dagestan, Ibadulaev, the chairman of Tuluy village soviet, entrusted Abdullah Salakhov, the local mullah, with the job of explaining *The Decree on Elections to the Supreme Soviet of the USSR*. In a number of conversations the mullah advised his audience to elect former kulaks and mullahs because they were 'the most literate'.

Some people in the soviets have been stupid enough to entrust churchmen with carrying out various public functions. For example, in the Dal'nekonstantinovsk region of Gor'ky *oblast'*, Sarlet, the village priest, duped the village soviet so effectively that they let him set up a defence-loan subscription scheme among the villagers.

I discovered from a correspondent in Mineral'nye Vody that a sexton, Fedorkin, lives in electoral district No. 7. Berfel'd, the chairman of the constituency electoral commission, came to trust this Fedorkin. He decided that Fedorkin, as an activist, could organize a pre-election meeting, and entrusted him with informing the citizens about this pre-election meeting. The wives of the workers proved to be much better at political vigilance. They said outright that this was a lapse in revolutionary vigilance. Instead of correcting his political mistake immediately, the chairman of the constituency electoral commission comrade Berfel'd stuck to his guns, saying, 'A priest has got voting rights. Why shouldn't we let the sexton do something in the district? What's wrong with that?'

[Source: *Antireligioznik* No. 5, 1938, pp. 15–16.]

Documents

Dramatis Personae:
Biographical Index

Aleksandrov (Mormonenko), Grigoriy Vasil'evich (1903–1983). Film producer, in agitprop in civil war, worked with Eisenstein 1920s and 1930s. Produced popular musicals and propaganda films. | 341

Aleksandrovich, P. (Dmitrievsky, V.A.) (1884–1918). Worker, internationalist SR during war, one of the Left SR leaders 1917–18. Deputy chairman of All-Russian Cheka 1918, involved in Left SR rising 6 July 1918. Executed without trial 7 July 1918. | 117

Alekseev, Mikhail Vasil'evich (1857–1918). General, professional soldier. Commanded various fronts in WWI, August 1915 appointed Chief of Staff of Commander-in-Chief. February 1917 helped persuade Nicholas to abdicate. 11 March 1917–22 May 1917 Commander-in-Chief. 1 September 1917 arrested Kornilov although sympathized with him. Formed anti-Red armies straight after October 1917. Died of heart disease. | 11, 120

Aleksey (Romanov, Aleksey Nikolaevich) (1904–1918). Tsarevich, executed by Cheka with rest of his family. | 12

Aleksiy. Archbishop of Khuta, 1927. | 256

Algasov (Burdakov), Vladimir Aleksandrovich (1887–1938). SR from 1905. Leading SR in Khar'kov after February 1917, one of the founders of the Left SRs. Elected to VTsIK at 2nd Soviet Congress. People's Commissar without portfolio December 1917–March 1918. Joined RKP(b) September 1918. In 1920s and 1930s higher education lecturer. Arrested and shot 1938. | 72, 88

Alkin, Ilias Said-Gireevich (1895–1937). Tatar politician. During WWI Menshevik, later SR. Chaired All-Russia Muslim Military Council 1917, supported Provisional Government. Elected to Constituent Assembly from Kazan'. Opposed Soviet power, supported Komuch, chaired its Ufa congress September 1918. Went over to Soviet side with Bashkir government, February 1919, joined RKP(b). Thereafter in academic work. Arrested and shot 1937. | 113

Anatoliy (Grisyuk, Andrey Grigor'evich) (1880–1938). Bishop and Archbishop of

Samara, 1922–24. Imprisoned on Solovki 1924–27. Shot 1938. | 256

Andreev. Academician, victimized in 'Academicians' Case', 1929–30 | 343

Andreev, Andrey Andreevich (1895–1971). Metalworker, Bolshevik from 1914, participant in October 1917 rising in Petrograd. Thereafter held numerous party and trade-union posts. In 1931 deputy chair of Sovnarkom, People's Commissar of Worker-Peasant Inspectorate, chair of CPSU CCC. | 281, 283

Andryukov. Urals labour camp administrator, 1930s. | 297

Antipov, Nikolay Kirillovich (1894–1938). Worker, joined Bolsheviks 1912. In Petrograd 1917, involved in factory committees and seizure of power in October. Involved in running Petrograd Cheka 1918–19, then held various trade-union and party posts. On CC from 1924. Ran Urals CP committee 1925. On Central Control Commission Presidium 1931–34. Arrested 1937, shot 1938. | 320

Antonov, Aleksandr Stepanovich (1889–1922). SR from around 1905, peasant leader. Involved in SR fighting organization, imprisoned 1909–17 for attempted assassination. Headed police in Kirsanov *uezd*, Tambov *guberniya* 1917–18. Organized armed peasant uprising in Tambov against Bolsheviks 1918–22. Killed in combat. | 139

Antonov-Ovseenko, Vladimir Aleksandrovich (1884–1939). Revolutionary from 1901, Menshevik from 1903, joined Bolsheviks May 1917. Participant in October 1917 rising in Petrograd. With Red Army throughout civil war, also involved in food requisitioning and suppression of Tambov rising 1921–22. In diplomatic posts from 1925, Soviet consul in Barcelona 1936–37. Arrested and shot. | 60

Arakcheev, Aleksey Andreevich (1769–1834). Count, General of Artillery, counsellor to Tsar Aleksandr I. Notorious for founding 'military settlements'—villages run on strict military lines. | 362

Argunov, Andrey Aleksandrovich (1866–1939). Revolutionary from 1890s, SR. Founder and editor of *Revolyutsionnaya Rossiya* from 1901. SR CC member from 1905. Several years in emigration or underground in Russia. Defencist in war, returned to Russia April 1917, sided with right wing of SRs. Involved in Provisional All-Russian Government autumn 1918. Arrested by Kolchak, exiled abroad, died in Prague. | 112

Arkhipov, I.M. Moscow Trotskyist, 1927. | 210–12

Astrov, Nikolay Ivanovich (1868–1934). Lawyer, judge, among founders and leaders of Kadet party. Worked for 1st and 2nd Duma. Among leaders of wartime Union of Cities. Mayor of Moscow March–June 1917. Attempted mediation between Kerensky and Kornilov September 1917. Worked in White Guard civil and political administration in South Russia 1918–20. Emigrated 1920. Died in Prague. | 107–08

Austrina. Kremlin telegram encoder, 1920s. | 251

Avanesov, Varlaan Aleksandrovich (Martirosov, Suren Karpovich) (1884–1930). Son of peasant, revolutionary from 1901, Social Democrat from 1903, Bolshevik from 1914. Studied medicine at Zurich. In Moscow and Petrograd Soviets 1917, elected to VTsIK October 1917, secretary and Presidium member 1917–19. Held various government, Cheka and economic posts in 1920s | 93

Avksent'ev, Nikolay Dmitrievich (1878–1943). SR leader. In Petrograd Soviet 1905, exiled north of Arctic Circle, escaped abroad 1907. Favoured legal party work and abandonment of terrorism. Defencist in war, returned to Russia after February 1917, chaired All-Russia Soviet of Peasant Deputies. July–September 1917 Minister of Internal Affairs. Member of 'Provisional All-Russia Government' in Ufa, 1918. Deposed by Kolchak, emigrated. | 107–08, 11

Bakhvalov. GPU agent, interrogated N. A. Berdyaev 1922. | 226–27

Bal'yan. Member of Andreev's commission on kulaks, 1931. | 283

Balzac, Honoré de (1799–1850). French novelist, noted for his originality, imagination and observation. | 218

Bazarov (Rudnev), Vladimir Aleksandrovich (1874–1939). Philosopher, translator, journalist and economist. Social Democrat from 1895. Bolshevik 1904–17, thereafter Social Democrat internationalist, non-party from 1918. Leader-writer on *Novaya zhizn'* 1917–18. Gosplan economist 1921–30. Arrested 1930 in connection with Menshevik trial, not tried. Died of natural causes. | 57, 346–47

Belen'ky, Abram Yakovlevich (1882–1941). Social Democrat from 1902, Bolshevik, in emigration 1904–17. In Cheka and successors from December 1917. Organized personal protection of political leadership. Arrested 1938, shot 1941. | 320

Beloborodov. RKP(b) functionary in the Don region, 1919. | 128

Belyakov. Member of Petrograd Bolshevik military organization, 1917. | 26

Berdyaev, Nikolay Aleksandrovich (1874–1948). Philosopher, attracted to Marxism as student, then turned to Christian 'mystical realism'. Contributor to *Vekhi*, blamed intelligentsia for Russia's 'spiritual crisis'. Welcomed fall of Tsarism, but then believed revolution being usurped by narrow class interests and urge towards social levelling. Expelled 1922. | 215–16, 224–29, 231

Berfel'd. Chairman of Mineral'nye Vody electoral commission, district No. 7, 1938. | 399

Beria, Lavrentiy Pavlovich (1899–1953). Party and state official, secret police chief. Bolshevik from 1917 or 1919, active in Caucasus. In secret police from 1921. First secretary of Georgian CP 1931–38. From 1938 head of NKVD. Arrested 26 June 1953, sentenced to death and shot. | 386

Bernstein, Eduard (1850–1932). German Social Democrat from 1871, Marxist theorist, journalist, Reichstag deputy 1902–06, 1912–18 and 1920–28. His critical analysis of Marx made him founder of 'revisionism'. Voted against war credits 1915, joined USPD, returned to SPD 1920. | 64

Bestuzhev-Ryumin, Konstantin Nikolaevich (1829–1897). Academician, historian, founded women's higher education ('Bestuzhev') courses in St Petersburg, 1878. | 98

Bitsenko (née Kameristaya), Anastasiya Alekseevna (1875–1938). SR from 1902, involved in assassination of General Sakharov. Released from prison 3 March 1917. In Soviet politics in Chita, then Moscow. Left SR, took part in Brest–Litovsk negotiations and Moscow local government 1918. Involved in Left SR rising July 1918. Late 1918 split from Left SRs into Party of Revolutionary Communism. Then joined RKP(b). Worked in Commissariat of Agriculture. Arrested and shot 1938. | 80

Bogdanov (Malinovsky), Aleksandr Aleksandrovich (1873–1928). Doctor, philosopher, scientist, journalist, economist, political activist. Social Democrat from 1896, Bolshevik 1904–09. Created original philosophical system 'empiriomonism'. Ally of Lenin to 1908, then split over political and philosophical differences. Developed organizational theory 'tektology'. Mobilized doctor in WWI, non-factional internationalist. Opposed Bolshevik seizure of power, helped organize *Proletkul't* cultural movement from 1917. Founded Blood Transfusion Institute 1926, died following experiment on self. | 68–70, 234

Boldyrev, Vasiliy Georgievich (1875–1933). Professional soldier, White Guard General. Arrested after October 1917, but soon released. Involved in Ufa Directory 1918, commanded its armed forces. Sent to Japan after Kolchak's takeover November 1918. Returned to Russia, amnestied 1923, worked in Siberian Planning Commission. Rearrested and shot 1933. | 107–08

Bonaparte, Charles Louis Napoléon (Napoleon III) (1808–1873). French politician, elected President 1848. Organized coup 1851 to become Emperor. Sought glory by material progress at home and aggression abroad. Captured at Sedan by Prussians 1870 and deposed. | 362

Bonch-Bruevich, Vladimir Dmitrievich (1873–1955). Social Democrat from 1895, Bolshevik from 1903. Worked legally in St Petersburg as publisher 1909–18. Active in February 1917 as journalist and in October as organizer. In Soviet administrative work until 1920, thereafter in academic work. | 88

Borisov, V. Correspondent for *Ural'skiy rabochiy*, 1929. | 394

Borodaevsky, Valerian Valerianovich (1874–1923). Poet. | 6

Brushvit, Ivan Mikhaylovich (1880–after 1956). SR, Constituent Assembly deputy from Samara, involved in *Komuch*. In SR emigration in Prague to 1946, when deported back to USSR and imprisoned until 1956. | 113

Bubnov, Andrey Sergeevich (1883–1938). Social Democrat from 1903, Bolshevik, organizer in industrial areas. On CC from 1917, involved in October seizure of power. Leftist until 1923, thereafter defender of Stalin. Held various party and Red Army posts. Wrote history of Bolsheviks. Arrested 1937, shot 1938. 25, | 320

Budberg, Aleksey Pavlovich (1869–1945). Professional soldier, White Guard General. Chief of Staff of 10th Army in WWI, then left Russia for Japan and Harbin, China. Fought with White armies 1919 and 1920. Thereafter active in White emigration. | 130

Budov, A.M. Anti-Stalin student, Donetsk, 1935. | 367

Bukharin, Nikolay Ivanovich (1888–1938). Journalist, economist, political activist. Social Democrat from 1906, Bolshevik. In emigration 1911–17, worked closely with Lenin. Editor of *Pravda* 1918–29, of *Izvestiya* 1934–37. Ally of Stalin 1923–28, then accused of 'right deviation' for opposing forced collectivization, removed from top CPSU and Comintern positions. Arrested 27 February 1937, main defendant in show trial March 1938. Shot. | 80, 206, 316, 324
—and campaign against Trotsky | 201–03, 208–09
—defeat by Stalin | 263–64, 266–67, 270–73, 275, 331, 337, 382–85
—and intelligentsia | 214, 234, 236–39, 331
—and NEP | 150, 166–71, 180
Bukharina, Nadezhda. N.I. Bukharin's first wife. | 382–83
Bukhvalov. Director of Zaikovo Machine Tractor Station, Urals, 1933. | 304
Bulat, I.L. Candidate CPSU CC member in 1930. | 320
Bulgakov, Mikhail Afanas'evich (1891–1940). Writer, satirist and dramatist. Published in private literary and trade-union press. Many works rejected by censors. Best known for satirical novel *The Master and Margarita*. | 344–45
Cagliostro, Count Alessandro (Balsamo, Giuseppe) (1743–1795). Conman, conjuror, from poor Sicilian background. Posed as count, miracle healer, sooth-sayer, etc., very successful in pre-revolutionary Paris society. | 362
Chakhotin, Sergey Stepanovich (1883–1974). Writer, professor, biologist. Participated in White movement, emigrated 1919, by 1921 in Berlin, partici-pated in *Smena vekh*. Worked in Soviet trade mission in Berlin, moved to France 1933, active against Hitler. Returned to USSR 1958, worked in Academy of Sciences. | 219, 226
Chamberlain, Sir Joseph Austen (1863–1937). British politician, MP 1892–1937. Initially Liberal, then Conservative. Chancellor of Exchequer 1919–21, Foreign Secretary 1924–29. | 257
Chayanov, Aleksandr Vasil'evich (1888–1937). Agronomist and agrarian economist, non-aligned socialist, advocate of peasant co-operation and agrarian reform. In food apparatus in WWI, after February 1917 active in government, soviet and co-operative food organs. Opposed Bolshevik seizure of power, but continued working in state and co-operative bodies. 1921–30 worked in Agriculture Commissariat and Gosplan. Denounced by Stalin, arrested 1930, shot 1937. | 233–34, 347, 350
Chaykovsky, Nikolay Vasil'evich (1850–1926). Narodnik from 1869, emigrated 1874, SR 1904–08. Returned to Russia 1907. After year in prison involved in non-party public organizations. On EC of Petrograd Soviet 1917, on its right wing. Opposed Bolshevik seizure of power, participated in various anti-Soviet governments and movements, emigrated again 1919. | 107–08
Chekhov, Anton Pavlovich (1860–1904). Author, playwright, leading exponent of realism in Russian literature. Trained as a doctor, and practised during 1880s. | 218

1st, 2nd and 4th Dumas. In 1917 on Menshevik CC, EC of Petrograd Soviet and VTsIK. Opened 2nd Soviet congress October 1917. From end 1917 led Mensheviks along with Yu.O. Martov. Imprisoned 1921–22, then exiled. Led Menshevik delegation abroad, one of the editors of *Sotsialisticheskiy vestnik*. Died in USA. | 52–53, 56, 61, 66, 135–36

Denikin, Anton Ivanovich (1872–1947). Professional soldier, General from 1916, in 1917 assistant to Chief of Staff at GHQ. Sympathized with Kornilov revolt, arrested. Helped form White 'volunteer' army in South Russia 1918, Commander-in-Chief from October. 'Supreme Ruler of the Russian State' from January 1920, emigrated April. | 114, 120, 134

Denisov, I.Kh. *Torgprom* member, 1920s. | 349

Didkovsky, Boris Vladimirovich (1883–1938). Geologist, political activist, Bolshevik from 1917, active in Urals. 1921–23 rector of newly founded Urals University. Then in Urals planning bureau, lecturer at Sverdlovsk Mining Institute, director of Urals Geological Trust. Denounced by G.E. Osipov, arrested. | 370–71

Dosov, Abulkhair. Deputy secretary of All-Russia TsIK, 1929. | 393

Dostoevsky, Fedor Mikhaylovich (1821–1881). Writer, most famous for *Crime and Punishment* (1866). First works published 1846, arrested 1849 for involvement in Petrashevtsy socialist circle, imprisoned and exiled to Siberia, later amnestied. Abandoned socialism for monarchism and Orthodoxy, argued Russia's uniqueness. | 215–16

Druzhinin, Vasiliy Grigor'evich (1859–1937). Historian, specialist on Orthodox Church schism. Corresponding member of Academy of Sciences from 1920. Purged 1929 in connection with 'Academicians' Case'. Arrested and released several times, disappeared. | 343

Dumbadze, Vladimir. On Georgian CP CC, 1922. | 186

Dutov, Aleksandr Il'ich (1879–1921). Professional soldier, Cossack leader. Chairman of All-Russia Cossack Congress June 1917, *ataman* (chieftain) of Orenburg *voysko* (Cossack community) from September. Commanded Orenburg Cossack troops in Kolchak's army 1918–19. Emigrated to China, killed there. | 71, 113

Dzerzhinsky, Feliks Edmundovich (1877–1926). From minor Polish nobility, Social Democrat from 1895, follower of Rosa Luxemburg. Mainly active in Poland, but exiled and imprisoned in Russia. Freed 1 March 1917 from Butyrki Prison by soldiers, active in Moscow and Petrograd. Helped organize Bolshevik seizure of power. From 7 December 1917 head of Cheka, organized Red Terror. Held other party and state posts, from 1924 also head of VSNKh, where favoured retaining NEP and defended non-party specialists. Died suddenly after speaking at CPSU CC meeting. | 25, 117, 173–74, 194, 206, 248–49

Eastman, Max (1883–1969). US journalist, socialist before WWI, wrote for *The Masses* 1912–18, then *The Liberator*. Favoured Trotsky in 1920s, translated his works. Became anti-communist in WWII, McCarthyite in 1950s. | 208

Efimov, P. Writer in *Antireligioznik*, 1938. | 399

Ehrenburg, Il'ya Grigorevich (1891–1967). Writer and journalist. Took part in 1905 events in Moscow, joined social-democratic organization, imprisoned in 1908. In Paris 1908–17, mixed with artists, wrote for Russian press. Returned to Russia 1917, wrote for SR press, in Ukraine and Crimea 1918–20, thereafter in Moscow and abroad as correspondent. Reported on Spanish Civil War and WWII. | 388

Eisenstein, Sergey Mikhaylovich (1898–1948). Artist, film director. Worked in *Proletkul't* theatre 1920. Films include *Strike* (1925), *Battleship Potemkin* (1925) and *October* (1927). Lectured at state film institute. | 339, 341

Eliava, Shalva Zurabovich (1883–1937). Georgian revolutionary, Bolshevik from 1904. In 1905 revolution in Tblisi and Kutaisi. Exiled. In Vologda 1917, headed *guberniya* EC. In Moscow end 1918, then on eastern front, headed VTsIK Turkestan commission. 1921–30 on CPSU Caucasus bureau, held leading posts in Georgia and Transcaucasian Federation. In 1930s in economic work. | 186, 320

Engels, Friedrich (1820–1895). German socialist theoretician, economist and historian, collaborator with Karl Marx. | 54, 178

Enukidze, Avel' Safronovich (1877–1937). Georgian Bolshevik, joined RSDRP 1898. Worked on railways in Baku 1900, established Baku RSDRP and underground press. Active in numerous places. Conscripted 1916, in Petrograd February 1917, on Petrograd Soviet and EC. Secretary of VTsIK Presidium 1918–35, held other party and state posts. Noted for debauched lifestyle, expelled from CPSU 1935, arrested and shot 1937. | 186, 224, 286, 288, 320, 367

Eremek. Camp prisoner, Urals, 1930s. | 297

Ermakov. Urals *oblast'* Corrective Labour Administration deputy director, OGPU plenipotentiary, 1930s. | 296–97

Ermirov. Worker at Il'ich factory, 1928. | 334

Eshba, Efrem Alekseevich (1893–1939). Caucasian Bolshevik from 1914, in Sukhumi party and soviet organizations 1917–18. Responsible for party work among Caucasus mountain peoples from 1918. Imprisoned in Menshevik Georgia 1919–20, secretary of Georgian CP 1922–24. Sympathized with Trotsky, expelled from CPSU 1927, readmitted 1928. In 1930s CPSU secretary in Chechnya. Arrested 1936, shot 1939. | 186

Evdokimov, Efim Georgievich (1891–1940). Party activist, secret policeman. Anarcho-syndicalist from 1911, in RKP(b) from 1918. In Red Army 1918, joined Cheka 1919. Specialized in rooting out subversive organizations. Oversaw investigation and trial of alleged sabotage group in Shakhty 1928. On CPSU CC from 1934, arrested 1938, shot 1940. | 202, 283, 289–90, 337–38

Evlogiy (Georgievsky, Vasiliy Semenovich) (1868–1946). Churchman and public figure. Bishop of Lublin 1902, Archbishop of Kholm 1912, of Volynya 1914. In 2nd and 3rd Dumas. Emigrated 1920, in charge of all Russian Orthodox churches in western Europe. Joined Supreme Monarchist Council at conference in Berlin 1921. | 257

Eydenov. Moscow CPSU member, attacked Trotskyist demonstration, 1927. | 211

Ezerskaya (Vol'f), Romana Davidovna (1899–1937). Secretary to Cheka and GPU presidiums 1921–23, then in other GPU and CPSU jobs. Shot. | 227

Ezhov, Nikolay Ivanovich (1895–1940). Worker's son, worked in factories and workshops in western Russia, at Putilov works 1914–15, conscripted. In Vitebsk 1917, joined Bolsheviks. Held Red Army political posts in civil war. Held numerous local party administrative positions 1920s. CPSU CC candidate 1930–34, full member 1934–39. Commissar for Internal Affairs 26 September 1936 to 25 November 1938—period of greatest repression. Arrested 1939, shot 1940. | 359, 370, 372, 374, 379, 381–82, 386, 397

Fedokin. Sexton, Mineral'nye Vody, 1938. | 399

Fedorovich, Florian Florianovich (1877–1928). SR from 1902, on SR CC from 1917, Constituent Assembly deputy from Penza, in *Komuch* 1918, opposed Kolchak's coup, Chairman of Irkutsk 'Political Centre' 1920. Arrested 1921, sentenced in SR show trial 1922. In internal exile from 1926. | 113

Figatner, Yuriy Petrovich (Yakov Isaakovich) (1889–1937). Bolshevik from 1903, abroad 1906–09. Arrested in Moscow 1909, released 1917. Chaired Kislovodsk Soviet 1917, after October held party posts in Caucasus, then Siberia. Organized 'Academicians' Case' purge of Academy of Sciences, 1930. On Andreev commission on kulaks 1931. Arrested and shot 1937. | 283, 341–43

Filipp. Archbishop of Zvenigorod, 1927. | 256

Flakserman, Galina K. Bolshevik, worked in Bolshevik CC secretariat 1917. Wife of N.N. Sukhanov. | 346–47

Flaubert, Gustave (1821–1880). French realist novelist, author of *Madame Bovary* (1857). | 218

Fomin, Nil Valerianovich (1890–1918). SR journalist and politician, Constituent Assembly deputy from Eniseysk, member of *Komuch*, killed in custody by Kolchak supporters after coup, 23 November 1918. | 113

Fotieva, Lidiya Aleksandrovna (1881–1975). Bolshevik from 1904. After October 1917 secretary to Sovnarkom, Council of Labour and Defence, and Lenin. Worked in Lenin Museum from 1938. | 155, 222, 232

France, Anatole (Thibault, Jacques Anatole) (1844–1924). Prolific French novelist, seen as continuing tradition of French eighteenth century. | 218

Fredericks, Vladimir Borisovich (1838–1927). Baron, count from 1908. Long military career, thereafter in court, assistant to Nicholas II. Signed abdication papers 2 March 1917. Permitted to leave Russia 1924. | 12

Frenkel', Zakhariy Grigor'evich (1869–1970). Doctor, academic, publicist, political activist. On CC of Kadet party 1906–17. Mainly concerned with public health, continued working in that sphere until 1953. | 40–41

Frinovsky, Mikhail Petrovich (1898–1940). Red Guard in 1917, Bolshevik from 1918, made career in secret police and armed forces from 1919. Deputy Commissar for Internal Affairs 16 October 1936 to 8 September 1938, Commissar

state positions until 1972. | 329

Gorky, Maksim (Peshkov, Aleksey Maksimovich) (1868–1936). Writer, political activist. Orphaned in childhood. In Narodnik circles from 1884. Engaged in revolutionary propaganda. Published short stories and plays from 1890s. Associated with Social Democrats 1900s, financed newspapers, raised funds. In Italy 1906–13. Internationalist in WWI, founded *Novaya zhizn'* 1917. Very critical of Bolsheviks 1917–18, then more favourable. In Italy 1921–33, then returned to USSR. Wrote in defence of Stalin regime. | 67–68, 356–57

Gorshenin, Konstantin Petrovich (1907–1978). Lawyer, academic and politician. In Komsomol and soviet work from 1927, in CPSU from 1930. Headed various law schools. RSFSR Justice Commissar 1940–43, USSR Procurator from 1943, USSR Justice Minister from 1948. From 1956 again headed law schools. | 329–30

Gots, Abram Rafailovich (1882–1940). Revolutionary from 1896, SR leader. In SR Fighting Organization from 1906, imprisoned for eight years from 1907. 'Siberian Zimmerwaldist' in WWI. On Petrograd Soviet EC from March 1917, led SR faction. After October chaired Committee to Save the Motherland and Revolution, advocated armed resistance to Bolsheviks. Defendant in 1922 SR trial, death sentence commuted to five years. Frequently arrested, died in camp 1940. | 66

Gregory VII (Hildebrand) (d. 1085). Catholic cleric-politician of humble origins, very powerful by 1050s, appointed Pope 1073. Zealous reformer, energetically promoted clerical celibacy, advocated crusades against Turks. Received capitulation of Henry IV at Canossa, 1077. Canonized in 1728. | 219

Grigor'ev, N.A. (Servetnik, Nikifor?) (1878–1919). Army officer in WWI. In civil war formed own band in Ukraine, which changed sides several times. Noted for brutal anti-Semitism and pogroms. Finally went over to anarchist Makhno, who shot him. | 131–32, 292

Grimm, David Davidovich (1864–1941). Professor of law, journalist, political activist. Held posts at St Petersburg and Khar'kov universities. Prominent in Kadet party. April–July 1917, deputy education minister. Emigrated after 1919, continued academic career in Prague and Tartu. | 40

Groman, Vladimir Gustavovich (1874–1932?). Economist, statistician, political activist. Social Democrat from mid-1890s, Menshevik. Became zemstvo statistician when exiled from St Petersburg. Union of Cities economist in WWI. In Soviet food apparatus from March 1917, advocate of strict state monopoly and regulation. From 1921, leading Gosplan economist. Opposed Stalin's rapid industrialization. Arrested 1930, in 'Menshevik' show trial 1931. | 348, 350

Grum-Grzhimaylo, Vladimir Efimovich (1864–1928). Industrial metallurgist, mining engineer, worked in Urals steelworks from 1885. Appointed lecturer 1907 and professor 1911 at St Petersburg Polytechnical Institute. Hostile to Bolshevism, but remained in Russia after 1917 as leading metallurgist. | 174–75, 335–36

Guchkov, Aleksandr Ivanovich (1862–1936). Major capitalist, among founders in 1905 of 'Union of 17 October', party chief from 1906. Elected member of State Council, chaired 3rd State Duma for a year. Headed Central War Industries Committee from summer 1915. Involved in conspiracies against Nicholas II from autumn 1916. War and Naval Minister in 1st Provisional Government to 30 April 1917. After October, subsidized and backed White armies. Died in France. | 9

Gukasov, Abram Osipovich (1858–?). Oil magnate, head of several major oil companies before 1917. Then in emigration, active in *Torgprom*, published newspaper *Vozrozhdenie*. | 349

Haase, Hugo (1863–1919). German SPD leader, lawyer. Reichstag deputy 1897–1907 and 1912–19. Opposed WWI, but initially followed party line voting for war credits. Co-founder 1917 of USPD. Fatally wounded by lunatic 1919. | 64

Henry IV (1050–1106). King of Germany, Holy Roman Emperor from c.1070–1108. Conflicted with Pope Gregory VII over appointment of bishops, capitulated at Canossa 1077. | 219

Hermogen (Dolganov, Georgiy Efremovich) (1858–1918). Churchman. Bishop from 1901. Noted for Black Hundred views, opposed church liberalization. Quarrelled with Rasputin 1912, tried to exclude him from court. Appointed Bishop of Tobol'sk, 8 March 1917. In secret contact with Tsar's family after October. Led religious processions against Soviet government, Tobolsk, April 1918, arrested. Drowned by Reds in civil war. | 123

Herostratus. Ephesian arsonist, burned down Temple of Artemis 356 BC to ensure historical immortality. | 362

Herzen, Aleksandr Ivanovich (1812–1870). Russian writer and revolutionary. Utopian socialist in 1830s, first exiled in 1834 to Perm' and Vyatka. Leading 'westernizer', disputed with 'Slavophiles', although believed Russian socialism would be based on peasant commune. Published exile literature *Polyarnaya zvezda* and journal *Kolokol* in London 1850s. Inspired numerous younger revolutionaries. | 218

Hitler, Adolf (1889–1945). Ideologist and leader of German National Socialism, dictator of Germany 1933–45. | 373–74, 384

Ibadulaev. Chairman of Tuluy village soviet, Dagestan, 1938. | 399

Il'enkov, Vasiliy Pavlovich (1897–1967). Noted Soviet writer of proletarian origin. | 313

Ioffe, Adol'f Abramovich (1883–1927). Political activist, publicist, doctor, diplomat. Joined RSDRP 1902. Spent time abroad in medical training. Worked with Trotsky in Vienna from 1908, became firm ally. In Russian prison or exile in WWI, opposed war. Joined Bolsheviks July 1917 with *Mezhrayontsy*, held Soviet and party posts. In Brest peace talks, supported Trotsky. Ambassador to Germany April–November 1918, then held series of party, state and diplomatic posts. Shot self in protest at Trotsky's expulsion from CPSU. | 80

Bolshevik from 1903. Leading Bolshevik in Petrograd from March 1917, initially opposed Lenin's April Theses. Favoured all-socialist coalition government November 1917. In Brest–Litovsk negotiations 1918. In party and state work thereafter. 1922–24 formed bloc with Zinoviev and Stalin against Trotsky. From 1925 in opposition to Stalin, defeated and expelled from party 1927. Readmitted and expelled twice more. Arrested December 1934, falsely charged with complicity in Kirov murder. In show trial August 1936, shot. | 57–58, 65–66, 122, 178, 198, 201–02, 205–07, 210–12, 266, 273, 366, 370, 372

Karelin, Vladimir Aleksandrovich (1891–1938). SR from 1907, journalist. Among leaders of large leftist Khar'kov SR organization, 1917, elected chairman of Khar'kov City Duma. Elected to Presidium at 2nd All-Russia Soviet congress. Among leaders of Left SR party. December 1917–March 1918 held various positions in Sovnarkom, then left for Ukraine. After July 1918 in and out of prison, left politics 1921, although maintained contacts with other Left SRs. Arrested 1937, appeared as witness in Bukharin trial March 1938, shot September. | 72, 80

Karklin, Otto Yanovich (1875–1937). Latvian Social Democrat, lawyer, arrested and sentenced to 8 years' hard labour 1908. After 1917 on revolutionary tribunals, member of USSR Supreme Court, 1920s. | 252

Karsky. Priest in Urals, 1929, allegedly former White Guard officer. | 391

Kartashev, Anton Vladimirovich (1875–1960). Theologian, public figure, political activist. From 1909 chairman of St Petersburg Religious–Philosophical Society. Joined Kadets early 1917. In 2nd coalition Provisional Government as Procurator of Holy Synod, then Minister of Faiths, declared Synod autonomous. Supported Kornilov. After October supported Whites, moved to Finland 1919, then in emigration. | 40–41, 53

Kaufman, Aleksandr Arkad'evich (1864–1919). Economist, statistician, public figure. In 1880s–90s studied peasant economy in Siberia. Helped devise Kadet party agrarian programme 1905. Believed peasant commune was viable, but did not idealize it. On Kadet CC in 1917, after October worked in Soviet statistical institutions. | 40–41

Kautsky, Karl (1854–1938). German Social Democrat, politician, theoretician, among most authoritative leaders of 2nd International. Editor of *Neue Zeit*. Ceased voting for war credits in Reichstag 1916, split from SPD with others 1917 to form Independent SPD (USPD). Regarded by Bolsheviks as 'centrist', i.e., between reformism and revolution. | 64

Kedrov, Mikhail Sergeevich (1878–1941). Social Democrat from 1901, Bolshevik. Active in various parts of European Russia. Supplied arms to Moscow insurgents 1905. In Switzerland 1912–16. In 1917 in Bolshevik military organization, Petrograd, edited *Soldatskaya pravda*. After October in military work, from 1918 in Cheka, from 1919 on its collegium. Noted for harshness. Thereafter combined secret police, Supreme Court and economic responsibilities. Arrested 1939, acquitted by court 1941, shot on Beria's instruction. | 25

Kerensky, Aleksandr Fedorovich (1881–1970). Lawyer, journalist, politician. Sympathized with SRs 1905. Made name as defence lawyer in political trials. Elected to 4th Duma 1912, led *Trudovik* group. Joined Provisional Government as Justice Minister 2 March 1917. May–September 1917 Army and Naval Minister, Prime Minister from 8 July 1917, Commander-in-Chief from 30 August 1917. Overthrown by Bolsheviks, emigrated 1918. | 8–10, 33, 37–38, 42–49, 51–52, 56–57, 59, 61, 64–65, 67, 107, 233, 237

Kerzhentsev (Lebedev), Platon Mikhaylovich (1881–1940). Bolshevik from 1904, deputy to 1st Duma, in emigration 1912–18. Returned to Soviet Russia, worked on *Izvestiya*, headed Soviet news agency ROSTA 1919–20. In foreign commissariat and diplomatic work 1920s, also in literary, cultural and censorship bodies 1920s and 1930s. Advocated scientific organization of labour; headed government body to promote this 1923–25. | 160–61

Khitrov. Member of Petrograd Bolshevik military organization, 1917. | 25

Khlestakov. Hero of Gogol's *Government Inspector*, boorish conman who pretends to be a government official to borrow money from gullible townsfolk. | 362

Kirov (Kostrikov), Sergey Mironovich (1886–1934). Social Democrat from 1904, Bolshevik. In Vladikavkaz, 1917, displayed great political flexibility. Replaced Zinoviev as head of Leningrad CPSU 1926. Very popular within CPSU, assassinated 1934 in dubious circumstances. | 186, 202, 341–42, 365–67, 375

Kiselev, Aleksey Semenovich (1879–1937). Textile worker, joined RSDRP 1898, Bolshevik. Active in various parts of European Russia, arrested several times. Lived underground in Siberia 1914–17. Chaired Ivanovo–Voznesensk Soviet 1917. After October held various party, state and trade-union posts. Headed textile syndicate 1918, on VSNKh Presidium. Candidate party CC member 1917–19, 1921–23 and 1925–34. Arrested and shot 1937. | 320

Kitaev, G.G. Alleged former White Guard, named by G.E. Osipov, 1936. | 371

Kizevetter, Aleksandr Aleksandrovich (1866–1933). Historian, academic, among founders of Kadets and CC member. Active in journalism and Kadet politics 1917–18. Arrested several times by Bolshevik authorities, deported 1922. | 229

Klembovsky, Vladislav Napoleonovich. Professional soldier, General of infantry, Chief of Staff spring 1917, later in Red Army, dismissed in Soviet–Polish War for unreliability. | 43–44

Knorin, Vil'gel'm Georgievich (1890–1938). Peasant's son, worked as shepherd as boy. Revolutionary from 1905, Bolshevik from 1910. Active in St Petersburg and Baltic provinces. In Minsk 1917, secretary of Minsk Soviet EC. After October in Soviet and party work in Belorussia and Lithuania. Secretary of CP Belorussia central bureau 1920–22. Then in CPSU propaganda, educational and Comintern work. On CC from 1927. Arrested and shot 1938. | 320

Koestler, Arthur (1905–1983). Hungarian-born novelist and journalist. Zionist in 1920s, German communist in 1930s, captured by Franco's forces in Spain, wrote

Spanish Testament (1937). Broke with communism, wrote *Darkness at Noon*, based on Moscow show trials of 1930s. Thereafter largely concerned with philosophy and mysticism. | 382

Kogan. Member of Andreev commission on kulaks, 1931. | 283

Kokoshkin, Fedor Fedorovich (1871–1918). Law professor, among initiators of Kadet party, member of 1st Duma. Held various posts in Provisional Government. Imprisoned after October, murdered by sailors 6 January 1918. | 40, 42

Kolchak, Aleksandr Vasil'evich (1873–1920). Tsarist Admiral, former commander of Black Sea Fleet. Took supreme power in Siberia in coup 18 November 1918. Organized White army, controlled all Siberia and Urals early 1919. Pushed back by Reds from May. January 1920 captured near Irkutsk, shot February. | 110–15, 120, 130–31, 134

Kollontai (née Domontovich), Aleksandra Mikhaylovna (1872–1952). Revolutionary from 1890s, Social Democrat. Particularly involved in educating women workers. Sided with Mensheviks 1906–15, thereafter Bolshevik. In exile in Germany, Sweden, Norway 1908–17. Returned to Petrograd March 1917. Drafted family law reforms of early Soviet government. Generally took leftist positions within Bolshevik party. From early 1920s in diplomatic work. | 30, 89

Komarov, Nikolay Pavlovich (Sobinov, Fedor Evgen'evich) (1886–1937). Worker, son of landless peasant, Bolshevik from 1909. Headed factory committee in Petrograd 1917. After October in military defence of Petrograd and Cheka. Organized suppression of Kronstadt revolt, 1921. Chaired Leningrad party committee and *guberniya* soviet EC 1926–29. Full CPSU CC member 1921–22, 1923–30; candidate 1922–23, 1934–37. Arrested and shot. | 320

Kondrat'ev, Nikolay Dmitrievich (1892–1938). Economist, agronomist, sociologist and political activist. SR 1905–19. Participated in February 1917 events, involved in Soviet and government food distribution bodies. Hostile to Bolshevik seizure of power, but worked in Soviet Commissariat of Agriculture after leaving SRs. In 1920s headed Conjuncture Institute and devised economic plans to revive agriculture. Arrested on false charges 1930, shot 1938. | 347–48, 350

Konovalov, Aleksandr Ivanovich (1875–1948). Manufacturer of cotton goods, politician. Belonged to Progressivist party in 4th Duma, critic of Nicholas's regime during war. Minister of Trade and Industry 2 March to 18 May and 25 September to 25 October 1917. Pessimistic about economic and military prospects 1917, favoured separate peace. Emigrated to France 1918, active in émigré circles. | 9–10

Konstantin. Bishop of Sumy, head of Khar'kov diocese 1927. | 256

Korets, Moisey Abramovich. Physicist, co-author of anti-Stalin leaflet, imprisoned 1935 and 1938–53, later worked on journal *Priroda*. | 384

Kornilov, Lavr Georgievich (1870–1918). Cossack, career soldier, General. Served in Central Asia and Russo-Japanese war. Commanded frontline infantry divisions from 1914. Captured 1915, famed in Russia after daring escape 1916.

Commander of Petrograd military district March–May 1917. Commander-in-Chief from 19 July 1917. Favoured restoring army discipline and reintroducing capital punishment. Led confused revolt against Provisional Government end August 1917, arrested. Escaped November 1917, helped form first White army. Killed in action. | 42–48, 54–56

Korolev. Moscow CPSU member, attacked Trotskyist demonstration 1927. | 211

Kosarev, Aleksandr Vasil'evich (1903–1939). Komsomol official, worker's son. Joined Komsomol 1918, RKP(b) 1919. Volunteer in civil war, then in various leading Komsomol posts, including general secretary 1929–38. On CPSU CC as candidate 1930–34, full member 1934–38. Arrested 1938, shot 1939. | 320

Kostyunenkos. Peasants in Nekrasovo village, 1917. | 97

Kozintsev, Grigoriy (1905–1973). Film producer, most noted for production of *Hamlet*. Among those who passed resolution on culture, 1928. | 341

Krasikov, Petr Anan'evich (1870–1939). Revolutionary from 1892, Social Democrat, Bolshevik from 1903, arrested several times. Studied law at St Petersburg, barrister. After October 1917 in Soviet justice system, helped draft first penal code. Involved in combating organized religion. From 1924 USSR Supreme Court procurator, 1933–38 deputy chairman. | 350–51

Krasin, Leonid Borisovich (1870–1926). Electrical engineer, Social Democrat from 1890, Bolshevik c. 1905–12. Involved in illegal party fundraising, accused by Lenin of embezzlement 1909. From 1913 head of Siemens and Schuckert's enterprises in Russia. Returned to Bolsheviks after October 1917. Held various leading posts in Soviet economic and foreign trade apparatus. | 150

Krasnov, Petr Nikolaevich (1869–1947). Professional soldier, journalist, monarchist, counter-revolutionary. Distinguished officer in WWI. Took part in Kornilov revolt 1917. Supported Kerensky against Bolsheviks October 1917. Arrested but released. Raised Don Cossack army 1918. Emigrated. Collaborated with Nazis in WWII, formed anti-Soviet Cossack bands. Captured 1945, hanged 1947. | 120

Krinitsky, Aleksandr Ivanovich (1894–1937). Bolshevik from 1915, in Tver' 1917. From 1918 Red Army political worker. Early 1920s held series of medium-level party jobs. Headed Belorussia CP from 1925, CPSU agitprop department 1926–29. Candidate CC member from 1924, full member from 1934. Arrested and shot 1937. | 320

Krupskaya (Ul'yanova), Nadezhda Konstantinovna (1869–1939). Daughter of army officer, Marxist from 1890, agitated amongst St Petersburg workers. Married Lenin 1898, assisted him throughout political life. Exiled 1898–1901, in emigration 1901–05 and 1907–17. Secretary of RSDRP CC 1905–07. Studied western European education methods. After October 1917 involved in education commissariat, literacy campaigns and library censorship. Conflicted with Stalin 1922–23, supported opposition 1925, thereafter loyal. | 97–99, 198, 205–07, 320

Krylenko, Nikolay Vasil'evich (1885–1938). Bolshevik from 1904, student leader

1905–08. Then teacher, in army, in exile until conscripted 1916. Involved in soldiers' committees, arrested after July Days, 1917. After October in military work, conserving army and helping build Red Army. Then in revolutionary tribunals and justice commissariat. USSR Procurator from 1928, involved in falsified economic show trials 1928–33. From 1936 USSR Commissar of Justice. Arrested and shot. | 124, 308–09, 341, 343

Krzhizhanovsky, Gleb Maksimovich (1872–1959). Engineer, economist, planner, songwriter. Marxist from 1891, arrested 1895. In prison and exile wrote 'Varshavyanka' and other revolutionary anthems. Involved in 2nd RSDRP congress 1903, abandoned politics after 1907 but occasionally assisted Bolsheviks. Returned to political activity 1917. In Soviet economic apparatus from 1918, headed GOELRO commission 1920 and Gosplan 1921–23 and 1925–30. On CPSU CC 1924–39. | 343

Kshesinskaya, Mariya-Matil'da Feliksovna (1872–1971). Ballerina, ballet teacher. Daughter of famous ballet master Feliks Kshesinsky. Performed at Mariinsky Theatre 1890–1917. Favourite of Nicholas II, who had palace built for her in Petersburg. Palace occupied by revolutionary soldiers early 1917, used by Bolsheviks and others. Emigrated to France 1920. | 29

Kubyak, Nikolay Afanas'evich (1881–1937). Worker's son. In RSDRP from 1898, Bolshevik. Active 1905–07, in prison and exile 1907–15. In 1917 chaired Sestoretsk Soviet. Head of Petrograd *guberniya* RKP(b) from 1918. Close ally of Zinoviev, helped organize Red Terror. In Far East 1922–26. On CPSU CC 1923–34, candidate 1934–37. Arrested and shot 1937. | 320

Kulikhins. Nekrasovo peasants, 1917. | 97

Kursky, Dmitriy Ivanovich (1874–1932). Studied law at Moscow University, joined RSDRP 1904, Bolshevik. In 1905 Moscow rising. Conscripted 1914, ensign. In 1917 chaired 4th army soldiers' soviet, October on Odessa Military-Revolutionary Committee. RSFSR justice commissar 1918–28, 1st Soviet Procurator-General. Ambassador to Italy from 1928. | 122

Kuskova (née Esipova), Ekaterina Dmitrievna (1869–1958). Political activist, journalist, educationalist. In study circles from 1885, involved with Narodnik revolutionaries, moved to Marxism 1890s. Married S.N. Prokopovich 1895. In 1899 set out views in so-called *Credo*, sharply criticized by Lenin. In Kadet circles 1905. Favoured co-operation of all left forces. Defencist in WWI. Opposed both Reds and Whites in civil war. Involved in famine relief 1921, expelled from Russia 1922. Active in émigré circles. | 233–34

Kutyuk. Senior camp orderly, Urals, 1930s. | 296

Kuybyshev, Valerian Vladimirovich (1888–1935). Joined RSDRP 1904, while at cadet school. Active in 1905, Bolshevik, arrested and exiled several times. Industrial worker in WWI, in Samara before 1917, headed Samara workers' soviet. Held numerous party and state posts after 1917, especially in economic apparatus. From 1924, supporter of Stalin. Headed VSNKh 1926–30, and

Lianozov, Stepan Georgievich (1872–1951). Oil magnate, organized syndicate to compete with other oil companies. Supported Whites, headed Yudenich's 'North-Western Government' 1919. Formed *Torgprom* with other exiles 1920 to defend the interests of Russian capitalists abroad. │ 257

Liber (Gol'dman), Mikhail Isaakovich (1880–1937). Bund leader from 1897, on RSDRP CC from 1907, Menshevik. Frequently arrested and exiled. Defencist during WWI. On Petrograd Soviet EC and VTsIK Presidium 1917. One of sharpest opponents of Bolsheviks among Menshevik leaders. Remained in Russia, arrested several times after 1923, shot 1937. │ 56

Liebknecht, Karl (1871–1919). German left Social Democrat, in SPD from 1900, Reichstag deputy 1912–16. First deputy to vote against war credits, December 1914. Imprisoned 1916 for organizing anti-war May Day demonstration. Involved with Independent SPD and Spartakusbund, one of the founders of the Communist Party of Germany, 1918. Murdered by officers following attempted rising, January 1919. 64, │ 82

Lipkin. Worker at Paris Commune factory, 1928. │ 354

Loboda, Fedosiy Matveevich. 'Resettled' former 'kulak', 1932. │ 291–94

Lockhart, Sir Robert Bruce (1887–1970). British civil servant, banker, journalist and diplomat. Vice-consul in Moscow 1915–17, special envoy to Soviet Russia 1918. Arrested 3 September 1918, released 1 October 1918 in exchange for M. Litvinov. │ 120–21

Lomov, A. (Oppokov, Georgiy Ippolitovich) (1888–1937). Bolshevik from 1903. Studied law at St Petersburg. In 1905 at Saratov, commanded RSDRP fighting detachment. In Moscow 1917, deputy chair of Moscow Soviet, on Military-Revolutionary Committee. First Commissar of Justice, 1917–18. Then mainly in economic work, in VSNKh and Gosplan. On CPSU CC 1927–34. Arrested and shot 1937. │ 320

Lunacharskaya, Anna Aleksandrovna (1883–1959). Wife of A.V. Lunacharsky, sister of A.A. Bogdanov. Author of several works of science fiction. │ 27–28, 60–61

Lunacharsky, Anatoliy Vasil'evich (1875–1933). Revolutionary from schooldays, Social Democrat from 1895. Studied in Zurich under positivist philosopher

Avenarius. Bolshevik from 1904, in emigration 1906–17. Fell out with Lenin over philosophy. Internationalist in WWI, rejoined Bolsheviks with *Mezhrayonka* 1917. In Petrograd City Duma, deputy mayor 1917. Education commissar 1917–29, founder of Soviet education system. Appointed ambassador to Spain 1933, died en route. | 27–29, 60–61, 68, 213, 221, 234, 236, 341, 343

Luxemburg, Rosa (1871–1919). German, Polish and international socialist, economist, theoretician, opponent of militarism and nationalism. Founder of Spartakusbund with Karl Liebknecht in WWI. Among founders of German CP end 1918. Killed by army officers following defeat of January 1919 rising. | 82

Luzyanin. Nizheturinsk camp assistant director of education, 1930s. | 297

L'vov, Georgiy Evgen'evich (1861–1925). Prince, landowner, zemstvo activist, Tolstoyan. In 1st Duma. Elected Moscow mayor 1913, vetoed by government. Organized Union of Towns and Zemstvos in WWI. Head of Provisional Government March–July 1917. Arrested February 1918, escaped to Omsk, then to USA, raised funds for White cause. | 9–10, 30

L'vov, Vladimir Nikolaevich (1872–1934). Landowner, politician, Octobrist, in 3rd and 4th Dumas. From 2 March 1917 Procurator of Holy Synod in Provisional Government. Involved in Kornilov affair as messenger between Kornilov and Kerensky. Emigrated after October, became *Smena vekh*-ist 1921. Returned to Russia 1922, in church administration, supported 'Renovationists'. Arrested 1927, exiled to Tomsk. Remained there until death. | 9–10, 43, 45–46

Lyapunov. Nizheturinsk camp director, 1930s. | 297

Lyubimov, Isidor Evstigneevich (1882–1937). In RSDRP from 1902, Bolshevik. In 1917 in Minsk and Ivanovo–Vosnesensk (mayor of latter city from August 1917). On Turkestan front in civil war, then in political and economic work in Ukraine. On VSNKh Presidium mid-1920s, light industry commissar 1932–37. CPSU CC candidate member 1925–27, full member 1927–37. | 320

Machiavelli, Niccolò (1469–1527). Florentine public servant and author, much decried for his perceptive analyses of political power. | 247

Makhno, Nestor Ivanovich (Bat'ko) (1888–1934). Son of peasant, anarchist communist from 1906. Active in home region of Gulyay–Pole, Ukraine. Robbed the rich. Imprisoned several times, including 1911–17 in Butyrki, where studied anarchist theory. On 23 March 1917 returned to Gulyay–Pole, where played dominant political role. After October organized armed band to fight Ukrainian Rada, Germans, Whites, Cossacks. Collaborated with Red Army against Whites, then clashed with Reds. Fought way out to Romania 1921, died in France. | 102–04, 131, 292

Makushin, A.I. (1856–1927). Doctor, banker, Kadet, 1st Duma deputy, CC member in 1917. | 40

Mal'kov, Pavel Dmitrievich (1887–1965). RSDRP member from 1904. Worked under Military Revolutionary Council direction in October 1917. Commandant of Smol'ny Institute 29 October 1917–March 1918, thereafter of Kremlin until

1920. | 59–60

Manuil'sky, Dmitriy Zakharovich (1883–1959). Social Democrat from 1903, participant in 1905 events, in emigration 1907–12 and 1913–17. Joined Bolsheviks with *Mezhrayonka* July 1917. After October in party and state work in Petrograd and Ukraine. On CPSU CC 1924–52, in Comintern apparatus 1922–43. | 320

Manuylov, Aleksandr Apollonovich (1861–1929). Journalist, economist, historian, academic, politician. Kadet from 1905, on CC. Rector of Moscow University 1908–11. Minister of Education in Provisional Government until July 1917. Soon after October declared willingness to work with Soviet power, worked in Commissariats of Finance, Agriculture and State Bank. | 9–10

Martov (Tsederbaum), Yuliy Osipovich (1873–1923). Political activist, writer, historian, Social Democrat from 1892, founder (1903) of Menshevik faction. In emigration 1901–05 and 1906–17. Internationalist during WWI. In 1917 on far left wing of Mensheviks, 1918–23 again central figure. On and off VTsIK 1917–19. Maintained principled criticism of Bolshevik policies. Allowed abroad 1920, died in Germany. | 51, 55, 61, 65, 124, 133–35, 206

Marx, Karl Heinrich (1818–1883). German socialist economist, sociologist, philosopher. Author of *Das Kapital*, ideological inspirer of social-democratic and communist movements. | 58, 164, 166, 216, 242, 339

Matsievich, Arseniy. Defrocked priest, 1920s. | 259

Maykovsky. White General, 1919. | 130

Mdivani, Budu Gurgenovich (1877–1937). Georgian, Bolshevik from 1903, active in Transcaucasia. On RKP(b) Caucasus bureau 1920–21. Head of Tiflis Revolutionary Committee and Transcaucasian Soviet Republic 1921–23. Then in diplomatic and economic work. Arrested. | 186, 192

Medvedev, Efim Grigor'evich (1886–1938). Mineworker, electrican, Social Democrat from 1904. In Khar'kov 1917, chairman of the All-Ukraine TsIK, December 1917–March 1918. Took part in Brest-Litovsk peace negotiations. Left Bolsheviks for Ukrainian Borot'bist party 1918. Arrested 1938. | 80

Mekhonoshin, Konstantin Aleksandrovich (1889–1938). Revolutionary from 1906, Bolshevik from 1913. In army from 1915, served in Petrograd. In Bolshevik military organization from April 1917. Arrested July, freed October. Involved in creating Red Army. Clashed with Stalin in civil war. Thereafter in military education, Red Sport International, and Gosplan. Arrested and shot 1937. | 25–26

Menzhinsky, Vyacheslav Rudol'fovich (1874–1934). Trained lawyer, in RSDRP from 1902, Bolshevik from 1903. Involved in 1905–07 events, then abroad until 1917. Helped organize Red Guard. Took part in October seizure of power, made Commissar of Finance, took over banks. Consul in Berlin 1918–19. In Cheka from 1919, deputy head 1923–26, then GPU/OGPU head until death. Involved in choreographing show trials 1928–33. | 25, 88, 348–50

Messing, Stanislav Adamovich (1889–1937). Polish revolutionary, Social Democrat from 1908, close to F.E. Dzerzhinsky and I.S. Unshlikht. In army in WWI. In

Moscow Cheka from end 1917, helped organize Red Terror. Prominent in GPU/OGPU to 1931, then in foreign-trade apparatus to 1937, when arrested and shot. | 231–32

Meyerhol'd(-Raykh), Vsevolod Emil'evich (1874–1940). Theatre producer. In Moscow Arts Theatre troupe from 1898, from 1902 organizing own company. Worked in leading St Petersburg theatres. In Crimea after 1917, arrested by Denikin. Creator and leader of new revolutionary theatre 1920–38. Theatre closed in 1938, Meyerhol'd arrested 1939. | 387–89

Mezhlauk, Valeriy Ivanovich (1893–1938). Ukrainian revolutionary, Menshevik 1907–17, then Bolshevik. Active in Khar'kov 1917. In civil war in Ukraine and Don, then in economic and transport work, planner in VSNKh and Gosplan. CPSU CC candidate member 1927–34, full member 1934–37. Arrested and shot. | 320, 336

Michael (Romanov, Mikhail Aleksandrovich) (1878–1918). Grand Duke, last Emperor of Russia (appointed 2 March 1917, abdicated 3 March1917), brother of Nicholas. Guards officer 1898–1911, commanded cavalry divisions in WWI. Arrested and shot 1918. | 342

Mikhaylov, P.Ya. Left Socialist-Revolutionary, People's Commissar 1917–18. | 72

Mikoyan, Anastas Ivanovich (1895–1978). Armenian revolutionary, Bolshevik from 1915. Only survivor of twenty-seven Baku commissars arrested 1918. Held numerous Soviet government posts, especially in economy and trade. After death of Stalin, loyal supporter of Khrushchev to 1964. On CPSU CC 1923–76, on Politburo 1935–66. | 271–73

Miller, Evgeniy Karlovich (1867–1937). Professional soldier, White Guard General. Chief of Staff of 5th Army in WWI, promoted to Lt-Gen. Resisted disintegration of Russian army 1917. Became Governor General and Commander-in-Chief of troops of Northern region during Allied intervention. After defeat by Reds, emigrated; from 1930 head of White émigré organization ROVS. Kidnapped by NKVD 1937. | 114

Milovanov. Nizheturinsk regional OGPU head, 1930s. | 296

Milyukov, Pavel Nikolaevich (1859–1943). Historian of Russia, journalist, public figure. Liberal views led to problems with authorities. Imprisoned briefly 1902. Lectured and studied in Bulgaria, UK, France, USA. Returned to Russia 1905, founder and leader of Kadet party, editor of *Rech'*. In 3rd and 4th Dumas, specialized in foreign affairs. Initiated formation of Progressive Bloc 1915. Denounced government in Duma 1 February 1916. Foreign affairs minister in 1st Provisional Government, strong supporter of Tsar's WWI treaties. Sided with Whites after October 1917, then in emigration in France. | 8–10, 12–13, 40–42, 349–50

Milyutin, Vladimir Pavlovich (1884–1937). Economist and political activist. Menshevik 1903–10, thereafter Bolshevik. Economist, agriculture commissar in 1st Soviet government. Deputy chairman of VSNKh 1918–21. Headed USSR statistical bureau 1928–34. Loyal supporter of party line. Arrested and shot 1937.

| 34

Mirbach, Count Wilhelm (1871–1918). German diplomat, ambassador in Moscow April–July 1918. Killed by Left SR Chekists in course of failed rising 6 July 1918. | 105, 117

Mironov, Filipp Kuz'mich (1872–1921). Professional Cossack soldier, dismissed from army 1905 for participation in revolution. In army in WWI. Fought with Reds in civil war, but opposed anti-Cossack policies. Joined RKP(b) 1920, arrested by Don Cheka and killed 1921. | 128

Mirov. *Oblast'* prison doctor, Nizheturinsk, 1930s. | 297

Molass. Academician, victimized in 1929–30. | 343

Molchanov. Worker at spirits factory 1940. | 330

Molchanov, Nikolay. Nekrasovo peasant, 1917. | 97

Molotov (Skryabin), Vyacheslav Mikhaylovich (1890–1986). Soviet politician. Bolshevik from 1906, in Petrograd early 1917, led party work there before Lenin's return. Took part in October seizure of power, thereafter in party and state work. On CPSU CC 1921–57. CC secretary 1921–30, chair of Sovnarkom 1930–41, foreign commissar/minister 1939–49, 1953–56. Loyal Stalinist, defeated by Khrushchev 1957, expelled from CPSU 1962, readmitted 1984. | 151, 177–78, 243, 247, 249, 251, 263, 265, 267, 275, 286, 288, 301, 305, 320, 347–49, 353, 386–89

Mostakova, U.P. Acquaintance of N.K. Krupskaya. | 97–99

Mrachkovsky, Sergey Vital'evich (1888–1936). Bolshevik from 1905. In military work in civil war and subsequently, commander in Urals, Volga region and Western Siberia. Thereafter in economic work, headed construction of Baikal–Amur railway 1932–33. Arrested and tried with Zinoviev and Kamenev in 'Trotskyite-Zinovievite Terrorist Centre' show trial, shot. | 370–71

Muralov, Nikolay Ivanovich (1877–1937). Bolshevik from 1903, involved in Moscow rising 1905, then fled to native Don. In army 1914–17. In 1917 helped organize Moscow Soviet soldiers' section, on Military-Revoltionary Committee, helped lead Moscow rising November. Commanded troops in civil war, thereafter in military and economic posts. Criticized campaign against opposition at 15th CPSU congress, expelled. Arrested and tortured 1936, in 1937 show trial, shot. | 210–12

Mussolini, Benito (1883–1945). Ideologist and leader of Italian Fascism, ruler of Italy 1922–43. | 384

Nabokov, Vladimir Dmitrievich (1869–1922). State official, jurist, academic, journalist, politician. Founding member of Kadet party, in 1st Duma, served three months in prison for signing Vyborg declaration 1906. In WWI worked at military HQ. Active in February 1917, helped secure Mikhail's abdication. Worked in Provisional Government apparatus, electoral commission for Constituent Assembly. Justice minister in Crimea government 1918, emigrated 1919. Died protecting P.N. Milyukov from attempted assassination. | 40, 42

Natanson, Mark Andreevich (1850–1919). Revolutionary from early 1870s, Narodnik, frequently arrested and exiled. Emigrated to Switzerland 1904. SR from 1905. In charge of party finances. Favoured union of all socialist parties, maintained links with Social Democrats. Internationalist in WWI. Returned to Russia May 1917. On EC of All-Russia Soviet of Peasants' Deputies. Favoured left opposition in SR party, joined Left SRs November 1917. Member of VTsIK Presidium after October 1917. Joined Party of Revolutionary Communism September 1918. Left Russia for medical treatment, died in Berne. | 55

Naumov, Mikhail. Nizheturinsk camp guard, 1930s. | 297

Nazaretyan, Amayak Makarovich (1889–1937). Bolshevik from 1905. In Tiflis party organization 1917–18, labour commissar of Terek republic 1918–19. Helped organize rising against Georgian Menshevik government. On Central Control Commission presidium from 1926. Arrested and shot 1937. | 186, 320

Nechaev. Doctor at Timiryazev hospital, 1928. | 335

Nekrasov, Nikolay Vissarionovich (1879–1940). Politician, active in co-operative movement. Joined Kadets 1905, on party CC 1909–17, led its left wing. In 3rd and 4th Dumas 1907–17, active in Progressive Bloc, in WWI favoured working with defencist socialists. Involved in conspiracies against Nicholas II, favoured declaring Russia republic March 1917. Served in Provisional Government to end August. Early 1918 changed name, worked incognito in co-operatives, then openly 1921–30. Arrested in connection with Menshevik case 1931, released 1933, rearrested 1939, shot 1940. | 9–10

Nero (37–68 AD). Roman Emperor 54–68 AD. Particularly noted for persecution of Christians, alleged to have ordered burning of Rome. | 362

Nevsky, Vladimir Ivanovich (Krivobokov, Feodosiy Ivanovich) (1876–1937). Political and military activist, journalist, historian. From rich merchant's family, revolutionary from 1895, Social Democrat from 1897, Bolshevik. In 1917 in Petrograd, in party military organization. Involved in Bolshevik seizure of power October 1917, then in creation of Red Army. Held various state posts, closely involved in *Istpart* party history commission. Defended objectivity in historical methods, fell from favour 1930s. Arrested 1935, shot 1937. | 25–26

Nicholas II (Romanov, Nikolay Aleksandrovich) (1868–1918). Emperor 1894–1917. Powers limited after 1905, abdicated March 1917, shot with family in Urals 17 July 1918. | 3–5, 11–12, 42, 117, 125, 151, 342

Nikolaev. Member of Andreev's commission on 'kulaks', 1931. | 283

Nikolaeva, Klavdiya Ivanovna (1893–1944). Worker's daughter, Bolshevik from 1909, active in printers' union. In St Petersburg 1917, among editors of *Robotnitsa*. Then in party work, especially agitprop. Full CPSU CC member 1924–25 and 1934–44, candidate member 1925–34. In WWII organized medical services and evacuation. | 320

Nobel', G.A. One of the founders of *Torgprom*, 1920s. | 349

Nogin, Viktor Pavlovich (1878–1924). Social Democrat from 1898, Bolshevik from

1903, professional revolutionary, arrested eight times, escaped from exile six times. In Moscow 1917, deputy chair, from September chair of Moscow Soviet. Involved in seizure of power but favoured coalition with other socialist parties. Thereafter worked in economic apparatus. | 65–67

Novikov, Mikhail Mikhaylovich (1876–1965). Zoologist, academic, public figure. Educated Moscow and Heidelberg. Lectured at Moscow University. Kadet deputy in 4th Duma. Rector of Moscow University 1919–20, continued lecturing there until deported 1922. Thereafter in Prague, Bratislava, New York. | 224, 229

Obolensky. Construction brigade leader, Urals, 1930s. | 313

Obraztsova, A. and **Pelageya**. Nekrasovo peasants, 1917. | 97

Okhlopkov, Nikolay Pavlovich (1900–1967). Celebrated actor and producer, in V.M. Meyerhol'd's theatre from 1923, head of Realist theatre 1930–37. Among those named by Meyerhol'd under NKVD torture. | 388

Okudzhava. CC member, Georgian CP, 1922. | 186

Ol'denburg, Sergey Fedorovich (1863–1934). Academician, ethnographer, specialist on Eastern peoples, public figure. On Kadet party CC. In Academy of Sciences from 1900, secretary of academy 1904–29. Minister of Education July–September 1917. After October, devoted self to academic work. | 40, 342–43

Olesha, Yuriy Karlovich (1899–1960). Ukrainian journalist and novelist, worked in press bureaus in Ukraine and Moscow. Author of children's novel *Three Fat Men* (1928). Had plays produced in Meyerhol'd's theatre. Among those named by Meyerhol'd under NKVD torture. | 388

Oleynikov. Kuznetskstroy clerk of works, 1931. | 312–13

Orakhelashvili, Ivan (Mamiya) Dmitrievich (1881–1937). Georgian, Bolshevik from 1903, active in St Petersburg, from 1908 worked as doctor in Transcaspian region, army doctor in WWI. Imprisoned by Georgian government 1918–20, led its overthrow 1921. From February 1921 on Revolutionary Committee of Georgia, secretary of Georgian CP. Then in leading posts in Transcaucasian Republic and USSR. Arrested and killed 1937. | 186

Ordzhonikidze, Grigoriy (Sergo) Konstantinovich (1886–1937). Georgian Social Democrat from 1903, active in Georgia, Baku. Exiled, escaped to Iran, then France. Bolshevik from c. 1911. Imprisoned in Russia 1912, exiled from 1915 to Yakutia. Around October 1917 in Caucasus. In civil war, then involved in imposing Soviet rule in Georgia. Held various party and state posts, heavy-industry commissar from 1932. Committed suicide. | 186, 192–93, 206, 342–43, 351, 353, 372

Oshchurkov. Nizheturinsk head of camp supplies, 1930s. | 297

Osinsky, N. (Obolensky, Valerian Valerianovich) (1887–1938). Political activist, journalist, economist. Marxist from early youth, in RSDRP from 1907, Bolshevik. After October 1917 in economic work, first chairman of VSNKh, also in State Bank from 1917 and Gosplan from 1925. Shot. | 320

Osipov, G.E. Denouncer of B.V. Didkovsky, 1936. | 370–71

Osorgin (Il'in), Mikhail Andreevich (1878–1942). Writer and journalist, published from 1895. Joined SRs 1904, arrested and exiled 1905, fled to Italy 1907, correspondent in Russian press. Returned to Russia 1916. Hostile to Bolsheviks, after October 1917 called for general strike. Active in Writers' and Journalists' Unions. Expelled from USSR with other oppositional intellectuals 1922. | 228–29

Panferov, Fedor Ivanovich (1896–1960). Writer, journalist, secret policeman. Son of peasants. Worked with Cheka after October 1917. First published 1918. Edited *Krest'yanskaya gazeta* 1925–27, pushed collective farming. Wrote novels, plays, etc., glorifying economic transformation of USSR. | 313

Panina, Sof'ya Vladimirovna (1871–1957). Countess, political activist, public figure. Very rich, noted for philanthropy for liberal, artistic and other causes. On Kadet CC from May 1917, worked in Provisional Government. After October attempted to resist Bolsheviks, orchestrated state employees' strike, imprisoned briefly. Assisted White cause until 1920, then in emigration in Europe and USA. | 40

Pashukanis, Evgeniy Bronislavovich (1891–1937). Soviet legal theorist, wrote on state and international law. USSR deputy justice commissar 1936. Arrested and shot 1937. | 309

Pasternak, Boris Leonidovich (1890–1960). Noted poet and writer. Studied music and philosophy in youth. In 1920s close to Mayakovsky, wrote poems and novels. In 1930s produced mainly translations. In 1950s worked on celebrated *Doctor Zhivago*, condemned in USSR, awarded Nobel prize. | 388

Pavel (Borisovsky, Pavel Petrovich) (1867–1938). Vyatka churchman, Archbishop from 1924. Arrested and exiled 1923. Shot at Yaroslavl'. | 256

Pavlov. Colonel, acting head of First Special Section of USSR MVD, 1953. | 360

Perepechko. CPSU CC candidate member from 1930. | 320

Perepelkin, Petr Mikhaylovich (1890–1921). Kronstadt sailor, member of Kronstadt Provisional Revolutionary Committee, sometime secretary. Shot. | 145

Petlyura, Simon Vasil'evich (1879–1926). Ukrainian social-democratic and nationalist politician. Joined Ukrainian Revolutionary Party (later Ukrainian Social Democratic Workers' Party) 1900. Russian patriot during WWI. Involved in Kiev Rada 1917. Opposed Bolsheviks. In charge of Ukrainian military end 1917, allied with emerging White forces. De facto Ukrainian leader spring 1918 and 1919–20. Emigrated October 1920. Assassinated in Paris in revenge for pogroms in Ukraine. | 131

Petrichenko, Stepan Maksimovich (1892–1947). Worker, conscripted into navy 1914. Joined RKP(b) 1919, then left. Head of Kronstadt Provisional Revolutionary Committee March 1921, fled to Finland on suppression of rising. Re-established links with Soviet authorities 1922. Recruited into Soviet intelligence in Finland, provided valuable information in WWII. Arrested by Finns 1941, freed 1944, arrested by Red Army 1945, died in Soviet captivity. | 145

Petrov, Grigoriy. Defrocked priest, 1920s. | 258

Petrov-Vodkin, Kuz'ma Sergeevich (1878–1939). Artist and writer, leading Russian exponent of symbolism in painting. From 1918 involved in reorganizing teaching of art. | 4

Petrovsky, Grigoriy Ivanovich (1878–1958). Ukrainian revolutionary, Social Democrat from 1897, Bolshevik. Among leaders of Ekaterinoslav Soviet 1905. Elected to 4th Duma, chair of Bolshevik group. Exiled 1915–17. RSFSR internal affairs commissar November 1917–March 1919. Chaired Ukrainian TsIK 1919–38. On CPSU CC 1921–39. Sacked from all top positions 1939 but not killed. | 88, 97–99, 120

Petrovykh. Camp administrator, Nizhneturinsk, 1930s. | 297

Pisarev, L. Professor, White supporter, 1918. | 112

Platonov, Sergey Fedorovich (1860–1933). Historian. Professor of Russian history at St Petersburg University from 1890, specialist in 16th and 17th centuries. Opposed to ideology in historiography. Wrote standard school textbook on Russian history, 1909. Hostile to Bolshevik take-over, but remained in Russia, helped preserve libraries and archives. Academician from 1920, arrested 1930 on fabricated 'Academic Case'. Died of heart failure. | 341–43

Plekhanov, Georgiy Valentinovich (1856–1918). Founder of Russian Marxism, Narodnik from 1876, emigrated 1880, became Marxist. Founded 'Emancipation of Labour' group 1883. Author of numerous political and philosophical works. Took neither side in RSDRP split 1903, later closer to Mensheviks. Staunch defencist in war, formed 'Edinstvo' social-democratic group, to right of all Menshevik factions. Returned to Russia 1917, defended Provisional Government. Denounced Bolshevism. Already very ill, died in Finland. | 63–65

Podvoysky, Nikolay Il'ich (1880–1948). Revolutionary from 1898, Bolshevik from 1903. In Petrograd Bolshevik organization 1917, initiated courses for agitators among soldiers, edited Bolshevik soldiers' papers. One of the organizers of the Petrograd Military-Revolutionary Committee, took direct part in seizure of power. Among initiators and organizers of Red Army, 1918. Thereafter in party and military work. | 25–26, 60, 88

Pokrovsky. Academician, victimized in 1929–30. | 343

Pokrovsky, Mikhail Nikolaevich (1868–1932). Historian, political activist, Bolshevik 1905–10, then non-factional. Emigrated to France after 1907. Internationalist during WWI, returned to Bolsheviks, agitated among Russian soldiers in France 1917, returned to Russia in September. Involved in Bolshevik seizure of power in Moscow. Deputy commissar of education from May 1918, headed Socialist Academy and Institute of Red Professors. In Academy of Sciences from 1929. 'Pokrovsky school' of historians formed around him. | 80, 342, 343

Polonsky, Vladimir Ivanovich (1893–1937). Worker from Tobol'sk, Bolshevik from 1912, trade unionist. Secretary of Moscow metalworkers' union 1917, after October held numerous party, state and trade-union posts. Candidate member

Pyatakov, Georgiy (Yuriy) Leonidovich (1890–1937). Son of owner of sugar factory near Kiev, revolutionary from 1904, Social Democrat from 1910. Arrested 1912, exiled 1914, escaped to North America, headed Kiev Bolshevik organization on return 1917. Left communist 1918. Worked underground in Ukraine 1918, then in Red Army. Held various party, state and economic posts in 1920s but sided with Trotskyist oppositions. Recanted 1928, deputy heavy industry commissar 1931–36. Arrested 1936, in show trial 1937, shot. | 273, 320, 371

Rakovsky, Khristian Georgievich (Stanchev, Christiu) (1873–1941). Balkan revolutionary, Social Democrat from 1889, follower of Plekhanov. Active among Bulgarian, Romanian and Russian Social Democrats, internationalist in war. Joined Bolsheviks end 1917, leading Bolshevik in Ukraine. Among founders of Comintern. Soviet ambassador to UK 1923–25, to France 1925–27. Supported Trotsky, did not recant until 1934. Arrested 1937, in show trial 1938, sentenced to twenty years, shot. | 210

Ramzin, Leonid Konstantinovich (1887–1948). Scientist, heating engineer and planner. Professor from 1920, in Gosplan from 1921. Arrested and tried in fabricated case of 'Industrial Party' 1930, released soon after and allowed to continue scientific work. Developed special industrial boiler which bore his name. | 346–50

Rapoport, Grigoriy Yakovlevich (1890–1938). Son of petty trader, member of Poalei-Zion (Workers of Zion) party 1904–05, fought pogromists 1905, then spent four years in USA. Returned to Russia, held various jobs. In Cheka from May 1918, joined Bolsheviks September 1918. Made career in secret police. OGPU Urals representative 1931–33. Sacked 1936, shot 1938. | 294–95

Raskol'nikov (Il'in), Fedor Fedorovich (1892–1939). Political activist, writer, diplomat and military commander. From a priest's family, Bolshevik from 1910, in navy in WWI. Based at Kronstadt after February 1917. Among organizers of July Days demonstrations in Petrograd, held in Kresty prison, released October. Held naval and party posts, arrested by British ship on reconnaissance December 1918, held at Brixton prison, exchanged for British officers. Thereafter in army and diplomatic posts. Sacked 1938 while abroad, refused to return to USSR and denounced Stalin. Died in mysterious circumstances. | 29

Remizov, Aleksey Mikhaylovich (1877–1957). Writer and playwright. Born to merchant, educated at Moscow University. Involved in labour movement until early 1900s, spent six years in prison and exile. Specialized in re-telling folk tales and legends. Hostile to Soviet government, emigrated 1921. | 4–5

Reshetov, I. Head of 4th section of GPU secret department, 1922. | 227–29

Rodos, Boris Veniaminovich. NKVD interrogator, noted for viciousness. Interrogated Meyerhol'd. | 389

Rodzyanko, Mikhail Vladimirovich (1859–1924). Politician and major landowner. In army to 1885, thereafter in public administration in Ekaterinoslav. Founded local Union of 17 October group 1905, in 3rd and 4th Dumas 1907–17. Opponent in WWI of Rasputin circle, attempted to influence Nicholas rather than protest publicly. As head of Duma Committee prominent in February 1917, helped persuade Nicholas and Mikhail to abdicate. Thereafter less prominent. Supported White cause, emigrated to Yugoslavia. | 4–5, 8, 10–11

Romanov, Dmitriy Konstantinovich (1860–1919). Grand Duke. Director of state stud farm. Stood apart from palace affairs. Shot as hostage in prison. | 124

Romanov, Georgiy Mikhaylovich (1863–1919). Grand Duke, General, attached to Stavka in WWI. Noted numismatist. Shot as hostage in prison. | 124

Romanov, Nikolay Mikhaylovich (1859–1919). Grand Duke, historian. In military service 1884–1903. Chairman of Russian Historical Society 1909–17. Wrote on early nineteenth century with abundant documentary material. Shot as hostage in prison. | 124–25

Romanov, Nikolay Nikolaevich (the younger) (1856–1929). Grand Duke, cavalry General. Commander-in-Chief 1914–August 1915, then commanded on Caucasus front. In emigration from 1919, pretender to vacant Russian throne. | 257

Romanov, Pavel Aleksandrovich (1860–1919). Grand Duke, cavalry General, commanded Life Guards and Guards Corps 1890s. Noted supporter of horse-breeding. Shot as hostage in prison. | 124

Room, Abram Matveevich (1894–1976). Theatre and film producer, lecturer. Made several films from 1920s to 1970s, largely political. CPSU member from 1949. Won several state prizes. | 341

Roshal', Semen Grigor'evich (1896–1917). Bolshevik from 1914, arrested December 1915, released February 1917. Sent by party to Kronstadt, arrested after July 1917 demonstrations. Freed after October 1917, sent to Romanian Front as Sovnarkom representative. Arrested and executed by White Guard forces December 1917. | 29

Royzenman, Boris Anisimovich (Isaak Anshelevich) (1878–1938). Ukrainian Social Democrat from 1902, Bolshevik, active in Cherkassy and Ekaterinoslav. Conscripted 1916. In 1917 on Ekaterinoslav Soviet, involved in establishing Soviet power there December 1917. In supply apparatus in civil war. From 1923 in party and Soviet control apparatus, on Central Control Commission presidium 1924–34. | 320

Rozanov, Sergey Nikolaevich. General, served in Red Army, defected to *Komuch* summer 1918. Chief of Staff of Ufa Directory Commander-in-Chief October 1918, Kolchak's representative in Krasnoyarsk 1919. | 129

Rozhkov, Nikolay Aleksandrovich (1868–1927). Academic, historian and economist, Social Democrat from 1905, Bolshevik to 1911, thereafter Menshevik. Internationalist in WWI. Deputy Posts and Telegraphs Minister May–June 1917. Left Menshevik in 1917, opposed Bolshevik take-over, but worked in Soviet institutions. Arrested 1921 and 1922, broke with Mensheviks under threat of deportation. Until his death, museum curator, lecturer. | 100–01, 231–32

Ryabushinsky, Pavel Pavlovich (1871–1924). Industrialist, financier, publisher, politician. From Old Believer background. Octobrist in 1905, split with Guchkov, helped found Progressivist Party 1912. Favoured uniting liberal and socialist opposition against Tsar's government in WWI. In 1917 opposed socialist participation in Provisional Government, grain monopoly and power sharing with soviets. Abroad after October, founded émigré capitalist organization *Torgprom*. | 38–39, 348–49

Rykov, Aleksey Ivanovich (1881–1938). Social Democrat from 1898, active in Saratov, Kazan', Moscow, etc. Arrested and exiled several times. Active in St Petersburg and Moscow 1905 and 1917, took part in October 1917 seizure of power. First internal affairs commissar. Thereafter in party, state and economic work, 1923–24 chair of VSNKh, 1924–30 chair of USSR Sovnarkom. Fell from favour along with others, denounced as 'right deviationist' after 1929. Full party CC member 1905–07, 1917–18, 1920–34; candidate 1907–12, 1934–37. Arrested 1937, in show trial with Bukharin and others. 1938, shot. | 264, 334, 337, 343, 348

Ryutin, Martem'yan Nikitich (1890–1937). Worker, Bolshevik from 1914. Ensign in army in Far East WWI. Fought around Irkutsk in civil war. Held various party posts, in Moscow from 1924. From mid-1920s supported various oppositions to Stalin. Involved in collectivization 1929, criticized excesses. Arrested 1930, freed 1931. Rearrested 1932 following 'Ryutin platform', sentenced to ten years, shot 1937. | 362–65, 367

Sabashvili. CP Georgia CC secretary, 1922. | 186

Sadovsky, Vladimir. Arch-priest, White Guard supporter 1918. | 112

Sakulin, Pavel Nikitich (1868–1930). Philologist, literary critic and historian of ideas. Lectured at Moscow University 1902–11 and from 1917. Author of books on Lomonosov, Turgenev, Odoevsky, and others. | 235–38

Salakhov, Abdullah. Mullah in Tuluy village, Dagestan, 1938. | 399

Saltykov-Shchedrin (Saltykov), Mikhail Evgrafovich (1826–1889). Writer, state official, noted satirist and author of short stories. Combined state service with work on oppositional journals *Sovremennik* (1862–64) and *Otechestvennye zapiski* (1884–88). Used experiences as provincial official as raw material for stories. | 345

Samsonov, Timofey Petrovich (1888–1956). Secret policeman. In RKP(b) from 1919. Headed Moscow Cheka special department from 1919, and secret division 1920–23. | 227

Sarlet. Village priest, Dal'nekonstantinovsk, 1930s. | 399

Savinkov, Boris Viktorovich (1879–1925). Political activist, journalist, writer, military conspirator. SR 1903–17, in SR Fighting Organization, organized assassinations. In France 1911–17, served in French army in WWI. In Russian war ministry 1917, worked with Kerensky, favoured war to victory. Sympathized with Kornilov, resigned. After October supported Whites, worked with Poles 1920. Returned to USSR 1924, arrested. Died in detention, circumstances unclear. | 45–46, 226

Shlyapnikov, Aleksandr Gavrilovich (1885–1937). Industrial worker from age 11, Social Democrat from early 1900s, strike leader, union organizer. Arrested several times. Worked in western European factories, active in socialist movement. Internationalist in WWI. On Bolshevik CC from 1915, liaised with leaders and foreign socialists. Moved between Russia and Sweden 1914–17. Headed Petrograd Bolsheviks February 1917. Held various state, party and trade-union posts after October. Headed 'workers' opposition' 1921, thereafter out of favour. Wrote histories of revolutionary movement. Arrested and exiled 1930s, shot 1937. | 88

Shostakovich, Dmitriy Dmitrievich (1906–1975). Composer, trained at Leningrad Conservatoire. Composed highly acclaimed symphonic, opera, ballet, film and other music. Periodically out of favour with authorities, but won numerous prizes. | 388

Shteynberg (Steinberg), Isaak-Nakhman Zakharovich (1888–1957). Writer and lawyer, SR theoretician. Joined SRs 1906, exiled 1907, studied law in Germany. In Ufa 1917. Joined Left SRs. People's Commissar of Justice December 1917–March 1918. Arrested several times up to 1923, emigrated. Thereafter in Jewish socialist circles in Germany, Britain and USA. Author of books on Russian revolution, memoirs, etc. | 72, 118

Shusharin. Tractor driver, Urals, 1930s. | 304

Shvarts, I.I. Bolshevik, on CC from 1924. | 320

Shvartsman, L.L. NKVD Colonel, 1930s. Interrogated Meyerhol'd. | 389

Shvernik, Nikolay Mikhaylovich (1888–1970). Metalworker, Bolshevik from 1905. Active in party and trade unions in European Russia. In Samara pipeworks 1917, on factory committee and local soviet. In party, Red Army and trade-union work after October. On CPSU CC from 1925. Supreme Soviet deputy 1937–66, chaired its presidium from 1946. | 270, 320

Sil'vestr. Archbishop of Omsk, White Guard supporter 1918. | 112

Sil'vestr (Bratanovsky, Aleksandr Alekseevich) (1871–1931? 1932?). Bishop of Perm' and Solikamsk 1920–24. From 1925 Vologda Archbishop. | 256

Sirotkin. Assistant Urals *oblast'* procurator, 1930s. | 297

Skoropadsky, Pavel Petrovich (1873–1945). Ukrainian, professional soldier. Cossack *ataman* (chieftain) from October 1917. Resisted Bolshevik take-over in Ukraine 1917–18. With German support proclaimed *Hetman* (ruler) of Ukraine 29 April 1918. Overthrown 14 December 1918, emigrated to Germany. Collaborated with Nazis, killed in bombing raid in Bavaria. | 103, 131

Smirnov, Aleksandr Petrovich (1878–1938). Worker, railwayman's son, Social Democrat from 1896, Bolshevik. Active in NW Russia, arrested several times. After October 1917 deputy internal affairs commissar. On CPSU CC from 1922, RSFSR agriculture commissar mid-1920s, held numerous other posts. RSFSR Sovnarkom deputy chairman 1928–30. Expelled from CPSU 1934, arrested 1937, shot 1938. | 393

Smirnov, Ivan Nikitich (1881–1936). Peasant's son, railway worker, joined RSDRP

1899, Bolshevik. Active in numerous cities, arrested several times. Conscripted 1916, served in Tomsk, on executive of Tomsk soviet 1917. Active in civil war on Eastern front. In Petrograd 1921–22, close to Zinoviev. In VSNKh. In Trotskyist opposition 1923–29, expelled from CPSU 1927, readmitted 1930. Rearrested 1933. In Zinoviev–Kamenev trial 1936, shot. | 361, 370

Smol'yaninov. Member of Andreev commission on 'kulaks', 1931. | 283

Sokol'nikov (Brilliant), Grigoriy Yakovlevich (1888–1939). Bolshevik from 1905, arrested several times, abroad 1909–17, active in Moscow and Petrograd 1917, involved in seizure of power, October. Headed delegation to sign Brest peace, 1918. From 1921 in finance commissariat, headed it 1923–26, organized currency stabilization. In opposition from 1926. Ambassador to UK 1929–31. Arrested 1936, in show trial 1937, shot. | 127, 162, 186, 320

Solodovnikov, Gavrila Gavrilovich (1826–1901). Merchant of the 1st guild, manufacturer, landlord, landowner, philanthropist. Financed hospitals, theatres, etc. Left over 20 million rubles to good causes and only 815,000 to descendants. | 175

Solov'evs, Nekrasovo peasants, 1917. | 97

Sol'ts, Aron Aleksandrovich (1872–1945). Studied law at St Petersburg University. Social Democrat from 1898, Bolshevik. Took part in revolutionary events 1905–07. Arrested and exiled several times. In Moscow 1917. From 1920 on party's Central Control Commission, on its presidium 1923–34. Member of Supreme Court from 1921. Acquired reputation as CPSU's 'conscience'. | 320

Sosnovsky, Lev Semenovich (1886–1937). Bolshevik from 1904, worked underground in party and trade-union organizations, spent time in prison and exile. In Urals in 1917. Editor of *Bednota* 1918–24. Headed Khar'kov party organization 1919–20, head of RKP(b) agitprop 1921, then in state service and journalism. Expelled from party 1927, arrested. Shot 1937. | 134

Spiridonova, Mariya Aleksandrovna (1884–1941). Revolutionary from schooldays, SR, terrorist, imprisoned for life 1906 for assassinating Tambov official Luzhenovsky. Freed by Kerensky March 1917. On far left of SR party, founder of Left SRs. On VTsIK after October. Involved in Left SR assassination of German ambassador Mirbach. Thereafter frequently arrested, exiled, imprisoned on political charges. Sentenced to twenty-five years 1938, shot 1941. | 55

Sreznevsky (possibly Vyacheslav Izmaylovich) (1849–1937). Academician, among those persecuted in 1930. | 343

Stadnitsky, Avksentiy Georgievich (Metropolitan Arseniy) (1862–1936). Metropolitan of Novgorod and Old Russia. Took part in 1917–18 Church Council. Member of Holy Synod and Supreme Church Council. Arrested 1922, exiled to Bukhara for three years, 1924. | 342

Stakhanov, Aleksey Grigor'evich (1905–1977). Celebrated shock worker. Farm labourer 1914–26, from 1927 miner. In 1935 set records for coal digging in orchestrated stunt, initiated mass emulation 'Stakhanovite' campaign. In CPSU from 1936. Thereafter given leading posts beyond his abilities. | 315

Stalin (Dzhugashvili), Iosif Vissarionovich (1878? 1879?–1953). Georgian Social
Democrat from 1898, Bolshevik from 1903. Active in Caucasus RSDRP, and in
1905–07 events. Involved in fund-raising bank robberies. Wrote *Marxism and the
National Question* 1913. In internal exile 1913–17, in Petrograd March 1917.
Initially conciliatory towards Provisional Government, then supported Lenin.
Involved in October seizure of power, first nationalities commissar. Held
numerous party and state organizational posts, RKP(b) General Secretary from
1922. Made this the key party post, became personal dictator of USSR until his
death. | 25, 177–78, 298, 317, 324, 369
—and agriculture | 263–64, 266–68, 270–71, 273, 331, 382, 385
—campaign against Trotsky | 180, 198, 201–03, 208–10, 276, 361, 370, 385
—and culture | 339, 341–45, 355
—and industrialization | 181–83, 273, 306, 320–21
—and intelligentsia | 231–32, 316, 351, 353
—investigates Cheka activities 1918. | 121–22
—and Lenin's 'Testament' | 203–08
—and national question | 186–89, 191–94
—and show trials | 337, 345–51, 353
—and 'socialism in one country' | 163, 165–66
—and terror | 359, 361–63, 365–66, 370, 372–75, 380–82, 384, 386–87, 397
Steklov, Yuriy Mikhaylovich (Nakhamkis, Ovshiy Moiseevich) (1873–1941).
Journalist and political activist, Social Democrat from 1893, associate of Lenin
from 1900, Bolshevik from 1903. In emigration 1894–1905, and from 1910. On
EC of Petrograd Soviet 1917, editor of *Izvestiya* 1917–25. Wrote books on history
of Marxism. Arrested 1938, died in prison. | 6, 19, 149–50, 231, 232
Stepanov. Camp doctor, Urals, 1930s. | 296–97
Stolypin, Petr Arkad'evich (1862–1911). Russian statesman and administrator, from
old nobility. Worked in interior ministry from 1889, governor of Grodno 1902,
of Saratov 1903–06, repressed peasant rebels. Interior Minister and Prime
Minister 1906–11. Dissolved 2nd Duma 1907, fixed electoral law to ensure right-
wing dominance. Combined repression with reform; his new agrarian law sought
to destroy village commune institutions. Assassinated 1911. | 151
Strievsky, Konstantin Konstantinovich (1885–1938). Worker, in RSDRP from
1902, Bolshevik. Active in 1905–07. Arrested and exiled several times.
Conscripted 1916, politically active in Petrograd garrison. On Petrograd Soviet
1917. Petrograd food commissar 1918–19, thereafter in economic, party and
trade-union work. CPSU CC full member 1927–34, candidate member
1924–27, 1934–38. | 320
Struve, Petr Berngardovich (1870–1944). Political activist, publicist, economist,
philosopher. Theoretician of 'legal Marxism' in 1890s, author of 1st RSDRP
programme, 1898. Liberal from 1900, founder member of Kadet party 1905, on
CC. In 2nd Duma. Supported Stolypin reforms. Among authors of *Vekhi*, 1909.

After October 1917 active on White side, worked with Wrangel' and Denikin, from 1920 in emigration. | 215

Sukhanov (Gimmer), Nikolay Nikolaevich (1882–1940). Journalist, economist, memoirist and political activist. SR from 1903, involved in Moscow rising 1905. Wrote on peasant economy. Internationalist non-party Social Democrat in WWI, Menshevik 1917–21. Helped found Petrograd Soviet 1917, writer on *Novaya zhizn'*. In Soviet economic apparatus from 1918. Wrote memoir of 1917, *Notes on Revolution*. Arrested 1930, defendant in Menshevik show trial 1931. Released 1935, rearrested 1937, shot 1940. | 346–47

Sulimov, Daniil Egorovich (1890–1937). Worker's son, Bolshevik from 1905. Conscripted into army 1915, in soldiers' soviets 1917. From 1918 in management of Urals regional industry and Red Army political work. Leading figure in Urals *oblast'* CPSU to 1927, then USSR deputy transport commissar. Chair of RSFSR Sovnarkom from 1930. On CPSU CC from 1923. Arrested and shot 1937. | 320

Svatikov, Sergey Grigor'evich (1880–1942). Publicist, political activist, Social Democrat around 1900, thereafter favoured unity of all anti-Tsarist forces. Closely involved in February 1917 overthrow of Tsarism and establishment of new authorities. Roving emissary debriefing Tsarist agents abroad 1917. Opposed Bolsheviks, sided with Whites, emigrated 1920. | 6

Sverdlov, Yakov Mikhaylovich (1885–1919). Social Democrat from 1901, Bolshevik. Arrested numerous times before 1917. Active in Urals in 1905. Active in Bolshevik seizure of power, October 1917. Chaired VTsIK from November 1917. Opened Constituent Assembly 5 January 1918 and oversaw its dispersal. Held numerous party and state posts until death from lung inflammation. | 25–26, 72, 93

Svidersky, Aleksey Ivanovich (1878–1933). Social Democrat from 1899, Bolshevik. Took part in 1905–07 events. In Ufa 1917–18, headed party and Soviet organizations. Then in food commissariat, organized requisitioning. In agriculture commissariat 1920s, from 1929 ambassador to Latvia, died in Riga. | 150

Swift, Jonathan (1667–1745). Irish author and journalist, most famous for *Gulliver's Travels*. | 218

Syrtsov, Sergey Ivanovich (1893–1937). Bolshevik from 1913. Active in Petrograd and Rostov-on-Don 1917. After October in Don region fighting White Cossacks. On Don RKP(b) bureau from 1918, active on southern front in civil war. Thereafter in other party work. Removed from party leadership end 1930 for 'factionalism'. Arrested and shot 1937. | 127–28

Tarle, Evgeniy Viktorovich (1874–1955). Historian. Educated at Kiev University, professor at St Petersburg. Sceptic with left sympathies. Worked on history of France. Welcomed fall of Tsarism. After October 1917 concentrated on history. From 1927 academician. Clashed with Pokrovsky, arrested 1930 in 'Academicians' case', released 1932, semi-rehabilitated, wrote celebrated works on Napoleon, and others. | 341

Taylor, Frederick Winslow (1856–1915). US engineer, industrialist, theoretician of scientific management (Taylorism). | 151

Teodorovich, Ivan Adol'fovich (1875–1937). Social Democrat from 1895, Bolshevik from 1903, on RS-DLP CC from 1907. Arrested and exiled several times before 1917. Food commissar in 1st Soviet government, thereafter in agriculture commissariat posts. Headed Peasant International 1928–30. Arrested and shot 1937. | 348

Teplov. Clerk of works, Kuznetskstroy, 1931. | 312–13

Tereshchenko, Mikhail Ivanovich (1886–1956). Landowner, sugar magnate, publisher, politician. Non-party member of 4th Duma. Involved in anti-Nicholas plots. Minister of Finance, then of Foreign Affairs in Provisional Governments 1917. Arrested after October, released 1918, fled abroad, supported White movement. Later major financier in France, died in Monaco. | 9–10

Tikhon, Patriarch (Belavin, Vasiliy Ivanovich) (1865–1925). Russian Orthodox churchman. Bishop of Lublin from 1898, Archbishop of Yaroslavl' from 1907 and of Lithuania from 1914. Very conservative in politics, headed Yaroslavl' branch of Union of Russian People (Black Hundreds). Appointed Patriarch 21 November 1917. Initially actively opposed Bolsheviks, although did not support White armies. Later attempted reconciliation while defending Church independence. | 85–87, 89, 111, 122, 124, 246–49, 251–54, 257–58

Timiryazev, Kliment Arkad'evich (1843–1920). Natural scientist, biologist, agronomist, popularizer of science. Radical sympathies since youth. Among first advocates of Darwinism in Russia. Saw plant biology as key to rational agriculture. Welcomed Bolshevik victory 1917, worked in education commissariat and Socialist Academy. | 237

Timofeev, Aleksandr Yakovlevich. On Kadet CC 1917. | 40

Tomsky (Efremov), Mikhail Ivanovich (1880–1936). Worker, trade unionist. Bolshevik from 1904, active in Moscow, Revel, etc. Arrested 1909, imprisoned 1911, exiled to Irkutsk 1916, in Petrograd and Moscow from April 1917, active in Bolshevik, Soviet and trade-union organizations. From 1918 mainly in trade-union work, head of trade-union organization 1918–29. On CP CC from 1919, Politburo from 1921. Supported Bukharin 1928–29, fell from favour. Shot self following implication at Zinoviev–Kamenev trial. | 264

Toroshelidze, Malakiya Georgievich (?–1937). On CC of Georgian CP 1922. Later head of Writers' Union in Georgia. Arrested and shot 1937. | 186

Trakhter. Director of Tagil'stroy, 1930s. | 284

Trauberg, Leonid Zakharovich (1902–1990). Film producer, worked at Lenfil'm from 1924 and Mosfil'm from 1943. Lectured on film-making. Signed resolution on need for Red culture 1928. | 341

Trotsky (Bronshteyn), Lev Davydovich (1879–1940). Revolutionary from end 1890s, joined RSDRP 1903–04, Menshevik. Briefly headed 1st Petersburg Soviet 1905, arrested, exiled, escaped to USA. Returned to Russia 1917, joined Bolsheviks

with *Mezhrayonka*. September 1917 chairman of Petrograd Soviet. Played key role in October seizure of power. War commissar 1918–24, founder of Red Army. On Politburo 1919–26. Expelled from CPSU 1927, deported 1929, assassinated 1940. | 49, 130, 139–40, 178, 180
—and anti-religious campaigns | 248–49, 251
—at Brest-Litovsk, 1918 | 78–80
—inner-party struggle | 198, 200–02, 209–12, 276, 361–62, 370, 372, 382
—and intelligentsia | 214, 228, 230, 232, 234
—in July Days, 1917 | 27, 29
—and Lenin's 'Testament' | 206, 208
—and October seizure of power | 58, 65–66, 68
Trutovsky, Vladimir Evgen'evich (1889–1937). Economist and journalist, specialist on local government, SR from 1908. Leading Left SR 1917, after October on VTsIK. December 1917–March 1918 People's Commissar for Local Government Affairs. In hiding after 6 July 1918. Frequently arrested thereafter, as maintained Left SR connections, especially in Ukraine. Final arrest 1937, shot October. | 72, 88
Tsereteli, Irakliy Georgievich (1881–1959). Georgian and all-Russia politician, Social Democrat from 1903, Menshevik. Led social-democratic faction in 2nd Duma 1906–07. Exiled to Siberia. In WWI 'Siberian Zimmerwaldist', after February 1917 on EC of Petrograd Soviet. May–July Minister of Posts and Telegraphs, June–October on Presidium of Soviet VTsIK. Left for Georgia 1918, member of Georgian parliament declaring independence 26 May 1918. Emigrated 1921. | 19–21, 33, 41, 55, 63
Tsintsadze, Kote. On Georgian CP CC, 1922. | 186
Tskhakaya, Mikhail (Mikha) Grigor'evich (1865–1950). Georgian revolutionary, Social Democrat from 1892. In leadership of Transcaucasian SFSR 1923–30, then head of state of Georgian SSR. | 186
Tsyurupa, Aleksandr Dmitrievich (1870–1928). Son of civil servant, revolutionary from early 1890s, in RSDRP from 1898, Bolshevik from 1903. Worked as zemstvo statistician and agronomist. In Ufa 1917, in October on Ufa Military-Revolutionary Committee. Head of food commissariat from 1918, organized requisitioning system. In economic and state work during NEP. | 96, 150, 155, 222
Tuchkov. Deputy plenipotentiary of Urals OGPU, 1930s. | 304
Tukhachevsky, Mikhail Ivanovich (1893–1937). Professional soldier, Lieutenant in WWI. In RKP(b) and Red Army, successful against Kolchak, Denikin, Kronstadt and Tambov rebellions, failed in Poland. Worked on military theory and modernization of Red Army 1920s and 1930s. Made Marshal of USSR 1937. Arrested and shot 1937. | 374
Turgenev, Ivan Sergeevich (1818–1883). Celebrated writer. Studied philosophy in Moscow, St Petersburg and Berlin, travelled in western Europe, associated with radical intellectuals Bakunin, Herzen, Belinsky, and others. Wrote for

Sovremennik and *Kolokol*. Spent much of his later life in France. Most famous novel *Fathers and Sons* (1862). | 218

Tyrkova (Tyrkova-Williams), Ariadna Vladimirovna (1869–1962). Political activist and publicist. In liberation movement, left Russia 1904 to avoid imprisonment. Kadet from 1905, on right of party. In WWI active in Union of Cities. Sceptical about February 1917, active opponent of Bolshevik rule after October, helped organize White volunteers, worked in Denikin's propaganda section. Thereafter active in emigration, wrote memoirs. | 40–41

Ufimtsev, S.I. Alleged Trotskyist, denounced by G.E. Osipov, 1936. | 371

Ul'yanova, Mariya Il'inichna (1878–1937). Sister of V.I. Lenin. In RSDRP from 1898. Involved in 1905–07 events and seizure of power in October 1917. Worked on *Pravda* 1917–29. Closely involved with Lenin during his final illness. On CPSU Central Control Commission 1925–34. | 203–05, 320

Unshlikht, Iosif Stanislavovich (1879–1938). Social Democrat from 1900, in RSDRP from 1906, Bolshevik. Active in Russian Poland. On Petrograd Soviet 1917, took part in October seizure of power. In Lithuanian and Belorussian party and Red Army work 1919–21. Thereafter in military, secret police and civil defence work. Arrested 1937, shot 1938. | 227, 248–49, 320

Uritsky, Moisey Solomonovich (1873–1918). Social Democrat from mid-1890s, Menshevik from 1903, associate of Trotsky. Internationalist during WWI, in *Mezhrayonka* in 1917, joined Bolsheviks. Took part in October rising, became leading figure in Cheka. Assassinated by L.S. Kanegisser. | 119–20

Ushinsky, Konstantin Dmitrievich (1823? 1824?–1870). Educationalist, inspector of schools under more liberal Alexander II from 1855, reformed Russian education and wrote textbooks, especially for teaching Russian language. | 236–37

Valentinov (Vol'sky), Nikolay Vladislavovich (1879–1964). Economist, political activist, journalist, Social Democrat from early 1900s. Bolshevik 1903–04, knew Lenin in Geneva. Increasingly unorthodox Menshevik 1905–17. Opposed Bolshevik seizure of power, worked in Soviet economic institutions from 1922. Worked as journalist in Soviet trade delegation in Paris from 1928, defected 1930. Wrote several books of memoirs. | 149–51

Vareykis, Iosif Mikhaylovich (1894–1939). Worker's son, Bolshevik from 1913. Held various party and state posts from 1917. Led suppression of Left SR rising July 1918. On CPSU CC from 1930. Arrested 1937, shot 1939. | 150

Vasil'ev, Pavel Dmitrievich. Chairman of Kronstadt Soviet on eve of rising, 1921. | 146

Veniamin. Simbirsk archbishop, White Guard supporter 1918. | 112

Verkhovsky, Aleksandr Ivanovich (1886–1938). Professional soldier, Lieutenant-Colonel in WWI. On Black Sea coast February 1917, advocated that his officers accept and welcome revolution. Sympathized with SRs. Although favoured order in army, opposed Kornilov revolt. Appointed war minister 30 August 1917, promoted to Major-General. Advocated peace with Germany October 1917. In

September. Supported Kolchak's coup November, in his government to 1919. Emigrated to China. | 107–08, 112

Vol'sky, Vladimir Kazimirovich (1877–1937). Revolutionary from 1897, SR from 1903. Journalist and co-operator. Defeatist in WWI. In Tver' 1917, active in peasant soviets and SR leadership. In *Komuch* 1918. After Kolchak's coup, reconciled to Soviet power. Arrested several times in 1920s and 1930s, shot. | 112–13

Voronin, Aleksandr Ivanovich (1908–?). Secret policeman. From 1920s in Komsomol and party work, joined NKVD as trainee 1937, interrogated Meyerhol'd 1940, made career in state security, retired 1962. | 389

Voroshilov, Kliment Efremovich (1881–1969). Soviet military and political leader. Factory worker from 1895, arrested for strike activity, joined Bolsheviks 1904, strike leader in 1905. Arrested several times. Factory worker in Petrograd February 1917, from March in party and Soviet work in Lugansk. In civil war active in Don Basin, on Tsaritsyn front, at Khar'kov. On RKP(b) CC from 1921, Politburo from 1925. Promoted in Red Army and state by Stalin. Demoted in WWII. | 357

Vostrotin, Stepan Vasil'evich (1864–after 1937). Entrepreneur, ocean explorer, politician. City chief of Eniseysk 1885–99. Kadet, on CC, in 3rd and 4th Dumas. Deputy agriculture minister in Provisional Government 1917. After October moved to Far East and Harbin, China. Visited Japan to raise support for intervention. Involved with Kolchak's forces. Returned to Harbin 1920. | 40

Wilhelm II (Hohenzollern, Wilhelm) (1859–1941). Last Kaiser of Germany, reigned 1888–1918. Deposed by political revolution at end of WWI, fled to Netherlands. | 101

Wrangel', Baron Petr Nikolaevich (1878–1928). Major-General, ruler of South Russia 1920. Evacuated from Crimea 1920, headed Russian All-Military Union from 1923. | 234

Yagoda, Genrikh Grigor'evich (Enokh Gershenovich) (1891–1938). Bolshevik from 1907, exiled for two years 1911, drafted into army 1915. In Bolshevik military organization 1917, worked on *Soldatskaya pravda*, took part in seizure of power. In Red Army 1918, Cheka from 1919, second deputy GPU/OGPU head 1923–26 and 1931–34, first deputy head 1926–31. NKVD head from 1934. Used prisoners' labour for massive economic projects. Fabricated Zinoviev–Kamenev trial 1936, himself tried and executed with Bukharin and others. 1938. | 282–83, 304, 320, 366

Yakovlev (Epshteyn), Yakov Arkad'evich (1896–1938). Bolshevik from 1913. In 1917 secretary of Ekaterinoslav party committee. Took part in October seizure of power, Petrograd. Worked underground in Ukraine, then in Ukrainian Bolshevik leadership. Edited peasant papers 1920s. Appointed USSR agriculture commissar 1929, oversaw collectivization. On CPSU CC from 1930. Arrested 1937, shot 1938. | 320

Yaroslavsky, Emel'yan Mikhaylovich (Gubel'man, Miney Izrailevich) (1878–1943).

Social Democrat from 1898, Bolshevik. Active in numerous places, in 1906 in Moscow party organization, in 1917 chaired Yakutsk Soviet. October 1917 on Moscow Military-Revolutionary Committee. Held numerous party and state posts. On Central Control Commission presidium 1923–34. Led campaigns against Church. Wrote historical works strictly to party line. | 260, 320, 390

Yermolova, Mariya Nikolaevna (1853–1928). Actress, trained at Maly Theatre, very popular amongst radical youth in 1870s. Honoured by Soviet state in 1920s. | 67

Yudenich, Nikolay Nikolaevich (1862–1933). Professional soldier, White Guard commander. Distinguished service in Russo-Japanese War and WWI on Caucasian front. Dismissed May 1917 for opposing Provisional Government. Emigrated to Finland 1918, organized anti-Soviet army. Some military success in 1919, but not supported by Baltic states. Emigrated to Britain, abandoned politics. | 114

Yurenev, Petr Petrovich (1874–1943). Railway engineer, political activist. Kadet from 1906, on CC from 1911. In 2nd Duma, thereafter in Moscow local government and on War Industries Committees, etc. Minister of Transport in 2nd-coalition Provisional Government 1917. Worked with Whites in civil war, emigrated. Finally in France, where worked as peasant, butter salesman, laundry worker and night-watchman. | 40

Yurovsky, Leonid Naumovich (1884–1938). Economist, journalist. Studied economics at St Petersburg and Munich, worked as journalist and lecturer. Conscripted 1915. Welcomed fall of Tsarism, worked as statistician in Provisional Government. Hostile to Bolshevik take-over, later worked in statistical office and finance commissariat. Involved in creating *chervonets* stable currency. Arrested 1930, charged with membership of Working Peasants' Party. Released 1934, rearrested 1937, shot 1938. | 172, 350

Yutkevich, Sergey Iosifovich (1904–1985). Artist, film producer. Studied under Meyerhol'd, 1920s. Produced numerous films, many on political themes. Developed ciné-collage technique combining animation and acting, 1960s. Signed resolution on need for Red culture 1928. | 341

Zalomov, Petr Andreevich (1877–1955). Worker, revolutionary from 1892, founded Sormovo RSDRP group 1902. Model for character Pavel Vlasov in Gorky's novel *Mother*. Arrested following demonstration, used court as tribune. Exiled, escaped 1905. In 1905 revolution. Abandoned politics 1906 owing to illness. In Soviets in Kursk 1917. Arrested and tortured by Whites in civil war. Peasant in 1920s. Joined CPSU 1925, took part in collectivization. | 170

Zamoshchina, Zhenya. Schoolgirl correspondent of Lenin, 1918. | 84–85

Zamyatin, Evgeniy Ivanovich (1884–1937). Writer and shipyard worker. Took part in 1905 revolution, lived undergound until 1911. First published 1908. Prosecuted for anti-war article 1914. Worked in shipyards in England 1916–17, returned to Russia. Wrote most famous anti-utopian novel *We* in 1920, not published in Russia. Permitted to emigrate 1931, lived in Paris. | 160, 217–18

Zaporozhets, A.E. Komsomol member, Naumovka, 1926. | 179

Zarudny, Aleksandr Sergeevich (1863–1934). Lawyer, defended radical cases. Joined People's Socialists 1917, deputy justice minister in Provisional Government until May, then on Constituent Assembly elections commission. Favoured working with bourgeois parties and co-operation with Kornilov. Left politics 1918, worked in Soviet apparatus. | 48

Zaytsev, Boris Konstantinovich (1881–1972). Writer. In Moscow literary circles from early 1900s. Works noted for optimistic world view. Elected president of Writers' Union 1921, involved in *Pomgol*, arrested, soon released. Granted permission to emigrate 1922, from 1924 lived in Paris. | 231

Zelensky, Isaak Abramovich (1890–1938). Worker, Bolshevik from 1906, active in many places, often arrested. In Moscow 1917, involved in taking power. In food commissariat 1918. Head of Moscow party organization from 1920. On CPSU CC from 1922. Held various party posts. From 1931 head of co-op organization. Arrested 1937, in 1938 Bukharin–Rykov trial. Shot. | 320

Zenzinov, Vladimir Mikhaylovich (1880–1953). Merchant's son, educated in western Europe, where joined SR circles. Returned to Russia 1904, in Moscow SR group. On SR CC from 1905. Joined SR Fighting Organization 1906. Exiled four years 1910. Defencist in WWI, became close colleague of A.F. Kerensky. Leading SR 1917, involved in *Komuch* and Ufa Directory 1918, emigrated 1919. Active in émigré circles. | 107, 112

Zhdanov, Andrey Aleksandrovich (1896–1948). Soviet politician, in revolutionary movement from 1912, RSDRP(b) from 1915. In soldiers' soviets 1917. Soviet and party leader in Tver' 1918–24, Nizhniy Novgorod 1924–34, Leningrad from 1934. Close ally of Stalin. On CPSU CC from 1927. Specialized in enforcing party control over culture. | 355

Zhdanov, Mikhail Afanas'evich (1903–?). In RKP(b) from 1920. Secretary of Nadezhdin town committee 1933, denounced and expelled from party 1934, rehabilitated 1935, then in economic work. | 294–95

Zhukov, N. Soldier, correspondent for *Soldatskaya pravda* 1917. | 17

Zinoviev, Grigoriy Evseevich (Radomysl'sky, Evsey Aronovich) (1883–1936). Social Democrat from 1901, Bolshevik from 1903. Mainly abroad to 1917, returned to Russia with Lenin. Opposed idea of rising, October 1917, but took part. End 1917 to end 1925, head of Petrograd/Leningrad Soviet and party organization. Head of Comintern 1919–26. In bloc with Stalin against Trotsky 1923–25, then with Trotsky against Stalin 1925–27. Removed from all important positions. Recanted 1927. Arrested end 1934 on (false) charge of complicity in Kirov murder. Main defendant in show trial August 1936, shot. | 29, 57–58, 65–66, 178, 198, 201–05, 207, 210, 212, 232, 276, 366, 370, 372

Zonov, K.I. OGPU agent in North Caucasus 1928, secured confessions for Shakhty trial. | 337–38

Zubarov, P. Secretary of Urals *oblast'* CPSU committee, 1930. | 278

Zyryanov. Labour camp administrator, Urals, 1930s. | 297

General Index

in Red Terror, 112, 124–25
releases, 1917, 4, 9
treatment of, 295–97
see also camps, forced labour
Procuracy
All-Union, 298, 300–01, 323, 332, 344, 350–53
regional, 29, 296–97, 326, 329
proletariat, *see* workers
Proletkul't, 68, 160, 234
Protestant churches, 83, 398
Provisional Council of the Republic, *see* Pre-Parliament
Provisional Government, 17–19, 21, 33–34, 37, 39–40, 65, 70, 75, 83, 90, 100, 236, 347
agrarian policy, 13–15, 32
collapse, 49, 52–54
economic policies, 13, 31–32, 35, 39, 49–50
foreign and military policy, 15, 31
formation of, 8–11
forms Directory, September, 48–49
and July crisis, 24–32
and Kornilov revolt, 42–48, 54
overthrow by Bolsheviks, 55–62
and Whites, 106–09
Provisional Government of Estonia, 1918, 108
Provisional Siberian Government, 1918, 106, 108
purges, verification of party cards, 370

rabfaki, workers' faculties, 221
Rabochaya gazeta (Urals paper, 1930s), 314
railways, 17, 73, 76, 94, 116, 140, 155, 164, 187, 193, 284, 291
railway workers, 56–57, 65–66, 152
railway workers' union, 67
rationalization of production, 310–12, 333, 352
rationing, 13–14, 69, 91, 101, 109, 145, 222, 229, 271, 287, 290, 315, 317, 323
Red Army
in civil war, 107, 114, 117, 129, 131, 133–34, 136, 138–39, 152–54, 219–20
formation, 75, 77
in GULAG system, 380
and Kronstadt revolt, 145–46
during NEP, 214, 243, 275, 291–92, 332, 357
Red Guards, 1917, 53, 59
religious sectarians, 374, 376, 393–95, 397–99
requisitioning of grain
after 1928 264, 275, 281, 285
abandoned by Soviets, 149, 152–54
by Bolsheviks and Red Army, 90, 92, 94, 101, 114, 135, 137–42, 144
by Provisional Government, 13–14, 41

by Whites, 115–16, 129
see also Old Believers
revolutionary tribunals, 117, 124, 249, 360–61
'Right deviation', 267–70, 316, 323, 337, 362
roadblock detachments, 145, 155
Rossiya, 219
Rubezhansky Institute of Chemical Technology, 367
Russian Academy of Artistic Sciences, 225
Russian Orthodox Church, 73, 83–89, 111–12, 242–60, 390–99
All-Russia Church Council, 1917–1918, 83, 85, 87–88, 122, 259
Diocesan Council, 246
disestablishment, 87–88, 325
émigré Church Council, 252
Holy Synod, 9, 43, 45, 83, 225, 246, 253–54, 256, 259
Patriarchate, 85, 255–56, 259
Rural and Parish Council, 246
Supreme Church Council, 246
Synod-in-exile, 255
Russian Social-Democratic Labour Party, *see* Bolsheviks, Communist Party, Mensheviks
Russkoe slovo, 57
Ryutin platform, 'Union of Marxist-Leninists', 1932, 362–65, 367

sabotage, 35, 66, 233, 270, 288, 290, 300, 316, 332–33, 336–38, 346, 353, 358, 371–75, 386, 393–94
sailors
in July 1917, 28–30
in October revolution, 54, 59, 60, 66
in Kronstadt revolt, 1921, 144–46
'Savage' Division, 44
schools, 97–98, 221–22, 288, 292, 301–02, 325, 385, 396
and the Church, 83–88, 260, 390, 394, 398
fees, 357
in Ukraine, 195
'scissors' crisis, 1923, 163
Second International, 80–81
Shakhty case, 1928, 332–39, 345–46, 351
'shock' workers, 310–15, 319
see also Stakhanovites
show trials, 241, 316, 330, 345–346, 349, 354, 381–382, 385
see also SR trial, Shakhty case, Industrial Party, Menshevik trial, Metro-Vickers Trial, Trotskyite-Zinovievite United Centre, Anti-Soviet Trotskyite Centre, Bloc of Rights and Trotskyites
sixty-six, declaration of, Ukraine, 1923, 195, 197
Smena vekh ('Change of Landmarks'), *smen-*

Place Index